International Finance

Also by Keith Pilbeam

Finance and Financial Markets
Exchange Rate Management: Theory and Evidence

International Finance

Third Edition

Keith Pilbeam

First edition 1992
Reprinted 5 times
Second edition 1998
Reprinted 6 times
Third edition 2006

Published by
PALGRAVE MACMILLAN
Houndmills, Basingstoke, Hampshire RG21 6XS and
175 Fifth Avenue, New York, N.Y. 10010
Companies and representatives throughout the world

PALGRAVE MACMILLAN is the global academic imprint of the Palgrave
Macmillan division of St. Martin's Press, LLC and of Palgrave Macmillan Ltd.
Macmillan® is a registered trademark in the United States, United Kingdom
and other countries. Palgrave is a registered trademark in the European
Union and other countries.

ISBN-13: 978–1–4039–4837–3
ISBN 10: 1–4039–4837–2

This book is printed on paper suitable for recycling and made from fully
managed and sustained forest sources.

A catalogue record for this book is available from the British Library.

Library of Congress Cataloging-in-Publication Data

Pilbeam, Keith
   International finance / Keith Pilbeam.—3rd ed.
      p. cm.
   Includes bibliographical references and index.
   ISBN 1–4039–4837–2 (paper)
      1. International finance. I. Title.
   HG3881 .P4845
   332'.042—dc22   2005051546

10   9   8   7   6   5   4   3   2   1
15   14 13 12 11 10 09 08 07 06

Printed and bound in China

To the children and workers
SOS Tibetan Children's Village, Pokhara, Nepal

Brief Contents

Contents

List of Tables

List of Figures

List of Boxes

Acknowledgements

In writing this book, I owe a heavy intellectual debt to the many people that have stimulated my interest and guided me through the field of international economics over the years; Ali El-Agraa, Tony Jones, Mike Stephenson, Theo Peeters, Loukas Tsoukalis, Jean-Paul Abraham, Paul De Grauwe, Alfred Steinherr, Francisco Torres, Emil-Maria Claassen and Wolfgang Gebauer. Feedback from numerous people on the second edition has been gratefully received and I am particularly indebted to four anonymous reviewers of the second edition who made many helpful suggestions for this new edition. I should especially like to thank Professor Laurence Harris and staff at the Centre for Economics and Financial Management Studies at the School of Oriental and African Studies for invaluable comments and ensuring healthy world-wide adoptions! Henk Jager kindly gave some useful comments at the production phase. Many thanks are due to the undergraduate and postgraduate students at City University, Cass Business School, Boston University, the European University Institute in Florence and participants in courses at the Executive Development Centre. They were subjected to the contents of the book and their questions and demands for further clarifications significantly influenced the contents. I should also like to thank *The Financial Times*, the International Monetary Fund, the Organisation for Economic Co-operation and Development, the Bank for International Settlements and the World Bank for use of their data. Much of the work for this new edition was carried out while I was on sabbatical leave at the European University Institute in Florence and thanks are due to the Head of Department, Massimo Motta, for offering me a most pleasant environment within which to work. I should like to thank the original commissioning editor Stephen Rutt, and his replacement Stephen Wenham, for their enthusiastic and excellent support throughout all three editions of this text; I share the middle name Stephen with them and they have been a pleasure to work with. Finally, I also share my first name with Keith Povey, who has copy-edited all three editions, and I should like to thank him for his superb assistance throughout the production phase.

KEITH PILBEAM

Introduction

The subject matter of international finance

The subject matter of international finance is, broadly speaking, concerned with the monetary and macroeconomic relations between countries. International finance is a constantly evolving subject that deals very much with real world issues such as balance of payments problems and policy, the causes of exchange rate movements and the implications of macroeconomic linkages between economies.

Many economists had predicted that the adoption of generalized floating in 1973 would lead to a demise of interest in the subject. They believed that exchange rate adjustments would eliminate balance of payments concerns. As is the case with many economists' predictions, they were proved wrong! Floating exchange rates did not eliminate balance of payments preoccupations, and in recent years the record US balance of payments deficits have become a mounting concern for the global economy. Floating exchange rates have been characterized by high volatility and substantial deviations from purchasing power parities. Exciting new theories were developed to explain these phenomena and these theories have been subjected to close empirical scrutiny. While the more recent literature has emphasized that purchasing power parity (PPP) may still be a valid run phenomenon, the speed with which deviations from PPP are corrected has become a source of recent controversy.

The quadrupling of oil prices at the end of 1973 and doubling in 1979 caused considerable turbulence to the world economy. There were dramatic divergences in economic performance; the United Kingdom and Italy experienced substantial rises in their inflation rates, while the Japanese and German economies managed to keep the lid on inflation. In such a turbulent world, a widespread desire to create a zone of currency stability between the currencies of countries belonging to the European Community led to the setting up of the European Monetary System in 1979. Contrary to much initial scepticism and the odd speculative attack, the system survived until the end of 1998, and on 1 January 1999 the European Union achieved the holy grail of Economic and Monetary Union (EMU) with 11 founding members. Greece was admitted into the Monetary Union on 1 January 2001 and was thereby able to fully participate when the euro finally arrived at street-level on 1 January 2002. The advent of European Monetary Union is probably the most significant development in the international monetary system since the breakdown of the Bretton Woods system in the early 1970s. The euro, although only five years in existence at the time of writing, has had a turbulent time in the foreign exchange markets falling from an initial value of $1.17/€1 to an all-time low of around $0.82/€1 in October 2000 before making a remarkable recovery to be trading around $1.25/€1 by mid-August 2005.

The dollar itself has had a turbulent history since the breakdown of Bretton Woods; it generally depreciated against its major trading partners in the 1970s but between 1981 and 1985 a massive and sustained real appreciation of the dollar was largely blamed on divergences in macroeconomic policies internationally. The United

States had an ever-growing fiscal deficit with rising real interest rates, while the European and Japanese economies were adopting much tougher fiscal policies. The resulting appreciation of the dollar led to trade frictions between the United States and its trading partners. To limit these damaging policy divergences, there were calls for a greater coordination of macroeconomic policies and much discussion in the economic literature over the potential gains to be had from such coordination.

In August 1982 the International Debt Crisis exploded on the scene with the announcement of the Mexican moratorium, and sparked off major concerns about stability of the international banking system. Resolving the worst of the crisis took up the best part of 15 years, and despite its supposed resolution there have been major economic crises in three of the four major debtors, notably Mexico in 1994/95, Brazil in 1999 and Argentina declaring a debt moratorium in December 2001 and ending its peso currency-board peg to the US dollar in January 2002.

Over the past couple of decades, the Southeast Asian economies have grown rapidly and their economic importance to the world economy has increased enormously. However, in July 1997 a devaluation of the Thai baht marked an abrupt ending of the 'Asian miracle' and the start of the so-called 'Asian financial crisis'. For the best part of a year and a half there was unprecedented turbulence in Asian financial markets with their currencies and stockmarkets both falling significantly in value and exhibiting enormous volatility. The turbulence in the financial markets was reflected in large output falls in many Asian economies and indeed a questioning of their economic systems. The economies have since stabilized and the economic profession has been busy analysing the implications of channels of trade and financial contagion, moral hazard and herding behaviour ever since in an attempt to rationalize the crisis. More recently, there have been moves to set up early-warning systems designed to detect potential crises before they develop.

Another major development in the past 35 years has been the exponential growth in trading in derivative instruments such as futures, options and swaps. These instruments have enabled firms to hedge risks but have also been the centre of concern in that some authorities, companies and banks have run up enormous losses either through a lack of understanding of the instruments or the taking of unduly risky positions. The $2 billion losses of Orange County in the United States and the remarkable losses run up by Barings bank due to trading by the infamous Nick Leeson are just two of the well-publicized cases.

Not surprisingly, in response to many of the foregoing developments, the literature and the importance of the subject has mushroomed. Although there are a number of very good texts covering many of these topics it is extremely hard to find a core book to recommend. Some books are very strong on theory but pay little attention to empirical issues. Others are excellent on recent exchange rate theory but presume a reasonable background in traditional exchange rate and balance of payments theory. Older texts, while good on traditional theories, inevitably do not cover the modern literature. The first two editions of this text were designed to provide a single core book giving an accessible and up-to-date introduction to the field of international finance. The market success of the previous two editions and events such as the achievement of EMU in Europe, the Asian financial crises and new theoretical and empirical developments in the subject area inevitably led to demands for a third edition which we present here. Economics is increasingly a profession where the tail (mathematics and econometrics) is wagging the dog (economics); I like to think this is a book where the dog is wagging the tail and it is written in this spirit.

Distinguishing features of this text

The main distinguishing features of this text can be summarized as:

- **Full scope of theory covered**. The text presents both traditional and modern theories in the field. To the extent possible, the presentation follows a chronological order that gives students an impression of the development of the literature.
- **Real-world data**. The text is not purely theoretical but presents students with a reasonable overview of the empirical evidence relating to the theories discussed.
- **Considerate use of maths**. The technical expertise required of students is kept to a fairly low level. However, rather than exclude some important topics that require a more technical exposition, a basic knowledge of mathematics and statistics is assumed.
- **Visual features**. Extensive use is made of diagrams, tables and graphs to illustrate the arguments in the text.
- **Full coverage of recent developments**. A number of important recent developments and subjects are given an extensive and up-to-date rather than cursory treatment. Most notably, there are entire chapters devoted to International Policy Coordination, Currency Derivatives, European Monetary Union, the International Debt Crisis and the Asian Financial Crisis. Among the issues discussed are, *inter alia*, exchange rate 'overshooting,' the problem of time inconsistency, game theory, currency crisis and moral hazard. The addition of a new chapter on the Asian financial crises reflects not just the growth of recent literature in this area, but also the increasing attention being paid by policy-makers and financial-market participants to this region of the world.
- **Updated further reading**. At the end of each chapter there is a selective own-list of further reading and references. It was felt that this would be considerably more useful to students and lecturers than a general bibliography at the end of the book. A list of very useful texts in the field is provided at the end of the book.
- **Web resources**. Reflecting the increasing use of the web by both students and lecturers, I have included a number of useful web urls that are pertinent to the world of international finance. These websites frequently provide access to invaluable information, data and the latest research in the subject area. In addition, the book now has its own companion website from which there are PowerPoint slides of all the figures and tables from the text. There is also a set of exercises with outline solutions for lecturers. I have also included some useful weblinks.

Appropriate courses for the text

The coverage and level of technical expertise expected of students makes the text suitable for use as a main text on a variety of degree courses. These include undergraduate and one-year postgraduate courses in international economics, international monetary economics and international finance. Much of the material covered makes the book particularly useful for the international finance component of MBA courses. Some of the chapters in the book are relevant to courses in intermediate macroeconomics and international relations.

Presentation and contents

In writing the text, it soon became apparent that there are a bewilderingly wide range of models that could be presented. At the same time it is extremely difficult to present the various theories as a subset of some general model, since that model would quickly become intractable. In the end, it was decided to concentrate on the models that have dominated the literature, even though the assumptions underlying the models in different chapters can differ greatly. It is hoped that the clear statement of the different assumptions underlying the theories at the beginning of each chapter and the contrasts drawn between the various models will facilitate student understanding.

The book is divided into three parts. The opening part is concerned with balance of payments theory and policy. The second part is devoted to theories of exchange rate determination and policy including an examination of the empirical exchange rate literature. The final part of the book traces the evolution and development of the international monetary system, and the major features of the current system are analysed.

Broadly speaking, an attempt has been made to present each part of the book in a chronological order that will give students a perspective on the development of the literature. A brief overview of the chapters is given below.

Part 1: balance of payments theory and macroeconomic policy in an open economy

The opening chapter provides an introduction to the foreign exchange market and provides an essential background to the study of the remaining chapters in the book. Chapter 2 provides an introduction to balance of payments statistics and their interpretation. Chapter 3 presents some national income and balance of payments identities and then examines the traditional elasticity and absorption approaches to devaluation that were developed in the 1930s to 1950s. Chapter 4 analyses macroeconomic policy in an open economy using the Keynesian IS–LM–BP model which dominated policy discussion in the 1960s. This framework is then used to examine the effectiveness of fiscal, monetary and exchange rate policies in achieving internal and external balance. This is then followed in Chapter 5 by an examination of the distinctive monetary approach to the balance of payments which emerged in the late 1960s and early 1970s.

At the outset, it is worth noting that there are considerable differences between the Keynesian model of Chapter 4 and the monetary model of Chapter 5. The Keynesian model is based upon fixed domestic prices and assumes a horizontal aggregate supply schedule, so that variations in aggregate demand translate into changes in output and not prices. This contrasts with the monetary model which assumes a vertical aggregate supply schedule at the full employment level of output so that changes in aggregate demand translate into changes in prices rather than output. The Keynesian model also takes a flow view of capital movements and assumes imperfect goods substitutability; whereas the monetary model takes a stock view of capital movements and assumes perfect goods substitutability.

Part 2: exchange rate determination theory, evidence and policy

Chapter 6 commences with the purchasing power parity (PPP) literature which is one of the earliest theories of exchange rate determination. PPP has not proved to be a reliable indicator of floating exchange behaviour, and some of the explanations that have been put forward to explain its failure are discussed. A new section dealing with measurement of per capita GDP and the relative size of different economies using PPP-exchange rates shows the relevance of the concept of PPP to understanding the world economy. In Chapter 7 there is an exposition of the modern monetary theories of exchange rate determination that were developed in the 1970s, and these emphasize the importance of monetary factors in explaining exchange rate behaviour. We deal first with the 'flexible price' monetary model, followed by the 'sticky price' Dornbusch model and finally the Frankel 'real interest rate differential model'. The chapter also introduces the risk premium and portfolio-balance approach to exchange rate determination. The portfolio-balance exchange rate model which was developed at the same time as the monetary models is discussed more fully in Chapter 8. The portfolio-balance model emphasizes that risk factors, and current account imbalances may have an important role to play in exchange rate determination.

Chapter 9 covers the empirical literature on floating exchange rates which only really got under way at the end of the 1970s and has mushroomed ever since. Three major empirical issues are examined; the first is whether or not the foreign exchange market can be regarded as efficient; the second concerns whether modern theories of exchange rates satisfactorily model observed exchange rate behaviour; and the third concerns the formation of exchange rate expectations. We include a discussion of some important recent results which suggest that economic fundamentals may still be useful for predicting longer-run exchange rates. Chapter 10 concentrates on exchange rate policy, beginning with a review of the traditional debate over the relative merits of fixed and floating exchange rates. This is then followed by an assessment using the more modern approach to analysing exchange rate policy, which compares the stabilizing properties of the two regimes within the context of a formal macroeconomic model.

Part 3: the international monetary system

Chapter 11 provides an overview of the development of the post-Second World War international monetary system. It commences with the operation and eventual breakdown of the Bretton Woods system, and then surveys the major developments since the adoption of generalized floating. Chapter 12 examines the Eurocurrency and Eurobond markets that have become ever more significant and are important vehicles for the globalization of international finance. Chapter 13 examines the basics of derivative instruments and explains the differences between options, futures and swaps as well as the principles behind the pricing of these instruments. Chapter 14 provides an overview of the literature on international policy coordination, a topic of which there has been a great deal of research since 1985 and which remains an area of considerable controversy. Chapter 15 is devoted to an analysis of many of the issues raised by the international debt crisis, covering the origins and management of the crisis, the Mexican 1994/95 crisis, the Brazilian devaluation of 1999 and the Argentinian debt default in December 2001 and the ending of its currency board in January 2002. Chapter 16 looks at the achievement of Economic and Monetary Union in Europe, fully updated to reflect the achievement of EMU, the framework within which the European Central Bank operates, controversy over the stability and growth pact and the issues raised by the recent accession countries that in principle should be joining EMU at some point in the future. Chapter 17 is a new chapter covering the recent currency crisis literature; there is coverage of first, second and third-generation models and a special focus on how these might be useful in analysing the East Asian financial crisis, as well as coverage of the recent literature on early-warning systems.

Use of the book

The scope of the book is sufficiently wide that there is considerable flexibility for lecturers to design courses that reflect their own interests. Chapters 1–5 probably provide the backbone to most courses in this field. Chapter 6 on purchasing power parity is a core chapter on exchange rate theory and floating exchange rate experience. Thereafter, the degree to which modern exchange rate theory is covered will be dependent on the length and priority of the course. Chapter 7 covers the modern monetary models. There is no doubt that the Dornbusch model of exchange rate over-shooting represents such a significant contribution to our understanding of exchange rate behaviour that getting over its message is highly desirable. The problem is that a formal presentation is sometimes too advanced for some courses in international finance. For this reason, I have split up the presentation of the Dornbusch model into two parts: one is a simple explanation of the model without recourse to the use of equations; this is followed by a more formal presentation for more advanced classes. I hope that this approach enables most students to gain at least an intuitive grasp of the ideas underlying modern exchange rate theory and at the same that it satisfies the demands of more rigorous courses.

Chapter 8 on the portfolio balance model can easily be omitted if the course does not go into great detail on exchange rate theory. With regard to the empirical evidence on exchange rates it is quite possible to omit the coverage of exchange market efficiency tests and just recommend sections 9.6 to 9.10 for an overview of how well modern exchange rate theories perform empirically. In Chapter 10 it is possible to cover the traditional debate on fixed and floating exchange rate regimes without having to cover the more modern approach; although I have found the modern approach that compares the two regimes within an aggregate supply and demand framework to be very popular with students. Part 3 of the book offers a range of topics that can be chosen to reflect the emphasis of the particular course.

PART 1

The Balance of Payments and Macroeconomic Policy in an Open Economy

1

The Foreign Exchange Market

1.1 Introduction

When studying open economies that trade with one another, there is a major difference in the transactions between domestic and foreign residents as compared to those between residents of the same country; namely, that differing national currencies are usually involved. A US importer will generally have to pay a Japanese exporter in yen, a German exporter in euros and a British exporter in pounds. For this reason, the US importer will have to buy these currencies with dollars in what is known as the foreign exchange market. The foreign exchange market is not a single physical place, rather it is defined as a market where the various national currencies are bought and sold. Exactly what factors determine how much domestic currency has to be given in exchange to obtain a unit of foreign currency, the behaviour of exchange rates and the impact of exchange rate changes on the economy is one of the major fields of study in international economics and is the subject matter of later chapters of this book.

In this chapter, we look at some preliminary issues; we examine the various participants in the foreign exchange market and the basic forces that operate in the market.

We then examine the basic determinants of exchange rate behaviour. The chapter proceeds to examine various exchange rate definitions and their economic significance. We then look at the basic operational differences between fixed and floating exchange rate regimes. The chapter finishes by examining the relationship between the spot and forward exchange rate.

One of the most fascinating things about the foreign exchange market is the huge sums of money that are exchanged on a daily basis, **Table 1.1** shows the result of surveys carried out by the Bank for International Settlements (BIS). The main centre for foreign exchange trading is London, with some $753 billion worth of foreign exchange traded on a daily basis, quite a lot when one considers that the annual gross domestic product of the United Kingdom is slightly over twice that amount. Other important foreign exchange centres are New York with $461 billion, Tokyo with $199 billion, Singapore $125 billion, Paris $64 billion and Frankfurt $118 billion. The net volume of foreign exchange dealing globally was in April 2004 estimated to be in excess of $2.4 trillion per day.

Table 1.1 Foreign exchange market turnover

| | Daily average (US$ billions) | | | | |
	April 1992	April 1995	April 1998	April 2001	April 2004
United Kingdom	291	464	637	504	753
United States	167	244	351	254	461
Japan	120	161	136	147	199
Singapore	74	105	139	101	125
Hong Kong	60	90	79	67	102
Switzerland	66	87	82	71	79
Germany	55	76	94	88	118
France	33	58	72	48	64
Other	210	287	368	339	507
Total	1,076	1,572	1,958	1,619	2,408

| | Geographic composition (% share) | | | | |
	April 1992	April 1995	April 1998	April 2001	April 2004
United Kingdom	26	27	30	31	31
United States	16	16	16	16	19
Japan	15	11	10	9	8
Singapore	8	7	7	6	5
Hong Kong	7	6	6	4	4
Switzerland	8	6	5	4	3
Germany	5	5	5	5	5
France	3	4	4	3	3
Other	12	18	17	13	13
Total	100	100	100	100	100

Notes: The above are net figures having been adjusted to allow for double counting.
Source: Bank for International Settlements.

Exchange rate definitions

The exchange rate is simply the price of one currency in terms of another, and there are two methods of expressing it:

1   Domestic currency units per unit of foreign currency – for example, taking the pound sterling as the domestic currency, on 14 January 2005 there was approximately £0.5319 required to purchase one US dollar, that is £0.5319/$1.
2   Foreign currency units per unit of the domestic currency – again taking the pound sterling as the domestic currency, on 14 January 2005 approximately $1.88 were required to obtain one pound, that is $1.88/£1.

The reader will note that the second method is merely the reciprocal of the former. While it is not important which method of expressing the exchange rate is employed, it is necessary to be careful when talking about a rise or fall in the exchange rate because the meaning will be very different depending upon which definition is used. A rise in the pounds per dollar exchange rate from say £0.5319/$1 to £0.625/$1 means that more pounds have to be given to obtain a dollar, this means that the pound has depreciated in value or, equivalently, the dollar has appreciated in value. If the second definition is employed, a rise in the exchange rate from $1.88/£1 to say $2/£1 would mean that more dollars are obtained per pound, so that the pound has appreciated or equivalently the dollar has depreciated.

Important note

For the purposes of this chapter, we shall define the exchange rate as foreign currency units per unit of domestic currency. This is the definition most commonly employed in the UK where the exchange rate is quoted as, for example, dollars or yen per pound and is the definition most frequently employed when compiling real and nominal exchange rate indices (see section 1.6) for all currencies. However, in other chapters of the book we shall normally be using the first definition which is the definition most often employed in the theoretical economic literature. It is important when reading newspapers, articles or other textbooks that readers familiarize themselves with the particular exchange rate definition being employed. There is no real way around this problem, up until 1 January 1999 British foreign exchange dealers were used to seeing market quotations as foreign currency per pound, for example dollars per pound, but since the advent of the euro they have had to get used to that particular rate being quoted in the market as pounds per euro!

    Table 1.2 shows the exchange rates of a variety of currencies as at 4 January 2005 against the major three currencies the pound, the US dollar and the euro. In **Table 1.2** we have given only the mid-point quotations of the currencies, while in reality there are bid-offer spreads to consider. For sterling the mid-point is $1.8834/£1, but in the market there will be two prices quoted – $1.8836 (bid) and $1.8832 (offer) – a spread of 4 bips. The bid rate is the rate at which a bank will buy sterling, while the offer rate is the rate at which the bank will sell sterling in exchange for dollars. The difference is known as the bid–offer spread and represents the gross profit margin of the bank. In the case of sterling, in our example, this spread is equal to $100 \times [(1.8836 - 1.8832)/1.8834] = 0.02\%$. The spread will vary from bank to bank, and from currency to currency and according to market conditions. Thinly traded currencies tend to have

Table 1.2　Exchange rate quotations at close of business, 4 January 2005 (closing mid-points)

	Foreign currency per £	Foreign currency per $	Foreign currency per €
Argentina	5.5914	2.9688	3.9462
Australia	2.4508	1.3012	1.7297
Brazil	5.1030	2.7095	3.6016
Canada	2.3049	1.2238	1.6268
Czech Republic	43.1620	22.9170	30.4625
Denmark	10.5334	5.5928	7.4342
Europe	1.4169	0.7522	1.0000
Hong Kong	14.6628	7.7852	10.3485
India	81.8431	43.4550	57.7626
Japan	196.542	104.355	138.714
Kenya	148.1290	78.6500	104.546
Mexico	21.3304	11.3255	15.0544
New Zealand	2.6702	1.4177	1.8845
Poland	5.8145	3.0872	4.1037
Russia	52.2079	27.7200	36.8469
Singapore	3.1313	1.7132	2.0910
South Africa	11.0268	5.8548	7.7824
Sweden	12.8210	6.8075	9.0488
Switzerland	2.1972	1.1666	1.5508
United States	1.8834	1.0000	1.3293
United Kingdom	1.0000	0.5310	0.7058

Source: *Financial Times*, 5 January 2005.

the largest spread, and the spread usually increases if the risks of trading in a particular currency are perceived to have risen.

1.3　Characteristics and participants of the foreign exchange market

The foreign exchange market (see **Figure 1.1**) is a worldwide market and is made up primarily of commercial banks, foreign exchange brokers and other authorized agents trading in most of the currencies of the world. These groups are kept in close and continuous contact with one another and with developments in the market via telephone, computer terminals, telex and fax.

Easily the most heavily traded currency is the US dollar which is known as a vehicle currency – because the currency is widely used to denominate international transactions. Oil and many other important primary products such as tin, coffee and gold all tend to be priced in dollars. Indeed, because the dollar is so heavily traded it is usually cheaper for a French foreign exchange dealer wanting Mexican pesos to first purchase US dollars with euros and then sell the dollars to purchase pesos rather than directly purchase the pesos with euros. The main participants in the foreign exchange market can be categorized as follows:

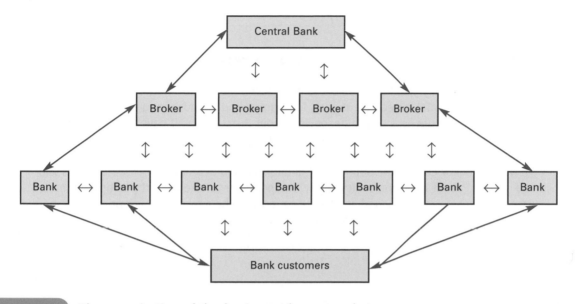

Figure 1.1   The organization of the foreign exchange market

- **Retail clients** – these are made up of businesses, international investors, multinational corporations and the like who need foreign exchange for the purposes of operating their businesses. Normally, they do not directly purchase or sell foreign currencies themselves rather they operate by placing buy/sell orders with the commercial banks.
- **Commercial banks** – the commercial banks carry out buy/sell orders from their retail clients and buy/sell currencies on their own account (known as proprietary trading) so as to alter the structure of their assets and liabilities in different currencies. The banks deal either directly with other banks or through foreign exchange brokers. In addition to the commercial banks, other financial institutions such as merchant banks are engaged in buying and selling currencies both for proprietary purposes and on behalf of their customers in finance-related transactions.
- **Foreign exchange brokers** – often banks do not trade directly with one another, rather they offer to buy and sell currencies via foreign exchange brokers. Operating through such brokers is advantageous because, since they collect buy and sell quotations for most currencies from many banks, the most favourable quotation is obtained quickly and at very low cost. One disadvantage of dealing though a broker is that a small brokerage fee is payable which is not incurred in a straight bank to bank deal. Each financial centre normally has just a handful of authorized brokers through which commercial banks conduct their exchanges.
- **Central banks** – normally the monetary authorities of a country are not indifferent to changes in the external value of their currency, and even though exchange rates of the major industrialized nations have been left to fluctuate freely since 1973 central banks frequently intervene to buy and sell their currencies in a bid to influence the rate at which their currency is traded. Under a fixed exchange rate system the authorities are obliged to purchase their currencies when there is excess supply, and sell the currency when there is excess demand.

> **Box 1.1**
>
> **Bulls and bears in the foreign exchange market**
>
> Speculators are usually classified as bulls and bears according to their view on a particular currency. If a speculator expects a currency, for example the pound (spot and forward), to appreciate in the future he is said to be 'bullish' about the currency. It pays the speculator to take a **long position** on the pound, that is, to buy the pound spot or forward at a cheap price today in the hope that he can sell it at a higher price in the future.
>
> If the speculator expects the pound (spot and forward) to depreciate in the future he is said to be 'bearish' about the currency. It will pay the speculator to take a **short position** on the currency, that is, to sell the pound at what he considers to be a relatively high price today in the hope of buying it back at a cheaper rate sometime in the future.

1.4 Arbitrage in the foreign exchange market

One of the most important implications deriving from the close communication of buyers and sellers in the foreign exchange market is that there is almost instantaneous arbitrage across currencies and financial centres. Arbitrage is the exploitation of price differentials for riskless guaranteed profits. To illustrate what is meant by these two types of arbitrage we shall assume that transaction costs are negligible and that there is only a single exchange rate quotation, ignoring the bid–offer spread.

Financial centre arbitrage ensures that the dollar–pound exchange rate quoted in New York will be the same as that quoted in London and other financial centres. This is because if the exchange rate is $1.89/£1 in New York but only $1.87/£1 in London, it would be profitable for banks to buy pounds in London and simultaneously sell them in New York and make a guaranteed 2 cents for every pound bought and sold. The act of buying pounds in London will lead to a depreciation of the dollar in London, while selling pounds in New York will lead to an appreciation of the dollar in New York. Such a process continues until the rate quoted in the two centres coincides at, say, $1.88/£1.

Cross currency arbitrage. To illustrate what is meant by currency arbitrage let us suppose that the exchange rate of the dollar is $1.88/£1 and the exchange rate of the dollar against the euro is $1.30/€1. Currency arbitrage implies that the exchange rate of the euro against the pound will be €1.4462/£1 (1.88/1.30 = 1.4462). If this were not the case, say there was 1.50 euros per pound, then a UK dealer wanting dollars would do better to first obtain 1.50 euros which would then buy $1.95 making nonsense of a $1.88/£1 quotation. The increased demand for euros would quickly appreciate its rate against the pound to the €1.4462/£1 level. **Table 1.3** shows a set of cross rates for the major currencies.

Table 1.3 Foreign exchange cross rates at close of business, 4 January 2005

		C$	DKr	€	Yen	NKr	SKr	SFr	£	US$
Canada	(C$)	1	4.570	0.615	85.27	5.086	5.563	0.953	0.434	0.817
Denmark	(DKr)	2.188	10	1.345	186.6	11.13	12.17	2.086	0.949	1.788
Euro zone	(€)	1.627	7.434	1	138.7	8.274	9.049	1.551	0.796	1.329
Japan	(¥)	1.173	5.359	0.721	100	5.965	6.523	1.118	0.509	0.958
Norway	(NKr)	1.966	8.985	1.209	167.6	10	10.94	1.874	0.853	1.607
Sweden	(SKr)	1.798	8.216	1.105	153.3	9.144	10	1.714	0.780	1.469
Switzerland	(SFr)	1.049	4.794	0.645	89.45	5.336	5.835	1	0.455	0.857
United Kingdom	(£)	2.305	10.53	1.417	196.5	11.72	12.82	2.197	1	1.883
United States	($)	1.224	5.593	0.752	104.4	6.225	6.808	1.167	0.531	1

Note: The exchange rate is the units of the currency in the top row, per unit of the currency listed in the left--hand column, where the following applies to the units in the left-hand column: yen per 100, Danish kroner per 10, Norwegian kroner per 10, Swedish kronor per 10.
Source: *Financial Times*, 5 January 2005.

1.5 The spot and forward exchange rates

Foreign exchange dealers not only deal with a wide variety of currencies but they also have a set of dealing rates for each currency which are known as the spot and forward rates.

The spot exchange rate is the quotation between two currencies for immediate delivery. In other words, the spot exchange rate is the current exchange rate of two currencies *vis-à-vis* each other. In practice, there is normally a two-day lag between a spot purchase or sale and the actual exchange of currencies to allow for verification, paperwork and clearing of payments.

The forward exchange rate. In addition to the spot exchange rate it is possible for economic agents to agree today to exchange currencies at some specified time in the future, most commonly for 1 month (30 days), 3 months (90 days), 6 months (180 days), 9 months (270 days) and 1 year (360 days). The rate of exchange at which such a purchase or sale can be made is known as the forward exchange rate. Exactly why economic agents may engage in forward exchange transactions and how the forward exchange rate quotation is determined is a subject we shall look at later in this chapter.

1.6 Nominal, real and effective exchange rates

Policy-makers and economists are very much concerned about analysing the implications of exchange rate changes for the economy and the balance of payments. The exchange rate itself does not convey much information, and to analyse the effects and implications of exchange rate changes economists compile indices of the nominal, real and effective exchange rates. Since most national and international authorities quote such rates as foreign currency per unit of domestic currency, we shall compile some hypothetical nominal, real and effective exchange rates using this definition.

This means that a rise of the nominal, real or effective exchange rate index represents an appreciation of the currency being indexed.

Nominal exchange rate. The exchange rate that prevails at a given date is known as the nominal exchange rate, and is the amount of US dollars that will be obtained for one pound in the foreign exchange market. Similarly, if the euro quotation is €1.40/£1, this is again a nominal exchange rate quotation. The nominal exchange rate is merely the price of one currency in terms of another with no reference made to what this means in terms of purchasing power of goods/services. The nominal exchange rate is usually presented in index form; if at the base period the exchange rate is $2/£1 and one period later the exchange rate is $1.80/£1 the nominal index of the pound will change from the base period value of 100 to 90. A depreciation or appreciation of the nominal exchange rate does not necessarily imply that the country has become more or less competitive on international markets, for such a measure we have to look at the real exchange rate.

Real exchange rate. The real exchange rate is the nominal exchange rate adjusted for relative prices between the countries under consideration. The real exchange rate is normally expressed in index form algebraically as:

$$S_r = S \frac{P}{P*}$$

where S_r is the index of the real exchange rate, S is the nominal exchange rate (foreign currency units per unit of domestic currency) in index form, P the index of the domestic price level and $P*$ is the index of the foreign price level.

Table **1.4** illustrates the compilation of hypothetical nominal and real exchange rate indices for the pound, and shows what exactly changes in the real exchange rate measure. In the first period the real exchange rate index is set equal to 100. A basket of UK goods priced at £100 will cost a US resident $200, while a basket of US goods priced at $100 would cost a UK resident £50. Between period 1 and period 2 there is no change in the nominal exchange rate which remains at $2/£1; however, the UK price index rises while the US index remains the same. This means that there has been

Table 1.4 Construction of nominal and real exchange rate indices

Period	Nominal exchange rate	Nominal exchange index	UK price index	US price index	Real exchange index of £
1	$2.00/£1	100	100	100	100
2	$2.00/£1	100	120	100	120
3	$2.40/£1	120	120	120	120
4	$1.80/£1	90	130	117	100
5	$1.50/£1	75	150	125	90

Note: The real exchange rate index is constructed by multiplying the nominal exchange rate index by the UK price index and dividing this by the US price index.

a real appreciation of the pound, UK goods now become relatively more expensive for US residents as they now have to use $240 dollars to purchase the original bundle of UK goods which now cost £120; the bundle of US goods costs a British citizen £50. This decreased British competitiveness is picked up by the real exchange rate appreciation of the pound from 100 to 120. Clearly, since the nominal exchange rate index has remained at 100 it has failed to pick up the change in competitiveness.

Between periods 2 and 3, UK prices remain unchanged while US prices increase; however, the pound appreciates sufficiently that the UK gains no competitive advantage. Between periods 3 and 4 UK prices rise and US prices fall but the competitive disadvantage to the UK is offset by a substantial depreciation of the pound, so that there is a real depreciation of the pound meaning an improvement in UK competitiveness. Finally, between periods 4 and 5, although UK prices rise much more than US prices making the UK less competitive, this is offset by a large nominal depreciation of the pound and overall there is a real depreciation of the pound. From this example it is clear that the real exchange rate monitors changes in a country's competitiveness. Real exchange rate indices unlike nominal exchange rate indices are not publishable on a daily basis because the price indices used are normally only published monthly.

Figures 1.2 and 1.3 show the evolution of the dollar–pound and dollar–yen nominal and real exchange rate indices between 1980 and 2005, compiled using quarterly data and consumer price indices. The figures show that there have been very substantial movements in both nominal and real exchange rates over this period.

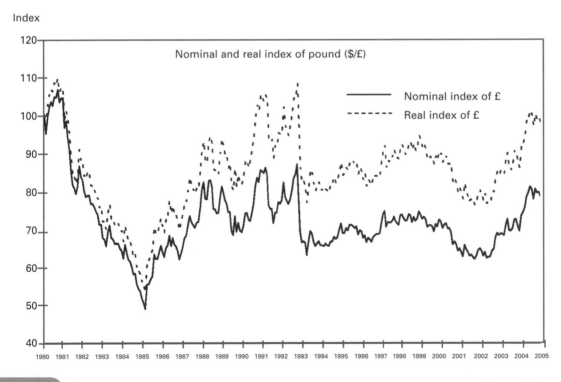

 Figure 1.2 The evolution of the dollar–pound nominal and real exchange rate, 1980–2005

Index

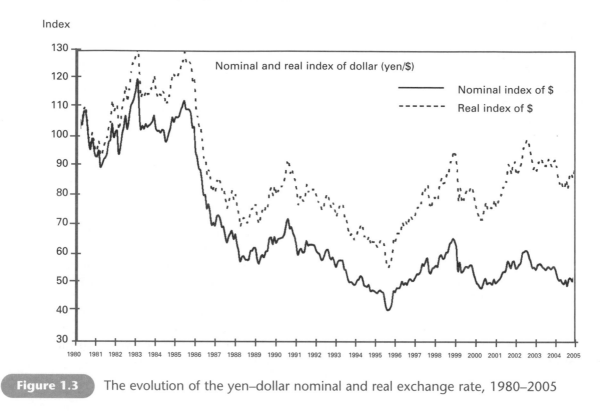

Figure 1.3 The evolution of the yen–dollar nominal and real exchange rate, 1980–2005

Effective exchange rate

Since most countries of the world do not conduct all their trade with a single foreign country, policy makers are not so much concerned with what is happening to their exchange rate against a single foreign currency but rather what is happening to it against a basket of foreign currencies with which the country trades. The effective exchange rate is a measure of whether or not the currency is appreciating or depreciating against a weighted basket of foreign currencies. In order to illustrate how an effective exchange rate is compiled consider the hypothetical case of the UK conducting 30% of its foreign trade with the US and 70% of its trade with Europe. This means a weight of 0.3 will be attached to the bilateral exchange rate index with the dollar, and 0.7 to the euro.

Table 1.5 shows movements of a hypothetical effective exchange rate index for the pound. The US dollar has a 30% weight and the euro a 70% weight. Between periods 1 and 2 the pound appreciates 10% against the dollar but depreciates 10% against the euro. Since the euro has a greater weight than the dollar the effective exchange rate index indicates an overall depreciation of 4%. Period 3 leads to further appreciation against the US dollar and no change against the euro, and the resulting appreciation of the effective exchange rate is consequently less marked than the appreciation against the dollar. In period 4, the pound depreciates against both the dollar and euro and consequently there is a depreciation of the effective exchange rate. Finally, in period 5 the pound depreciates against the US dollar and appreciates to a lesser extent against the euro; however, the effective exchange rate depreciates only marginally

Table 1.5 Construction of a nominal effective exchange rate index

Period	Nominal exchange rate index of $/£	Nominal exchange rate index of €/£	Effective exchange rate index of £
1	100	100	100
2	110	90	96
3	120	90	99
4	90	80	83
5	75	85	82

Note: The effective exchange rate index is constructed by multiplying the $/£ index by 0.3 and the €/£ index by 0.7.

because more weight is attached to the appreciation against the euro than to the depreciation against the dollar.

While the nominal effective exchange rate is easy to compile on a daily basis and normally provides a reasonable measure of changes in a country's competitive position for periods of several months, it does not take account of the effect of price movements. In order to get a better idea of changes in a country's competitive position over time we would need to compile a real effective exchange rate index. For this, we would first of all compile the real exchange rate index against each of the trading partners' currencies, and then use the same procedure as for compiling the nominal effective exchange rate index. **Table 1.6** shows the nominal effective exchange rate indexes for the major industrialized countries since 1980, derived from the International Monetary Fund's multilateral exchange rate model (MERM), while **Table 1.7** shows the real effective exchange rate indices for the major industrialized countries using consumer price indices for calculation purposes.

1.7 A simple model of the determination of the spot exchange rate

Since the adoption of floating exchange rates in 1973 there has developed an exciting new set of theories attempting to explain exchange rate behaviour, generally known as the modern asset-market approach to exchange rate determination. We shall be looking in some detail at these theories in Chapters 7–9. For the time being, we shall look at a simple model of exchange rate determination which was widely used prior to the development of these new theories. Despite its shortcomings the model serves as a useful introduction to exchange rate determination and is a prerequisite for the understanding of Chapters 1–6 of the book. The basic tenet of the model is that the exchange rate (the price) of a currency can be analysed like any other price by a resort to the tools of supply and demand. The exchange rate of the pound will be determined by the intersection of the supply and demand for pounds on the foreign exchange market.

The demand for foreign exchange

The demand for pounds in the foreign exchange market is a derived demand; that is, the pounds are not demanded because they have an intrinsic value in themselves, but

Table 1.6 Nominal effective exchange rate indices, 1980–2004 (annual averages)

	United States	Canada	Japan	United Kingdom	Germany	Italy	France
1980	100.0	100.0	100.0	100.0	100.0	100.0	100.0
1981	109.5	99.7	112.1	102.7	96.1	90.6	93.9
1982	121.3	99.1	104.8	99.0	101.8	85.0	86.9
1983	125.6	100.3	114.8	92.9	106.9	83.0	82.0
1984	134.3	96.8	121.0	89.5	106.4	79.6	79.3
1985	138.9	92.3	123.7	89.4	106.9	75.5	80.4
1986	113.0	86.4	158.0	81.5	116.1	76.6	82.6
1987	99.8	88.2	171.6	79.8	122.7	76.4	82.6
1988	93.0	94.0	190.2	84.6	122.1	73.8	80.9
1989	97.1	98.9	181.9	82.2	121.1	74.5	80.1
1990	92.6	99.2	163.9	80.3	126.4	75.6	83.5
1991	91.2	100.8	177.6	81.0	125.2	74.6	82.1
1992	89.4	94.9	186.5	77.8	120.0	72.2	84.7
1993	92.1	89.5	223.8	71.4	134.1	60.7	87.7
1994	90.4	84.0	241.3	71.7	134.4	58.1	88.5
1995	85.0	82.3	253.1	68.2	141.3	52.4	91.2
1996	89.4	83.7	219.9	69.3	137.6	57.3	91.1
1997	96.7	83.9	206.8	80.8	131.3	57.7	88.1
1998	101.4	78.9	193.8	83.5	131.6	57.5	88.6
1999	98.9	78.4	226.4	83.3	129.0	56.5	87.3
2000	102.9	79.3	252.1	86.4	123.7	54.6	84.5
2001	109.6	76.2	227.7	84.9	124.5	54.8	84.8
2002	108.5	75.5	215.9	85.2	125.8	55.3	85.5
2003	95.9	82.9	216.5	80.5	130.9	57.1	88.4
2004	88.1	87.4	220.8	83.8	133.1	57.9	89.6

Notes: The above are the nominal effective exchange rates derived from the International Monetary Fund's multilateral exchange rate model.
Source: IMF, International Financial Statistics.

rather because of what they can buy. **Table 1.8** shows the derivation of a hypothetical demand for pounds schedule with respect to changes in the exchange rate. As the pound appreciates against the dollar, that is moves from $1.60/£1 towards $2/£1, the price of the UK export to US importers increases, which leads to a lower quantity of exports and with it a reduced demand for pounds. Hence, the demand curve (D) for pounds which is depicted in **Figure** 1.4 slopes down from left to right.

In this simple model, the demand for pounds depends upon the demand for UK exports. Any factor which results in an increase in the demand for UK exports, that is column 4 in **Table 1.8** will result in an increased demand for pounds and a shift to the right of the demand curve for pounds. Among factors that result in a right-ward shift of the demand schedule for pounds are a rise in US income, a change in US tastes in favour of UK goods, and a rise in the price of US goods. All these factors would result in an increased demand for UK exports and hence pounds. The effect of an increase in the demand for pounds is to shift the demand schedule to the right.

Table 1.7   Real effective exchange rate indices, 1980–2004

	United States	Canada	Japan	United Kingdom	Germany	Italy	France
1980	100.0	100.0	100.0	100.0	100.0	100.0	100.0
1981	110.0	105.0	106.7	102.9	91.3	97.6	95.4
1982	123.1	112.1	96.8	99.3	92.9	98.8	91.1
1983	128.9	117.0	104.7	91.2	93.5	104.2	87.7
1984	136.8	114.8	109.3	87.2	89.4	105.1	86.3
1985	141.6	110.8	112.1	88.9	87.0	104.7	88.4
1986	119.0	100.2	143.7	82.7	92.1	112.1	91.6
1987	107.1	100.4	151.3	82.6	95.1	115.4	92.7
1988	100.9	105.8	161.5	89.2	92.7	114.3	90.6
1989	104.2	113.3	147.9	89.6	90.5	116.9	88.7
1990	99.8	112.0	131.4	92.6	93.3	122.4	91.8
1991	99.3	115.7	141.7	95.8	84.1	125.2	90.3
1992	97.0	106.3	146.1	92.4	88.3	121.5	91.6
1993	100.3	99.6	172.5	82.8	92.0	102.8	92.7
1994	99.2	90.7	181.5	83.1	92.3	99.8	92.4
1995	95.9	87.8	184.5	80.1	96.4	93.0	94.9
1996	100.0	89.3	155.5	81.9	93.3	103.8	94.7
1997	107.4	90.5	146.5	96.5	88.7	104.3	90.7
1998	115.0	86.5	141.1	102.5	89.2	106.7	91.0
1999	114.3	85.6	163.2	102.2	86.2	104.5	88.4
2000	119.7	87.2	175.3	105.6	81.0	100.3	84.0
2001	128.6	86.4	156.8	103.8	81.6	101.7	84.0
2002	128.1	85.7	145.5	104.5	82.7	104.0	85.3
2003	117.5	93.1	142.7	100.8	86.4	109.7	89.4
2004	112.5	97.8	145.8	106.0	85.6	109.8	89.0

Notes: The above are the real effective exchange rates derived from the International Monetary Fund's multilateral exchange rate model using consumer price indices.
Source: IMF, International Financial Statistics.

Table 1.8   The demand for pounds

Price of UK export good in £s	Exchange rate $/£	Price of UK export good in $s	Quantity of UK exports	Demand for pounds
10	$1.60/£1	16	1,800	18,000
10	$1.80/£1	18	1,500	15,000
10	$2.00/£1	20	1,200	12,000

The supply of foreign exchange

The supply of pounds is in essence the UK demand for dollars, **Table 1.9** sets out the derivation of a hypothetical supply of pounds schedule. As the pound appreciates, the cost of US exports becomes cheaper for UK residents. As such, they demand more US exports and this results in an increased demand for dollars which are purchased by

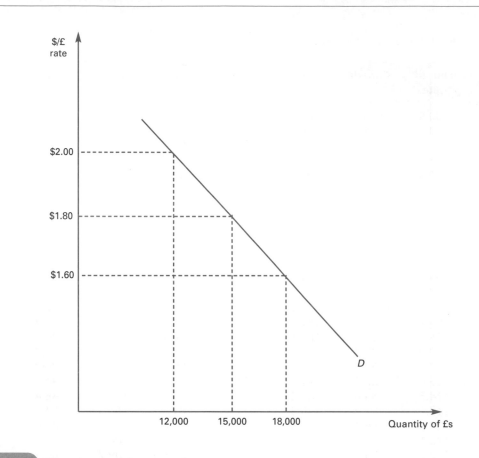

Figure 1.4   The demand for pounds

Table 1.9   The supply of pounds

Price of US export good in dollars	Exchange rate $/£	Price of US export in £s	Quantity of US exports	Demand for dollars	Supply of pounds
20	$1.60/£1	12.50	1,000	20,000	12,500
20	$1.80/£1	11.11	1,350	27,000	15,000
20	$2.00/£1	10.00	1,700	34,000	17,000

increasing the amount of pounds supplied in the foreign exchange market, and this yields an upward-sloping supply of pounds (**Figure 1.5**).

The supply of pounds schedule (S) depends upon the UK demand for US exports; its position will shift to the right if there is an increase in UK income, a change in British tastes in favour of US goods or a rise in UK prices. All these factors imply an increased demand for US goods and dollars which is reflected in an increased supply of pounds.

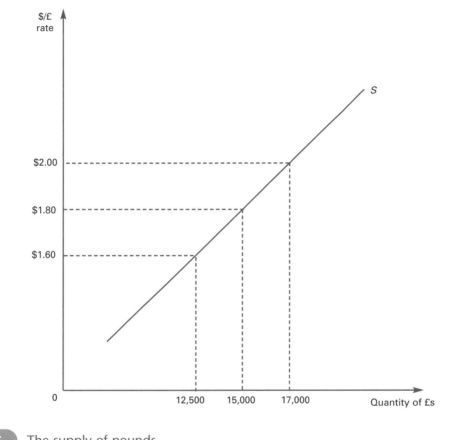

Figure 1.5   The supply of pounds

Since the exchange market is merely a market which brings together those people that wish to buy a currency (which represents the demand) with those that wish to sell the currency (which represents the supply), then the spot exchange rate can most easily be thought of as being determined by the interaction of the supply and demand for the currency. **Figure 1.6** illustrates the determination of the dollar–pound exchange rate in the context of such a supply and demand framework. The figure depicts the supply and demand for pounds in the foreign exchange market. The equilibrium exchange rate is determined by the intersection of the supply and demand curves (*S* and *D*) to yield a dollar–pound exchange of $1.80/£1. When the exchange rate is left to float freely it is determined by the interaction of the supply and demand curves.

1.8 ▎ **Alternative exchange rate regimes**

At the Bretton Woods conference of 1948 the major nations of the Western world agreed to a pegged exchange rate system, each country fixing its exchange rate against the US dollar with a small margin of fluctuation around the par value. In 1973 the

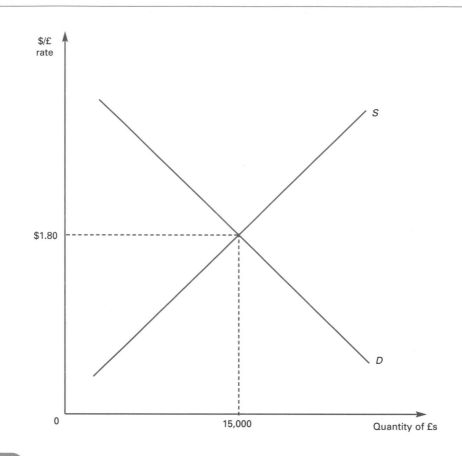

Figure 1.6   Determination of the dollar–pound exchange rate

Bretton Woods system broke down and the major currencies were left to be determined by market forces in a floating exchange rate world. The basic differences between the two regimes can be highlighted using the supply and demand framework.

Floating exchange rate regime

Under a floating exchange rate regime the authorities do not intervene to buy or sell their currency in the foreign exchange market. Rather, they allow the value of their currency to change due to fluctuations in the supply and demand of the currency. This is illustrated in **Figure 1.7**.

   In **Figure 1.7(a)** the exchange rate is initially determined by the interaction of the demand (D_1) and supply (S_1) of pounds at the exchange rate of $1.80/£1. There is an increase in the demand for UK exports which shifts the demand curve from D_1 to D_2, and this increase in the demand for pounds leads to an appreciation of the pound from $1.80/£1 to $2.00/£1. **Figure 1.7(b)** examines the impact of an increase in the supply of pounds due to an increased demand for US exports and therefore dollars. The increased supply of pounds shifts the S_1 schedule to the right to S_2 resulting in a

(a) Increase in demand   (b) Increase in supply

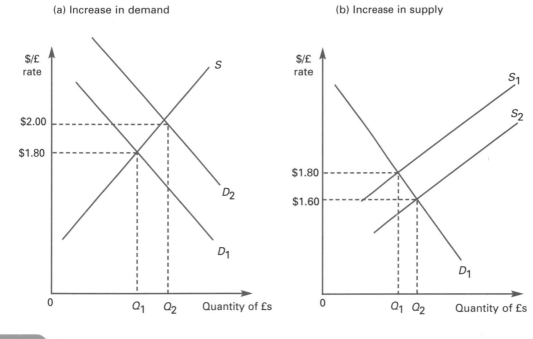

 Figure 1.7   Floating exchange rate regime

depreciation of the pound to $1.60/£1. The essence of a floating exchange rate is that the exchange rate adjusts in response to changes in the supply and demand for a currency.

Fixed exchange rate regime

In **Figure 1.8(a)** the exchange rate is assumed to be fixed by the authorities at the point where the demand schedule (D_1) intersects the supply schedule (S_1) at $1.80/£1. If there is an increase in the demand for pounds which shifts the schedule from D_1 to D_2, there is a resulting pressure for the pound to be revalued. To avert an appreciation it is necessary for the Bank of England to sell $Q_1 Q_2$ of pounds to purchase dollars in the foreign exchange market, these purchases shift the supply of pounds from S_1 to S_2. Such intervention eliminates the excess demand for pounds so that the exchange rate remains fixed at $1.80/£1. The intervention increases the Bank of England's reserves of US dollars while increasing the amount of pounds in circulation.

Figure 1.8(b) depicts an initial situation where the exchange rate is pegged by the authorities at the point where the demand schedule (D_1) intersects the supply schedule (S_1) at $1.80/£1. An increase in the supply of pounds (increased demand for US dollars) shifts the supply schedule from S_1 to S_2. The result is an excess supply of pounds at the prevailing exchange rate. This means that there will be pressure for the pound to be devalued. To avoid this, the Bank of England has to intervene in the foreign exchange market to purchase $Q_1 Q_2$ pounds to peg the

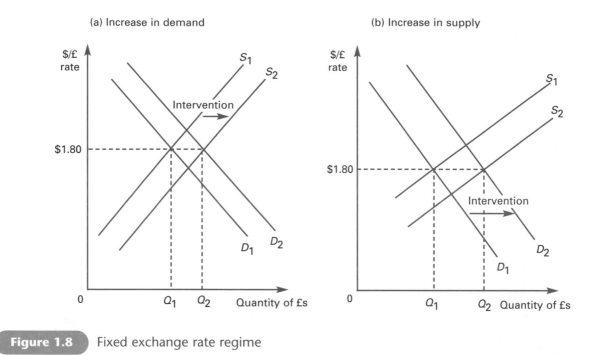

Figure 1.8 Fixed exchange rate regime

exchange rate. This intervention is represented by a rightward shift of the demand schedule from D_1 to D_2. Such intervention removes the excess supply of pounds so that the exchange rate remains pegged at $1.80/£1. The intervention leads to a fall in the Bank of England's reserves of US dollars and a fall in the amount of sterling in circulation.

1.9 The determination of the forward exchange rate

The forward exchange market is where buyers and sellers agree to exchange currencies at some specified date in the future. For example, a UK trader who has to pay $17,500 to his US supplier at the end of August may decide on 1 June to buy $17,500 dollars for delivery on 31 August of the same year at a forward exchange rate of $1.75/£1. The question that naturally arises is, why should anyone wish to agree today to exchange currencies at some specified time in the future? To answer this question we need to look at the various participants in the forward exchange market. Traditionally economic agents involved in the forward exchange market are divided into three groups, distinguished by their motives for participation in the foreign exchange market.

1   **Hedgers** are agents (usually firms) that enter the forward exchange market to protect themselves against exchange rate fluctuations which entail exchange rate risk. By exchange risk we mean the risk of loss due to adverse exchange rate movements. To illustrate why a firm may engage in a forward exchange rate transaction, consider the example of a UK importer who is due to pay for goods from the USA

to the value of $17,500 in one year's time. Let us suppose that the spot exchange rate is $1.80/£1 while the one-year forward exchange rate is $1.75/£1. By buying dollars forward at this rate the trader can be sure that he only has to pay £10,000. If he does not buy forward today, he runs the risk that in one year's time the spot exchange rate may be worse than $1.75/£1, such as $1.50/£1, which would mean him having to pay £11,667 ($17,500/1.50). Of course, the spot exchange rate in one year's time may be more favourable than $1.75/£1, such as $2/£1 in which case he would only have had to pay £8,750 ($17,500/2) which would *ex post* have been better than engaging in a forward exchange contract. However, by engaging in a forward exchange contract the trader can be sure of the amount of sterling he will have to pay for the imports, and as such he can protect himself against the risk entailed by exchange rate fluctuations.

It may be asked why the importer does not immediately buy US $17,500 dollars spot at $1.80/£1 and hold the dollars for one year. One reason is that he may not at present have the necessary funds for such a spot purchase and is reluctant to borrow the money knowing that he will have the funds in one year's time because of money from sales of goods. By engaging in a forward contract he can be sure of getting the dollars he requires at a known exchange rate even if he does not yet have the necessary sterling.

In effect, hedgers avoid exchange risk by matching their assets and liabilities in the foreign currency. In the above example, the UK importer buys $17,500 forward (his asset) and will have to pay $17,500 for the imported goods (his liability).

2 **Arbitrageurs** are agents (usually banks) that aim to make a riskless profit out of discrepancies between interest rate differentials and what is known as the forward discount or forward premium. A currency is said to be at a forward premium if the forward exchange rate quotation for that currency represents an appreciation for that currency compared to the spot quotation. Whereas a currency is said to be at a forward discount if the forward exchange rate quotation for that currency represents a depreciation for that currency compared to the spot quotation. The forward discount or premium is usually expressed as a percentage of the spot exchange rate; that is:

$$\text{Forward discount/premium} = \frac{F - S}{S} \times 100$$

where F is the forward exchange rate quotation and S is the spot exchange rate quotation.

The presence of arbitrageurs ensures that what is known as the **covered interest parity** (CIP) condition holds continually – the covered interest parity condition is the formula used by banks to calculate their forward exchange quotation and is given by:

$$F = \frac{(r^* - r)S}{(1 + r)} + S \tag{1.1}$$

where F is the one-year forward exchange rate quotation in foreign currency per unit of domestic currency, S is the spot exchange rate quotation in foreign currency per unit of domestic currency, r is the one-year domestic interest rate and r^* is the one-year foreign interest rate.

Table 1.10 The $/£ forward exchange quotations and UK and US interest rates, 11 August 2004

	Dollar–pound exchange rate	Sterling eurocurrency interest rate	Dollar eurocurrency interest rate
Spot rate	1.8277		
1 month	1.8228	4.8125	1.59375
3 month	1.8132	4.9375	1.71875
6 Month	1.7998	5.0625	1.93750
12 month	1.7761	5.2500	2.28125

Notes:
The spot sterling exchange rate is 1.8227 dollars per pound.

The one-month forward exchange rate is calculated as:

$$\frac{[(0.0159375 - 0.048125)/12]}{[1 + (0.048125/12)]} 1.8277 + 1.8277 = \$1.8228/£1$$

The three-month forward exchange rate is calculated as:

$$\frac{[(0.0171875 - 0.049375)/4]}{[1 + (0.049375/4)]} 1.8277 + 1.8277 = \$1.8132/£1$$

The six-month forward exchange rate is calculated as:

$$\frac{[(0.019375 - 0.050625)/2]}{[1 + (0.050625/2)]} 1.8277 + 1.8277 = \$1.7988/£1$$

The one-year forward exchange rate is calculated as:

$$\frac{[(0.0228125 - 0.0525)]}{[1 + 0.0525])} 1.8277 + 1.8277 = \$1.7761/£1$$

Source: *Financial Times*, 12 August 2004.

The above formula has to be amended by dividing the three-month interest rates by four to calculate the three-month forward exchange rate quotation, and by dividing the six-month interest rates by two to calculate the six-month forward exchange rate. **Table 1.10** shows how the calculation works in practice using the dollar–sterling exchange rate and data from the *Financial Times*.

Numerical Example

Calculation of the forward exchange rate
Suppose that the one-year dollar interest rate is 5%, the sterling interest rate is 8% and the spot rate of the dollar against the pound is $1.80/£1. Then the one-year forward exchange rate of the pound is:

$$F = \frac{(0.05 - 0.08)}{1.08} 1.80 + 1.80 = \$1.75/£1$$

and

$$\frac{F-S}{S} = \frac{1.75 - 1.80}{1.80} \times 100 = -2.78$$

so that the one-year forward rate of sterling is at an annualized forward discount of 2.78%.

To understand why CIP must be used to calculate the forward exchange rate, consider what would happen if the forward rate was different to that calculated in the example; say it was $1.90/£1. In this instance, a US investor with $100 could earn the US interest rate and at the end of the year have $105, but by buying pounds spot (at $1.80/£1) and simultaneously selling pounds forward (at $1.90) he would have £55.55 earning the UK interest rate of 8% giving him £60.00 (£55.55 × 1.08) at the end of one year, which he would sell at a forward price of $1.90/£1 giving $114.00. Clearly, it pays a US investor to sell pounds forward. With a sufficient numbers of investors doing this, the forward rate of the pound would depreciate until such arbitrage possibilities were eliminated. With a spot rate of $1.80/£1, only if the forward rate is at $1.75/£1 will the guaranteed yields in US and UK time deposits be identical, since £60 times $1.75 equals $105. Only at this forward exchange rate are there no riskless arbitrage profits to be made.

Since the denominator in equation (1.1) is typically very close to unity, the equation can be simplified to yield an approximate expression for the forward premium/discount:

$$\frac{F-S}{S} \approx r^* - r \tag{1.2}$$

This approximate version of CIP says that if the domestic interest rate is higher than the foreign interest rate, then the domestic currency will be at a forward discount by an equivalent percentage. While if the domestic interest rate is lower than the foreign interest rate the currency will be at a forward premium by an equivalent percentage. In our example, the US interest rate of 5% less the UK interest rate of 8% indicates an annual forward discount on the pound of 3%, which is an approximation to the actual 2.78% discount obtained using the full CIP formula.

3 **Speculators** are agents that hope to make a profit by accepting exchange rate risk. Speculators engage in the forward exchange market because they believe that the future spot rate corresponding to the date of the quoted forward exchange rate will be different to the quoted forward rate. Consider, if the one-year forward rate is quoted at $1.75/£1 and a speculator feels that the spot rate will be $1.60/£1 in one year's time, in this instance he may sell £1,000 forward at $1.75/£1 to obtain $1,750 and hope to change the dollars back into pounds in one year's time at $1.60/£1 to obtain £1,093.75, making £93.75 profit. Of course, the speculator may be wrong and finds that in one-year's time the spot exchange rate is above $1.75/£1, say $1.90/£1 in which case his $1,750 are worth £921.05 implying a loss of £78.95. A speculator hopes to make money by taking an 'open position' in the

foreign currency. In our example, he has a forward asset in dollars which is not matched by a corresponding liability of equal value.

1.10 The interaction of hedgers, arbitrageurs and speculators

The forward exchange rate is determined by the interaction of traders, hedgers and speculators. One of the conditions that must hold in the forward exchange market is that for every forward purchase there must be a forward sale of the currency so that the excess demand for the currency sums to zero:

$$NDH + NDA + NDS = 0$$

where NDH is the net demand of hedgers, NDA is the net demand of arbitrageurs and NDS is the net demand of speculators.

The forward exchange rate and volume of forward transactions is determined jointly by the actions of arbitrageurs traders and speculators and is jointly determined with the spot exchange rate. This is illustrated in **Figure 1.9** that depicts the simultaneous determination of the spot and forward exchange rates. **Figure 1.9(a)** shows the supply and demand situation in the spot market, and **Figure 1.9(b)** the supply and demand schedules in the forward market. The AA schedule reflects the forward exchange rate consistent with CIP. In effect, this is the net supply and demand of forward exchange of arbitrageurs for a given interest differential. Since the pound is at a forward discount, the interest rate in the UK is above that in the USA.

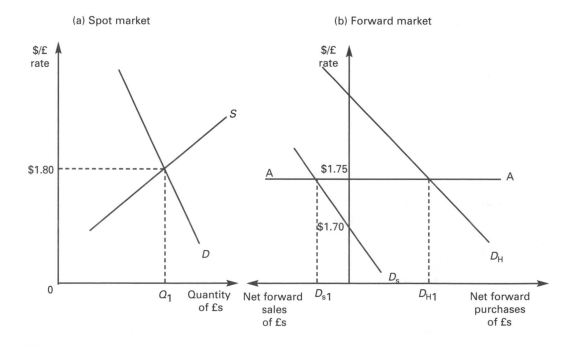

Figure 1.9 The joint determination of the spot and forward exchange rate

The D_H schedule is the *net* demand for pounds of hedgers in the forward exchange market, as the pound depreciates in the forward market then hedgers' net demand for pounds rises.

The D_s schedule is the demand schedule for forward exchange of speculators, it cuts the vertical axis at $1.70 per pound. This means that $1.70 represents the average forecast of speculators since at this rate speculators would be neither net purchasers or sellers of forward pounds. However, because speculators on average expect the pound to depreciate more than is indicated by the forward exchange rate, they are net sellers of pounds forward if the rate is above $1.70/£1 (because they expect to be able to buy pounds in the future at a better rate than they sold them) and net purchasers of pounds forward if the rate is below $1.70/£1 (because they expect to be able to sell in the future at a better rate than they purchased them).

At the end of the day the arbitrage formula as given by CIP is crucial to the forward rate which is determined along the arbitrage schedule AA at $1.75/£1. At this rate, hedgers happen to be net purchasers of pounds given by D_{H1} while speculators happen to be net sellers of pounds given by D_{S1}. Since the net purchases of hedgers exceed the net sales of speculators, then there is pressure for the forward rate to rise above $1.75/£1, which induces arbitrageurs to be net sellers of pounds forward (constituting net sales equal to $D_{H1} - D_{S1}$) so as to clear the forward exchange market.

Speculators are at work in both the spot and forward exchange markets; if they decide that the current spot rate is overvalued they may sell spot so that the currency depreciates, if interest rates do not change then both the spot and forward exchange rates depreciate. Similarly, if speculators feel that the currency is overvalued forward then they will sell forward and both the forward and spot exchange quotations will depreciate. Hence, arbitrage ties the spot and forward exchange market quotations together via the CIP condition. Speculation and hedging may be thought of as determining the level of the spot and forward exchange quotations.

1.11 Conclusions

The need for a foreign exchange market arises because international trade in goods/services and financial assets almost always involves the exchange of differing national currencies. Were the world economy to have a single currency, then a foreign exchange market would not exist. The modern foreign exchange market is truly a global market and is characterized by a huge volume of daily transactions.

Much of the topic of international finance is about the forces that determine exchange rate movements and on the implications of these movements for trade and economic growth and the development of the world economy. When conducting an economic analysis of the effects of exchange rate changes, it proves useful to distinguish between the real and nominal exchange rates and between bilateral and effective exchange rates, depending upon the purpose of the particular analysis being undertaken.

Governments are not indifferent to movements in the value of their currencies in the foreign exchange market, and on occasions they intervene in an attempt to influence the rate of exchange at which their currencies are traded. Indeed, many governments have for various reasons decided to peg their exchange rates, such as the Hong Kong dollar and Chinese renminbi both of which are tied to the US dollar. However, in July 2005 the Chinese announced a scheme whereby the US dollar peg would be changed to targeting the exchange rate of the renminbi against a basket of foreign currencies.

Although exchange rates may move quite substantially at times, this is not necessarily disruptive to international trade as companies can protect themselves against exchange risk by hedging in the forward exchange market. For many countries, the depreciation or devaluation of their currencies is an important mechanism for maintaining their international competitiveness and trade volumes.

Further reading and resources

Pilbeam, K.S. (2005) *Finance and Financial Markets* (Basingstoke: Palgrave Macmillan).

Shamah, S. and Shamah, S.A. (2003) *Foreign Exchange Primer* (New York: Wiley).

Walmsley, J. (2000) *The Foreign Exchange and Money Markets Guide*, 2nd edn (New York: Wiley).

2

The Balance of Payments

2.1 Introduction

In this chapter we look at one of the most important economic indicators for policy-makers in an open economy, namely, the balance of payments. What is happening to a country's balance of payments often captures the news headlines and can become the focus of attention. A good or bad set of figures can have an influential effect on the exchange rate and can lead policy-makers to change the content of their economic policies. Deficits may lead to the government raising interest rates or reducing public expenditure to reduce expenditure on imports. Alternatively, deficits may lead to calls for protection against foreign imports or capital controls to defend the exchange rate.

Before considering various policy options that may be devised to deal with perceived problems in the balance of payments, we need to consider in some detail exactly what the balance of payments figures are and what is meant by the notion of a balance of payments surplus or deficit. In this chapter, we shall look at what is contained in the balance of payments statistics, how they are compiled and at various possible economic interpretations of the statistics. We also look at how the current account of the balance of payments can be interpreted within the framework of the national income accounts and the effects of changes in governments' expenditure and exports on the balance of payments.

2.2　What is the balance of payments?

The balance of payments is a statistical record of all the economic transactions between residents of the reporting country and residents of the rest of the world during a given time period. The usual reporting period for all the statistics included in the accounts is a year. However, some of the statistics that make up the balance of payments are published on a more regular monthly and quarterly basis. Without question the balance of payments is one of the most important statistical statements for any country. It reveals how many goods and services the country has been exporting and importing and whether the country has been borrowing from or lending money to the rest of the world. In addition, whether or not the central monetary authority (usually the central bank) has added to or reduced its reserves of foreign currency is reported in the statistics.

A key definition that needs to be resolved at the outset is that of a domestic and foreign resident. It is important to note that citizenship and residency are not necessarily the same thing from the viewpoint of the balance of payments statistics. The term residents comprises individuals, households, firms and the public authorities. There are some problems that arise with respect to the definition of a resident, for example multinational corporations are by definition resident in more than one country. For the purposes of balance of payments reporting, the subsidiaries of a multinational are treated as being a resident in the country in which they are located even if their shares are actually owned by domestic residents. Another problem concerns the treatment of international organizations such as the International Monetary Fund, the World Bank, United Nations, the European Commission and so forth. These institutions are treated as being foreign residents even though they may actually be located in the reporting country. For example, although the International Monetary Fund is located in Washington, contributions by the US government to the Fund are included in the US balance of payments statistics because they are regarded as transactions with a foreign resident. Tourists are regarded as being foreign residents if they stay in the reporting country for less than a year.

The criterion for a transaction to be included in the balance of payments is that it must involve a transaction between a resident of the reporting country and a resident from the rest of the world. Purchases and sales between residents from the same country are excluded.

2.3　Collection, reporting and presentation of the balance of payments statistics

The balance of payments statistics record all of the transactions between domestic and foreign residents, be they purchases or sales of goods, services or of financial assets such as bonds, equities and banking transactions. Reported figures are normally in the domestic currency of the reporting country. Obviously, collecting statistics on every transaction between domestic and foreign residents is an impossible task. The authorities collect their information from the customs authorities, surveys of tourist numbers and expenditures, and data on capital inflows and outflows are obtained from banks, pension funds, multinationals and investment houses. Information on government expenditures and receipts with foreign residents is obtained from local authorities and central government agencies. The statistics are based on reliable sampling techniques but nevertheless, given the variety of sources, the figures provide only an estimate of the actual transactions. The responses from the various sources are compiled by government statistical agencies. In the United States, the statistics are compiled by the US Department of Commerce and in the United Kingdom by the Department of Trade and Industry.

There is no unique method governing the presentation of balance of payments statistics and there can be considerable variations in the presentations of different national authorities. However, the International Monetary Fund provides a set of guidelines for the compilation of balance of payments statistics published in its Balance of Payments manual. In addition, the Fund publishes the balance of payments statistics of all its member countries in a standardized format facilitating inter-country comparisons. These are presented in two publications – the *Balance of Payments Statistics Yearbook* and the *International Financial Statistics*.

In the USA, the value of exports and imports is compiled on a monthly basis and likewise in the UK. The monthly figures are subject to later revision and two sets of statistics are published; the seasonally adjusted figure and the unadjusted figure. The seasonally adjusted figures correct the balance of payments figures for the effect of seasonal factors which influence the balance of payments to reveal underlying trends.

2.4 Balance of payments accounting and accounts

An important point about a country's balance of payments statistics is that in an accounting sense it always balances. This is because it is based upon the principle of double-entry bookkeeping. Each transaction between a domestic and foreign resident has two sides to it, a receipt and a payment, and both of these are recorded in the balance of payments statistics. Each receipt of currency from residents of the rest of the world is recorded as a credit item (a plus in the accounts), while each payment to residents of the rest of the world is recorded as a debit (a minus in the accounts).

Before considering some examples of how different types of economic transactions between domestic and foreign residents get recorded in the balance of payments, we need to consider the various sub-accounts that make up the balance of payments. Traditionally, the statistics are divided into two main sections – the current account and the capital account with each part being further sub-divided. The reason for dividing the balance of payments into these two main parts is that the current account items refer to income flows, while the capital account records changes in assets and liabilities. A simplified example of the annual balance of payments accounts for Europa is presented in **Table 2.1**.

Table 2.1 Balance of payments of Europa (€ millions)

Current Account			
(1)	Exports of goods	+ 150	
(2)	Imports of goods	– 200	
(3)	**Trade Balance**	**– 50**	sum rows (1) + (2)
(4)	Exports of services	+ 120	
(5)	Imports of services	– 160	
(6)	Interest, profits and dividends received	+ 20	
(7)	Interest, profits and dividends paid	– 10	
(8)	Unilateral receipts	+ 30	
(9)	Unilateral payments	– 20	
(10)	**Current account balance**	**– 70**	sum (3) to (9) inclusive
Capital Account			
(11)	Investment Abroad	– 30	
(12)	Short term lending	– 60	
(13)	Medium and long term lending	– 80	
(14)	Repayment of borrowing to ROW	– 70	
(15)	Inward Foreign investment	+ 170	
(16)	Short term borrowing	+ 40	
(17)	Medium and long term borrowing	+ 30	
(18)	Repayments on loans received from ROW	+ 50	
(19)	**Capital account balance**	**+ 50**	sum (11) to (18)inclusive
(20)	Statistical error	+ 5	zero minus [(10) + (19) + (24)]
(21)	**Official settlements balance**	**–15**	sum (10) + (19) + (20)
(22)	Change in reserves rise (–), fall (+)	+ 10	
(23)	IMF borrowing from (+) repayments to (–)	+ 5	
(24)	**Official financing balance**	**+ 15**	(22) + (23)

Notes: ROW stands for rest of the world. The official financing balance is equal in magnitude but opposite in sign to the official settlements balance.

2.5 An overview of the sub-accounts in the balance of payments

The trade balance

The trade balance is sometimes referred to as the visible balance because it represents the difference between receipts for exports of goods and expenditure on imports of goods which can be visibly seen crossing frontiers. The receipts for exports are recorded as a credit in the balance of payments, while the payment for imports is recorded as a debit. When the trade balance is in surplus this means that country has earned more from its exports of goods than it has paid for its imports of goods.

The current account balance

The current account balance is the sum of the visible trade balance and the invisible balance. The invisible balance shows the difference between revenue received for exports of services and payments made for imports of services such as shipping, tourism, insurance, banking. In addition, receipts and payments of interest, dividends and profits are recorded in the invisible balance because they represent the rewards for investment in overseas companies, bonds and equity, while payments reflect the rewards to foreign residents for their investment in the domestic economy. As such, they are receipts and payments for the services of capital that earn and cost the country income just as do exports and imports.

The reader will note that there is an item referred to as unilateral transfers included in the invisible balance; these are payments or receipts for which there is no corresponding quid pro quo. Examples of such transactions are migrant workers' remittances to their families back home, the payment of pensions to foreign residents, and foreign aid. Such receipts and payments represent a redistribution of income between domestic and foreign residents. Unilateral payments can be viewed as a fall in domestic income due to payments to foreigners and so are recorded as a debit, while unilateral receipts can be viewed as an increase in income due to receipts from foreigners and consequently are recorded as a credit.

The capital account balance

The capital account records transactions concerning the movement of financial capital into and out of the country. Capital comes into the country by borrowing, sales of overseas assets and investment in the country by foreigners. These items are referred to as capital inflows and are recorded as credit items in the balance of payments. **Capital inflows are, in effect, a decrease in the country's holding of foreign assets or an increase in liabilities to foreigners**. The fact that capital inflows are recorded as credits in the balance of payments often presents students with difficulty. The easiest way to understand why they are pluses is to think of foreign borrowing as the export of an IOU. Similarly, investment by foreign residents is the export of equity or bonds, while sales of overseas investments is an export of those investments to foreigners. Conversely, capital leaves the country due to lending, buying of overseas assets and purchases of domestic assets owned by foreign residents. These items represent capital outflows and are recorded as debits in the capital account. **Capital outflows are, in effect, an increase in the country's holding of foreign assets or a decrease in liabilities to foreigners**. These items are recorded as debits as they represent the purchase of an IOU from foreigners, the purchase of foreign bonds or equity and the purchase of investments in the foreign economy.

Items in the capital account are normally distinguished according to whether they originate from the private or public sector and whether they are of a short-term or long-term nature. The summation of the capital inflows and outflows as recorded in the capital account gives the capital account balance.

Official settlements balance

Given the huge statistical problems involved in compiling the balance of payments statistics, there will usually be a discrepancy between the sum all the items recorded in the current account, capital account and the balance of official financing (see below) which in theory should sum to zero. To ensure that the credits and debits are equal it is necessary to incorporate a **statistical discrepancy** for any difference between the sum of credits and debits. There are several possible sources of this error. One of the most important is that it is an impossible task to keep track of all the transactions between domestic and foreign residents; many of the reported statistics are based on sampling estimates derived from separate sources, so that some error is unavoidable. Another problem is that the desire to avoid taxes means that some of the transactions in the capital account are underreported. Moreover some dishonest firms may deliberately under-invoice their exports and over-invoice their imports so as to artificially deflate their profits. Another problem is one of 'leads and lags'. The balance of payments records receipts and payments for a transaction between domestic and foreign residents, but it can happen that a good is imported but the payment delayed. Since the import is recorded by the customs authorities and the payment by the banks, the time discrepancy may mean that the two sides of the transaction are not recorded in the same set of figures.

The summation of the current account balance, capital account balance and the statistical discrepancy gives the official settlements balance. The balance on this account is important because it shows the money available for adding to the country's official reserves or paying off the country's official borrowing. A central bank normally holds a stock of reserves made up of foreign currency assets, principally US treasury bonds (the US authorities hold mainly euro and yen treasury bonds). Such reserves are held primarily to enable the central bank to purchase its currency should it wish to prevent it depreciating. Any official settlements deficit has to be covered by the authorities drawing on the reserves, or borrowing money from foreign central banks or the IMF (recorded as a plus in the accounts). If, on the other hand, there is an official settlements surplus then this can be reflected by the government increasing official reserves or repaying debts to the IMF or other sources overseas (a minus since money leaves the country).

The fact that reserve increases are recorded as a minus, while reserve falls are recorded as a plus in the balance of payments statistics is usually a source of confusion. It is most easily rationalized by thinking that reserves increase when the authorities have been purchasing the foreign currency because the domestic currency is strong. This implies that the other items in the balance of payments are in surplus, so reserve increases have to be recorded as a debit to ensure overall balance. Conversely, reserves fall when the authorities have been supporting a currency that is weak, that is, all other items sum to a deficit so reserve falls must be recorded as a plus to ensure overall balance.

2.6 Recording of transactions in the balance of payments

To understand exactly why the sum of credits and debits in the balance of payments should sum to zero we consider some examples of economic transactions between domestic and foreign residents. There are basically five types of economic transactions that can take place between domestic and foreign residents:

1   An exchange of good/services in return for a financial asset.
2   An exchange of goods/services in return for other goods/services. Such trade is known as barter or countertrade.
3   An exchange of a financial item in return for a financial item.
4   A transfer of goods or services with no corresponding *quid pro quo* (for example military and food aid).
5   A transfer of financial assets with no corresponding *quid pro quo* (for example, migrant workers remittances to their families abroad, a money gift).

We now look at how each transaction is recorded twice, once as a credit and once as a debit. **Table 2.2** considers various types of transactions between US and UK residents and shows how each transaction is recorded in each of the two countries' balance of payments. The exchange rate for all transactions is assumed to be $2/£1.

The examples in **Table 2.2** illustrate in a simplified manner the double-entry nature of balance of payments statistics. Since each credit in the accounts has a corresponding debit elsewhere, the sum of all items should be equal to zero. This naturally raises the question as to what is meant by a balance of payments deficit or surplus?

Table 2.2 Examples of balance of payments accounting

Example 1 Boeing of the United States exports a $100 million aircraft to the United Kingdom which is paid for by British Airways debiting its US bank deposit account by a like amount.

US balance of payments current account		UK balance of payments current account	
Exports of goods	+$100m	Import of goods	−£50m
Capital account		**Capital account**	
Reduced US bank liabilities to UK residents	−$100m	Reduction in US bank deposit assets	+£50m

Example 2 The US exports $2,000 of goods to the UK in exchange for $2,000 of services.

US balance of payments current account		UK balance of payments current account	
Merchandise exports	$2,000	Exports of services	£1,000
Imports of services	−$2,000	Imports of goods	−£1,000

Example 3 A US investor decides to buy £500 of UK Treasury bonds and to pay for them by debiting his US bank account and crediting the account of the UK Treasury held in New York.

US balance of payments capital account		UK balance of payments capital account	
Increase in UK treasury bond holdings	−$1000	Increased bond liabilities to US residents	£500
Increased in US bank liabilities	+$1000	Increased US bank deposit	−£500

Example 4 The US makes a gift of £1 million of goods to a UK charitable organization.

US current account		UK current account	
Exports	$2m	Imports	−£1m
Unilateral payment	−$2m	Unilateral receipt	+£1m

Example 5 The US pays interest, profits and dividends to UK investors of $100 million by debiting US bank accounts which are then credited to UK residents' bank accounts held in the US.

US current account		UK current account	
Interest, profits, dividends paid	−$100m	Interest, profits, dividends received	+£50m
US capital account		**UK capital account**	
Increased US bank liabilities	+$100m	Increase in US bank deposits	−£50m

2.7 What is meant by a balance of payments surplus or deficit?

As we have seen in **Table 2.2**, the balance of payments always balances since each credit in the account has a corresponding debit elsewhere. However, while the overall balance of payments always balances this does not mean that each of the individual accounts that make up the balance of payments is necessarily in balance. For instance, the current account can be in surplus while the capital account is in deficit. When talking about a balance of payments deficit or surplus economists are really saying that a subset of items in the balance of payments are in surplus or deficit.

When referring to a balance of payments deficit or surplus economists make a distinction between autonomous (above the line items) and accommodating (below the line) items. The autonomous items are transactions that take place independently of the balance of payments, whilst the accommodating items are those transactions which finance any difference between autonomous receipts or payments. A surplus in the balance of payments is defined as an excess of autonomous receipts over autonomous payments, while a deficit is an excess of autonomous payments over autonomous receipts.

Autonomous receipts > Autonomous payments = Surplus
Autonomous receipts < Autonomous payments = Deficit

The issue that then arises is which specific items in the balance of payments should be classified as autonomous and which as accommodating. Disagreement on which items qualify as autonomous leads to alternative views on what constitutes a balance of payments surplus or deficit. The difficulty over classifying items as autonomous or accommodating arises because it is not easy to identify the motive underlying a transaction. For example, if there is a short-term capital inflow in response to a higher domestic interest rate, it should be classified as an autonomous item. If, however, the item is an inflow to enable the financing of imports then it should be classified as an accommodating item. The difficulty of deciding which items should be classified as accommodating and autonomous items has led to several concepts of balance of payments disequilibrium. We shall now review some of the most important of these concepts and consider their usefulness as economic indicators.

2.8 Alternative concepts of surplus and deficits

The trade account and current account

These two accounts derive much of their importance because estimates are published on a monthly basis by most developed countries. Since the current account balance is concerned with both visibles and invisibles it is generally considered to be the more important of the two accounts. What really makes a current account surplus or deficit important is that a surplus means that the country as a whole is increasing its stock of claims on the rest of the world; while a deficit means that the country is reducing its net claims on the rest of the world. Furthermore, as we shall see in Chapter 3, the current account can readily be incorporated into economic analysis of an open economy. More generally, the current account is likely to quickly pick up changes in other economic variables such as changes in the real exchange rate, domestic and foreign economic growth and relative price inflation.

The basic balance

This is the current account balance plus the net balance on long-term capital flows. The basic balance was considered to be particularly important during the 1950s and 1960s period of fixed exchange rates because it was viewed as bringing together the stable elements in the balance of payments. It was argued that any significant change in the basic balance must be a sign of a fundamental change in the direction of the balance of payments. The more volatile elements such as short-term capital flows and changes in official reserves were regarded as below-the-line items.

Although a worsening of the basic balance is supposed to be a sign of a worsening economic situation, having an overall basic balance deficit is not necessarily a bad thing. For example, a country may have a current account deficit that is reinforced by a large long-term capital outflow so that the basic balance is in a large deficit. However, the capital outflow will yield future profits, dividends and interest receipts that will help to generate future surpluses on the current account. Conversely, a surplus in the basic balance is not necessarily a good thing. A current account deficit which is more than covered by a net capital inflow so that the basic balance is in surplus could be open to two interpretations. It might be argued that because the country is able to borrow long-run that there is nothing to worry about since the country is regarded as viable by those foreigners who are prepared to lend money long-run to the country. Another interpretation could argue that the basic balance surplus is a problem because the long-term borrowing will lead to future interest, profits and dividend payments which will worsen the current account deficit.

Apart from interpretation, the principal problem with the basic balance concerns the classification of short and long-term capital flows. The usual means of classifying long-term loans or borrowing is that they be of at least 12 months to maturity. However, many long-term capital flows can be easily converted into short-term flows if need be. For example, the purchase of a five-year US treasury bond by a UK investor would be classified as a long-term capital outflow in the UK balance of payments, and as a long-term capital inflow in the US balance of payments. However, the UK investor could very easily sell the bond back to US investors any time before its maturity date. Similarly, many short-term items with less than 12 months to maturity automatically get renewed so that they effectively become long-term assets. Another problem that blurs the distinction between short-term and long-term capital flows is that transactions in financial assets are classified in accordance with their original maturity date. Hence, if after four and a half years a UK investor sells his five-year US treasury bond to a US citizen it will be classified as a long-term capital flow even though the bond has only six months to maturity.

The official settlements balance

The official settlements balance focuses on the operations that the monetary authorities have to undertake to finance any imbalance in the current and capital accounts. With the settlements concept, the autonomous items are all the current and capital account transactions including errors, while the accommodating items are those transactions that the monetary authorities have undertaken as indicated by the balance of official financing. The current account and capital account items are all regarded as being induced by independent households, firms, central and local government and are regarded as the autonomous items. If the sum of the current and capital accounts is negative, the country can be regarded as being in deficit as this has to be financed by the authorities drawing on their reserves of foreign currency, borrowing from foreign monetary authorities or the International Monetary Fund.

The official settlements concept of a surplus or deficit is not as relevant to countries that have floating exchange rates as it is to those with fixed exchange rates. This is because if exchange rates are left to float freely the official settlements balance will tend to zero because the central authorities neither purchase or sell their currency and so there will be no changes in their reserves. If the sales of a currency exceed the purchases, then the currency will depreciate and if sales are less than purchases the currency appreciates. The settlements concept is, however, very important under fixed exchange rates because it shows the amount of pressure on the authorities to devalue or revalue the currency. Under a fixed exchange rate system a country that is running an official settlements deficit will find that sales of its currency exceed purchases, and to avert a devaluation of the currency authorities have to sell reserves of foreign currency to purchase the home currency. Whereas, under floating exchange rates and no intervention the official settlements balance automatically tends to zero as the authorities do not buy or sell the home currency since it is left to appreciate or depreciate.

Even in a fixed exchange rate regime the settlements concept ignores the fact that the authorities have other instruments available with which to defend the exchange rate such as capital controls and interest rates. Also, it does not reveal the real threat to the domestic currency and official reserves represented by the liquid liabilities held by domestic and foreign residents that might switch suddenly out of the currency.

Although in 1973 the major industrialized countries switched from a fixed to floating exchange rate system, many developing countries continue to peg their exchange rate to the US dollar and consequently attach much significance to the settlements balance. Indeed, to the extent that industrialized countries continue to intervene in the foreign exchange market to influence the value of their currencies, the settlements balance retains some significance and news about changes in the reserves of the authorities is of interest to foreign exchange dealers as a guide to the amount of official intervention in the foreign exchange market.

The IMF provides an annual summary of the balance of payments statistics using these alternative concepts of balance of payments disequilibrium, and balance of payments statistics for the seven major industrialized nations in 2002 are presented in **Table 2.3**. **Table 2.4** summarizes the key balance of payments concepts.

Having looked at the balance of statistics we now proceed to analyse the record US balance of payment deficits and how the current account is an integral part of the national income accounts. We also examine the impact of changes in government expenditure and exports upon both the economy and the current account.

2.9 Do the record United States current account deficits matter?

Since 1982 the United States current account has moved from a position of a small surplus to ever-increasing deficits both in absolute terms and as a percentage of gross domestic product. The plain fact is that for close to 25 years the United States' economy as a whole has been consistently spending abroad more than it has been earning from abroad; the country as a whole also spending more than it has been producing and making up the difference by borrowing from abroad. The ever-increasing size of

Table 2.3 IMF balance of payments summary: the United States, Japan, Germany, France, Italy, Canada and the United Kingdom, 2002 (US$ billions)

	USA	Japan	Germany	France	Italy	Canada	UK
A Current Account	**-480.86**	**112.45**	**46.59**	**25.74**	**-6.74**	**14.91**	**-14.41**
Merchandise exports (f.o.b)	685.38	395.58	615.02	305.62	253.68	264.08	279.33
Merchandise imports (f.o.b)	-1,164.76	-301.75	-492.84	-296.63	-237.15	-227.24	-332.38
Balance on Goods	-479.38	93.83	122.18	8.99	16.53	36.84	-53.05
Exports Services	288.72	65.71	106.00	86.74	60.25	37.20	125.46
Imports Services	-227.38	-107.94	-150.49	-68.95	-63.54	-42.48	-104.25
Income credit (IPD)	255.54	91.48	103.26	80.75	43.30	20.17	185.55
Income debit (IPD)	-259.51	-25.71	-109.26	-67.93	-57.85	-37.69	-154.30
Current transfers credit	11.50	10.04	15.83	20.39	20.87	4.46	16.85
Current transfers debit	-70.35	-14.96	-40.94	-34.25	-26.31	-3.59	-30.68
B Capital and Financial Account	**530.39**	**-66.70**	**-77.31**	**-33.54**	**11.93**	**-8.62**	**13.39**
Capital account credit/debit	-1.29	-3.32	-0.23	-0.18	0.74	3.07	1.68
Direct investment abroad	-137.84	-32.02	-25.30	-62.73	-17.25	-28.86	-7.46
Direct investment in the nation	39.63	9.09	37.30	52.02	14.70	20.50	28.19
Portfolio investment assets	15.80	-85.93	-63.32	-77.37	-15.26	-15.84	2.46
Portfolio investment liabilities	421.44	-20.04	98.70	61.32	32.93	13.45	92.11
Financial Derivatives	...	2.48	-0.79	5.33	-2.71	...	17.91
Other investment assets	-53.27	36.41	-151.21	-36.08	4.16	-6.90	-202.93
Other investment liabilities	245.91	26.63	27.55	24.15	-5.38	5.96	81.44
C Net errors and omissions	**-45.84**	**0.39**	**28.74**	**3.83**	**-2.02**	**6.47**	**0.39**
D Official Settlements Balance	**3.69**	**46.13**	**-1.98**	**-3.97**	**3.17**	**-0.18**	**-0.63**
E Reserves and related items	**-3.69**	**-46.13**	**1.98**	**3.97**	**-3.17**	**0.18**	**0.63**
Reserve assets	-3.69	-46.13	1.98	3.97	-3.17	0.18	0.63
Use of IMF credit and loans	...	...	...	...	...	...	...
Exceptional Financing	...	...	...	...	...	...	...

Note: Other investment is mainly short-term.
Source: International Monetary Fund, *Balance of Payments Yearbook* (Washington DC: IMF, 2003).

Table 2.4   Summary of key balance of payments concepts

Trade Balance
+ Exports of goods
– Imports of goods
= Trade balance

Current Account
Trade balance
+ Exports of services
+ Interest, dividends and profits received
+ Unilateral receipts
– Imports of services
– Interest, dividends and profits paid
– Unilateral payments abroad
= Current account balance

Basic Balance
Current account balance
+ Balance on long-term capital account
= Basic balance

Official Settlements Balance
Current account balance
+ Balance on capital account
+ Statistical error
= Official settlements balance

Table 2.5   United States current account

	1990	1992	1994	1996	1998	1999	2000	2001	2002	2003	2004	2005
Billions of dollars	–79	–48	–118	–120	–210	–297	–413	–385	–473	–530	–669	–761
As a % of GDP	–1.4	–0.8	–1.7	–1.5	–2.4	–3.2	–4.2	–3.8	–4.5	–4.8	–5.7	–6.2

Source: OECD *Economic Outlook*; the 2004 figure is a provisional estimate, and that for 2005 is a forecast value.

the current account deficits and their significance and sustainability has provoked an intense debate between economists about the desirability and sustainability of these deficits. As can be seen in **Table 2.5**, the size of these deficits has widened dramatically in recent years both in absolute terms and as a percentage of GDP.

In 1982 the United States was the world's biggest creditor nation, but is now the world's biggest debtor nation, its net international investment position (NIIP) at the end of 2004 being a negative $3.3 trillion or around 28% of US GDP, up from only 5% of GDP in 1997 and now standing at around 290% of the annual value of US exports (see **Table 2.6**). The NIIP is the stock of accumulated foreign claims on the USA (debt and equity) minus the stock of US claims on the rest of the world, since the US position is negative, claims of the rest of the world on the USA exceed US holdings of foreign assets.

Table 2.6 United States net international investment position (NIIP)

	1982	1985	1990	1995	2000	2001	2002	2003	2004
NIIP $billions	+236	+97	−165	−306	−1589	−2314	−2553	−2651	−3320
NIIP % GDP	7.3	2.3	−4.6	−4.1	−16.2	−22.9	−24.4	−24.1	−28.4
NIIP % exports	83	32	−48	−38	−145	−231	−262	−260	−291

Note: The reported NIIP is measured at market values.
Sources: Roubini and Setser, November 2004, Bureau of Economic Analysis and author's own calculations.

At any point in time, the United States NIIP figure is affected by three factors: (1) the size of the US current account – a current account deficit means the NIIP will worsen by the amount of the current account deficit since it needs to borrow the equivalent sum from foreign residents; (2) changes in the local currency values of US assets and liabilities, for example the value of foreign stocks and bonds held by US residents (US assets) and the value of US stocks and bonds held by foreign residents (US liabilities) – if US holdings of foreign stocks and bonds rise in price more than foreign holdings of US stocks and bonds this helps to improve the United States NIIP; and (3) changes in the dollar exchange rate, for example a depreciation of the dollar against the euro will raise the dollar value of US residents' holdings of euro-denominated assets and thereby help improve the United States NIIP. Roubini and Setser (2004) show that US claims are very concentrated in Europe and the dollar decline against the euro 2001–4 has to some extent helped mitigate the negative effects of the US current account deficits on the United sates NIIP.

Another problem for the United States, as Catherine Mann (2002) points out, is that its income elasticity of demand for imports appears to be quite high at 1.80, while the foreign income elasticity of demand for US exports is quite low at 0.8. This asymmetry of how US economic growth affects imports and how world economic growth affects US exports means that if the US economy and the rest of the world grow at the same rate, the current account deficit will continue to widen unless the exchange rate of the dollar persistently depreciates (see also Obstfeld and Rogoff, 2000).

Roubini and Setser also show that in recent years there has been a decreased appetite for US investments on the part of the foreign private sector in terms of less willingness to hold US stocks and bonds. However, this lack of private sector demand has been replaced by heavy central bank intervention by Asian central banks attempting to prevent their currencies appreciating against the dollar. In particular, the Bank of Japan and the Bank of China have been large purchasers of US dollar Treasury securities; Asian bank holdings of US Treasury bonds increased from $1,069 billion in 2000 to an estimated $2,445 billion by the end of 2004. Without such heavy purchases the dollar might have fallen quite significantly on a trade-weighted basis and this may also account for why US Treasury bond yields have been quite low over this period despite large bond sales by the Bush administration to finance its large and growing fiscal deficit.

Clearly, however, there is a limit to the amount that foreign central banks will be willing to purchase of US-denominated assets since the more they purchase the greater their losses could be should the dollar depreciate or US interest rates rise. Should such purchases cease, then it would be difficult for the United States to attract the capital inflow required to finance its current account deficits without either a large depreciation of the dollar making US assets look cheap to purchase and/or a rise in US interest rates to attract foreign investors.

Some economists, such as Cooper (2001), are less worried about the US deficits, arguing that the United States is a strong highly productive economy which is dynamic and innovative, with well-functioning goods, labour and capital markets (with liquid securities) combined with political stability that will make good use of the borrowed money over time providing foreign investors with a relatively 'high and reliable' return on their investments. Cooper (2001 pp. 219–20) states,

> The language of current account deficits is unfortunate: it reverses the economic logic and suggests that in the U.S. case a deficit is undesirable, even though it reflects a vote of confidence by the rest of the world in the United States, or at least in claims on Americans. Put another way, the United States has demonstrated strong comparative advantage in exporting stocks, bonds, bank deposits, and other claims on such U.S. assets as real estate and U.S.-domiciled firms under foreign management control (that is, foreign direct investment) . . . Nearly half of all foreign claims on the United States are interest bearing, and U.S. interest rates in recent years have been higher than those in Europe, and much higher than in Japan. This has allowed the United States to attract and hold funds from those areas and elsewhere. Other parts of the world have been through financial crises, resulting in higher interest rates, but also in much greater uncertainty about their exchange rates and even the prospect of repayment.

McKinnon (2001) also argues that because the dollar is a vehicle currency widely used for trade invoicing, by financial markets, financial institutions and by central banks, the demand for US dollar-denominated assets will remain strong: 'This status of the dollar as international money, providing the central currency in the world system, is a natural monopoly' (2001, p. 229). Even if private-sector demand for the dollar were to wane, McKinnon is confident the slack would be taken up by foreign central banks keen to prevent their currencies appreciating against the dollar:

> Absent monetary instability in the center country, the dollar standard is robust and could continue without the United States running up against significant borrowing constraints from the rest of the world. Any incipient run on the dollar would be offset by foreign central banks accumulating dollar reserves in order to prevent their currencies from appreciating, because to do otherwise would impose a loss on their countries' international mercantile competitiveness. (2001, p. 237)

There are examples of other advanced economies accumulating net international debt of over 50% of GDP without obvious adverse effects. Australia's net international investment position in 2004 was a negative 64% of GDP, with both New Zealand and Canada also having substantial negative NIIPs. Others, such as Roubini and Sester (2004) are far more sceptical pointing out that the USA is a large economy and is consuming a disproportionate amount of world savings to finance its current account deficit. In addition, Catherine Mann (2002, p. 149) warns:

> The global investor may continue for a time to increase holdings of U.S. assets, particularly if the relative risk-reward profile holds up. At some point, however,

global investors will reach, or even go beyond, the desired proportion of U.S. assets in their portfolios. If the current account deficit continues to be large at a time when global investors no longer wish to add more U.S. assets to their portfolio, the current account deficit will not be sustainable, and an economic adjustment must occur.

Several mechanisms could lead to an eventual correction of the US current account deficit: (1) a rise in real US interest rates which would lead to more private savings and less private investment, with an accompanying slowdown in the US economy and net imports; (2) a depreciation of the dollar in trade-weighted terms which over time should increase US exports and decrease imports; (3) a decrease in the US budget deficit via a mixture of tax rises and/or a decrease in government expenditure which would again slow the US economy and decrease imports; and (4) an increase in economic growth rates in countries like Japan and Europe which would increase the demand for US exports.

One advantage that the USA does have over many other countries is that its external debt is denominated in its own currency, unlike typical emerging market economies that often have much of their external debt denominated in foreign currencies; hence it can always print the money to service and redeem its debts, for example US Treasury bonds held by foreign central banks. In this sense the USA has a large advantage over most emerging market economies, a rapid depreciation of the dollar would not increase the real cost to the United States of servicing its debt, whereas currency crises in emerging markets leading to the depreciation of their currencies against the dollar had major adverse consequences for many of their companies and banks that had dollar-denominated debts. There are clearly significant risks to foreign holders of US assets, such as the Bank of Japan and the Bank of China that have large holdings of US securities and would suffer substantial losses if US interest rates rise and/or the dollar depreciates. Since US liabilities are around $10.5 trillion there are potentially substantial losses to foreigners; from each 10% decline of the dollar they would lose approximately $1 trillion as measured in their own currencies. Roubini and Setser (2004, p. 6) warn:

No doubt the dollar's position as the world's reserve currency and the depth of U.S. financial markets creates an intrinsic source of demand for both dollars and dollar denominated assets. However, this could prove to be mixed blessing. The dollar's privileged position could increase the risk that the world will finance large U.S. trade deficits for too long, leading to excessive U.S. debt accumulation. This will let the U.S. delay needed adjustment, but increase the cost of the adjustment when it finally happens.

In the longer run, it is clear that the US current account deficits do matter, since increasing external indebtedness raises the interest payments the US has to make to the rest of the world which implies less money to buy goods/services in the future. A large structural current account deficit also acts as a constraint on economic growth since strong economic growth leads to even bigger current account deficits (unless it is export-led economic growth). Also increased external indebtness over time increases the probability of there being a sharp correction at some point in the future, which would imply a significant fall in the dollar, a rise in US interest rates and possibly a prolonged and significant recession for the US economy. There is also the risk of a financial crisis resulting from a loss of confidence on the part of financial markets and foreign central banks about the potential for a large depreciation of the US dollar. Finally, of course, there is the threat of protectionism; the larger the US current account deficits and the correspondingly greater the bilateral surpluses of Japan and China, the greater the risks that protectionist elements in the USA will surface.

2.10 Some open economy identities

In an open economy, gross domestic product (GDP) differs from that of a closed economy because there is an additional injection, export expenditure which represents foreign expenditure on domestically produced goods. There is also an additional leakage, expenditure on imports which represents domestic expenditure on foreign goods and raises foreign national income. The identity for an open economy is given by:

$$Y = C + I + G + X - M \tag{2.1}$$

where Y is national income, C is domestic consumption, I is domestic investment, G is government expenditure, X is export expenditure and M is import expenditure.
If we deduct taxation T from the right hand side of equation (2.1) we have:

$$Y_d = C + I + G + X - M - T \tag{2.2}$$

where Y_d is disposable income.
If we denote private savings as $S = Y_d - C$ we can rearrange equation (2.2) to obtain:

$$
\underset{\substack{\text{Current account} \\ \text{balance}}}{(X - M)} \quad = \quad \underset{\substack{\text{Net saving/} \\ \text{dissaving of the} \\ \text{private sector}}}{(S - I)} \quad + \quad \underset{\substack{\text{Government} \\ \text{deficit/surplus}}}{(T - G)} \tag{2.3}
$$

Equation (2.3) is an important identity, it says that a current account deficit has a counterpart in either private dissaving, that is private investment exceeding private saving and/or in a government deficit, that is government expenditure exceeding government taxation revenue. The equation is merely an identity and says nothing about causation. Nonetheless, it is often stated that the current account deficit is due to the lack of private savings and/or the government budget deficit. However, it is possible that the causation runs the other way, and it is the current account deficit that may be responsible for the lack of private savings or budget deficit. The identity has been much talked about since the 1980s (see **Box 2.1**).

Box 2.1

Current accounts and government fiscal policies

The fact that a country's current account (CA) is made up of the government budget surplus/deficit and net private savings/dissavings has led to very different perspectives on current account imbalances. **Table 2.7** shows the relevant components for the United States, the United Kingdom, Germany and Japan. CA stands for current account balance.

→

→

| Table 2.7 | Budget deficits/surpluses and current account balances (percentage of GDP) |

	United States			United Kingdom		
Year	(T – G)	(S – I)	CA	(T – G)	(S – I)	CA
1980	−1.4	+1.5	0.1	−3.4	+4.6	+1.2
1982	−3.5	+3.1	−0.4	−2.5	+4.2	+1.7
1984	−3.0	+0.4	−2.6	−3.9	+4.4	+0.5
1986	−3.5	+0.1	−3.4	−2.4	+2.2	−0.2
1988	−3.6	+1.2	−2.4	+0.5	−4.7	−4.2
1990	−4.2	+2.8	−1.4	−1.6	−2.4	−4.0
1992	−5.8	+5.0	−0.8	−6.5	+4.6	−2.1
1994	−3.6	+1.9	−1.7	−6.8	+5.8	−1.0
1996	−2.2	+0.7	−1.5	−4.2	+3.3	−0.9
1998	+0.4	−2.8	−2.4	+0.1	−0.6	−0.5
2000	+1.6	−5.8	−4.2	+3.8	−6.3	−2.5
2002	−3.8	−0.7	−4.5	−1.7	0	−1.7
2004	−4.4	−1.3	−5.7	−3.2	+1.0	−2.2
2006	−4.2	−2.2	−6.4	−3.3	+1.1	−2.2

	Germany			Japan		
Year	(T – G)	(S – I)	CA	(T – G)	(S – I)	CA
1980	−2.9	+1.3	−1.6	−4.4	+3.4	−1.0
1982	−3.3	+4.1	+0.8	−3.6	+4.2	+0.6
1984	−1.9	+3.6	+1.7	−2.1	+4.9	+2.8
1986	−1.3	+5.9	+4.6	−0.9	+5.2	+4.3
1988	−2.0	+6.1	+4.1	+1.1	+1.6	+2.7
1990	−2.0	+4.9	+2.9	+2.1	−0.6	+1.5
1992	−2.6	+1.6	−1.0	+0.8	+2.1	+2.9
1994	−2.4	+1.0	−1.4	−3.8	+5.1	+2.7
1996	−3.4	+2.8	−0.6	−5.1	+6.5	+1.4
1998	−2.2	+1.6	−0.6	−5.5	+8.5	+3.0
2000	+1.3	−2.7	−1.4	−7.5	+10.0	+2.5
2002	−3.7	+5.8	+2.1	−7.9	+10.7	+2.8
2004	−3.9	+7.2	+3.3	−6.5	+10.0	+3.5
2006	−2.7	+7.4	+4.7	−6.3	+10.0	+3.7

Notes: The (S – I) figure is an implied figure. The 2004 figure is a provisional estimate and that for 2006 is a forecast figure.
Source: OECD *Economic Outlook*, vol. 76, no. 2.

Interesting comparisons were made between the current account deficits of the USA and the UK in the 1980s. Many economists blamed the rapidly growing US current account deficit from 1982 onwards as due to the steep rise in the US budget deficit from 1.4% of GNP in 1980 to an average 3.5% of GDP in 1986. The UK current account moved into a heavy deficit from 1987 onwards; however, because the UK government was running a budget surplus,

→

➜

the government claimed that the current account position was primarily a private-sector phenomenon due to high investment and there was no need for remedial action by the government. The contrasts naturally led economists to propose different solutions to the deficits in both countries. Much of the US policy debate was concerned with reducing the federal budget deficit, while discussion in the UK focused upon measures designed to encourage private-sector savings (reducing private consumption) and reduce investment. The UK government pursued a tight monetary policy with a significant rise in UK interest rates.

The United States economy current account has worsened considerably since 1998, and by 2004 the US current account deficit had reached record proportions of 5.7% of GDP. Much focus has again been on the size of the budget deficits, following President Bush's tax cuts, but also on low savings and the pick-up in investment resulting from the extremely low short-term interest rate policy pursued by the Federal Reserve following the large falls in its stockmarket and the bust of 'dot com' stocks (the Federal Reserve cut the Feds fund rate from 6.5% in June 2000 to a mere 1% in July 2003).

Many economists believe that the reason why Germany and Japan had such persistent surpluses in their current accounts in the 1980s was that they have had much higher savings ratios. Following German reunification, however, the German current account position deteriorated noticeably due to a combination of worsening public finances bought on by the huge cost of propping up the former East German economy, and a consumer boom as East Germans went on a spending spree following the conversion of their East German ostmarks into German marks at a very generous one to one parity.

One must, however, be careful not to imply causation from what is in fact merely an accounting identity. This is clearly illustrated by comparing the fiscal deterioration in the cases of both the United States and Japan. In the USA the fiscal deterioration from 2000 onwards, due to a combination of tax cuts and a slowing economy, is clearly associated with a widening current account deficit; while in Japan post-1994 there is a significant worsening of the fiscal position which is accompanied by an improvement in the Japanese current account! From the mid-1990s, the Japanese fiscal position deteriorated noticeably but the Japanese current account remained in surplus due in part to even higher savings on the part of the Japanese worried about the effects of economic recession. Indeed, from 1998 onwards as the Japanese fiscal deficit increased, it seems that Japanese consumers possibly worried about the implications of these large fiscal deficits for their prospective future tax liabilities saved even more ensuring that the current account remained in surplus.

Equation (2.3) can be rearranged to yield:

$$I + G + X = S + T + M \tag{2.4}$$

This shows that the equilibrium level of national income is determined where injections (the variables on the left-hand side of 2.4) are equal to leakages (the variables on the right-hand side of 2.4). Injections are all those factors that work to raise national income, while leakages are those factors that work to lower national income. Equation (2.4) is an important identity to which we shall return in Chapter 4.

2.11 Open economy multipliers

John Maynard Keynes in his classic work *The General Theory of Employment, Interest and Money* published in 1936 pioneered the use of multiplier analysis to examine the effects of changes in government expenditure and investment on output and employment. However, his work was concerned almost exclusively with a closed economy. It was not long, however, before the ideas of Keynes' work were applied to an analysis of open economies, most notably by Fritz Machlup (1943).

The assumptions underlying basic multiplier analysis are: (i) both domestic prices and the exchange rate are fixed, (ii) the economy is operating at less than full employment so that increases in demand result in an expansion of output, and (iii) the authorities adjust the money supply to changes in money demand by pegging the domestic interest rate. This latter assumption is important, increases in output that lead to a rise in money demand would with a fixed money supply lead to a rise in the domestic interest rate; it is assumed that the authorities passively expand the money stock to meet any increase in money demand so that interest rates do not have to change. There is no inflation resulting from the money supply expansion because it is merely a response to the increase in money demand.

The starting point for the analysis is the identity of equation (2.1) repeated below as (2.5):

$$Y = C + I + G + X - M \tag{2.5}$$

Keynesian analysis proceeds to make assumptions concerning the determinants of the various components of national income. Government expenditure and exports are assumed to be exogenous, government expenditure being determined independently by political decision, and exports by foreign expenditure decisions and foreign income. Domestic consumption is partly autonomous and partly determined by the level of national income. This is denoted algebraically by the equation:

$$C = C_a + cY \tag{2.6}$$

where C_a is autonomous consumption, c is the marginal propensity to consume, that is the fraction of any increase in income that is spent on consumption. In this simple model, consumption is assumed to be a linear function of income. An increase in consumers' income induces an increase in their consumption.

Import expenditure is assumed to be partly autonomous and partly a positive function of the level of domestic income,

$$M = M_a + mY \tag{2.7}$$

where M_a is autonomous import expenditure and m is the marginal propensity to import, that is the fraction of any increase in income that is spent on imports. In this simple formulation import expenditure is assumed to be a positive linear function of income. There are several justifications for this, on the one hand increased income leads to increased expenditure on imports and also more domestic production normally requires more imports of intermediate goods. Since we have assumed that domestic prices are fixed this means that income Y also represents real income.

If we substitute equations (2.6) and (2.7) into equation (2.5) we obtain:

$$Y = C_a + cY + I + G + X - M_a - mY$$

Therefore:

$$(1 - c + m)Y = C_a + I + G + X - M_a$$

Given that $(1 - c)$ is equal to the marginal propensity to save, s, that is the fraction of any increase in income that is saved, then we obtain:

$$Y = \frac{1}{s + m} (C_a + I + G + X - M_a) \tag{2.8}$$

Equation (2.8) can be transformed into difference form to yield:

$$dY = \frac{1}{s + m} (dC_a + dI + dG + dX - dM_a) \tag{2.9}$$

where d in front of a variable represents the change in the variable. From equation (2.9) we can obtain some simple open economy multipliers.

The government expenditure multiplier

The first multiplier of interest is the government expenditure multiplier, which shows the increase in national income resulting from a given increase in government expenditure. This is given by:

$$\frac{dY}{dG} = \frac{1}{s + m} > 0 \tag{2.10}$$

Equation (2.10) says that an increase in government expenditure will have an expansionary effect on national income, the size of which depends upon the marginal propensity to save and the marginal propensity to import. Since the sum of the marginal propensity to save and import is less than unity, an increase in government expenditure will result in an even greater increase in national income. Furthermore, the value of the open economy multiplier is less than the closed economy multiplier which is given by $1/s$. The reason for this is that increased expenditure is spent on both domestic and foreign goods rather than domestic goods alone and the expenditure on foreign goods raises foreign rather than domestic income.

Numerical Example

Assume that the marginal propensity to save is 0.25 and the marginal propensity to import is 0.15. The effect of an increase in government expenditure of £100 million on national income is given by:

$$dY = \frac{1}{s+m} dG = \frac{1}{0.25 + 0.15} £100m = 2.5 \times £100m = £250m$$

Hence, an increase of government expenditure of £100m will raise eventual national income by £250m. This is because 60% of the £100m will get spent giving a further £60 million increase in incomes of which 60% will get spent giving a further £36 million increase in incomes and so on. The limit of such a series of expenditure rounds is £250 million.

The foreign trade or export multiplier

In this simple model, the multiplier effect of an increase in exports on national income is identical to that of an increase in government expenditure, and given by $dY/dX = 1/(s+m)$. In practice, it is often the case that government expenditure tends to be somewhat more biased to domestic output than private consumption expenditure, implying that the value of m is smaller in the case of the government expenditure multiplier than in the case of the export multiplier. If this is the case, an increase in government expenditure will have a more expansionary effect on domestic output than an equivalent increase in exports.

Numerical Example

Assume that the marginal propensity to save is 0.25 and the marginal propensity to import is 0.15. The effect of an increase in exports of £100 million on national income is given by:

$$dY = \frac{1}{s+m} dX = \frac{1}{0.25 + 0.15} £100m = 2.5 \times £100m = £250m$$

The effects of either an increase in government expenditure or increase in exports is illustrated in **Figure 2.1**.

In **Figure 2.1**, on the vertical axis we have injections/leakages and on the horizontal axis national income. The savings plus import expenditures $(s + m)$ are assumed to increase as income rises, reflected by the upward slope of the injections schedule. Because the sum of the marginal propensity to import and save is less than unity this schedule has a slope less than unity. Injections are assumed to be exogenous of the level of income and consequently this schedule is a horizontal line. The equilibrium level of national income is determined where injections into the economy (investment plus exports) equal leakages (savings and imports), which is initially at income level Y_1. An increase in exports or government expenditure or investment results in an upward shift of the injections schedule from $(G + I + X)_1$ to $(G + I + X)_2$ and this rise in income induces more saving and import expenditure but overall the increase in income from Y_1 to Y_2 is greater than the initial increase in injections. The lower are

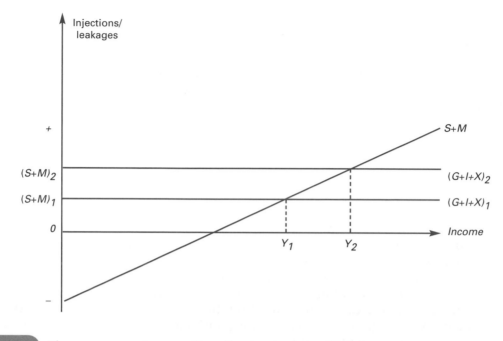

The government expenditure/foreign trade multiplier

the marginal propensities to save and invest, the less steep the leakages schedule and the greater the increase in income.

In practice, it is often the case that government expenditure tends to be somewhat more biased to domestic output than private consumption expenditure, implying that the value of m is smaller in the case of the government expenditure multiplier than in the case of the export multiplier. If this is the case, an increase in government expenditure will have a more expansionary effect on domestic output than an equivalent increase in exports.

The current account multipliers

The other relationships of interest are the effects of an increase in government expenditure and of exports on the current account (CA) balance. Rearranging equation (2.5) we have:

$$Y - C - I - G + M - X = 0$$

Substituting in equations (2.6) and (2.7) yields:

$$Y - cY + mY - C_a + M_a - I - G - X = 0$$

Since $Y(1 - c + m) = Y(s + m)$ we have:

$$Y(s + m) - C_a + M_a - I - G - X = 0$$

Multiplying by $m/(s + m)$ yields:

$$mY - \frac{m}{s + m}(C_a - M_a + I + G + X) = 0$$

Adding M_a and X to each side, recalling that $M = M_a + mY$ and rearranging yields:

$$CA = X - M = X - M_a - \frac{m}{s + m}(C_a - M_a + I + G + X) \tag{2.11}$$

Equation (2.11) can now be expressed in difference form as:

$$dCA = dX - dM_a - \frac{m}{s + m}(dCa - dM_a + dI + dG + dX) \tag{2.12}$$

From equation (2.12) we can derive the effects of an increase in government expenditure on the current account balance which is given by $dCA/dG = -m/(s + m) < 0$. That is, an increase in government spending leads to a deterioration of the current account balance which is some fraction of the initial increase in government expenditure. This is because economic agents spend part of the increase in income on imports.

Numerical Example

Assume that the marginal propensity to save is 0.25 and the marginal propensity to import is 0.15. The effect of an increase in government expenditure of £100 million on the current account is given by:

$$dCA = -\frac{-m}{s + m} dG = \frac{-0.15}{0.25 + 0.15} £100m = -0.375 \times £100m = -£37.5m$$

That is, an increase in government expenditure leads to an eventual deterioration in the current account of £37.5m. The reason is that the increased government expenditure of £100 million because of the open economy multiplier increases national income by £250m. Since the marginal propensity to import is 0.15, the £250m increase in income leads to a $0.15 \times £250 = £37.5m$ increase in imports which corresponds to the deterioration in the current account.

The other multiplier of interest is the effect of an increase in exports on the current balance. This is given by the expression:

$$\frac{dCA}{dX} = 1 - \frac{m}{s + m} = \frac{s + m}{s + m} - \frac{m}{s + m} = \frac{s}{s + m} > 0$$

Since $s/(s + m)$ is less than unity, an increase in exports leads to an improvement in the current balance that is less than the original increase in exports. The explanation for this is that part of the increase in income resulting from the additional exports is offset to some extent by increased expenditure on imports.

> **Numerical Example**
>
> Assume that the marginal propensity to save is 0.25 and the marginal propensity to import is 0.15. The effect of an increase in exports of £100 million on the current account is given by:
>
> $$\frac{dCA}{dX} = \frac{s}{s+m} = \frac{0.25}{0.25+0.15} \text{ £100m} = \text{£62.5m}$$
>
> The explanation is that the £100m increase in exports initially improves the current account by a like amount. However, it also generates an eventual increase of national income of £250m which induces an increase in imports of £37.5m, so the net improvement in the current account is limited to £62.5m.

The simple multiplier analysis that we have looked at here shows that Keynesian income effects are an essential part of balance of payments analysis, and that the current account of the balance of payments is an integral part of macroeconomic equilibrium for an open economy. Another important conclusion is that an analysis of macroeconomic fluctuations for an open economy requires consideration of what is happening in foreign economies; increases in foreign income raise the exports and income of the home economy. The foreign trade multiplier analysis deals with what happens to the balance of payments when income changes, assuming that prices are held constant.

2.12 Conclusions

From the discussion we can see that there are a variety of concepts of balance of payments disequilibrium. The very fact that there is no single agreed upon definition is not surprising; the choice of which concept is most relevant depends upon the exchange rate regime and the particular purpose of the analysis being undertaken. Each of the concepts has a different information content and, taken together, they provide an important indicator about the macro performance of an open economy. In the short run, however, it is inevitable the trade and current account balances capture the attention of macro economic policy-makers because they are published so frequently. Furthermore, it is not what happens so much in any given quarter's balance of payments that is significant, but what the statistics reveal over a period of time about the direction of an economy.

An important point to be borne in mind is that it is necessary to bring in a time dimension when analysing balance of payments statistics. A deficit is not necessarily a bad thing if it is likely to be followed by future surpluses and *vice-versa*. In this respect, it can be argued that it is necessary to look at the composition of goods that a country is importing. If the imported goods are predominantly consumer goods like cars and consumer electronics, then it might be argued that the deficit is more worrying than when the imports are plant and machinery that could be important in generating future exports.

Another point that needs to be borne in mind when considering if a current account deficit or surplus is a significant problem, is whether or not the country concerned is a net creditor or debtor *vis-à-vis* the rest of the world. A current account deficit means that the country concerned is increasing its indebtedness or reducing its claims on the rest of the world. If the country is a net creditor it can usually afford to do this, whereas if it is a net debtor the deficit may be regarded as a more serious problem. This is why the deficits of the United States have caused some concern because the USA has become the world's largest debtor. By contrast, there was much less concern about the German current account deficits resulting from German reunification because past German surpluses have made it a net creditor *vis-à-vis* the rest of the world.

Another factor to bear in mind when looking at a country's current account position is the potential cause of the deficit or surplus. If a country has a large deficit due to a large government budget deficit, then the remedy may well require reducing government expenditure and/or raising taxes. If, however, the deficit is due to high investment, then there is a good chance that future export growth will reduce the deficit and corrective policy action may not be necessary. Alternatively, the current account deficit may be due to a consumer boom (reflected in low savings) and a tightening of monetary policy in the form of higher interest rates may be needed. Whatever, some sort of analysis of causes is crucial to appraising whether a deficit or surplus is a policy problem.

Finally, when analysing a country's balance of payments statistics and attempting to assess whether the country is facing or is likely to face problems in the near future, it is important to remember that whatever concept of balance of payments disequilibrium is used it gives only a partial view of the economy. If a country has a current account deficit, high inflation and low economic growth, then the balance of payments problem is more worrying than if the deficit is accompanied by high economic growth and low inflation.

Further reading

Cooper, R.N. (2001) 'Is the U.S. Current Account Deficit Sustainable? Will it be Sustained', Brookings Papers on Economic Activity, vol. 1, pp. 217–25.

Kemp, D.S. (1987) 'Balance of Payments Concepts – What Do They Really Mean?', in *Readings in International Finance*, Federal Reserve Bank of Chicago, Chicago.

Machlup, F. (1943) *International Trade and the National Income Multiplier* (Philadelphia: Blakston).

Mann, C. (2002) 'Perspectives on the U.S. Current Account Deficit and Sustainability', *Journal of Economic Perspectives*, vol. 16, no. 3, pp. 131–52.

McKinnon, R. (2001) 'The International Dollar Standard and the Sustainability of the U.S. Current Account Deficit', Brookings Papers on Economic Activity, vol. 1, pp. 227–39.

Obstfeld, M. and Rogoff, K. (2000) 'Perspective on OECD Economic Integration: Implications for US Current Account Adjustment', *Global Economic Integration: Opportunities and Challenges*, Federal Reserve Bank of Kansas City, pp. 168–209.

Roubini, N. and Setser, B. (2004) 'The US as a Net Debtor: The Sustainability of the US External Imbalances', New York University mimeo.

Stern, R.M. *et al.* (1977) 'The Presentation of the United States Balance of Payments: A Symposium', Princeton Essays in International Finance, no. 123, Princeton University.

Thirwall, A.P. (1986) *Balance of Payments Theory and the United Kingdom Experience* (London: Macmillan – now Palgrave Macmillan).

3

Elasticity and Absorption Approaches to the Balance of Payments

3.1 Introduction

In the opening two chapters we have introduced the exchange rate and the balance of payments. In this chapter, we investigate the relationship between the exchange rate and the balance of payments. In particular, we shall be studying two models that investigate the impact of exchange rate changes on the current account position of a country. These two approaches are popularly known as the elasticity approach and the absorption approach. Both models were designed to tackle one of the most important questions in international economics – will a devaluation (or depreciation) of the exchange rate lead to a reduction of a current account deficit? The answer to this question is of crucial importance because if an exchange rate change cannot be relied upon to ensure adjustment of the current account, then policy-makers will have to rely on other instruments to improve the position.

We start the chapter by examining the impact of exchange rate changes according to the elasticity approach which looks at the impact of exchange rate changes assuming domestic and foreign prices are fixed. This is followed by an analysis of the absorption model which examines the effects of the exchange rate in terms of its impact on domestic income and spending. The chapter concludes by analysing the similarities and differences between the two models. For simplicity, throughout this chapter we shall ignore the complications of unilateral transfers and interest, profit and dividends on the current account balance and concentrate on the export and import of goods and services. *Throughout this chapter, the exchange rate is defined as domestic currency units per unit of foreign currency, so that a devaluation/depreciation of the currency is represented by a rise in the exchange rate.*

3.2 | **The elasticity approach to the balance of payments**

The elasticity approach to the balance of payments provides an analysis of what happens to the current account balance when a country devalues its currency. The analysis was pioneered by Alfred Marshall (1923) and Abba Lerner (1944), and later extended by Joan Robinson (1937) and Fritz Machlup (1939). At the outset, the model makes some simplifying assumptions; the model focuses on demand conditions and assumes that the supply elasticities for the domestic export good and foreign import good are perfectly elastic, so that changes in demand volumes have no effect on prices. In effect, these assumptions mean that domestic and foreign prices are fixed so that changes in relative prices are caused by changes in the nominal exchange rate.

The central message of the elasticity approach is that there are two direct effects of a devaluation on the current balance, one of which works to reduce a deficit, whilst the other actually contributes to making the deficit worse than before. Let us consider these two effects in some detail:

The current account balance when expressed in terms of the domestic currency is given by:

$$CA = P X_v - S P^* M_v \tag{3.1}$$

where P is the domestic price level, X_v is the volume of domestic exports, S is the exchange rate (domestic currency units per unit of foreign currency), P^* is the foreign price level and M_v is the volume of imports. We shall set the domestic and foreign price levels at unity; the value of domestic exports ($P X_v$) is given by X; while the foreign currency value of imports ($P^* M_v$) is given by M. Using these simplifications equation (3.1) becomes:

$$CA = X - S M \tag{3.2}$$

In difference form equation (3.2) becomes:

$$dCA = dX - S \, dM - M \, dS \tag{3.3}$$

Dividing equation (3.3) by the change in the exchange rate dS, we obtain:

$$\frac{dCA}{dS} = \frac{dX}{dS} - S\frac{dM}{dS} - M\frac{dS}{dS} \tag{3.4}$$

At this point we introduce two definitions; the price elasticity of demand for exports ηx, is defined as the percentage change in exports over the percentage change in price as represented by the percentage change in the exchange rate, giving:

$$\eta x = \frac{dX/X}{dS/S}$$

so that

$$dX = \frac{\eta x \, dS \, X}{S} \tag{3.5}$$

and the price elasticity of demand for imports ηm, is defined as the percentage change in imports over the percentage change in their price as represented by the percentage change in the exchange rate (we place a negative as we wish to express elasticity as a positive number):

$$\eta m = - \frac{dM/M}{dS/S}$$

so that

$$dM = - \frac{\eta m \, dS \, M}{S} \tag{3.6}$$

Substituting equations (3.5) and (3.6) into equation (3.4) we obtain:

$$\frac{dCA}{dS} = \frac{\eta x \, X}{S} + \eta m \, M - M$$

and dividing by M

$$\frac{dCA}{dS} \frac{1}{M} = \frac{\eta x \, X}{S \, M} + \eta m - 1 \tag{3.7}$$

Assuming that we initially have balanced trade, $X/SM = 1$, and rearranging equation (3.7) yields:

$$\frac{dCA}{dS} = M(\eta x + \eta m - 1) \tag{3.8}$$

Equation (3.8) is known as the Marshall–Lerner condition and says that starting from a position of equilibrium in the current account, a devaluation will improve the current account, that is $dCA/dS > 0$ only if the sum of the foreign elasticity of demand for exports and the home country elasticity of demand for imports is greater than unity; that is, $(\eta x + \eta m) > 1$. If the sum of these two elasticities is less than unity, then a devaluation will lead to a deterioration of the current account.

Table 3.1 Devaluation and the balance of payments

| Description | Before devaluation the current account is in balance | | | |
	Volume	Price	Sterling value	Dollar value
UK exports	100	£1	£100	$200
UK imports	40	$5	£100	$200
Current account			£0	$0
Case 1 devaluation leads to a current account deficit				
UK exports	105	£1	£105	$157.5
UK imports	36	$5	£120	$180
Current account			–£15	–$22.5

Approximate elasticities: $\eta_x = 0.05/0.33 = 0.15$, $\eta_m = 0.1/0.33 = 0.3$, $\eta_x + \eta_m = 0.45$

Case 2 devaluation leaves the current account unaffected				
UK exports	120	£1	£120	$180
UK imports	36	$5	£120	$180
Current account			£0	$0

Approximate elasticities: $\eta_x = 0.20/0.33 = 0.60$, $\eta_m = 0.10/0.33 = 0.30$, $\eta_x + \eta_m = 0.9$

Case 3 devaluation leads to a current account surplus				
UK exports	130	£1	£130	$195
UK imports	30	$5	£100	$150
Current account			+£30	+$45

Approximate elasticities: $\eta_x = 0.30/0.33 = 0.9$, $\eta_m = 0.25/0.33 = 0.75$, $\eta_x + \eta_m = 1.65$

The economic explanation of this result is illustrated in **Table 3.1** which shows the pre-devaluation and three possible post-devaluation scenarios. Before devaluation the sterling–dollar exchange rate is £0.50/$1 ($2/£1), whereas after the devaluation the sterling–dollar exchange rate is £0.666/$1 ($1.50/£1). The price of one unit of UK exports is £1 and the price of one unit of US exports is $5.

There are two effects in play once a currency is devalued:

1 **The price effect** – exports become cheaper measured in foreign currency: a UK export earns only $1.50 post-devaluation compared to $2 prior to devaluation. Imports become more expensive measured in the home currency, each unit of imports costs £2.50 prior to the devaluation but costs £3.33 post-devaluation. The price effect clearly contributes to a worsening of the UK current account.

2 **The volume effect** – the fact that exports become cheaper should encourage an increased volume of exports, and the fact that imports become more expensive should lead to a decreased volume of imports. The volume effect clearly contributes to improving the current balance.

The net effect depends upon whether the price or volume effect dominates. In **Table 3.1** case 1, the increase in export volumes and decrease in import volumes are not sufficient to outweigh the fact that less is received for exports and more has to be paid for imports. The result is that the current account balance move from balance into deficit. Approximate elasticities sum to 0.45. In case 2, the increased export volumes and decreased volume of imports exactly match the decreased earnings per unit of exports and increased expenditure per unit of imports so that the current balance is unchanged. Approximate elasticities sum to 0.9 which is close to unity. In case 3, the increased volume of export sales and decreased volume of imports are sufficient to outweigh the price effects so that the current balance improves following a devaluation. Approximate elasticities sum to 1.65 which fulfils the critical Marshall–Lerner condition for a successful devaluation.

A more complicated formula can be derived which allows for supply elasticities of exports and imports of less than infinity. Given the assumption of less than infinite supply elasticity conditions and assuming initially balanced trade, Stern (1973, pp. 64–7) has shown that a more complicated condition needs to be satisfied; namely, the balance of payments will improve following a devaluation if:

$$\frac{\varepsilon x(\eta x - 1)}{\varepsilon x + \varepsilon m} + \frac{\eta m(\varepsilon m + 1)}{\eta m + \varepsilon m} > 0 \tag{3.9}$$

where εx is the domestic supply elasticity of the exports good and εm is the foreign supply elasticity for its export good (the domestic country's imports). The effect of less than infinite supply elasticities is to make the required demand elasticities less stringent in the sense that the current account may improve even if the sum of the demand elasticities is less than unity. If the supply elasticities of exports and imports are less than infinite, an increase in demand for exports will lead to some rise in the domestic price of exports which will give an additional boost to export revenues (when demand is inelastic). Similarly, the fall in the demand for foreign imports will have the effect of reducing the foreign currency price of imports so lowering import expenditure. Both these effects are absent under the infinite supply elasticities we have assumed.

3.3 Empirical evidence on import and export demand elasticities

The possibility that a devaluation may lead to a worsening rather than improvement in the balance of payments led to much research into empirical estimates of the elasticity of demand for exports and imports. Economists divided up into two camps popularly known as 'elasticity optimists' who believed that the sum of these two elasticities tended to exceed unity, and 'elasticity pessimists' who believed that these elasticities tended to less than unity. It was argued that a devaluation may work better for industrialized countries than for developing countries. Many developing countries are heavily dependent upon imports, and their price elasticity of demand for imports was likely to be very low, while for industrialized countries that have to face competitive export markets the price elasticity of demand for their exports may be quite elastic. The implication of the Marshall–Lerner condition was that devaluation may be a cure for some countries' balance of payments deficits but not for others.

Table 3.2 The elasticity of demand for exports and imports of 15 industrial and 9 developing countries

	Elasticity of export demand	Elasticity of import demand	Sum
Industrial countries			
Austria	1.02	1.23	2.25
Belgium	1.12	1.27	2.39
Canada	0.68	1.28	1.96
Denmark	1.04	0.91	1.95
France	1.28	0.93	2.21
Germany	1.02	0.79	1.81
Iceland	0.83	0.87	1.70
Italy	1.26	0.78	2.04
Japan	1.40	0.95	2.35
Netherlands	1.46	0.74	2.20
Norway	0.92	1.19	2.11
Sweden	1.58	0.88	2.46
Switzerland	1.03	1.13	2.16
United Kingdom	0.86	0.65	1.51
United States	1.19	1.24	2.43
Average	1.11	0.99	2.10
Developing countries			
Argentina	0.6	0.9	1.5
Brazil	0.4	1.7	2.1
India	0.5	2.2	2.7
Kenya	1.0	0.8	1.8
Korea	2.5	0.8	3.3
Morocco	0.7	1.0	1.7
Pakistan	1.8	0.8	2.6
Philippines	0.9	2.7	3.6
Turkey	1.4	2.7	4.1
Average	1.1	1.5	2.6

Notes: The above estimates refer to price elasticities over a 2–3 year period. Estimates are based upon the results of a number of different studies. Individual studies give differing estimates depending on the time periods involved, the econometric methodology employed and the particular data-set used.
Source: Gylfason (1987), *European Economic Review*, vol. 31, p. 377.

There are enormous problems involved in estimating the elasticity of demand for imports and exports. A summary by Gylfason (1987) of 10 econometric studies undertaken between 1969 and 1981 has shown that the Marshall–Lerner condition was fulfilled for all of the 15 industrial and nine developing countries surveyed, and the results are shown in **Table 3.2**. The results are based on estimates of the elasticities over a two–three-year time horizon. As such, while the table demonstrates clearly that a devaluation will improve the current account over such a time span, it does not preclude an initial J-curve effect. Indeed, a study by Artus and Knight (1984) has shown that up to a period of six-months estimated price elasticities are invariably so low that the Marshall–Lerner conditions are not fulfilled. In a recent study, Hooper *et al.* (1998) examined the short and long-run price elasticities of demand for imports and exports of the G-7 countries from the mid-1950s through to the end of 1996. The total (import and export demand elasticities) for the short and long-run respectively were: Canada (0.6, 1.8), France (0.2, 0.6), Germany (0.3, 0.4), Italy (0.3, 1.3), Japan (0.6, 1.3), United Kingdom (0.2, 2.2) and United States (0.6, 1.8). The results show the difference between short and long-run elasticities and show clearly that in the short run the Marshall–Lerner condition does not hold, but in the longer run the condition is generally met (except in the cases of France and Germany).

A general consensus accepted by most economists is that elasticities are lower in the short run than in the long run, in which case the Marshall–Lerner conditions may not hold in the short run but may hold in the medium to long run. Goldstein and Kahn (1985) in an excellent survey of the empirical literature conclude that, in general, long-run elasticities (greater than two years) are approximately twice as great as short-run elasticities (0–6 months). Further, the short-run elasticities generally fail to sum to unity, while the long-run elasticities almost always sum to greater than unity.

The possibility that in the short run the Marshall–Lerner condition may not be fulfilled although it generally holds over the longer run leads to the phenomenon of what is popularly known as the J-curve effect which is illustrated in **Figure 3.1**.

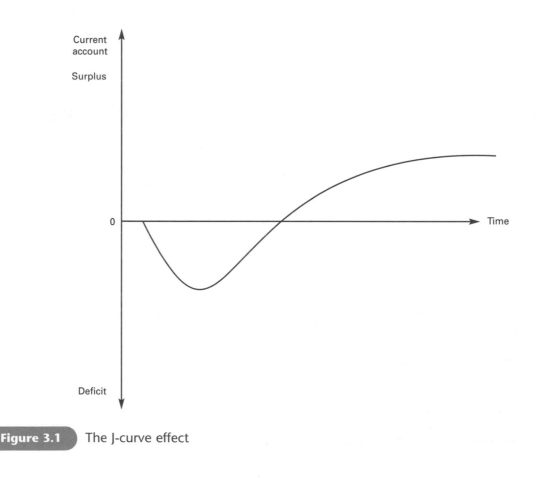

Figure 3.1   The J-curve effect

The idea underlying the J-curve effect is that in the short run export volumes and import volumes do not change much so that the country receives less export revenue and spends more on imports leading to a deterioration in the current balance. However, after a time lag export volumes start to increase and import volumes start to decline, and consequently the current deficit starts to improve and eventually moves into surplus. The issue then is whether the initial deterioration in the current account is greater than the future improvement so that overall devaluation can be said to work. Krugman (1991) in an analysis of the effects of a sharp depreciation of the US dollar during 1985–87 found a J-curve effect for the US current account; the deficit initially rose in both absolute terms and as a percentage of US gross national product, but after a lag of approximately two years it improved with long-run elasticities for imports and exports summing to 1.9 in excess of that required by the Marshall–Lerner condition.

There have been numerous reasons advanced to explain the slow responsiveness of export and import volumes in the short run and why the response is far greater in the longer run; three of the most important are:

- **A time lag in consumer responses**. It takes time for consumers in both the devaluing country and the rest of the world to respond to the changed competitive situation. Switching away from foreign imported goods to domestically produced goods inevitably takes some time because consumers will be worried about issues other than the price change, such as the reliability and reputation of domestic produced goods as compared to the foreign imports. While foreign consumers may be reluctant to switch away from domestically produced goods towards the exports of the devaluing country.
- **A time lag in producer responses**. Even though a devaluation improves the competitive position of exports, it will take time for domestic producers to expand production of exportables. In addition, the orders for imports are normally made well in advance and such contracts are not readily cancelled in the short run. Factories will be reluctant to cancel orders for vital inputs and raw materials. For example, the waiting list for a Boeing aeroplane can be over five years; it is most unlikely that a British airline will cancel the order just because the pound has been devalued. Also, the payments for many imports will have been hedged against exchange risk in the forward market and so will be left unaffected by the devaluation.
- **Imperfect competition**. Building up a share of foreign markets can be a time consuming and costly business. This being the case, foreign exporters may be very reluctant to lose their market share in the devaluing country and might respond to the loss in their competitiveness by reducing their export prices. To the extent that they do this, the rise in the cost of imports caused by the devaluation will be partly offset. Similarly, foreign-import-competing industries may react to the threat of increased exports by the devaluing country by reducing prices in their home markets, limiting the amount of additional exports by the devaluing country. These effects rely upon some degree of imperfect competition which gives foreign firms some super-normal profit margins enabling them to reduce their prices. If foreign firms were in a highly competitive environment they would only be making normal profits and so would be unable to reduce their prices.

In addition to the above effects it is unlikely that the price of exports as measured in the domestic prices will remain fixed. Many imports are used as inputs for exporting industries and the increased price of imports may lead to higher wage costs as workers seek compensation for higher import prices, this will to some extent lead to a rise in export prices reducing the competitive advantage of the devaluation.

3.4 The pass-through effect of a depreciation or appreciation

In the preceding analysis, we have assumed that a 10% depreciation/devaluation will lead to a rise in price of imports by 10%. In the real world this might not be valid, and economists use the term *pass through effect* to describe the extent to which a 1% depreciation (appreciation) leads to a rise (fall) in import prices. If there is complete pass-through, a 10% depreciation (appreciation) of the currency leads to a 10% rise (fall) in import prices. If, however, a 10% depreciation (appreciation) leads to only a 6% rise (fall) in import prices, then there is only a partial pass-through effect, with the elasticity of exchange rate pass-through being 0.6. There are numerous reasons advanced as to why an x% depreciation of the exchange rate may lead to a less than x% rise in prices in the short run. As noted previously, in a world of imperfect competition foreign firms may not be prepared to risk losing market share following a depreciation and decide to absorb part of the depreciation by reducing their foreign currency price of exports so that the price rise following the devaluation will be less than the x% devaluation. This may be a sensible strategy since firms may hesitate to risk losing market share following what might be a temporary depreciation in the exchange rate. Similarly, if a currency appreciates foreign firms may decide not to change their local currency prices since they will be able to increase their profits as measured in their local currency without having to invest to increase physical shipments to the country for what might be only a transitory appreciation.

A recent paper by Yang (1997) who studied as selection of 77 manufacturing industries in the United States for the period December 1980 until December 1991 found that the elasticity of pass-through was 0.3185 for one quarter of a year, suggesting that a 10% depreciation of the dollar leads to a rise in import prices of 3.185% on average. However, there was quite a bit of dispersion between different industries with the elasticity of pass-through being only 0.025 in hardwood veneer and plywood and 0.757 in printing trade machinery. As the time horizon increased, however, in all industries the elasticity of pass-through increased and often approached unity. One of the key factors determining the elasticity of pass-through being the degree of product differentiation; the greater the degree of product differentiation then the more the ability of foreign exporters to raise their prices presumably because firms in industries where the product is differentiated tend to face more price-inelastic demand for their product and so are able to pass on price rises with less fear of losing sales. In a recent study, Klitgaard (1999) looking at US imports from Japan in four major export industries (industrial machinery, transportations equipment, electrical machinery and precision equipment) during the 1990s found that when the dollar depreciated by 10% then the price of Japanese imports rose by only 6%, suggesting that Japanese exporters take a 4% offsetting change in their profit margin on exports in the short run.

To the extent that there is only a partial pass-through effect on the price of imports in the short run, the effect will be to dampen the size and complicate the dynamics and timing of the J-curve effect. This is because imports will not rise in price as much as suggested by the devaluation, which will tend to reduce import expenditure compared to complete pass-through in the very short run. However, as the exchange rate depreciation is increasingly passed on over time, this will tend to raise import expenditure so prolonging the initial deterioration of the J-curve.

3.5 The absorption approach

One of the major defects of the elasticity approach is that it is based upon the assumption that all other things are equal. However, changes in export and import volumes will by definition have implications for national income and consequently income effects need to be incorporated in a more comprehensive analysis of the effects of a devaluation. Alexander (1952) is one of the most important papers evaluating this effect; his paper focuses on the fact that a current account imbalance can be viewed as the difference between domestic output and domestic spending (absorption).

Taking the equation for national income:

$$Y = C + I + G + X - M \tag{3.10}$$

and defining domestic absorption as $A = C + I + G$, equation (3.10) can be rearranged as follows:

$$CA = X - M = Y - A \tag{3.11}$$

Equation (3.11) says that the current balance represents the difference between domestic output and domestic absorption. A current account surplus means that domestic output exceeds domestic spending, while a current account deficit means that domestic output is less than domestic spending. Transforming equation (3.11) into difference form yields:

$$dCA = dY - dA \tag{3.12}$$

What equation (3.12) implies is that the effects of a devaluation on the current balance will depend upon how it affects national income relative to how it affects domestic absorption. If a devaluation raises domestic income relative to domestic spending this current account improves. If, however, devaluation raises domestic absorption relative to domestic spending, the current account deteriorates. Understanding how devaluation affects both income and absorption is therefore central to the absorption approach to balance of payments analysis.

Absorption can be divided up into two parts: a rise in income will lead to an increase in absorption which is determined by the marginal propensity to absorb, a, but there will also be a 'direct effect' on absorption which is all the other effects on absorption resulting from devaluation denoted by A_d. Thus the change in total absorption dA, is given by:

$$dA = adY + dA_d \tag{3.13}$$

Substituting (3.13) into equation (3.12) yields:

$$dCA = (1 - a)dY - dA_d \tag{3.14}$$

Equation (3.14) reveals that there are three factors that need to be examined when considering the impact of devaluation. A devaluation can affect the current balance only by changing the marginal propensity to absorb, a, changing the level of income, dY, and by affecting direct absorption, dA_d. The condition for a devaluation to improve the current account is $(1 - a)dY > dA_d$, that is, any change in income not spent on absorption must exceed any change in direct absorption.

To consider whether the above condition is likely to be fulfilled it is worth distinguishing two possible states of an economy: below full employment so that income may rise, and full employment so that national income cannot rise.

3.6 The effects of a devaluation on national income

Clearly a relevant question if the economy is at less than full employment is whether a devaluation is likely to raise or lower national income. If the marginal propensity to absorb is less than unity then a rise in income will raise the income to absorption ratio and so improve the current account. Whereas, if income were to fall this would raise the absorption to income ratio (as absorption would fall by less than income) which would worsen the current account. There are two important effects on income that need to be examined, the employment effect and the terms of trade effect:

- **Employment effect**. If the economy is at less than full employment, then providing the Marshall–Lerner condition is fulfilled there will be an increase in net exports following a devaluation which will lead to an increase in national income via the foreign trade multiplier. However, if the Marshall–Lerner condition is not fulfilled, then net exports would fall implying that national income falls. Hence, it is not clear whether the employment effect will raise or lower national income.
- **Terms of trade effect**. The terms of trade are the price of exports divided by the price of imports, expressed algebraically as:

$$\frac{\text{Price of exports}}{\text{Price of imports}} = \frac{P}{S\,P^*}$$

where P is the domestic price index, P^* is the foreign price index and S is the exchange rate (domestic currency units per unit of foreign currency).

A devaluation (a rise in S) tends to make imports more expensive in domestic currency terms which is not matched by a corresponding rise in export prices; this means that the terms of trade deteriorate. A deterioration in the terms of trade represents a loss of real national income because more units of exports have to be given to obtain a unit of imports. Hence, the terms of trade effect lowers national income.

Overall, the effects of a devaluation on the income of the devaluing country are ambiguous. Even if there are increased net exports earnings (which relies on the Marshall–Lerner condition being fulfilled) the negative terms of trade effect works to reduce national income.

Even if income rises overall, it is still not clear what the implications of a rise in income are for the current account, as this will depend upon the value of the marginal propensity to absorb. If this is less than unity then an increase in income generated by the increase in net exports leads to an improvement in the current account because income rises by more than absorption. If, however, the marginal propensity to absorb is greater than unity then the increased income would lead to an even bigger rise in absorption resulting in a worsening of the current account. Although one may think that the marginal propensity to absorb will be less than unity this need not be the case. Alexander (1952) speculated that unemployed workers who obtain jobs are likely to have a high propensity to consume and that an increase in income may well stimulate a great deal of investment. Workers who obtain jobs may well be decide to spend more than their income by borrowing against future prospective income. Similarly, as the economy expands firms' expenditure may exceed their revenues as they undertake significant investment in the expectation of high future profits. Hence, it is conceivable in the short run that the marginal propensity to absorb could be greater than unity, so that a rise in income leads to a deterioration in the current account.

Of course, if the economy is at a position of full employment, an increase in income is not possible. In this instance for a devaluation to improve the current deficit would require a reduction in direct absorption. Income changes are only one of the factors influencing the current account, the other effect that we need to consider is the impact on direct absorption.

3.7 The effects of a devaluation on direct absorption

For the moment, let us assume that the net effect of a devaluation on income is zero. This being the case, we must consider the effect of the devaluation on direct absorption. If the devaluation reduces direct absorption, then a devaluation will lead to an improvement in the current balance, whereas if direct absorption increases then the effect on the current balance will lead to a deterioration of the current account. Let us now consider possible ways in which a devaluation can be expected to impact upon direct absorption.

Real balance effect

A simple formulation of the demand to hold money is that it is a demand to hold real money balances. If prices double then agents will demand twice as much money as before. Algebraically a money demand function can be expressed as:

$$M/P_I = k \tag{3.15}$$

where k is some constant and P_I is an aggregate price index defined as:

$$P_I = \alpha P + (1 - \alpha) S P^* \tag{3.16}$$

where α is the percentage of expenditure on domestic goods, P is the price of the domestic good, P^* is the price of the foreign import good, and S is the exchange rate defined as domestic currency units per unit of foreign currency.

For example, assume that the price of the domestic good, P, is £1 while the price of the foreign good, P^*, is $5 and the pre-devaluation exchange rate is £0.5/$1. Further, that domestic consumers spend 80% of their money on domestic goods, $\alpha = 0.8$, then the average price level is:

$$P_I = 0.8 \; £1 + 0.2 \; \$5 \; (£0.5/\$1) = £1.30$$

If the pound is devalued to £0.666/\$1 then the average price level then becomes:

$$P_I = 0.8 \; £1 + 0.2 \; \$5 \; (£0.666/\$1) = £1.47$$

Hence, a 33% devaluation of the pound will raise the average price index facing UK consumers by approximately 12.8%.

Given an unchanged money stock and the assumption that economic agents aim to maintain a given amount of real money balances as depicted in equation (3.15), then a devaluation (rise in S) by raising the overall price index in equation (3.16) means that economic agents have to maintain their real balances by cutting down on direct absorption. Economic agents will attempt to increase their money balances by selling bonds which pushes down the price of bonds and raises the domestic interest rate. The rise in interest rates will reduce investment and consumption, so reducing direct absorption.

For the real balance effect to come into play, it must be emphasized that the authorities must not accommodate the increased money demand by increasing the money supply in line with the increased money demand. If they raise the money supply, this would leave the ratio M/P_I constant so that the real balance effect will not come into play.

Income redistribution effect

The rise in the general price index (equation 3.16) resulting from a devaluation is likely to have a number of effects on the income distribution. To the extent that it redistributes income from those with a low marginal propensity to absorb to those with a high marginal propensity to absorb this will increase direct absorption. While to the extent the reverse is true, it will lower direct absorption. A few possibilities in this respect are:

(a) The rise in the general price index will tend to reduce the real income of those with fixed incomes, but if overall income is unchanged then those with variable incomes will have gained. It tends to be the case that the group on fixed incomes are the poor who have a high propensity to absorb, while those on variable incomes are better off and have a lower propensity to absorb. To the extent that income is redistributed from those with fixed incomes to those with variable incomes, this income redistribution effect will tend to reduce direct absorption.

(b) A devaluation often leads to an improvement of company profits through increased sales in export and import-competing industries, while real wages are reduced by the rise in the aggregate price index and take time to catch up. The effect on direct absorption of this redistribution is not clear, while firms may have a lower tendency to absorb than workers this will be very much dependent on their expectations about the future. If these expectations are very favourable then the devaluation and profits rise may stimulate investment and even raise direct absorption.

(c)   There may be considerable income adjustments within groups of companies and workers. Some companies' profits will benefit from a devaluation as export sales rise, however, some firms that are reliant on imported inputs may find that the costs increases reduce their profit margins. Similarly, some workers will be able to protect themselves against the induced price rise because they are represented by strong trade unions, while others with no union representation may not secure compensating rises. The overall effect on direct absorption will then depend on whether the companies and workers that gain have a higher propensity to absorb than those that lose.

Overall, it is extremely difficult to say whether the income redistribution effects will raise or lower direct absorption.

Money illusion effect

It is possible that even though prices rise because of the devaluation, consumers suffer money illusion and buy exactly the same bundle of goods as before, even though their real spending power has been reduced. If this is the case they are actually spending more on direct absorption than before. However, the money illusion effect may work in reverse and consumers, because of the price rises, may actually decide to cut back direct absorption in more than proportion to the price rise so that direct absorption falls. Whatever way the money illusion effect works it is unlikely to be very significant and is most probably only a temporary rather than a permanent factor.

Expectational effects

It is possible that economic agents regard the price rises induced by devaluation as likely to spark further price rises. This would lead to an increase in direct absorption which would worsen the balance of payments. However, against this it can be argued that inflationary expectations may reduce investment which lowers direct absorption.

Laursen–Metzler effect

Laursen and Metzler (1950) noted that the deterioration in the terms of trade following a devaluation will have two effects on absorption. An income effect and a substitution effect. While the deterioration in the terms of trade lowers national income and thereby income-related absorption, it also makes domestically produced goods relatively cheaper compared to foreign produced goods, which implies a substitution effect in favour of increased consumption of domestically produced goods. If the positive substitution effect outweighs the negative income effect Laursen–Metzler noted that a devaluation which results in a deterioration of the terms of trade could actually lead to a rise in absorption.

Hence, the effects of a devaluation on direct absorption are ambiguous. While the real money balance effect works to lower direct absorption, all the other effects may raise or lower direct absorption. Since we do not know if the marginal propensity to absorb is greater or less than unity, if income rises or falls, nor if direct absorption rises or falls, the effects of a devaluation are indeterminate. Indeed, the picture will become much more complex once it is recognized that all the differing effects take place at different speeds over time and that some effects will be more significant in certain economies than in others. Overall, the approach suggests that a devaluation will have many diverse and often conflicting effects on the current account.

Nonetheless, the absorption approach has some important lessons for policy-makers. Its central message is that raising domestic income relative to domestic absorption will improve the current balance. In this respect, a devaluation is more likely to succeed if it is accompanied by economic policy measures that concentrate on raising income while constraining absorption.

3.8 A synthesis of the elasticity and absorption approaches

Initially, it was believed that the absorption approach was an alternative to the elasticities approach; the elasticity approach concentrating on price effects while the absorption approach concentrated on income effects. However, authors such as Tsiang (1961) and Alexander (1959) showed that the two models are not substitutes, rather they are complementary.

To understand this complementarity, consider the effects of a devaluation on income. Exports will increase more than imports, so raising income only if the Marshall–Lerner elasticities condition is fulfilled. If the Marshall–Lerner condition is not fulfilled, then exports will rise by less than imports implying that income will fall. Hence, the Marshall–Lerner condition is clearly relevant to the absorption approach. Similarly, when account is taken of income effects the necessary elasticity condition for a devaluation to improve the current balance is affected. This is because if the elasticities sum to greater than unity, so that there is an initial improvement in the current balance, this improvement leads to an increase in income which induces a larger increase in imports than in the absence of such an income effect. For this reason, the initial improvement in the current account has to be more pronounced than in the absence of such income effects. This implies that the sum of elasticities needs to be somewhat greater than the unity value derived from the elasticity approach. Thus, the absorption approach is relevant to the elasticity approach.

3.9 Conclusions

We have seen that the absorption approach, like the elasticity approach, does not provide an unambiguous answer to the question of whether a devaluation leads to an improvement in the current account. At issue is how economic agents respond to the change in relative prices that is implied by a devaluation. The two analyses are not alternative theories, but rather provide complementary insights into the processes at work.

Although, the two models are comparative static in nature, they both point to the importance of dynamic forces and a time dimension to the eventual outcome. Demand elasticities are higher in the long run than in the short run, leading to a possible J-curve effect and the effects of a devaluation on income and absorption will be spread over time. Even in these simple models, it is seen that there are likely to be a variety of forces at work. No doubt even greater ambiguity would emerge as a result of including time lags, wealth effects and an explicit treatment of expectations.

Despite their simplistic assumptions, ambiguous conclusions and deficiencies the two approaches have remained influential because they contain clear and useful messages for policy-makers. A devaluation is more likely to succeed when elasticities of demand for imports and exports are high and when it is accompanied by measures such as fiscal and monetary restraint that boost income relative to domestic absorption.

The overwhelming weight of empirical estimates suggests that at two years and above time horizons the Marshall–Lerner conditions are fulfilled, suggesting that exchange rate adjustments are an influential tool in eliminating current account deficits. One should not expect a devaluation to work in the same manner for all countries. The effects of a devaluation will in part be determined by whether or not the economy is at or below full employment and on the structural parameters of the particular economy under consideration. Finally, it should be remembered that both models assume that foreign countries do not react to the competitive advantage gained by the devaluing country. To the extent that they react by devaluing their currencies, this will undermine the effectiveness of a devaluation policy.

Further reading

Alexander, S. (1952) 'Effects of a Devaluation on a Trade Balance', IMF Staff Papers, pp. 263–78, reprinted in R.E. Caves and H.G. Johnson (eds) (1968), *Readings in International Economics* (Homewood, Illonois: Irwin).

Alexander, S. (1959) 'Effects of Devaluation: A Simplified Synthesis of Elasticities and Absorption Approaches', *American Economic Review*, vol. 49, pp. 22–42.

Artus, J.R. and Knight, M.D. (1984) 'Issues in the Assessment of the Exchange Rates of Industrial Countries', IMF Occasional Paper, no. 29.

Goldstein, M. and Kahn, M.S. (1985) 'Income and Price Effects in Foreign Trade', in R.W. Jones and P.B. Kenen (eds), *Handbook of International Economics*, Vol. II (Amsterdam: Elsevier).

Gylfason, T. (1987) 'Does Exchange Rate Policy Matter?', *European Economic Review*, vol. 30, pp. 375–81.

Hooper, P., Johnson, K. and Marquez, J. (1998) 'Trade Elasticities for G-7 Countries', International Finance Discussion Papers no. 609, Board of Governors of the Federal Reserve System.

Johnson, H.G. (1976) 'Elasticity, Absorption, Keynesian Multiplier, Keynesian Policy and Monetary Approaches to Devaluation Theory: A Simple Geometric Exposition', *American Economic Review*.

Klitgaard, T. (1999) 'Exchange Rates and Profit Margins: The Case of Japanese Exporters', Federal Reserve Bank of New York, Economic Policy Review, vol. 5, no. 1, pp. 41–54.

Krugman, P. (1991) 'Has the Adjustment Process Worked?', in F.C. Bergsten (ed.), *International Adjustment and Financing, The Lessons of 1985–1991* (Washington: Institute for International Economics).

Laursen, S. and Metzler, L.A. (1950) 'Flexible Exchange Rates and the Theory of Employment', *Review of Economics and Statistics*.

Lerner, A. (1944) *The Economics of Control* (London: Macmillan, now Palgrave Macmillan).

Marshall, A. (1923) *Credit and Commerce* (London: Macmillan, now Palgrave Macmillan).

Machlup, F. (1955) 'Relative Prices and Aggregate Spending in the Analysis of Devaluation', *American Economic Review* (June).

Meade, J. (1951) *The Theory of International Economic Policy, Vol. 1, The Balance of Payments* (London: Oxford University Press).

Robinson, J. (1937) 'The Foreign Exchanges', in J. Robinson, *Essays in the Theory of Employment* (Oxford: Basil Blackwell).

Stern, R.M. (1973) *The Balance of Payments: Theory and Economic Policy* (London: Macmillan, now Palgrave Macmillan).

Tsiang, S.C. (1961) 'The Role of Money in Trade Balance Stability: Synthesis of the Elasticity and Absorption Approaches', *American Economic Review*, vol. 51, pp. 912–36.

Yang, J. (1997) 'Exchange Rate Pass-Through in U.S. Manufacturing Industries', *Review of Economics and Statistics*, vol. 79, no. 1, pp. 95–104.

4

Macroeconomic Policy in an Open Economy

4.1   Introduction

In Chapter 3 we looked at some of the fundamental identities for an open economy and considered the possible effect of devaluation on the current account. It was noted that the ultimate impact of a devaluation will in large part be dependent upon the economic policies that accompany the devaluation. In this chapter we shall be examining how both exchange rate changes and macroeconomic policies impact upon an open economy. A fundamental difference between an open economy and a closed economy is that over time a country has to ensure that there is an approximate balance in its current account. This is because no country can continuously build up a stock of net liabilities to the rest of the world by running a continuous current account deficit. Conversely, it does not make sense for a surplus country to continuously build up a stock of net claims on the rest of the world. Eventually it will wish to spend those claims.

The need for economic policy-makers to pay attention to the implications of changes in monetary and fiscal policy on the balance of payments is an important additional dimension for consideration in the formulation of economic policy in an open economy. Ensuring a sustainable balance of payments position over time is an important economic objective to go along with those like high economic growth, low unemployment and low inflation.

One of the additional policy choices that has to be made by the authorities of an open economy is to decide whether to fix the exchange rate, allow it to float, or perhaps choose some arrangement between these two extremes. The choice between these two regimes is the focus of analysis of Chapter 10; in this chapter we concentrate upon how fiscal and monetary policy operate under both regimes.

4.2 The problem of internal and external balance

To appreciate the development of the postwar literature on open economies, readers need to bear in mind that between 1948 and 1973 the international monetary system was one of fixed exchange rates, with the major currencies being pegged to the US dollar. Only in cases of 'fundamental disequilibrium' were authorities allowed to devalue or revalue their currencies. This meant that there was considerable interest in the relative effectiveness of fiscal and monetary policies as a means of influencing the economy. Although economic policy-makers generally have many macroeconomic aims, the discussion in the 1950s and 1960s was primarily concerned with two objectives. The principal goal was one of achieving full employment for the labour force along with a stable level of prices which may be termed internal balance. Although governments were generally committed to achieving full employment it is widely recognized that expanding output in an open economy will have implications for the balance of payments. For instance, expanding output and employment will result in greater expenditure on imports and consequently lead to a deterioration of the current account. As authorities had agreed to maintain fixed exchange rates, they were interested in running an equilibrium in the balance of payments, that is, balance in the supply and demand for their currency. This latter objective can be termed external balance.

Changes in fiscal and monetary policies which aim to influence the level of aggregate demand in the economy are termed **expenditure changing** policies. Whereas policies such as devaluation/revaluation of the exchange rate which attempt to influence the composition of spending as between domestic and foreign goods are known as **expenditure switching** policies.

Much of the 1950s and 1960s literature was concerned with how the authorities might simultaneously achieve both internal and external balance. The policy problem of achieving both internal and external balance was conceptualized by Trevor Swan (1955) in what is known as the Swan diagram, which is illustrated in **Figure 4.1**. On the vertical axis is the real exchange rate, defined as domestic currency units per unit of foreign currency so that a rise represents a real depreciation which implies improved international competitiveness. On the horizontal axis we have the amount of real domestic absorption which represents the sum of consumption, investment and government expenditure.

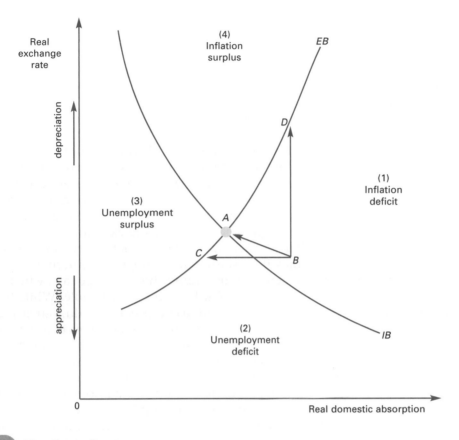

Figure 4.1 The Swan diagram

The IB schedule represents combinations of the real exchange rate and domestic absorption for which the economy is in internal balance, that is full employment with stable prices. The IB schedule is downward-sloping from left to right. This is because an appreciation (fall) of the real exchange rate will reduce exports and increase imports, therefore to maintain full employment it is necessary for there to be an increase in domestic expenditure. To the right of the IB schedule there are inflationary pressures in the economy because for a given exchange rate domestic expenditure is greater than that required to produce full employment, while to the left there are deflationary pressures because expenditure is short of that required to maintain full employment.

The EB schedule shows combinations of the real exchange rate and domestic absorption for which the economy is in external balance, that is equilibrium in the current account. The EB schedule is upward-sloping from left to right. This is because a depreciation of the exchange rate will increase exports and reduce imports, so to prevent the current account moving into surplus requires increased domestic expenditure to induce an offsetting increase in imports. To the right of the EB schedule domestic expenditure is greater than that required for current account equilibrium so the result is a current account deficit, while to the left there is a current account surplus.

Hence, the Swan diagram is divided into four zones depicting different possible states for an economy:

Zone 1 – a deficit and inflationary pressures.
Zone 2 – a deficit and deflationary pressures.
Zone 3 – a surplus and deflationary pressures.
Zone 4 – a surplus and inflationary pressures.

Only at point A where the IB and EB schedules intersect is the economy in both internal and external equilibrium. Suppose that the economy for some reason finds itself at point B in zone 1, experiencing both inflationary pressures and a current account deficit. If the authorities maintain a fixed exchange rate and try to reduce the current account deficit by cutting back real domestic expenditure they move the economy towards point C. While to achieve external balance by using expenditure-reducing policies alone would require such a cut-back in absorption that the economy would suffer and be pushed into recession with resulting unemployment. Alternatively, the authorities might try to tackle the deficit by devaluing the exchange rate, which has the effect of moving the economy towards point D on the EB schedule. While the devaluation has the effect of reducing the current account deficit it does so at the expense of adding further inflationary pressures to the economy. This is shown by the fact that the economy moves further away from the internal balance schedule.

A major lesson of this simple model is that the use of one instrument, be it fiscal policy or devaluation, to achieve two targets, internal and external balance, is most unlikely to be successful. To move from point B to point A, the authorities need to both deflate the economy and undertake a devaluation by appropriate amounts. The deflation combined with a devaluation will control inflation and improve the current account so that the two objectives can be met. The idea that a country generally requires as many instruments as it has targets was elaborated by the Nobel Prize-winning Dutch economist Jan Tinbergen (1952), and is popularly known as Tinbergen's instruments–targets rule.

While the Swan diagram provides a useful conceptual framework for economic policy discussion, it is rather simplistic in that the underlying economic relationships are not explicitly defined. Furthermore, there is no role for international capital movements that were an increasingly important feature of the post-Second World War international economy. In addition, there is no distinction made between monetary and fiscal policies as means of influencing aggregate demand and output in the economy. The so called Mundell–Fleming model to which we now turn attempts to integrate such features into a formal open economy macroeconomic model.

4.3 The Mundell–Fleming model

This model owes its origins to papers published by James Fleming (1962) and Robert Mundell (1962 and 1963). Their major contribution was to incorporate international capital movements into formal macroeconomic models based on the Keynesian IS–LM framework. Their papers led to some dramatic implications concerning the effectiveness of fiscal and monetary policy for the attainment of internal and external balance. We shall now examine the main implications of the Keynesian model and the results of Fleming's and Mundell's papers by using what is known as IS–LM–BP analysis. Firstly we derive the IS, LM and BP schedules that provide the framework for the analysis.

4.4 **Derivation of the IS schedule for an open economy**

The IS curve for an open economy shows various combinations of the level of output (Y) and the rate of interest that make leakages, that is savings and import expenditure ($S + M$), equal to injections, that is investment, government expenditure and exports ($I + G + X$). In an open economy we have he identity:

$$Y = C + I + G + X - M \tag{4.1}$$

where Y is national income, C is domestic consumption, I is domestic investment, G is government expenditure, X is export expenditure and M is import expenditure. This identity can be restated in terms of equality between leakages and injections. Since $Y - C = S$, where S is savings, we can rewrite equation (4.1) as:

$$S + M = I + G + X \tag{4.2}$$

For simplicity the following linear relationships are assumed:

$$S = S_a + sY \tag{4.3}$$

Here, savings S are equal to autonomous savings (S_a) plus savings which are a positive function of income, where s is the marginal propensity to save.

$$M = M_a + mY \tag{4.4}$$

Imports M are equal to autonomous imports (M_a) plus imports which are a positive function of increases in income, where m is the marginal propensity to import.

$$I = I(r) \qquad dI/dr < 0 \tag{4.5}$$

Equation (4.5) says that investment is assumed to be an inverse function of the rate of interest. As far as government expenditure and exports are concerned these are assumed to be autonomous with respect to the rate of interest and level of national income. The relationships above are illustrated in **Figure 4.2**.

Quadrant (1) depicts the relationship between leakages and income; it is an upward-sloping line because increases in income lead to increased savings and imports, and the slope of the line is given by $1/(s + m)$. At income level Y_1, the corresponding level of leakages is given by L_1, and likewise at income level Y_2 the corresponding level of leakages is given by L_2. The resulting volume of leakages is transferred to quadrant (2), which has a 45-degree line that converts any distance along the vertical axis to an equivalent distance on the horizontal axis which measures injections. Hence, the leakages L_1 are converted into an equivalent amount of injection In_1.

The injections schedule is depicted in quadrant (3) which shows that given the price level and state of expectations the rate of interest that leads to a level of injections In_1 is given by r_1. The injections schedule is downward-sloping from left to right because investment is inversely related to the rate of interest, while the level of government expenditure and exports are assumed to be independent of the rate of interest.

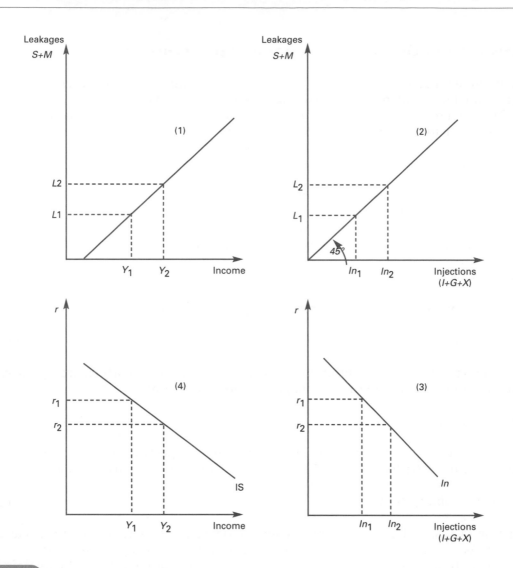

Figure 4.2 Derivation of the IS schedule

We now know that the income level Y_1 generates leakages L_1 which will be equal to injections In_1 if the interest rate is r_1. This means that in quadrant (4) we can depict a point on the IS curve for an open economy because at interest rate r_1 and income level Y_1 we know that leakages are equal to injections. We can repeat the same process for the income level Y_2 to obtain the rate of interest r_2 for which leakages are equal to injections. By repeating the process we can obtain a large number of income and interest rate levels for which leakages are equal to injections. By joining up these points we obtain the IS curve for an open economy. As can be seen in quadrant (4), the IS curve is downward-sloping from left to right in the interest rate/income level space. This is because higher levels of income generate higher levels of leakages requiring a fall in the interest rate to generate increased investment and maintain equality of injections an leakages.

4.5 Derivation of the LM schedule for an open economy

The LM schedule shows various combinations of the level of income and rate of interest for which the money market is in equilibrium; that is, for which money demand equals money supply. In the simplified model, we assume that money is demanded for only two reasons; transactions purposes and speculative purposes. With the transactions motive people hold money because there is not normally a synchronization between their receipt and expenditure of money. In general it is postulated that the higher an individuals' income the larger the amount of money that is held for transactions purposes. This is based on the presumption that the higher one's income the greater one's payments and correspondingly the greater the desired holdings of money for transaction purposes. As such, the transactions demand for money is assumed to be a positive function of income. This is expressed algebraically as:

$$M_t = M_t(Y) \qquad\qquad (4.6)$$

where M_t is the transactions demand for money.

The other reason for holding money is the speculative motive. It is assumed that any money balances held in excess of those required for transactions purposes are speculative balances. If the rate of interest rises then so does the opportunity cost of holding money. For instance, if the rate of interest is 5% per annum the opportunity cost of £100 is £5 per annum, but if the interest rate is 10% the opportunity cost is £10 per annum and consequently the demand to hold speculative balances will fall as the rate of interest rises. This inverse relationship between the demand for speculative balances and the rate of interest is expressed algebraically as:

$$M_{sp} = M_{sp}(r) \qquad\qquad (4.7)$$

where M_{sp} is the speculative demand for money.
In equilibrium, the money demand (M_d) made up of transactions and speculative balances is equal to the money supply (M_s). This is expressed algebraically as:

$$M_d = M_{sp} + M_t = M_s \qquad\qquad (4.8)$$

The derivation of the LM curve is illustrated in **Figure 4.3**. Quadrant (1) depicts the transactions demand for money as a positive function of income. As income rises from Y_1 to Y_2, the demand for transaction balances rises from M_{t1} to M_{t2}. The transactions balance figure is transferred to quadrant (2) which shows the distribution of the fixed money supply between transaction and speculative balances. The distance 0a represents the total money supply, so that if M_{t1} is held for transaction purposes, then 0a minus M_{t1} which is equal to M_{sp1} is held as speculative balances. Quadrant (3) shows the speculative demand for money schedule which is downward-sloping from left to right because the demand for speculative balances is inversely related to the rate if interest. The schedule reveals that speculative balances M_{sp1} are only willingly held at the interest rate r_1. We now have enough information to plot a point on the LM schedule; this is done in quadrant (4) which shows that at interest rate r_1 and income level Y_1 the demand for speculative and transaction balances is equal to the money supply.

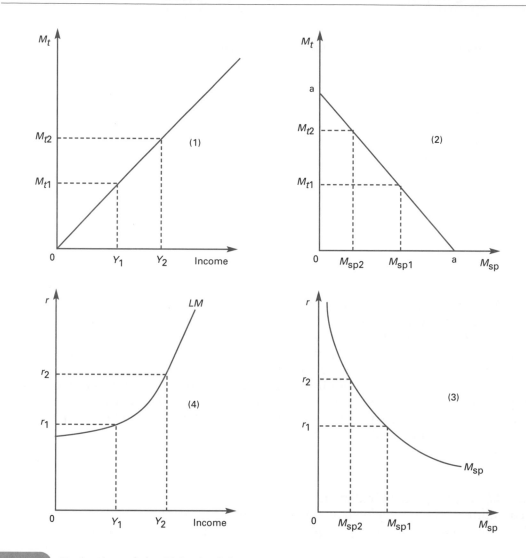

Figure 4.3 Derivation of the LM schedule

By taking another income level Y_2 we can by a similar process find a rate of interest r_2 which is compatible with money-market equilibrium. Other such derivations can be done and by joining them together we obtain the LM schedule. The LM schedule is upward-sloping from left to right. This is because high income levels require relatively large transaction balances which for a given money supply can only be drawn out of speculative balances by a relatively high interest rate.

4.6 Derivation of the BP schedule for an open economy

The balance of payments schedule shows different combinations of rates of interest and income that are compatible with equilibrium in the balance of payments. When referring to the balance of payments we divide it up into two sections; the current account and the capital account. Exports are assumed to be independent of the level of national income and the rate of interest, but imports are assumed to be positively related to income, expressed algebraically as:

$$M = M_a + mY \qquad (4.9)$$

Total imports (M) are a function of autonomous imports (M_a) and the level of income, where m is the marginal propensity to import.

We now need to remind ourselves of the constituent parts of the balance of payments. As we saw in Chapter 2, the overall balance of payments is made up of three major components; the current account (CA), the capital account (K) and the change in the authorities reserves (dR). By maintaining balance in the supply and demand for the currency – that is external balance – we mean that there is no need for the authorities to have to change their holdings of foreign exchange reserves. This implies that if there is a current account deficit there needs to be an offsetting surplus in the capital account so that the authorities do not have to change their reserves. Conversely, if there is a current account surplus there needs to be an offsetting deficit in the capital account to have equilibrium in the balance of payments.

Since exports are determined exogenously and imports are a positive function of income, the higher the level of national income the smaller will be any current account surplus or the larger any current account deficit. The net capital flow (K) is a positive function of the domestic interest rate. Assuming that the rate of interest in the rest of the world (r^*) is fixed, the higher the domestic interest rate (r) the greater the capital inflow into the country, or the smaller any capital outflow. This relationship is expressed algebraically as:

$$K = K(r - r^*) \qquad (4.10)$$

Since the balance of payments schedule shows various combinations of levels of income and the rate of interest for which the balance of payments is in equilibrium, then:

$$X - M + K = 0 \qquad (4.11)$$

A positive K indicates a net inflow of funds, whereas a negative K indicates a net outflow of funds.

The derivation of the BP schedule is illustrated in **Figure 4.4**. Quadrant (1) shows the relationship between the current account and level of national income. The current balance schedule slopes downwards from left to right because increases in income lead to a deterioration of the current account. At income level Y_1 there is a current account surplus of CA_1, whereas at income level Y_2 there is a current account deficit of CA_2. The current account surplus or deficit is transferred to quadrant (2) where the 45-degree line converts the current account position to an equal capital flow of the opposite sign. With a current account surplus CA_1 there is a required capital outflow K_1 to ensure balance of payments equilibrium, while a current account deficit CA_2 requires a capital inflow K_2. Quadrant (3) shows the rate of interest that is required for a given capital flow. The capital flow schedule is downward-sloping from left to right because high interest rates encourage a net capital inflow whereas low

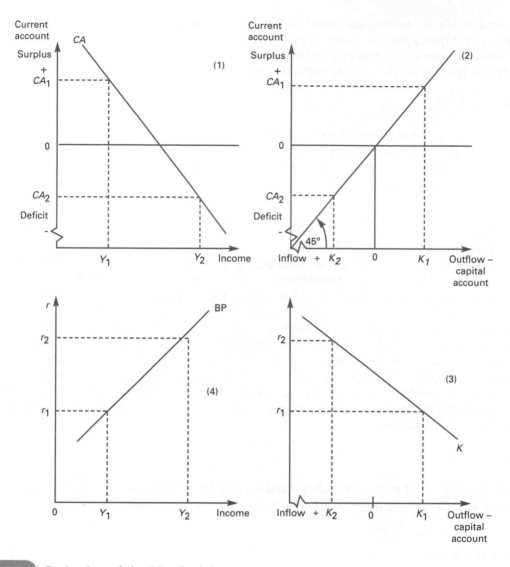

Figure 4.4 Derivation of the BP schedule

interest rates encourage a net capital outflow. To get a capital outflow of K_1 requires the interest rate to be r_1, while a capital inflow of K_2 requires a higher interest rate r_2.

Since income level Y_1 is associated with a balance of payments surplus, there has to be an offsetting capital outflow K_1 which requires an interest rate r_1; these coordinates give a point on the BP schedule that is depicted in quadrant (4). The BP schedule is upward-sloping because higher levels of income cause a deterioration in the current account, which necessitates a reduced capital outflow/higher capital inflow requiring a higher interest rate. Every point on the BP schedule shows a combination of domestic income and rate of interest for which the overall balance of payments is in equilibrium. At points to the left of the BP schedule the overall balance of payments is in surplus because for a given amount of capital flows the current account is better than that required for equilibrium as the level of income is lower. Conversely, to the right of the BP schedule the overall balance of payments is in deficit as the income level is higher than that compatible with overall equilibrium.

At this point it is worth noting that the slope of the BP schedule is determined by the degree of capital mobility internationally; the higher the degree of capital mobility then the flatter the BP schedule. This is because for a given increase in income which leads to a deterioration of the current account, the higher the degree of capital mobility the smaller the required rise in the domestic interest rate to attract sufficient capital inflows to ensure overall equilibrium. When capital is perfectly mobile, the slightest rise in the domestic interest rate above the world interest rate leads to a massive capital inflow making the BP schedule horizontal at the world interest rate. At the other extreme, if capital is perfectly immobile internationally then a rise in the domestic interest will fail to attract capital inflows making the BP schedule vertical at the income level that ensures current account balance. Between these two extremes, that is when we have an upward-sloping BP schedule, we say that capital is imperfectly mobile.

4.7 Equilibrium of the model

Figure 4.5 depicts all three schedules intersecting through a common point. The BP schedule is steeper than the LM schedule, but this need not always be the case. As we shall see later, changing the relative slope of the two schedules can lead to somewhat different policy prescriptions. All three schedules pass through a common point A which corresponds to the domestic interest rate r_1 and income level Y_1. The income level Y_1 is seen to be less than that of the full employment level of income Y_f, implying that there is some unemployment in the economy. Although the economy is not in internal equilibrium, the balance of payments is in equilibrium because the IS and LM schedules intersect at a point on the BP schedule.

The explanation as to why the IS–LM schedules do not intersect at the full employment level of income Y_f is that at Y_f planned leakages (savings and import expenditure) would exceed planned injections (government expenditure, exports and investment). This would imply a build up of stocks of unsold goods leading producers to reduce output. Only at output level Y_1 do planned leakages equal planned injections so that changes in stocks are avoided.

Figure 4.6 illustrates scenarios where there is a surplus or deficit in the balance of payments. In **Figure 4.6(a)**, because the IS and LM schedules intersect to the left of the BP schedule, there is a balance of payments surplus. This surplus comes about because the level of income is too low and/or the rate of interest is too high to be compatible with overall equilibrium. In **Figure 4.6(b)** there is a balance of payments deficit because the IS and LM schedules interest to the right of the BP schedule, which means that the income level Y_2 too high and/or the interest rate r_2 is too low, inducing an overall balance of payments deficit.

4.8 Factors shifting the IS–LM–BP schedules

In the analysis of the rest of this chapter we need to consider how changes in the exchange rate and monetary and fiscal policies affect the position of the various schedules.

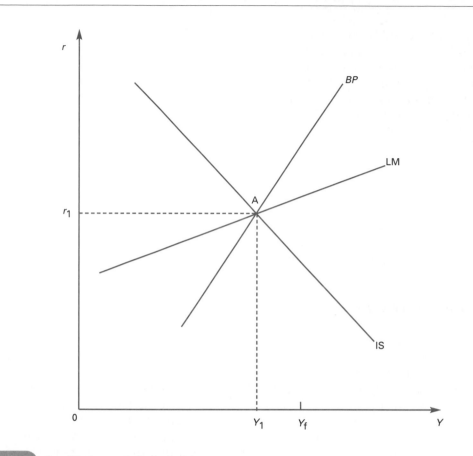

Figure 4.5 Equilibrium of the model

Factors shifting the IS schedule

The IS schedule will shift to the right if there is an increase in either investment, government expenditure or exports. This is because an increase in these injections requires a higher level of national income to induce a matching increase in leakages in the form of increased savings and imports. An autonomous fall in savings or imports will also require a rightward shift of the IS schedule because a higher level of income is required to induce more savings and import expenditure so as to maintain equality of leakages and injections. Another important factor that causes a rightward shift of the IS schedule is a depreciation or devaluation of the exchange rate, providing that the Marshall–Lerner condition holds; this is because a depreciation (rise) in the exchange rate leads to a reduction of import expenditure and an increase in export sales so that injections then exceed leakages requiring an increased level of income to bring them back into equality.

Factors shifting the LM schedule

The LM schedule will shift to the right if there is an increase in the domestic money supply because, for a given rate of interest, the increased supply will only be willingly

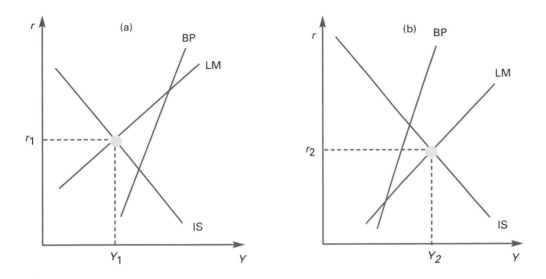

Figure 4.6 Surplus (a) and deficit (b) in the balance of payments

held if there is an increase in income which leads to a rise in the transactions demand for money. A depreciation of the exchange rate will lead to a rise in the aggregate price index, that is an index made up of a weighted basket of domestic and foreign imported goods (see equation 3.16), because it implies a rise in the price of imports. This means that real money balances will be reduced and there will be a resulting increase in the demand for money that can only be eliminated by reducing the transactions demand for money implying a lower level of income and leftward shift of the LM schedule.

Factors shifting the BP schedule

An autonomous increase in exports or an autonomous decrease in imports will lead to an improvement in the current account requiring a rightward shift of the BP schedule to induce a sufficient increase in imports to maintain balance of payments equilibrium. Another factor that can cause a rightward shift of the BP schedule is a depreciation/devaluation of the exchange rate, providing the Marshall–Lerner condition holds; the value of export sales will rise and the value of import expenditure decline. Hence, the only way to ensure overall balance of payments equilibrium is a rise in the level of domestic income.

Bearing in mind these shift factors we proceed to look at how this toolkit can be usefully applied to some key issues in the realm of open economy macroeconomic policy.

4.9 Internal and external balance

The Swan diagram showed that authorities generally need as many instruments as they have targets and revealed that the use of both expenditure switching and expenditure-changing policies can lead to the attainment of internal and external balance.

However, it was not possible to distinguish between the fact that fiscal and monetary policies are quite different and independent types of expenditure-changing policies. This begs the question as to whether or not it is feasible to achieve the twin objectives of internal and external balance by combining fiscal and monetary policies without the need to adjust the exchange rate?

Before attempting to answer this question we need to consider how monetary and fiscal policy may be used as policy instruments for achieving internal and external balance, and to consider how the two policies influence economic activity.

Monetary policy

When the authorities conduct an expansionary monetary policy they purchase bonds from the public, which pushes up the price of bonds, expands the money supply and leads to a fall in the domestic interest rate. The fall in the domestic interest rate will stimulate investment and so lead to a rise in output. As far as the balance of payments is concerned, the increased income leads to a deterioration of the current account and the lower interest rate will lead to increased capital outflows so that the balance of payments moves into deficit. Conversely, a contractionary monetary policy involves the authorities selling bonds, which pushes down the price of bonds, reduces the money supply and leads to a rise in the domestic interest rate. The rise in the interest rate leads to less investment and a fall in output. The balance of payments position will improve as imports fall and the higher interest rate attracts capital inflows.

Fiscal policy

With an expansionary fiscal policy, the government increases its expenditure and with pure fiscal policy finances this increased expenditure by selling bonds. The increased expenditure shifts the IS schedule to the right through the government expenditure multiplier effect examined in Chapter 3. However, the bond sales will depress the price of bonds thereby raising the domestic interest rate which will partially offset expansion in output. The precise effect of the fiscal expansion on the balance of payments is indeterminate because, while the expansion of output will worsen the current account, the rise in interest rates will improve the capital account. The converse reasoning holds for a contractionary fiscal policy. The money supply is not affected by the expansionary fiscal policy since the money raised by bond sales is used to finance the increased government expenditure.

Sterilized and non-sterilized intervention

One other policy which we need to clarify is the distinction between sterilized and non-sterilized intervention in the foreign exchange market. With sterilized intervention the authorities offset the money-base implications of their exchange market interventions to ensure that the changes in reserves due to intervention do not affect the domestic money base. Whereas with a policy of non-sterilized intervention the authorities allow the reserve changes resulting from their interventions to affect the monetary base.

We illustrate the distinction between sterilized and non-sterilized intervention by an example of what happens if there is a monetary expansion under fixed exchange rates; this is depicted in **Figure 4.7**. A monetary expansion shifts the LM schedule to

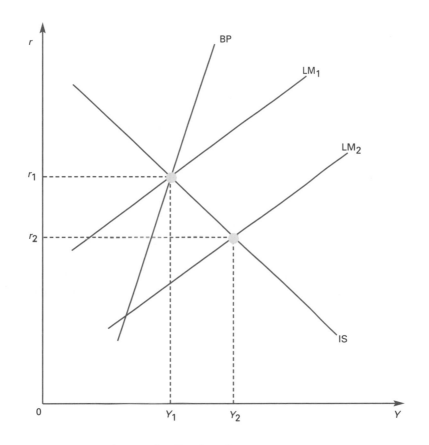

Figure 4.7 A monetary expansion under fixed exchange rates

the right from LM_1 to LM_2. This causes a fall in the interest rate to r_2 and a rise in domestic income to Y_2, the result is a balance of payments deficit as both the current and capital account deteriorate. The deficit means that there is an excess supply of the currency on the foreign exchange market and to maintain a fixed exchange rate the authorities have to purchase the home currency with reserves.

Ordinarily, the purchases of the home currency by the authorities would start to shift the LM schedule back to the left from LM_2 back towards LM_1. This is an example of non-sterilized intervention, that is the authorities allow their interventions in the foreign exchange market to influence the money supply. However, if the authorities pursue a policy of sterilization of reserve changes, the reserve falls which reduce the money supply are exactly offset by a further expansion of the money supply so that the LM schedule remains at point LM_2. A clear problem with a sterilization policy is that by remaining at LM_2 with interest rate r_2 and income level Y_2, the authorities will suffer a continuous balance of payments deficit and a continuous fall in reserves. Such a sterilization policy is only feasible in the short run because over the longer run reserves would eventually run out making a devaluation inevitable.

We can are now in a position to examine how fiscal and monetary policy and exchange rate policy can be combined in various combinations to simultaneously achieve internal and external balance.

4.10 Internal and external balance under fixed exchange rates

A situation of fixed exchange rates and unemployment is depicted in **Figure 4.8**. The economy is assumed to be at point A with interest rate r_1 and income level Y_1, which means that while the economy is in external balance the income level is below the full employment level of income Y_f.

The government attempts to eradicate the unemployment via a bond-financed fiscal expansion, which shifts the IS schedule to the right from IS_1 to IS_2. Domestic output expands from Y_1 to Y_2 and the economy would be at point B with interest rate r_2. In raising the level of output beyond the full employment level we find that the induced increase in imports moves the current account into deficit, and although the rise in the interest rate attracts some capital inflow the balance of payments is in overall deficit since the economy is to the right of the BP schedule. The authorities are forced to purchase the home currency in the foreign exchange market, but because they pursue a sterilization policy the LM schedule remains at LM_1. Hence, using only a single policy instrument, in this case fiscal policy, the government can temporarily achieve its internal objective at the expense of a sacrifice in the objective of external balance.

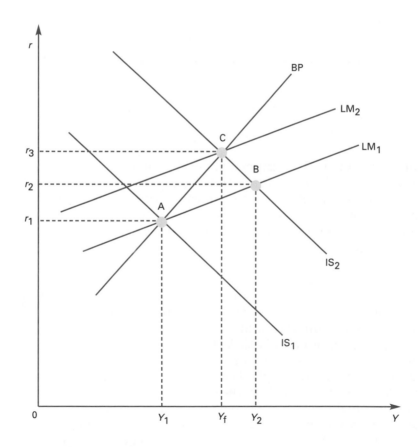

Figure 4.8 Internal and external balance under a fixed exchange rate

Ideally, however, the authorities would like to achieve both internal and external balance. This is possible if they combine the expansionary fiscal policy – IS_1 to IS_2 – with a contractionary monetary policy which shifts the LM schedule from LM_1 to LM_2 where it passes through point C on the BP schedule. The restrictive monetary policy raises interest rates further than in the case of a solely fiscal expansion to r_3, and in so doing attracts additional capital inflows so as to restore the balance of payments back to equilibrium. Hence, by combining an expansionary fiscal policy with a contractionary monetary policy the authorities can achieve both internal and external balance. An important lesson from this example is that the authorities can achieve both internal and external balance without the need to change the exchange rate; this is because they have two independent instruments, monetary and fiscal policy, and two targets.

4.11 Internal and external balance under floating exchange rates

According to our analysis of the Swan diagram, by combining an exchange rate change with an expenditure-changing policy it is possible to achieve both internal and external balance. An interesting issue that we can explore within the framework of our model is what are the likely differences of achieving internal and external balance by combining exchange rate changes with monetary policy as opposed to doing so by combining exchange rate changes with fiscal policy. To examine this issue we first consider the case of combining exchange rate adjustments with monetary policy, and then examine the implications of combining exchange rate adjustment with fiscal policy.

Figure 4.9 considers the case of monetary expansion under floating exchange rates. Initial equilibrium is at point A with interest rate r_1 and output level Y_1. The authorities adopt an expansionary monetary policy and this shifts the LM schedule from LM_1 to LM_2. The combination of a fall in the interest rate and increase in income leads to a balance of payments deficit at point B. However, the exchange rate is allowed to depreciate and this leads to a rightward shift of the IS schedule from IS_1 to IS_2, and a rightward shift of the BP schedule from BP_1 to BP_2. However, it also leads to a leftward shift of the LM schedule until all three schedules intersect at a common point such as C, with new income level Y_2 and interest rate r_2. Hence, by using monetary policy in conjunction with exchange rate changes, it is possible to raise real output to the full employment level and achieve external balance simultaneously.

Overall, the money-supply expansion results in an exchange rate depreciation, a fall in the domestic interest rate and an increase in income. The lower interest rate implies a lower capital inflow/higher capital outflow than before the money supply expansion, while the increase in income worsens the current account. This implies that the depreciation improves the current account to exactly offset the preceding effects.

Fiscal expansion under floating exchange rates

The effects of a fiscal expansion on the exchange rate under floating rates depend crucially upon the slope of the BP schedule relative to the LM schedule. We shall consider two cases; in case 1 the BP schedule is steeper than the LM schedule, while in case 2 the reverse is true.

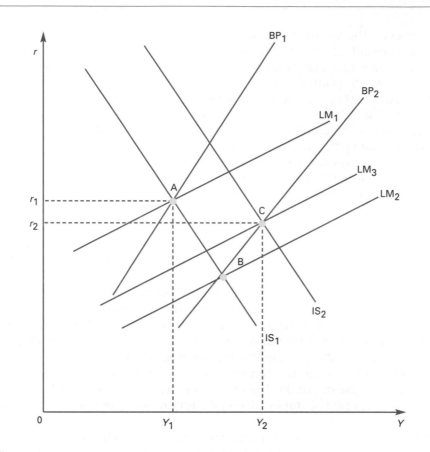

Figure 4.9 A monetary expansion under floating exchange rates

In **Figure 4.10** the BP schedule is steeper than the LM schedule, which means that capital flows are relatively insensitive to interest rate changes, while money demand is fairly elastic with respect to the interest rate. An expansionary fiscal policy shifts the IS schedule from IS_1 to IS_2. The induced rise of the domestic interest rate and domestic income has opposing effects on the balance of payments, the expansion in real output leads to a deterioration of the current account but the rise in interest rate improves the capital account. However, because capital flows are relatively immobile the former effect outweighs the latter so the balance of payments moves into deficit. In turn, the deficit leads to a depreciation of the exchange rate, this has the effect of shifting the BP schedule to the right from BP_1 to BP_2 and the LM schedule to the left from LM_1 to LM_2 and the IS schedule even further to the right from IS_2 to IS_3. Final equilibrium is obtained at point C, with interest rate r_2 and income level Y_2. Hence, the deterioration in the balance of payments resulting from the rise in real income is offset by a combination of a higher interest rate and an exchange rate depreciation.

In **Figure 4.11** an expansionary fiscal policy shifts the IS schedule from IS_1 to IS_2. In this case because capital flows are much more responsive to changes in interest rates the BP schedule is less steep than the LM schedule. The increased capital inflow more than offsets the deterioration in the current account due to the increase in income, and the balance of payments moves into surplus. The surplus induces an appreciation

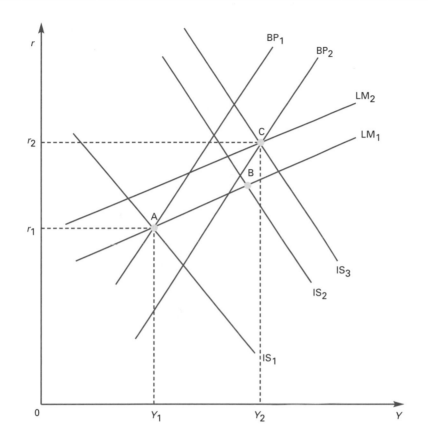

Figure 4.10 Case 1: A fiscal expansion under floating exchange rates

of the exchange rate, which moves the LM schedule to the right from LM_1 to LM_2, the BP schedule to the left from BP_1 to BP_2 and the IS schedule to the left from IS_2 to IS_3. Equilibrium is obtained at a higher level of output, higher interest rate and an exchange rate appreciation.

Hence a fiscal expansion can, according to the degree of international capital mobility, lead to either an exchange rate depreciation of an exchange rate appreciation.

4.12 A small open economy with perfect capital mobility

One prominent feature of the post-Second World War international monetary system has been the increasing integration of international capital markets. There has been a great deal of discussion about the desirability of these capital flows and how they might threaten the ability of authorities to conduct effective economic policies. In classic papers, Mundell (1962) and Fleming (1962) sought to examine the implications of high capital mobility for a small country that had no ability to influence world interest rates. Their papers showed that for such a country, the choice of exchange rate regime would have a radical implications concerning the effectiveness of monetary and fiscal policy in influencing the level of economic activity.

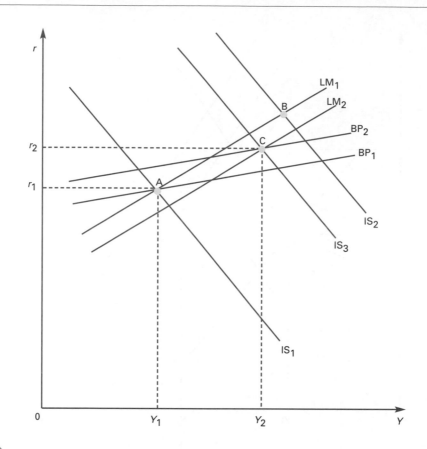

Figure 4.11 Case 2: A fiscal expansion under floating exchange rates

The model assumes a small country facing perfect capital mobility. Any attempt to raise the domestic interest rate leads to a massive capital inflow to purchase domestic bonds pushing up the price of bonds until the interest rate returns to the world interest rate. Conversely, any attempt to lower the domestic interest rate leads to a massive capital outflow as international investors seek higher world interest rates. Such massive bond sales mean that the domestic interest rate immediately returns to the world interest rate so as to stop the capital outflow. The implication of perfect capital mobility is that the BP schedule for a small open economy becomes a horizontal straight line at a domestic interest rate that is the same as the world interest rate.

Figure 4.12 depicts a small open economy with a fixed exchange rate; the initial level of income is where the IS–LM curves intersect at the income level Y_1 which is below the full employment level of income Y_f. If the authorities attempt to raise output by a monetary expansion the LM schedule shifts to the right from LM_1 to LM_2. There is downward pressure on the domestic interest rate and this results in a massive capital outflow. This capital outflow means that there is pressure for a devaluation of the currency; the authorities have to intervene in the foreign exchange market to purchase the home currency with reserves. Such purchases result in a reduction of the money supply in the hands of private agents. The purchases have to continue until the LM curve shifts back to its original position at LM_1 where the domestic interest

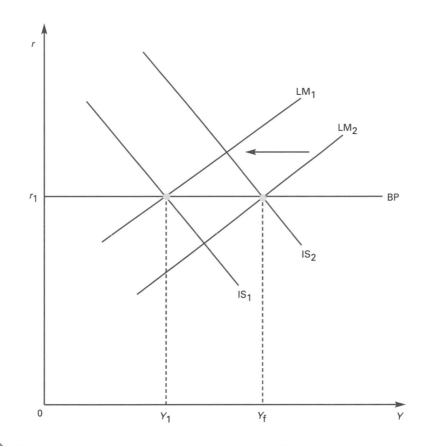

Figure 4.12 Fixed exchange rates and perfect capital mobility

rate is restored to the world interest rate. With perfect capital mobility, any attempt to pursue a sterilization policy leads to such large reserve losses that it cannot be pursued. Hence, with perfect capital mobility and fixed exchange rates monetary policy is ineffective at influencing output.

By contrast, if there is a fiscal expansion this shifts the IS schedule to the right from IS_1 to IS_2, which puts upward pressure on the domestic interest rate and leads to a massive capital inflow. To prevent an appreciation the authorities have to purchase the foreign currency with the domestic currency. This means that the amount of domestic currency held by private agents increases and the LM_1 schedule shifts to the right from LM_1 to LM_2. The increase in the money stock continues until the LM schedule passes through the IS_2 schedule at the initial interest rate. Hence, under fixed exchange rates and perfect capital mobility an active fiscal policy alone has the ability to achieve both internal and external balance. This is an exception to the instruments–targets rule, although monetary policy does have to passively adjust to maintain the fixed exchange rate.

Floating exchange rates and perfect capital mobility

In **Figure 4.13** initial equilibrium is at the income level Y_1 where the IS_1 schedule intersects the LM_1 schedule. In this case, we have a floating exchange rate. A monetary

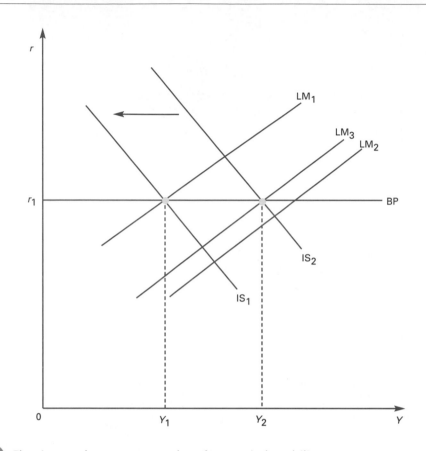

Figure 4.13 Floating exchange rates and perfect capital mobility

expansion shifts the LM schedule from LM_1 to LM_2 leading to downward pressure on the interest rate, a capital outflow and a depreciation of the exchange rate. The depreciation leads to an increase in exports and reduction in imports so shifting the IS curve to the right and the LM schedule to the left, so that final equilibrium is obtained at a higher level of income, say Y_2. Clearly with an appropriate initial monetary expansion the authorities could obtain both internal and external balance by monetary policy alone.

Suppose, instead, the authorities attempt to expand output by an expansionary fiscal policy. The increased government expenditure shifts the IS schedule to the right from IS_1 to IS_2, but the bond sales that finance the expansion lead to upward pressure on the domestic interest rate resulting in a massive capital inflow and an appreciation of the exchange rate. The appreciation of the exchange rate results in a reduction of exports and increase in imports, which forces the IS schedule back to its original position. Hence, with a floating exchange rates and perfect capital mobility fiscal policy is ineffective at influencing real output.

By contrast, a monetary expansion that shifts the LM schedule from LM_1 to LM_2 leads to a fall in the domestic interest rate and a depreciation of the exchange rate. This depreciation then leads to an increase in exports and reduction in imports that shifts the IS schedule to the right from IS_1 to IS_2 and some reduction of the real money stock shifting LM$_2$ to the left to, say LM$_3$, so that overall income rises to Y_2. In this instance, it is monetary policy alone which can achieve both internal and external balance, although the exchange rate adjusts passively to the change in the money stock.

The contrast between the effectiveness of fiscal and monetary policy with perfect capital mobility under different exchange rate regimes is one of the most famous results in international economics. Monetary policy is ineffective at influencing output under fixed exchange rates, while it alone can influence output under floating exchange rates. By contrast, fiscal policy alone is effective at influencing output under a fixed exchange rate, while it is ineffective under floating exchange rates.

Box 4.1

The macroeconomic trilemma

It has become very popular in recent debates about the international monetary system to speak about the 'macroeconomic trilemma' facing economic policy-makers. The trilemma is that the authorities have to make a choice out of two of the following three goals. Some have termed the trilemma the 'impossible trinity', reflecting the fact that is not possible to achieve all three goals simultaneously. The impossible three are:

1 monetary independence;
2 fixed exchange rates; and
3 free movement of international capital.

The three goals are sometimes captured on a diagram such as in **Figure 4.14.**

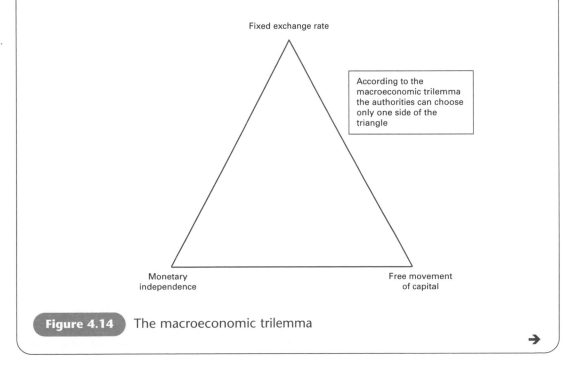

Figure 4.14   The macroeconomic trilemma

➜

The authorities could choose goals 1 and 2, but in order to do this they would need to sacrifice goal 3, that is enact capital controls. A prominent example of a country doing this is China, the Chinese authorities currently peg the Chinese renminbi to the US dollar and can raise or lower interest rates to meet domestic policy aims. However, they have to use capital controls to stop large inflows or outflows of capital that would otherwise undermine the fixed exchange rate to the US dollar. Some authorities choose goals 1 and 3, prime examples being the United States and the United Kingdom; these two countries are free to raise or lower domestic interest rates to achieve domestic macroeconomic goals such as inflation control and economic growth, and they permit free movement of capital into and out of the country. However, they have to forego the possibility of a fixed exchange rate in order to do this. For instance, an aggressive cut in short-term interest rates is likely to lead to large capital outflows and a depreciation of their currencies meaning that they cannot maintain a fixed exchange rate. The UK, which switched from the right-hand side to the base of the triangle when its membership of the exchange rate mechanism ended in 1992, was free to cut interest rates as monetary policy autonomy was restored. The other possible combination is goals 2 and 3, which is the case when a country permits free movement of capital whilst maintaining a fixed exchange rate. A good example of this is Hong Kong which pegs the Hong Kong dollar rigidly to the US dollar and allows free movement of capital into and out of the country. The price, however, is that it gives up its monetary independence; if the Federal Reserve of the United States raises dollar interest rates then the Hong Kong Monetary Authority (HKMA) has to raise its rates or the Hong Kong dollar would come under speculative attack; conversely, if the US lowers its interest rates the HKMA more or less automatically lowers its interest rates.

The trilemma is particularly important for developing countries, many of which choose to fix their exchange rates, for example to the US dollar; but if they choose to do this then they must either give up control of their monetary policy or impose capital controls if they wish to have some degree of monetary autonomy. Imposing capital controls may give them some degree of monetary autonomy, but access to international capital markets is essential to the longer-term process of economic development. On the other hand, liberalization of capital flows will mean that they have to sacrifice their monetary autonomy and will have to raise or lower their interest rates if the Federal Reserve changes US short-term interest rates regardless of the state of their economies if they wish to maintain their fixed exchange rate.

4.13 The principle of effective market classification

While Tinbergen's instruments–targets rule shows us that we generally need two instruments to achieve both internal and external balance, it does not tell us which instrument should be assigned to which target. We have seen that we can use combinations of fiscal and monetary policy to achieve internal and external balance under fixed exchange rates, or we can use combinations of monetary or fiscal policy under floating exchange rates.

Mundell (1968) suggested that what he called the principle of effective market classification should be used by economic policy-makers in conjunction with Tinbergen's 'instruments–targets' rule. By the principle of effective market classification, Mundell stated that 'Policies should be paired with the objectives on which they have the most influence' (1962, p. 79). For instance, if monetary policy is the most effective instrument at controlling external balance and fiscal policy best at influencing output, then this is also the appropriate pairing of instruments to targets. The principle of effective market classification seems eminently sensible – by analogy a conductor should be assigned to conducting an orchestra and a doctor assigned to a hospital and not *vice-versa*! What makes the Mundell principle of effective market classification interesting, is the suggestion that if this principle is not adopted economies may suffer from cyclical instability.

The problem for economic policy-makers to determine which instruments to assign to which targets, is termed the 'assignment problem'. Mundell suggested that under fixed exchange rates monetary policy should be assigned to external balance and fiscal policy to internal balance.

An illustration of the assignment problem is shown in **Figure 4.15**, that illustrates internal and external balance schedules for various fiscal and monetary policy stances under a fixed exchange rate regime. On the vertical axis we have monetary policy which is neutral at point N_m, but expansionary above this while it is contractionary below. Similarly, the fiscal policy stance is neutral at point N_f and expansionary to the

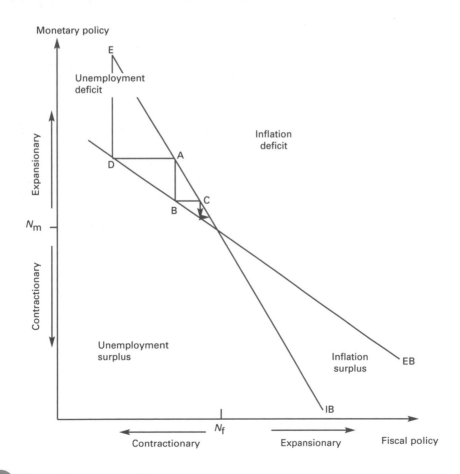

Figure 4.15 The assignment problem

right and contractionary to the left. The internal balance schedule has a negative slope, because if we start at full employment a contractionary monetary policy has to be accompanied by an expansionary fiscal policy to maintain full employment. To the right of the IB schedule the fiscal/monetary policy mix is so expansionary as to cause inflation, whereas to the left the fiscal/monetary policy mix is deflationary.

The external balance schedule may have a positive or negative slope, because an expansionary fiscal policy has two conflicting effects on the balance of payments as we saw in **Figures 4.10** and **4.11**. On the one hand, the increase in income leads to a deterioration in the current account which worsens the balance of payments, but on the other hand the rise in interest rates leads to an inflow of capital which improves the balance of payments. In **Figure 4.15** we have drawn the EB schedule with a negative slope meaning that an expansionary fiscal policy causes a net deterioration in the balance of payments (the current account effect dominates the capital account effect). This being the case, when fiscal policy is expansionary monetary policy has to be contractionary, which by raising the domestic interest rate increases capital inflows to ensure equilibrium in the balance of payments.

The IB schedule is drawn steeper than the EB schedule, which must be the case because a fiscal expansion which causes a rise in income of $x\%$ will cause less of a deterioration in the balance of payments than a monetary policy that increases income by $x\%$. This is because a fiscal expansion will lead to a rise in interest rates leading to partially offsetting capital inflows, while a money expansion leads to a fall in interest rates leading to an additional deterioration in the balance of payments above the income effect. Hence, monetary policy has more effect on external balance than fiscal policy. As monetary policy is relatively more effective at influencing external balance, then fiscal policy is relatively more effective with respect to internal balance.

According to Mundell's classification, if we are at point A with internal balance but a balance of payments deficit, a contractionary monetary policy moves the economy to say point B on the external balance curve but this leads to unemployment which is then tackled by an expansionary fiscal policy moving to point C on the internal balance curve. This pushes the economy back into deficit and this is then accompanied by a monetary contraction to achieve external balance. Each time we need less and less adjustment of monetary and fiscal policy. We have a stable assignment as we are clearly converging to the intersection of the internal and external balance schedules.

Suppose policy-makers get the assignment wrong and use fiscal policy to eradicate the balance of payments deficit and monetary policy for internal balance. In such circumstances, the fiscal contraction moves the economy from point A to point D; external balance is achieved but at the cost of high unemployment. If the authorities then use an expansionary monetary policy to achieve internal balance, the economy moves from point D to point E. Clearly, such a policy assignment proves to be unstable moving the economy away from the simultaneous achievement of internal and external balance. The danger exists that the authorities could get the assignment wrong and cause considerable damage to the economy before they eventually reverse their assignment to the correct one. Given this, it may be wise to try achieve targets gradually by adjusting policy instruments slowly to make sure they are having the intended effect.

Unfortunately, there is no unambiguous answer to the assignment problem. Consider, for example, our analysis of a small open economy under conditions of perfect capital mobility. We have seen that the effectiveness of fiscal and monetary policy at influencing output depends upon whether or not there is a fixed or floating exchange rate. If the exchange rate is fixed then fiscal policy should be paired with the objective of full employment, whereas if the exchange rate is floating then one should assign monetary policy. The assignment problem has no simple solution and is considerably more complicated once we have three targets and three instruments. The appropriate pairing of instruments and targets depending upon the structural parameters governing the behaviour of an economy. This includes, amongst others, the degree of capital mobility, the marginal propensity to save and import, income and interest elasticity of demand for money, the price elasticity of demand for imports and exports, and the responsiveness of investment to interest rate variations.

4.14 Limitations of the Mundell–Fleming model

The IS–LM–BP model has been a one of the major policy models underlying economic policy formulation for open economies in the last three decades. Given this, we need to look at some of the limitations of the model, not least because these criticisms were one of the reasons motivating the formulation of the monetary approach to the balance of payments and economic policy, that is the subject matter of Chapter 5. A number of the criticisms relate to the short-run nature of the model:

- **The Marshall–Lerner condition**. The model assumes that the Marshall–Lerner condition holds even though the model is essentially of a short-term nature, which is the time scale when the Marshall–Lerner conditions are least likely to be met.
- **Interaction of stocks and flows**. The model ignores the problem of the interaction of stocks and flows. According to the model a current account deficit can be financed by a capital inflow. While such a policy is feasible in the short run, a capital inflow over time increases the stock of foreign liabilities owed by the country to the rest of the world and this factor means a worsening of the future current account as interest is paid abroad. Clearly, a country cannot go on financing a current account deficit indefinitely as the country becomes an ever-increasing debtor to the rest of the world.
- **Neglect of long-run budget constraints**. In an excellent review of the Mundell–Fleming model, Frenkel and Razin (1987) highlight the fact that one of the major deficiencies of the model is that it fails to take account of long-run constraints that govern both the private and public sector. In the long run, private-sector spending has to equal its disposable income, while in the absence of money-creation government expenditure (inclusive of its debt-service repayments) has to equal its revenue from taxation. This means that in the long run the current account has to be in balance. One implication of these budget constraints is that a forward-looking private sector would realize that increased government expenditure will imply higher taxation for them in the future, and this will induce increased private-sector savings today that will undermine the effectiveness of fiscal policy.
- **Wealth effects**. The model does not allow for wealth effects that may help in the process of restoring long-run equilibrium. A decrease in wealth resulting from a fall in foreign assets will ordinarily lead to a reduction in import expenditure which

should help to reduce the current account deficit. While such an omission of wealth effects on the import expenditure function may be justified as being of small significance in the short run, the omission nevertheless again emphasizes the essentially short-term nature of the model.

- **Neglect of supply-side factors**. One of the obvious limitations of the model is that it concentrates on the demand side of the economy and neglects the supply side. There is an implicit assumption that supply adjusts in accordance with changes in demand. In addition, because the aggregate supply curve is horizontal up to full employment, increases in aggregate demand do not lead to changes in the domestic price level, rather they are reflected solely by increases in real output.

- **Treatment of capital flows**. One of the biggest problems of the model concerns the modelling of capital flows. It is assumed that a rise in the domestic interest rate leads to a continuous capital inflow from abroad. However, to expect such flows to continue indefinitely is unrealistic because, after a point, international investors will have rearranged the stocks of their international portfolios to their desired portfolios and once this happens the net capital inflows into the country will cease. The only way that the country could then continue to attract capital inflows would be a further rise in its interest rate until once again international portfolios are restored to desired portfolios. Hence, a country that needs a continuous capital inflow to finance its current account deficit has to continuously raise its interest rate. In other words, capital inflows are a function of the change in the interest differential rather than the differential itself.

- **Exchange rate expectations**. A major problem with the model is the treatment of exchange rate expectations. The model does not explicitly model exchange rate expectations and implicitly presumes that the expected change of the exchange rate is zero which is known as static exchange rate expectations. While this might not seem to be an unreasonable assumption under fixed exchange rates, it is less tenable under floating exchange rates. According to the model a monetary expansion leads to a depreciation of the currency under floating exchange rates – in such circumstances it seems unreasonable to assume that economic agents do not expect a depreciation as well. If agents expect a depreciation this may require a rise in the domestic interest rate to encourage them to continue to hold the currency which will have an adverse effect on domestic investment – implying a weaker expansionary effect of monetary policy than is suggested by the model.

- **Flexibility of policy instruments**. Another criticism is that the analysis is of a comparative static nature and it assumes that adjusting monetary and fiscal policy is a fairly simple matter. In the real world, the political process means that the degree of flexibility to adjust economic policy, especially fiscal policy, is hard to achieve.

4.15 Conclusions

In this chapter we have illustrated some important aspects concerning the conduct of economic policy in an open economy. While fiscal and/or monetary policy may be useful in achieving full employment, they will also have important implications for the balance of payments and exchange rate which will in turn have feedback effects on the domestic economy. Economic policy formulation in an open economy has to take into account many important additional considerations compared to a simple closed economy.

Among the most important lessons for economic policy-makers is that they generally need as many independent policy instruments as they have targets. This result is important because the idea the authorities can use a single policy instrument such as monetary policy alone to achieve all the targets of economic policy is highly questionable. Nevertheless, policy-makers still have a major policy problem in deciding which instrument to assign to which target. Since the structures of economies differ, no general rules exist to solve this problem. Theory warns that an incorrect assignment may provoke rather than limit instability in the economy.

In the real world the achievement of internal and external balance will be far more difficult that our theoretical analysis has suggested. Policy-makers face uncertainty over means–end relationships, there are time-lag problems, the authorities are in the possession of only limited information about the position of an economy, and economies are continually being subjected to new shocks as well adjusting to previous shocks. In practice, getting close to targets is likely to be the name of the game rather than actually achieving them.

We have seen that the relative effectiveness of fiscal and monetary policy is very much dependent upon the choice of exchange rate regime. In particular, with perfect capital mobility monetary policy is more effective under a floating exchange rate regime while fiscal policy is more effective under a fixed exchange rate. One of the crucial parameters determining the effectiveness of both of fiscal and monetary policy in an open economy is the degree of financial integration of an economy with the rest of the world as reflected by the mobility of capital internationally.

Although the Mundell–Fleming model has many limitations, it nonetheless focuses attention on the difficulties and dilemmas facing policy-makers in an open economy. Perhaps its most significant contribution to international economics is that it focuses on the important role that international capital flows can play in determining the effectiveness of macroeconomic policies under alternative exchange rate regimes.

Further reading

De Grauwe, P. (1983) *Macroeconomic Theory for the Open Economy* (London: Gower).

Fleming, J.M. (1962) 'Domestic Financial Policies Under Fixed and Floating Exchange Rates', IMF Staff Papers, vol. 9, pp. 369–80.

Frenkel, J.A. and Razin, A. (1987) 'The Mundell–Fleming Model a Quarter Century Later: A Unified Exposition,' IMF Staff Papers, vol. 34, pp. 567–620.

Kenen, P.B. (1985) 'Macroeconomic Theory and Policy: How the Closed Economy was Opened', in R.W. Jones and P.B. Kenen, *Handbook of International Economics*, Vol. II. (Amsterdam: Elsevier).

Mundell, R.A. (1962) 'The Appropriate Use of Monetary and Fiscal Policy for Internal and External Stability', IMF Staff Papers, vol. 9, pp. 70–9.

Mundell, R.A. (1963) 'Capital Mobility and Stabilization Policy Under Fixed and Flexible Exchange Rates', *Canadian Journal of Economic and Political Science*, vol. 29, pp. 475–85.

Mundell, R.A. (1968) *International Economics* (London: Macmillan, now Palgrave Macmillan).

Swan, T. (1955) 'Longer Run Problems of the Balance of Payments', reprinted in R.E. Caves and H.G. Johnson (eds) (1968), *Readings in International Economics* (London: Allen & Unwin).

Tinbergen, J. (1952) *On the Theory of Economic Policy* (Amsterdam: North Holland).

5

The Monetary Approach to the Balance of Payments

5.1 Introduction

In this chapter, we shall look at one of the most influential policy analyses of the balance of payments known as the monetary approach. This approach to balance of payments analysis was pioneered by Marina Whitman (1975), Jacob Frenkel and Harry Johnson (1976). The fundamental basis of the monetary approach is that the balance of payments is essentially a monetary phenomenon. Not only is the balance of payments a measurement of monetary flows, but such flows can only be explained by a disequilibrium in the stock demand for and supply of money.

There are several variants of the monetary approach to the balance of payments and not all advocates of the application of monetary concepts to balance of payments analysis necessarily accept all the assumptions used. We shall outline a simple model that captures the essential message of the monetary approach – that disequilibrium in the balance of payments reflect disequilibrium in the money market. Consequently, balance of payments analysis needs to focus on both the supply of and demand for money.

Within the context of the monetary model, we shall examine how a devaluation will impinge upon the balance of payments. We then proceed to examine how the model can be used to highlight some fundamentally different implications of fixed and floating exchange rates. We compare and contrast the effects of a money supply shock, a rise in domestic income and a foreign price shock under fixed and floating rates. We then summarize the policy implications of the monetary approach and consider how the model differs from the Keynesian model examined in Chapter 4.

5.2 A simple monetary model

There are three key assumptions that underlie the monetary model; these are a stable money demand function, a vertical aggregate supply schedule, and purchasing power parity (PPP).

Stable money demand runction

The most basic postulate of the monetary approach to the balance of payments is that there is a stable demand for money function that is made up of only a few variables. The monetarists use the quantity theory of money as the basis of the money demand function, which is written as:

$$M_d = kPy \qquad \text{where } k > 0 \tag{5.1}$$

where M_d is the demand for nominal money balances, P is the domestic price level, y is real domestic income, and k is a parameter that measures the sensitivity of money demand to changes in nominal income.

The demand for money is a positive function of the domestic price level, because the demand for money is a demand for real money balances. A rise in the domestic price level will reduce real money balances (M/P) and accordingly lead to an equiproportionate increase in the demand for money. The demand for money is positively related to real domestic income; a rise in real income will, *ceteris paribus*, lead to an increase in the transactions demand for money. The money demand function forms the basis of the aggregate demand schedule which is illustrated in the **Figure 5.1** for a simple monetary model.

From equation (5.1), if we hold the money supply/money demand fixed and assume that k is a fixed parameter, this means that an increase in y from y_1 to y_2 requires an equiproportionate fall in the price level from P_1 to P_2. Since $P_1 y_1 = P_2 y_2$ the aggregate demand schedule is a rectangular hyperbola given by AD_1. A fall in the price level from P_1 to P_2, given a fixed money supply, will create excess real money balances (M/P) and this leads to increased aggregate demand from y_1 to y_2. An increase in the money supply has the effect of shifting the aggregate demand schedule to the right from AD_1 to AD_2, because at any given price level there is an rise in real money balances which leads to increased aggregate demand.

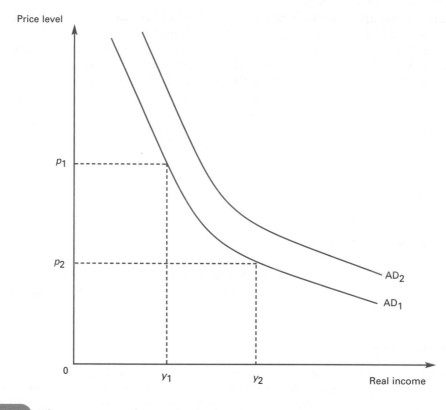

Price level

p_1

p_2

AD_2

AD_1

0

y_1

y_2

Real income

 Figure 5.1   The aggregate demand schedule

Vertical aggregate supply schedule

The simple monetary model assumes that the labour market is sufficiently flexible that the economy is continuously at a full employment level of output. In other words, wages are sufficiently flexible that they are constantly at the level that equates the supply and demand for labour. Furthermore, a rise in the domestic price level does not lead to an increase in domestic output because wages adjust immediately to the higher price level so that there is no advantage for domestic producers to take on more labour. This means that the aggregate supply schedule is vertical at the full employment level of output as shown in **Figure 5.2**.

Although the aggregate supply schedule AS_1 iis vertical at the full employment level of output y_1, this does not mean that output is always constrained to be fixed at y_1; the aggregate supply schedule may shift to the right to, say, AS_2 if there is an improvement in productivity due to technological progress which means that full employment is associated with a higher level of real output.

Purchasing power parity (PPP)

The final assumption that underpins the monetary model is the assumption of purchasing power parity. PPP theory is examined in much more detail in Chapter 6, but for the time being we can state that in its simplified version the theory

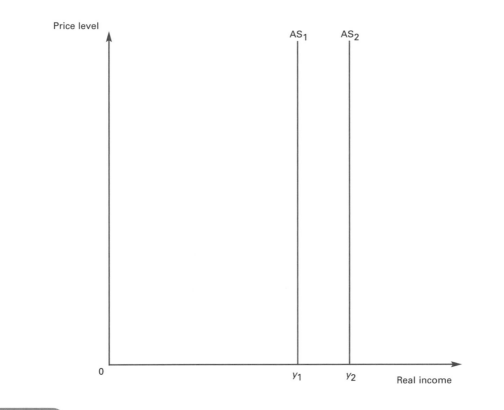

Figure 5.2 The aggregate supply schedule

says that the exchange rate adjusts so such as to keep the following equation in equilibrium:

$$S = \frac{P}{P^*} \qquad \text{that is, } P = SP^* \qquad\qquad (5.2)$$

where S is the exchange rate defined as domestic currency per unit of foreign currency, so that a rise is a depreciation while a fall is an appreciation of the domestic currency; P is the domestic price level in the domestic currency and P^* is the foreign price in the foreign currency.

Equation (5.2) says that if a basket of goods costs £100 in the UK, and the same basket costs $200 in the USA, then the £/$ exchange rate should be £0.50/$1. This means that the basket of goods has the same price in both countries. If the exchange rate were above £0.50/$1, say £0.60/$1, then the US bundle would cost a UK citizen $200 × 0.60 = £120, while the UK bundle would cost a US citizen £100/0.6 = $166.66. Conversely, an exchange rate below PPP, say at £0.40/$1, would mean the US bundle of goods would cost a UK citizen $200 × 0.4 = £80, while the UK bundle would cost a US citizen £100/0.40 = $250. According to the theory this would lead to a rush to buy US goods and a depreciation of the pound until it was restored to £0.50/$1.

Figure 5.3 depicts the PPP schedule which shows combinations of the domestic

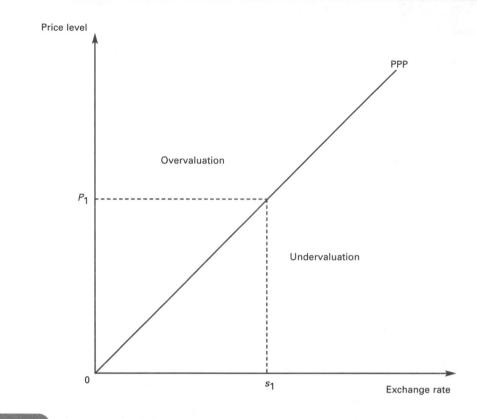

Figure 5.3 The PPP schedule

price level and exchange rate which are compatible with PPP, given the foreign price level P^*. It has a slope given by P^* and implies that a $x\%$ rise in the domestic price level requires an $x\%$ depreciation (rise) of the home currency to maintain PPP. Points to the left of the PPP schedule represent an overvaluation of the domestic currency in relation to PPP, whereas points to the right show undervaluation in relation to PPP.

The simple monetary model invokes the three assumptions set out above and then proceeds with the use of some accounting identities and behavioural assumptions to develop a theory of the balance of payments.

The domestic monetary supply in the economy is made up of two components:

$$M_s = D + R \qquad (5.3)$$

where M_s is the domestic money base, D is domestic bond holdings of the monetary authorities and R is the reserves of foreign currencies.

The monetary base can come into circulation in one of two ways: (1) the authorities may conduct an open-market operation, which involves the central bank purchasing treasury bonds held by private agents; this increases the central bank's monetary liabilities but increases its assets of domestic bond holdings which is the domestic component of the monetary base as represented by D. (2) The authorities may conduct a foreign exchange operation (FXO) which involves the central bank purchasing foreign currency assets (money or foreign treasury bonds) held by private agents

by the central bank. This again increases the central bank's liabilities but increases its assets of foreign currency and foreign bonds which are represented by R.

We can now rewrite equation (5.3) in difference form as:

$$dM_s = dD + dR \tag{5.4}$$

Equation (5.4) says that any increase (decrease) in the domestic money supply can come about through either an OMO as represented by dD or a FXO as represented by dR. The relationship between the money supply and reserves is illustrated in **Figure 5.4**.

In the figure, at point D_1 all the domestic money supply is made up entirely of the domestic component since reserves are zero. For convenience we set the exchange rate of the domestic to foreign currency equal to unity; this being the case an increase of 1 unit of foreign currency leads to an increase in the domestic money supply of 1 unit, so that when reserves are R_1 the money supply is M_1, that is $D_1 + R_1$.

An OMO will have the effect of shifting the M_s schedule by the amount of the increase in the increase central bank's domestic bond holdings. An OMO which increases the domestic component of the monetary base from D_1 to D_2 shifts the money supply schedule from M_{s1} to M_{s2} and the total money supply rises from M_1 to M_2 and is represented by a movement from point A to point C. By contrast, an expansion of the money supply due to a purchase of foreign currencies, that is an FXO, increases the country's foreign exchange reserves from R_1 to R_2. This, too, has the

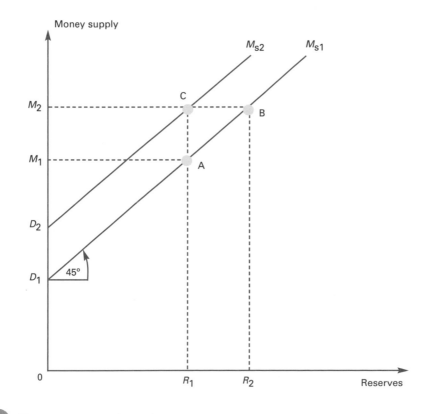

Figure 5.4 The money supply and reserves

effect of raising the money stock from M_1 to M_2 and is represented by a movement along the money supply schedule M_{s1} from point A to point B.

5.3 The monetarist concept of a balance of payments disequilibrium

The monetarists view balance of payments surpluses and deficits as monetary flow due to stock disequilibrium in the money market. A deficit in the balance of payments is due to an excess of the money supply in relation to money demand, while a surplus in the balance of payments is a monetary flow resulting from an excess demand for money in relation to the stock money supply. Thus a balance of payments disequilibrium is merely a reflection of a disequilibrium in the money market. In this sense the monetary flows are the 'autonomous' items in the balance of payments while the purchases and sales of goods/services and investments (long, medium and short-term) are viewed as the accommodating items. This is completely the reverse of the Keynesian approach which views the current account items as the autonomous and capital account and reserve changes as the accommodating items. This different way of looking at the balance of payments statistics is sometimes contrasted by saying that Keynesians look at the balance of payments statistics from the 'top down' (that is, the current account) while the monetarists look from the 'bottom up' (the change in reserves).

Monetarists observe that the overall balance of payments (BP) can be thought of as consisting of the current account balance, capital account balance and changes in the authorities' reserves. That is:

$$BP = CA + K + dR = 0$$

so that:

$$CA + K = -dR \tag{5.5}$$

where CA is the current account balance, K is the capital account balance and dR is the change in the authorities reserves. If the recorded dR in the balance of payments accounts is positive, this means that the combined current account and capital account are in deficit. This implies that reserves have fallen as the authorities have purchased the home currency with foreign currency reserves (see Chapter 1).

Equation (5.5) is a distinct way of viewing the balance of payments; increases in reserves due to purchases of foreign currencies constitute a surplus in the balance of payments surplus, while falls in reserves resulting from purchases of the domestic currency represent a deficit in the balance of payments. If the authorities do not intervene in the foreign exchange market, that is the currency is left to float, then reserves do not change and as far as the monetary view of the balance of payments is concerned the balance of payments is in equilibrium. Under a floating exchange rate regime a current account deficit must be financed by an equivalent capital inflow so that the balance of payments is in equilibrium.

With this concept of a balance of payments surplus/deficit in mind we can proceed to an analysis of the effects of various shocks under both fixed and floating exchange rates.

The model is in equilibrium when aggregate demand is equal to aggregate supply so that there is no excess demand for goods which is given by the intersection of the aggregate demand and supply schedules at price level P_1 and output level y_1 in **Figure 5.5(b)**. Also, PPP holds in the foreign exchange market so that at price level P_1 and the exogenous foreign price level P^* the exchange rate compatible with PPP is given by S_1 in **Figure 5.5(a)**. Finally, the money market is in equilibrium, so with the money supply M_1 made up of the domestic so component D_1 and reserve component R_1 is equal to money demand in **Figure 5.5(c)**. The M_s schedule M_{s1} cuts the money demand schedule M_{d1}. The precise position of the money demand schedule is determined by the domestic price level and domestic income level. Equilibrium in the money market also implies equilibrium in the balance of payments.

We are now in a position to examine the effects of various shocks within the context of the monetary approach to the balance of payments.

5.4 The effects of a devaluation

The monetary approach argues that a devaluation can only have an affect on the balance of payments by influencing the demand for money in relation to the supply of money. In **Figure 5.6** the immediate effect of a devaluation of the exchange rate from S_1 to S_2 is to make domestic goods competitive in relation to PPP. As domestic goods become more competitive compared to foreign goods there is an increase in the demand for the domestic currency as represented by a shift of the money demand schedule from M_{d1} to M_{d2}. This means that money demand M_2 exceeds the money supply M_1. The competitive advantage of the devaluation means that the balance of payments moves into surplus as domestic residents demand less foreign goods/services, while foreigners demand more domestic goods. To prevent the domestic currency appreciating, the authorities have to purchase the foreign currency with new domestic money base. This increases the reserves and leads to an expansion of the domestic money supply which in turn raises aggregate demand for domestically produced goods. The aggregate demand schedule shifts to the right from AD_1 to AD_2 and starts pushing up domestic prices until PPP is restored at price P_2.

Once the domestic price level is at P_2 and the money supply has increased to M_2, real money balances will be at their equilibrium level ($M_1/P_1 = M_2/P_2$) and the competitive advantage of the devaluation has been offset. The balance of payments will back in equilibrium as money supply is once again equal to money demand. In the long run, the effect of an $x\%$ devaluation is to lead to an $x\%$ rise in the domestic price level and $x\%$ increase in the domestic money stock. In other words, the surplus resulting from a devaluation is merely a transitory phenomenon.

The monetary approach emphasizes that a devaluation will have a transitory beneficial effect on the balance of payments only so long as the authorities do not simultaneously engage in an expansionary OMO. If the authorities immediately increase the money stock to M_2 via an OMO, there would be an immediate rise in aggregate demand and domestic prices to P_2 so that the competitive advantage conferred by a devaluation would be eliminated.

The important point derived from the monetary model concerning the effect of a devaluation is that exchange rate changes are viewed as incapable of bringing about a lasting change in the balance of payments. A devaluation or revaluation operates

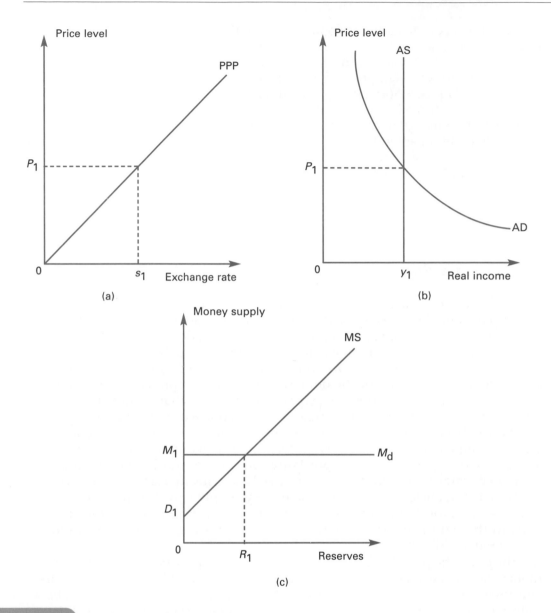

(a)

(b)

(c)

Figure 5.5   Equilibrium of the model

strictly by causing a disequilibrium in the money market, causing a deficit or surplus in the balance of payments which continues only until equilibrium is restored in the money market via reserve changes.

5.5 A monetary exchange rate equation

Before we compare and contrast the effects of various shocks under fixed and floating exchange rates we need to consider how the exchange rate is determined in the

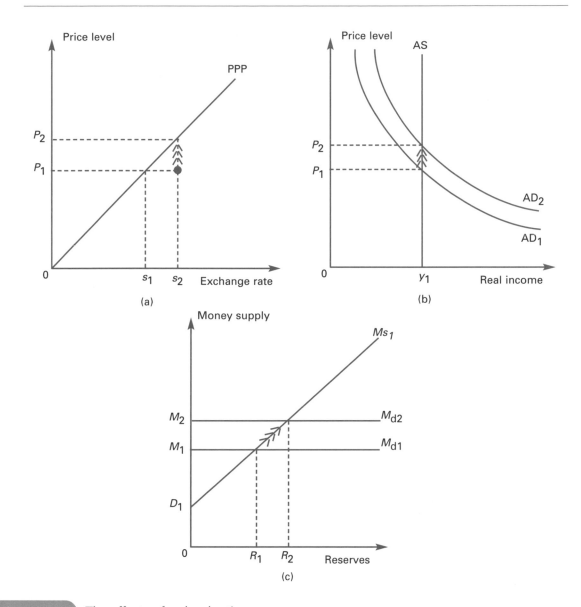

Figure 5.6 The effects of a devaluation

context of our simple monetary model. As we have seen in equation (5.1), which is repeated below as equation (5.6), the demand for money in the home country is given by:

$$M_d = kPy \tag{5.6}$$

This being the case, we can postulate that the demand for money in the foreign economy is of a similar type, given below as:

$$M_{d*} = k^*P^*y^* \tag{5.7}$$

where M_{d*} denotes foreign money demand, $k*$ the foreign nominal income elasticity of demand for money, $P*$ the foreign price level and $y*$ real foreign income. The exchange rate is determined by PPP so that:

$$S = \frac{P}{P*} \qquad (5.8)$$

In equilibrium, money demand is equal to the money supply in each country, so that:

$$M_s = M_d \text{ and } M_{s*} = M_{d*} \qquad (5.9)$$

This being the case, we can denote the relative money supply functions as equation (5.6) divided by (5.7), replacing M_d and M_{d*} with M_s and M_{s*} from equation (5.9):

$$\frac{M_s}{M_{s*}} = \frac{kPy}{k*P*y*} \qquad (5.10)$$

Since $P/P* = S$ because of PPP, then we can rewrite equation (5.11) as:

$$\frac{M_s}{M_{s*}} = \frac{kSy}{k*y*} \qquad (5.11)$$

Solving the above equation for the exchange rate yields:

$$S = \frac{M_s/M_{s*}}{ky/k*y*} \qquad (5.12)$$

Equation (5.12) says that the exchange rate is determined by the relative supply and demand for the different national money stocks. An increase in the domestic money stock relative to the foreign money stock will lead to a depreciation (rise) of the home currency, while an increase in domestic income relative to foreign income leads to an appreciation (fall) of the home currency exchange rate. The reason being that an increase in income leads to an increased transactions demand for the home currency leading to an appreciation. With this simple model of exchange rate determination in mind we can proceed to analyse in more detail the effects of money supply, income changes and changes in the foreign price level.

5.6 A money supply expansion under fixed exchange rates

If the exchange rate of a currency is fixed, this means that the authorities have to buy the currency when it is in excess supply and sell the currency when it is in excess demand in the foreign exchange market to avoid a currency depreciation or appreciation. When the authorities sell the domestic currency this leads to a rise in their reserves of foreign currency. If the authorities buy the domestic currency they do so with foreign currency and so their reserves fall.

Let us now consider what happens if their is an expansionary OMO under a fixed

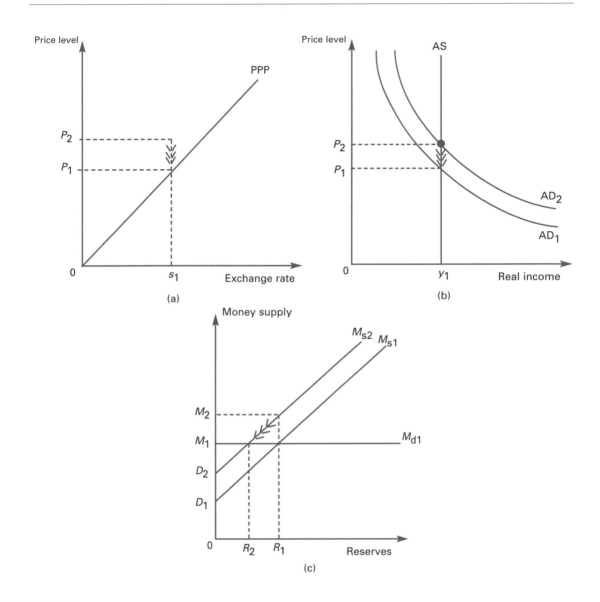

Figure 5.7   A monetary expansion under fixed exchange rates

exchange rate which raises the money supply by a central bank purchase of treasury bonds. In **Figure 5.7** an expansionary OMO shifts the money supply schedule from M_{s1} to M_{s2} and increases the domestic money supply from M_1 to M_2, the domestic component of the monetary base rising from D_1 to D_2. The immediate effect is that domestic residents have excess real money balances ($M_2/P_1 > M_1/P_1$), that is, the money supply M_2 exceeds money demand M_1. To reduce their excess real balances, residents increase aggregate demand for goods as represented by a shift of the aggregate demand schedule from AD_1 to AD_2, and this puts upward pressure on domestic goods prices whose price rises from P_1 to P_2. At price P_2 and fixed exchange rate S_1 the domestic economy is uncompetitive in relation to PPP as it finds itself to the left of the PPP schedule.

The uncompetitive nature of the economy moves the balance of payments into deficit. To prevent a devaluation of the currency, the authorities have to intervene to purchase the domestic currency and the authorities' reserves start to decline below R_1. The purchase back of the domestic money supply starts to reduce the excess money supply and at the same time aggregate demand starts to shift back from AD_2 towards AD_1. As the excess money balances are reduced, this puts downward pressure on the domestic price level which falls back to its original level P_1 so as to arrive back at PPP. Once the money supply returns to M_1 along the M_{s2} schedule the excess supply of money is eliminated and the economy is restored to equilibrium.

In the long run, the price level, output level and money stock return to their initial levels. Thus, an increase in the domestic component of the monetary base from D_1 to D_2 will, because of the foreign exchange intervention it necessitates to maintain a fixed exchange rate, lead to an equivalent fall in the reserves from R_1 to R_2. This fall in the reserves due to purchases of the home currency leads to a return of the money stock to its original level. The fact that the money supply has to return to its original level can be explained by reference to equation (5.12). As the parameters S, M_{s*}, ky and k^*y^* are all fixed, any rise in M_s must eventually be reversed for the equation to hold.

The monetary approach regards the balance of payments deficits resulting from the expansion in the money stock to be merely a temporary and self-correcting phenomenon. An expansion of the money supply causes a temporary excess supply of money and a current and capital account deficit which, to maintain the fixed exchange rate, necessitates intervention in the foreign exchange market which eventually eliminates the excess supply of the currency.

There are two circumstances under which a balance of payments deficit can become more than a transitory feature. One case is when the authorities practice sterilization of their foreign exchange operations. When the authorities intervene to purchase their currency to prevent it being devalued there is a reduction of the monetary base. The authorities could try to offset these money-base implications by conducting a further open market purchase of bonds from the public; however, as we have seen, such an open market operation causes a balance of payments deficit requiring a further foreign exchange intervention. Hence, sterilization policies can cause prolonged balance of payments deficits. The pursuit of such sterilization operations will be limited by the extent of a country's reserves.

Another factor that can lead to a continuous deficit would be if the surplus countries were prepared to purchase the deficit country's currency and hold it in their reserves. In such circumstances, the deficit country will have its exchange rate fixed by foreign central bank intervention and such a process can continue so long a foreign central banks are prepared to accumulate the home-country's currency in their reserves. Although in this case reserve changes are zero, the deficit is reflected as an increase in liabilities to foreign authorities.

5.7 A money supply expansion under floating exchange rates

Under floating exchange rates the monetary approach maintains that there is no such thing as a balance of payments deficit or surplus as the authorities do not intervene to purchase or sell the domestic currency. Since there are no changes in international

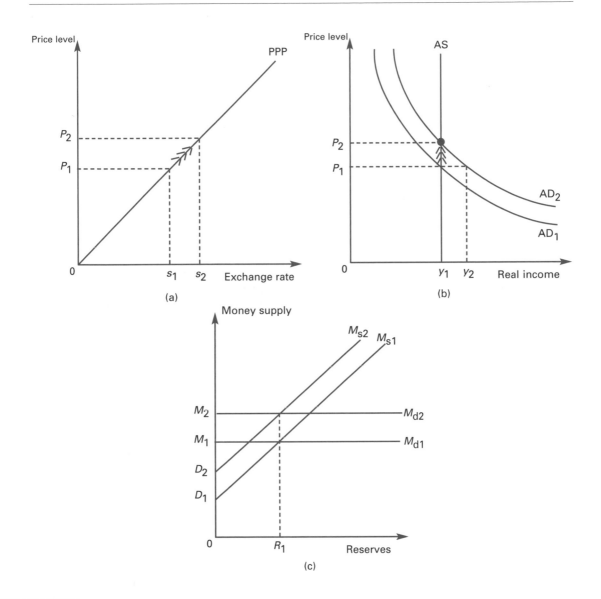

Figure 5.8 A monetary expansion under floating exchange rates

reserves there is no balance of payments surplus or deficit. Referring to equation (5.6), as the change in reserves is zero any current account deficit (surplus) has to be offset by a net capital inflow (outflow) of a like amount. **Figure 5.8** illustrates the effects of a monetary expansion under floating exchange rates.

An expansionary OMO leads to a rise in the money stock from M_1 to M_2 and creates excess money balances. The result is that the aggregate demand shifts from AD_1 to AD_2 with demand y_2 exceeding domestic output y_1. The excess demand for goods translates into increased expenditure on foreign goods/services and investments leading to a depreciation of the exchange rate. As a result of the excess demand for goods the domestic price level begins to rise and this leads to an increase in money demand as reflected by an upward shift of the money demand function from M_{d1} towards M_{d2}. As the domestic price level rises this increase the demand for money leading to a contraction of aggregate demand along the AD_2 schedule until equilibrium price level P_2 is achieved.

In the long run, the effect of an x% increase in the money stock is an x% depreciation of the exchange rate and an x% increase in the domestic price level. The rise in the price level induces a rise in the demand for money so that the excess money balances created by the OMO are eliminated. With reference to equation (5.12) we can see that with the parameters M_{s*}, ky and k^*y^* all fixed, any rise in M_s leads to a rise in the exchange rate S for the equation to hold.

The case of floating exchange rates provides a clear contrast with the fixed exchange rate case. Under fixed exchange rates an expansionary OMO leads to a disequilibrium in the money market which is resolved by adjustment in the balance of payments and reserves held by the authorities. Under floating exchange rates an expansion in the monetary base leads to a depreciation of the exchange rate and a rise in domestic prices. Under fixed exchange rates the authorities can no longer retain independent control of the money supply, the quantity of money returns to its original level due to a gradual fall in the international reserves held by the authorities. Whereas under floating exchange rates they can determine the amount of the money supply, money market equilibrium is restored by changes in money demand brought about by changes in the domestic price level and exchange rate. One of the arguments against fixed exchange rates is that the authorities can no longer conduct independent monetary policies, while with floating exchange rates the authorities are free to expand and contract the money supply to their desired levels.

Having contrasted the effects of a money supply expansion under both exchange rate regimes, we now consider the contrasting effects of changes in domestic income and a foreign price level changes.

5.8 The effects of an increase in income under fixed exchange rates

Within the context of the monetary approach to the balance of payments an increase in domestic income can only have an effect on the balance of payments by influencing money demand in relation to the money supply. **Figure 5.9** shows the effects of an increase in domestic income under fixed exchange rates. The increase in real domestic income is represented by a rightward shift of the aggregate supply schedule from AS_1 to AS_2. As a result of the increase in domestic income the demand to hold money increases which shifts the money demand function from M_{d1} to M_{d2}. The result is that money demand M_2 exceeds the money supply M_1. The result is reduced expenditure on both domestic and foreign goods/services and this leads to a fall in the domestic price level from P_1 to P_2. The fall in the domestic price level means that at the fixed exchange rate S_1 the country gains a competitive advantage and the current and capital account move into surplus. To prevent an appreciation of the currency the authorities have to purchase the foreign currency with newly created money base, and as a result of the intervention in the foreign exchange market there is a rise in the reserves and in the domestic money supply. The increase in the money supply shifts the aggregate demand schedule from AD_1 to AD_2, which leads to a rise the domestic price level back towards its purchasing

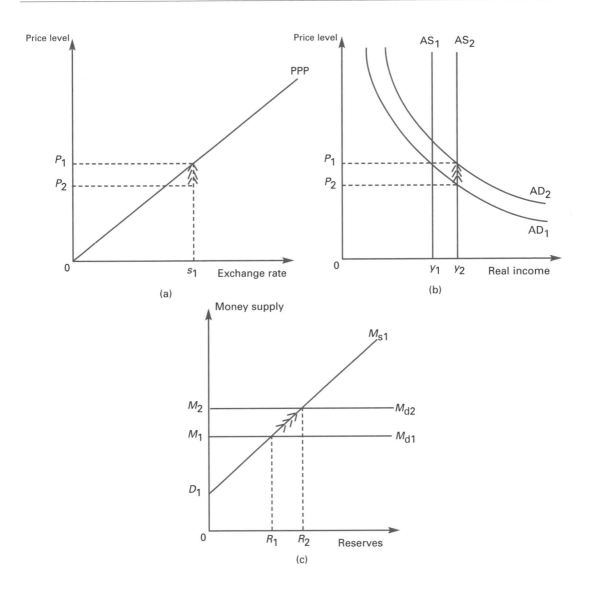

Figure 5.9 An increase in income under fixed exchange rates

power parity value P_1. Once the money stock has risen to M_2 the excess money balances are eliminated.

Notice that in the long run, while the price level has returned to its original level P_1, the money stock has risen from M_1 to M_2 because of the transitory balance of payments surplus. This means that real money balances are greater than before; that is, M_2/P_1 is greater than M_1/P_1. The reason why this is possible is that all the increased money stock is willingly held as transactions balances due to the increase in domestic income. In terms of equation (5.12), given that S, M_{s*} and $k*y*$ are all fixed, the increase in domestic income is offset by the rise in the domestic money supply.

5.9 The effects of an increase in income under floating exchange rates

An increase in income under floating exchange rates has its impact on the exchange rate by influencing the demand for money in relation to the supply of money as shown in **Figure 5.10**. An increase in income leads to an increase in the transactions demand for money and implies an excess supply of goods ($y_2 > y_1$) at the existing price level P_1. This means that there is a downward pressure on the domestic price level which falls from P_1 to P_2 so as to equate aggregate demand and supply. As the

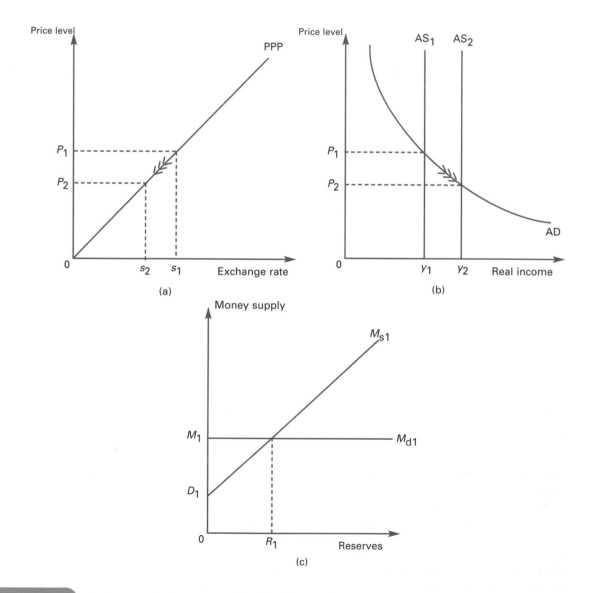

Figure 5.10 An increase in income under floating exchange rates

price level falls, the exchange rate appreciates so as to maintain PPP. Eventually, new equilibrium is obtained at a lower domestic price level P_2 and an exchange rate appreciation from S_1 to S_2.

In the long run, we note that there has been an increase in real money balances as M_1/P_2 is greater than M_1/P_1. Again, the reason for this is that the increase in real domestic income raises the demand for transaction balances, so that the increased real money balances are willingly held. Overall, the money demand schedule did not shift because while the fall in domestic prices leads to less money demand, this is exactly offset by the rise in money demand due to the increase in real income. In terms of equation (5.13) the fixed parameters are M_s, M_{s*} and $k*y*$, a rise in ky due to an increase in income therefore implies an appreciation (fall) in S.

Under fixed exchange rates with an increase in domestic income, eventual adjustment was obtained via an increase in the domestic money supply and reserves so as to satisfy the increased money demand; while under a floating exchange rate equilibrium is obtained by an appreciation of the exchange rate and fall in the domestic price level (to maintain PPP) with the domestic money supply unchanged.

5.10 An increase in foreign prices under fixed exchange rates

The effects of an increase in the foreign price level under fixed exchange rates are shown in **Figure 5.11**. An increase in the foreign price level means that the PPP line swivels upwards from PPP_1 to PPP_2. This is because at the exchange rate S_1, a rise in the foreign price level means that at price level P_1 the domestic economy is now more competitive than PPP. Accordingly, to maintain PPP at the exchange rate S_1 requires a rise in the domestic price level to P_2.

The initial effect of the rise in foreign prices is to make domestic goods at price P_1 more competitive compared to foreign goods. This results in reduced consumption of foreign goods creating a balance of payments surplus and an increase in the demand for the domestic currency which is shown by a shift of the money demand schedule from M_{d1} to M_{d2}. To prevent an appreciation of the currency the authorities have to purchase foreign currencies with newly created domestic money base. The reserves rise from R_1 to R_2 and the money supply rises from M_1 to M_2. The increased money supply and undervaluation of the currency in relation to PPP lead to a shift to the right of the aggregate demand schedule from AD_1 to AD_2 which pushes up domestic prices from P_1 towards P_2 where PPP is restored. Once, PPP is restored the balance of payments surplus ceases.

An important point that emerges from this analysis is that by choosing to peg its exchange rate the country also has to eventually accept that movements in its domestic price level will be determined by changes in the world price level. A country that decides to peg its exchange rate therefore runs the risk of imported inflation/deflation. If foreign inflation is determined by changes in the foreign money supply, the monetary approach suggests that a country that opts to fix its exchange rate must change its money supply in line with changes in the foreign money supply. Hence, countries that opt to fix their exchange rates give up their monetary autonomy. As we shall see in the next section, this is not the case with floating exchange rates.

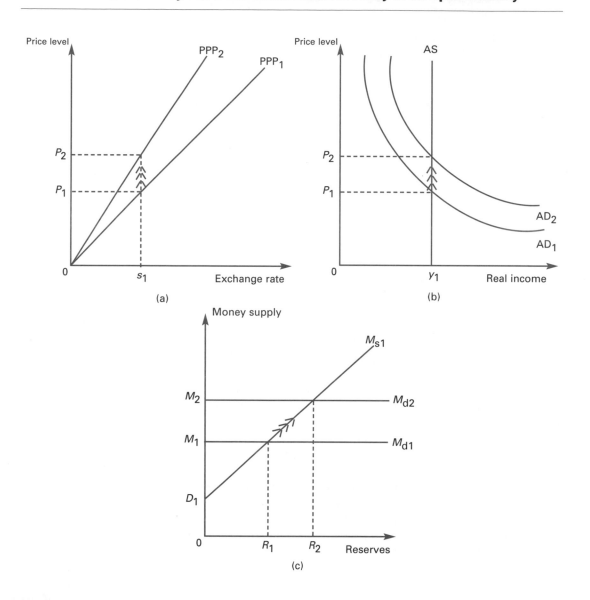

Money supply

Figure 5.11 An increase in foreign prices under fixed exchange rates

5.11 An increase in foreign prices under floating exchange rates

The effects of a rise in the foreign price level when the exchange rate is left to float freely are depicted in **Figure 5.12**. A rise in the foreign price level leads to a swivel of the PPP line from PPP_1 to PPP_2. With a floating exchange rate the competitive advantage to the domestic economy is offset by an appreciation of the currency from S_1 to S_2 to maintain PPP at the existing domestic price level P_1. Hence, with a floating exchange rate, the domestic price level and aggregate demand and output are left unaffected by the foreign price shock.

The insulation of the domestic economy from the foreign price shock under floating

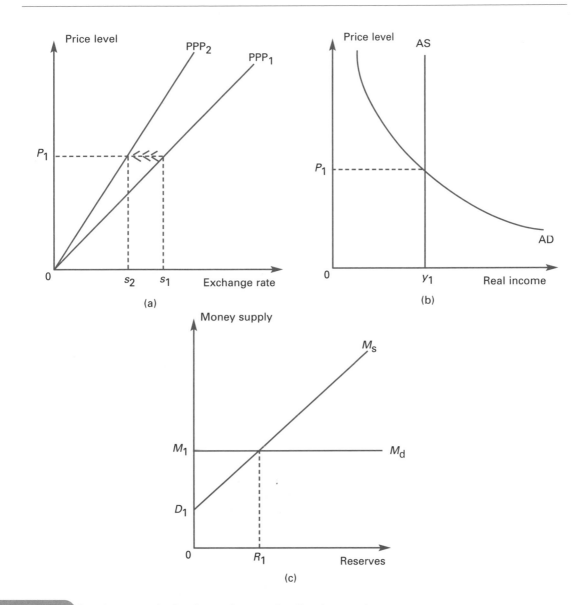

Figure 5.12 An increase in foreign prices under floating exchange rates

exchange rates with the authorities able to operate an independent monetary policy stands in contrast to the imported inflation experienced under fixed exchange rates. One of the most powerful arguments made by the proponents of floating exchange rates is that it gives the authorities the ability to avoid imported inflation/deflation. In effect a floating exchange rate enables the authorities to pursue an independent monetary policy. The exchange rate will adjust to offset an inflation differential and maintain PPP. Under fixed exchange rates the need to maintain PPP means that an economy has to accept an inflation rate determined by the rate of growth of the foreign money supply, monetary independence is lost. However, this independence of monetary policy depends crucially upon the exchange rate adjusting in line with PPP.

5.12 Implications of the monetary approach

The distinctive feature of the monetary approach to the balance of payments is that money market disequilibrium is seen as a crucial factor in provoking balance of payments disequilibrium. It is maintained that the crucial decision of private agents concerns the level of their real money balances. With real output fixed, aggregate expenditure is viewed as a function of real money balances rather than income. In the monetary model agents decide firstly upon the amount of real balances they wish to hold and then spend accordingly and not the other way round. In this sense, it is money decisions that matter and not the expenditure ones.

The core of the monetary approach is that the demand for money function is a stable and predictable function of a relatively few variables. Variables such as the price elasticities of demand for goods and services and foreign exchange are not considered to be important.

A major implication of the monetary approach is that in a fixed exchange rate regime the authorities have to accept a loss of control over their domestic monetary policy as the price of fixing the exchange rate. As we have seen, any attempt to expand the domestic money supply under fixed exchange rates leads to a balance of payments deficit and the need to purchase back the currency on the foreign exchange market. If foreign prices rise then so does the domestic money supply and domestic price level. Under fixed exchange rates the authorities lose the ability to pursue an independent monetary policy. The only thing that the authorities can do is to control the composition of the monetary base between its domestic and foreign components. With a fixed exchange rate, an increase in the domestic component of the monetary base leads to an equivalent fall in the foreign component.

A further implication of the monetarist approach is that from the viewpoint of the balance of payments it is irrelevant whether the change in the money supply results from an OMO or a FXO. As far as monetarists are concerned both operations can bring about disequilibrium in the money market. An expansion of the domestic monetary base under fixed exchange rates whether arising from a purchase of domestic bonds or a purchase of foreign currencies causes an excess of real money balances. The result is a balance of payments deficit which requires the authorities to intervene to support their currency, the reserves decline until the money supply is brought back to its original level and excess balances are eliminated.

The contrast between a fixed and floating exchange rates in the monetary model is pronounced. Under fixed exchange rates monetary policy is endogenously determined by the need to peg the exchange rate, while with a floating exchange rate the country can exogenously determine its money supply because it is the exchange rate and not monetary changes that restore equilibrium.

There is a split in the monetarist camp over the desirability of fixed as opposed to floating exchange rates. Some monetarists argue that because balance of payments deficits and surpluses are necessarily transitory and self-correcting, then countries should agree to permanently fix their exchange rates and enjoy the benefits of stable exchange rates. On the other hand, Milton Friedman has long advocated that authorities should allow exchange rates to float so that countries are left free to determine their own rates of inflation and monetary policies independently of other countries. Many other arguments are brought into play in the fixed versus floating exchange rate debate and these are examined in more detail in Chapter 10.

5.13 Empirical evidence on the monetary approach

Much of the empirical evidence on the monetary approach attempts to measure the so called 'offset coefficient'. The offset coefficient measures the extent to which an increase in the domestic component of the money base leads to a fall in reserves of a like amount in a fixed exchange rate regime as postulated by the monetary approach. To validate the monetary model, empirical estimates of the offset coefficient under fixed exchange rates require that it be equal to minus one, that is, an increase in domestic component of the monetary base leads to an exactly offsetting fall in the reserves. Some of the better-known estimates of the offset coefficient covering various countries and periods of the fixed exchange rate system that prevailed prior to 1973 are presented in **Table 5.1**.

As we can see, the empirical evidence on the monetary approach is somewhat mixed. In the Bean (1976) and Kouri and Porter (1974) studies the offset coefficient is of the correct sign and statistically different from minus unity. One explanation that may help to explain the lower than expected offset coefficient was put forward by Magee (1976) who pointed out that exchange rates were not rigidly fixed under the Bretton Woods system. This being the case, part of a increase in the domestic component of the monetary base may be absorbed by a depreciation of the exchange rate rather than a fall in the reserves.

Nonetheless, Obstfeld (1982) pointed out that the estimates of Kouri and Porter (1974) and Bean (1976) were likely to have been over estimates of the offset coefficient because of the frequent practice of sterilization of foreign exchange interventions by

Table 5.1 Empirical estimates of the offset coefficient

Study	Country	Estimation period	Offset coefficient
Bean (1976)	Japan	1959–70	–0.67 (–8.32)
Genberg (1976)	Sweden	1959–70	–1.11* (–3.00)
Kouri and Porter (1974)	Australia	1961–72	–0.47 (–5.29)
	Germany	1960–70	–0.77 (–18.40)
	Italy	1964–70	–0.43 (–4.36)
	Netherlands	1960–70	–0.59 (–7.58)
Obstfeld (1982)	Germany	1961–67	0.003 (0.001)
Taylor (1990)	UK	1965–71	–0.49 (–5.44)

Notes: (a) The hypothesis is that the offset coefficient is equal to –1. (b) An asterisk by the reported estimate indicates that it is statistically in line with the hypothesis. (c) The *t*-statistics are in parentheses.

central banks. Suppose a country expands the domestic component of the monetary base; there would be pressure for the currency to depreciate and the authorities would then have to buy the domestic currency with a fall in their reserves. To prevent a fall in the money supply, authorities typically tried to sterilize the fall by further purchases of domestic bonds. To the extent that purchasing domestic bonds (which will tend to lower domestic interest rates) does not induce further outflows, the offset coefficient will be greater than minus unity; that is, the expansion of domestic component of the money base is greater than the fall in reserves. Since in the Kouri and Porter and Bean studies their estimation procedures did not take into account sterilization practices, they require reestimation using more sophisticated econometric procedures. In his study, Obstfeld (1982) found that the offset coefficient for Germany changed from –0.55 to an insignificant 0.003 when sterilization practices were accounted for. Obstfeld's result therefore casts grave doubt on the monetary approach.

All the empirical estimates need to be treated with caution even if the simultaneous-equation bias problem has been accounted for by using appropriate econometric estimation techniques. This is because all the studies assume that the price level, real output and interest rates are exogenous and unaffected by changes in the money supply. Such assumptions have no grounding in economic theory and are most unlikely to be fulfilled in the real world.

5.14 Criticisms of the monetary approach

We need to emphasize that the monetary model presented in this chapter is not necessarily a model which all advocates of the monetary approach to the balance of payments would be in full agreement with. There is a wide spectrum of views that can be categorized within the monetarist camp. Some monetarists argue that an increase in the domestic money supply might not be reflected exclusively in an equivalent fall in the reserves under fixed exchange rates. For instance, if there is unemployment an expansionary monetary policy may lead to some increase in output (reflected in a positive-sloping aggregate supply function) which by raising money demand will reduce the devaluation pressures on the home currency. In this instance, reserves would not need to fall in exact proportion as the initial rise in the money supply as some of the expansion would be willingly held as transactions balances.

Some critics have argued that to regard the balance of payments as a monetary phenomenon is only true in the sense that the balance of payments measures monetary flows between domestic and foreign residents. They argue that it is quite wrong to regard the balance of payments deficits and surpluses as exclusively due to monetary decisions because the question of causation is an open issue. If suddenly economic agents decide to hold spend more on foreign goods/services and foreign investments under a fixed exchange rate system there will be a transitory deficit in the balance of payments. The deficit then forces the authorities to buy the domestic money base in the foreign exchange market. The cause of the deficit is the expenditure decision not a decrease in money demand which then leads to excess real money balances and a balance of payments deficit. In other words, causation can easily lead from expenditure decisions to changes in money demand rather than changes in money demand inducing changes in expenditure behaviour.

A survey of the monetary approach by Boughton (1988) has argued that nearly every assumption made by the proponents is empirically open to question. There is ample evidence that money demand functions can be highly unstable, economies are rarely at full employment and purchasing power parity is useless as a guide to exchange rate movements (see Chapter 6). Although these assumptions hold reasonably well in the longer run, they are very rarely fulfilled in the short run. The empirical violation of these key assumptions must bring into question the policy relevance of the monetary approach.

The proponents of the monetary approach argue that it provides an insight into the short-run disequilibrium in the balance of payments. Yet, since its assumptions of full employment and purchasing power parity and a stable money demand function are highly questionable in the short run, there is clearly something wrong with using assumptions that may be valid in the long run to explain what is happening in the short run. In this sense, the monetary model's conclusions about the long-run consequences of changes in economic policy are probably more insightful than its postulates about the short-run consequences.

Another criticism of the monetary approach is that no attention is paid to the composition of a deficit and surplus. If there is a large deficit in the current account which is financed by an offsetting surplus in the capital account the monetarists argue that this means that there is no need for any policy concern with regard to the balance of payments. Indeed, because any surplus or deficit is necessarily a transitory feature representing a stock disequilibrium in the money market which is necessarily self-correcting, a policy with regard to the balance of payments is unnecessary. Such an approach ignores the dangers of increasing indebtedness due to current account deficits being financed by capital inflows. In the real world it is the increase in such indebtedness that causes much concern for policy-makers of the countries concerned.

5.15 Conclusions

The monetary approach provides a distinctive and clear analysis of the effects of a devaluation and monetary expansion on the balance of payments. Its emphasis on disequilibrium in the balance of payments as being a flow response to stock disequilibrium in the money market represents an important contribution to the research on international economics.

Another significant contribution of the monetary approach is that it provides a rich set of policy recommendations. A country that opts to fix its exchange rate will lose its monetary autonomy and a monetary expansion can lead to temporary balance of payments deficits, whereas a country that allows its currency to float will have monetary autonomy but a monetary expansion then leads to a depreciation of its currency. Hence, it provides a warning to policy-makers that reckless monetary expansion can lead to balance of payments problems under fixed exchange rates or a currency problem under floating exchange rates.

With regard to the effects of a devaluation of a currency, starting from a position of equilibrium, the monetary approach suggests that there be an unambiguous transitory surplus in the balance of payments. This stands in contrast to the elasticity and absorption approaches which suggest that the effects are ambiguous. It must be borne in mind, however, that the monetary model is referring to both the current and capital account whereas the latter two are concerned exclusively with the current account. Finally, it needs to be remembered that the monetary approach does not specify precisely how temporary the resulting surplus is, presumably this varies on a country by country basis.

Further reading

Bean, D. (1976) 'International Reserve Flows and Money Market Equilibrium, the Japanese Case,' in J.A. Frenkel and H.G. Johnson (eds), *The Monetary Approach to the Balance of Payments* (London: Allen & Unwin).

Boughton, J.M. (1988) 'The Monetary Approach to Exchange Rates: What Now Remains?', *Princeton Essays in International Finance*, Princeton, no. 171.

Copeland, L.S. (2004) *Exchange Rates and International Finance* (CFT: Prentice Hall).

Frankel, J.A. (1979) 'On the Mark: A Theory of Floating Exchange Rates Based on Real Interest Rate Differentials', *American Economic Review*, vol. 69, pp. 610–22.

Frenkel, J.A. and Johnson, H.G. (eds) (1976), *The Monetary Approach to the Balance of Payments* (London: Allen & Unwin).

Genberg, H. (1976) 'Aspects of the Monetary Approach to Balance of Payments Theory: An Empirical Study of Sweden', in J.A. Frenkel and H.G. Johnson (eds), *The Monetary Approach to the Balance of Payments* (London: Allen & Unwin).

Johnson, H.G. (1976) 'The Monetary Theory of Balance of Payments Policies', in J.A. Frenkel and H.G. Johnson (eds), *The Monetary Approach to the Balance of Payments*. (London: Allen & Unwin).

Johnson H.G. (1977) 'The Monetary Approach to the Balance of Payments: A Nontechnical Guide', *Journal of International Economics*, vol. 7, pp. 251–68.

Kouri, P.J.K. and Porter, M.G. (1974) 'International Capital Flows and Portfolio Equilibrium', *Journal of Political Economy*, vol. 82, pp. 443–67.

Kreinin, M.E. and Officer, L.H. (1978) 'The Monetary Approach to the Balance of Payments: A Survey', *Princeton Studies in International Finance*, no. 43.

Magee, S.P. (1976) 'The Empirical Evidence on the Monetary Approach to the Balance of Payments and Exchange Rates', *American Economic Review, Papers and Proceedings*, vol. 66, pp. 163–70.

Obstfeld, M. (1982) 'Can We Sterilize? Theory and Evidence', *American Economic Review, Papers and Proceedings*, vol. 72, pp. 45–50.

Officer, L. (1976) 'The Purchasing Power Parity Theory of Exchange Rates: A Review Article', *IMF Staff Papers*, vol. 23, pp. 1–61.

Rabin, A. and Yeager, L. (1982) 'Monetary Approaches to the Balance of Payments and Exchange Rates', *Princeton Essays in International Finance*, no. 148.

Sarno, L. and Taylor, M.P. (2002) *The Economics of Exchange Rates* (Cambridge: Cambridge University Press).

Taylor, M.P. (1990) *The Balance of Payments* (Aldershot: Edward Elgar).

Whitman, M.V.N. (1975) 'Global Monetarism and the Monetary Approach to the Balance of Payments', *Brookings Papers on Economic Activity*, vol. 2, pp. 491–536.

PART 2

Exchange Rate Determination: Theory, Evidence and Policy

Part 2

6

Purchasing Power Parity and Floating Exchange Rate Experience

6.1 Introduction

In Chapter 1, we looked at what exactly the foreign exchange market is, introduced a number of differing exchange rate concepts and examined a simple current account model of exchange rate determination. In this chapter we look at one of the earliest and simplest models of exchange rate determination known as purchasing power parity (PPP) theory. An understanding of PPP is essential to the study of international finance. PPP theory has been advocated as a satisfactory model of exchange rate determination in its own right, and also provides a point of reference for the long-run exchange rate in many of the modern exchange rate theories which we examine in later chapters.

Having looked at PPP theory, we proceed to examine how well-suited this theory is to explaining actual exchange rate behaviour since the adoption of generalized floating in 1973. As we shall see, PPP theory does not provide an adequate explanation of some of the observed features of floating exchange rates. Some of the possible explanations for the failure of PPP are then discussed.

6.2 Purchasing power parity theory and the law of one price

PPP is generally attributed to Gustav Cassell's writings in the 1920s, although its intellectual origins date back to the writings of the nineteenth-century British economist David Ricardo. The basic concept underlying PPP theory is that arbitrage forces will lead to the equalization of goods prices internationally once the prices of goods are measured in the same currency. As such the theory represents an application of the 'law of one price'.

The law of one price

The law of one price simply says that in the presence of a competitive market structure and the absence of transport costs and other barriers to trade, identical products which are sold in different markets will sell at the same price when expressed in terms of a common currency.

The law of one price is based on the idea of perfect goods arbitrage. Arbitrage occurs where economic agents exploit price differences so as to provide a riskless profit. For example, if a car costs £15,000 in the UK and the identical model costs $30,000 in the USA, then according to the law of one price the exchange rate should be £15,000/$30,000, which is £0.50/$1. If the exchange rate were higher than this, say at £0.60/$1, then it would pay a US resident to purchase a car in the UK because with $25,000 he would obtain £15,000 which could then be used to purchase a car in the UK saving $5,000 compared to purchasing in the USA. According to the law of one price, US residents will exploit this arbitrage possibility and start purchasing pounds and selling dollars. Such a process will continue until the pound appreciates to £0.50/$1 at which point arbitrage profit opportunities are eliminated. Conversely, if the exchange rate is £0.4/$1 then a UK car would cost a US resident £15,000/0.4 = $37,500, while a US car would cost UK residents $30,000 × 0.4 = £12,000, the pound is overvalued. Hence, US residents will not buy UK cars and UK residents will buy US cars (saving £3,000) so the pound will depreciate on the foreign exchange market to its PPP value of £0.50/$1.

The proponents of PPP argue that the exchange rate must adjust to ensure that the 'law of one price' which applies only to individual goods, also holds internationally for identical **bundles** of goods.

6.3 Absolute and relative PPP

Purchasing power parity theory comes in two forms; one is based on a strict interpretation of the law of one price and is termed absolute purchasing power parity, while the other is a 'weaker' variation known as relative purchasing power parity. We shall first examine the absolute version of the theory and then consider the relative version.

Absolute PPP

The absolute version of PPP holds that if one takes a bundle of goods in one country and compares the price of that bundle with an identical bundle of goods sold in a foreign country converted by the exchange rate into a common currency of measurement, then the prices will be equal. For example, if a bundle of goods costs £100 in the UK and the same bundle costs $200 in the USA, then the exchange rate defined as pounds per dollar will be £100/$200 = £0.50/$1. Algebraically, the absolute version of PPP can be stated as:

$$S = \frac{P}{P^*} \tag{6.1}$$

where S is the exchange rate defined as domestic currency units per unit of foreign currency, P is the price of a bundle of goods expressed in the domestic currency, and P^* is the price of an identical bundle of goods in the foreign country expressed in terms of the foreign currency.

According to absolute PPP, a rise in the home price level relative to the foreign price level will lead to a proportional depreciation of the home currency against the foreign currency. In our example, if the price of the UK bundle rises to £160 while the price of the US bundle remains at $200, then according to absolute PPP the pound will depreciate to £0.80/$1.

Relative PPP

The absolute version of PPP is, even proponents of the theory generally acknowledge, unlikely to hold precisely because of the existence of transport costs, imperfect information and the distorting effects of tariff and non-tariff barriers to trade.

Nonetheless, it is argued that a weaker form of PPP known as relative purchasing power parity can be expected to hold even in the presence of such distortions. Put simply, the relative version of PPP theory argues that the exchange rate will adjust by the amount of the inflation differential between two economies. Algebraically this is expressed as:

$$\%\Delta S = \%\Delta P - \%\Delta P^* \tag{6.2}$$

where $\%\Delta S$ is the percentage change in the exchange rate, $\%\Delta P$ is the domestic inflation rate, and $\%\Delta P^*$ is the foreign inflation rate.

According to the relative version of PPP, if the inflation rate in the UK is 10% whilst that in the United States is 4%, the pounds per dollar exchange rate should be expected to depreciate by approximately 6%. The absolute version of PPP does not have to hold for this to be the case. For example, the exchange rate may be £0.5/$1 while the UK bundle of goods costs £120 and the US bundle of identical goods costs $200 so that absolute PPP is not holding (this requires a rate of £0.60/$1). But if UK prices go up 10% to £132 and the US bundle goes up 4% to $212, the relative version of PPP predicts the pound will depreciate 6% to £0.53/$1 (even though absolute PPP requires £0.622/$1=£132/$212).

A generalized version of PPP

One of the major problems with PPP theory as we have so far examined it, is that it suggests that PPP holds for all types of goods. However, a more generalized version of PPP that provides some useful insights makes a distinction between traded and non-traded goods. Traded goods are goods that are susceptible to the rigours of international competition, be they exports or import-competing industries such as most manufactured goods. Non-traded goods are those that cannot be traded internationally at a profit, such as houses and certain services such as a haircut, or restaurant food.

The point of the traded/non-traded goods distinction is that on *a priori* grounds PPP is more likely to hold for traded than for non-traded goods. This is because the price of traded goods will tend to be kept in line by international competition, while the price of non-traded goods will be determined predominately by domestic supply and demand considerations. For example, if a car costs £15,000 in the UK and $30,000 in the USA, arbitrage will tend to keep the pound–dollar rate at £0.50/$1. However, if the price of a house costs £150,000 in the UK and $80,000 in the USA and the exchange rate is £0.50/$1, arbitrage forces do not easily come into play (unless fed-up UK citizens emigrate to America pushing up US house prices and lowering UK prices). Similarly, if a haircut costs £10 in the UK but $10 in the USA and the exchange rate is £0.50/$1, only insane people in the UK will travel to the USA for a haircut knowing that they can save £5 because of the time and transport costs involved.

We now consider the importance of the tradables/non-tradables distinction for PPP when aggregate price indices made up of both tradables and non-tradables are considered. In the first instance, we assume that PPP holds for tradables goods, which means:

$$P_T = S P_{T*} \tag{6.3}$$

where S is the exchange rate defined as domestic currency units per unit of foreign currency, P_T is the price of traded goods in the domestic country measured in terms of the domestic currency, and P_{T*} is the price of traded goods in the foreign country measured in terms of the foreign currency.

The aggregate price index (P_I) for the domestic economy is made up of a weighted average of the price of both tradable (P_T) and non-tradable goods (P_N) priced in the domestic currency. Likewise, the foreign aggregate price index (P_{I*}) is made up of a weighted average of the price on tradables (P_{T*}) and non-tradables (P_{N*}) priced in the foreign currency. This gives:

$$P_I = \alpha P_N + (1 - \alpha)P_T \tag{6.4}$$

where α is the proportion of non-traded goods in the domestic price index;

$$P_{I*} = \beta P_{N*} + (1 - \beta)P_{T*} \tag{6.5}$$

where β is the proportion of non-traded goods in the foreign price index. Dividing equation (6.4) by (6.5) we obtain:

$$\frac{P_I}{P_{I*}} = \frac{\alpha P_N + (1 - \alpha)P_T}{\beta P_{N*} + (1 - \beta)P_{T*}} \tag{6.6}$$

If we divide the numerator by P_T and the denominator by SP_{T*} which, because of the assumption of PPP for tradable goods, are equivalent expressions (see equation 6.3) we obtain:

$$\frac{P_I}{P_I^*} = S \times \left[\frac{\alpha(P_N/P_T) + (1 - \alpha)}{\beta(P_{N*}/P_{T*}) + (1 - \beta)} \right] \tag{6.7}$$

This can be rearranged to give the solution for the exchange rate as:

$$S = \frac{P_I}{P_{I*}} \times \left[\frac{\beta(P_{N*}/P_{T*}) + (1 - \beta)}{\alpha(P_N/P_T) + (1 - \alpha)} \right] \tag{6.8}$$

Equation (6.8) is an important modification to our simple PPP equation, because PPP no longer necessarily holds in terms of aggregate price indices due to the multiplicative term on the right-hand side. Furthermore, the equation suggests that the relative price of non-tradables relative to tradables will influence the exchange rate. If the domestic price of non-tradables rises relative to tradables this will lead to an appreciation (fall) of the home currency. The reason is that PPP holds only in terms of tradable goods. A rise in the relative price of non-tradables while keeping the aggregate price index constant implies that the price of tradables must have fallen which will then induce an appreciation of the exchange rate (to maintain PPP for tradable goods) even though the aggregate price index has remained unchanged. Conversely, a rise in the price of tradables while holding the aggregate price index constant leads to a depreciation of the exchange rate to maintain PPP for tradable goods.

The tradable/non-tradable distinction serves as a warning when testing for PPP. Testing for PPP using price indices based on tradable goods prices is likely to lead to better results than when using aggregate price indices made up of both types of goods. Exchange rate movements induced by changes in the relative prices between tradable and non-tradable goods represent real exchange rate changes. Among the factors that can lead to such relative price changes are differing rates of productivity in the traded and non-traded sectors of the economy, and changing consumer demand patterns.

6.5 Measurement problems in testing for PPP

Many of the proponents of PPP argued prior to the adoption of floating exchange rates that exchange rate changes would be in line with levels predicted by purchasing power parity theory. Before examining some of the empirical evidence on PPP theory, it is worth considering some of the practical problems involved in testing for PPP. One of the major problems is to decide whether or not the theory is supposed to be applicable to both traded goods and non-traded goods, or applicable to only one of those categories. At first sight PPP theory seems more readily applicable to traded goods, but some authors have argued that the distinction between the two categories is fuzzy and there are mechanisms linking both traded and non-traded goods prices. For example, some traded goods are used as inputs into the production of non-traded goods, and *vice-versa* (for example shop rents differ in price from the USA compared to say Mexico).

The argument over whether or not PPP should be applied to traded goods only or whether a more general price index made up of both traded and non-traded goods should be used is important for the empirical testing of PPP theory. If the theory is supposed to be applicable to traded goods only, then the price index used for testing the theory needs to be made up only of traded goods. Conversely, if the theory is applicable to both traded and non-traded goods then a more general price index should be employed. In practice, researchers who test PPP theory for traded goods typically use wholesale or manufacturing price indices which are normally dominated by traded goods, while if the test involves both traded and non-traded goods then consumer price indices which weight both classes of goods are generally used. An overall problem facing researchers, whichever price index they decide to employ, is that PPP is only expected to hold for similar baskets of goods, but national price indices typically attach different weights to different classes of goods. For instance, consumer price indices in underdeveloped economies typically have a high weighting for food, while those in developed countries have a lower weighting for food and a higher weighting for consumer goods.

Another statistical problem in testing for PPP is that the base period for the test should ideally be one where PPP held approximately. In addition, there are divergences of view over the time span during which PPP can be expected to assert itself; a strong version of PPP would suggest it holds on a monthly basis whereas progressively weaker versions would argue that it can be expected to hold only on a quarterly, six monthly or yearly and beyond basis. Bearing in mind some of these practical problems we proceed to look at some of the empirical evidence on PPP theory.

6.6 Empirical evidence on PPP

There are a variety of methods of testing for PPP, including graphical evidence, simplistic data analysis and more sophisticated econometric evidence. We first look at the graphical evidence.

Graphical evidence on PPP

Figure 6.1 plots the actual exchange rate and the exchange rate that would have maintained PPP, for various currencies, and shows that the exchange rate has diverged considerably from that suggested by purchasing power parity.

In **Figure 6.1(a)** it can be seen that PPP does not do at all well in tracking the dollar–pound rate – it performs reasonably well up to 1977 but between mid-1976 and mid-1981 there is a dramatic appreciation of the pound while PPP would have predicted a depreciation (due to higher UK inflation). A massive dollar appreciation after 1981 leads to the restoration of PPP in early 1984. Thereafter the pound has a brief period of undervaluation in relation to PPP and from late 1985 to 2005 the pound becomes rather overvalued in relation to PPP. Neither is the deutschmark–dollar rate (**Figure 6.1(b)**) explained by PPP, with the dollar generally undervalued in relation to PPP up to early 1981. Thereafter the dollar becomes substantially overvalued in relation to PPP up until mid-1986 when it once again becomes undervalued in relation to PPP. Again with the yen–dollar (**Figure 6.1(c)**) there are sustained and marked departures from PPP. **Figure 6.1(d)** shows that PPP does a poor job at tracking the yen–deutschmark parity.

(a) Dollar–pound rate and PPP rate

$/£ rate

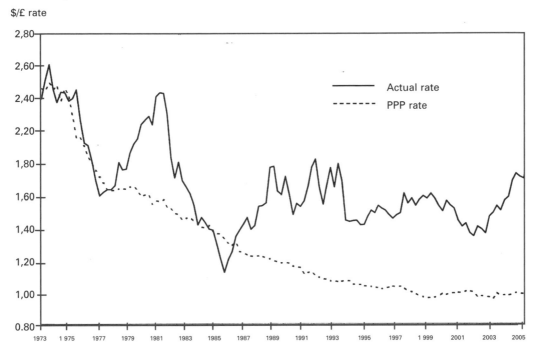

(b) Deutschmark–dollar rate and PPP rate

DM/$ rate

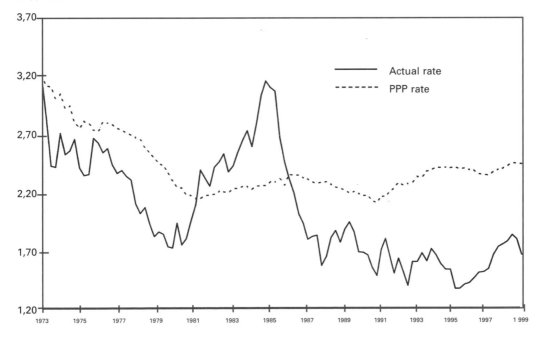

 Figure 6.1 The actual exchange rate and the PPP exchange rate for different currency pairs

(c) Yen–dollar rate and PPP rate

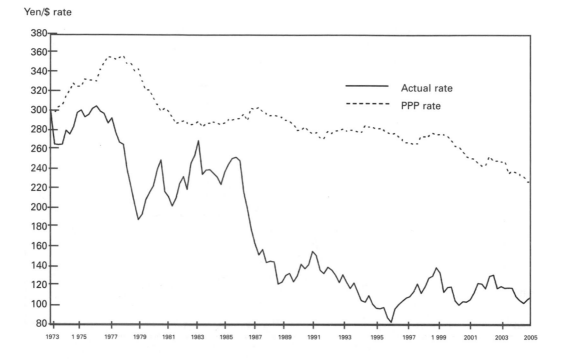

(d) Yen–deutschmark rate and PPP rate

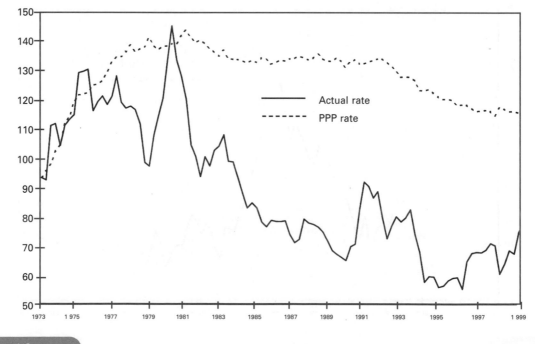

Figure 6.1 cont.

(e) French franc–deutschmark rate and PPP rate

FF/DM rate

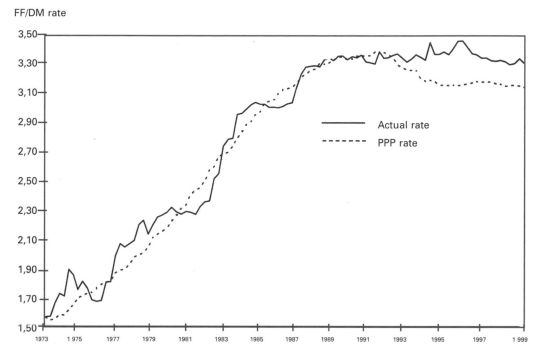

(f) Lira–deutschmark and PPP rate

Lira/DM rate

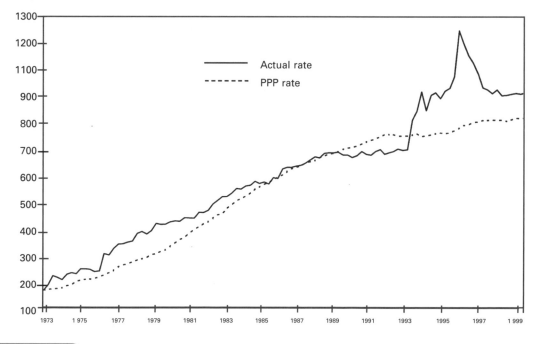

Figure 6.1 cont.

(g) Deutschmark–pound rate and PPP rate

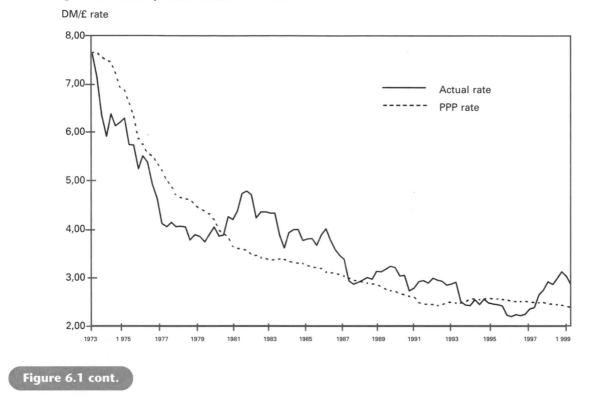

Figure 6.1 cont.

When it comes to tracking the lira, French franc and pound against the deutschmark (**Figures 6.1(e–g)**) the plots reveal that although there are deviations from PPP, the order of magnitude is much smaller than against the dollar and that PPP does a reasonable job. This is not that surprising since transport costs and trade barriers between France, Italy, the UK and Germany are small because of their geographical proximity, and membership of the European Union prohibits the use of trade barriers between its members. These conditions facilitate the goods-market arbitrage that PPP is so heavily dependent on.

It is noticeable in all the plots that although the exchange rate is frequently far from PPP it does have a tendency to go back towards the PPP rate over the longer run. This provides some evidence that PPP may be a useful guide for the determination of the long run exchange rate.

Econometric evidence on PPP

Apart from comparing the exchange rate that would have maintained PPP with the actual exchange rate, we can test for PPP by use of regression analysis. In log form the two simple hypotheses may be expressed as follows:

Absolute PPP: $\ln S_t = a_1 + a_2(\ln P_t - \ln P_{t*}) + u_t$

Relative PPP: $\Delta\ln S_t = a_1 + a_2(\Delta\ln P_t - \Delta\ln P_{t*}) + u_t$

where Δ is the one-period change in the variable, $\ln S_t$ is the log of the domestic exchange rate per unit of foreign currency, $\ln P_t$ is the log of domestic tradable goods prices, $\ln P_{t*}$ is the log of foreign tradable goods prices, and u_t is a random error with zero mean and normal distribution.

In both cases, for PPP to hold the regression estimates would yield $a_1 = 0$ and $a_2 = 1$. The price and exchange rate variables are put into log form because the change in the log of a variable approximates to the percentage change in the variable. **Table 6.1** contains some empirical estimates of the relative version of PPP using quarterly data (having the system in first-difference form makes the validity of the test somewhat superior as it has the effect of detrending the data).

The regression estimates provide additional support for the graphical analysis in the case of the relative PPP version. For the pound–dollar rate the coefficient a_2 is wrongly-signed and statistically insignificant. For the dollar–deutschmark the coefficient a_2 is well-below the hypothesized value of unity and is not significantly different from zero leading to a clear rejection of PPP. PPP does not help much with the yen–dollar rate either, in the two sub-periods the coefficient a_2 is not significantly different from zero in the first sub-period and the point estimate is 2.79 in the second sub-period, although over the entire period it performs all right. PPP does somewhat better for the lira–dollar rate. All currencies (except the dollar) perform better in PPP tests against the German deutschmark than they do against the dollar. However, the results are very mixed; the coefficient a_2 is alright in some sub-periods but not in others, and it is frequently not significantly different from zero.

The overall evidence on the PPP hypothesis is not very supportive; the graphical evidence and econometric results show that for some rates the deviations from PPP are both substantial and prolonged. This is especially the case for the major currencies against the US dollar, where PPP performs abysmally. While PPP has a better explanatory power for a number of currencies against the German mark, the results are still not that supportive, as the estimates for the coefficient a_2 can differ substantially in sub-periods and are often not significantly different from zero. In sum, there is much more to exchange rate determination than PPP. For an excellent review of the literature on PPP the reader is referred to Sarno and Taylor (2002).

6.7 Summary of the empirical evidence on PPP

1   Our results are very much in line with those presented by Frenkel (1981), that shows PPP performs better for countries that are geographically close to one another and where trade linkages are high. This is also borne out in the graphical plots – the biggest divergences between the actual and PPP exchange rates are between the pound, deutschmark and yen against the dollar; while the lira and French franc rates against the deutschmark are quite accurately tracked by PPP. Not only are France, Italy and Germany in close proximity to one another, minimizing transport costs, but they are also members of the European Union so that there exist no tariff impediments to restrict trade among them.
2   The plots of the exchange rates and PPP rates show that there have been both substantial and prolonged deviations from PPP which have frequently been reversed.

Table 6.1 Relative purchasing power parity tests

Rate	Relative PPP Period	$\Delta \ln S_t = a_1 + a_2(\Delta \ln P_{t*} - \Delta \ln P_t) + u_t$		SE	DW
		a_1	a_2		
Pound/dollar	73Q1–81Q4	0.01	−0.17	0.050	1.83
		(0.56)	(−0.46)		
	81Q4–90Q3	0.00	−0.21	0.059	1.85
		(0.03)	(−0.26)		
	73Q1–90Q3	0.00	−0.01	0.054	1.87
		(0.41)	(−0.04)		
Deutschmark/dollar	73Q1–81Q4	0.00	0.53	0.069	1.79
		(−0.25)	(0.89)		
	81Q4–90Q3	−0.01	0.48	0.062	1.96
		(−0.76)	(0.59)		
	73Q1–90Q3	−0.01	0.46	0.064	1.88
		(−0.80)	(1.00)		
Yen/dollar	73Q1–81Q4	0.00	0.82	0.051	1.94
		(−0.43)	(1.82)		
	81Q4–90Q3	0.01	2.79	0.063	2.01
		(0.93)	(3.67)		
	73Q1–90Q3	0.00	1.22*	0.058	1.95
		(−0.26)	(3.15)		
Lira/dollar	73Q1–81Q4	0.01	0.68*	0.053	1.99
		(0.74)	(2.25)		
	81Q4–90Q3	−0.01	0.78*	0.055	1.90
		(−0.70)	(1.07)		
	73Q1–90Q3	0.00	0.73*	0.055	1.98
		(−0.05)	(2.36)		
French franc/deutschmark	73Q1–81Q4	0.00	0.77*	0.034	1.89
		(0.21)	(1.29)		
	81Q4–90Q3	0.00	0.76*	0.021	1.91
		(0.59)	(1.35)		
	73Q1–90Q3	0.00	0.71*	0.027	2.00
		(0.53)	(1.90)		
Lira/deutschmark	73Q1–81Q4	0.01	0.51*	0.054	1.80
		(1.32)	(1.64)		
	81Q4–90Q3	0.00	0.55*	0.017	1.88
		(0.56)	(2.39)		
	73Q1–90Q3	0.00	0.68*	0.040	1.79
		(0.87)	(3.51)		
Pound/deutschmark	73Q1–81Q4	0.01	0.16	0.057	1.95
		(0.91)	(0.39)		
	81Q4–90Q3	−0.01	1.32*	0.045	1.97
		(−0.71)	(2.63)		
	73Q1–90Q3	0.01	0.40	0.051	1.96
		(0.83)	(1.32)		
Yen/deutschmark	73Q1–81Q4	0.00	0.90*	0.061	1.99
		(−0.25)	(1.84)		
	81Q4–90Q3	0.00	1.18*	0.039	1.97
		(0.10)	(2.81)		
	73Q1–90Q3	0.00	0.93*	0.050	1.99
		(−0.15)	(2.78)		

Notes: Hypothesis is $a_2 = 1$. An asterisk by a variable indicates that it is both of the correct sign and statistically equal to its hypothesized value. The t-statistics are in parentheses.
Source: Author's own estimates.

Per cent change

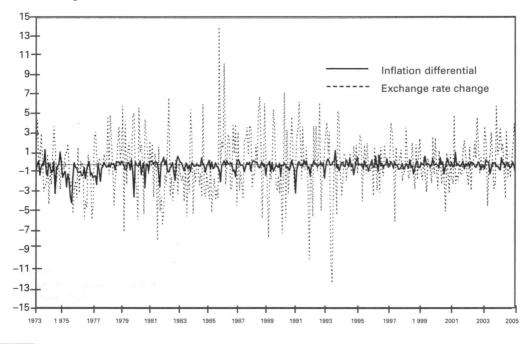

Monthly per cent changes in the dollar–pound ($/£) exchange rate and monthly inflation differentials (US–UK)

3   Exchange rates have been much more volatile than the corresponding national price levels (see Frenkel and Mussa (1980), and MacDonald (1988)). This again is contrary to the PPP hypothesis in which exchange rates are only supposed to be as volatile as prices. **Figure 6.2** shows that the monthly volatility of the $/£ exchange rate is significantly higher than the difference in the monthly changes in the US and UK price indices.

4   Empirically, PPP holds better in the long run than in the short run. A study by Lothian (1997) using data from 22 OECD countries covering the period 1974–91 found that although there have been substantial and prolonged short-run deviations from relative PPP, it cannot be rejected over the longer run between three to six years. This long-run validity of PPP has also been supported by Sarno and Taylor (2002) using the latest econometric techniques.

5   The currencies of countries that had very high inflation rates relative to trading partners, such as Israel, Brazil and Argentina in the 1980s, experienced rapid depreciations reflecting their relatively high inflation rates. This suggests that PPP was the dominant force in determining their exchange rates during that period.

6   Overall, PPP holds better for traded goods than for non-traded goods, and this is confirmed in a study by Officer (1986). In addition, a striking and major empirical regularity is that the price of non-traded goods tends to be more expensive in rich countries than in poor countries once prices are converted into a common currency; we investigate this phenomenon further in section 6.10. This observation also has important implications about how we measure per capita GDP (see section 6.10).

Box 6.1

The hamburger standard

In 1986, *The Economist* magazine launched a Big Mac index; the 'McDonald standard' is based upon the concept of PPP, the price index for measuring PPP being simply the price of a Big Mac hamburger. In May 2004 the average price of a Big Mac in the USA was $2.90 and in Mexico the price was 24 pesos; dividing the peso price by the US dollar price ($2.90) yields an implied PPP of 8.28 pesos per dollar compared with an actual exchange rate of 11.57 pesos per dollar, yielding a 28% undervaluation of the peso. **Table 6.2** presents the measurements of over/undervaluation of the dollar in terms of PPP against various other currencies using hamburger prices. According to the table, the second-most undervalued currency is the Chinese yuan (a Beijing Big Mac costs only $1.26), while Philippines is the most undervalued currency (a big Mac costs $1.23) and the most overvalued currency is the Swiss franc (a Zurich Big Mac costs a beefy $4.90).

Table 6.2   Hamburgers and purchasing power parity

| Country | Big Mac prices | | Implied PPP of the dollar* | Actual $ exchange rate | Local currency under(−)/over(+) valuation (%) |
	in local currency	in dollars			
USA	$2.90	$2.90	–	–	–
Argentina (peso)	4.35	1.48	1.50	2.96	−49
Australia (A$)	3.25	2.27	1.12	1.43	−22
Brazil (real)	5.40	1.70	1.86	3.18	−41
Britain (£)	1.88	3.37	1.54**	1.79	+16
Canada (C$)	3.20	2.33	1.10	1.37	−20
Chile (peso)	1400	2.18	483	642	−25
China (yuan)	10.40	1.26	3.59	8.25	−56
Czech Re (CKr)	56.55	2.13	19.50	26.55	−27
Denmark (DKr)	27.75	4.46	9.57	6.22	+54
Egypt	10.00	1.62	3.45	6.17	−44
Euro Area (€)	2.74	3.28	1.06***	1.20	+13
HongKong (HK$)	12.00	1.54	4.14	7.79	−47
Hungary (forint)	531	2.52	183	210	−13
Indonesia (rupiah)	16,100	1.77	5,552	9,096	−39
Japan (yen)	262	2.33	90.3	112.4	−20
Malaysia (M$)	5.05	1.33	1.74	3.79	−54
Mexico (peso)	24.00	2.08	8.28	11.54	−28
New Zealand (NZ$)	4.35	2.65	1.50	1.64	−9
Peru	9.00	2.57	3.10	3.50	−11
Philippines	69.00	1.23	23.8	56.1	−58
Poland (zloty)	6.29	1.63	2.17	3.86	−44
Russia (rouble)	42.05	1.45	14.5	29.0	−50
Singapore (S$)	3.30	1.92	1.14	1.72	−34
South Africa (rand)	12.40	1.86	4.28	6.67	−36
S.Korea (won)	3,200	2.72	1,103	1,176	−6
Sweden (SKr)	29.90	3.94	10.3	7.59	+36
Switzerland (SFr)	6.30	4.90	2.17	1.29	+68
Taiwan (NT$)	75.10	2.24	25.9	33.5	−23
Thailand (baht)	58.90	1.45	20.3	40.6	−50
Venezuela	4,400	1.48	1,517	2,973	−49

Local currency prices and actual exchange rates are inferred by the author from data presented in *The Economist*. 'Euro Area' is a weighted average price based on the price in the 12 Eurozone countries. * PPP is the local price divided by the price in the United States, ** dollars per pound, *** dollars per euro.
Source: The Economist, 27 May 2004.

7 A number of recent papers have estimated the half-life of corrections of deviations from PPP. The half-life is the time it takes in years to correct 50% of a deviation from PPP, and in an influential paper by Rogoff (1996) was estimated to be three to five years. This shows that deviations from PPP are not speedily corrected. Rogoff (1996, p. 647) refers to the PPP Puzzle, 'The purchasing power puzzle is this. How can one reconcile the enormous short run volatility of real exchange rates with the extremely slow rate at which shocks appear to damp out?' However, Sarno and Taylor (2002) dispute the validity of the half-lives reported by Rogoff in the case of large deviations from PPP, which they argue are far more speedily corrected.

8 In a recent study, Xu (2003) emphasizes the importance of using the correct price index in PPP tests. PPP is much less likely to hold if one uses consumer price indices (CPI), than if wholesale price indices (WPI) are used; significantly better is the use of a tradables price index (TPI). In his study Xu estimates the half-life of deviations from PPP to be somewhat lower than Rogoff's three–five-years; he calculates the half life to be around two years if CPI or WPI indices are used and as low as one year if a TPI index is used.

6.8 Explaining the poor performance of purchasing power parity theory

There have been many explanations put forward to explain the general failure of exchange rates to adjust in line with PPP theory, and we proceed to look at some of the most important.

Statistical problems

We have seen that PPP theory is based upon the concept of comparing identical baskets of goods in two economies. An important problem facing researchers in this respect is that different countries usually attach different weighs to various categories of goods and services when constructing their price indices, which means it is difficult to compare 'like with like' when testing for PPP. This factor is probably very significant when testing for PPP between developed and developing economies which have vastly different consumption patterns. People in developing countries usually spend a high proportion of their income on basics such as food and clothing, while these take up a much smaller proportion of people's expenditure in developed economies.

Differing consumption baskets are not of such significance when comparing most industrialized economies since consumers have fairly similar consumption baskets in these economies. Even between developed economies, however, there is a problem posed by the differing quality of goods consumed. Although British and German consumers both spend roughly the same proportion of their incomes on cars, the Germans tend to drive German makes like BMW while the British tend to drive Fords and Japanese cars. We do not necessarily expect PPP to hold in terms of cars between the two countries because once again we are not comparing like with like.

Transport costs and trade impediments

Studies such as Frenkel (1981), which note that PPP holds better when the countries concerned are geographically close and trade linkages are high, can partly be explained by transport costs and the existence of other trade impediments such as tariffs. If a bundle of goods costs £100 in the UK and $200 in the USA, PPP would suggest an exchange rate of £0.50/$1. If transport costs are £20 then the exchange rate could lie anywhere between £0.40/$1 and £0.60/$1 without bringing arbitrage forces into play. Nonetheless, since transport costs and trade barriers do not change dramatically over time they are not sufficient explanations for the failure of the relative versions of PPP.

Imperfect competition

One of the notions underlying purchasing power parity is that there is sufficient international competition to prevent major departures of the price of a good in one country exceeding that in another. However, it is clear that there are considerable variations in the degree of competition internationally, and these differences mean that multinational corporations can often get away with charging different prices in different countries. In fact, the conditions necessary for successful price discrimination, namely differences in the willingness to pay of different sets of consumers, the ability to prevent resale from the low-cost to high-cost market and some degree of monopoly power, are for the most part more likely to hold between rather than within countries.

Differences between capital and goods markets

Purchasing power parity is based upon the concept of goods arbitrage and has nothing to say about the role of capital movements. In a classic paper which we shall be looking at in more detail in Chapter 7, Rudiger Dornbusch (1976) hypothesized that in a world where capital markets are highly integrated and goods markets exhibit slow price adjustment, there can be substantial prolonged deviations of the exchange rate from PPP. The basic idea is that in the short run goods prices in both the home and foreign economies can be considered as fixed, while the exchange rate adjusts quickly to new information and changes in economic policy. This being the case, exchange rate changes represent deviations from PPP which can be quite substantial and prolonged.

Productivity differentials

As mentioned, one striking empirical observation that is well-documented is that when prices of similar baskets of both traded and non-traded goods are converted into a common currency, the aggregate price indices tend to be higher in rich countries than in poor countries. In other words, a dollar buys more goods in say Mexico than in the United States. Further, evidence shows that prices of tradable goods are nowhere as dissimilar internationally as those of non-traded goods. Consequently the overall higher price index in rich countries is mainly due to the fact that non-tradable goods prices are higher in developed than developing countries.

An explanation for the lower relative price of non-tradables in poor countries has been put forward separately by Bela Balassa (1964) and Paul Samuelson (1964), and is worth considering in detail. As we shall see, the model argues that the lower price of goods in the non-traded sector in developing countries is mainly due to lower labour productivity in the tradables sector compared to developed countries. Or, equivalently, the higher price of non-traded goods in a developed nation (compared to non-traded goods in the developing country) is mainly due to higher labour productivity in the traded sector compared to labour productivity in the tradables sector of developing countries.

6.9 ## The Balassa–Samuelson model

Balassa (1964) and Samuelson (1964) argue that labour productivity in rich countries is higher than labour productivity in poor countries. Furthermore, this productivity differential occurs predominately in the tradables rather than the non-tradables sector. A Mexican barber tends to be as efficient as his American counterpart (as measured by haircuts per day), but a Mexican car worker is less efficient than his American counterpart (as measured by cars produced per day). Wages are assumed to be the same in the tradables and non-tradables sectors within each economy and positively related to productivity. Prices are determined positively by wages and inversely by productivity. These assumptions lead to the following set of relationships:
In the poor country:

$$P_N = W_N/Q_N \quad \text{and} \quad P_T = W_T/Q_T \tag{6.9}$$

In the rich economy:

$$P_{N*} = W_{N*}/Q_{N*} \qquad P_{T*} = W_{T*}/Q_{T*} \tag{6.10}$$

where P_N represents non-tradables prices, P_T represents traded goods prices, Q_N is output per worker in the tradables sector, Q_T is output per worker in the non-tradables sector, and an asterisk denotes a high income (high productivity) economy.
   Wage rates are the same in both the industries in each of the two economies:

$$W_N = W_T \quad \text{and} \quad W_{N*} = W_{T*} \tag{6.11}$$

Productivity is higher in the rich economy's tradables sector than in the poor country's, but in the non-tradables sector productivity in the rich and poor countries are the same. This means that:

$$Q_{T*} > Q_T \quad \text{and} \quad Q_{N*} = Q_N \tag{6.12}$$

Finally, PPP is assumed to hold only for traded goods:

$$S = P_T/P_{T*} \tag{6.13}$$

The price ratio of traded to non-traded goods in each country is given by:

$$\frac{P_N}{P_T} = \pi \tag{6.14}$$

and

$$\frac{P_{N^*}}{P_{T^*}} = \pi^* \tag{6.15}$$

Since there is higher productivity in the rich economy's tradables sector, then the relative price of non-tradables to tradables will be higher in the rich country making $\pi^* > \pi$.

Rewriting equations (6.14) and (6.15) as:

$$\frac{P_N}{P_T} = \pi \tag{6.16}$$

and

$$\frac{SP_{N^*}}{SP_{T^*}} = \pi^* \tag{6.17}$$

Since PPP holds for the tradables sector, making $P_T = S\,P_{T^*}$, then the denominator of equations (6.16) and (6.17) are the same. Consequently, since $\pi^* > \pi$, the price of non-tradables in the rich economy exceeds the price of non-tradables in the developing country, that is, $S\,P_{N^*} > P_N$; that is, PPP does not work for non-traded goods. The reason is that low wages in the developing country due to low productivity in its traded sector also lead to a relatively low price for its non-traded goods even though its productivity in this sector is the same as in developed countries; while high productivity in the rich country's tradables sector leads to high wages in its non-tradables sector, even though it is no more efficient than the poor country in that sector. Consequently, when we use the exchange rate to examine non-tradable goods prices we find that they are higher in developed countries than developing countries.

The Balassa–Samuelson model is helpful in explaining why it is that rich countries tend to have overall high price indices and poor countries low price indices when aggregate baskets of traded and non-traded goods are converted into a common currency such as the US dollar. Furthermore, it helps explain why the ratio of non-traded to traded prices tends to be higher in developed economies than developing countries.

It is clear that PPP based on tradable goods alone will undervalue the purchasing power and living standards of people in poor countries because they can purchase more non-traded goods per dollar than can people in rich countries, even if PPP holds for traded goods (see section 6.10). This means that when comparing per capita income levels between countries such as Mexico and the United States in dollar terms this should not be done at the PPP rate for tradables goods; rather, the proportion of Mexican expenditure on non-tradables should be valued at US non-tradables prices thereby raising the value of Mexican incomes in US dollar terms.

The productivity differential theory may also have some application in explaining divergences from PPP in terms of aggregate price indices between developed countries. For instance, since the Second World War Japan has consistently had higher productivity in its tradables sector than the United States. According to the Balassa–Samuelson model, this means that the real value of the yen should appreciate against the dollar as the higher productivity of Japanese tradables workers leads to a fall in Japanese traded goods prices relative to US traded goods prices, and therefore an appreciation of the yen to maintain PPP for tradable goods. Richard Marston (1986) found evidence that in the period 1973–83, Japanese productivity growth in its tradables sector outstripped US tradables productivity. During that period the yen appreciated by some 9% in real terms against the dollar.

Although the Balassa–Samuelson model helps explain why PPP does not necessarily hold in terms of aggregate price indices, it is only a partial explanation. By assumption the theory cannot explain the failure of PPP to hold for traded goods!

6.10 Per capita income levels, the relative sizes of economies and the importance of PPP estimates

The World Bank keeps a very keen eye on the per capita income levels of developing countries, since the poorest countries in the world are often deemed to be the countries that policy-makers wish to direct aid towards and provide access to cheap finance for developmental purposes. The fact that PPP tends not to hold, especially between developed and developing nations, is of considerable importance in this respect. It is well-documented that, in particular, the price of non-tradable goods and services in developing countries is significantly lower in developing countries than in developed countries. This means that $100 will tend to buy far more haircuts, restaurant meals, hotel time and many other goods and services when transferred into the local currency of a developing country than in a developed nation like the United States, the United Kingdom or Japan, simply because PPP is not holding. In particular, the exchange rates of developing countries tend to be noticeably undervalued in terms of purchasing power for goods and services. Consider the case of the Chinese renminbi versus the US dollar; the official exchange rate in 2004 was 8.6 renminbi per US dollar. Imagine, however, that when we change $100 into renminbi to obtain 860 renminbi we are then able to buy five times more goods and services in China than in the USA. The appropriate PPP exchange rate in terms of goods and services would then be 8.6/5 = 1.72 renminbi per dollar. If the exchange rate was at the calculated PPP rate then $100 would convert to 172 renminbi which would purchase the same bundle of goods and services in China as $100 buys in the USA. Think now of the implications for calculations of GDP per capita. If the United States GDP per capita was $35,000 while the Chinese per capita income was 8,600 renminbi, then using the market exchange rate the Chinese income per capita is only $1,000 which is a mere 1/35th of that of the United States. However, if $1,000 buys five times more goods and services in China, then we need to multiply the Chinese income by five to get a PPP per capita income which is $5,000 (which is the same as dividing the Chinese GDP per capita of 8,600 renminbi by the PPP rate of 1.72). This would suggest that Chinese income levels are 'only' 1/7th of those of the United States. The GDP per capita based on PPP is therefore a more reliable guide (albeit highly imperfect!) to relative living standards in the two countries than using the market exchange rate which does not reflect purchasing power parity.

The previous example calculation is by no means far from reality in the case of the United States and China, as **Table 6.3** shows gross national income (GDP) per capita according to the World Bank using the both the Atlas method and the PPP method. The Atlas method mainly uses an average of market exchange rates over the past three years to calculate income per capita in terms of US dollars, making some allowance for recent inflation (this methodology helps to iron out sudden changes in relative figures

Table 6.3 GDP per capita using the Atlas and PPP methods

	Atlas method (US dollars)	PPP method (PPP dollars)
Luxembourg	43,940	54,430
Norway	43,450	37,300
Switzerland	39,880	32,030
United States	37,610	37,300
Japan	34,510	26,620
Denmark	33,650	31,210
Sweden	28,840	26,620
United Kingdom	28,350	27,650
Finland	27,020	27,100
Ireland	26,960	30,450
Netherlands	26,310	28,600
Belgium	25,820	28,930
Germany	25,250	27,460
France	24,770	27,460
Canada	23,930	29,740
Australia	21,650	28,920
Italy	21,560	26,760
Singapore	21,230	24,180
Spain	16,990	22,020
Greece	13,720	19,920
Slovenia	11,830	19,240
Czech Republic	6,740	15,650
Hungary	6,330	13,780
Mexico	6,230	8,950
Poland	4,960	11,450
Malaysia	3,780	8,940
Argentina	3,650	10,920
Venezuela	3,490	4,740
Turkey	2,790	6,690
South Africa	2,780	10,270
Brazil	2,710	7,480
Russia	2,610	8,920
Egypt	1,390	3,940
China	1,100	4,990
India	530	2,880
Kenya	390	960
Mozambique	210	1,070

Source: World Bank, figures are for 2003.

due merely to large year-to-year exchange rate changes compared to using purely current market exchange rates), and these are compared to the estimates of GDP per capita using PPP estimates in the second column.

Not only do PPP adjustments make a significant difference to GDP per capita estimates, they also make a big difference to the importance of the relative size of different economies. As **Table 6.4** shows, the largest economy in 2003 using market exchange

Table 6.4 The sizes of different economies as measured by their GDPs

Rank using market rates		$millions	Rank using PPP rates		$millions PPP
1	United States	10,881,609	1	United States	10,871,095
2	Japan	4,326,444	2	China	6,435,838
3	Germany	2,400,655	3	Japan	3,582,515
4	United Kingdom	1,794,858	4	India	3,096,239
5	France	1,747,973	5	Germany	2,279,134
6	Italy	1,465,895	6	France	1,632,119
7	China	1,409,852	7	United Kingdom	1,606,853
8	Spain	836,100	8	Italy	1,559,321
9	Canada	834,390	9	Brazil	1,371,655
10	Mexico	626,080	10	Russia	1,318,827
11	Korea (South)	605,331	11	Canada	963,550
12	India	598,966	12	Mexico	934,553
13	Australia	518,382	13	Spain	915,072
14	Netherlands	511,556	14	Korea	858,028
15	Brazil	492,338	15	Indonesia	721,583
16	Russia	433,491	16	Australia	579,662
17	Switzerland	309,465	17	Turkey	477,256
18	Belgium	302,217	18	Netherlands	476,912
19	Sweden	300,795	19	South Africa	475,215
20	Austria	251,456	20	Iran	474,383

Source: World Bank, figures are for 2003.

rates was the United States with Japan second and China seventh. If, however, we measure the relative sizes of economies based upon PPP exchange rate estimates then China becomes the second largest economy in the world, with India jumping from twelfth to fourth and Brazil jumping from fifteenth to ninth!

6.11 Conclusions

At the time of the adoption of floating exchange rates it was widely believed that they would adjust in line with changes in national price levels as predicted by PPP theory. However, the experience with floating rates has shown that there can be substantial and prolonged deviations of exchange rates from PPP. A clear conclusion is that in the short to medium term, international goods arbitrage is nowhere near as powerful as proponents of PPP had presupposed.

There are many possible explanations for these deviations from PPP. Among the strongest candidates is that the theory relies too heavily on goods arbitrage and has no role for the international capital movements which have grown enormously in scale since the end of the Second World War. Such capital movements are heavily influenced by prospective returns and therefore agents' expectations about the future. As expectations change, then so will exchange rates regardless of whether goods prices are changing. In the following chapters we shall be looking at some of the most recent theories that attempt to take into account the implications of such capital movements.

Nonetheless, the fact that PPP does not hold very well in the short to medium term does not mean that it has no role to play in exchange rate determination. Over- or undervaluation of currencies in relation to PPP induce changes in current-account positions which will eventually lead to exchange rate changes. It is the case that deviations from PPP do have a habit of reversing themselves over the longer run. Furthermore, although exchange rates may diverge substantially from PPP, if the break in this link becomes too large the forces of goods arbitrage do start to come into play and move the exchange rate towards its PPP value. More recent evidence shows that PPP may be a useful guide to the long-run exchange rate and should not therefore be abandoned altogether.

Further reading

Balassa, B. (1964) 'The Purchasing Power Parity Doctrine: A Reappraisal', *Journal of Political Economy*, vol. 72, pp. 584–96.

Cassell, G. (1928) *Post-war Monetary Stabilization* (New York: Columbia University Press).

Dornbusch, R. (1976) 'Expectations and Exchange Rate Dynamics', *Journal of Political Economy*, vol. 84, pp. 1161–76.

Dornbusch, R. (1987) 'Purchasing Power Parity', in the *New Palgrave Dictionary of Economics* (London: Palgrave Macmillan).

Frenkel, J.A. (1981) 'The Collapse of Purchasing Power Parities During the 1970s', *European Economic Review*, vol. 16, pp. 145–65.

Frenkel, J.A. and Mussa, M. (1980) 'The Efficiency of Foreign Exchange Markets and Measures of Turbulence', *American Economic Review*, vol. 70, pp. 375–81.

Genberg, H. (1978) 'Purchasing Power Parity under Fixed and Flexible Exchange Rates', *Journal of International Economics*, vol. 8, pp. 247–76.

Hakkio, C.S. (1984) 'A Re-examination of Purchasing Power Parity', *Journal of International Economics*, vol. 17, pp. 265–77.

Isard, P. (1977) 'How Far Can We Push the Law of One Price?', *American Economic Review*, vol. 67, pp. 942–8.

Katseli, L. and Papaefstratiou, L.T. (1979) 'The Re-emergence of the Purchasing Power Parity Doctrine in the 1970s', *Princeton Special Papers in International Economics*, no. 13.

Lothian, J. (1997) 'Multi-Country Evidence on the Behaviour of Purchasing Power Parity under the Current Float', *Journal of International Money and Finance*, vol. 16, no. 1, pp. 19–35.

MacDonald, R. (1988) *Floating Exchange Rates: Theory and Evidence* (London: Unwin Hyman).

Manzur, M. (1990) 'An International Comparison of Prices and Exchange Rates: A New Test of Purchasing Power Parity', *Journal of International Money and Finance*, vol. 9, pp. 75–91.

Marston, R.C. (1986) 'Real Exchange Rates and Productivity Growth in the United States and Japan', Working Paper no. 1922, National Bureau of Economic Research.

Officer, L. (1976) 'The Purchasing Power Parity Theory of Exchange Rates: A Review Article', *IMF Staff Papers*, vol. 23, pp. 1–61.

Officer, L. (1986) 'The Law of One Price Cannot be Rejected: Two Tests Based on the Tradeable/Non Tradeable Goods Dichotomy', *Journal of Macroeconomics*, vol. 8, pp. 159–82.

Rogoff, K. (1996) 'The Purchasing Power Parity Puzzle', *Journal of Economic Literature*, vol. 34, no. 2, pp. 647–68.

Samuelson, P. (1964) 'Theoretical Notes on Trade Problems', *Review of Economics and Statistics*, vol. 46, pp. 145–54.

Sarno, L. and Taylor, M.P. (2002) 'Purchasing Power Parity and the Real Exchange Rate', *International Monetary Fund Staff Papers*, vol. 49, pp. 65–105.

Xu, Z. (2003) 'Purchasing Power Parity, Price Indices and Exchange Rate Forecasts', *Journal of International Money and Finance*, vol. 22, pp. 105–130.

7

Modern Models of Exchange Rate Determination

7.1 Introduction

The purchasing power parity theory outlined in Chapter 6 is far from a satisfactory explanation of observed exchange rate behaviour. In particular, it is very much concerned with goods arbitrage and has nothing to say about capital movements internationally. During the post-Second World War era there has been an enormous growth of capital markets, meaning that it is possible for international investors to switch huge amounts money out of one currency into another very speedily. This being the case, speculators will tend to move their money between currencies based on the expected rate of return of being in one currency compared to another. What people expect to happen to the exchange rate will be a crucial part in determining which currencies to buy and sell – if a currency is expected to depreciate, then agents will tend to switch out of that currency into currencies that they expect to appreciate. In this chapter, we look at some more recent and sophisticated exchange rate models that have been developed in an attempt to model exchange rate behaviour more successfully.

The common thread to the models that we analyse in this chapter is that they all emphasize the important role of relative money supplies in explaining the exchange rate. The monetary models start from the observation that the exchange rate is the price of one money in terms of another. However, the monetary models go beyond this simple observation to argue that exchange rate movements can be explained by changes in the supply and demand for national money stocks. There are a variety of models put forward by monetarists to explain exchange rate behaviour and we deal with three of the most important versions in this chapter. The 'flexible-price' monetary model, the 'sticky-price' monetary model and the 'real interest rate differential' model. The monetarist exchange rate models make an assumption that domestic and foreign bonds are perfect substitutes, there developed a brand of models known as portfolio balance models that allow for differences in riskiness between domestic and foreign bonds. We shall spend some time looking at the implications of imperfect asset substitutability between domestic and foreign bonds by looking at a more general model that allows for a portfolio balance effect.

7.2 Asset prices

Since international investors can quickly and easily switch out of domestic assets into foreign assets and *vice-versa*, the exchange rate can be viewed as a relative asset price. The fundamental characteristic of an asset price is that its present value will be largely influenced by its expected rate of return. To illustrate this, imagine an investor that has money to invest and two alternative investment possibilities, asset A or asset B. If the price of asset A is £100 and he expects that one year later he can sell asset A for £120, the expected rate of return on asset A is given by the formula:

$$\text{Expected rate of return on asset A} = \frac{\text{Expected sale price} - \text{Purchase price}}{\text{Purchase price}} \times 100$$

$$= \frac{120 - 100}{100} \times 100 = 20\%$$

Note that the rate of return refers to a specific time period. If asset A is expected to increase in price by 20% over two years, then the rate of return per year is slightly less than 10% per annum. Similarly, if the price of asset B is £200 and an investor expects that in one year's time he can sell asset B for £240, then the expected rate of return on asset B is given by:

$$\text{Expected rate of}\atop\text{return on asset B} = \frac{\text{Expected sale price} - \text{Purchase price}}{\text{Purchase price}} \times 100$$

$$= \frac{240 - 200}{200} \times 100 = 20\%$$

In other words, although they differ in price, assets A and B offer identical expected returns to the investor. If the investor regards both assets A and B as equally risky investments then he will be indifferent between investing in asset A or asset B so long as their expected rate of returns are equal. Suppose the investor changes his view about what he expects to sell asset A at, instead of £120 he expects to sell it at £132. The new expected rate of return on asset A is then:

$$\text{Expected rate of}\atop\text{return on asset A} = \frac{\text{Expected sale price} - \text{Purchase price}}{\text{Purchase price}} \times 100$$

$$= \frac{132 - 100}{100} \times 100 = 32\%$$

Since asset A is equally as risky as asset B, it no longer makes sense for investors to invest their money in B, instead there will be an increased demand for asset A which will push up the price of A. The price of A will be bid up until the expected rate of return on A is the same as the return on B, which occurs at a price of £110.

$$\text{Expected rate of}\atop\text{return on asset A} = \frac{\text{Expected sale price} - \text{Purchase price}}{\text{Purchase price}} \times 100$$

$$= \frac{132 - 110}{110} \times 100 = 20\%$$

Hence, a change in expectations concerning the future price of asset A from £120 to £132 will lead to a change in the current price from £100 to £110 so as to equalize the expected rate of return in relation to another equally risky asset B. Clearly what people expect to happen to future prices of assets will be crucial in determining their current prices.

7.3 Uncovered interest rate parity

Imagine the case of an international investor who has the option of investing his money in UK bonds or US bonds of similar risk and maturity. If he regards the bonds as equally risky and can switch between the two assets instantaneously, the only difference between the bonds is their currency of denomination and possibly the interest rate attached to them. There will be two factors that international investors will bear in mind when considering which to purchase, the rates of interest on UK bonds and US bonds and what they expect to happen to the pound–dollar exchange rate. We can write that:

$$E\dot{s} = r_{uk} - r_{us} \tag{7.1}$$

where $E\dot{s}$ is the expected rate of depreciation of the exchange rate of the pound, defined as pounds per dollar, r_{uk} is the UK interest rate and r_{us} is the US interest rate. Equation (7.1) is known as the uncovered interest parity condition (UIP). UIP says that the expected rate of depreciation of the pound against the dollar is equal to the interest rate differential between UK and US bonds. For example, if the interest rate in the UK is 10% per annum while the interest rate in the USA is 4% per annum, then on average international investors expect the pound to depreciate by 6% per annum.

With an initial pound per dollar exchange rate of £0.50/$1. Investing £1,000 in UK bonds will yield the investor £100 return (10%) at the end of the year. If he expects the pound to depreciate by 6% during the year, he expects the pound–dollar exchange rate to be £0.53/$1. Hence, he could purchase £1,000 worth of dollars today at £0.50/$1 which gives him $2,000 which will earn the US interest rate of 4% meaning he will then have $2,080 which he expects to convert back into pounds at £0.53/$1 giving him £1,102.4. This implies an expected return of £102.4 (approximately 10%) from investing in US bonds is approximately equal to the expected return on UK bonds. Hence, the UIP condition implies that the expected rate of return on domestic and foreign bonds are equal.

If the expected rate of depreciation of the pound was 10% then according to UIP the UK interest rate will have to be 10% higher than the US interest rate to ensure the equalization of expected yields on UK and US bonds. Crucially, for the uncovered interest rate parity condition to hold continuously requires that capital is **perfectly mobile** so that investors can instantly alter the composition of their international investments. In addition, they have to regard UK and US bonds as equally risky – were this not the case then investors that are risk-averse would require a higher expected return on the riskier asset. For example, if risk-averse UK investors viewed the risk on UK bonds as being greater than the risk on US bonds, they would require a higher expected rate of return on UK bonds than US bonds so that the uncovered interest parity condition no longer holds.

When there is both perfect capital mobility and equal riskiness of domestic and foreign bonds, UK and US bonds are said to be **perfect substitutes**. Perfect substitutability of domestic and foreign bonds implies that the uncovered interest rate parity condition will hold on a continuous basis. The monetarist models that we examine in this chapter make a crucial assumption that domestic and foreign bonds are perfect substitutes.

Box 7.1

The UIP condition and changes in exchange rate expectations

According to the UIP condition, changes in the future expected exchange rate can exert a significant effect on the spot exchange rate. In **Figure 7.1** we illustrate the UIP condition for the dollar–pound parity. The spot exchange rate is assumed to be £0.50/$1, the UK interest rate is 10% per annum and the US interest rate is 4% per annum. According to the UIP condition, the pound should be expected to depreciate by 6% per annum; that is, to £0.50/$1 × 1.06 = £0.53/$1. The resulting equalisation of expected yield is illustrated in **Figure 7.1**. In **Figure 7.1(a)** the expected year-end total is £110 regardless of whether the money is left in sterling or converted into $200 spot which becomes $208 which is expected to be converted back to at the end of the year at £0.53/$1 × $208 = £110.24.

→

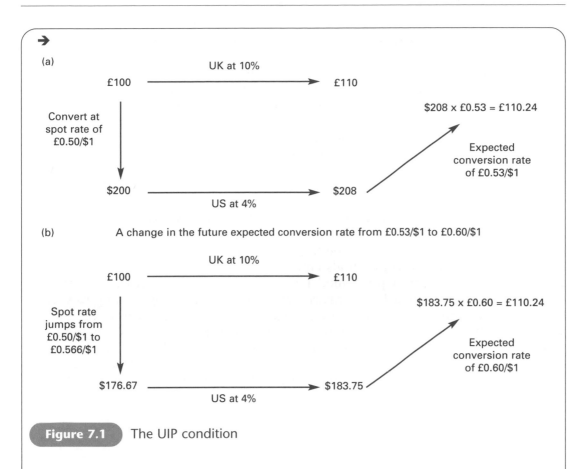

(a)

UK at 10%

£100 ──────────────────→ £110

Convert at
spot rate of
£0.50/$1

$208 x £0.53 = £110.24

Expected
conversion rate
of £0.53/$1

$200 ──────────────────→ $208
          US at 4%

(b)   A change in the future expected conversion rate from £0.53/$1 to £0.60/$1

UK at 10%

£100 ──────────────────→ £110

Spot rate
jumps from
£0.50/$1 to
£0.566/$1

$183.75 x £0.60 = £110.24

Expected
conversion rate
of £0.60/$1

$176.67 ──────────────────→ $183.75
          US at 4%

Figure 7.1 The UIP condition

An interesting question concerns what would happen if for some reason there is some bad economic news or adverse market sentiment against the pound that, while leaving UK and US interest rates unchanged, leads market participants to change their view of the expected future exchange rate of the pound–dollar parity from £0.53/$1 to say £0.60/$1? The answer is shown in **Figure 7.1(b)**. Clearly the spot exchange rate cannot remain at $0.50/£1, for this would mean that the expected proceeds from switching from pounds into dollars spot, that is $200 earning the US interest rate and converting the proceeds $208 back into sterling, that is $208 × £0.6/$1 = £124.8, are higher than just leaving the money in sterling, that is £110. In such circumstances, everyone would be selling pounds spot today so the pound would depreciate today. It is fairly straightforward to calculate the new spot rate that will satisfy the UIP condition, since the interest rate differential is 6% in favour of sterling, the spot rate needs to be 6% below the new expected future spot rate of £0.60/$1. Hence, the spot rate needs to depreciate from £0.50/$1 to £0.566/$1 (£0.60/$1 divided by 1.06). At this spot exchange rate, £100 can be converted into $176.67 dollars spot which will earn the 4% US interest rate and by the end of the year this will become $183.75 ($176.67 × 1.04) which the investor expects to convert at £0.60/$1 yielding £110.24 ($183.75 × £0.60/$1). The expected return is hence equalized as required by the UP condition. The important point about this exercise is that a perceived worsening of the expected sterling parity in one year's time from £0.53/$1 to £0.60/$1 leads to a depreciation of the sterling spot rate. Changes in expectations about the future are potentially powerful forces in determining the spot exchange rate.

7.4 The monetary models of exchange rate determination

Having provided the basic background to the monetary models of exchange rate determination we now proceed to examine the specific characteristics and predictions of three of the major monetarist models of exchange rate determination. These are commonly termed the 'flexible-price', 'sticky-price' and 'real interest rate differential' monetary models. A common characteristic of these models is that the supply and demand for money are the key determinants of exchange rates.

Another common starting point is that all the models employ the UIP condition; that is, they assume that domestic and foreign bonds are equally risky so that their expected rates of returns are equalized.

Beyond this similarity there are some significant differences between the models. The 'flexible-price' monetary model argues that all prices in the economy, be they wages, prices or exchange rates, are perfectly flexible both upwards and downwards in both the short and the long run. It also incorporates a role for the effect of inflationary expectations. The 'sticky-price' model, first elaborated by Rudiger Dornbusch (1976a), is a monetary model that argues that in the short run wages and prices tend to be sticky and only the exchange rate changes in response to changes in economic policy. Only in the medium to long run do wages and prices adjust to changes in economic policy and economic shocks. In the Dornbusch model, inflationary expectations are not explicitly dealt with. The 'real interest rate differential' model combines the role of inflationary expectations of the flexible-price monetary model with the sticky prices of the Dornbusch model.

7.5 The flexible-price monetary model

The flexible-price monetary model was developed by Frenkel (1976), Mussa (1976) and Bilson (1978) and assumes that purchasing power parity holds continuously. It represents a valuable addition to exchange rate theory, however, because it explicitly introduces relative money stocks into the picture as determinants of the relative prices which in turn determine the exchange rate.

We start by assuming that there is a conventional money demand function given by:

$$m - p = \eta y - \sigma r \tag{7.2}$$

where m is the log of the domestic money stock, p is the log of the domestic price level, y is the log of domestic real income and r is the nominal domestic interest rate. Equation (7.2) says that the demand to hold real money balances is positively related to real domestic income due to increased transactions demand, and inversely related to the domestic interest rate. A similar relationship holds for the foreign money demand function which is given by:

$$m^* - p^* = \eta y^* - \sigma r^* \tag{7.3}$$

where m^* is the log of the foreign nominal money stock, p^* is the log of the foreign price level y^* is the log of foreign real income and r^* is the foreign interest rate. It is assumed that purchasing power parity holds continuously, expressed as:

$$s = p - p^* \tag{7.4}$$

where s is the log of the exchange rate defined as domestic currency units per unit of foreign currency.

The monetarist models make a crucial assumption that domestic and foreign bonds are perfect substitutes. This being the case, the uncovered interest parity condition holds:

$$E\dot{s} = r - r^* \tag{7.5}$$

where $E\dot{s}$ is the expected rate of depreciation of the home currency.
Equation (7.5) says that the expected rate of depreciation of the home currency is equal to the interest rate differential between domestic and foreign bonds.

We can rearrange equations (7.2) and (7.3) to give solutions for the domestic and foreign price levels:

$$p = m - \eta y + \sigma r \tag{7.6}$$

$$p^* = m^* - \eta y^* + \sigma r^* \tag{7.7}$$

We then substitute equations (7.6) and (7.7) into equation (7.4) to obtain:

$$s = (m - m^*) - \eta(y - y^*) + \sigma(r - r^*) \tag{7.8}$$

Equation (7.8) is what is known as a 'reduced-form' exchange rate equation. The spot exchange rate (the dependent variable) on the left-hand side is determined by the variables (explanatory variables) listed on the right-hand side of the equation.

What does equation (7.8) predict about the effect of a change in one of the right-hand variables on the exchange rate?

(a) Relative money supplies affect exchange rates
A given percentage increase in the home money supply leads to an exactly equivalent depreciation of the currency, while a given percentage increase in the foreign money supply leads to an exactly equivalent percentage appreciation of the domestic currency. The rationale behind this is that a 10% increase in the home money supply leads to an immediate 10% increase in prices, and because PPP holds continuously this also implies a 10% depreciation of the currency. Conversely, a 10% increase in the foreign money supply leads to a 10% rise in foreign prices and for PPP to hold this means the domestic currency appreciates 10%.

(b) Relative levels of national income influence exchange rates
If domestic income were to rise, this increases the transactions demand money, the increased demand for money means that if the money stock and interest rates are held constant the increased demand for real balances can only come about through a fall in domestic prices (see equation 7.2). The fall in domestic prices then requires an appreciation of the currency to maintain purchasing power parity. On the other hand, an increase in foreign income leads to a fall in the foreign price level and therefore a depreciation of the home currency to maintain PPP.

(c)   Relative interest rates affect exchange rates

An increase in the domestic interest rate leads to a depreciation of the domestic currency. The rationale behind this is that a rise in the domestic interest rate leads to a fall in the demand for money and hence a depreciation of the domestic currency. Another rationalization for this effect can be made by expressing the nominal interest rate as made up of two components, the real interest rate and the expected inflation rate; that is:

$$r = i + P\dot{e}$$

where i is the real rate of interest and $P\dot{e}$ is the expected rate of price inflation. Similarly the foreign nominal interest rate is given by:

$$r^* = i^* + P\dot{e}^*$$

Assuming that the real rate of interest is constant and identical in both countries ($i = i^*$), an increase in the domestic nominal interest rate is due to increase in domestic price inflation expectations. Such increased inflation expectations lead to a decreased demand for money and increased expenditure on goods, which in turn leads to a rise in domestic prices. The rise in domestic prices then requires a depreciation of the currency to maintain PPP. Conversely, a rise in the foreign price level reduces foreign-erss money demand leading to increased expenditure on foreign goods and a rise in the foreign price level, requiring an appreciation of the home currency to maintain PPP.

Equation (7.8) can be rewritten using price inflation expectations differentials instead of interest rate differentials as:

$$s = (m - m^*) - \eta(y - y^*) + \sigma(P\dot{e} - P\dot{e}^*) \tag{7.9}$$

The flexible price monetary model is based upon the premise that all prices in an economy are fully flexible; bonds are perfect substitutes and what matters for exchange rate determination is the demand for money in relation to the supply of money. In such circumstances, countries with high monetary growth rates will have high inflationary expectations which leads to reduction in the demand to hold real money balances, increased expenditure on goods, a rise in the domestic price level and a depreciating currency in order to maintain PPP. There have been many tests of the monetarist models but, given that the theory is based upon PPP, it is not surprising that it has not performed well empirically (empirical tests of this and other exchange rate models are dealt with in Chapter 9).

Despite its shortcomings and reliance on PPP, the flexible-price monetarist model is an important addition to exchange rate theory because it introduces the role of money supplies and inflationary expectations and economic growth as determinants of exchange rate changes.

7.6 The Dornbusch sticky-price monetarist model

One of the major deficiencies of the flexible-price monetarist model is that it assumes that purchasing power parity holds continuously and that prices are as flexible upwards and downwards as exchange rates. Indeed, it is price changes that are supposed to induce exchange rate changes via the PPP condition. As such, the model is of no use in explaining the observed prolonged departures from PPP since the adoption of floating exchange rates. In a classic article, Rudiger Dornbusch (1976a) proposed a monetary exchange rate model that could explain large and prolonged departures of the exchange rate from PPP.

The model outlined by Dornbusch is termed the 'sticky-price' monetarist model and introduces the concept of exchange rate 'overshooting'. The basis underlying the model is that prices in the goods market and wages in the labour market are determined in 'sticky-price' markets and they only tend to change slowly over time in response to various shocks such as changes in the money supply. Prices and wages are especially resistant to downward pressure. However, the exchange rate is determined in a 'flex-price' market, and can immediately appreciate or depreciate in response to new developments and shocks. In such circumstances, exchange rate changes are not matched by corresponding price movements and there can be persistent and prolonged departures from PPP.

As the Dornbusch overshooting model represents such an important contribution to exchange rate theory and understanding exchange rate behaviour, we shall first consider a simple explanation of the model without recourse to the use of mathematics to grasp the essential ideas. Only then shall we proceed to a more formal presentation of the model.

7.7 A simple explanation of the Dornbusch model

In the Dornbusch model the UIP condition is assumed to hold continuously; that is, if the domestic interest rate is lower than the foreign interest rate then there needs to be an equivalent expected rate of appreciation of the domestic currency to compensate for the lower domestic interest rate. This is because there is perfect arbitrage of expected returns in capital markets. By contrast, goods prices adjust only slowly over time to changes in economic policy partly because wages are only adjusted periodically and partly because firms are slow to adjust their prices upwards or downwards, so we have 'sticky' domestic prices.

In such an environment, imagine that everyone believes that the long-run exchange rate is determined by PPP. Also, that the economy is initially in full equilibrium with a domestic interest rate r_1 equal to the world interest rate, so that there is no expected appreciation or depreciation of the currency. Such a situation is illustrated in **Figure 7.2**. The domestic money stock is given by M_1 which gives a domestic price level of P_1 and an exchange rate S_1 which given the foreign price level corresponds to PPP. Let us now suppose that at time t_1, the authorities unexpectedly expand the domestic money supply by 20% from M_1 to M_2.

In the long run everyone knows that a 20% rise in the domestic money supply will lead to a 20% rise in domestic prices from P_1 to $\bar{P}$ and therefore a 20% depreciation of the domestic currency from S_1 to $\bar{S}$ to maintain long-run PPP. However, in the short run the Dornbusch model shows that things will be very different.

In the short run, because domestic prices are sticky they remain at P_1. The unexpected increase in the domestic money supply will mean that at price level P_1 there is now an excess supply of money that will only willingly be held if the domestic interest rate falls from r_1 to r_2. As then the domestic interest rate is now lower than the

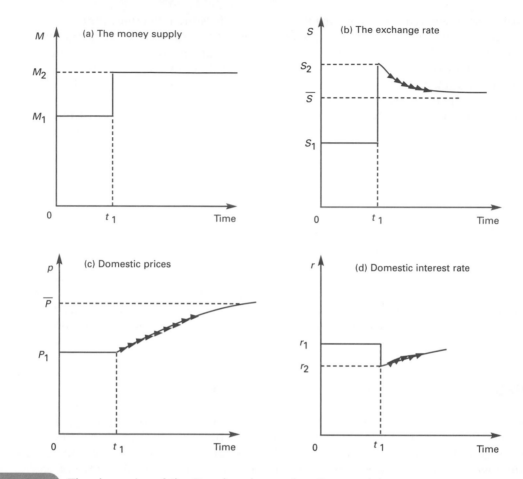

Figure 7.2   The dynamics of the Dornbusch overshooting model

world interest rate, this means that speculators will require an expected appreciation of the domestic currency to compensate. For this reason, the domestic currency jump depreciates at time t_1 from s_1 to s_2, overshooting its long-run equilibrium value $\bar{S}$. The exchange rate has to 'overshoot' its long-run equilibrium value because it is only by depreciating by more than 20% that there can be an expected appreciation of the domestic currency to compensate for the lower rate of interest on domestic bonds.

After the initial response of the exchange rate and interest rate to the increase in the money stock, there are a number of forces that come into play to move the economy to its long-run equilibrium. As a result of the fall in the domestic interest rate and the depreciation of the domestic currency, there is an increase in the demand for domestic goods. As output is assumed to be fixed, this excess demand for domestic goods starts to drive up domestic prices from P_1. The increased demand for domestic goods by foreigners leads to an exchange rate appreciation. From S_2 towards $\bar{S}$ (thus the expected appreciation is matched by an actual appreciation). At the same time, the rise in the domestic price level leads to an increase in domestic money demand and a rise in the domestic interest rate to maintain money-market equilibrium. Over time the domestic price level rises from P_1 to $\bar{P}$ by the same percentage as the increase in the money supply; the exchange rate appreciates from S_2 to $\bar{S}$ which corresponds to a restoration of PPP. Meanwhile, the domestic interest rate rises from r_2 to its original level r_1, so that once again there is neither an expected appreciation or depreciation of the domestic currency.

Having outlined the principal idea we now proceed to a more formal exposition of the Dornbusch model of exchange rate 'overshooting'. Those readers that wish to skip this can proceed straight to section 7.13.

7.8 A formal explanation of the Dornbusch model

In the model outlined, we focus upon a 'small country' in the sense that it faces a fixed world interest rate r^* which it cannot influence. The demand to hold money in the home country is given by a conventional money demand function:

$$m - p = \eta y - \sigma r \qquad (7.10)$$

where m is the log of the domestic money stock, p is the log of the domestic price level, y is the log of domestic real income and r is the nominal domestic interest rate. We again assume that domestic and foreign bonds are perfect substitutes so that the UIP condition holds, that is:

$$E\dot{s} = r - r^* \qquad (7.11)$$

where $E\dot{s}$ is the expected rate of depreciation of the home currency.
The major difference between the sticky-price and flexible-price monetary models is that the sticky-price model assumes that PPP holds only in the long run, not continuously as assumed in the flexible-price monetary model. The hypothesis that the long-run exchange rate is determined by PPP yields:

$$\bar{s} = \bar{p} - \bar{p}^* \qquad (7.12)$$

where $\bar{s}$ is the log of the long-run equilibrium exchange rate, $\bar{p}$ is the log of the long-run domestic price level, and $\bar{p}^*$ is the log of the long-run foreign price level.
Since the model allows for departures from PPP, it is necessary to specify an equation for the expected rate of change of the exchange rate. The Dornbusch model specifies a regressive exchange given by:

$$E\dot{s} = \Theta(\bar{s} - s) \text{ where } \Theta > 0 \qquad (7.13)$$

Equation (7.13) says that the expected rate of depreciation of a currency is determined by the speed of adjustment parameter Θ, and the gap between the current exchange rate s and its long-run equilibrium value $\bar{s}$. If the spot rate is above $\bar{s}$, then the exchange rate of the domestic currency will be expected to appreciate (that is, $E\dot{s}$ is negative), whereas if the spot rate s is below $\bar{s}$ then the exchange rate of the domestic currency is expected to depreciate (that is, $E\dot{s}$ is positive).

We now proceed to derive the two schedules vital to the Dornbusch model: the goods-market equilibrium schedule which shows equality of aggregate demand and supply for goods, and the money-market equilibrium schedule which shows equality between the demand and supply of money.

7.9 Derivation of the goods-market equilibrium schedule

The goods-market equilibrium schedule shows the equality of demand and supply for goods in the price–exchange rate plane. The model postulates that the rate of price inflation in the model is determined by the gap between aggregate demand and aggregate supply. That is:

$$\dot{p} = \pi(d - y) \tag{7.14}$$

where $\dot{p}$ is the rate of domestic price inflation, π is the speed of adjustment of prices and d is the log of aggregate demand.

Aggregate demand is assumed to be a function of exogenous expenditure β, a positive function of the real exchange rate expressed in log form as $(s - p + p^*)$, a positive function of domestic income and a negative function of the domestic nominal interest rate, which yields:

$$d = \beta + \alpha(s - p + p^*) + \varphi y - \lambda r \tag{7.15}$$

Substituting equation (7.15) into equation (7.14) we obtain:

$$\dot{p} = \pi[\beta + \alpha(s - p + p^*) + (\varphi - 1)y - \lambda r] \tag{7.16}$$

Along the goods-market equilibrium schedule (GG) the equality of supply and demand for goods means that there is zero inflation, that is $\dot{p} = 0$. To find the slope of the goods-market schedule we must substitute a solution for r from equation (7.10), into equation (7.16) to obtain:

$$\dot{p} = \pi[\beta + \alpha(s - p + p^*) + (\varphi - 1)y - \lambda/\sigma(p - m + \eta y)] \tag{7.17}$$

Then by setting equation (7.17) to zero we find the slope of the GG schedule in the price level–exchange rate plane. Along the GG schedule aggregate demand equals aggregate supply, implying zero price inflation. The slope of the GG schedule is given by:

$$\left. \frac{dp}{ds} \right|_{\dot{p} = 0} = \frac{\alpha}{\alpha + \lambda/\sigma} \tag{7.18}$$

From equation (7.18) we can see that the GG schedule is upward-sloping from left to right and has a slope of less than unity as shown in **Figure 7.3**.

The rationale behind the GG schedule is that a depreciation (rise) of the exchange rate leads to an increased demand for exports, and this increase in demand can only be offset by a rise in the domestic price level which negates the competitive advantage of the depreciation. However, because the rise in the price level increases money demand, it is accompanied by a rise in interest rates which further reduces demand.

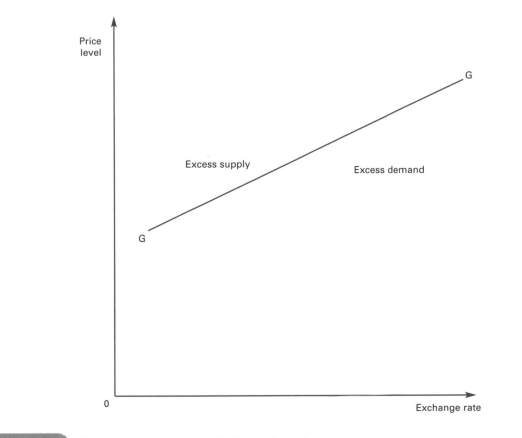

Figure 7.3   The goods-market equilibrium schedule

This means that the percentage depreciation of the exchange rate has to exceed the percentage rise in the price level to keep aggregate demand in line with aggregate supply.

To the left of the GG schedule there is an excess supply of goods due to the fact that assuming output to be fixed for any given price level, an exchange rate appreciation (fall) reduces aggregate demand. The excess supply of goods will put downward pressure on prices. Conversely, to the right of the GG schedule for any given price level, the exchange rate depreciation (rise) leads to an excess demand for domestic goods causing and upward pressure on prices.

7.10 Derivation of the money-market equilibrium schedule

The money market schedule shows different combinations of the price level and exchange rate that are consistent with equilibrium in the money market; that is, equilibrium of the supply and demand for money. To derive the money-market schedule we first of all invert the money demand function (7.10) to solve for the domestic interest rate, which yields:

$$r = \frac{p - m + \eta y}{\sigma} \tag{7.19}$$

We then substitute the solution for $E\dot{s}$ in equation (7.11) into equation (7.13) and replace the solution for r in equation (7.19) to obtain:

$$s = \bar{s} - \frac{1}{\sigma\Theta} [p - m + \eta y - \sigma r^*] \tag{7.20}$$

which means that for slope of the money market schedule is given by:

$$\frac{dp}{ds} = -\sigma\Theta \tag{7.21}$$

Hence the MM schedule is shown to have a negative slope in the price-level–exchange-rate plane as shown in **Figure 7.4**.

The explanation is that for a given money stock a fall in the price level implies a relatively high real money stock, and high real money balances will only be willingly

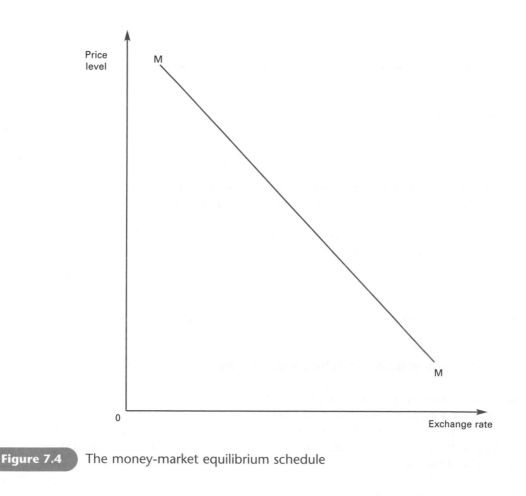

Figure 7.4 The money-market equilibrium schedule

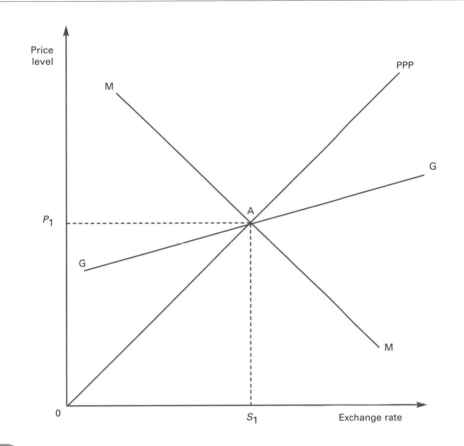

Figure 7.5 Equilibrium in the Dornbusch model

held if the domestic interest rate falls. A fall in the domestic interest rate requires an expected appreciation of the currency to compensate holders of the domestic currency. Given that exchange rate expectations are regressive, such an expected appreciation can only occur if the exchange rate depreciates.

Equilibrium of the model occurs when both the goods and money markets are in equilibrium and the exchange rate is at its PPP value as shown in **Figure 7.5**.

The PPP line is depicted as a ray from the origin indicating that if the domestic price level increases by $x\%$ then the exchange rate must also depreciate by $x\%$ to maintain PPP. The GG schedule as we have seen is less steep than the PPP line because an $x\%$ rise in the price level needs to be accompanied by a greater than $x\%$ depreciation of the exchange rate. The money-market schedule is given by MM, and it is assumed that the money market is in continuous equilibrium so that the economy is always somewhere on the MM schedule. The economy is in full equilibrium when the exchange rate corresponds to PPP, aggregate supply equals aggregate demand and there is asset-market equilibrium, this occurs where all three schedules intersect at point A.

We are now in a position to consider the effects of an economic shock such as an increase in the domestic money supply in the Dornbusch model.

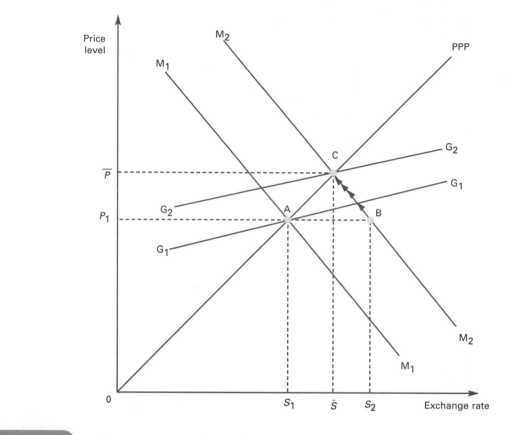

Figure 7.6   Exchange rate overshooting

7.11 A money supply expansion and exchange rate 'overshooting'

The effects of an $x\%$ increase in the money supply in the context of the Dornbusch model are illustrated in **Figure 7.6**.

Initially the economy is in full equilibrium at point A where the G_1G_1 schedule intersects the M_1M_1 schedule. Let us now suppose that the authorities unexpectedly expand the money supply by $x\%$. Before examining the short-run effects of the money expansion it is worth considering what will be the long-run effects. In the long run, we know that domestic prices will rise by the same percentage as the rise in the money stock, which gives a long-run price of p which is $x\%$ above p_1. As PPP holds in the long run, a rise in the domestic price level of $x\%$ requires a depreciation of the exchange rate by $x\%$, which gives a long-run exchange rate $\bar{s}$. Bearing this in mind we can now consider the short-run effects of the monetary expansion.

In the short run, the $x\%$ increase in the money supply results in a rightward shift of the M_1M_1 schedule to M_2M_2. We know that the M_2M_2 schedule must pass through the long-run equilibrium price $\bar{p}$ and long-run exchange rate $\bar{s}$ at point C. The major feature of the Dornbusch model is that in the short run, domestic prices are sticky, while money markets are in continuous equilibrium as indicated by the UIP condition. In the context of **Figure 7.6** this means that the economy is always on the new money market equilibrium schedule M_2M_2. As domestic prices do not initially change, the price level remains at p_1 and this is consistent with a jump in the exchange rate from s_1 to s_2 on the money-market equilibrium schedule M_2M_2. The fact that the short-run equilibrium exchange rate s_2 exceeds the long-run equilibrium rate $\bar{s}$ is known as the phenomenon of exchange rate 'overshooting'.

The reason why in the short run the exchange rate overshoots its long-run equilibrium value is as follows. Given that domestic prices are fixed in the short run, the money supply expansion creates an excess of real money balances which (given a fixed output level) are only willingly held at a lower domestic interest rate. According to the UIP condition, a fall in the domestic interest rate means that international investors will require an expected appreciation of the domestic currency to compensate for the lower domestic interest rate. An expected appreciation of the domestic currency is only possible if the exchange rate depreciation in the short run exceeds the required long-run depreciation. This is shown in **Figure 7.6** by the fact that the exchange rate jump depreciates from s_1 to s_2, overshooting the long-run equilibrium exchange rate $\bar{s}$. The exchange rate is then expected to appreciate from s_2 to $\bar{s}$.

Having had a short-run jump in the exchange rate to point B on the M_2M_2 schedule, forces come into play to move the economy along the M_2M_2 schedule over time from point B to the long-run point C. There are two factors at work in the movement from B to C during which time the currency appreciates from s_2 to its long-run equilibrium value $\bar{s}$ and the price level rises from p_1 to its long-run value $\bar{p}$. First, the reduced domestic interest rate will encourage increased expenditure. Second, the undervaluation of the currency in relation to its PPP value will mean that domestic goods become relatively cheap as compared to foreign goods, and this leads to a substitution of world demand in favour of domestic goods which Dornbusch (1976b) identifies as the 'arbitrage effect'. These two factors work to shift up the goods market expenditure schedule from G_1G_1 to G_2G_2 and drive up the domestic price level and appreciate the exchange rate until the long-run equilibrium is established at point C. During the transition, the rise in the price level reduces real money balances requiring a rise in the domestic interest rate until at $\bar{p}$ the original interest rate is restored and there is no expected change in the exchange rate.

7.12 Importance of the sticky-price monetary model

The sticky-price monetary model represented a major advance in the exchange rate literature and it has had lasting appeal. The major innovation of the model is its emphasis on capital-market rather than goods-market arbitrage being the major determinant of exchange rates in the short run. Goods-market arbitrage is viewed as relevant to exchange rate determination only in the medium to long run, while the desire of investors to equalize expected yields on their international portfolios is viewed as the major determinant of the short-run exchange rate.

The model provides an intuitively appealing explanation of why exchange rate movements have been large relative to movements in international prices and changes in international money stocks. Furthermore, it explains such movements as the outcome of a rational foreign exchange market that produces an exchange rate that deviates from PPP based on economic fundamentals, not in isolation from them. Most economists find it hard to accept the notion that observed divergences of exchange rates from PPP have been due to irrational speculation. The existence of models such as Dornbusch's that explain such deviations as the result of rational speculation provide considerable comfort.

Another important point that comes from the Dornbusch model is that it helps explain why observed exchange rates are usually even more volatile than supposed determinants such as the money supply. Since the exchange rate initially depreciates by more than *x*% in the short run in response to an *x*% increase in the money supply, it follows that the exchange rate will be more volatile than domestic monetary policy.

7.13 The Frankel real interest rate differential model

The sticky-price monetary model of Dornbusch represents a major advance on the flexible price monetary exchange rate model, but unlike the former the Dornbusch model does not explicitly take into account inflationary expectations. However, the 1970s period of floating exchange rates was dominated by inflation. In a bid to combine the inflationary expectations element of the flexible-price monetary model with the insights of the sticky-price model, Frankel (1979) developed a general monetary exchange rate model that accommodates the 'flexible-price' and 'sticky-price' monetarist models as special cases.

As in the other monetarist models, there is a conventional money demand function:

$$m - p = \eta y - \sigma r \qquad (7.22)$$

where *m* is the log of the domestic money stock, *p* is the log of the domestic price level, *y* is the log of domestic real income and *r* is the nominal domestic interest rate. Similar relationships are postulated for the rest of the world as represented by the foreign country:

$$m^* - p^* = \eta y^* - \sigma r^* \qquad (7.23)$$

where an asterisk represents a foreign variable.

For simplicity it is also assumed that elasticities (η and σ) are identical across countries. Combining equations (7.22) and (7.23) yields:

$$(m - m^*) = (p - p^*) + \eta(y - y^*) - \sigma(r - r^*) \qquad (7.24)$$

Like the other monetarist models the theory assumes that domestic and foreign bonds are perfect substitutes so that the uncovered interest parity condition holds:

$$E\dot{s} = r - r^* \qquad (7.25)$$

where $E\dot{s}$ is the expected rate of depreciation of the home currency.

As in the Dornbusch model, it is assumed that the expected rate of depreciation of the exchange rate is a positive function of the gap between the spot rate *s* and the long-run equilibrium rate $\bar{s}$. In addition it is also a function of the expected long-run inflation differential between the domestic and foreign economies. This yields:

$$E\dot{s} = \Theta(\bar{s} - s) + P\dot{e} - P\dot{e}^* \qquad (7.26)$$

where Θ is the speed of adjustment to equilibrium, $P\dot{e}$ is the expected long-run domestic inflation rate and $P\dot{e}*$ is the expected long-run foreign inflation rate. Equation (7.26) states that in the short run, the spot exchange rate as given by s is expected to return to its long-run equilibrium value $\bar{s}$ at a rate Θ. In the long run, since $s = \bar{s}$ the expected rate of depreciation of the currency is equal to the difference of the domestic to foreign inflation via the relative PPP condition.

Combining equations (7.25) and (7.26) yields:

$$s - \bar{s} = -\frac{1}{\Theta}\,[(r - P\dot{e}) - (r* - P\dot{e}*)] \tag{7.27}$$

Equation (7.27) states that the gap between the current real exchange rate and its long-run equilibrium value is proportional to the real interest rate differential as given by the term in brackets. Thus, if the real rate of interest on domestic bonds is greater than the real rate of interest on foreign bonds, there will be a depreciation of the domestic currency until the real interest rates are equalized in the long-run steady state.

By invoking long-run PPP, the long-run equilibrium exchange rate $\bar{s}$ can be expressed in log form as the difference between the long-run price levels:

$$\bar{s} = \bar{p} - \bar{p}* \tag{7.28}$$

In the long run the expected real rates of interest are equalized so that any long-run nominal interest rate differentials are explained by differences in the steady-state inflation rates:

$$r - r* = P\dot{e} - P\dot{e}* \tag{7.29}$$

By combining equations (7.29) and (7.28) with equation (7.24) we can obtain an expression for the long-run steady-state equilibrium exchange rate given by:

$$\bar{s} = (m - m*) - \eta(y - y*) + \sigma(P\dot{e} - P\dot{e}*) \tag{7.30}$$

Equation (7.30) states that the long-run equilibrium exchange rate is determined by the relative supply $(m - m*)$ and relative demands as given by $\eta(y - y*) + \sigma(P\dot{e} - P\dot{e}*)$ of the two national money stocks. The reader will note that equation (7.30) which refers to the long-run exchange rate is identical to equation (7.9) of the flexible-price monetarist model for the short-run exchange rate. However, the solution for the short-run exchange rate in the Frankel model differs because of sticky prices in the short run. We now proceed to find the solution for the short-run exchange rate in the Frankel model.

In the Frankel generalization of the Dornbusch model, the speed of adjustment of the goods market is relevant to the determination of the short-run exchange rate, so that equation (7.27) has to be taken into account when solving for the short-run exchange rate. Combining equation (7.30) with (7.27) and rearranging terms yields the following solution for the short-run exchange rate:

$$s = (m - m*) - \eta(y - y*) + \sigma(P\dot{e} - P\dot{e}*) - \frac{1}{\Theta}\,[(r - P\dot{e}) - (r* - P\dot{e}*)] \tag{7.31}$$

The Frankel formulation makes clear that if there is a disequilibrium set of real interest rates, then the exchange rate will deviate from its long-run equilibrium value. If the real domestic interest rate is below the real foreign interest rate then the exchange rate of the domestic currency will be undervalued in relation to its long-run equilibrium value, so that there is an expected appreciation of the real exchange rate of the domestic currency to compensate.

The fully flexible price monetarist school argues that all markets clear instantaneously so that the speed of adjustment parameter Θ in equation (7.31) is infinite, so that the solution for the short-run exchange rate is given by equation (7.9). In the real interest model as portrayed by equation (7.31), the goods and labour market prices are assumed to be slow to adjust to shocks so the speed of adjustment parameter Θ is finite. Thus, rational expectations holds for the foreign exchange market but not for domestic markets. In such circumstances, an unanticipated monetary expansion leads to a fall in the real domestic interest rate relative to the real foreign interest rate while the domestic price level is initially unchanged but expected to rise. The result according to equation (7.31) is that the short-run exchange rate overshoots its long-run equilibrium value, depreciating proportionately more than the increase in the money stock so that there are expectations of a future appreciation of the currency to compensate for the lower real rate of return on domestic bonds.

7.14 Implications of the monetary views of exchange rate determination

Whichever monetarist model that one adopts, a clear implication is that monetary policy is the only predictable and effective means of influencing the exchange rate. Furthermore, because domestic and foreign bonds are assumed to be perfect substitutes there is no distinction to be made between the effects of an open market operation (OMO) and a foreign exchange market operation (FXO). An expansionary OMO is a purchase of domestic treasury bonds, while an expansionary FXO is a purchase of foreign bonds. As far as the monetary model is concerned, if they increase the money supply by a like amount they have identical exchange rate effects. What matters for the exchange rate is the supply of money in relation to the demand for it, the source of creation of the money stock is irrelevant.

From the above, it follows that there is no scope for the authorities to pursue a sterilized foreign exchange operation (SFXO) that will have exchange rate effects. An SFXO is an exchange of domestic for foreign bonds that leaves the supply of money in relation to the demand for it unaffected. Within the context of the monetary approach to exchange rate determination, because the two assets are perfect substitutes and the money supply is left unchanged, an SFXO cannot exert exchange rate effects.

In the flexible-price monetarist model, while the authorities can influence the nominal exchange in a predictable fashion by monetary policy, they cannot do likewise with the real exchange rate. If there is a once and for all $x\%$ increase in the money supply this will lead to a once and for all $x\%$ depreciation of the home currency and a simultaneous $x\%$ increase in both the domestic price level and wages. This is a case of complete neutrality of monetary policy with respect to the real economy; monetary policy influences only nominal not real variables.

Within the context of the 'sticky-price' monetarist approach, the authorities can exploit the finite speed of adjustment of domestic markets to influence the real exchange rate in the short run, provided that real output is fixed. For example, if there is an unexpected increase in the domestic money stock, we have seen that with domestic prices sticky in the short run there will be a depreciation of the real exchange rate. The Frankel model makes clear that the overshooting of the exchange rate is proportional to the deviation of the real domestic interest rate from its equilibrium value.

The possibility of real exchange rate overshooting due to the adoption of an expansionary or contractionary monetary policy has strengthened the arguments of those that call for 'gradualism' in the implementation of monetary policy. The basis of their claim is that economic agents in the goods and labour markets take time to adjust to a new monetary policy regime because they need convincing that the authorities mean what they say. For this reason, domestic wage restraint is unlikely to follow immediately following the adoption of a tighter monetary policy. If this is the case, then the real exchange rate will appreciate in the short run and thereby place pressure on the tradables sector of the economy. Gradualists argue that if the authorities implement their policy of restraint gradually, then economic agents will have time to observe that the authorities are implementing their stated policy and wage behaviour will then adjust without the high cost imposed upon the economy of overshooting.

Whichever monetarist view that one adheres to, the clear implication is that monetary policy is the most effective means of managing the exchange rate. Furthermore, in the long run the authorities should abandon any attempt to influence the real exchange rate because it is determined by real and not monetary factors. Thus, in the long run (short run in the flexible-price version) the authorities should direct exchange rate management at stabilizing the domestic price level. Whether stabilizing the domestic price level will stabilize the nominal exchange rate depends upon the stability of the foreign price level and therefore upon the monetary policies of foreign countries. The authorities should not seek to stabilize the nominal exchange rate by monetary policy because this may involve destabilizing the domestic price level if the foreign authorities are not pursuing stable monetary policies.

Box 7.2

New open economy macroeconomics: a challenge to the Mundell–Fleming and Dornbusch overshooting models?

Obstfeld and Rogoff (1995) started what has become known as the literature on new open economy macroeconomics (NOEM), recent contributions in this area include Chari *et al.* (1998), Lane (2001), Corsetti and Pesenti (2001) and Sarno (2001), and an excellent exposition of many issues is contained in Mark (2001, Chapter 9). While this literature is technically quite advanced, it is important to understand how it differs from the Mundell–Fleming and Dornbusch overshooting models. The new open economy macroeconomics is based on microeconomic foundations and is intertemporal in nature, a representative consumer maximizes their utility over their (infinite!) lifetime, this utility depends positively upon current and future consumption, positively upon their real money balances and negatively on work effort (and since work effort is positively related to output, then utility is negatively related to output). The model assumes that both PPP and UIP hold at all times, that goods produced at home and abroad are differentiated (a market structure based on monopolistic competition) and since

→

➔

producers have monopolistic price-setting powers there is a sub-optimal level of real output. Economic agents are assumed to be interested in smoothing their consumption over time in both the home and foreign economies, and their interactions are explicitly modelled and money demand is positively related to consumption rather than positively to income.

The main focus of the Obstfeld and Rogoff (1995) 'Redux' paper is on analysing the impacts of a monetary shock. They show that when goods prices are perfectly flexible, a permanent increase in the money supply produces no dynamics and that prices increase in exact proportion to the increase in the money supply and the exchange rate depreciates by a like amount, so monetary policy has no role in correcting the sub-optimal level of output. If, however, one allows for price stickiness in the goods markets in the short run, then things are very different; an increase in the money supply will lead to a fall in the domestic interest rate and a depreciation of the currency, the depreciation however makes domestic goods cheaper relative to foreign goods and leads to an increase in domestic output since increases in demand will encourage monopolistic producers to raise output even with fixed short-run domestic prices. Although output rises, consumption rises by less; since consumers wish to smooth consumption over time they save part of the increase in output, hence the current account moves into surplus, this surplus then raises domestic wealth due to an accumulation of foreign assets which over time reduces their work effort. In the long run, the level of domestic output is permanently higher than before the monetary expansion (though lower than the initial level of output induced by the monetary shock) so that money is non-neutral in the long run.

In the short run, while the exchange rate depreciates it does not overshoot as in the Dornbusch model, because the foreign interest rate also declines following the home monetary expansion, the lower interest rate and improved terms of trade for the foreign economy raise consumption in the foreign economy. It is not clear what happens to foreign output because while the increase in foreign consumption will tend to raise its output, the appreciation of its currency will tend to work in the opposite direction. In any case, the increase in foreign consumption is greater than any output rise (or fall) resulting in a current account deficit for the foreign economy.

A remarkable result of the Obstfeld and Rogoff paper is that the monetary expansion raises domestic and foreign welfare by equal amounts despite the differing output effects on the two economies; this is because the fall in the interest rate generates equivalent increases in consumption in both the domestic and foreign economies. There is an improvement in world welfare as global output rises following the monetary shock. There is one big problem with the new open economy models, however, and it is that they are extremely sensitive to the particular model specification. For example, Corsetti and Pesenti (2001) show that under a different model specification, a monetary shock does not lead to a current account surplus (in fact it stays in balance) and the long-run output effects of a monetary expansion are neutral. The Obstfeld and Rogoff paper did not allow for the presence of physical capital, but Chari *et al.* (1998) argue that it is essential to allow for capital since a monetary expansion by lowering the domestic interest rate may lead to an investment boom and a short-run current account deficit rather than the surplus of the Obstfeld and Rogoff paper. Lane (2001) shows that for a small open economy exchange rate overshooting still occurs since the fall in the domestic interest rate does not lead to a fall in the interest rate in the large economy. Similarly, as outlined in Mark (2001), if firms price to market then it is also possible to get exchange rate overshooting in the *Redux* model.

There is no doubt that the new open economy macroeconomic offers some new and important insights, particularly the emphasis on the microfoundations and the importance of market structure. As Lane (2001, p. 236) points out: ➔

→

This approach offers several attractions. The presentation of explicit utility and profit maximisation problems provides welcome clarity and analytical rigour. Moreover, it allows the researcher to conduct welfare analysis, thereby laying the groundwork for credible policy evaluation. Allowing nominal rigidities and market imperfections alters the transmission mechanism for shocks and also provides a more potent role for monetary policy. In this way, by addressing issues of concern to policymakers, one goal of this new strand of research is to provide an analytical framework that is relevant for policy analysis and offers a superior alternative to the Mundell–Fleming model that is still widely employed in policy circles as the theoretical reference point.

Although the new open economy models are rigorous and allow for rich dynamics, the outcome of the models can prove very sensitive to, *inter alia*, the specification of the utility function, elasticities between current and future consumption, and between domestic and foreign goods, whether price stickiness originates from the labour or goods markets, the type of market structure assumed, whether the economy is small or large, the size of the monetary shocks and whether allowance is made for traded and non-traded goods. As Sarno and Taylor (2002, p. 165) put it:

> Agreeing on a particular new open economy model is hardly possible at this stage. This is the case not least because it requires agreeing on assumptions which are often difficult to test empirically (such as the specification of the utility function) or because they concern issues about which many economists have strong beliefs on which they are not willing to compromise (such as whether nominal rigidities originate from the goods market or the labour market or whether nominal rigidities exist at all) . . . While the profession shows some convergence towards a *consensus approach* in macroeconomic modelling (where the need for micro foundations, for example, seems widely accepted), it seems very unlikely that a *consensus model* will emerge in the foreseeable future.

Hence, because of their diverse predictions and sensitivity of their results to parameter values and particular model specifications, the results of the new open economy macro models must at this stage be treated with extreme caution when it comes to making policy recommendations. The new approach is, nonetheless, clearly a major threat to the established Mundell–Fleming paradigm that has dominated international macroeconomic thinking and modelling since the early 1960s.

7.15 Allowing for imperfect substitutability between domestic and foreign bonds

The monetary models of exchange rate determination we have so far examined make the crucial assumption that domestic and foreign bonds are perfect substitutes. This implies that the expected yields on domestic and foreign bonds are equalized via the uncovered interest rate parity condition. In effect, apart from their currency of denomination, domestic and foreign bonds are regarded by international investors as the same. In this section, we examine the portfolio balance effect which breaks up the uncovered interest rate parity condition by introducing a risk premium. The portfolio balance model distinguishes itself from the monetary models because it allows for the possibility that international investors may regard domestic and foreign bonds as having different characteristics other than their currency of denomination, in particular, they might for various reasons regard one of the bonds as being more risky than the other. This being the case they will generally require a higher expected return on the bond that are considered more risky to compensate for the additional risk it entails. For a risk premium to exist, all of the following three conditions must be fulfilled (see Isard 1983):

1   There must be perceived differences in risks between domestic and foreign bonds – the essence of a risky asset being that its expected real rate of return is uncertain. Either domestic bonds are viewed as relatively risky compared to foreign bonds, or *vice-versa*. If the two bonds were equally as risky then with perfect capital mobility they must be perfect substitutes.
2   There has to be risk-aversion on the part of economic agents to the perceived differences in risk. The principle of risk-aversion is that investors will only be prepared to take on increased risk if there is a sufficient increase in expected real returns to compensate. If investors were not risk-averse then they would not expect a higher return on relatively risky bonds.
3   Given the different risks on domestic and foreign bonds there is a theoretical portfolio known as the risk-minimizing portfolio which would minimize the risks facing private agents. There must be a difference between the risk-minimizing portfolio and the actual portfolio forced at market clearing prices into investors' portfolios. However, the amount of domestic and foreign bonds held by private agents is determined by the respective authorities that issue them. If the risk-minimizing portfolio is not held, then agents will demand a risk premium to compensate.

If all three of the above conditions are fulfilled, then the uncovered interest parity condition will not hold due to the existence of a risk premium which represents the compensation required by private agents for accepting risk exposure above the minimum possible. When a risk premium exists, then the UIP condition no longer holds, and instead a more relevant equation is given by:

$$r - r^* = E\dot{s} + RP \tag{7.32}$$

where RP is the risk premium on the domestic currency.

According to equation (7.32) the UIP condition may no longer hold due to the existence of a risk premium. Imagine that domestic bonds require a 2% risk premium over foreign bonds. Then a possible numerical example of equation (7.32) is as follows:

$$10\% - 5\% = 3\% + 2\%$$

That is, the domestic bonds have an expected return of 10%, while foreign bonds have an expected return of only 8% (that is 5% interest plus a 3% expected appreciation of the foreign currency (that is, a 3% expected depreciation of the domestic currency). The reason being that domestic bonds are regarded as more risky by investors, which is reflected by a 2% risk premium on the domestic bonds. In principle, of course, there is no real reason why domestic bonds need to be considered more risky than foreign bonds; it may well be the reverse, which would be reflected by a negative risk premium on the domestic bonds such that the expected rate of return on domestic bonds is lower than on foreign bonds.

The most simple formulation of the risk premium on the domestic currency is to say that it is positively related to the supply of domestic bonds and negatively related to the supply of foreign bonds. One means of expressing such a function in log form is given by:

$$RP = \frac{-\alpha}{\beta} + \frac{b - s - f}{\beta} \tag{7.33}$$

α is a constant, b is the log of domestic bonds in the hands of private agents, s is the log of the exchange rate, f is the log of foreign currency denominated bonds in the hands of private agents, and β is a coefficient measuring the degree of substitutability between domestic and foreign bonds.

The first element α is a constant term; when it is positive it means that there is a preference for domestic bonds, but if it is negative there is a preference for foreign bonds. The more interesting is the second part of the equation, which suggests that when we increase the holdings of domestic bonds in private agents' portfolios the risk premium on the domestic currency rises (or risk premium on the foreign currency falls), because there will be an increase in the proportion of domestic bonds in agents' portfolios which increases the domestic risk to agents' portfolios and requires a rise in the risk premium on the domestic currency to compensate investors for the increased risk exposure to domestic bonds in their portfolios. On the other hand, a depreciation of the exchange rate (rise in s) will lead to a fall in the risk premium required on domestic bonds (or a rise on risk premium on foreign bonds), because a depreciation of the domestic currency increases the domestic currency value of foreign bonds held in private agents' portfolios and so increases the risk exposure to foreign bonds so lowering the risk premium required on domestic bonds. Similarly, a rise in foreign bond holdings will lead to a fall in the risk premium required on domestic bonds, because this results in a rise in the proportion of foreign bonds held in private agents' portfolios and so increases the risk exposure to foreign bonds so lowering the risk premium required on domestic bonds (or raising the risk premium on foreign bonds). The parameter β is crucial as it is a measure of the degree of substitutability between domestic and foreign bonds; as we raise the value of β, domestic and foreign bonds become closer substitutes and this lowers the risk premium, and in the limiting case when β approaches infinity then domestic and foreign bonds are perfect substitutes so that the risk premium vanishes as can be readily verified in equation (7.33).

If we insert equation (7.33) into equation (7.32) we obtain:

$$r - r = E\dot{s} - \frac{\alpha}{\beta} + \frac{b - s - f}{\beta} \tag{7.34}$$

which can be rewritten as

$$b - s - f = \alpha + \beta(r - r^* - E\dot{s}) \tag{7.35}$$

Equation (7.35) makes it clear that in order to hold more domestic currency denominated bonds, domestic investors would require either a rise in the interest rate differential in favour of domestic bonds, and/or an expected appreciation of the domestic currency, that is, $E\dot{s} < 0$. Allowing for domestic and foreign bonds to have different characteristics is potentially very important, because money market and foreign exchange operations that influence the exchange rate affect the composition of domestic and foreign bonds in agents' portfolios in different ways. We shall be using equation (7.35) in the synthesis exchange rate model that follows, hence it is important to understand the rationale behind equation (7.35).

7.16 A synthesis portfolio balance model

Jeffrey Frankel (1983 and 1984) extended his monetary synthesis equation (1979) to incorporate a portfolio balance effect. The basic derivation of his synthesis exchange rate equation is as follows (see Frankel, 1983). One begins with a conventional domestic money demand function given by:

$$m = p + \eta y - \sigma r \tag{7.36}$$

where m is the log of the domestic money supply, p is the log of the domestic price level, y is the log of domestic real income, η is money demand elasticity with respect to income, and σ is money demand semielasticity with respect to the interest rate.

A similar money demand function is postulated for the foreign country, and assuming identical elasticities for the foreign economy we have:

$$m^* = p^* + \eta y^* - \sigma r^* \tag{7.37}$$

where an asterisk represents a foreign variable.

Taking the difference of the two equations yields the relative money demand function:

$$(m - m^*) = (p - p^*) + \eta(y - y^*) - \sigma(r - r^*) \tag{7.38}$$

By invoking long-run PPP the long-run equilibrium exchange rate $\bar{s}$ can be expressed in log form as the difference between the long-run price levels:

$$\bar{s} = \bar{p} - \bar{p}^* \tag{7.39}$$

where $\bar{p}$ is the log of the long-run domestic price level, and $\bar{p}^*$ is the log of the long-run foreign price level.

Substituting equation (7.39) into equation (7.38) and rearranging gives the following expression for the long-run equilibrium exchange rate:

$$\bar{s} = (m - m^*) - \eta(y - y^*) + \sigma(r - r^*) \tag{7.40}$$

Rather than assume uncovered interest rate parity which is inconsistent with a portfolio balance framework, we use equation (7.35) repeated here as equation (7.41):

$$b - s - f = \alpha + \beta(r - r^* - E\dot{s}) \tag{7.41}$$

where α is a constant, b is the log of domestic bonds in the hands of private agents, and f is the log of foreign currency denominated bonds in the hands of private agents. That is, in order to hold more domestic currency denominated bonds domestic investors would require either a rise in the interest rate differential in favour of domestic bonds and/or an increased expected appreciation of the domestic currency (expected fall in the exchange rate). The parameter β measures the degree of substitutability; if β is equal to infinity then moving it and α to the left-hand side yields the UIP condition.

The expected change in the exchange rate is given by the following expression:

$$E\dot{s} = \Theta(\bar{s} - s) + P\dot{e} - P\dot{e}* \qquad (7.42)$$

where Θ is the speed of adjustment to equilibrium, $P\dot{e}$ is the expected long-run domestic inflation rate, and $P\dot{e}*$ is the expected long-run foreign inflation rate. That is, the expected rate of change in the exchange rate is determined by the speed of adjustment to the long-run equilibrium rate Θ, the gap between the current and long-run exchange rate and the expected inflation differential.

Solving for $E\dot{s}$ in equation (7.41) we find that:

$$E\dot{s} = \frac{-b + s + f + \alpha}{\beta} + r - r* \qquad (7.43)$$

Thus, substituting (7.43) into (7.42) and rearranging we find that:

$$s - \bar{s} = \frac{b - s - f - \alpha}{\Theta\beta} + \frac{1}{\Theta}[(r* - P\dot{e}*) - (r - P\dot{e})] \qquad (7.44)$$

Finally, substituting our expression for the long-run equilibrium exchange rate given by equation (7.40) into equation (7.44), and after some algebraic manipulation, we obtain an exchange rate equation that synthesizes both the monetary and portfolio balance approaches to exchange rate determination, given by:

$$s = \frac{-\alpha}{\Theta\beta + 1} + \frac{\Theta\beta}{\Theta\beta + 1}(m - m*) - \frac{\eta\Theta\beta}{\Theta\beta + 1}(y - y*) + \frac{\beta(\sigma\Theta + 1)}{\Theta\beta + 1}(P\dot{e} - P\dot{e}*)$$

$$- \frac{\beta}{\Theta\beta + 1}(r - r*) + \frac{1}{\Theta\beta + 1}(b - f) \qquad (7.45)$$

Equation (7.45) can be rewritten as:

$$s = \frac{-\alpha}{\Theta\beta + 1} + \frac{1}{1 + 1/\Theta\beta}(m - m*) - \frac{\eta}{1 + 1/\Theta\beta}(y - y*) + \frac{\sigma + 1/\Theta}{1 + 1/\Theta\beta}(P\dot{e} - P\dot{e}*)$$

$$- \frac{1}{\Theta + 1/\Theta\beta}(r - r*) + \frac{1}{\Theta\beta + 1}(b - f) \qquad (7.46)$$

The fully flexible price monetarist version postulates that as both the parameters Θ and β approache infinity, this reduces equation (7.46) to the flexible-price monetary equation (7.8). The sticky-price monetarist school holds that Θ is less than infinite while β is infinite so we end up with the real interest differential equation (7.31). Whereas, the sticky-price portfolio balance model holds that both the parameters β and Θ are less than infinite, so that relative bond supplies have an impact on the exchange rate and the relevant equation is therefore (7.46).

7.17 The importance of the portfolio balance model

The portfolio balance model is an important contribution to the exchange rate literature because it allows a role for changes in perceived risk or risk-aversion in the determination of the exchange rate. For example, an increase in the perceived riskiness of foreign bonds compared to domnestic bonds can lead to both a fall in the domestic interest rate and an appreciation of the domestic currency as private agents rebalance their portfolios. While an increase in the perceived riskiness of domestic bonds can lead to a depreciation of the domestic currency and/or a rise in the domestic interest rate. These effects accord with intuition and are frequently invoked to explain observed exchange rate changes. Such an effects are, however, absent from the monetary models which assume that domestic and foreign bonds are perfect substitutes.

Another important contribution of the portfolio balance model is that there is a significant role for the current account to play in the determination of the exchange rate over time. A current account surplus implies an accumulation of foreign assets (for example foreign bonds) and an increase in domestic wealth, the result is a larger proportion of foreign bonds in investors' portfolios than they desire. In turn, this leads to purchases of domestic bonds and a resulting appreciation of the domestic currency which will, over time, work to reduce a current account surplus.

Another contribution of the portfolio balance model is that it permits a relatively easy discussion of the role of fiscal policy in determining the exchange rate. A bond-financed fiscal expansion has an ambiguous effect on the exchange rate. This is because while a higher proportion of domestic bonds in agents' portfolios will lead to an increase in the demand for foreign bonds, the higher domestic interest rate will lead to a fall in the demand for foreign bonds. If the former effect is greater than the latter, the exchange rate depreciates, but if the reverse is true the exchange rate appreciates.

A significant policy implication that emerges from the portfolio balance model is that a given change in the money stock has a more powerful effect on the exchange rate when carried out by a purchase of foreign assets (a FXO) than when achieved via a purchase of domestic assets (an OMO). To understand this, consider a foreign exchange operation whereby the central bank purchases foreign currency bonds, which increases the domestic money supply but by reducing private agents' holdings of foreign bonds induces them to sell domestic bonds and purchase foreign bonds, placing additional pressure for the domestic currency to depreciate. If, however, the central bank undertakes an open market operation and expands the money supply by purchasing domestic bonds, then the exchange rate will depreciate due to the rise in the relative money supply but the purchases of domestic bonds create a shortage of these in private agents' portfolios which they will try to offset by selling some foreign bonds to purchase domestic bonds which will to some extent reduce the depreciation of the domestic currency compared to an FXO.

Another important result that comes from the portfolio balance model is that when domestic and foreign bonds are imperfect substitutes, then a sterilized foreign exchange operation (SFXO) has the potential to exert exchange rate effects which cannot happen in the monetarist models. If the authorities buy foreign bonds with the domestic currency and then mop up the increase in the money supply by selling domestic bonds, then they have effectively reduced private agents' holdings of foreign bonds while increasing their holdings of domestic bonds with the money supply remaining unchanged. According to the portfolio balance model, the increase in the supply of domestic bonds and decrease in the supply of foreign bonds held by the private sector will induce agents to attempt to restore equilibrium in their portfolios by selling domestic bonds to purchase foreign bonds, leading to a depreciation of the currency which will help in the process of rebalancing their portfolios since it will lead to an increase in the domestic currency value of foreign bonds in their portfolios. Hence, if domestic and foreign bonds are imperfect substitutes, then foreign exchange intervention that leaves the domestic money supply unchanged may still affect the exchange rate. The potential for sterilized foreign exchange to exert exchange rate effects is an important theoretical and empirical issue because it suggests that to some extent authorities might be able to keep the money supply level unchanged and yet still move the exchange rate.

7.18 Conclusions

A common characteristic of the three monetary models of exchange rate determination examined in this chapter is that what matters for the exchange rate is the money supply in relation to money demand in both the home and foreign countries. The exchange rate is the relative price of two national monies and is consequently a monetary phenomenon.

All the monetary models build upon PPP. The flexible-price monetary model assumes that PPP holds continuously and maintains that the price level adjusts instantaneously to changes in the supply and demand for money. This then leads to immediate exchange rate adjustment to maintain PPP. Changes in real income and inflation expectations induce changes in the exchange rate because they affect the demand for money. In the sticky-price monetary models the asymmetric speeds of adjustment in goods and asset markets can lead to divergences from PPP in the short run, although PPP reasserts itself in the long run.

The sticky-price monetary models provide an explanation of both exchange rate volatility and misalignment. Exchange rates can become misaligned in relation to PPP because of the phenomenon of exchange rate 'overshooting', while instability in monetary policies can result in even greater instability in exchange rates. An important point made by the sticky-price model is that both divergences from PPP and highly volatile exchange rates can be explained by rational speculation and are not necessarily the result of 'irrational' foreign exchange speculation.

Perhaps the most noticeable omission of the monetary models of exchange rate determination is an explicit role for the current account to influence the exchange rate. Furthermore, domestic and foreign bonds are regarded as perfect substitutes; that is, they are regarded as equally risky so there is no role for risk perceptions to play a part in the determination of exchange rates. By contrast, the portfolio balance model of exchange rate determination has an explicit and important role for both of these factors to influence exchange rates.

One issue that is not explicitly dealt with by the portfolio balance model is the precise reason for the perceived differences in risks between domestic and foreign bonds. This can be caused amongst other things by unstable economic policies and differing perceived political risks. In the circumstance where unstable economic policies create the risks, it may be best for the authorities to stabilize their economic policies. In the case where political risks are concerned the authorities might consider ways of reducing the perceived risks. In sum, reducing perceived risks may be an important mechanism for reducing exchange rate fluctuations.

Further reading

Bilson, J.F.O. (1978a) 'Rational Expectations and the Exchange Rate', in J.A. Frenkel and H.G. Johnson (eds), *The Economics of Exchange Rates* (Reading: Addison-Wesley).

Bilson, J.F.O. (1978b) 'The Monetary Approach to the Exchange Rate: Some Empirical Evidence', *IMF Staff Papers*, vol. 25, pp. 48–75.

Bilson, J.F.O. (1979) 'Recent Developments in Monetary Models of Exchange Rate Determination', *IMF Staff Papers*, vol. 26, pp. 201–23.

Chari, V., Kehoe, P.J. and McGratten, E.R. (1998) 'Can Sticky Price Models Generate Volatile and Persistent Real Exchange Rates?', *Review of Economic Studies*, vol. 69 no. 3, pp. 533–63.

Corseti, G. and Pesenti, P. (2001) 'Welfare and Macroeconomic Interdependence', *Quarterly Journal of of Economics*, vol. 116, pp. 421–45.

Dornbusch, R. (1976a) 'Expectations and Exchange Rate Dynamics', *Journal of Political Economy*, vol. 84, pp. 1161–76.

Dornbusch, R. (1976b) 'The Theory of Flexible Exchange Rate Regimes and Macroeconomic Policy', *Scandinavian Journal of Economics*, vol. 84, pp. 255–75.

Dornbusch, R. (1983) 'Flexible Exchange Rates and Interdependence', *IMF Staff Papers*, vol. 30, pp. 3–30.

Frankel, J.A. (1979) 'On the Mark: A Theory of Floating Exchange Rates Based on Real Interest Rate Differentials', *American Economic Review*, vol. 69, pp. 610–22.

Frankel, J.A. (1983) 'Monetary and Portfolio Balance Models of Exchange Rate Determination', in J.S. Bhandari and B.H. Putnam (eds), *Economic Interdependence and Flexible Exchange Rates* (Cambridge, Mass.: MIT Press).

Frankel, J.A. (1984) 'Tests of Monetary and Portfolio Balance Models of Exchange Rate Determination', in J.F.O. Bilson and R.C. Marston *Exchange Rate Theory and Practice* (Chicago: University of Chicago Press).

Frenkel, J.A. (1976) 'A Monetary Approach to the Exchange Rate: Doctrinal Aspects and Empirical Evidence', *Scandinavian Journal of Economics*, vol. 78, pp. 169–91.

Frenkel, J.A. and Johnson, H.G. (eds) (1976) *The Monetary Approach to the Balance of Payments* (London: Allen & Unwin).

Isard, P. (1978) 'Exchange Rate Determination: A Survey of Popular Views and Recent Models', *Princeton Studies in International Finance*, no. 42.

Isard, P. (1983) 'An Accounting Framework and some Issues for Modelling How Exchange Rates Respond to News', in J.A. Frenkel (ed.), *Exchange Rates and International Macroeconomics* (Chicago: University of Chicago Press).

Lane, P. (2001) 'The New Open Economy Macroeconomics: A Survey', *Journal of International Economics*, vol. 54, pp. 235–66.

MacDonald, R. and Taylor, M.P. (1989) 'Economic Analysis of Foreign Exchange Markets: An Expository Survey', in R. MacDonald and M.P. Taylor, *Innovations in Open Economy Macroeconomics* (Oxford: Basil Blackwell).

Mark, N. (2001) *International Macroeconomics and Finance: Theory and Econometric Methods* (Oxford: Basil Blackwell).

Mussa, M. (1976) 'The Exchange Rate, the Balance of Payments, and Monetary and Fiscal Policy Under a Regime of Controlled Floating', *Scandinavian Journal of Economics*, vol. 78, pp. 229–48.

Obstfeld, M. and Rogoff, K. (1995) 'Exchange Rate Dynamics Redux', *Journal of Political Economy*, vol. 103, pp. 624–60.

Sarno, L. (2001) 'Towards a New Paridigm in Open Economy Modelling: Where Do We Stand?', *Federal Reserve Bank of St Louis Review*, vol. 83, pp. 21–36.

Sarno, L. and Taylor, M.P. (2002) *The Economics of Exchange Rates* (Cambridge: Cambridge University Press).

8

The Portfolio Balance Model

8.1 Introduction

The monetary models of exchange rate determination make the crucial assumption that domestic and foreign bonds are perfect substitutes. This implies that the expected yields on domestic and foreign bonds are equalized. In effect, apart from their currency of denomination domestic and foreign bonds are regarded by international investors as the same. As we saw, however, in Chapter 7 the portfolio balance model is distinguished from the monetary models because it allows for the possibility that international investors may regard domestic and foreign bonds as having different characteristics other than their currency of denomination. In particular, they might for various reasons regard one of the bonds as being more risky than the other. This being the case they will generally require a higher expected return on the bond that is considered more risky to compensate for the additional risk it entails.

Allowing for domestic and foreign bonds to have different characteristics is potentially very important because operations that influence the exchange rate affect the composition of domestic and foreign bonds in agents' portfolios in different ways. In this chapter we use the portfolio balance model to examine three operations that are commonly used to influence the exchange rate:

1   An open market operation (OMO) which is defined as an exchange of domestic money base for domestic bonds or *vice-versa*.
2   A foreign exchange operation (FXO) which is an exchange of domestic money for foreign bonds or *vice-versa*. Such foreign exchange market intervention affects the domestic money supply and is termed a non-sterilized intervention in the foreign exchange market.
3   A sterilized foreign exchange operation (SFXO) which is an exchange of domestic bonds for foreign bonds or vice versa leaving the domestic money base unchanged.

The interesting thing about an SFXO is that it represents the difference between an OMO and FXO. An expansionary FXO means that the authorities purchase foreign bonds with domestic money, which means that the public holds more money and less foreign bonds. If the authorities decide they wish to keep the money supply at its original level they can conduct a contractionary monetary policy by selling domestic bonds to the public so that the money held by the public returns to its original level. If they conduct such a sterilization operation, the net effect is that the public holds less foreign bonds and more domestic bonds with the money supply unchanged.

   In the monetary models the only thing that matters for the exchange rate is money supply in relation to money demand, the source of money creation being unimportant. This means that in such models there is no difference in the exchange rate and interest rate effects of an FXO or OMO that change the money supply by like amounts. The reason being, that in the monetary models there is no distinction between domestic and foreign bonds. Within the context of the monetary models an SFXO will have no exchange rate or interest rate effects because it leaves money supply unchanged and is merely the exchange of domestic for foreign bonds which are perfect substitutes.

   In this chapter we look at the portfolio balance model in more detail than was considered in Chapter 7. In particular, we examine the concept of a risk premium as crucial to the portfolio balance approach to exchange rate determination. We then look at different types of risks that may make domestic and foreign bonds imperfect substitutes and outline a simple version of the portfolio balance model and use this to examine the differing effects of OMOs, FXOs and SFXOs. We then look at the results in the light of their effects on the risk premium. Finally, we consider some of the dynamic features of the portfolio balance model.

8.2   The concept of a risk premium

The distinguishing feature of the portfolio balance model is that investors no longer regard domestic and foreign bonds as perfect substitutes. This being the case the expected returns on the two assets no longer have to be equal. In other words, the uncovered interest parity condition which was a key condition in the monetary models generally no longer holds. For example, if investors are risk-averse and regard domestic bonds as being relatively risky as compared to foreign bonds, they will require a higher expected return on domestic bonds than foreign bonds. This additional expected return on the relatively risky as compared to the less risky bond is known as the 'risk premium'. For a risk premium to exist, all of the following three conditions must be fulfilled (see Isard, 1983):

1   There must be perceived differences in risks between domestic and foreign bonds – the essence of a risky asset being that its expected real rate of return is uncertain. Either domestic bonds are viewed as relatively risky compared to foreign bonds, or *vice-versa*. If the two bonds were equally risky then with perfect capital mobility they must be perfect substitutes.

2   There has to be risk-aversion on the part of economic agents to the perceived differences in risk – the principle of risk-aversion is that investors will only be prepared to take on increased risk if there is a sufficient increase in expected real returns to compensate. If investors were not risk-averse then they would not expect a higher return on relatively risky bonds.

3   Given the different risks on domestic and foreign bonds there is a theoretical portfolio known as the risk-minimizing portfolio which would minimize the risks facing private agents. There must be a difference between the risk-minimizing portfolio and the actual portfolio forced at market clearing prices into investors' portfolios. However, the amount of domestic and foreign bonds held by private agents is determined by the respective authorities that issue them. If the risk minimising portfolio is not held then agents will demand a risk premium to compensate.

If all three of the above conditions are fulfilled, then the uncovered interest parity condition will not hold due to the existence of a risk premium which represents the compensation required by private agents for accepting risk exposure above the minimum possible.

$$r - r^* = E\dot{s} + RP \tag{8.1}$$

where r is the domestic interest rate, r^* is the foreign interest rate and $E\dot{s}$ is the expected rate of depreciation of domestic currency defined as domestic currency units per unit of foreign currency, and RP is the risk premium required on domestic bonds which may be either positive or negative.

The difference between equation (8.1) and the uncovered interest parity condition (equation 7.1) is the risk-premium expression. The expected rate of return on domestic bonds may be higher (a positive risk premium) or lower (a negative risk premium) when compared to foreign bonds. For example, if domestic bonds are regarded as more risky than foreign bonds and if the domestic interest rate is 10%, the foreign interest rate 6% and the expected rate of depreciation of the domestic currency is only 3%, then there is a 1% risk premium on the domestic currency. Foreign assets have an expected yield of 9%, the 6% interest and 3% expected appreciation of the foreign currency, which is lower than the 10% yield on domestic bonds. The 1% positive risk premium on the domestic currency is a negative 1% risk premium on the foreign currency.

An issue that we need to briefly examine concerns what types of risk may cause the emergence of a risk premium?

8.3 Different types of risk

When analysing risk, economists make some postulates about economic agents. Investors are assumed to be rational in that they wish to maximize their expected utility which is a positive function of expected real returns and a negative function of the perceived level of risk. The basis of investors' portfolio decisions is choosing an optimum combination of expected rate of return and risk given their risk–return preferences (degree of risk-aversion). The less risk-averse investors are, the more they will be prepared to take on risk. Conversely, the more risk-averse they are the less risk they will be prepared to take on.

In the first instance we need to define a risky asset. The definition of a risky asset is that its expected real rate of return is uncertain. In other words, economic agents for various reasons cannot be sure what the value of the return in terms of purchasing power will be.

Typically risks fall into one of two main categories (see Wihlborg 1978), 'currency risks' and 'country risks'. Currency risks arise because domestic and foreign bonds are denominated in different currencies, while country risks arise because they are issued by countries with different legal jurisdictions and different political regimes.

Currency risks

There are two types of currency risk that we shall consider, one is called 'inflation risk' and the other is termed 'exchange risk'.

- **Inflation risk**. This type of risk occurs because the inflation rates in the domestic and foreign economies are uncertain. If PPP were to hold continuously, the real rate of return on the domestic bond is given by the nominal interest rate less the expected domestic inflation rate ($P\dot{e}$). If the latter is uncertain then so will be the real return on the asset considered. Similarly, the expected real rate of return on foreign bonds is given by the nominal foreign interest rate less the expected foreign inflation rate ($P\dot{e}*$), if the latter is also subject to uncertainty then so will be the real return on foreign bonds.

    If PPP holds continuously and the expected domestic price inflation rate rises, this reduces the expected real rate of return on domestic bonds but does not increase the expected real rate on foreign bonds because the currency will depreciate by the same amount as the expected inflation rate. The risk of holding a domestic bond can therefore be represented as a positive function of the variance in the domestic inflation rate while the risk of holding a foreign bond can be represented as a positive function of the variance of the foreign inflation rate. A greater variance of the expected domestic inflation rate raises the relative riskiness of domestic as compared to foreign bonds and *vice-versa*.

- **Exchange risk**. If PPP holds continuously, then inflation risk would be the sole currency risk facing international investors. However, we saw in Chapter 6 that the overwhelming weight of empirical evidence since the advent of floating exchange rates rejects the use of PPP as a valid approximation of short-run exchange rate determination. This being the case, then one has to take into account deviations from PPP when calculating the expected real rate of return on domestic and foreign bonds during the holding period. While the expected real rate of return on domestic bonds is given by the nominal interest rate minus the expected rate of inflation, the expected rate of return from holding foreign bonds is now given by the foreign interest rate less the expected rate of inflation plus the expected deviation of the exchange rate from PPP. For simplicity, let us assume that inflation and domestic and foreign interest rates are equal and exchange rates are initially at PPP. In this case an expected real depreciation of the currency in terms of PPP means that there is an expected appreciation of the foreign currency implying an increased expected return from holding foreign bonds. The expected real rate of return on domestic bonds is, however, unaffected by such deviations from PPP.

The expected deviation of the exchange rate from PPP causes a risk specific to foreign bonds given by the variance of the expected deviation from PPP. That is, fluctuations in the exchange rate that cause deviations from PPP constitute a risk specific to foreign investments which is called 'exchange risk'. Exchange rate changes only cause exchange risk to the extent that they represent deviations from PPP. If exchange rate changes ensure that PPP holds, then they do not constitute exchange risk. Theoretically, therefore, exchange rate fluctuations are an incorrect measure of exchange risk. It is fluctuations of the exchange rate around PPP that constitutes exchange risk.

Country risks

Country risks are somewhat less amenable to economic analysis than currency risks. Nevertheless, since the definition of a risky asset is that its expected real rate of return is uncertain, it is not difficult to conceptualize country risks. Country risks can be divided into three types – exchange control risk, political risk and default risk.

- **Exchange control risk.** This is a type of country risk whereby investors face uncertain real rates of return. The real rate of return on domestic and foreign bonds may be uncertain due to the risk of the imposition of a tax on the interest element during the holding period. This risk may be greater or less for domestic as compared to foreign bonds.
- **Default risk.** Another, more serious, country risk is 'default risk' whereby a government refuses to pay the interest and sometimes the principal on bonds issued by them and denominated in a foreign currency. Note that the bonds need to be denominated in foreign currency because a government will not default on bonds issued in its own currency because in that case it could always print the money to redeem the bonds.
- **Political risk.** This risk covers an extremely broad range of scenarios, but basically refers to the danger that investors face because the political environment in a country could cause them to lose part or all of their investment including returns due; or, find costly restrictions imposed on how they may manipulate their investments.

From the above discussion we can see that there are a variety of reasons why domestic and foreign bonds may have different relative riskiness which is a necessary precondition for making them imperfect substitutes. What matters to produce imperfect asset substitutability and a risk premium is perceived differences in risks between domestic and foreign bonds. If assets are regarded as equally risky, then with perfect capital mobility they must be perfect substitutes.

8.4 A portfolio balance model

The portfolio balance model of exchange rates was pioneered by William Branson (1976, 1977, 1984) and Pennti Kouri (1976) and has been subsequently modified and extended in various directions by Maurice Obstfeld (1980), Girton and Henderson (1977), Allen and Kenen (1980) and Kenen (1982). The model we shall look at is based upon Branson (1976) and Kouri (1976). This model is a simple version of many portfolio balance models because it utilizes the assumption of static exchange rate expectations; that is, the exchange rate is not expected to change. The $E\dot{s}$ expression in equation (8.1) is assumed to be zero.

In the model outlined we assume that domestic prices and output are fixed following a policy disturbance. This means the focus of the analysis is on the accumulation or decumulation of foreign assets resulting from imbalances in the current account following an operation to influence the exchange rate. A current account surplus means that the country is building up a stock of claims on the rest of the world as represented by an increased holdings of foreign bonds; while a deficit in the balance of payments corresponds to a decline in foreign bond holdings. The operation of the portfolio balance model is shown in **Figure 8.1**.

An OMO, FXO or SFXO creates a disturbance in asset-holders' portfolios requiring a change in the exchange rate and domestic interest rate. These changes then lead to effects on output and the current account. A current account surplus/deficit leads to an accumulation/decumulation of foreign assets, which leads to further changes in assets-holders' portfolios with implications for the exchange rate and domestic interest rate, and so on until the model is restored to long-run equilibrium.

In the model that follows, we can distinguish between OMOs and FXOs because domestic and foreign bonds are assumed to be imperfect substitutes. This means that a SFXO which represents the difference of a FXO and OMO becomes feasible. The model follows the portfolio balance framework developed by William Branson (1976, 1977, 1984), and the analysis focuses on a 'small country' in the sense that it can influence its real exchange rate without provoking a reaction from the rest of the

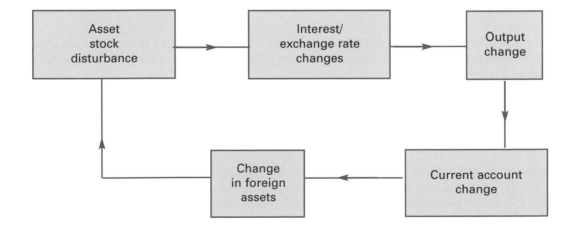

Figure 8.1   The operation of the portfolio balance model

world. This assumption enables the derivation of some concrete results; the point that the foreign country's reaction may reinforce or offset the policy pursued by the home country is self-evident. In addition, because the domestic economy is small, its assets are assumed not to be of any interest to the rest of the world and hence they are held only by domestic residents.

There are a number of simplifying assumptions that we shall make at the outset, that both the domestic and foreign price levels are fixed and that real domestic output is also fixed. We do, however, discuss the possible implications of OMOs, FXOs and SFXOs on real output in section 8.11.

The model

There are assumed to be three assets that are held in the portfolios of private agents and the authorities:

(a)   domestic monetary base, M;
(b)   domestic bonds denominated only in the domestic currency, B; and
(c)   foreign bonds denominated only in the foreign currency, F.

Domestic bonds may be held by either domestic private agents or the authorities. Thus, we may denote the net supply of domestic bonds which is assumed to be fixed as:

$$\bar{B} = B_p + B_a \qquad (8.2)$$

where $\bar{B}$ is the fixed net supply of domestic bonds, B_p is the domestic bond holdings of private agents and B_a is the domestic bond holdings of the authorities.

Similarly, the country's net holding of foreign bonds is held by private agents and the authorities which we assume in our analysis to be positive in both cases and equal to the summation of previous current account surpluses. Unlike the stock of domestic bonds, the holdings of foreign assets may be increased or decreased over time via a current account surplus or deficit. Thus, we have:

$$F = F_p + R \qquad (8.3)$$

where F is the net foreign bond holdings of the country, F_p is the foreign bond holdings of private agents R is the stock of foreign bonds held by the authorities as foreign exchange reserves.

The domestic monetary base liability of the authorities is equivalent to the assets of the authorities so that:

$$M = B_a + SR \qquad (8.4)$$

where S is the exchange rate defined as domestic currency units per unit of foreign currency. For simplicity it is assumed that capital gains or losses to the authorities as a result of exchange rate changes do not affect the monetary base.

Total private financial wealth (W) at any point in time is given by the identity:

$$W = M + B_p + SF_p \qquad (8.5)$$

An important point concerning equation (8.5) is that the domestic currency value of foreign bonds is given by the value of foreign bonds times the exchange rate defined as domestic currency units per unit of foreign currency; that is, SF_p. This means that an excess demand for foreign bonds can be partly met by a depreciation (rise) of the domestic currency which raises the domestic currency value of foreign bond holdings.

The demand to hold money by the private sector is inversely related to the domestic interest rate, inversely related to the expected rate of return on foreign bonds, and positively to domestic income and wealth. This yields:

$$M = m(r, E\dot{s}, Y, W) \; m_r < 0, \; m_{\dot{s}} < 0, \; m_y > 0 \text{ and } m_w > 0 \tag{8.6}$$

where r is the domestic nominal interest rate, $E\dot{s}$ is the expected rate of depreciation of the domestic currency, Y is domestic nominal income m_r, $m_{\dot{s}}$, m_y and m_w are partial derivatives.

The demand to hold domestic bonds as a proportion of private wealth is positively related to the domestic interest rate, inversely related to the expected rate of return on foreign assets and inversely related to domestic nominal income and positively to wealth. This yields:

$$B_p = b(r, E\dot{s}, Y, W) \; b_r > 0, \; b_{\dot{s}} < 0, \; b_y < 0 \text{ and } b_w > 0 \tag{8.7}$$

where b_r, $b_{\dot{s}}$, b_y and b_w are partial derivatives.

The demand to hold foreign bonds is inversely related to the domestic interest rate, positively related to the expected rate of return from holding foreign bonds and inversely related to domestic nominal income and positively to wealth. This yields:

$$SF_p = f(r, E\dot{s}, Y, W) \; f_r < 0, \; f_{\dot{s}} > 0, \; f_y < 0 \text{ and } f_w > 0 \tag{8.8}$$

where f_r, $f_{\dot{s}}$, f_y and f_w are partial derivatives.

Since any increase in wealth is held as either money, bonds or foreign bonds, then the sum of the partial elasticities with respect to wealth must sum to unity, this is known as the balance sheet constraint and is given by the identity:

$$m_w + b_w + f_w = 1 \tag{8.9}$$

The balance sheet identity is coupled with the assumption that assets are gross substitutes, implying the following constraints on the partial derivatives:

$$m_r + b_r + f_r = 0 \tag{8.10}$$

$$m_{\dot{s}} + b_{\dot{s}} + f_{\dot{s}} = 0 \tag{8.11}$$

From equation (8.10), it can be inferred that the demand for domestic bonds is more responsive to the domestic interest rate than foreign bond demand, while the demand for domestic bonds is less responsive to the foreign bond yield than foreign bond demand. Also from equation (8.11) it can be inferred that the demand for domestic bonds is less responsive to the expected rate of return on foreign bonds than foreign bond demand.

The current account balance is crucial to the dynamics of the system because the current account surplus gives the rate of accumulation of foreign assets. That is:

$$C = \frac{dF_p}{dt} = \dot{F}_p = T + r^* \ (F_p + R) \tag{8.12}$$

where C is the current account surplus measured in foreign currency, T is the trade balance measured in foreign currency, and r^* is the foreign interest rate.

The current account is made up of two components; the revenue from net exports (the trade balance), and interest rate receipts from net holdings of foreign assets. Net exports are assumed to be a positive function of the real exchange rate, inversely related to domestic income via the marginal propensity. This yields:

$$T = T(S/P, Y,) \ T_s > 0 \text{ and } T_y < 0 \tag{8.13}$$

where P is the domestic price level, T_s and T_y are partial derivatives.

The assumption that net exports are a positive function of the real exchange rate is quite strong because it rules out the possibility that there may be an initial J-curve effect on the trade balance (see Chapter 3), the assumption implies that the Marshall–Lerner condition always holds.

8.5 Derivation of the asset demand functions

We now proceed to analyse the effects of OMOs, FXOs and SFXOs on the exchange rate and domestic interest rate using a comparative static framework. To make things easier we set the initial value of the exchange rate S and level of wealth equal to unity. Taking the total differential of equation (8.5) we obtain:

$$dW = dM + dB + F_p \ dS + S \ dF_p \tag{8.14}$$

Taking the total differentials of the asset market functions given by equations (8.6) to (8.8) we obtain:

$$dM = m_r \ d_r + m_{\dot{s}} \ dE\dot{s} + m_w \ (dM + dB_p + F_p \ dS + S \ dF_p) \tag{8.15}$$

$$dB_p = b_r \ dr + b_{\dot{s}} \ dE\dot{s} + b_w \ (dM + dB_p + F_p \ dS + S \ dF_p) \tag{8.16}$$

$$dSF_p = f_r \ dr + f_{\dot{s}} \ dE\dot{s} + f_w \ (dM + dB_p + F_p \ dS + S \ dF_p) \tag{8.17}$$

Setting the left-hand side of the above equations to zero and noting that because of static exchange rate expectations $dE\dot{s} = 0$, we can obtain the slope of the various asset market schedules in the interest rate–exchange rate plane.

The money market schedule

The money market (MM) schedule shown in **Figure 8.2** shows various combinations of the domestic interest rate for which money supply is equal to money demand. Keeping the money supply fixed ($dM = O$) and since $dE\dot{s} = 0$ from equation (8.15) we find that the money market schedule has a positive slope given by:

$$\frac{dr}{dS} = \frac{-m_w F_p}{m_r} > 0 \qquad (8.18)$$

The bond market schedule

The bond market schedule (BB) in **Figure 8.2** shows various combinations of the domestic interest rate and exchange rate for which the private bond supply is equal to private bond demand. Keeping the private bond supply fixed ($dB_p = O$) and since $dE\dot{s} = 0$ from equation (8.16) we find that the bond market schedule has a negative slope given by:

$$\frac{dr}{dS} = \frac{-b_w F_p}{b_r} < 0 \qquad (8.19)$$

The foreign bond schedule

The foreign bond market schedule (FF) in **Figure 8.2** shows various combinations of the domestic interest rate and exchange rate for which the private holding of the foreign bond supply is equal to private foreign bond demand. Keeping the private foreign bond supply fixed ($dFp = O$) and since $dE\dot{s} = 0$ from equation (8.17) we find that the foreign bond market schedule has a negative slope given by:

$$\frac{dr}{dS} = \frac{(1 - f_w)F_p}{f_r} < 0 \qquad (8.20)$$

8.6 Equilibrium of the model

The asset market of the model is in equilibrium when all three asset markets, that is the money markets and the domestic and foreign bond markets clear at the appropriate domestic interest rate and exchange rate. This is illustrated in **Figure 8.2**.

The MM schedule depicts equilibrium in the domestic money market, and is upward-sloping from left to right in the interest rate–exchange rate plane. The reason for this is that a depreciation (rise) of the exchange rate leads to a increase in the value of domestic residents' wealth as it raises the domestic currency value of their holdings of foreign bonds. This being the case, they will wish to hold more domestic money, but given the existing money stock the increased money demand can only be offset by a rise in the domestic interest rate. An increase in the money supply for a given exchange rate requires a fall in domestic interest rate to be willingly held, implying a rightward shift of the MM schedule.

The BB schedule depicts equilibrium in the domestic bond market, and is downward-sloping from left to right. A depreciation by raising domestic wealth also leads to an increased demand for domestic bonds which, given the existing stock of domestic bonds, can only be offset by a fall in the domestic interest rate which will reduce their attractiveness to investors. An increase in the domestic bond supply for a given exchange rate requires a rise in the domestic interest rate for the bonds to be willingly held, implying a rightward shift of the BB schedule.

Finally, the FF schedule depicts equilibrium in the foreign bonds market, and slopes downward from left to right. A rise in the interest rate on domestic bonds makes them

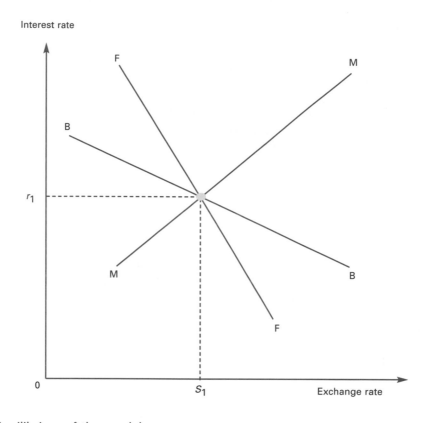

Figure 8.2 Equilibrium of the model

relatively more attractive as compared to foreign bonds, inducing agents to sell foreign bonds to purchase domestic bonds leading to an appreciation of the domestic currency. An increase in the supply of foreign bonds, given the assumption of a fixed foreign interest rate and a given exchange rate, requires a fall in the domestic interest rate for the foreign bonds to be willingly held, implying a leftward shift of the FF schedule.

The FF schedule is steeper than the BB schedule on the assumption that changes in the domestic rate of interest affect the demand for domestic bonds more than they influence the demand for foreign bonds. The different slopes of the BB and FF schedules shows that the two assets are regarded by private agents as different.

We now proceed to examine the short-run effects of an FXO, OMO and SFXO respectively. In each case, we shall assume that the operation is designed to produce a depreciation of the exchange rate to improve the international competitiveness of the country.

8.7 The effects of a foreign exchange operation

With an expansionary FXO, the authorities purchase foreign bonds from the private sector with newly created monetary base. This means that there is an increase in the

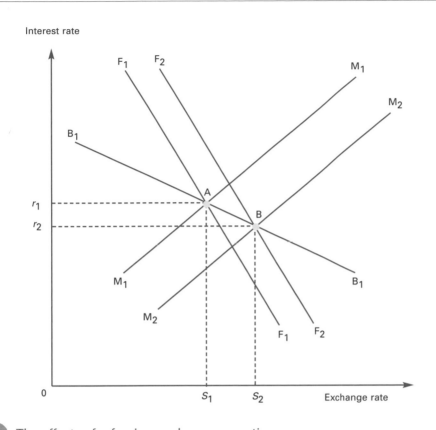

Interest rate

Figure 8.3 The effects of a foreign exchange operation

private sector's holdings of money and an equivalent fall in their holdings of foreign bonds ($dM = -SdF_p = SdR$). The short-run effects of an FXO are shown in **Figure 8.3**.

An FXO is an exchange of domestic money for foreign assets, and will lead to a rightward shift of the MM and FF schedules. Since agents hold less foreign assets than before the operation, we know that the exchange rate will have depreciated to S_2 and the domestic interest rate must have fallen to r_2 at point B on the unchanged BB schedule. The exchange rate depreciation is required because the FXO creates a shortage of foreign assets in agents portfolios which can only be satisfied in the short run by a depreciation which raises the domestic currency value of agents remaining holdings of foreign assets; while the fall in the interest rate is required to encourage agents to hold the increased money stock.

8.8 The effects of an open market operation

With an expansionary OMO, the authorities increase the private sector holdings of money and decrease its holdings of domestic bonds by an equivalent amount; that is, $dM = -dB_p = dB_a$. The effects of an OMO are shown in **Figure 8.4**.

In contrast to an FXO, an OMO leaves the FF schedule unchanged while leading to a rightward shift of the money supply schedule from M_1 to M_2 and a leftward shift of

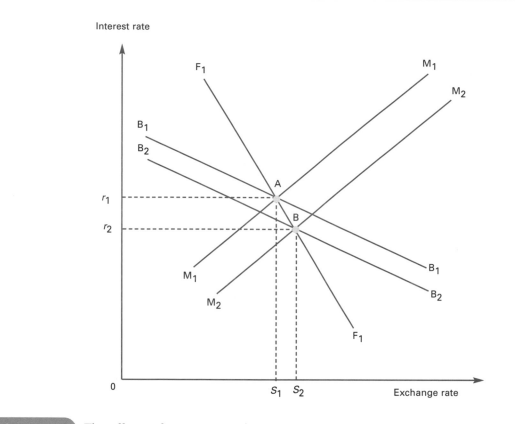

Figure 8.4 The effects of an open market operation

the BB schedule from B_1 to B_2. This means that there is a depreciation of the exchange rate and a fall in the domestic interest rate. The is because the OMO creates an excess supply of money in agents' portfolios which leads to an increased demand for both domestic and foreign bonds, which results in a fall in the domestic interest rate and a depreciation of the currency which raises the value of foreign bond holdings.

8.9 The effects of a sterilized foreign exchange operation

One means of comparing the relative effects of an OMO and FXO in the model is to combine the two operations by having an expansionary FXO and a contractionary OMO of an equivalent amount. That is, the authorities first purchase foreign assets with domestic money base then offset the increase in the monetary base by selling domestic bonds. Such an operation represents a sterilized intervention in the foreign exchange market since it leaves the domestic monetary base unchanged ($dM = -SdF_p$ and $-dM = dB_p$ so that $-SdF_p = dB_p$), and is tantamount to the authorities altering the currency composition of bonds held in private portfolios. The effects of an SFXO are illustrated in **Figure 8.5**.

The SFXO has the effect of increasing the supply of domestic bonds shifting the BB schedule to the right from B_1 to B_2, whilst decreasing agents' holdings of foreign assets

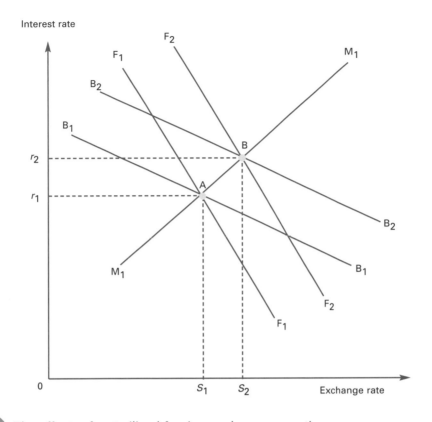

Figure 8.5 The effects of a sterilized foreign exchange operation

shifting the FF schedule to the right from F_1 to F_2; the MM schedule remains unchanged because the domestic money base is left unaffected. The net effect of the operation is a depreciation of the exchange rate and a rise in the rate of interest. The exchange rate depreciates because the SFXO causes a shortage of foreign assets in agents' portfolios requiring an exchange rate depreciation to achieve the desired hold-ings. The interest rate rises because the excess supply of domestic bonds in agents' portfolios depresses domestic bond prices.

The fact that an SFXO can have exchange rate and interest rate effects in the portfolio balance model stands in marked contrast to the monetary models examined in Chapter 7. In the monetary models, domestic and foreign bonds are perfect substitutes, so a swap of domestic for foreign bonds by the authorities is an exchange of identical assets as far as private agents are concerned. Hence, there is no need for interest or exchange rate changes. In contrast, in the context of the portfolio balance model domestic and foreign bonds are regarded by economic agents as different assets, and this being the case an SFXO that increases agents' holdings of domestic bonds while decreasing agents' hold-ings of foreign bonds causes a disequilibrium in agents' portfolios. Agents find them-selves with more domestic bonds than they want and less foreign bonds, which means that their portfolio is more exposed to domestic risks. Equilibrium for agents' portfolios is restored by a higher domestic interest rate which compensates for the increased risk due to increased domestic bond holdings, and a depreciation of the exchange rate which reduces risk exposure by revaluing the remaining holdings of foreign assets.

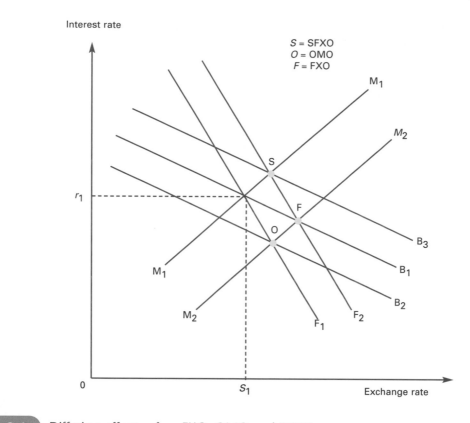

Figure 8.6 Differing effects of an FXO, OMO and SFXO

8.10 A comparison of an FXO, OMO and SFXO

Having analysed all three operations separately, we can compare and contrast the short-run effects of the three operations together as shown in **Figure 8.6**.

In the figure we can see the contrasting effects of the three operations. The effects of an OMO and FXO on the domestic interest rate and exchange rate are qualitatively similarly; however, an FXO leads to a larger depreciation of the exchange rate, while an OMO leads to a larger fall in the domestic interest rate. The rationale for this result is that an FXO leads to a fall in agents' holdings of foreign bonds, while an OMO does not, consequently an FXO creates a greater excess demand for foreign bonds which is satisfied only by a stronger depreciation of the exchange rate. By contrast, an OMO creates a greater shortage of domestic bonds creating a greater excess demand for bonds which is offset only by a larger fall in the domestic interest rate.

In the model, real output has been assumed to be fixed and while this has the advantage of yielding some clear and useful insights, it is also worth briefly considering the effects of an OMO and FXO on real output. Dan Lee (1980) analysed the dynamics of an FXO and OMO in a model where the level of output in the short run is endogenously determined. The question he attempted to answer was whether an OMO or FXO would have a more expansionary effect on domestic output. Using a portfolio balance framework he, too, found that an expansionary OMO lowers the domestic interest rate more than an FXO, while the latter leads to a larger depreciation of the exchange rate. He assumed that domestic investment is inversely related to the real domestic interest rate and net exports are positively related to the real exchange rate.

Lee found that because an OMO has more effect on the domestic interest rate, its expansionary effect on output depends relatively more than a FXO on the responsiveness of investment to the fall in the real interest rate that follows the operation; while the effect of a FXO on real output depends relatively more than an OMO on the effect of the real exchange rate depreciation on the trade account balance. Overall, an expansionary OMO may or may not have a greater effect on output than an expansionary FXO. If the response of the trade balance to changes in the real exchange rate is relatively weak and slower than that of investment to interest rate changes, it will be the case that an OMO has a stronger effect on output. If, however, the foreign sector is large and highly responsive to the real exchange rate we may be able to say the opposite. Thus, Lee concluded that at the theoretical level one cannot say whether an FXO or OMO will have a more expansionary effect on output without imposing restrictions on the relevant parameters.

When comparing an FXO with an SFXO we find that an SFXO has a relatively weaker effect on the exchange rate than in the case of an FXO, and the interest rate effects are opposite in sign. The reason for these differing effects is that an FXO increases the money stock which, by lowering the domestic interest rate, encourages a greater excess demand for foreign assets leading to a greater depreciation. By contrast, an SFXO increases the stock of domestic bonds requiring a higher domestic interest rate which by reducing the attractiveness of holding foreign bonds limits the exchange rate depreciation.

In contrast to an FXO, the effects of an SFXO on real output will be ambiguous. This is because while the exchange rate depreciation will encourage net exports, the rise in the domestic interest rate will discourage domestic investment. Even if the former outweighs the latter effect, so that there is a net increase in domestic output, the expansion will be less than in the case of an FXO because the exchange rate effect is weaker.

8.11 The dynamics of the model

To distinguish between short run and long-run equilibrium in the model we should note that in the long run the current account should be in balance and the rate of change of the exchange rate should also be zero. This means that the country is neither increasing nor decreasing its foreign bond holdings and the exchange rate is at its equilibrium value. **Figure 8.7** illustrates the dynamics of the exchange rate and current account in the model following an OMO, FXO or SFXO that cause an exchange rate depreciation assuming that real output remains fixed.

At time t_1 there is an OMO, FXO or SFXO that causes a depreciation of the exchange rate from S_1 to S_2, with prices fixed this means that there has been a real exchange rate depreciation. The resulting improvement in the country's international competitiveness moves its current account into surplus. A counterpart to the current account surplus is that the country starts to accumulate more foreign bonds. This increases the proportion of foreign assets in investors' portfolios and to reduce this risk exposure they start to purchase domestic assets (most probably domestic bonds

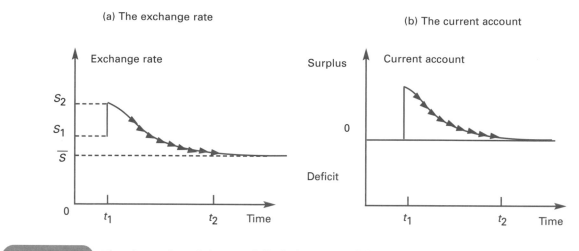

Figure 8.7   The dynamics of the portfolio balance model

rather than money) leading to an appreciating exchange rate. In turn, the exchange rate appreciation erodes the country's competitive advantage and so reduces the current account surplus. The dynamics come to an end when the exchange rate has appreciated sufficiently that the current account is brought back into balance.

One of the features of the model is that it is long-run non-neutral with respect to the real exchange rate, since the long-run exchange rate $\bar{S}$ lies below the initial exchange rate S_1. This is because the current account surplus that follows an operation results in an accumulation of foreign assets and an accompanying increase in the contribution of interest rate receipts from the holding of foreign assets on the service component of the current account. As such, it is necessary for the real exchange rate to have appreciated in the long-run equilibrium so that there is a deterioration of the trade account to offset the improvement in the service account and so ensure that the current account is restored to balance in the long run.

During the transition from the short run to the long run, the economy experiences an appreciating currency and a current account surplus, Kouri (1983) labels this link the 'acceleration hypothesis'. It is worth noting that the stable transition to equilibrium we have described depends crucially upon certain stability conditions being fulfilled. Following an operation that causes an exchange rate depreciation which moves the current account into surplus, there are two conflicting effects at work on the current account. The surplus will induce an exchange rate appreciation which will work to eliminate the surplus. However, the current account surplus also implies an accumulation of foreign assets and with it increased interest rate receipts which improves the surplus. Consequently, for the appreciation of the exchange rate to reduce the surplus it is necessary that the fall in net exports exceed the increased interest receipts.

8.12 The effects of a change in risk perceptions

A key feature of the portfolio balance model is that it provides a role for risk factors to influence exchange rates which may account for some of the exchange rate changes

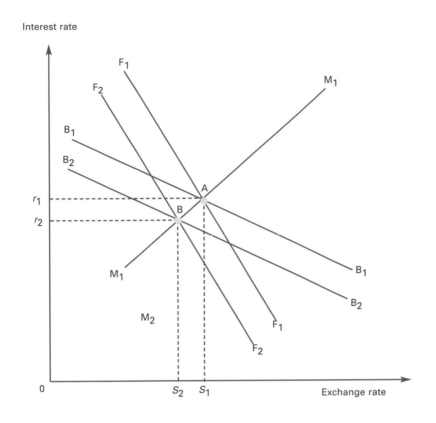

Figure 8.8   Foreign bonds become more risky

experienced under floating exchange rates. Consider the case where for some reason investors perceive that foreign bonds have become more risky as compared to domestic bonds. The effects of such a change in perceptions is illustrated in **Figure 8.8**.

As a result of the perceived increase in risks attached to holding foreign bonds there is a decreased demand for foreign bonds and an increased demand for domestic bonds. Both the foreign bond schedule F_1 and the domestic bonds schedule B_1 shift to the left and the new schedules F_2 and B_2 intersect at point B. The increased demand for domestic bonds is reflected in an appreciation of the exchange rate from S_1 to S_2 and a fall in the domestic interest rate from r_1 to r_2.

The exchange rate appreciation leads to a current account deficit, which in turn leads to a decline in foreign asset holdings which creates a shortage of foreign bonds in agents' portfolios and consequently agents try to purchase foreign bonds leading to a depreciation of the exchange rate. Over time, the depreciation improves the country's international competitiveness so reducing the current account deficit.

8.13 Money versus bond-financed fiscal expansion

There are two ways that authorities may try to finance increased government expenditure; one is by simply printing extra money and using the money to directly finance its expenditure, the other is to finance expenditure by borrowing, that is by selling bonds to economic agents. We now proceed to examine short-run implications of these two alternative methods of financing increased government expenditure within the context of the portfolio balance model. In the analysis we shall ignore the possible expansionary effects of the increased expenditure on national income since this considerably complicates the picture.

Money-financed expenditure

An increase in public expenditure financed by printing money means that investors will find that their wealth has risen because they will hold more money and the same amounts of domestic and foreign bonds. The problem is that they will find that they have a larger proportion of money in their portfolios, and for this reason they will demand more domestic bonds and more foreign bonds; the results of this portfolio adjustment are shown in **Figure 8.9**.

The increased money supply is reflected in a rightward shift of the money market schedule from M_1 to M_2. It is worth noting that this shift is less than in the case of an OMO which increases the money by a like amount because the money supply increases wealth and part of this is reflected in an increase in the demand for money. In addition, the increase in wealth leads to an increase in the demand for both

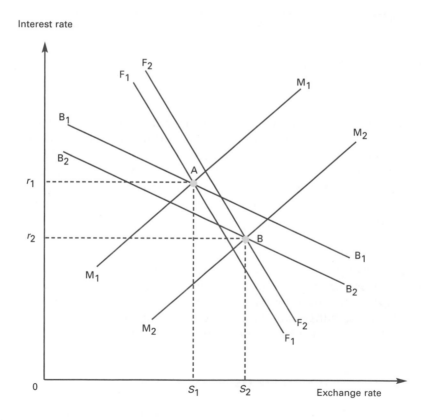

Figure 8.9 Money-financed expenditure

domestic and foreign bonds, the bond market schedule shifts to the left from B_1 to B_2, while the foreign bond schedule shifts to the right. The net effect of the money-based expansion is a depreciation of the exchange rate and a fall in the domestic interest rate.

Bond-financed expenditure

An increase in public expenditure financed by borrowing will again increase investors' wealth because they will hold more bonds and the same amounts of domestic money and foreign bonds. While the bond sales reduce the publics holdings of money, the money is then put back into private agents' hands by increased government expenditure. In this instance, agents will find that they have a larger proportion of domestic bonds in their portfolios than desired, which will lead investors to demand more money and foreign bonds; the results of this portfolio adjustment are shown in **Figure 8.10**.

The increase in the supply of bonds will shift the BB schedule to the right from B_1 to B_2. Since investors are holding more bonds and the same amount of money and foreign bonds their wealth must have increased. This increase in wealth will lead to an increase in the demand for bonds so reducing the extent of the rightward shift of the bond schedule and an increase in the demand for money represented by a leftward shift of the MM schedule. The net effect on the demand for foreign bonds is uncertain. While the rise in wealth will lead to increased foreign bond demand leading to a shift of the foreign bond schedule to the right, the rise in the domestic interest rate will lead to a substitution of demand away from foreign bonds.

If the wealth effect dominates, the FF schedule moves to the right as in **Figure 8.10(a)** and equilibrium is obtained at a higher interest rate and an exchange rate depreciation. Conversely, if the interest rate effect dominates, the FF schedule moves to the right as in **Figure 8.10(b)** but equilibrium is obtained at a higher interest rate

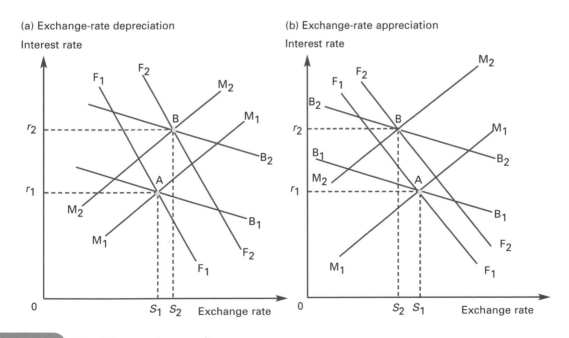

(a) Exchange-rate depreciation

(b) Exchange-rate appreciation

Figure 8.10 Bond-financed expenditure

and an exchange rate appreciation. Thus, fiscal policy will have an ambiguous effect on the exchange rate.

In this section we have seen that the impact of fiscal expansion on the interest rate and exchange rate depends not only on the size of the expansion but on how the policy is financed. If it is financed by printing money this leads to a short-run depreciation and a fall in interest rates; while if it is financed by borrowing the effect is a rise in interest rates and the exchange rate may depreciate or appreciate. It is important to remember that these are only the short-run results. The money-financed fiscal expansion is likely to translate quickly into inflation as the expansionary fiscal policy will be further boosted by the exchange rate depreciation and fall in the domestic interest rate. While a bond-financed fiscal expansion effects on prices and output are likely to be less inflationary because in the case where the exchange rate depreciates the expansion of demand will be reined back to some extent by the rise in interest rates. Demand will be even further restrained if the fiscal expansion leads to an exchange rate appreciation. In sum, a bond-financed fiscal expansion will be less inflationary than a money-financed expansion.

Before concluding this section, it is worth remembering that the rising US budget deficit in the early 1980s was primarily financed by US government bond sales, a rising US interest rate and an appreciating dollar. In the context of the portfolio balance model this would suggest that the substitution effect of rising US interest rates dominated the wealth effect.

8.14 The risk premium, imperfect and perfect substitutability

The portfolio balance model that we have examined in this chapter has been based upon the assumption that domestic and foreign bonds are imperfect substitutes. This is shown by the fact that although the foreign interest rate is fixed and exchange rate expectations are static, the domestic interest rate could diverge from the foreign interest rate. The reason being that the differing operations influence the risk premium, allowing the domestic interest rate to diverge from the foreign rate. This point is illustrated as follows.

In the portfolio balance model the domestic interest rate can diverge from the foreign interest rate not only because of exchange rate expectations, but also because of the risk premium in accordance with equation (8.1) which is repeated below as equation (8.21):

$$r - r^* = E\dot{s} + RP \tag{8.21}$$

This can be expressed in difference form as:

$$dr - dr^* = dE\dot{s} + dRP \tag{8.22}$$

Throughout we have been assuming static exchange rate expectations ($dE\dot{s} = 0$) and a fixed foreign interest rate so that $dr^* = 0$. Substituting in these values into equation (8.22) we find:

$$dr = dRP \tag{8.23}$$

Hence, all changes in the domestic interest rate can be interpreted as due to changes in the risk premium. A rise in the interest rate reflects a rise in the risk premium on domestic assets, while a fall in the domestic interest rate reflects a fall in the risk premium. In the case of perfect substitutability there is no risk premium, so the uncovered interest parity condition is the relevant equation, that is:

$$r - r^* = E\dot{s} \tag{8.24}$$

In difference form:

$$dr - dr^* = dE\dot{s} \tag{8.25}$$

With static expectations and a fixed foreign interest rate this means:

$$dr = 0 \tag{8.26}$$

For this to be the case, both the BB and FF schedules must coincide and be horizontal at the world interest rate r^*, as illustrated in **Figure 8.11**.

In the figure, the BB and FF schedules are horizontal and coincide as represented by the schedule BF; only changes in monetary policy as reflected by shifts in the MM

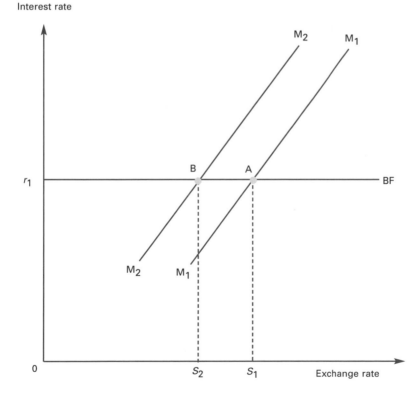

Figure 8.11 Perfect substitutability

schedule can influence the exchange rate. There is no distinction to be made between an OMO or FXO on the exchange rate. An SFXO leaves the MM schedule unchanged and the BF schedule remains in the same position so it has no exchange rate or interest rate effects. A bond-financed fiscal expansion will in this special case have an unambiguous effect. Although the BF schedule remains at BF, the increased wealth resulting from the increased supply of bonds will raise money demand causing a leftward shift of the MM schedule and an exchange rate appreciation.

8.15 Conclusions

The portfolio balance model represents an important contribution to the exchange rate literature because it allows a role for changes in perceived risk or risk-aversion in the determination of the exchange rate. An increase in the perceived riskiness of domestic bonds compared to foreign bonds can lead to both a rise in the domestic interest rate and a depreciation of the currency; while an increase in the perceived riskiness of foreign bonds can lead to an appreciation of the domestic currency and a fall in the domestic interest rate. These effects accord with intuition and are frequently invoked to explain observed exchange rate changes. Such an effects are, however, absent from the monetary models which assume that domestic and foreign bonds are perfect substitutes.

Another important contribution of the portfolio balance model is that there is a significant role for the current account to play in the determination of the exchange rate over time. A current account surplus implies an accumulation of foreign assets and an increase in wealth, and the result is a larger proportion of foreign bonds in investors portfolios than they desire. In turn, this leads to purchases of domestic bonds and money and a resulting appreciation of the exchange rate which works to reduce the current account surplus.

Another contribution of the portfolio balance model is that it permits a relatively easy discussion of the role of fiscal policy in determining the exchange rate. A bond-financed fiscal expansion has an ambiguous effect on the exchange rate, because while a higher proportion of domestic bonds and an increase in asset-holders' wealth will lead to an increase in the demand for foreign bonds, the higher domestic interest rate will lead to a fall in the demand for foreign bonds. If the former effect is greater than the latter the exchange rate depreciates, but if the reverse is true the exchange rate appreciates.

A significant policy implication that emerges from the portfolio balance model is that a given change in the money stock has a more powerful effect on the exchange rate when carried out by a purchase of foreign assets (an FXO) than when achieved via a purchase of domestic assets (an OMO). It is only in the limiting case when domestic and foreign bonds are perfect substitutes that the effects become identical. This is an important result because it at least provides a rationale for the observed interventions of authorities in foreign exchange markets. Another result that emerges is that it is only by assuming that domestic and foreign bonds are imperfect substitutes that an SFXO can exert exchange rate effects. However, even if an SFXO can affect the exchange rate, it will have a relatively weaker effect on the exchange rate than an FXO. The lesson for policy-makers is that non-sterilized intervention has a more powerful effect on the exchange rate than sterilized intervention.

One issue that is not explicitly dealt with by the portfolio balance model is the precise reason for the perceived differences in risks between domestic and foreign bonds. This can be caused amongst other things by unstable economic policies and differing perceived political risks. In the circumstance where unstable economic policies create the risks, it may be best that the authorities stabilize their economic policies. In the case where political risks are concerned the authorities might consider ways of reducing the perceived risks. In sum, reducing perceived risks may be an important mechanism for reducing exchange rate fluctuations.

Further reading

Allen, P.R. and Kenen, P.B. (1980) *Asset Markets, Exchange Rates and Economic Integration* (Cambridge: Cambridge University Press).

Branson, W.H. (1976) 'Asset Markets and Relative Prices in Exchange Rate Determination', *Institute for International Economic Studies, Seminar Paper*, no. 66, Stockholm.

Branson, W.H. (1984) 'A Model of Exchange Rate Determination with Policy Reaction: Evidence from Monthly Data', in P. Malgrange and P.A. Muets (eds), *Contemporary Macroeconomic Modelling* (Oxford: Basil Blackwell).

Branson, W.H. and Henderson, D.W. (1985) 'The Specification and Influence of Asset Markets', in P.B. Kenen and R.W. Jones (eds) *Handbook of International Economics* (Amsterdam: North-Holland).

Branson, W.H., Huttunen, H. and Masson, P. (1977) 'Exchange Rates in the Short Run: Some Further Results', *European Economic Review*, vol. 12, pp. 395–402.

Frankel, J.A. (1982) 'A Test of Perfect Substitutability in the Foreign Exchange Market', *Southern Economic Journal*, vol. 49, pp. 406–16.

Frankel, J.A. (1983) 'Monetary and Portfolio Balance Models of Exchange Rate Determination', in J.S. Bhandari and B.H. Putnam (eds), *Economic Interdependence and Flexible Exchange Rates* (Cambridge, Mass.: MIT Press).

Girton, L. and Henderson, P.W. (1977) 'Central Bank Operations in Foreign and Domestic Assets Under Fixed and Flexible Exchange Rates', in P.B. Clark, D.E. Logue and R.J. Sweeny (eds), *The Effects of Exchange Rate Adjustment* (Washington: Government Printing Office).

Isard, P. (1983) 'An Accounting Framework and some Issues for Modelling how Exchange Rates Respond to News', in J.A. Frenkel (eds), *Exchange Rates and International Macroeconomics* (Chicago: University of Chicago Press).

Kenen, P.B. (1982) 'Effects of Intervention and Sterilization in the Short Run and the Long Run', in R.N. Cooper, P.B. Kenen, J.B. Macedo and J.V. Ypersele, *The International Monetary System Under Flexible Exchange Rates*. (Cambridge Mass.: Ballinger).

Kouri, P.J.K. (1976) 'The Exchange Rate and the Balance of Payments in the Short Run and the Long Run: A Monetary Approach', *Scandinavian Journal of Economics*, vol. 78, pp. 280–304.

Kouri, P.J.K. (1983) 'The Balance of Payments and the Foreign Exchange Market: A Dynamic Partial Equilibrium Model', in J.S. Bhandari and B.H. Putnam (eds), *Economic Interdependence and Flexible Exchange Rates* (Amsterdam: North Holland).

Lee, D. (1983) 'Effects of Open Market Operations and Foreign Exchange Market Operations Under Flexible Exchange Rates', in M. Darby and J.R. Lothian (eds), *The International Transmission of Inflation* (Chicago: University of Chicago Press).

Obstfeld, M. (1980) 'Imperfect Asset Substitutability and Monetary Policy Under Fixed Exchange Rates', in M. Darby and J.R. Lothian (eds), *The International Transmission of Inflation* (Chicago: University of Chicago Press).

Wihlborg, C. (1978) 'Currency Risks in International Finance Markets', *Princeton Studies in International Finance*, no. 44.

9

Empirical Evidence on Exchange Rates

9.1 Introduction

We have so far considered the exchange rate literature from a predominately theoretical viewpoint, but the exchange rate field has also been rich in empirical research. Apart from investigations into the validity of PPP theory which we examined in Chapter 6, empirical research on exchange rates has addressed three other key questions:

1 Is the foreign exchange market efficient?
2 What model best predicts exchange rate movements?
3 How can we model exchange market participants' expectations?

Answers to these questions are of enormous importance from a policy viewpoint. If it can be shown that the foreign exchange market is 'efficient' then the case for government intervention in that market would be considerably undermined. While if we can identify a model that successfully explains exchange rate determination, it would be possible for the authorities to determine the best way to influence exchange rates and limit exchange rate volatility. Furthermore, the consequences of alternative economic policy measures could be better evaluated as their implications for the exchange rate would be understood. Finally, if we understood how exchange market participants form their views on exchange rates, then policy-makers may be able to use such information to help them in the process of stabilizing those rates.

9.2 What is an efficient market?

Following Eugene Fama, an efficient market is conventionally defined as one 'in which prices always "fully reflect" available information' (1970, p. 383). In the specific application to the foreign exchange market this implies that market participants use all relevant available information bearing on the appropriate value of the exchange rate to produce a set of exchange rates – spot and forward – that does not provide an opportunity for unusual *ex ante* profit opportunities. In other words, unusual profit cannot be made by speculators who make exchange rate forecasts on a similar information set. In connection with this broad definition, there are two key concerns (i) is new information instantaneously and fully reflected in the exchange rate? and (ii) what is relevant and what is irrelevant information?

There are a number of tests that have been proposed to determine whether or not the foreign exchange market is efficient. One of the most popular has been to see if the forward exchange rate systematically over- or underpredicts the future spot exchange rate, if it were to do so then this would be indicative of foreign exchange market inefficiency.

For example, suppose that the forward exchange rate were to systematically underpredict the value of the future spot rate of a currency. There would be simple rule which could yield a speculator abnormal profits; the rule being to buy the currency forward today knowing that he can sell it when the contract is due at a higher value. A numerical example will illustrate the point. Suppose the three-month forward rate of the pound against the dollar is £0.60/$1 but speculators know that the forward rate systematically underpredicts the future rate by 5%. This means that the future spot exchange rate in three months' time will be above £0.60/$1 at £0.63/$1. Hence, by buying dollars forward today for £0.60/$1 a speculator will know that in three months' time when he is due to pay the £0.60/$1, for each dollar purchased he can immediately expect £0.63/$1 for each dollar sold.

According to the efficient market hypothesis (EMH) the scenario depicted above would not persist because the opportunity for abnormal profits would lead to massive purchases of dollars forward. This would leads to a rise in the forward rate above £0.60/$1 towards £0.63/$1 until any abnormal profits are eliminated.

However, there is a major problem with exchange market efficiency tests. Even if one were to discover that the forward rate systematically over- or under-predicted the future spot rate, this discrepancy is not necessarily a sign of foreign exchange market inefficiency, it could be indicative of the existence of a risk premium in the foreign exchange market. If the forward exchange rate of a currency were to systematically underpredict its future spot exchange rate, as in our numerical example, this may be due to the existence of a positive risk premium attached to the foreign currency. In our numerical example, the difference between the forward rate of £0.60/$1 and the actual/expected future spot rate of £0.63/$1 may be viewed as a £0.03 risk premium on the dollar; that is, speculators will only buy dollars forward if they expect to be able to sell them in the future and make £0.03 profit. This profit represents the compensation required by speculators to buy dollars forward which are regarded as more risky than pounds.

Hence, any expected excess profits to be earned on buying the foreign currency forward are merely the compensation required by an efficient foreign exchange market to compensate for the risks associated with holding the foreign currency forward. If the forward exchange rate of the foreign currency is systematically undervalued in relation to the future spot exchange rate, this may be evidence of the existence of a positive risk premium attached to the foreign currency. That is, international investors require a higher expected return on the foreign currency as compared to the domestic currency because they regard it as a relatively risky asset to hold compared to the domestic currency. A positive risk premium on the foreign currency corresponds to a negative risk premium on the domestic currency, and *vice-versa*.

9.3 Exchange market efficiency tests

The rational expectations hypothesis (REH) is particularly useful when examining the concept of exchange market efficiency. This is because like the EMH it presumes that economic agents do not make systematic errors when making their predictions. According to the REH, economic agents have a good knowledge of the economic model relevant to predicting a variable so that they do not persistently over- or under-predict the future value of that variable. Applying rational expectations to the prediction of the future exchange rate we find:

$$s_{t+1} = Es_{t+1} + u_{t+1} \qquad (9.1)$$

where s_{t+1} is the log of the actual spot exchange rate in one period's time defined as domestic currency units per unit of foreign currency, Es_{t+1} is the log of the expected exchange rate in one period's time and u_{t+1} is a random error term with a normal distribution and mean of zero.

Equation (9.1) says that the actual future exchange rate corresponds to that which was anticipated by economic agents plus or minus some random error. The next step is to assume that investors are risk-neutral (that is, there is no risk premium) and consequently and so they set the forward rate at a level that corresponds to the expected future spot exchange rate this gives:

$$f_t = Es_{t+1} \qquad (9.2)$$

where f_t is the log of the forward exchange rate at time t, defined as domestic currency units per unit of foreign currency. Substituting equation (9.2) into equation (9.1) we obtain:

$$s_{t+1} = f_t + u_{t+1} \qquad (9.3)$$

Equation (9.3) says that providing economic agents have rational expectations and there is no risk premium in the foreign exchange market, then the future spot rate should be equal to today's quoted forward rate plus a random error. In other words, on average the forward rate should neither over- or underpredict the actual exchange rate.

Equation (9.3) constitutes a joint test of both exchange market efficiency and no risk premium. The forward rate may systematically over- or underpredict the future actual exchange rate not because of exchange market inefficiency, but because there is a positive or negative risk premium on the domestic currency. If a risk premium is present we have to modify equation (9.2) to yield:

$$Es_{t+1} = f_t + RP_t \qquad (9.4)$$

where RP_t is the risk premium on the foreign currency.

Substituting equation (9.4) into (9.1) yields:

$$s_{t+1} = f_t + RP_t + u_{t+1} \qquad (9.5)$$

Equation (9.5) says that the forward rate may systematically over- or underpredict the future spot rate because of the presence of a risk premium. If there is a positive risk premium on the foreign currency (negative risk premium on the domestic currency) the one-period-ahead forward rate of the domestic currency will systematically over-value the domestic currency as compared to its actual rate one period ahead; whereas if there is a negative risk premium on the foreign currency (positive risk premium on the domestic currency) then the one-period-ahead forward rate of the domestic currency will systematically undervalue the currency compared to its actual rate one period ahead.

The early tests (see for example Levich, 1978, and Frenkel, 1982a) of exchange market efficiency were based on equation (9.3) and set out as follows:

$$s_{t+1} = a_1 + a_2 f_t + u_{t+1} \qquad (9.6)$$

According to this test, if the foreign exchange market is efficient in the sense that the exchange rate (spot and forward) incorporates all currently available information and there is no risk premium in the foreign exchange market, then the forward rate will be an unbiased predictor of the future spot exchange rate. Hence, the expected sign of a_1 is zero, if it were non-zero then the forward exchange rate would systematically over- or underpredict the future spot exchange rate and rational economic agents could use this information to make systematic profits. The coefficient a_2 will be equal to unity showing that the forward exchange rate on average correctly predicts the future spot exchange rate. Finally, the error term (u_t) will possess the classical ordinary least squares (OLSQ) properties. In particular, errors will be serially uncorrelated. By no serial correlation we mean that there is no statistically significant relationship between the errors of one period and errors made in other periods. One cannot forecast future errors on the basis of past errors. If agents could predict future errors on the basis of past errors this would be a sign of foreign exchange market inefficiency; that is, there would be unexploited profit opportunities. The results of some of the studies of Levich and Frenkel for equation (9.6) are reported in **Table 9.1**.

Table 9.1 Risk premium/market efficiency test

Study	Rate	Estimated equation $s_{t+1} = a_1 + a_2 f_t + u_{t+1}$ Period	a_1	a_2	DW	$\bar{R}^2$
Levich (1978)	Pound	73M3–78M5	0.02* (0.17)	0.98* (9.33)	1.51	0.81
	French franc	73M3–78M5	0.00* (1.00)	0.86 * (5.05)	1.79	0.59
	Deutschmark	73M3–78M5	0.00* (1.00)	1.00* (110.78)	1.40	0.99
Frenkel (1982)	Pound	73M6–79M7	0.03 (1.67)	0.96* (38.44)	1.74	0.95
	French franc	73M6–79M7	–0.24 (–2.95)	0.84 (15.92)	2.24	0.78
	Deutschmark	73M6–79M7	–0.02 (–0.78)	0.97* (30.41)	2.10	0.93

Notes: The hypothesis is that $a_1 = 0$ and $a_2 = 1$. An asterisk by a variable indicates that it is both of the correct sign and not statistically different from its hypothesized value. All rates are against the US dollar. The *t*-statistics are in parentheses.

The results presented in the table were interpreted by the two authors as highly supportive of the joint hypothesis of foreign exchange market efficiency and no risk premium. The coefficient a_1 does not differ significantly from zero, while the coefficient a_2 does not differ significantly from unity. In addition, the Durbin–Watson statistic reveals that there is no first-order serial correlation in the residuals. The adjusted $\bar{R}^2$ for the entire sample period is generally high, suggesting that most information is incorporated in the forward rate. The implication of these results is that the foreign exchange market is efficient and there is no risk premium.

Nevertheless, other authors such as Hansen and Hodrick (1980), Meese and Singleton (1982) and Cumby and Obstfeld (1984) have pointed out that the Levich/Frenkel regression is inappropriate if exchange rates follow a non-stationary process – that is, there is some trend exchange rate appreciation or depreciation in the exchange rate. In this case, it is necessary to detrend the data in order for the regression estimates to be unbiased. Cumby and Obstfeld argue that we should reestimate the previous equation by running the following regression:

$$(s_{t+1} - s_t) = a_1 + a_2 (f_t - s_t) + u_{t+1} \tag{9.7}$$

where s_t = the log of the spot exchange rate.

Equation (9.7) detrends equation (9.3) and as such constitutes a more powerful test of the EMH. It says that a currency that is at a forward discount $(f_t - s_t)$ of x% should on average depreciate by x%, whereas a currency that is at a forward premium $(s_{t+1} - s_t)$ of x% should on the average appreciate by x%.

If the foreign exchange market is efficient and characterized by rational expectations, so that we can substitute the actual exchange rate for the expected exchange rate, along with the assumption that there is no risk premium, then one would

Table 9.2 Risk premium/exchange market efficiency test with detrended data

| Exchange rate | Period | Estimated equation $(s_{t+1} - s_t) = a_1 + a_2 (f_t - s_t) + u_{t+1}$ | |
		a_1	a_2
Canadian dollar	70M7–81M12	0.0005*	–0.389
		(0.55)	(–0.71)
French franc	73M8–81M12	–0.0066*	–1.838
		(–1.74)	(–2.10)
German mark	73M6–81M12	0.0021*	–0.533
		(0.41)	(0.38)
Italian lira	73M6–81M12	–0.0106	–0.4786
		(–2.41)	(–1.01)
Japanese yen	73M6–81M12	0.0008*	–0.480
		(0.26)	(–1.01)
UK Pound	73M6–81M12	–0.006*	–1.533
		(–1.62)	(–1.82)

Note: Hypothesis is: $a_1 = 0$ and $a_2 = 1$. An asterisk by a variable indicates that it is both of the correct sign and not statistically different from its hypothesised value. All currencies are against the US dollar. *t*-statistics are in brackets.
Source: Boothe and Longworth (1986, p. 139).

again expect a_1 to be zero and the coefficient a_2 to not differ significantly from unity, indicating that on average the realized change in the exchange rate is correctly forecast by the forward premium/discount. **Table 9.2** reports the results of Boothe and Longworth on equation (9.7) for a variety of currencies against the US dollar.

The results of Boothe and Longworth (which confirm the findings of Cumby and Obstfeld) reported in **Table 9.2** show that one can decisively reject the null hypothesis of exchange market efficiency. Similar findings have been found for the period March 76–July 86 by Taylor (1988). These results reveal that once we take account of the trend in the exchange rate, market participants have on average mispredicted the direction of movement of the exchange rate. As MacDonald and Torrance (1989) note in a survey of these tests, the coefficient a_2 is usually closer to minus one than the hypothesized value of unity!

The tests of equation (9.7) suggest that on average currencies that were at a forward discount actually appreciated, while those at a forward premium actually depreciated! This is a clear rejection of the joint market efficiency test because it suggests that there exists a fairly simple rule for investors to make excessive profits – simply put your money in a currency that is at a forward discount (because of the relatively high interest rate in that country) and you will not only benefit from the higher interest rate but also an exchange rate appreciation of that currency. This is a clear violation of uncovered interest parity.

A major problem with these decisive rejections is that because they are a joint test of exchange market efficiency (rational expectations) and the non-existence of a risk premium, there is no clear-cut interpretation. It may be evidence of exchange market inefficiency (that is, REH does not hold) or be indicative of the existence of a risk premium (possibly time-varying) in the foreign exchange market.

> ### Box 9.1
>
> ## Exchange market efficiency and the distinction between anticipated and unanticipated economic policy
>
> The efficient market hypothesis has some important implications for exchange rate dynamics in response to changes in economic policy. Let us consider the case of monetary policy. When the foreign exchange market is efficient it is only unanticipated monetary expansion that can cause discrete jumps in the exchange rate. If a monetary expansion is anticipated to occur, market efficiency implies that there would be no discrete jump in the exchange rate when the money supply expansion takes place because it has already been appropriately discounted in advance. **Figure 9.1** contrasts the effects of unanticipated and anticipated money expansions in the context of the 'overshooting' exchange rate model.
>
> **Figure 9.1(a)** illustrates what happens if a money supply expansion takes place unannounced at time t_2, leading to a sudden discrete jump of the exchange rate from S_1 to S_2 which represents an 'overshoot' leading from its long-run equilibrium rate $\bar{S}$; thereafter, the exchange rate heads towards its long-run value $\bar{S}$. This contrasts to the dynamics of the exchange rate when the authorities announce at time t_1 that they will expand the money supply at time t_2, which is shown in **Figure 9.1(b)**. In this case, there would be an immediate initial depreciation at the time of the announcement t_1 to S_2 which is followed by a gradual depreciation of the exchange rate to S_3 so that at time t_2 when the money expansion actually takes place the exchange rate is there is no discrete jump of the exchange rate, thereon it appreciates smoothly to its long run value $\bar{S}$.
>
> The lack of a discrete exchange rate jump when the money supply expansion is anticipated (because of the prior announcement) follows from the EMH. If the exchange rate did not depreciate until the expansion actually took place at time t_2, this would imply a large discrete depreciation of the exchange rate at that time. However, since the money expansion was expected such a discrete jump would imply a missed abnormal *ex ante* profit opportunity as speculators could easily have sold the currency in advance of the depreciation. As the foreign
>
>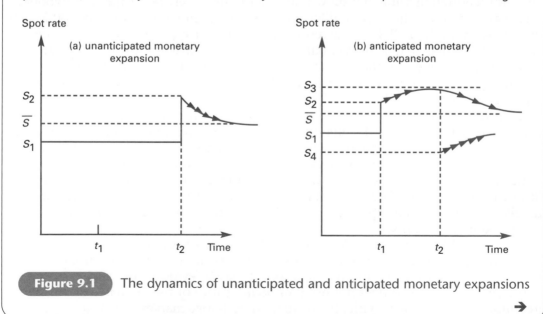
>
> ### Figure 9.1   The dynamics of unanticipated and anticipated monetary expansions

→

exchange market is efficient the expectation of a money supply expansion leads to a smaller discrete depreciation of the rate (reflecting the news of future monetary expansion) at the time of the announcement, with a smooth depreciation followed by an appreciation thereafter. In this way, all anticipated disturbances are fully discounted and therefore unusual *ex ante* profit opportunities eliminated.

An interesting issue concerns what would happen if we arrive at time t_2 and the authorities fail to carry out the announced money expansion? This itself represents a further piece of news to the foreign exchange market. The exchange rate will jump appreciate back to the exchange rate S_4, so that there is a period of an overvalued exchange rate to correct for the previous unjustified undervaluation. Hence, it is possible that much of the exchange rate volatility witnessed under floating is due to the failure of authorities to carry out their stated policy intentions.

This EMH has implications for exchange rate movements generally. The announcement of bad economic news like a large deficit in the current account will only cause an exchange rate depreciation to the extent that it is worse than what the market was anticipating prior to the announcement. If a large current account deficit is not as bad as the market was expecting it could lead to an exchange rate appreciation!

9.4 Alternative tests of the efficient market hypothesis

According to the EMH, the forward rate is supposed to embody all the relevant information concerning the future expected spot exchange rate. This implies that it should not be possible to add a further variable available at time *t* to regression (9.3) which proves to be statistically significant. Were it to do so, this can be taken as evidence that the forward exchange rate does not contain all relevant information concerning the future spot exchange rate. An example of a regression that tests to see if another variable can improve the fit of regression (9.3) is:

$$s_{t+1} = a_1 + a_2 f_t + a_3 f_{t-1} + u_{t+1} \tag{9.8}$$

where f_{t-1} is the log of the forward rate in the previous period.

According to the EMH a variable such as the previous period's forward exchange rate should not contain any additional information relevant to the future exchange rate (that is, a_3 should not be statistically different from zero). Using monthly data (July 73 to September 1979) for the pound–dollar, French franc–dollar, lira–dollar and deutschmark–dollar, Edwards (1983b) found that the coefficient a_3 is not statistically different from zero, suggesting that f_{t-1} contains no useful additional information. Edwards' study is very supportive of exchange market efficiency.

Another test of efficient market hypothesis concerns an examination of the errors between the expected future exchange rate and the actual future exchange rate. If the foreign exchange market is efficient then it should not be possible to predict these errors on the basis of information available at the time the forecast is made. That is:

$$u_{t+1} = a_1 + a_2 I_t + v_{t+1} \tag{9.9}$$

where u_{t+1} is the forecast error, that is $s_{t+1} - f_t$, I_t is a subset of information available at time *t* and v_{t+1} is a random error term with a normal distribution and mean of zero.

If the foreign exchange market is efficient then the coefficient a_2 should be equal to zero. That is, we can not put in any relevant economic variables at time t, such as the current spot exchange rate s_t, the previous periods spot s_{t-1} or lagged forward rate f_{t-1} or any other known variable at time t and use this to predict the error. This efficiency test is known as the orthogonality property and it implies that agents use all relevant information in making their forecasts so as to avoid predictable forecast errors. The EMH holds that the forecast error u_{t+1} is due to unpredictable shocks and will be unrelated to any information available at the time expectations are formed. Among the other information available at time t is the previous period's forecast errors u_t. As such, a test of the orthogonality assumption would be to see if the forecast error $s_{t+1} - f_t = u_{t+1}$ is independent of the previous period's forecast error, $s_t - f_{t-1} = u_t$. That is:

$$s_{t+1} - f_t = a_1 + a_2(s_t - f_{t-1}) + v_{t+1} \tag{9.10}$$

where v_{t+1} is a random normally distributed error.

Equation (9.10) can be rearranged to yield:

$$s_{t+1} = a_1 + a_2(s_t - f_{t-1}) + a_3 f_t + v_{t+1} \tag{9.11}$$

According to the efficient market hypothesis if there is no risk premium and the foreign exchange market uses all information efficiently then $a_1 = 0$, $a_2 = 0$ and $a_3 = 1$. Frankel (1980) produces results for the French franc–dollar, pound–dollar and Italian lira–dollar for the period July 1974–April 1978 using weekly data that lead to a rejection of the efficient market hypothesis.

Other tests of the efficient market hypothesis have been variations on the traditional tests. Most notably they have involved using alternative proxies for the future expected exchange rate Es_{t+1} other than the actual exchange rate at time $t + 1$. In addition, more sophisticated estimation techniques have been used, and two studies of particular note are those of Clarida and Taylor (1997) and Clarida et al. (2003). Clarida and Taylor (1997), using a linear framework, find that information from a series of forward exchange rates (4, 13, 26 and 52 weeks) can help to beat a random walk forecast (that is, a forecast that the exchange rate one-period hence will be the same as the current spot rate) by a margin of up to 40%. Clarida et al. (2003), using a series of forward rates (4, 13, 26 and 52 weeks) and non-linear techniques, show that there is information useful to forecasting the future spot exchange rate and they are able to beat a random walk forecast by a margin of 27–31% at the four-week horizon and 5–68% at the 52-week horizon, improving upon the linear framework of the Clarida and Taylor (1997) study. Finally, in tests of the orthogonality property, authors have used a wider range of variables in the information set.

9.5 Summary of findings on exchange market efficiency

There has been a great deal of testing of the joint hypothesis of foreign exchange market efficiency and the non-existence of a risk premium. The problem with all these tests is that even when the joint hypothesis is rejected there is no means of knowing whether this is due to the existence of a risk premium or due to the failure of foreign exchange market efficiency.

Overall, the results of the various exchange market efficiency tests are fairly mixed depending upon the currency and the particular test considered. Nonetheless, there is an accumulation of evidence suggesting that for certain periods and certain rates the joint hypothesis does not hold. Specifically, tests of EMH using the forward premium/discount as a prediction for the future appreciation/depreciation of the currency convincingly reject the joint hypothesis.

Accepting that the joint hypothesis does not hold, then the big issue left to resolve is whether or not the rejection is due to the existence of a risk premium or the existence of inefficiency/non-rational expectations in the foreign exchange market. At the theoretical level Frankel (1986) has argued that the risk premium if it does exist is likely to be too small to account for the failure of exchange market efficiency tests. In addition, Frankel (1986) and Rogoff (1986) test to see if the risk premium behaves as predicted by the portfolio balance model; that is, if it increases with the supply of domestic bonds and decreases with the supply of foreign bonds. In both studies the relevant coefficients to prove statistically insignificant.

A tentative suggestion is that the more likely candidate for the failure is not the existence of a risk premium but rather non rational expectations in the foreign exchange market. Indeed, Frankel and Froot (1987) suggest that neither the rational expectations hypothesis or alternative expectations hypotheses correctly specify exchange market expectations, while preliminary research into this question by MacDonald and Torrance (1989) and Taylor (1989) suggests that both the existence of a risk premium and non-rational expectations are to blame. However, the recent success of papers such as Clarida and Taylor (1997) and Clarida et al. (2003) suggests there may be information in the series of forward exchange rates that is useful for predicting the future path of the spot exchange rate suggesting non-rational use of information.

9.6 Empirical tests of exchange rate models

As we saw in Chapter 7, there are a variety of models of exchange rate determination for the authorities to choose from with radically different implications for the conduct of exchange rate policy. In particular, the monetary and portfolio balance models have very different implications concerning the effectiveness of sterilized intervention.

Predictably, some authors have conducted empirical tests of their exchange rate model and found evidence to support it, while others using either different time periods or different bilateral exchange rates have found evidence against a given model. Another problem is that some authors have taken the empirical evidence to support their exchange rate model when the same predictions are also made by rival theories. As we saw in Chapter 7, in an attempt to overcome this latter problem, Jeffrey Frankel (1983 and 1984) extended his monetary synthesis equation (1979) to incorporate a portfolio balance effect. We repeat the synthesis equation (7.46) below:

$$s = \frac{-\alpha}{\Theta\beta + 1} + \frac{1}{1 + 1/\Theta\beta}(m - m^*) - \frac{\eta}{1 + 1/\Theta\beta}(y - y^*) + \frac{\sigma + 1/\Theta}{1 + 1/\Theta\beta}(\dot{P}e - \dot{P}e^*)$$

$$- \frac{1}{\Theta + 1/\Theta\beta}(r - r^*) + \frac{1}{\Theta\beta + 1}(b - f) \tag{9.12}$$

The fully flexible price monetarist version postulates that both the parameters Θ and β approach infinity, this reduces equation (9.22) to the flexible price monetary equation (7.9) of Chapter 7. The sticky price monetarist school holds that Θ is less than infinite while β is infinite so we end up with the real interest differential equation (7.31), whereas the sticky price portfolio balance model holds that both the parameters β and Θ are less than infinite so that relative bond supplies have an impact on the exchange rate and the relevant equation is therefore (7.46) or (9.12).

Equation (9.22) yields the following reduced form regression for the exchange rate:

$$s = a_1 + a_2 (m - m^*) + a_3 (y - y^*) + a_4 (r - r^*) + a_5 (P\dot{e} - P\dot{e}^*) + a_6 (b - f) + ut \qquad (9.13)$$

Table 9.3 reveals the conflicting predictions of the four main models of exchange rate determination derived from equation (9.13).

The Frankel formulation shows that the theoretical predictions of the main models of exchange rate determination are sufficiently different that a resort to empirical testing should allow us to discriminate between the various theories. Frankel tests his synthesis equation for the US dollar against the deutschmark using monthly data for the period January 1974–October 1978. In a similar vein, Pilbeam (1991) tests the Frankel equation for the US dollar against the pound for the period January 1973 to December 1984. Results from these two studies are reported in **Table 9.4**.

The results reported in the table rate are typical examples of most exchange rate tests. As we can see from the reported regressions, the results rather than favouring any particular model of exchange rate determination are not favourable to any. In the Frankel study the only variable to be significant is the equation for relative bond supplies but this is of the wrong sign! In the Pilbeam study, the only variable to be significant is the money stock but this is a prediction common to all three models. The coefficient for real output is correctly signed in the Pilbeam study, but incorrectly signed in the Frankel study, and statistically insignificant in both. As for the nominal interest rate differential and expected inflation differential the actual estimated coefficients were not significantly different from zero, revealing that there is no clear cut empirical relation between interest rates and price expectations for either the dollar–deutschmark or the dollar–pound exchange rate. The regression coefficient for the portfolio balance parameter is wrongly signed in both studies.

Table 9.3 Predictions of exchange rate models

Model	a_2 $(m - m^*)$	a_3 $(y - y^*)$	a_4 $(r - r^*)$	a_5 $(P\dot{e} - P\dot{e}^*)$	a_6 $(b - f)$
Flexible price monetary model	+	−	0	+	0
Sticky-price Dornbusch monetary model	+	−	−	0	0
Real interest differential monetary model	+	−	−	+	0
Sticky-price portfolio model	+	−	−	+	+

$m - m^*$ is the log of relative money supply; $y - y^*$ is the log of relative income; $r - r^*$ is the nominal interest rate differential; $P\dot{e} - P\dot{e}^*$ is the expected inflation differential; $b - f$ is the log of relative bond supplies.

Table 9.4   Test of exchange rate models

Frankel (1983) estimation for dollar–deutschmark
   Estimated equation:

$$s = a_1 + a_2\ (mus - mg) + a_3\ (yus - yg) + a_4\ (rus - rg) + a_5\ (\dot{P}eus - \dot{P}eg) + a_6\ (bus - bg) + ut$$

Sample period	a_1	a_2	a_3	a_4	a_5	a_6	$\bar{R}^2$
1974M1 1978M9	−0.26	−0.01	−0.13	−0.40	0.85	−0.40	0.93
	(−1.13)	(−0.03)	(−0.06)	(−0.79)	(0.21)	(−4.37)	

Source: Frankel (1983), p. 104.

Pilbeam (1991) estimation for dollar–pound
   Estimated equation:

$$s = a_1 + a_2\ (mus - muk) + a_3\ (yus - yuk) + a_4\ (rus - ruk) + a_5\ (\dot{P}eus - \dot{P}euk) + a_6\ (bus - buk) + ut$$

Sample period	a_1	a_2	a_3	a_4	a_5	a_6	$\bar{R}^2$
1973Q1 1984Q4	3.85	0.64*	−0.50	0.16	0.02	−0.28	0.93
	(3.67)	(2.79)	(−1.01)	(0.40)	(0.21)	(−1.56)	

Source: Pilbeam (1991), p. 155.

Notes: Hypotheses are: $a_2 > 0$; $a_3 < 0$; $a_4 < 0$; $a_5 > 0$; $a_6 > 0$. An asterisk by a variable indicates that it is both of the correct sign and not statistically different from its hypothesized value.

9.7   Exchange rate models: a forecasting analysis

From the regression coefficients reported in **Table 9.4**, it is not possible to rank any of the alternative theories derived from the Frankel synthesis equation. Although the regression coefficients provide very little support for any of the theories this does not rule out the possibility that one of the exchange rate models may prove useful for forecasting purposes. In two important papers, Meese and Rogoff (1983a, 1983b) have tested the forecasting accuracy of popular exchange rate models. Their test procedures and results have been replicated by Pilbeam (1991) for the dollar–pound exchange rate and it is the results of that study which are reported here.

   Three models are tested, the flexible-price monetary model, the real interest rate model and the sticky-price portfolio balance model. For the purposes of forecasting the exchange rate, the three models are tested by using the variables which are deemed to be of interest from the Frankel synthesis equation regardless of whether the coefficients proved statistically significant or not. Pilbeam tests the forecasting accuracy of the models for the period 1979:1 to 1988:3 using a quarterly data set.

   In order to forecast the one-period-ahead exchange rate, a rolling regression technique was used, which meant reestimating the regression coefficients for each period t to forecast the exchange rate in time $t + 1$. For example, to forecast the 1979:1 exchange rate a regression for the period 1973:1 to 1978:4 was undertaken using the coefficients deemed to be relevant by a given theory; these estimated coefficients were then used to forecast the 1979:1 exchange rate. Next, to forecast the 1979:2 exchange rate the regression was redone using data from 1973:1 to 1979:1 to reestimate the coefficients and these new estimates were then used to forecast the 1979:2 period exchange rate, and so on. For the purposes of forecasting the exchange rate in time $t + 1$, the actual values of the exogenous (right-hand side) variables in time $t + 1$ were used. This latter point is important because it means that forecasts for one period ahead will not be based on the wrong moneys supplies, interest rates etc so that any forecasting error is due to the weakness of the models rather than inaccurate forecasting of the fundamentals.

It is important to emphasize that for the purposes of forecasting it was the regression estimates of coefficients that were employed and that these rarely corresponded to the theoretical values. For instance, the fully flexible monetarist model predicts that the coefficient a_2 for the money stock will be unity but in the regressions it hovered between 0.2 and 0.55, while for the portfolio balance model the coefficient for relative bond supplies was persistently wrong signed. The purpose of the exercise was to see if any of the three models could be empirically useful devices to forecast the exchange rate. Meese and Rogoff (1983b) used plausible theoretical coefficient values as opposed to the estimated coefficients for forecasting purposes, but their results were largely the same as using the above procedure which is the basis of their (1983a) study. **Table 9.5** shows the forecast values of the exchange rate of the three alternative models tested in the Pilbeam study and the actual exchange rate.

For the purposes of ranking the forecasting accuracy of the three models, a commonly used statistical measure known as the root-mean-squared error (RMSE) criterion was used. The RMSE criterion compares the predicted exchange rate with the actual exchange rate using the following formula:

$$\text{Mean-squared error (MSE)} = \frac{1}{n} \sum_{i=1}^{n} \frac{(s_{t+i*} - s_{t+i})^2}{s_{t+i}}$$

where n is the number of forecast, s_{t+i*} is the predicted exchange rate for period $t + i$ at time t and s_{t+i} is the actual exchange rate in period $t + i$.

$$\text{Root-mean-squared error (RMSE)} = \sqrt{\text{MSE}}$$

The lower the RMSE, the better the forecasting capability of the model. The results of the RMSE test for the three alternative exchange rate models are printed below, and these results are compared with the RMSE of a simple random-walk model of the exchange rate whereby the current exchange rate at time t is used as the forecast for the exchange rate in period t + 1. In other words, a random-walk forecast involves a speculator saying that the exchange rate forecast for one period's time (in this case three months) will be the same as it is today. Anyone without any knowledge of economics can make a random-walk forecast simply by opening the daily newspaper!

Root mean squared error	
Flexible-price monetary model	0.0806
Real interest differential model	0.0882
Sticky-price portfolio model	0.0870
Random walk model	0.0769

Note that the above results are based on the values of the exchange rate listed in **Table 9.5**. The reported results are in line with those of Meese and Rogoff (1983a and

Table 9.5 Exchange rate forecasts of different exchange rate models

Period	Flexible-price monetary model	Real interest differential model	Sticky-price portfolio model	Actual
1979Q1	1.9981	1.9888	2.0070	2.0688
1979Q2	2.1120	2.0954	2.1274	2.1684
1979Q3	2.1019	2.0884	2.1055	2.1976
1979Q4	2.1866	2.1789	2.1817	2.2240
1980Q1	2.2065	2.2577	2.2561	2.1668
1980Q2	2.1481	1.9965	2.0439	2.3620
1980Q3	2.3588	2.3897	2.3762	2.3883
1980Q4	2.3192	2.3307	2.3286	2.3850
1981Q1	2.3578	2.3547	2.3158	2.2442
1981Q2	2.2105	2.2136	2.2849	1.9428
1981Q3	1.9287	1.9147	1.9122	1.8005
1981Q4	1.7940	1.7911	1.7628	1.9080
1982Q1	1.9412	1.9654	1.9534	1.7817
1982Q2	1.7749	1.7746	1.7762	1.7383
1982Q3	1.7474	1.7409	1.7245	1.6927
1982Q4	1.7306	1.7340	1.7141	1.6145
1983Q1	1.6492	1.6509	1.6576	1.4790
1983Q2	1.4641	1.4638	1.4565	1.5304
1983Q3	1.5609	1.5610	1.5543	1.4957
1983Q4	1.4949	1.4946	1.4888	1.4506
1984Q1	1.4490	1.4497	1.4293	1.4426
1984Q2	1.4298	1.4284	1.4273	1.3527
1984Q3	1.3631	1.3622	1.3538	1.2480
1984Q4	1.2440	1.2416	1.2310	1.1565
1985Q1	1.1630	1.1630	1.1851	1.2430
1985Q2	1.2177	1.2163	1.2300	1.2951
1985Q3	1.3465	1.3523	1.3408	1.4010
1985Q4	1.4108	1.4159	1.3822	1.4445
1986Q1	1.4483	1.4509	1.4693	1.4853
1986Q2	1.5148	1.5124	1.5031	1.5303
1986Q3	1.5239	1.5305	1.5144	1.4500
1986Q4	1.4865	1.4862	1.4664	1.4745
1987Q1	1.4278	1.4250	1.4443	1.6050
1987Q2	1.6476	1.6482	1.6374	1.6100
1987Q3	1.6159	1.6161	1.5815	1.6297
1987Q4	1.6130	1.6131	1.6162	1.8715
1988Q1	1.9464	1.9482	–	1.8798
1988Q2	1.8681	1.8681	–	1.7093
1988Q3	1.6390	1.6400	–	1.6855

Notes: The above figures are dollar–pound rates.
Source: Pilbeam (1991), p. 158.

1983b) in showing that a simple random-walk model has a superior forecasting power than any of the popular models of exchange rate determination. Such a result is quite devastating for professional forecasters who use sophisticated econometric models, because it suggests that anyone by opening a newspaper can on average outperform a sophisticated exchange rate model designed by groups of professional forecasters (this leaves us with the puzzle of explaining those forecasters' high salaries!). In addition to the poor root-mean-squared errors, **Table 9.5** shows that none of the models does very well at forecasting the exchange rate at the three month horizon. In fact, in the Meese and Rogoff studies, it is shown that it is only at the 12-months plus horizon that exchange rate models start (in some instances) to outperform the random-walk model. The abysmal performance of the theories requires some explanation which is attempted in the next section.

9.8 Explaining the poor results of exchange rate models

In addition to the Meese and Rogoff studies and the Pilbeam study, other researchers comparing existing exchange rate models with varying degrees of econometric technicality have shown that exchange rate models perform poorly empirically. (See for example, Frankel (1984) who tests his synthesis equation for the deutschmark, yen, pound, French franc and Canadian dollar against the US dollar; Bakus (1984) who concentrates on the Canadian–US dollar rates; Leventakis (1987) who concentrates on the deutschmark–US dollar; and Hacche and Townend (1981) who failed in their attempt to model sterling's effective exchange rate.) Although some authors such as MacDonald and Taylor (1993) have managed to beat the random walk model using a relatively sophisticated dynamic specification of the monetary model for forecasting the deutschmark–dollar parity, they only manage to do so by a very small margin and their results could be time-specific and a result of the application of very sophisticated techniques. Overall, the empirical studies reveal that the failure of existing exchange rate models is quite general.

No doubt one could engage in a data-mining exercise looking at particular sub-periods, a variety of bilateral exchange rates using different estimation techniques, and present evidence (by excluding results that do not support your model!) favouring a given theory. However, it is surely better to recognize that there is no clear-cut empirical support for any given theory. This failure to satisfactorily account for exchange rate behaviour does not mean that the exchange rate models are necessarily wrong, rather it probably reflects the enormous econometric problems of modelling exchange rate behaviour. In fact, the exchange rate theories provide many reasons as to why exchange rates will be difficult to model empirically. Among the more important are:

- Exchange rates are determined not simply by the stance of monetary policy, but depend in a complex and as yet little understood manner upon the monetary/fiscal policy mix and the interactions of these macroeconomic policies between countries.
- The theoretical literature on exchange rate determination since the advent of floating exchange rates has made it abundantly clear that the current exchange rate depends not only upon the present fundamentals, but also upon the expected future course of those fundamentals. For this reason, new information which alters perceptions about the future course of these fundamental factors will have an impact upon the current exchange rate. It is extremely difficult to identify and model changes in new information and how they are discounted into the current exchange rate.
- Another related problem has become known in the literature as the 'Finance Minister Problem' or 'Peso Problem'. Even if we have a correct model of

exchange rate determination and an event relevant to the exchange rate is widely expected to occur at some time in the future (the appointment of a new finance minister or increase in the money supply) this will affect the current exchange rate. However, if the expected event does not materialize (the finance minister is not appointed or the money supply is not increased) then the movements in the exchange rate will appear unrelated to the supposed underlying determinants. The model itself would not be wrong but the empirical test would not verify it.

- Another closely related problem was illustrated in **Box 9.1**. The dynamic path of the exchange rate will be completely different depending upon whether a given shock or policy disturbance has been anticipated or unanticipated. As we shall see in section 9.10, while some empirical progress has been made in identifying anticipated and unanticipated exchange rate movements, it is has so far not been possible to accurately integrate such effects into an empirically testable exchange rate model.

- All modern asset-market models of exchange rate determination are in agreement that expectations are crucial to the determination of the current exchange rate. However, both in theory and when it comes to the empirical test of a theory, the econometrics requires that we adopt some major simplifications. In the first instance, most theories assume that expectations are homogeneous when in the real world they are clearly heterogeneous as taking the predictions for the future spot exchange rate from professional forecasters will testify. Also, when it comes to empirical implementation it becomes necessary to adopt further radical simplifications. Some models assume perfect foresight on the part of foreign exchange market participants, so that expectations are fully consistent with the underlying theoretical model, while other models assume that exchange rate expectations are static or follow a regressive expectations scheme. It is unlikely that any of these expectation mechanisms properly specifies expectations formation in an uncertain world (see section 9.10). Until we are able to more realistically model exchange rate expectations we shall remain unable to satisfactorily model exchange rate behaviour.

- Another problem that may be particularly acute is that it has not only been changes in the supply of money that have been important in explaining the exchange rate, but also instability in the demand-for-money schedules. Theoretically such shifts are as important in determining the exchange rate as changes in the money stock. In an attempt to study the problem of shifts in money demand Frankel (1984) found that taking account of such shifts could improve the performance of the monetary model.

- A particularly acute problem in attempts to model exchange rate behaviour since the advent of floating rates is to incorporate into the empirical model the role of real shocks on exchange rate movements.

- A final problem worth mentioning and probably of considerable importance has been the enormous changes in the financial and real structure of economies. These have had important implications for the performance of economies and thereby on the exchange rate.

This list of reasons as to why it may prove empirically difficult to verify existing exchange rate models is rather formidable. The implication is that a given theory may be correct, but it may not pass an empirical test.

9.9 The 'news' approach to modelling exchange rates

Although models of exchange rate determination measured in terms of levels have not proved particularly successful, some success has been achieved with modelling exchange rate behaviour in a 'news' context. An attractive feature of the 'news' approach is that it combines the concept of exchange market efficiency with modern models of exchange rate determination, and for this reason it is worth considering the approach in some detail.

Authors such as Dornbusch (1980) and Frenkel (1981) have suggested that the correct way to model exchange rate movements is to presume that the foreign exchange market is efficient, in the sense that all *ex ante* profit opportunities are eliminated. This being the case, movements in exchange rates will be due to the arrival of new information. As we shall see, the way that the two authors model news is somewhat different, but their results do provide some support for the 'news' approach.

The basic tenet of the news approach is that if the foreign exchange market is efficient then any difference between the forward rate and the corresponding rate that later transpires must in an efficient market (with no risk premium) be due to the arrival of new information. In other words, unanticipated exchange rate movements are due to unexpected changes in the fundamentals. A typical specification of a 'news' model of exchange rates is the following:

$$s_t - f_{t/t-1} = a_1 + a_2 uX_t + a_3 uY_t + a_4 uZ_t + u_t \qquad (9.14)$$

where s_t is the log of the spot exchange rate at time t, $f_{t/t-1}$ is the log of the forward exchange rate for time t at time $t - 1$, uX_t, uY_t and uZ_t are the log of unexpected changes in the fundamental variables X, Y and Z.

The main problem for the news-type models is obtaining a proxy for the unexpected change in the fundamentals (right-hand side of equation (9.14)). While the actual change in the selected fundamentals is known, the problem is to devise proxies for what was the expected change. By deducting from the actual change in a variable the proxy for the expected change in that variable, we are left with the unexpected change.

In devising a proxy for the unexpected change in the exchange rate we can invoke the EMH. In other words, the expected spot rate is given by the forward exchange rate in the previous period. Hence, by deducting from the actual exchange rate the previous period's forward rate we have a proxy for the unexpected change in the exchange rate.

As for the unexpected change in the fundamentals, one has to firstly decide what are the fundamental variables X_t, Y_t and Z_t and so on. This choice will obviously be dependent upon the exchange rate model selected. Having selected the model it is then necessary devise the proxies for the unexpected change in the variables chosen. There are several alternative methods for devising such proxies:

1 Use publicly available forecasts – this is the approach taken by Dornbusch (1980), who takes the six-monthly forecasts of the OECD as broadly representative of informed opinion about expected economic growth rates and current account balances. By deducting these forecasts from what subsequently occurred, he obtains a proxy for the unexpected change in these variables.

2   Use regression analysis. We can take a fundamental variable X make it a dependent variable and make a forecast of what X will be the next period on the basis the expected values of its supposed determinants. That is:

$$X_{t/t-1} = a_1 + a_2 L_{t/t-1} + a_3 M_{t/t-1} + a_4 N_{t/t-1} + \ldots + u_t$$

where $X_{t/t-1}$ is the forecast value for the fundamental variable X_t at time $t-1$, $L_{t/t-1}$, $M_{t/t-1}$ and $N_{t/t-1}$ are the expected values for the fundamental variables L, M and N for time t at time $t-1$ that are supposed to be useful for predicting variable X one period ahead.

The above regression would then yield a forecast (expected) value for X_t that could be deducted from the actual value to yield the unexpected change. This method is not very popular because it depends on having a good explanatory model for the variable X. This is very rarely the case in economics!

3   Use a time series methodology known as autoregression. With this method the forecast value of fundamental variable X is determined purely by a regression of past values of X. That is:

$$X_{t/t-1} = a_1 + a_2 X_{t-1} + a_3 X_{t-2} + a_4 X_{t-3} + \ldots + ut$$

where X_{t-1}, X_{t-2}, and X_{t-3} etc are increasingly previous values of the variable X. This method is a fairly popular way of generating a forecast for the value of X as one is effectively extrapolating from the current and past values of X in order to generate an expected value of X.

In the Dornbusch (1980) and Frenkel (1981) studies that pioneered the 'news' approach, the results were found to be highly supportive. Generally, the unexpected changes in the fundamentals (that is, the news items) were found to be significant determinants of the unexpected change in the exchange rate and the coefficients of the expected sign. However, the choice of fundamental variables in the studies was rather *ad hoc*, not involving tests of formal exchange rate models.

In a test of the news version of the real interest rate differential model, Edwards (1982) runs the following regression:

$$s_t = a_1 f_{t/t-1} + a_2(um - um^*)_t + a_3(uy - uy^*)_t + a_4(ui - ui^*)_t + ut$$

where $f_{t/t-1}$ is the one-period-ahead forward exchange rate at time $t-1$, um is the log of unexpected change in domestic money supply, uy is the unexpected increase in domestic income and ui is the unexpected change in the domestic real interest rate. An asterisk denotes the corresponding unexpected change in the foreign variable.

The expected signs in the coefficients are $a_1=1$ as the forward rate is an unbiased predictor of the future spot rate (that is EMH); a_2 is positive so that a relative unexpected rise in the domestic money supply leads to a unexpected depreciation; a_3 should be negative as an unexpected rise in relative domestic income leads to an unexpected appreciation; a_4 should be negative as an unexpected rise in domestic real interest should lead to an unexpected appreciation. The results of the Edwards study are reported in Table 9.6.

These results provide mixed support for the 'news' approach. As can be seen, the unexpected money supply coefficient is correctly signed and significant for two of the

Table 9.6   Test of the news exchange rate model

| Rate | Estimated equation $s_t = a_1 f_{t/t-1} + a_2 (um - um^*)_t + a_3 (uy - uy^*)_t + a_4 (ui - ui^*)_t + u_t$ | | | | |
	a_1	a_2	a_3	a_4	DW
Pound/dollar	0.97*	0.10	0.01	0.01	1.85
	(48.5)	(0.67)	(3.00)	(0.39)	
French franc/dollar	0.95*	0.36*	0.18	−0.01	1.88
	(25.70)	(2.53)	(7.91)	(−0.33)	
Deutschmark/dollar	0.96*	0.37*	0.24	0.01	2.09
	(45.60)	(2.04)	(1.40)	(0.48)	

Notes: Hypothesis is: $a_1 = 1$; $a_2 > 0$; $a_3 < 0$; $a_4 < 0$. An asterisk by a variable indicates that it is both of the correct sign and not statistically different from its hypothesised value. All currencies are against the US dollar. *t*-statistics are in parentheses.
Source: Edwards (1982) June 73–Sept 79.

currencies, while the coefficient for expected output is significant but of the wrong sign! However, the unexpected change in the real interest differential is not statistically significant.

Apart from the original Dornbusch and Frenkel studies, MacDonald (1983) tested a news-type model for six currencies against the US dollar over the period 1972:Q1 to 1979:Q4. He found that monetary developments are sometimes statistically important but occasionally with the wrong sign!

An interesting finding by both Edwards (1983) and MacDonald (1983) is that in some regressions past news (that is, lagged news terms) can have a significant effect on the unexpected exchange rate change. Such an effect is incompatible with the concept of exchange market efficiency. Edwards argues that this effect may be due to a lag in the publication of data. MacDonald also finds that lagged news terms can be statistically significant even with a lag of up to four periods. This is something of a mystery because while publication lags may account for significant one-period lags, it is difficult to rationalize two or three-period lags. In sum, although some of the news items move exchange rates in the direction predicted, the results are not particularly robust across different currencies and the news items are sometimes statistically significant but wrong signed! Furthermore, the fact that lagged news items can be significant for more than one period does not tie in with the concept of exchange market efficiency. Although results using lagged news effects are not particularly robust.

In a recent study, Ehrmann and Fratzscher (2004) examine the impact of news using daily data for the dollar–deutschmark (euro) for the period January 1993 to February 2003. They subtract the median money market survey views of the likely announcement for a set of 25 macro variables (such as GDP growth, money supply growth, inflation, unemployment, trade balance, retail sales and so on) from the actual announced values to find the news element and find that they can successfully explain 73% of the direction of exchange rate movements. In their study, they find that it is important to use real-time data when examining the impact of news, that is data actually released at the time rather than vintage data – revised data is often released months after the original data typically used in exchange rate studies. When they use vintage data they can only successfully predict 60% of the direction of exchange rate movements. They also find that the impact of news varies with market conditions; in particular, news has a greater impact in times when there is a high degree of market uncertainty and when previous exchange rate volatility has been large. Their study is not entirely successful, however; while an unexpected tightening of US monetary policy such as an unexpected 50 basis points rise in the Federal funds interest rate leads to a 0.8% appreciation of the dollar, an unexpected interest rate hike by the Bundesbank or European central bank did not seem to have a similar effect on the deutschmark/euro. One final point from the study is that while they find that the news approach is good at explaining the direction of exchange rate movements, it tends to explain only around 40% of the magnitude of exchange rate movements that have actually occurred. The authors hypothesise that this might be due to an overreaction on the part of market participant to news announcements.

Overall, the news approach which combines the concept of exchange market efficiency with conventional exchange rate models has proved a relatively fruitful area for exchange rate research. Nonetheless, given that the empirical evidence on exchange market efficiency and conventional exchange rate models both have little empirical support, it is not surprising that the news approach which combines the two concepts has somewhat mixed empirical support.

9.10 The longer-run predictability of exchange rate movements

Given the failure of models to successfully predict exchange rate movements in the short run, there has been more emphasis in the recent literature on trying to predict exchange rate movements over the longer run. An interesting paper in this respect is that of Nelson Mark (1995). The basic approach taken by Mark is to run regressions of the following equation:

$$s_{t+k} - s_t = \alpha_k + \beta_k (z_t - s_t) + u_{t+k} \text{ where } k, 1, 4, 8, 12, 16 \tag{9.15}$$

where s_{t+k} is the k-step ahead exchange rate forecast, s_t is the spot exchange rate, z_t is a fundamental variable significant for exchange rate determination, for example, $z_t = [(m_t - m_t^*) - \eta(y_t - y_t^*)]$ from the monetary model, it should be noted that Mark imposes the restriction that the income elasticity of money demand (η) is equal to unity and u_{t+k} is a random error.

If the fundamental equation is useful at predicting exchange rates, then we would expect to find $\beta_k > 0$ and significant, and that it should increase with the time horizon k; whereas if $\beta_k = 0$ then there is mean reversion in the exchange rate and it is unrelated to economic fundamentals. Note that lagged fundamentals are being used to predict the future exchange rate this arises from the error correction mechanism methodology employed. Mark estimates equation (9.15) using quarterly data for the period 1973:Q2 to 1991:Q4 for the Canadian dollar, the deutschmark, yen and Swiss franc against the dollar using 1, 4, 8, 12, and 16 quarters ahead.

As shown in **Table 9.7**, the point estimates of β_k are all positive and increase with time k as does the explanatory power of the regression as reflected in the R^2 statistic, and except in the case of the Canadian dollar the significance of the estimates of β_k improve with time. One negative result from the Mark study, however, is that the estimated β_k coefficients are not statistically different from zero, although Mark argues that this may be due mainly to the small sample size available. More positively, in a forecasting exercise Mark finds that he is able to beat a random-walk forecast using the

Table 9.7   Tests of the validity of the monetary model under floating exchange rates

Estimated equation $s_{t+k} - s_t = \alpha_k + \beta_k (z_t - s_t) + u_{t+k}$ where k, 1, 4, 8, 12, 16					
	Canadian dollar			Swiss Franc	
k	β_k	R^2	k	β_k	R^2
1	0.040	0.059	1	0.074	0.051
4	0.155	0.114	4	0.285	0.180
8	0.349	0.351	8	0.568	0.265
12	0.438	0.336	12	0.837	0.538
16	0.450	0.254	16	1.086	0.771
	Deutschmark			Yen	
1	0.035	0.015	1	0.047	0.020
4	0.205	0.104	4	0.263	0.125
8	0.554	0.265	8	0.575	0.301
12	0.966	0.527	12	0.945	0.532
16	1.324	0.762	16	1.273	0.694

Note: The data set employed covers the period 1973:Q2 to 1991:Q4.
Source: Mark (1995).

deutschmark, yen and Swiss franc at the four-year horizon using the monetary model, but in the case of the Canadian dollar the random-walk model still wins out. Overall, Mark's results seem to suggest that economic fundamentals and the monetary model contain significant information for the determination of the long-run exchange rate.

In a follow-up study, Mark and Sul (2001) using quarterly data for a panel of 19 countries for the period 1973:Q1 to 1997:Q1 find further support for the monetary model in the long run and suggest that it is better than the use of PPP as a modelling device for the long-run exchange rate. They show that in an out-of-sample forecasting exercise for 13 out of 18 currencies, the monetary model can (very marginally) improve forecasts of exchange rates at the one-period-ahead quarterly forecast horizon compared to a random-walk forecast. In addition, the PPP model can also be shown to very marginally improve upon a random-walk forecast at the quarterly investment horizon. At the 16-quarter investment horizon, the monetary model is able to decisively beat the random walk for 17 of the 18 currencies, as does the PPP model. However, a word of caution is introduced in the Mark and Sul (2001) study in that the beating of the random-walk forecast is valid when either the dollar or Swiss franc are used as the *numeraire* currency. If, instead, the Japanese yen is used as the *numeraire* currency, the random walk beats the monetary model at the quarterly investment horizon and, more importantly, the random walk even beats both the monetary and PPP models even at the 16-quarter horizon! Another note of caution is that Faust *et al.* (2003) show that if one uses original released data (that is data available at the time forecasts are made) rather than fully revised data (which was not available to market participants at the time), their results undermine to some extent Mark's (1995) study especially for the yen and deutschmark parities against the dollar. They also show that exchange rate forecasts are generally much better using real-time data rather than fully revised *ex post* data as has been done in virtually all exchange rate studies including the classic Meese and Rogoff studies.

Table 9.8 Cross-section estimates of the long-run monetary model

	Estimated equation $\overline{\Delta s_t} = \beta + \beta_1\,(\overline{\Delta m_t}) + \beta_2\,(\overline{\Delta y_t}) + u_t$			$\bar{R}^2$
	β	β_1	β_2	
US dollar	−0.004	1.039	−2.229	0.78
	(0.001)	(0.178)	(0.754)	
German Deutschmark	0.005	1.024	−1.953	0.77
	(0.001)	(0.168)	(0.725)	

Notes: Hypothesis is $\beta_1 = 1$ and $\beta_2 < 0$ (−1 in monetarist theory). Standard errors are in parentheses.
Source: Groen (2000).

Further support for the monetary model as a long-run description of the data is provided by Groen (2000), who tests the following exchange rate model using both cross-sectional data and pooled panel-data methods (a mixture of time series and cross-sectional data) for a group of 14 countries for the period 1973:Q1 to 1994:Q4. Using either the dollar or the deutschmark as the *numeraire* currency provides long-run support for the monetary model. Using cross-sectional data, Groen estimates if the average exchange rate change $\overline{\Delta s_t}$ is related to the average differential money $\overline{\Delta m_t}$ supply growth rate and the average differential change in real income $\overline{\Delta y_t}$ as given by equation (9.26)

$$\overline{\Delta s_t} = \beta + \beta_1\,(\overline{\Delta m_t}) + \beta_2\,(\overline{\Delta y_t}) + u_t \tag{9.16}$$

where the expected sign for the coefficients is $\beta_1 = 1$ and $\beta_2 < 0$.

The results reported by Groen are quite favourable to the monetary model as a long-run description of the data with the following two regressions as reported in **Table 9.8**.

As can be seen, the cross-sectional estimates show that as an average long-run description of the data for the 14 currencies the monetary model seems to perform very well; the estimated β_1 coefficient is significant and one cannot reject the hypothesis that it is equal to unity as predicted by the monetary model. Furthermore, the income elasticity of money demand is negative and significant as predicted by the model (although more negative than the −1 predicted in many monetary models). In addition, using a more sophisticated pooled panel data methodolgy, Groen obtains estimates for β_1 and β_2 that are ($\beta_1 = 0.664$, $\beta_2 = -1.335$) for the dollar and ($\beta1 = 0.923$, $\beta2 = -1.832$) for the deutschmark. All this shows that the monetary model seems to have quite good long-run predictive powers for explaining exchange rate movements.

In an interesting paper, Rapach and Wohar (2002) take a different approach to Mark (1995) and test the monetary model for 14 currencies against the US dollar. They test the validity of the monetary model using very-long-run data using annual data covering the period 1880–1995 (in most cases). Their results show considerable support for the monetary model for France, Italy, Netherlands and Spain, moderate support for Belgium, Finland and Portugal and only weak support for Switzerland. However, they fail to find support for Australia, Canada, Denmark, Norway, Sweden and the UK. One problem with using relatively long periods of data is that the test covers many

Table 9.9 Long-run tests of the monetary model

| Country | Estimated equation $s_t = \beta + \beta_1 (m_t - m_t^*) + \beta 2(y_t - y_t^*) + u_t$ | |
	$\beta 1$	$\beta 2$
Australia (1880–1995)	0.45	–0.41
	(0.3)	(0.63)
Belgium (1880–1989)	0.93	–1.06
	(0.25)	(0.23)
Canada (1880–1995)	0.20	0.08
	(0.08)	(0.08)
France (1880–1989)	1.03	–0.09
	(0.14)	(0.54)
Italy (1880–95)	0.98	–1.87
	(0.02)	(0.25)
Spain (1901–95)	0.85	–1.05
	(0.04)	(0.l4)
Switzerland (1880–1995)	1.59	–2.42
	(0.52)	(0.61)
United Kingdom (1880–1995)	0.31	–0.71
	(0.13)	(0.16)

Notes: The hypothesis is that $\beta_1 = 1$ and $\beta_2 < 0$ (–1 in monetarist theory). We report only a selection of the Johansen maximum likelihood estimates from the paper. Standard errors are in parentheses.
Source: Rapach and Wohar (2002).

different exchange rate regimes including the gold standard, the Bretton Woods system and the recent period of floating. A key test in the paper is as follows:

$$s_t = \beta + \beta_1 (m_t - m_t^*) + \beta_2(y_t - y_t^*) + u_t \qquad (9.17)$$

According to the monetary model then we would expect $\beta_1 = 1$ and $\beta_2 = -1$. A summary of the results for some of the currencies is shown in **Table 9.9**.

Other recent studies such as Kilian (1999) and Kilian and Taylor (2003) based on long-run regressions produce more mixed results, but the latter study using a simple purchasing power parity-based model of fundamentals, that is setting $z_t = s_t = (p_t - p_t^*)$ as in the Mark (1995 study) and allowing for non-linearity in the data-generating process, find strong evidence in favour of longer-term predictability of the nominal exchange rate suggesting that PPP is a valid long-run proposition. Kilian and Taylor (2003) argue that one reason for the failure of existing exchange rate models is that they are based on linear relationships between macro determinants and exchange rates. This means that they may be missing important non-linear relationships between exchange rates and macro fundamentals. In particular, the long-run funda- mentals are represented by PPP and Kilian and Taylor allow for a non-linear adjust- ment mechanism of exchange rate deviations from PPP to their PPP values. They look at seven bilateral dollar parities using quarterly data, and while their forecasts fail to beat the random walk in the short run they find that for six of the seven pari- ties they are able to beat a random-walk forecast at a time horizon of two to three years. However, they are unable to beat the random-walk model in periods of six months or less, suggesting that the Meese and Rogoff (1983) results remain robust at the short-term horizon. Indeed, they are unable to decisively refute the Meese and Rogoff results in an out-of-sample test at even longer-term horizons, although this is in due part to the low power of the statistical tests given the amount of forecasts that they are able to make.

It now seems that there is now an accumulation of recent quite sophisticated econometric evidence that suggests that *long-run* exchange rates can in large part be modelled on the basis of economic fundamentals such as the monetary model of exchange rate determination. The evidence is somewhat mixed and the success of the monetary model in the long run cannot yet be categorized as a 'stylized fact'. However, it is becoming a stylized fact that economic fundamentals are proving better for both modelling and forecasting the long-run exchange rate than the short-run exchange rate.

9.11 Modelling exchange rate expectations

Given the importance of future expected exchange rates for the current exchange rate, any satisfactory model of exchange rates must model exchange rate expectations. The problem is that modelling economic agents' expectations is an area of considerable controversy in economics. There are a variety of alternative but plausible methods of modelling expectations, and in this section we briefly look at some of the popular hypotheses used and summarise some of the recent empirical research in this area.

There are six plausible theoretical methods for modelling the expected future exchange rate: static expectations, adaptive expectations, regressive expectations, rational expectations and perfect foresight!

Static expectations

$$Es_{t+1/t} = s_t$$

The expected exchange rate in one period's time ($Es_{t+1/t}$) is equal to the current exchange rate (s_t). In other words, the average expectation is that the exchange rate will not change. Such an average exchange rate expectation could be rationalized by assuming that economic agents consider that there is an equal probability of the exchange rate appreciating or depreciating by a given percentage. In other words, if the current exchange rate is £0.50/$1, the exchange rate expected one year hence is also £0.50/$1.

Adaptive expectations

$$Es_{t+1/t} = \alpha s_t + (1 - \alpha)Es_{t/t-1} \qquad 0 < \alpha < 1$$

The expected exchange rate in one period's time is equal to a weighted average of the current exchange rate and the exchange rate that was expected to be the current exchange rate one period before ($Es_{t/t-1}$). Thus, if the current exchange rate exceeds the previously anticipated current exchange rate then agents will revise upwards their forecasts as compared to previous periods' forecasts. For instance, if the current pound–dollar rate is £0.50/$1, but agents had one year previously thought it would be £0.40/$1, their forecast for the pound in one year's time will be above £0.40/$1 but below £0.50/$1. How close it is to the current rate will depend on the weight attached to the current exchange rate (the larger is α).

Extrapolative expectations

$$Es_{t+1/t} = s_t + m(s_t - s_{t-1}) \qquad m > 0$$

The expected exchange rate in one period's time is equal to the current exchange rate plus some multiple (m) of the change in the exchange rate during preceding period. If the current exchange rate is £0.50/$1 and one year previously the pound stood at £0.40/$1 (that is it depreciated by £0.10/$1 over the previous year), the expected exchange rate one year hence will be somewhere above £0.50/$1. If m is less than one it will be between £0.50/$1 and £0.60/$1, while if m is greater than 1 it will be above £0.60/$1. In other words, if the pound depreciated the previous year it is expected to depreciate in the forthcoming year.

Regressive expectations

$$Es_{t+1/t} = \alpha s_t + (1 - \alpha)s^* \qquad 0 < \alpha < 1$$

The expected exchange rate in one period's time is a weighted function of the current exchange rate and agents' estimate of the long-run equilibrium exchange rate (s*). If the current exchange rate is different to the long-run equilibrium exchange rate, the expected exchange rate in the next period will lie closer to the equilibrium rate than the current exchange rate. For example, if the current exchange rate is £0.50/$1 but the underlying long-term equilibrium rate is believed to be £0.60/$1, then the expected exchange rate one year hence will lie between £0.50/$1 and £0.60/$1. In other words, the exchange rate is expected to converge towards its long-run equilibrium exchange rate.

Rational expectations

$$Es_{t+1/t} = s_{t+1} + u_{t+1}$$

The expected exchange rate in the next period will on average equal the actual exchange rate (s_{t+1}), although it may deviate by a random error of u_{t+1}; the average of u_{t+1} being zero. On average the exchange rate that is expected to materialize is the exchange rate that materializes. The rational expectations hypothesis is that on average, over a number of time periods, economic agents do not systematically over- or underpredict the exchange rate. They may make forecast errors but these mistakes consist of sometimes overpredicting the future exchange rate and sometimes underpredicting it.

Perfect foresight

$$Es_{t+1/t} = s_{t+1}$$

The expected exchange rate in the next period is equal to the actual exchange rate that materializes in the next period. This suggests that economic agents have a complete knowledge of the model underlying exchange rate determination so that they do not make any errors concerning the future exchange rate.

Which expectations hypothesis is best?

All of the above expectations mechanisms have some degree of plausibility; however, the static expectation, adaptive expectation and extrapolative expectation mechanisms are somewhat arbitrary because they say that the future exchange rate can be predicted entirely on the basis of current and past values of the exchange rate. As such, no attention is paid to other information that may be relevant to the future exchange rate such as domestic and foreign inflation rates, interest rates, fiscal and monetary policy stance, and so on.

The regressive expectations mechanism, rational expectations and perfect foresight models are from a theoretical viewpoint much better suited to dealing with exchange rates because they all allow for economic agents using a far wider set of information. The regressive expectations mechanism requires that economic agents form a view concerning the appropriate long-run equilibrium exchange rate, while the rational expectations hypothesis suggests that although agents do not always get the exact exchange rate right, they nevertheless do not systematically get things wrong. Finally, the perfect foresight model implies that economic agents actually have the correct model of exchange rate determination and thereby they do not make errors with regard to the future exchange rate. While this latter case may seem unrealistic, it does have the major advantage that the exchange rate implications from models that employ perfect foresight are purely due to the structure of the model itself and not because of an arbitrary specification of exchange rate expectations.

9.12 Empirical tests of different expectations mechanisms

There are great difficulties in modelling exchange rate expectations; in particular market expectations concerning the expected future spot rate are not directly observable and if one uses the forward rate as a proxy then this constitutes a joint test of the rational expectations hypothesis and the non-existence of a risk premium. Fortunately, sets of survey data concerning market participants' forecasts for the future exchange rate do exist; such data sets are made up of forecasts from various market participants such as economists, bankers, corporate treasurers, forecasting agencies, central bankers, investment managers and the like.

Dominguez (1986) using Money Market Services data for the period 1983–85 rejects the rational expectations hypothesis for modelling one-week, one-month and three-month expectations for all currencies studied. Frankel and Froot (1987) use survey data to examine extrapolative, adaptive and regressive expectations mechanisms and find a difference between short-run and long-run expectations. In particular, they find evidence that for short-term horizons of one week to one month, that expectations tend to be extrapolative. However, in the longer run of 6 to 12 months they find expectations tend to be regressive with the exchange rate moving towards its long-run value as proxied by PPP. They argue that this may reflect the fact that market participants use chartist and technical analysis in the short run, whereas economic fundamentals are more widely used for longer-run forecasting. However, Liu and Maddala (1992) using the cointegration technique find that the rational expectations hypothesis cannot be rejected at the one-week-ahead forecasting horizon, although they reject the rational expectations hypothesis at the one-month-plus time horizon. Meanwhile, Allen and Taylor (1990) are unable to reject the null hypothesis of static expectations for very-short-term forecasts. Finally, Cavaglia *et al.* (1994) reject the hypothesis of rational expectations and indeed find some evidence that expectations are irrational.

In sum, the empirical evidence concerning which expectations mechanisms are best for modelling exchange rates expectations is very mixed. The most plausible story is that the appropriate expectations mechanism is itself time-variant, with market participants sometimes having static expectations, sometimes extrapolative expectations, sometimes regressive expectations, and so on. The rational expectations mechanism, while theoretically highly plausible, seems to be far from the complete story. Furthermore, it must also be recognized that the studies tend to take the median forecast of various market participants' forecasts for the purpose of empirical testing of the various expectation hypotheses; however, authors such as MacDonald and Marsh (1996) have shown that there is usually a high degree of heterogeneity in market participants' forecasts, suggesting that economic agents process information differently and that any individual expectations hypothesis is unlikely to capture the actual diversity present in the marketplace.

9.13 Alternative approaches to modelling exchange rates: the role of chartists and fundamentalists

Partly due to the failure of existing exchange rate models to satisfactorily account for exchange rate behaviour, a number of recent papers such as Goodhart (1987), Allen and Taylor (1989), Frankel and Froot (1990), De Grauwe and Vansanten (1991) and Pilbeam (1995) have started to analyse the role played by various groups in the foreign exchange market. Two groups that have attracted an increasing amount of attention are the so-called 'chartists' and 'fundamentalists'.

Chartists claim to be able to successfully predict the future behaviour of a variable such as the exchange rate merely by examining a variety of recent charts of the exchange rate. Chartists claim that certain patterns of behaviour repeat themselves and that by detecting the relevant pattern in play, considerable success can be had in predicting the future exchange rate. Many of the patterns are given names such as 'head and shoulders', 'triple bottom', 'ascending triangle', and 'double top', and Feeny (1989) provides an excellent summary of chartist methodology. The important point about chartists is that the only information they require to predict exchange rates is the recent past behaviour of the exchange rate itself; 'economic fundamentals' such as money supplies, interest rates, the balance of payments position are not required. Critics of chartists are inclined to accuse them of 'having long rulers and small brains!'

Fundamentalists are economists that argue that the best way to predict the future course of exchange rates is to look at the prospectives for underlying economic fundamentals such as the future interest rates, balance of payments prospects, inflation rates and so forth. The important thing about fundamentalists is that they believe that the foreign exchange market is efficient, so past behaviour of the exchange rate will be of little use in predicting the course of the exchange rate. What matters for the exchange rate is the prospective development of the economic fundamentals.

Frankel and Froot (1990) argue that much exchange rate behaviour may be explained by the fact that at certain times chartists have the upper hand in determining the exchange rate, while at other times the fundamentalists have the upper hand. In periods of high uncertainty over the course of economic fundamentals, chartists tend to be the predominant force in the exchange market; while at times when economic fundamentals strongly point to a certain path for the exchange rate, the fundamentalists become the predominant force.

There are a wide range of views within both chartism and fundamentalism. Allen and Taylor (1989) conducted a survey of the influence of chartism on the London foreign exchange market, and they found that chartism is widely used as an input for short-term forecasting, while fundamental analysis is mainly used for longer-term forecasting. On each Tuesday during the period June 1988 to March 1989 they asked a sample of chartists for their exchange rate forecasts for the sterling–dollar, dollar–mark and dollar–yen for both one week and one month ahead. It was noted that there was a tendency for chartists to underpredict a rise in the exchange rate and overpredict in a falling market. This suggests that chartists' 'elasticity of expectations' is less than unity – that is, a 1% rise (fall) in the exchange rate appears to induce a less than 1% expected rise (fall) in the following period. However, one chartist codenamed 'Mr M' did manage to consistently outperform the random-walk model. Allen and Taylor found that there were significant differences in the forecasts between individual chartists, and chartist forecasts were generally worse than a random-walk forecast. It seems that chartists are just as bad as economists in forecasting exchange rates.

Given the variety of chartist and fundamental methods that could be used to forecast the exchange rate, an obvious question arises as to which method is most profitable. In a study of this issue, Pilbeam (1995) using quarterly data from January 1973 to the end of 1994 conducted a study of the relative investment performance of three groups of hypothetical traders; chartists, fundamentalists and simpletons. The chartist group was made up of three traders that come up with different forecasts merely by using past movements of the exchange rate to forecast the future exchange rate. Similarly, the fundamentalist group was made up of three traders that use different exchange rate models for forecasting the future exchange rate, namely the flexible-price monetary model, the Frankel sticky-price monetary model and the portfolio balance model. Finally, a group of three simpleton traders was introduced that merely uses simple trading rules when investing their funds. For example, a 'foreign simpleton' places all his money into the foreign currency and leaves it there to earn the foreign interest rate plus (less) any appreciation (depreciation) of the foreign currency; a 'highest simpleton' places his funds into the currency that provided the highest return (interest rate and exchange rate return) in the previous quarter; while, finally, a 'random-walk simpleton' who believes the exchange rate follows a random walk merely places his funds in the currency with the highest international interest rate since he expects no gain to be made on the average from exchange rate movements. The key results from the Pilbeam study are shown in **Table 9.10** – the respective group yields and standard deviations derived by taking the average of the three traders associated with each group for the period 1974–94.

The study shows that there is no clear-cut winner in terms of profitability and could not reject the hypothesis that the annualized yields achieved by chartists, fundamentalists and simpletons were equal for any of the individual parities or for the group currency averages. While there were statistical differences in the variability of yields between the various groups, no robust pattern emerged. For instance, for the pound parity the fundamentalists had a statistically significant lower variability than the simpletons, while the reverse held for the yen parity. The clear result that emerges

Table 9.10 Group averages of annual yields and standard deviations, 1974–94

	Pound	Yen	Deutschmark	Franc	Group average
Chartists	11.61	11.58	9.82	11.49	11.13
	(8.34)*	(9.49)*	(9.93)	(9.38)*	(9.29)*
Fundamentalists	10.80	11.08	11.39	9.34	10.65
	(6.81)**	(10.52)	(9.76)	(9.03)*	(9.03)*
Simpletons	11.58	11.60	9.71	11.15	11.01
	(10.43)	(8.50)**	(9.62)	(11.18)	(9.93)

Notes: An *F*-test of the null hypothesis of equality of the quarterly yields between the various groups could not reject the hypothesis at the 95% confidence level for any of the above exchange rates or group currency averages. A single asterisk indicates that an *F*-test showed the group's standard deviation to be significantly lower from the group with the highest standard deviation. A double asterisk indicates that an *F*-test showed the group's standard deviation to be significantly lower than both the other groups.
Source: Pilbeam (1995).

from the Pilbeam study is that at the quarterly investment horizon there is no real difference between trading using past movements of the exchange rate or using economic fundamentals, indeed even naive trading strategies seem to perform as well as trading on charts or fundamentals.

9.14 Conclusions

In contrast to the exciting advances in the theoretical modelling of exchange rates, empirical tests of these theories have been notoriously unrewarding, especially at the short-term horizon. None of the major theories stands up well to empirical examination. In large part, the empirical failure of the models reflects the enormous econometric problems involved in modelling exchange rates. However, recently the use of more sophisticated econometric techniques while not greatly improving short-term modelling has begun to suggest that there are predictable long-run relationships between exchange rate movements and economic fundamentals.

There is quite a substantial amount of empirical evidence that rejects the joint test of exchange market efficiency and no risk premium; that is, uncovered interest parity in the short run. This is particularly damaging for the monetarist models which assume both. Although the portfolio balance model allows for departures from uncovered interest parity due to the existence of a risk premium, there is little empirical evidence to support it as an alternative to the monetary models. Attempts to explain the risk premium in terms of its theoretical underlying determinants have failed. In sum, the possibility that the modern theories of exchange rate determination are very incomplete explanations of short to medium-term exchange rate movements cannot be ruled out.

On the other hand, empirical rejection of the models does not necessarily mean that they are wrong because tests of exchange rate models do little justice to the complexities of the various theories. Thus, policy-makers should not ignore the theories but it may be unwise to base policy on any single theory. In this respect, most theories emphasize the importance of pursuing stable monetary policies in order to avoid disruptive exchange rate movements.

In all probability many of the major empirical issues concerning exchange rate determination in the short to medium run are likely to remain unresolved in the foreseeable future, although recent studies have suggested better success in modelling long-run exchange rate behaviour. Recent research focusing on the role played by different groups such as chartists and fundamentalists in the determination of the exchange rate is yielding new and useful insights. However, this approach is most unlikely to yield a significant improvement in the empirical modelling of short and medium-term exchange rate behaviour. The core of the problem lies in the fact that all sides accept that expectations are crucial to the modelling of the exchange rate, but as we have seen we currently have no satisfactory method of measuring these expectations. Until we can more satisfactorily model expectations we shall be unable to satisfactorily model short to medium-run exchange rate behaviour.

Further reading

Allen, H.L. and Taylor, M.P. (1989) 'Charts and Fundamentals in the Foreign Exchange Market', *Bank of England Discussion Papers*, no. 40.

Allen, H.L and Taylor, M.P. (1990) 'Charts, Noise and Fundamentals in the Foreign Exchange Market', *The Economic Journal*, vol. 100, supplement, pp. 49–59.

Backus, D. (1984) 'Empirical Models of the Exchange Rate: Separating the Wheat from the Chaff', *Canadian Journal of Economics*, vol. 17, pp. 824–46.

Bailey, M.J., Tavlas, G.S. and Ulan, M. (1986) 'Exchange Rate Variability and Trade Performance: Evidence for the Big Seven Industrial Countries', *Weltwirtschafliches Archiv*, vol. 122, pp. 466–77.

Boothe, P. and Longworth, D. (1986) 'Foreign Exchange Market Efficiency Tests: Implications of Recent Empirical Findings', *Journal of International Money and Finance*, vol. 5, pp. 135–52.

Brooks, S., Cuthbertson, K. and Mayes, D. (1986) *The Exchange Rate Environment*, (Kent: Croom Helm).

Cavaglia, S., Vershoor, W. and Wolff, C. (1994) 'On the Unbiasedness of Foreign Exchanges: Irrationality or a Risk Premium?', *Journal of Business*, vol. 67, no. 3, pp. 321–43.

Caves, D. and Feige, E. (1980) 'Efficient Foreign Exchange Markets and the Monetary Approach to Exchange Rate Determination', *American Economic Review*, vol. 70, 120–34.

Clarida, R.H. and Taylor, M.P. (1997) 'The Term Structure of Forward Exchange Premiums and the Forecastability of Spot Exchange Rates: Correcting the Errors', *Review of Economics and Statistics*, vol. 79, pp. 353–61.

Clarida, R.H., Sarno, L., Taylor, M.P. and Valente, G. (2003) 'The out of Sample Success of Term Structure Models as Exchange Rate Predictors: A Step Beyond', *Journal of International Economics*, vol. 60, pp. 61–83.

Cooper, R.N. (1982) 'Flexible Exchange Rates 1973–80: How Bad Have they Really Been?', in R.N. Cooper, P.B. Kenen, J.B. Macedo and J.V. Ypersele (eds), *The International Monetary System under Flexible Exchange Rates* (Cambridge Mass.: Ballinger).

Cumby, R.E. and Obstfeld, M. (1984) 'International Interest Rate and Price Level Linkages under Flexible Exchange Rates: A Review of Recent Evidence', in J.F.O. Bilson and R.C. Marston (eds), *Exchange Rate Theory and Practice* (Chicago: University of Chicago Press).

De Grauwe, P. (1991) 'Speculative Dynamics and Chaos in the Foreign Exchange Market', in *Finance and the International Economy: 4*. (Oxford: Oxford University Press).

De Grauwe, P. and Vansanten, K. (1990) 'Deterministic Chaos in the Foreign Exchange Market', CEPR, Discussion Paper, no. 446.

Dominguez, K.M. (1986) 'Are Foreign Exchange Forecasts Rational? New Evidence from Survey Data', *Economic Letters*, vol. 21, pp. 277–81.

Dornbusch, R. (1980) 'Exchange Rate Economics: Where Do We Stand?', *The Brookings Papers on Economic Activity*, vol. 1, pp. 143–85.

Dornbusch, R. (1987) 'Exchange Rate Economics: 1986', *The Economic Journal*, vol. 97, pp. 1–18.

Edwards, S. (1982) 'Exchange Market Efficiency and New Information', *Economic Letters*, vol. 9, pp. 211–24.

Edwards, S. (1983a) 'Exchange Rates and "News": A Multi-Currency Approach', *Journal of International Money and Finance*, vol. 3, pp. 211–24.

Edwards, S. (1983b) 'Floating Exchange Rates, Expectations and New Information', *Journal of Monetary Economics*, vol. 11, pp 321–36.

Ehrmann, M. and Fratzcher, M. (2004) 'Exchange Rates and Fundamentals: New Evidence from Real Time Data', European Central Bank Working Paper Series, no. 365.

Evans, G.W. (1986) 'A Test for Speculative Bubbles and the Sterling–Dollar Rate. 1981–84', *American Economic Review*, vol. 76, pp. 621–36.

Fama, E. (1970) 'Efficient Capital Markets: A Review of Theory and Empirical Work', *Journal of Finance*, vol. 25, pp. 383–417.

Faust, J., Rogers, J. and Wright, J. (2003) 'Exchange Rate Forecasting: The Errors We've Really Made', *Journal of International Economics*, vol. 60, no. 1, pp. 35–59.

Feeny, M. (1989) 'Charting the Foreign Exchange Markets', in C. Dunis and M. Feeny (eds), *Exchange Rate Forecasting* (Cambridge: Woodhead-Faulkner.)

Frankel, J.A. (1979) 'On the Mark: A Theory of Floating Exchange Rates Based on Real Interest Rate Differentials', *American Economic Review*, vol. 69, pp. 610–22.

Frankel, J.A. (1980) 'Tests of Rational Expectations in the Forward Exchange Market', *Southern Economic Journal*, vol. 46, pp. 1083–1101.

Frankel, J.A. (1982a) 'In Search of the Exchange Risk Premium: A Six Currency Test Assuming Mean Variance Optimization', *Journal of International Money and Finance*, vol. 1. pp. 275–84.

Frankel, J.A. (1982b) 'A Test of Perfect Substitutability in the Forward Exchange Market', *Southern Economic Journal*, vol. 48, pp. 406–16.

Frankel, J.A. (1983) 'Monetary and Portfolio Balance Models of Exchange Rate Determination', in J.S. Bhandari and B.H. Putnam (eds), *Economic Interdependence and Flexible Exchange Rates* (Cambridge, Mass.: MIT Press).

Frankel, J.A. (1984) 'Tests of Monetary and Portfolio Balance Models of Exchange Rate Determination', in J.F.O. Bilson and R.C. Marston (eds), *Exchange Rate Theory and Practice* (Chicago: University of Chicago Press).

Frankel, J.A. (1986) 'The Implications of Mean Variance Optimization for Four Questions in International Macroeconomics', *Journal of International Money and Finance*, vol. 5, pp. 53–75.

Frankel, J.A. and Froot, K.A. (1987) 'Using Survey Data to Test Standard Propositions Regarding Exchange Rate Expectations', *American Economic Review*, vol. 77, pp. 133–53.

Frankel, J.A. and Froot, K.A. (1989) 'Chartists, Fundamentalists, and Trading in the Foreign Exchange Market', *American Economic Review Papers and Proceedings*, vol. 80, pp. 181–5.

Frankel, J.A. and Froot, K.A. (1990) 'Chartists, Fundamentalists, and the Demand for Dollars', in A.S. Courakis and M.P. Taylor (eds), *Policy Issues for Interdependent Economies* (Oxford: Clarendon Press).

Frenkel, J.A. (1982) 'Flexible Exchange Rates, Prices and the Role of "News": Lessons from the 1970s', in R.A. Batchelor and G.E. Wood (eds), *Exchange Rate Policy* (London: Palgrave Macmillan).

Frenkel, J.A. and Mussa, M. (1980) 'The Efficiency of Foreign Exchange Markets and Measures of Turbulence', *American Economic Review*, vol. 70, pp. 374–81.

Goodhart, C. (1988) 'The Foreign Exchange Market: A Random Walk with a Dragging Anchor', *Economica*, vol. 55, pp. 437–60.

Groen, J. (2000) 'The Monetary Exchange Rate Model as a Long Run Phenomenon', *Journal of International Economics*, vol. 52, pp. 219–319.

Hacche, G. and Townend, J. (1981) 'Exchange Rates and Monetary Policy: Modelling Sterling's Effective Exchange Rate 1972–1980', in W.A. Eltis and P.J.N. Sinclair (eds), *The Money Supply and the Exchange Rate* (Oxford: Clarendon).

Hansen, L.P. and Hodrick, R.J. (1980) 'Forward Exchange Rates as Optimal Predictors of Future Spot Rates: An Econometric Analysis', *Journal of Political Economy*, vol. 88, pp. 829–53.

Isard, P. (1987) 'Lessons from Empirical Models of Exchange Rates', *IMF Staff Papers*, vol. 34, pp. 1–28.

Kilian, L. (1999) 'Exchange Rates and Monetary Fundamentals: Evidence on Long-Horizon Predictability', *Journal of Applied Econometrics*, vol. 14, pp. 491–510.

Kilian, L. and Taylor, M.P. (2003) 'Why Is it so Difficult to Beat a Random Walk Forecast of Exchange Rates', *Journal of International Economics*, vol. 60, pp. 85–107.

Leventakis, J.A. (1987) 'Exchange Rate Models: Do they Work?', *Weltwirtschafliches Archiv*, vol. 123, pp. 363–76.

Levich, R.M. (1978) 'Tests of Forecast Models of Market Efficiency in the International Money Market', in J.A. Frenkel and H.G. Johnson (eds), *The Economics of Exchange Rates* (Reading: Addison-Wesley).

Levich, R.M. (1985) 'Empirical Studies of Exchange Rates, Price Behaviour, Rate Determination and Market Efficiency', in R.W. Jones and P.B. Kenen (eds), *Handbook of International Economics*, Vol. II (Amsterdam: Elsevier).

Liu, P.C. and Maddala, G.S. (1992) 'Using Survey Data to Test Market Efficiency in the Foreign Exchange Markets', *Empirical Economics*, vol. 17, pp. 303–14.

Longworth, D. (1981) 'Testing the Efficiency of the Canadian–US Exchange Market under the Assumption of No Risk Premium', *Journal of Finance*, vol. 36, pp. 43–9.

MacDonald, R. (1983) 'Some Tests of the Rational Expectations Hypothesis in the Foreign Exchange Market', *Scottish Journal of Political Economy*, vol. 30, pp. 255–50.

MacDonald, R. (1988) *Floating Exchange Rates: Theories and Evidence* (London: Unwin Hyman).

MacDonald, R. (1992) 'Exchange Rate Survey Data: A Disaggregated G-7 Perspective', *The Manchester School of Economic and Social Studies*, vol. 40, pp. 33–42.

MacDonald, R. and Marsh, I. (1996) 'Currency Forecasters are Heterogeneous Confirmation and Consequences', *Journal of International Money and Finance*, vol. 15, no. 5, pp. 665–85.

MacDonald, R. and Taylor, M.P. (1992) 'Exchange Rate Economics: A Survey', *IMF Staff Papers*, vol. 39, no. 1, pp. 1–57.

MacDonald, R. and Taylor, M.P. (1993) 'The Monetary Approach to the Exchange Rate', *IMF Staff Papers*, vol. 40, no. 1, pp. 89–107.

MacDonald, R. and Torrance, T.S. (1989) 'Some Survey Based Tests of Uncovered Interest Parity', in R. MacDonald and M.P. Taylor (eds), *Exchange Rates and Open Economy Macroeconomic Models* (Oxford: Basil Blackwell).

Mark, N. (1995) Exchange Rates and Economic Fundamentals: Evidence on Long Run Predictability', *American Economic Review*, vol. 85, no. 1, pp. 201–18.

Mark, N. and Sul, D. (2001) 'Nominal Exchange Rates and Monetary Fundamentals: Evidence from a Small Post Bretton Woods Panel', *Journal of International Economics*, vol. 53, pp. 29–52.

Meese, R. and Rogoff, K. (1983a) 'Empirical Exchange Rate Models of the Seventies: Do they Fit Out of Sample?', *Journal of International Economics*, vol. 14, pp. 3–24.

Meese, R. and Rogoff, K. (1983b) 'The out of Sample Failure of Empirical Exchange Rate Models: Sampling Error or Misspecification', in J.A. Frenkel (ed.) *Exchange Rates and International Economics* (Chicago: University of Chicago Press).

Meese, R. and Singleton P. (1982) 'On Unit Roots and Empirical Modelling of Exchange Rates', *Journal of Finance*, vol. 37, pp. 1029–35.

Mussa, M. (1979) 'Empirical Regularities in the Behaviour of Exchange Rates and Theories of the Foreign Exchange Market', in K. Brunner and A.H. Meltzer (eds), *Policies for Employment, Prices and Exchange Rates*, Carnegie-Rochester Conference Series on Public Policy (Amsterdam: North Holland).

Pilbeam, K.S. (1991) *Exchange Rate Management: Theory and Evidence* (London: Palgrave Macmillam).

Pilbeam, K.S. (1995) 'The Profitability of Trading in the Foreign Exchange Market: Chartists, Fundamentalists, and Simpletons', *Oxford Economic Papers*, vol. 47, no. 2, pp. 437–52.

Rapach, D.E. and Wohar, M.E. (2002) 'Testing the Monetary Model of Exchange Rate Determination: New Evidence from a Century of Data', *Journal of International Economics*, vol. 58, pp. 359–85.

Rogoff, K. (1984) 'On the Effects of Sterilized Intervention: An Analysis of Weekly Data', *Journal of Monetary Economics*, vol. 14, pp. 133–50.

Sarno, L. and Taylor, M.P. (2002) *The Economics of Exchange Rates* (Cambridge: Cambridge University Press).

Taylor, M.P. (1988) 'A DYMIMIC Model of Forward Foreign Exchange Risk with Estimates for Three Major Exchange rates', *The Manchester School*, vol. 56, pp. 55–68.

Taylor, M.P. (1989) 'Expectations, Risk and Uncertainty in the Foreign Exchange Market: Some Results Based on Survey Data', *The Manchester School*, vol. 57, no. 2, pp. 142–53.

Wasserfallen, W. and Kyburz, H. (1985) 'The Behaviour of Flexible Exchange Rates in the Short Run – A Systematic Investigation', *Weltwirtschaftliches Archiv*, vol. 121, pp. 646–60.

10

Fixed, Floating and Managed Exchange Rates

10.1 Introduction

Prior to the move to generalized floating in 1973, the adoption of floating exchange rates had long been advocated by eminent economists such as Milton Friedman (1953), Egon Sohmen (1961) and Harry Johnson (1970). However, the experience with floating rates has not been the panacea that many advocates had presupposed, and this has led many economists to propose schemes designed to limit exchange rate flexibility.

In this chapter, we examine the traditional and more recent arguments for and against fixed and floating exchange rates. We start by looking at the traditional debate over the two regimes, based upon evaluating the arguments for and against each of the regimes. As we shall see, the traditional debate is inconclusive, with floating rates having some advantages and disadvantages as compared to fixed exchange rates. The failure of the traditional debate stimulated an alternative method of evaluating these regimes based upon comparing which regime best stabilizes the economy in the face of various shocks within the context of a formal macroeconomic model. To give a flavour of the insights gained by this more modern approach we use a simple macro-economic model to evaluate the two regimes.

Although exchange rates have been allowed to float since 1973, authorities have frequently intervened in the foreign exchange market in a bid to influence the exchange rate at which their currency is traded, hence the term 'managed' floating. We look at the economic rationale behind discretionary intervention in the foreign exchange market. The chapter also includes **Box 10.1** which takes a brief look at an important strand of international economic literature known as optimal currency area theory, which attempts to find a set of criteria for determining the optimal size of area for a single currency. This is a particularly important issue as the European countries have recently given up 12 national currencies for a single currency, the euro, and questions arise as to, how many countries should the euro encompass and what set of criteria does economics offer as to whether a country should be admitted to the euro?

10.2 The case for fixed exchange rates

The case for fixed exchange rates usually has two sides to it; on the one hand there are some positive arguments in favour of fixed exchange rates, and on the other there are arguments against floating exchange rates. One needs to be careful with this approach because arguments against floating exchange rates are not necessarily arguments in favour of fixed rates, they may well constitute arguments for some degree of exchange rate management rather than for fixed parities. In this spirit, let us consider both the positive arguments in favour of fixed rates and the argument against floating rates.

Fixed exchange rates promote international trade and investment

The proponents of fixed exchange rates argue that fixed parities provide the best environment for the conduct of international trade and investment. It is argued that just as a single currency is the best means of promoting economic activity at the national level, fixed exchange rates are the best means of promoting international trade and investment at the international level. Exchange rate fluctuations cause additional uncertainty and risk in international economic transactions and inhibit the growth and development of such transactions.

Fixed exchange rates provide discipline for macroeconomic policies

An argument frequently put forward in favour of fixed exchange rates is that the commitment to a fixed exchange rate regime provides a degree of discipline to domestic macroeconomic policy that is absent if exchange rates are allowed to float. If the authorities are in a fixed rate regime, the pursuit of reckless macroeconomic policies (such as excessive monetary growth) will lead to pressure for a devaluation of the currency necessitating intervention by the authorities to defend their currency and a fall in their reserves. If the pressures continue, the authorities would eventually have to devalue the currency which would be taken as a sign by economic agents that the authorities have mismanaged the economy. Such an unpleasant scenario should encourage governments to resist adopting unsound expansionary macroeconomic policies which they are invariably tempted to undertake prior to elections and in their attempts to reconcile conflicting demands.

Fixed exchange rates promote international cooperation

Another argument in favour of fixed exchange rates is that they necessitate a degree of international cooperation and coordination between countries that is generally absent under floating exchange rates (see Chapter 13 for more on international policy coordination). Countries that agree to peg their exchange rates generally have to agree on measures to be undertaken when the agreed exchange rate parity comes under pressure. At a minimum, fixed exchange rates require an agreement to avoid conflicting exchange rate targets ruling out the dangers of competitive devaluation scenarios such as occurred in the 1930s. The enhanced degree of international cooperation should bring benefits and lead to a more stable environment for the conduct of international trade and investment.

Speculation under floating rates is likely to be destabilizing

The major argument advanced against floating exchange rates is that they are likely to be characterized by destabilizing private speculation producing the 'wrong' exchange rate, the wrong exchange rate being an exchange rate that is sub-optimal from the viewpoint of resource allocation. There are several ways in which private speculation can bring about the wrong exchange rate. Some of the arguments depend on 'irrational' speculation while others depend upon uncertainty.

One example of 'irrational' speculation frequently cited is that the foreign exchange market can be **too risk-averse**. It often attaches too high a probability to the possibility of a depreciation of a 'weak' currency or, equivalently, too high a probability to the possibility of an appreciation of a 'strong' currency, even when this is not justified by the fundamentals. That is, one currency, say the pound sterling, is regarded as 'too risky' while another, say the US dollar, is regarded as 'safe' – market participants are basing their exchange rate forecasts not only on currently available information but also past performance. The result is that there may be an unjustified reluctance to move out of dollars and to hold pounds, so that there is a larger depreciation of the pound than is justified by the fundamentals required as a premium by speculators to hold the pound. As a result, the dollar becomes overvalued while the pound becomes undervalued. The argument does not imply that risk-aversion is an inefficient feature of the foreign exchange market, but rather that excessive risk-aversion unjustified by the fundamentals is. Instability of a country's economic policies may well create uncertainty and therefore risk concerning estimates about the correct value of its currency. Excessive risk-aversion, however, implies that part of the risk premium required by the market is unjustified by the fundamentals.

Another case where irrational private speculation can produce the wrong rate is via the **'bandwagon' effect**. The idea is that there is too much self-generating speculation detached from the fundamentals, 'speculation feeding upon speculation' rather than the fundamentals. A possible scenario involving the 'bandwagon effect' is when some news hits the market, say an unexpected increase in the UK money supply, which then sets off unjustified speculation that the eventual rate of monetary growth will be even greater bringing with it an unduly pessimistic inflation forecast. Assuming that the rate of growth of the money supply contained in the news turns out to be the actual rate, the depreciation of the pound will turn out to have been greater than was justified by the news and this will then reverse itself when it becomes evident that a bandwagon effect has been in play.

The excessive risk-aversion and bandwagon effect arguments presuppose that foreign exchange speculators do not use all the information and news available to them efficiently, and consequently speculation produces the wrong exchange rate until eventually fundamentals reassert themselves. Authors such as Dornbusch (1983) have emphasized reasons as to why even rational speculators can produce the 'wrong' exchange rate. These explanations are all based upon the concept of exchange rate uncertainty.

One reason why rational speculators may produce the wrong exchange rate is that in a world of uncertainty they do not know the correct exchange rate model, and as such they use a **seriously defective model**. Their expectations based on the wrong (irrelevant) exchange rate model will then generally lead to the wrong exchange rate. This point is important because market participants may be impressed by a plausible but relatively unimportant fundamental variable and make their expectations based upon movements in that variable come true. Furthermore, changes in irrelevant variables may lead to significant exchange rates movements. A further danger is that economic agents may shift their attention between many irrelevant pieces of information, causing excessive exchange rate variability and even major exchange rate collapses.

Another reason why rational speculators may produce the wrong exchange rate is known as the **'Peso Problem'**. Exchange rates are determined not only by what is held to be the underlying fundamentals today, but by what is expected to happen to those fundamentals in the future. Even if the speculators' model of the underlying fundamentals is correct, their perceptions about the future can prove to be seriously wrong. In such cases, the exchange rate moves immediately in anticipation of events that do not materialize. Such *ex post* unjustified exchange rate movements can seriously interfere with the conduct of macroeconomic policy and, with it, macroeconomic stability.

Blanchard (1979) proposed another reason for rational speculation producing the wrong rate, known as a **'rational bubble'**. An exchange rate bubble exists when holders of a currency realize that it is overvalued but they are nevertheless willing to hold it, since they believe that the appreciation will continue for a while longer and that there is only a limited risk of a serious depreciation during a given holding period. So speculators expect to be able to sell eventually at an exchange rate that will provide them with a sufficient capital gain to compensate them for running the risk of a sudden collapse. Such speculation both prolongs an exchange overvaluation and aggravates the macroeconomic costs associated with it.

Hence, there are a variety of arguments as to why private speculation may be destabilizing, and such destabilizing speculation is often used as an argument for a fixed exchange rate and against a floating exchange rate. However, we have to be extremely careful here because a fixed exchange rate can be fixed at the wrong rate, just as a floating rate can float to one. Even if a fixed exchange rate is initially fixed at the optimal exchange rate, when the economic fundamentals change the fixed parity then becomes the wrong rate.

10.3 The case for floating exchange rates

The case for floating exchange rates is a mixture of positive arguments in favour of floating and arguments against fixed exchange rates. Again caution is warranted with the arguments against fixed exchange rates because they do not necessarily constitute arguments for completely floating exchange rates.

Floating exchange rates ensure balance of payments equilibrium

Proponents of floating exchange rates argue that in a floating regime the exchange rate automatically adjusts to ensure continuous equilibrium between the demand for and supply of the currency. If a country is running an unsustainable current account deficit, its exchange rate will depreciate which will reduce imports and increase exports until the balance of payments is restored to a sustainable level. Conversely, a structural surplus in the balance of payments will lead to an exchange rate appreciation that will reduce the surplus to sustainable levels.

In other words, floating exchange rates ensure a balance between the demand for and supply of a currency, excess demand leads to an appreciation whereas excess supply leads to a depreciation. This contrasts to the scenario under fixed exchange rates where an overvalued rate leads to an excess supply and thereby a fall in the authorities' reserves, while fixing it at an undervalued rate leads to excess demand and increase in the authorities' reserves. Even if by chance the authorities initially peg the exchange rate at the point where supply equals demand, that rate will soon become inappropriate when a change in the economic fundamentals affects the supply or demand for the currency. Exchange rate adjustments by taking care of the balance of payments deficits relieve the authorities of having to adopt unpopular alternatives such as deflation or resort to protectionism which could even provoke a damaging trade war.

Floating exchange rates ensure monetary autonomy

One of the major arguments put forward in favour of floating exchange rates is that they enable each country to operate an independent monetary policy; that is, they restore **monetary autonomy** enabling each country to determine its own inflation rate. Countries that prefer low inflation rates are free to adopt tight macroeconomic policies experiencing appreciating currencies, while countries that pursue expansionary macroeconomic policies will suffer higher inflation and depreciating currencies. This contrasts with what happens under fixed exchange rates where the need to have common inflation rates to maintain competitiveness constrains countries to pursue similar monetary policies.

Floating exchange rates insulate economies

A further argument put forward in favour of floating exchange rates is that they can **insulate** the domestic economy from foreign price shocks. If there is an increase in foreign prices under floating exchange rates, provided the exchange rate moves roughly in line with PPP the domestic currency would merely appreciate so preventing the country importing foreign inflation. This contrasts to what happens under fixed exchange rates where a foreign price rise makes the home economy overcompetitive leading to a balance of payments surplus which necessitates purchases of the foreign currency with newly created domestic currency to peg the exchange rate. The increase in the domestic money supply leads to an accompanying rise in domestic prices ending the surplus. Hence, fixed exchange rates lead to the importing of foreign price inflation/deflation (see Chapter 5).

Floating exchange rates promote economic stability

A forceful argument put forward by Milton Friedman (1953) in favour of flexible exchange rates is that it is better to let exchange rates adjust in response to shocks to economy than fix the exchange rate and force the adjustment onto other economic variables. He argued that floating exchange rates are more conducive to economic stability. The exchange rate is a variable which can easily rise or fall whereas domestic prices tend to be very difficult to reduce. Hence, if there is a loss of international competitiveness it is better to allow the exchange rate (one price) to depreciate rather than maintain a fixed exchange rate and require deflationary policies to restore international competitiveness. Since the domestic price level is resistant to downward pressure, it may require quite severe deflationary policies with associated high unemployment to induce the fall in domestic wages and prices necessary to restore international competitiveness.

Private speculation is stabilizing

The advocates of floating exchange rates argue that private speculators are a stabilizing rather than destabilizing force. It is in the interests of speculators to move the exchange rate to its fundamental economic value. Speculators will attempt to buy the currency at a low value, and sell it at a high value and in so doing reduce the gap between the low and high values. Of course, occasionally speculators will make mistakes and buy a currency which they think has depreciated sufficiently and find that it continues to depreciate but such destabilizing speculation will involve losses. This being the case, there is every reason to suppose that private speculators will move the exchange rate towards its fundamental equilibrium value.

Many of the preceding arguments advanced for and against the two regimes are extremely difficult if not impossible to prove. No doubt there are elements of truth on both sides of the argument; Speculation can at times be stabilizing and at other times may be destabilizing. Fixed exchange rates can provide a stable framework for international trade but so too can floating rates by ensuring countries maintain their international competitiveness. Economic policies can be more or less stable under a fixed exchange rate regime as compared to a floating one.

Since the traditional advantages/disadvantages approach leaves plenty of scope for disagreement, this has stimulated an alternative more modern approach to evaluating the two regimes. In this approach, the relative merits of the two regimes is evaluated within the context of a formal macroeconomic model. We now look at the insights provided by this alternative approach by using a relatively simple macroeconomic model.

Box 10.1

The optimum currency area literature

Aside from the issue of fixed, floating and managed exchange rates, there is branch of economic literature that focuses on the issue of the relevant economic criteria for determining the optimum economic area for a single currency unit. Put simply, an optimum currency area is a region for which it is optimal to have a common currency and a common monetary policy. For example, the United States is a vast economic area; is it optimal for it to have only a single currency unit for that area or would it make more economic sense for it to have two currencies one, for the western part and one for the eastern part? The issue is particularly pertinent when it comes to the European Union that has recently moved from a situation where 12 of its

→

→

member countries with 12 different currencies have formed the eurozone area which has one currency, the euro, to serve those 12 countries. What is the optimum amount of countries that should join the euro and what criteria should be used to evaluate the suitability of a prospective member for joining the euro? Indeed, is a single currency optimal only for one country, a group of countries or all countries of the world? Determining a set of criteria to determine which countries should participate in a monetary union has been the subject matter of optimal currency area theory. In the literature on the subject there is no single set of criteria which is generally agreed upon, and for excellent surveys the reader is referred to Tavlas (1993) and Bayoumi and Eichengreen (1994). Nonetheless, it is worthwhile to briefly review some of the criteria that have been suggested for determining which countries should join a monetary union.

- **Degree of factor mobility internationally**. Mundell (1961) proposed that the higher the degree of factor mobility between countries, then the more beneficial a monetary union would be between them. The rationale behind this criterion is that if a country is in a monetary union and faces a fall in demand for its goods which pushes its balance of payments into deficit, high capital mobility will enable it to finance its deficit more easily without the need for an exchange rate depreciation. In addition, high labour mobility will mean that deficit regions can deflate their economies without fear of a large increase in unemployment since labour can migrate to other countries within the union. Conversely, if factor mobility is low, then an exchange rate depreciation is required to eliminate the deficit and maintain employment levels, and hence a monetary union would be undesirable.

- **Degree of financial integration**. This is connected with the degree of factor mobility mentioned above, but is specifically concerned with the ability of a country to gain access to external finance. If a country has a high degree of financial integration with other countries, then it will be more able to finance its deficits and less dependent on exchange rate changes. A small variation in its interest rates will attract the necessary capital flows to finance imbalances. If countries are financially integrated then a single currency is a more feasible option than in the absence of such integration.

- **Degree of openness**. McKinnon (1963) has argued that the more open the economy as measured by the size of its tradables relative to its non-tradables sector, the more profitable it is to join a currency union. The rationale is that if the economy has a large tradables sector it will be much more vulnerable to inflation from a depreciating currency and unemployment from an appreciating currency and therefore the less desirable exchange rate changes are. Indeed, the more important is trade for the country, the more potential it will have to benefit from the introduction of a single currency with its major trading partners. Also, the more open the economy the more the adjustment costs associated with changes in the exchange rate.

- **Degree of product diversification**. Kenen (1969) has suggested that the more diversified a country's range of exports and imports, the more it will benefit from monetary union. A diversified economy means less variability in its export earnings and import expenditure and more stability for its balance of payments. Accordingly, the less will be the need to resort to exchange rate changes. If, however, it has only a few export products it may experience much greater variability in its export earnings and will be more dependent upon exchange rate changes to maintain external equilibrium.

- **Degree of similarity of inflation rates**. The idea underlying this criterion is fairly straightforward. If countries have similar inflation rates then PPP theory suggests that there is

→

➔

no need for exchange rate changes and hence a monetary union is more feasible, whereas
if the countries have widely divergent propensities to inflate, then floating exchange rates
become necessary to ensure that the relatively high inflation countries maintains their international competitiveness.

Even if we ignore numerous criticisms that can be made of the individual criteria (see the
surveys by Tower and Willett (1976) and Ishyima (1975) and Goodhart (1975) Chapter 15), it
is clear that emphasizing one particular factor is hardly sufficient grounds for justifying monetary union. What happens if two countries score well under one of the criteria and poorly on all
the others? An index of the various criteria might offer a better solution, but there is plenty of
scope for disagreement over the appropriate weight to assign to each of the criteria and then
the total index value that would justify membership of a monetary union. Goodhart (1975)
emphasized that the need for a high degree of social cohesion appears to be a crucial determinant of the size of a single currency area in the real world rather than any clear-cut economic
criteria. In sum, the optimal currency area literature addresses an interesting question but the
various criteria that have been suggested are far from conclusive.

10.4 The modern evaluation of fixed and flexible exchange rate regimes

The modern exchange rate literature has attempted to evaluate the choice between
fixed and flexible exchange rates by seeing which regime best stabilizes the domestic
economy in the face of various shocks to the economy. The exchange rate regime that
provides the most stability to the domestic economy is deemed to be the preferred
regime. As we shall see, although more sophisticated, this literature does not provide
an unambiguous answer to the question of which is the best exchange rate regime.
What it shows is that the choice between the two regimes is crucially dependent upon
a multiplicity of factors. In our model, we highlight three of these factors; the specification of the objective function of the authorities as between price and output stability, the type of the shock impinging upon the economy, and the structural parameters
of the economy.

10.5 Specification of the objective function

There are many factors that the authorities have to take into account when designing
their policies. Most importantly, they have to decide what are their objectives and the
weight to be attached to each of them. For simplicity we shall deal with an economy
where the authorities have two objectives, price and output stability. The aim of the
authorities is viewed as being the minimization of fluctuations of the price level (P)
and output level (Y) around their target values. The authorities will wish to minimize
the value of the following objective function:

$$O(P, Y) = w (Y - Yn)^2 + (1 - w) (P - Pn)^2 \quad 0 \le w \le 1$$

where w is the relative weight attached to each of the two objectives in the overall objective function, Yn is the natural/target value for domestic real income, Pn is the natural/target value for the domestic price level.

The idea of incorporating a weighted objective function is that there may be a trade-off for the authorities as between income and price stability. Some authorities may attach a high weight to price stability, whereas others may attach a high priority to income stability and a weighted objective function allows for this possibility. A value of $w = 1$ means that the objective involves only domestic income stability, whereas if $w = 0$ the sole concern is with price stability.

10.6 The model

We now investigate the choice between fixed and flexible exchange rate regimes for an economy that is buffeted by various transitory shocks. The fact that the shocks are assumed to be transitory, that is self-reversing, the next period is an important assumption because it means that the economy is always expected to return to its natural price (Pn) and output level (Yn). In terms of the model, it means some simple rules can be made concerning expectations. If the exchange rate depreciates today it is expected to appreciate back to its normal level the next period. Similarly, if the price or output levels rise above their normal levels they will be expected to go back to their normal levels the next period. In the model that follows, we shall examine the performance of fixed and floating exchange rate regimes in the face of three types of transitory shocks, money demand, aggregate demand and aggregate supply. All variables except interest rates are expressed in logarithms.

The demand for the home country's money is a positive function of the aggregate price index, a positive function of real domestic income and inversely related to the domestic nominal interest rate. That is:

$$Md_t = Pi_t + \eta Y_t - \sigma r_t + Ut_1 \tag{10.1}$$

where Md_t is the demand to hold money in the current period t, Pi_t is the currently observable aggregate price index made up of a weighted average of the domestic and foreign price levels as set out in equation (10.1a), Y_t is real domestic income in period t, r_t is the domestic nominal interest rate in current period t which is a currently observable financial variable and Ut_1 is a transitory money demand shock term with zero mean and normal distribution.

The idea of incorporating the aggregate price index in the demand for money function is derived from the monetarist proposition that the demand to hold money is a demand for real balances related to the purchasing power of money. The aggregate price index is a weighted average of the domestic price level and the domestic price of the imported foreign good, which is equal to the exchange rate times the price of the foreign good. That is:

$$Pi_t = \alpha P_t + (1 - \alpha)(s_t + P_{t*}) \qquad 0 < \alpha < 1 \tag{10.1a}$$

where α is the weight of the domestic good in the overall consumption basket, s_t is the exchange rate defined as domestic currency per unit of foreign currency in the current period, P_t is the price of domestic good in the current period, and P_{t*} is the price of the imported foreign good in the foreign currency in the current period.

The demand for domestic output is a positive function of the real exchange rate and inversely related to the domestic real interest rate and a positive function of the natural level of income. That is:

$$Yd_t = \Theta(s_t + P_{t*} - P_t) - \beta(r_t + P_t - P_{t+1/t}) + \pi Yn + Ut_2 \qquad (10.2)$$

where $P_{t+1/t}$ is the expected price level in one periods time given the information available in the current period, Yn is the natural level of output, Ut_2 is a transitory aggregate demand shock term with zero mean and normal distribution.

The real exchange rate is given by the first bracketed expression; an appreciation of the exchange rate would reduce the demand for the domestic good. Similarly, the real domestic interest rate is given by the second bracketed expression and is equivalent to the nominal interest rate minus the expected rate of price inflation. A rise in the real interest rate will act to reduce the current demand for the domestic good.

The supply of domestic output depends upon the price at which producers are able to sell their output relative to the wage rate that they must pay per unit of labour. That is:

$$Ys_t = \varphi(P_t - W_t) + Ut_3 \qquad (10.3)$$

$$Ys_t = Ys_t(L_t) \text{ where } \delta Ys_t/\delta L_t > 0 \text{ and } \delta^2 Ys_t/\delta^2 L_t < 0 \qquad (10.3a)$$

where Ys_t is the supply of domestic good, L_t is labour input, Ut_3 is a transitory aggregate supply shock term with zero mean and normal distribution.

Equation (10.3) says that if the price of the domestic good rises relative to the wage rate, domestic producers will increase their output and employment levels as the real wage facing them falls. While equation (10.3a) says that output is a positive function of labour input but is subject to the law of diminishing returns. It is assumed that financial capital is perfectly mobile and that domestic and foreign bonds are perfect substitutes. As a result, the uncovered interest parity condition is assumed to hold continuously. That is:

$$r_t = r_{t*} + (s_{t+1/t} - s_t) \qquad (10.4)$$

where r_{t*} is the foreign interest rate in current period, $s_{t+1/t}$ is the expected exchange rate in period $t + 1$ given information available at time t. The expression $(s_{t+1/t} - s_t)$ gives the expected rate of depreciation of the currency.

The contracting arrangement that determines the setting of nominal wages is central to the behaviour of the model. The contracts have a duration of one period and establish a nominal base wage W_t. It is assumed that the base wage W_t is set at the level required to generate an expected level of output at the natural level Yn, which is also the target level of the authorities.

$$W_t = W_{t*} \qquad (10.5)$$

where W_{t*} is the wage rate that will in the absence of any shocks to the economy lead to full employment at the natural rate of output.

In order to close the model we require the simultaneous fulfilment of the following two equations: that money demand in the current period (Md_t) equals the current money supply (Ms_t), and that current aggregate supply equals current aggregate demand. That is:

$$Ms_t = Md_t \tag{10.6}$$

$$Ys_t = Yd_t \tag{10.7}$$

Under fixed exchange rates perfect capital mobility means that the domestic interest rate equals the foreign interest rate and the money supply is endogenously determined. While under floating exchange rates the money supply is exogenously determined and the domestic interest rate and exchange rate are endogenously determined but tied together via the uncovered interest rate parity condition. We now set out the model using a diagrammatic exposition.

10.7 Determining equilibrium

We use for exposition purposes aggregate supply and demand schedules defined by equations (10.2) and (10.3) respectively, and also make use of the money market curve as set out by equation (10.1). Initial equilibrium is found where all three schedules intersect as shown in **Figure 10.1**.

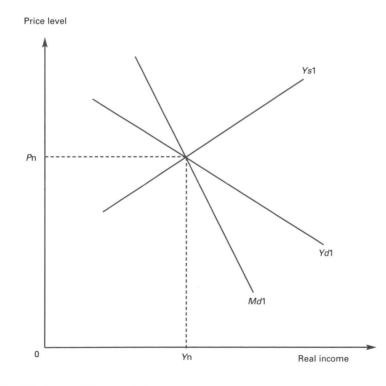

Figure 10.1 Equilibrium of the model

The aggregate demand schedule is given by Yd and is derived from equation (10.2), it is downward-sloping because a rise in the domestic price level leads to a fall in aggregate demand for the domestic good, *ceteris paribus*, for two reasons. Firstly by inducing a decline in net exports, and secondly since any rise in the domestic price level leads to a future expected return of the price to its target level, the expected rate of price inflation will be negative which raises the real interest rate. The absolute slope of the Yd schedule is given by the reciprocal of the summation of the elasticities of aggregate demand with respect to the real exchange rate and real interest rate, that is $1/(\Theta + \beta)$.

Md depicts the money demand schedule derived from equation (10.1) of the model, it also has a negative slope because a rise in the domestic price level increases the demand for money requiring a fall in real income to maintain money demand equilibrium. The absolute slope of the *Md* schedule is given by the income elasticity of money demand divided by the share of the domestic good in the aggregate price index, that is η/α.

The slope of the Yd schedule may be flatter or steeper than the Md schedule and this proves to be critical when comparing fixed and floating exchange rates in the face of an aggregate supply shock. The condition for the Yd schedule to be flatter than the Md schedule is that $\eta(\Theta + \beta) > \alpha$. For most of the analysis we shall assume that this condition is satisfied. Obviously, it is more likely to be satisfied the more open the economy (that is, the smaller is α) and the greater the elasticity of the demand for the home good with respect to the real exchange rate and real interest rate. However, in order to see the importance of the relative slopes, in the case of an aggregate supply shock both cases are examined.

The aggregate supply curve has a positive slope since a rise in the domestic price level for a fixed nominal wage reduces the real wage facing producers encouraging them to take on more workers which results in increased output. It has a positive slope given by $1/\varphi$.

Equilibrium of the system is determined by the simultaneous interaction of all three schedules through a common point. In the absence of unanticipated disturbances to the economy, output is at its natural level *Yn* and the price level at the natural level *Pn*. In the analysis, we shall also assume that these are the optimal target values of the authorities, so that the economy is initially in full equilibrium.

If the system is initially in full equilibrium, only unanticipated disturbances will cause the schedules to shift from their equilibrium levels, inducing corresponding adjustments in price and output. Under fixed exchange rates the money stock adjusts passively to shifts in the Ys and Yd schedules because the money stock is endogenously determined, whereas under floating exchange rates the exchange rate and interest rate adjust to equilibrate the system causing shifts in both the Md and Yd schedules. For example, an appreciation of the exchange rate shifts the Yd schedule to the left due to a loss of competitiveness with a resulting fall in exports, as well as the fact that an appreciation leads to an expected future depreciation as the shocks impinging upon the economy are known to be selfreversing. As a result, the domestic interest rate is forced up further to maintain uncovered interest parity shifting the Yd schedule to the left. The rise in the domestic interest rate to the extent that the demand for money is interest-elastic lowers the demand for money which for a given money stock requires a shift to the right of the Md schedule. We now compare the relative performance of fixed and floating exchange rates in the face of various shocks to the economy.

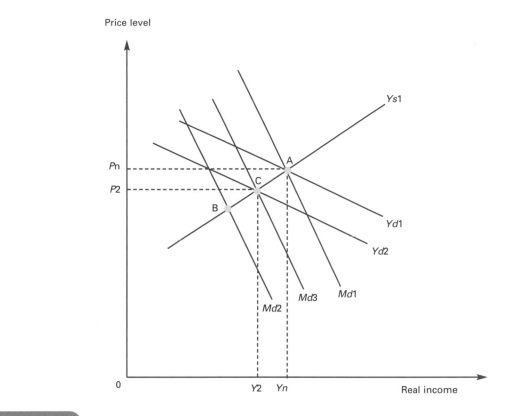

Figure 10.2 Money demand shock

10.8 Money demand shock

Suppose that there is an unanticipated rise in money demand, as depicted in **Figure 10.2**; this has the effect of shifting the *Md* schedule to the left. It is assumed that there are no other shocks impinging upon the economy.

An increase in money demand causes a shift to the left of the money demand schedule from *Md*1 to *Md*2. Under fixed exchange rates the excess demand for money will cause a tendency for the currency to appreciate, as a result the authorities have to purchase the foreign currency in the foreign exchange market which expands the domestic money stock the purchases continue until the *Md*2 schedule shifts back to *Md*1. Thus, short-run equilibrium remains at point A under fixed exchange rates with no disturbance to either domestic prices or domestic output. This means that fixed exchange rates prove optimal. In effect, all the authorities do is increase the money stock in line with the increased demand to hold money so that there are no required adjustments to price and output.

If we are in a floating exchange rate regime the appreciation of the exchange rate shifts *Yd*1 to the left to *Yd*2 due to the fall off in export demand and rise in the domestic interest rate as there is an expected future depreciation of the currency. The rise in the interest rate leads to a fall off in money demand shifting *Md*2 to *Md*3. Temporary equilibrium is attained where all three schedules intersect at point C. Thus, it can be seen that under floating exchange rates a rise in the demand to hold money leads to a fall in both the domestic price and output level. From this, it is obvious that whether the principal objective is price or output stabilization, fixed exchange rates are preferable for dealing with monetary shocks and in fact prove optimal.

10.9 Aggregate demand shock

Assume that there is an unanticipated increase in aggregate demand, as depicted in **Figure 10.3**; this has the effect of shifting the Yd schedule to the right.

An increase in aggregate demand shifts $Yd1$ to $Yd2$. This means that there is an excess demand for money which will cause the exchange rate to appreciate. As a result, the authorities have to intervene in the foreign exchange market to purchase the foreign money with newly created domestic money so that $Md1$ shifts to $Md2$ and the excess money demand is eliminated. Thus, under fixed exchange rates short run equilibrium is found at point B with rises in both the domestic price and output level to $P2$ and $Y2$ respectively.

If, however, the authorities allow the exchange rate to float, the excess demand for money will result in an appreciation of the domestic currency which will have two effects: The aggregate demand schedule will shift to the left from $Yd2$ to $Yd3$ due to

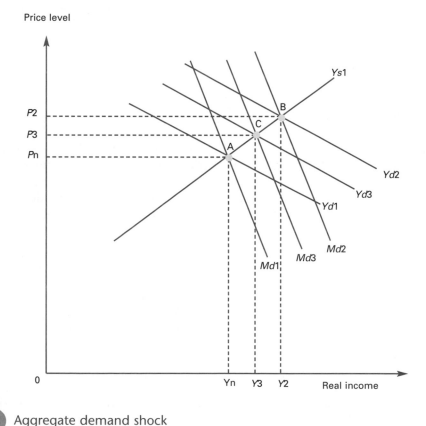

Figure 10.3 Aggregate demand shock

the fall off in exports, and the money demand schedule will shift to the right from *Md*1 to *Md*3 due to the rise in the domestic interest rate. Equilibrium of the system is obtained at point C with price *P*3 and output *Y*3.

From this, it is evident that in the case of an aggregate demand disturbance whether the objective of the authorities is price or output stability floating exchange rates outperform fixed rates.

10.10 Aggregate supply shock

Assume that there is an unanticipated fall in aggregate supply; this has the effect of shifting the aggregate supply schedule to the left. Here it is necessary to distinguish two cases; in case 1 the *Md* schedule is steeper than the *Yd* schedule, while in case 2 the Yd schedule is steeper than the *Md* schedule.

The economy is initially in equilibrium at point A in **Figure 10.4** with price *Pn* and output *Yn*. The economy is then hit by a transitory inflationary supply shock which shifts *Ys*1 to *Ys*2. In this case, point B corresponds to a position of excess supply of money, hence, there is a tendency for the currency to depreciate. In order to maintain a fixed exchange rate the authorities have to contract the money supply until the

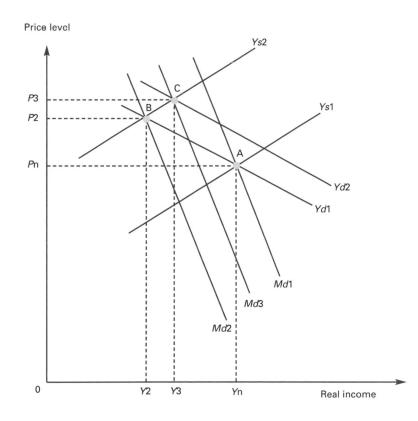

Figure 10.4 Aggregate supply shock, case 1: *Md* schedule is steeper than the *Yd* schedule, i.e. $\eta(\theta + \beta) > \alpha$

excess supply is eliminated, so the Md schedule shifts from $Md1$ to $Md2$. Thus, under fixed exchange rates the inflationary supply shock leads to a rise in price to $P2$ and a fall in output to $Y2$.

If, however, the authorities allow the exchange rate to float the excess supply of money resulting from the aggregate supply shock will lead to a depreciation of the currency. The depreciation shifts the aggregate demand schedule to the right from $Yd1$ to $Yd2$ since it results in increased export sales of the domestic good. Furthermore, the depreciation leads to an expected appreciation and therefore a fall in the domestic interest rate which leads to a increased demand to hold money which shifts the money demand schedule from $Md1$ to $Md3$. Equilibrium of the system under floating exchange rates is therefore obtained at point C with a rise in price to $P3$ and a fall in output to $Y3$.

From this, we notice that our evaluation of the choice between fixed and floating exchange rate regimes would depend primarily upon the objectives of the authorities. This is because fixed exchange rates favour price stability while floating exchange rates favour income stability. Clearly, if the objective function of the authorities is biased towards price stability the authorities would find fixed rates preferable to floating. If, however, the authorities are more concerned with output stability they would find floating rates preferable to fixed. This is a good illustration of the importance of the specification of the objective function. Since depending upon the weighting of the objective function either fixed or floating exchange rates could be deemed superior.

In **Figure 10.5** we again assume that there is a transitory inflationary aggregate supply shock that shifts the aggregate supply function from $Ys1$ to $Ys2$, this time, however, the money demand schedule is less steep than the aggregate demand schedule.

In this case, the aggregate supply shock under fixed exchange rates causes there to be an excess demand for money at point B, and consequently there is a tendency for the currency to appreciate. In order to avoid an appreciation of the currency the authorities intervene in the foreign exchange market to purchase the foreign currency resulting in an increase in the domestic money stock until the Md schedule shifts from $Md1$ to $Md2$. The end result under fixed exchange rates is that the domestic price level rises to $P2$ and output falls to $Y2$.

Under floating exchange rates, the excess demand for money resulting from the shock leads to an appreciation of the exchange rate. This has the effect of shifting the aggregate demand schedule to the left from $Yd1$ to $Yd2$. In addition, the appreciation leads to the expectation of a future depreciation which via the uncovered interest rate parity condition raises the domestic interest rate constituting an additional reason for the leftward shift of the Yd schedule. The rise in the domestic interest rate by reducing the demand for money shifts the Md schedule to the right from $Md1$ to $Md3$. The result is that short-run equilibrium under floating exchange rates is obtained at point C with a rise in the domestic price level to $P3$ and fall in domestic output to $Y3$.

In this case, we again observe a conflict when choosing between fixed and floating exchange rates. The difference is that in this instance fixed exchange rates favour output stability while floating exchange rates favour price stability.

The point of including this second case is that it illustrates the point that the choice between fixed and floating exchange rates is very closely related to the structural parameters of the economy. In the first case, greater output stability could be obtained by floating exchange rates while in the second case fixed exchange rates prove superior. From this, it follows that any policy recommendations should be based on a study of the characteristics of the particular economy. Even if economies

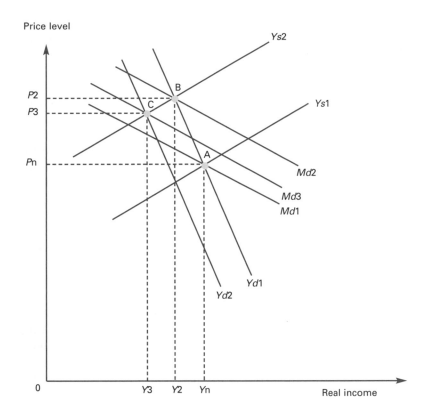

Figure 10.5 Aggregate supply shock, case 2: Yd schedule is steeper than the Md schedule, i.e. $\eta(\theta + \beta) < \alpha$

have similar objectives and face similar shocks we may be led to make different policy recommendations due to structural differences between economies. The results of the analysis of our model are summarized in **Table 10.1**.

Table 10.1 reveals that the choice between fixed and floating exchange rates is nowhere near as clear-cut as their advocates are prone to argue. The choice between the two regimes is seen to depend crucially upon the type of shock impinging upon

Table 10.1 Summary of the results under fixed and floating rates

Transitory shock	Floating rates		Fixed rates	
	Price stability	Output stability	Price stability	Output stability
Money demand	X	X	✔	✔
Aggregate demand	✔	✔	X	X
Aggregate supply Md steeper than Yd	X	✔	✔	X
Aggregate supply Yd steeper than Md	✔	X	X	✔

Note: ✔ – indicates performs best, X – indicates performs worst.

the economy, the objectives of the authorities and the structural parameters of the particular economy considered (the steepness of the *Md* schedule relative to the *Yd* schedule).

Before concluding this section it is worth reminding readers that the model set out is extremely simple. In practice, the choice between a fixed or floating exchange rate will be even more complex. We considered only the case of transitory shocks, but economies are subjected to both transitory and permanent disturbances. In addition, some economies have wage indexation while others do not, indexation will lead to wage adjustments following movements in the domestic price level or the exchange rate which can alter the ranking of the two regimes (see Pilbeam 1991). Finally, we have not touched upon the problem of interdependence; while a fixed exchange rate may be the preferred choice for one economy, its trading partners may prefer a floating regime. If this is the case, the appropriate exchange rate regime for the two countries is clearly greatly complicated.

10.11 Managed floating

Since the advent of floating exchange rates in 1973 it has become evident that authorities have not always let their currency float freely but rather they have frequently intervened to influence the exchange rate. A number of rationales have been put forward to justify such intervention and are worth consideration.

Before examining some the most frequently used arguments for intervention it is necessary to assume that the authorities can influence the nominal and or real exchange rate in their desired direction, without such an assumption no rationale for intervention can exist. Further, when assessing the validity of intervention policy it is necessary to compare exchange market intervention with alternative policies. Only if it can be demonstrated that intervention has a superior benefit to cost impact than other policies, or that constraints prevent the use of superior policies, can exchange market intervention be justified. It should be remembered throughout that exchange rate management by the authorities can vary in degree from occasional intervention to influence the exchange rate to a permanent pegging.

The arguments for some degree of discretionary intervention to some extent overlap but fall into three main categories: (i) the authorities can choose an exchange rate more in line with economic fundamentals than the market; (ii) Intervention is required to mitigate the costs of exchange rate 'overshooting'; and (iii) intervention is an appropriate instrument for smoothing necessary economic adjustments.

Authorities might be able to produce a more appropriate exchange rate

As we argued in section 10.2, for a variety of reasons the exchange rate produced by the market may be the wrong rate compared to underlying economic fundamentals. The market may use the wrong model, it may have the wrong perception about the future and will have difficulty in interpreting the implications of news relevant to the exchange rate. However, the fact that the market may produce the wrong rate does not justify intervention by the authorities; it is necessary to demonstrate that the authorities can choose a more appropriate rate.

There exists a case for intervention if the news or information available to the market is efficiently used but the news itself is either inadequate – increasing risk – or misleading, and the authorities are in possession of superior relevant information. Intervention in such circumstances can prove both stabilizing and profitable. However, it could be argued that a superior policy is for the authorities to abstain from intervention and release the relevant information to the market. Nevertheless, there may be circumstances under which such an information-release is not considered desirable, and even if the authorities were to release the relevant information to the market, there is no guarantee that the market would believe them.

Connected with the above argument is a far more convincing reason for the authorities to intervene. While it may be the case that the authorities do not know any more than the market regarding what is the correct rate, they should know better and sooner what they themselves are about to do (in most cases!). Since the exchange rate is an asset price it incorporates expectations concerning its future price appropriately discounted into the current price so that unusual *ex ante* speculative profits cannot be made. For example, if the money supply is expected to increase at a given date in the future, this implies a depreciation of the exchange rate; if the exchange rate did not depreciate until the expected increase in the money supply took place, this would imply a large discrete depreciation of the exchange rate at that time. However, since the depreciation was expected such a discrete jump would imply a missed abnormal *ex ante* profit opportunity. Since the foreign exchange market is efficient the expectation of a depreciation leads to a smaller discrete depreciation of the current rate (reflecting the news of future monetary expansion), with a gradual depreciation thereafter until the actual increase in the money supply takes place. In this way all anticipated disturbances are fully discounted and therefore unusual *ex ante* profit opportunities eliminated.

The point is that the authorities should be more capable than the market in predicting the future course of their policies and this is of relevance to the correct exchange rate. Given this, intervention in the foreign exchange market may be interpreted by the market as a commitment by the authorities to adopt a given course of action; if this is the case, economic agents may more readily lend their support to the new policy helping to make it more effective and more speedily so than would otherwise be the case. Thus, there exists a case for official intervention on the grounds that the authorities have a better knowledge of their future policy intentions than private market participants. Official intervention in the foreign exchange market may literally 'buy credibility' convincing economic agents that the authorities intend to fulfil their stated domestic policy targets by committing the assets of the central bank in support of its declared future policy. A key postulate of the rational expectations literature is that the authorities will only be able to achieve their short-run inflation objectives painlessly if economic agents are convinced that the authorities intend to carry out their stated objectives. The opportunity to purchase some credibility by intervening in the foreign exchange market could prove to be a useful policy tool.

To illustrate the above point, consider the case where there is news of an increase in the rate of growth of the money supply. This may be viewed as affecting speculators' expectations in at least three possible ways: it may be seen as only a transitory development of a countercyclical nature that will subsequently be reversed; or, it may be seen as a once and for all change in the money stock that will not be reversed but which will not affect the underlying rate of growth of the money stock; or alternatively it may be seen as heralding a more permanent increase in the rate of growth of the money stock. Each of the alternatives has different implications concerning the required depreciation of the currency, the greater the actual growth the greater the required depreciation. There is no *a priori* reason to believe that the market, in the short run at least, will on balance know what is the required depreciation; the authorities, however, should know and could indicate their feelings regarding the appropriate rate via an intervention policy.

Intervention needed to mitigate costs of exchange rate overshooting

The Dornbusch (1976) overshooting model examined in Chapter 7 showed that a move to monetary restraint can lead to a short-run real exchange rate appreciation, while an expansionary monetary policy can lead to a real depreciation. These real exchange rate movements (over and undervaluations in relation to PPP) will exert effects on the real economy. In what follows we shall refer to substantial and prolonged deviations from PPP as exchange rate misalignments.

Misaligned exchange rates distort the allocation of resources between tradables and non-tradables as well as consumption patterns between the two. Undervaluation by raising the domestic price level and placing downward pressure on real wages may spark off inflationary pressures, while overvaluation by squeezing the tradables sector may result in increased unemployment. Misalignment complicates and inhibits investment decisions because uncertainty as to the duration of the over/undervaluation will affect the profitability calculations concerning whether to invest in tradables or non-tradables, particularly inhibiting marginal investment decisions.

Misalignments almost certainly exert a ratchet effect on protectionism. In periods of undervaluation of the currency, resources that would ordinarily not be viable enter into the tradables sector but as the rate corrects itself they will come under increasing pressure and will then seek recourse to protection. Alternatively, if the currency is overvalued this will tend to lead to automatic protectionist cries due to the pressure on the tradables sector. It should also be remembered that undervaluation for one currency involves overvaluation for another and *vice-versa*, so that one could expect protectionism to be a global and persistent phenomenon so long as exchange rates are misaligned. Since an under/overvaluation must necessarily eventually be corrected, this will involve the various adjustment costs arising because of factor immobility occupationally and geographically; retraining of labour will involve costs and time, and absorption cannot be painlessly varied at will.

Foreign exchange intervention designed to reduce the costs and extent of exchange rate overshooting could be justified. It is worth noting that the case for intervention in this instance is not in any way due to inefficiency in the foreign exchange market. The rate produced by the market is the correct rate but because of 'sticky' goods prices there are short-run real exchange rate changes. If the price level increased (decreased) by $x\%$ immediately following an $x\%$ change in the money supply, as in the flexible price monetary model, there would be no overshooting of the exchange rate. This latter observation has led some authors to propose that rather than intervene in the foreign exchange market, the authorities should tackle the inefficiencies in the goods and labour markets. If these markets were made more flexible so that the rate of inflation adjusted quickly to changes in monetary policy, then this would reduce the amount of overshooting. The measures proposed would include anti-trust legislation, reductions in trade union power and the reduction of social security benefits, all of which would make goods and factor prices more flexible and thereby reduce the problem of overshooting. Not surprisingly, by comparison to the likely resistance and turmoil associated with such policies, exchange market intervention can prove a superior policy tool.

Intervention to smooth the economic adjustment process

There may exist a rationale for the authorities to intervene in the foreign exchange market to achieve a preferable exchange rate in the short run to permit a smoothing of the necessary adjustments that the economy must for various reasons undergo. The rationale for smoothing the adjustment process is that it is a painful process for those who have to adjust and is more acceptable at a controlled pace than a market-determined pace.

Suppose that a country has a persistent balance of payments surplus because the traded goods sector is too large relative to the non-traded sector. There will consequently be a tendency for an appreciation of the real exchange rate which will encourage factors to move from the traded goods sector to the non-traded sector. If the authorities are concerned about the possibility of large transitional unemployment resulting from such an appreciation, they may try to moderate the appreciation to allow time for the traded goods sector to contract and the non-tradables sector to expand, so as to avoid what they consider to be excessive transitional unemployment costs. Corden (1982) has coined the phrase 'exchange rate protection' to describe an exchange rate policy whereby a country protects its tradable goods sector relative to the non-tradables sector, by either devaluing the real exchange rate, allowing the exchange rate to depreciate by more than it otherwise would, or preventing an exchange rate appreciation that would otherwise take place.

The preceding case is only one variant of the need to switch resources in the economy; another may occur when the tradables sector itself is divided into 'booming' and 'lagging' sectors. The booming sector will cause the real exchange rate to have a tendency to appreciate, and in so doing will speed up the demise of the lagging sector. In either of the two cases cited, the case for exchange rate protection is clearly linked to the speed at which adjustment can take place, be it between the traded and non-traded sector or within the tradables sector.

Exchange market intervention can compare favourably to other methods of protection for the purpose of slowing down the necessary adjustment such as tariff protection. This is because exchange rate protection which involves influencing the real exchange rate and with it the accumulation of reserves must necessarily be a temporary method of protection, whereas tariffs and subsidies have a habit of becoming permanent features and, because of their explicit protective nature, tend to invite retaliation. Nevertheless, it is difficult to say that either form of protection is to be preferred, for while tariffs distort production patterns within the tradables sector in favour of the lagging (protected) sector, exchange rate protection protects all tradables whether they require assistance or not, and it could be argued that because it is a more widespread means of protection it is more likely to invite retaliation.

Another rationale for intervention may exist if the economy is caught in a 'vicious circle'. Consider, a country experiencing for whatever reason a current account deficit that it is trying to eliminate by permitting the depreciation of its currency. If wages adjust fully and instantaneously to the increased domestic price level implied by such a policy, and the authorities adopt an accommodating monetary policy to avoid an increase in unemployment, the country will be back where it started. A further depreciation will be necessary and via the same process this will again lead the country back where it started; the country will be caught in a vicious circle of depreciation, price rises and wage rises and further depreciation. Under such circumstances, intervention in the foreign exchange market may serve to slow down or even avoid the spiral, allowing the authorities to adopt a more appropriate policy designed to bring about the necessary reduction in real wages or to await productivity improvements in the economy which means that real wages do not have to fall.

It should be noted, however, that the real issue behind the vicious-circle argument for intervention concerns the effectiveness of different policy instruments in bringing about the ultimate reduction in real wages that is essential for adjustment (in the absence of productivity improvements), while minimizing the harmful consequences for other macro objectives such as the maintenance of full employment and reasonable price stability. Here one should recall Keynes' argument that price changes may prove a more acceptable method of reducing real wages because they hit the labour force more or less equally, and by so doing do not upset to any great extent wage differentials. The alternative policy of deflation may prove a lot more painful process of reducing real wages, especially with regard to the employment objective because it may require a large rise in unemployment before the principle of real wage cuts becomes accepted by the labour force. Thus, there may be a case in the vicious-circle argument for government intervention to slow down the rate of depreciation so that real wages are reduced only gradually at a more acceptable pace.

Before concluding this section, it is worth emphasizing that the adjustment arguments advanced for exchange rate management involve smoothing the adjustment process, not preventing it. Ideally, the exchange rate should be allowed to adjust towards its equilibrium rate at an optimum pace the determination of which is clearly a policy problem. It is the acceptance of the principle of exchange rate adjustment that ensures that the required changes in the economy do take place.

10.12 Conclusions

The clear result that emerges from this chapter is that neither the traditional advantages/disadvantages approach or modern literature provide a clear-cut reason to prefer fixed exchange rates to floating or *vice-versa*. Fixed exchange rates have some advantages and disadvantages as compared to floating exchange rates. Indeed, many of the proposed advantages can under some circumstance be viewed as disadvantages. For example, floating exchange rates restore monetary autonomy, but whether this is a good thing or bad thing will depend upon whether the authorities use the autonomy wisely.

The modern approach to evaluating the two regimes shows that only under very specific conditions can we say that one regime is better than the other. Our analysis has focused on three crucial factors determine the choice of exchange rate regime, the specification of the objective function, the type of shock impinging upon the economy and the structure of the economy. In particular, the analysis highlights the importance of the specification of the objective function and demonstrates how a slight modification to this can completely reverse the ranking of the regimes. Different countries even if they have similar economic structures and face similar shocks may well require different exchange rate regimes simply because their objectives differ.

There are a host of other factors that will complicate the choice of exchange rate regime such as the implications of wages indexation, the possibility of permanent shocks and relationships between various shocks. It should also be remembered that, in practice, it is extremely difficult to know if an economy is being afflicted by a supply or demand shock or a shock to money demand. Even if a shock is identified, there is the question as to whether or not it is a permanent or transitory phenomenon.

The lack of decisive arguments in favour of either fixed or floating exchange rates has frequently been taken as a rationale for some degree of exchange rate management between the two regimes. The argument being that such exchange rate management has the potential to combine the advantages of both regimes, while limiting the disadvantages. However, a demonstration that private speculation may produce the wrong rate, or that exchange rates are prone to 'overshoot', does not by itself justify intervention. It is necessary to demonstrate that the authorities can choose a more appropriate rate and that intervention can influence the exchange rate in the desired direction. In addition, it is necessary to demonstrate that intervention in the foreign exchange market is the best means of tackling the economic problem in hand. Instability of the exchange rate may merely be due to unstable macroeconomic policies by the country concerned and the best means for reducing such fluctuations is to stabilize domestic economic policies, not intervention in the foreign exchange market.

Since there is no unique case for exchange rate management there can be no unique set of rules expected to deal with the wide variety of circumstances that can arise. An appropriate intervention policy may involve reducing or exacerbating exchange rate movements, intervention may need to be temporary or prolonged, and the amount of intervention required will vary with the circumstances. In other words, even if intervention can be justified, the precise direction, duration and volume of intervention required need to be determined.

Finally, it should not be forgotten that we have examined the choice between alternative regimes within the context of a specific model specification of a small open economy. One of the implications of the analysis is that different countries may need to opt for different exchange rate regimes. It may be the case that the choice of exchange rate policy by one country may well be a crucial factor in determining the choice of exchange rate policy for other countries and this is an issue that merits further research.

Further reading

Argy, V. (1982) 'Exchange Rate Management in Theory and Practice', *Princeton Studies in International Finance*, no. 50.

Artus, J.R. and Crockett, A. (1978) 'Floating Exchange Rates and the Need for Surveillance', *Princeton Essays in International Finance*, no. 127.

Artus, J.R and Young, J.H. (1979) 'Fixed and Flexible Exchange Rates: A Renewal of the Debate', *IMF Staff Papers*, vol. 26, pp. 654–98.

Basevi, G. and De Grauwe, P. (1977) 'Vicious and Virtuous Circles. A Theoretical Analysis and a Policy Proposal for Managing Exchange Rates', *European Economic Review*, vol. 10, pp. 277–301.

Bayoumi, T. and Eichengreen, B. (1994) 'One Money or Many? Analysing the Prospects for Monetary Union in Various Parts of the World', *Princeton Studies in International Finance*, no. 76, Princeton, New Jersey.

Blanchard, O. (1979) 'Speculative Bubbles, Crashes and Rational Expectations', *Economic Letters*, vol. 3, pp. 387–9.

Claassen, E.M. (1976) 'World Inflation Under Flexible Exchange Rates', *Scandinavian Journal of Economics*, vol. 78, pp. 346–65.

Corden, M. (1982) 'Exchange Rate Protection', in R.N. Cooper, P.B. Kenen, J.B. Machedo and Y.V. Ypersele (eds), *The International Monetary System Under Flexible Exchange Rates* (Cambridge Mass.: Ballinger).

Dooley, M. (1981) 'An Analysis of Exchange Market Intervention of Industrial and Developing Countries', *IMF Staff Papers*, vol. 29, pp. 233–69.

Dornbusch, R. (1976) 'Expectations and Exchange Rate Dynamics', *Journal of Political Economy*, vol. 84, pp. 1161–76.

Dornbusch, R. (1983) 'Flexible Exchange Rates and Interdependence', *IMF Staff Papers*, vol. 29, pp. 233–69.

Frankel, J.A. (1999) 'No Single Currency Regime is Right for all Countries or at all Times', *Princeton Essays in International Finance*, no. 215, Princeton, New Jersey.

Friedman, M. (1953) 'The Case for Flexible Exchange Rates', M. Friedman, *Essays in Positive Economics* (Chicago: University of Chicago Press).

Goodhart, C.A.E. (1975) *Money, Information and Uncertainty* (London: Macmillan, now Palgrave Macmillan).

Ishiyama, Y. (1975) 'The Theory of Optimum Currency Areas: A Survey', *IMF Staff Papers*, vol. 22, pp. 344–83

Johnson, H.G. (1969) 'The Case for Flexible Exchange Rates, 1969', *Federal Reserve Bank of St Louis Review*, vol. 51, pp. 12–24.

Kenen, P.B. (1969) 'The Theory of Optimum Currency Areas: An Eclectic View', R. A. Mundell and A.K. Swoboda (eds), *Monetary Problems of the International Economy* (Chicago: University of Chicago Press).

Kenen, P.B. (1987) 'Exchange Rate Management: What Role for Intervention?', *American Economic Review Papers and Proceedings*, pp. 194–9.

Kenen, P.B. (1988) *Managing Exchange Rates* (London: Routledge).

McKinnon, R.I. (1963) 'Optimum Currency Areas', *American Economic Review*, vol. 53, pp. 717–25.

Mundell, R.A. (1961) 'A Theory of Optimum Currency Areas', *American Economic Review*, vol. 51, pp. 509–17.

Mussa, M. (1979) 'Macroeconomic Interdependence and the Exchange Rate Regime', R. Dornbusch and J.A. Frenkel (eds), *International Economic Policy* (Baltimore: John Hopkins University Press).

Mussa, M. (1981) 'The Role of Official Intervention', *Group of 30 Occasional Papers no. 6*, New York.

Nurkse, R. (1944) *International Currency Experience* (League of Nations, Columbia University Press).

Pilbeam, K.S. (1991) *Exchange Rate Management: Theory and Evidence* (London: Palgrave Macmillan).

Sohmen, E. (1961) *Flexible Exchange Rates* (Chicago: The University of Chicago Press).

Tavlas, G. (1993) 'The New Theory of Optimum Curency Areas', *World Economy*, vol. 16, pp. 211–38.

Tower, E. and Willet, T.D. (1976) 'The Theory of Optimum Currency Areas and Exchange Rate Flexibility', *Princeton Special Papers in International Finance*, no. 11, Princeton.

Turnovsky, S.J. (1984) 'Exchange Market Intervention in a Small Open Economy: An Expository Model', P. Malgrange and P.A. Muet (eds), *Contemporary Macroeconomic Modelling* (Oxford: Basil Blackwell).

PART 3

The Postwar International Monetary System

11

The International Monetary System

11.1 Introduction

The international monetary system is broadly defined as the set of conventions, rules, procedures and institutions that govern the conduct of financial relations between nations. In this chapter we look in some detail at the development of the post-Second World War international monetary system. An understanding of the historical, institutional and economic developments that have occurred since the end of the Second

World War are an essential background to the study of international finance. Many of the proposals for reform of the international monetary system have been based upon the desire to avoid the problems and mistakes of the past. There are many facets of the postwar system that merit attention and that are studied in this chapter. Among these are the Bretton Woods system and its eventual breakdown, the move to floating exchange rates, economic events of the 1970s including two oil shocks, and the economic policy divergences of the 1980s. The setting-up of the European Monetary System leading eventually to achievement on 1 January 1999 of Economic and Monetary Union in Europe is probably the most significant event to occur in the evolution of the international monetary system since the breakdown of the Bretton Woods system.

The 1990s witnessed considerable currency turmoil, firstly afflicting developed economies with speculative attacks launched against a number of EMS currencies including the British pound, the Italian lira and the Spanish peseta. The EMS crisis was followed by a series of currency and financial crises afflicting emerging market economies. In 1994–95 Mexico suffered what has become known as the 'Tequila crisis', but this proved to be merely a taster for the currency and financial turmoil that was to follow. In July 1997, a Thai baht devaluation marked an abrupt end to the 'Asian miracle' and the start of the 'Asian financial crisis' which involved roughly one and a half years of unprecedented turbulence in the region's financial and currency markets. Barely had the Asian crisis started to subside, when a new crisis broke out following an effective Russian default on its domestic and foreign currency debts; the Russian crisis was accompanied by concerns for the global capital markets when Long-Term Capital Management (LTCM), a hedge fund with massive speculative positions in the financial markets, was effectively bankrupted. The Russian crisis had a direct impact on Brazil which had its own currency crisis in 1999. The new century started out with its own set of crises, starting with a devaluation of the Turkish lira in 2001. This was followed by the largest ever default on $100 billion of external debt by Argentina in January 2002, and the ending of its experiment with a currency board system that had since 1991 pegged its currency at a one peso–one US dollar parity. The Argentinian crisis eventually impacted upon Uruguay which was forced to float its currency later in the year.

Much of the story of the postwar international monetary order is about the central role of the US dollar which, despite the birth of the euro, remains the major international currency. However, even the dollar has been subjected to considerable turbulence in the foreign exchange markets in recent years; it appreciated sharply and unexpectedly against the euro upon the latter's birth from $1.174/€1 in January 1999 to $0.827/€1 on 26 October 2000, where it steadied and began to depreciate and then rally back until 11 June 2001, when it started to depreciate from $0.843/€1. Mounting concerns about the size of the US current account deficits and cuts in US interest rates to historically low levels by the Federal Reserve led to substantial falls in the US dollar from mid-June 2001. The frequent currency crises and ever-increasing international movements have led some commentators to argue that there is no room for a halfway house when it comes to the choice of exchange rate regime. They have argued that the international monetary system will increasingly become bipolar with countries adopting the extremes of either a 'hard peg' or a floating exchange rate. This view has recently been challenged on empirical grounds and there have been a number of recent studies that attempt to empirically examine the relative merits of fixed, floating and intermediate exchange rate regimes on the basis of their association with economic performance, which we shall review. We conclude by examining some recent and older proposals for reform of the international monetary system.

11.2 The Bretton Woods system

The initial talks on reconstructing a postwar international monetary system started between the United States and United Kingdom as early as 1941. The lead negotiators were Harry Dexter White for the USA and John Maynard Keynes for the British. Given the US economic and political dominance at the end of the war, it is not surprising that the eventual system reflected more the US proposals. The system that emerged was ratified at an international monetary conference held at Bretton Woods, New Hampshire, attended by some 44 countries although some commentators dubbed the conference as a meeting of 1½ nations (the USA and the UK!).

The motivation behind creating a new international monetary order was the desire to avoid the breakdown in international monetary relations that had occurred in the 1930s. In the 1920s Germany witnessed hyperinflation and the US stockmarket collapse of 1929 heralded a worldwide recession. The 1930s were marked by major trade imbalances which in turn led to the adoption of widespread protectionism, the adoption of deflationary policies, competitive devaluations and the abandonment of the gold exchange standard. In an influential report for the League of Nations Ragnar Nurkse (1944) argued that experience with floating exchange rates had shown that they discouraged international trade, caused a misallocation of resources and were generally characterized by bouts of destabilizing speculation.

11.3 Features of the system

There were several important features to the system; a fixed but adjustable exchange rate and the setting up of two new international organizations. These were the International Monetary Fund (IMF) with the duty of monitoring and supervising the system, and the International Bank for Reconstruction and Development (IBRD) commonly known as the World Bank, charged initially with the role of assisting the reconstruction of Europe's devastated economies. In fact the World Bank is a pair of institutions – the IBRD and the International Development Association (IDA) which obtains money from developed nations and lends out the funds to the poorest less-developed countries (LDCs) at concessional terms. A third institution, the International Finance Corporation (IFC) is affiliated to the World Bank, and provides risk capital direct to the private sector of LDCs.

Fixed but adjustable exchange rates

Bretton Woods established a system of fixed but adjustable exchange rates. Under the Articles of Agreement of the IMF, each currency was assigned a central parity against the US dollar and was allowed to fluctuate by plus or minus 1% either side of this parity. The dollar itself was fixed to the price of gold at $35 per ounce.

The idea of fixing the dollar to the price of gold was to provide confidence in the system. In 1945 the US authorities held approximately 70% of the world's gold reserves. It was reasoned that foreign central banks would be more willing to hold dollars in their reserves if they knew that they could be converted into gold. The US authorities made a commitment to keep the dollar convertible into gold at $35 dollars per ounce, which in effect was a pledge on the part of the USA to preserve the purchasing power of dollars making the dollar 'as good as gold'.

A country was expected to preserve the par value of its currency *vis-à-vis* the dollar, but in the case of 'fundamental disequilibrium' in its balance of payments could devalue or revalue its currency. Providing the proposed change was less than 10% the IMF could not object, but larger realignments required the permission of the Fund. The ability of a country to alter its par rate as a last resort was seen as an essential part of the system; it offered countries an ultimate alternative to deflation or import controls as a means of correcting persistent balance of payments imbalances.

Under the Articles of Agreement of the Fund, the member governments committed themselves to make their currencies convertible for current account transactions as soon as was feasible. Convertibility for current account transactions meant that while governments could still employ capital controls, they could not prevent their residents or residents of other countries from buying or selling their currency for current account transactions. It is notable, however, that such a commitment to convertibility was not required with respect to capital account transactions. This omission reflected the widespread suspicion that capital movements were potentially highly destabilizing.

The IMF and credit facilities

The IMF was set up with its general objective being to oversee and promote international monetary cooperation and the growth of world trade. To these ends, one of the principal tasks of the Fund was to ensure the smooth functioning of the fixed exchange rate system. In particular, minimizing the need for countries to devalue and revalue their currencies by providing them with credit facilities with which to finance temporary balance of payments imbalances.

One of the major problems envisaged with the fixed exchange rate system was that countries facing a temporary balance of payments deficit would be forced to deflate their economies if they wished to maintain their exchange rate parity. As most governments had committed themselves to the maintenance of full employment, such a scenario was not particularly appealing. To avert this, a credit mechanism was set up to provide support for countries facing transitory balance of payments problems. Avoidance of deflationary policies was viewed as helpful in maintaining the volume of world trade.

Under the credit facility, each member of the IMF was allocated a quota, the size of the quota being related to its economic importance as reflected in the size of its subscription to the Fund. A country had to place one-quarter of its quota in reserve assets (mainly gold) and the remaining three-quarters in its own currency with the Fund. This gave the IMF a stock of funds which could be lent to countries facing balance of payments difficulties. A country facing difficulty could draw upon its quota should it need to do so. A country was entitled to the first 25% of its quota, known as its gold tranche, automatically and a further four tranches of 25%, known as credit tranches, could be drawn providing the country agreed to conditions set by the IMF which became increasingly austere with each tranche drawn. Thus, in total, a country could draw a maximum of 125% of its quota. The conditions attached to the latter tranches are known as IMF **conditionality** and generally constitute a set of measures designed to improve a country's balance of payments. The IMF commenced operations in March 1947 with the total sum of initial quotas available at $8.8 billion.

When drawing upon the IMF resources, a member purchases reserve assets (usually dollars) in exchange for further deposits of its currency. The Fund decides what assets and currencies the drawing country receives on the basis of the composition of its own resources. As a rule any borrowing from the Fund has to be repaid over a period of three–five years. When repaying the Fund a country buys back its currency with foreign reserves.

11.4 A brief history of the Bretton Woods system

When the system of fixed parities commenced operation in March 1947 currencies were not freely convertible, there were many restrictions on the amount of dollars that could be brought on the foreign exchange market as most authorities had insufficient reserves to meet the huge demand for dollars. In the immediate years after the Second World War, the USA ran healthy current account surpluses and the European economies large deficits. This was partly because the Europeans did not have strong exporting capabilities and partly because they were importing investment goods for reconstruction purposes and satisfying a pent-up consumer demand.

The setting-up of the Bretton Woods system did not *per se* provide the basis for the reconstruction of the European countries. One of the major problems confronting the Europeans was their lack of dollars for purchasing the vital capital goods required to rebuild their war-torn economies. In 1948, partly out of a desire to help the Europeans help themselves, the US Secretary of State George Marshall announced a massive package of aid to the European economies. The 'Marshall aid' package was a very significant contribution to European reconstruction and the development of the postwar world economy. Between mid-1948 and mid-1952, Marshall aid provided some $11.6 billion of grants and $1.8 billion in loans and this greatly relieved the problem of the dollar shortage. The funds enabled European countries to purchase the capital and raw materials necessary for reconstruction.

Marshall aid was made partly conditional on greater cooperation between the European economies. One sign of this cooperation was the setting up of the Organization for European Economic Cooperation (OEEC) which administered the Marshall aid funds; later this organization became the Organization for Economic Cooperation and Development (OECD) with the USA and Canada joining in 1961 and Japan in 1964. Another result of US encouragement to greater European cooperation was the European Payments Union (EPU) which commenced operations in 1950. The EPU enabled the European member countries to settle trade credits among themselves with the minimal use of dollars. This further relieved the dollar shortage and contributed to the faster liberalization and growth of intra-European trade as compared to extra-European trade.

In 1949 the European deficits led to a series of currency devaluations (UK, France, Scandinavian countries) which received the approval of the IMF. The Fund recognized that the parities that were fixed in 1944 overvalued the European currencies and that to not allow the devaluations would require a severe deflation in the European economies which would be undesirable as they sought to reconstruct their economies.

Furthermore, the funds that the IMF had available for financing these deficits were considered to be inadequate and should not to be used to finance the reconstruction of the European economies.

From the early 1950s onwards the US basic balance moved from its postwar surplus into deficits of approximately $1.5 billion per year. The counterpart of this was that the Europeans and Japanese started to run surpluses. Initially the US deficits caused no worries because its trading partners, notably West Germany and Japan, were experiencing export-led growth and were happy to build up dollar reserves. So long as the US deficits were of reasonable proportions and US gold reserves exceeded its dollar liabilities the system functioned well. The operation of the EPU, Marshall aid package and the improved health of the European economies in the 1950s enabled the Europeans to relax their trade and capital controls. In December 1958 the Europeans had acquired sufficient reserves that they were able to make their currencies convertible and abolish the EPU.

During the period 1958–61 there was a more rapid deterioration in the US balance of payments (see **Table 11.1**). Many of the dollars acquired were converted into gold by foreign central banks, and this gold drain provoked some concern in the US administration about the US deficit. In March 1961 there was a 5% revaluation of the deutschmark and the Dutch guilder. In addition, to forestall speculation against the dollar, the USA and nine other countries arranged a General Arrangement to Borrow (GAB). The GAB members who became known as the group of ten (G-10) agreed to lend additional funds to the IMF should one of the members require large-scale borrowing. The GAB arrangements were opened in October 1962 with potential lending commitments totalling $6 billion. In the event the USA never used the facility which was not activated until the UK used it at the end of 1964.

Table 11.1 The US balance of payments, 1959–73 (US$ billions)

Year	Trade balance	Current balance	Basic balance
1959	0.91	−2.14	−2.00
1960	4.89	1.80	−3.20
1961	5.57	3.07	−3.11
1962	4.52	2.46	−3.69
1963	5.22	3.20	−5.04
1964	6.80	5.79	−6.19
1965	4.95	4.29	−6.19
1966	3.82	1.94	−4.12
1967	3.80	1.54	−5.36
1968	0.64	0.96	−1.08
1969	0.61	−1.63	−2.27
1970	2.16	−0.32	−3.02
1971	−2.72	−3.91	−6.27
1972	−6.99	−9.81	−1.67
1973	0.62	0.67	−2.52

Source: US Department of Commerce, Survey of Current Business.

In 1954 the London gold bullion market reopened for private trading in gold. Around 1961, due to speculation of a US devaluation against gold, there was persistent upward pressure on the price of gold. Indeed, in 1962 there was such persistent upward pressure on the gold price that the central banks of the USA and seven other industrialized countries set up a 'gold pool'. The purpose of the pool was to increase the supply of gold on the private market when there was an upward pressure on its price so as to keep it in line with the official price of $35 per ounce.

In 1965, President De Gaulle made a speech extolling the virtues of gold as compared to the dollar, and the French started to covert dollars into gold with the US authorities. By mid-1967 it was becoming apparent that with US dollar liabilities exceeding its gold reserves any attempt by central banks to convert their dollar reserves into gold would lead to a breakdown of the system. This led to an agreement by central banks not to convert their dollar reserves into gold. In addition, the authorities decided to give up their sales of gold to the private market in a bid to prevent its price rising. A two-tier market for gold was established with the official rate remaining at $35 per ounce while the private market price was allowed to rise.

During the early 1960s the US balance of payments position stabilized but by the mid-1960s, with US involvement in the Vietnam War, the US balance of payments began to deteriorate more noticeably as may be seen in **Table 11.1**. There was a growing feeling that the dollar was overvalued in relation to other currencies. Things started coming to a head in 1967 when, after a series of current account deficits, the UK authorities decided to devalue the pound by 14.6%. In 1969 problems with the French balance of payments and the fall of De Gaulle led to an 11% devaluation of the franc and a 9.3% revaluation of the deutschmark. These devaluations reminded speculators that exchange rates were adjustable and that considerable profits could be made in anticipating and selling currencies which would be devalued.

Little action was taken to reduce the size of the US balance of payments deficits which continued to rise. By 1971 it became increasingly apparent to speculators that the dollar was overvalued and the deutschmark and yen were undervalued. In April 1971, the US trade balance went into deficit for the first time that century, which led to a massive capital outflow from the dollar in anticipation of a dollar devaluation. During May the speculation against the dollar was so immense that the Bundesbank had to purchase some $2 billion in just two days. Speculation became so intense that foreign exchange trading was halted for a week. When trading recommenced, the deutschmark was revalued by 7% and the Austrian schilling by 5%.

The revaluations were not considered to be sufficient, and with the private market price of gold exceeding the official price speculators felt that a devaluation of the dollar was inevitable. Massive speculation against the dollar continued with speculators buying yen and deutschmark in anticipation of quick short-term profits from a dollar devaluation. With continued massive speculation against the dollar, on the 15 August 1971 President Nixon officially announced that the dollar was no longer convertible into gold. In addition, he announced an emergency 10% tariff on all US imports as an interim measure until US trading partners agreed to revalue their currencies against the dollar. Nixon also announced some domestic polices designed to stabilize the US inflation rate; these included price and wage controls.

The motivation behind the Nixon measures was to prompt other countries to revalue their currencies against the dollar; the US authorities did not feel that devaluing the dollar against gold was a desirable course of action. One reason was that the administration believed it would be a break of faith with foreign central banks that had been persuaded to hold dollars rather than gold. Furthermore, a devaluation of the dollar against gold would not improve US competitiveness if other countries continued to peg against the dollar. The hope was that the Nixon measures would encourage other countries to revalue their currencies against the dollar and so restore US competitiveness.

The immediate response of foreign governments to the Nixon measures was along the lines sought by the US administration. Foreign governments allowed their exchange rates to float and agreed to a further liberalization of trade barriers. In a bid to restore the pegged exchange rate system, the G-10 nations met in December at the Smithsonian Institute in Washington. They tried to tackle the problem of the overvalued dollar by devaluing it against gold from $35 to $38 and revaluing currencies against the dollar by an average of 8%. In addition, the margin by which other currencies could fluctuate against the dollar was widened from ±1 to ±2.25%. In return for the revaluations, the USA agreed to remove its 10% import tariff. Although President Nixon hailed the package as 'the most significant monetary agreement in the history of the world' it was in tatters within 15 months. The devaluation and increased flexibility were really a case of too little too late, especially as inflation rate differentials between the industrialized countries began to diverge (see **Table 11.6**). The devaluation did little to remedy the US balance of payments which reached record proportions in 1972.

By mid-1972 the UK ran into further balance of payments difficulties, and in June the UK authorities decided to let the pound float. The worsening US deficit led to further speculation against the dollar and in January 1973 the Swiss authorities announced that the Swiss franc was to float against the dollar, soon followed in February by the Japanese decision to allow the yen to float despite a further 10% dollar devaluation on 12 February. With further speculation against the dollar at the beginning of March, the foreign exchange markets again had to be closed and when they reopened on 19 March the European currencies began a joint float against the dollar known as the 'Snake in the Tunnel', an arrangement which meant that many Europeans currencies were allowed to fluctuate a maximum of ±1.125% against one another (the Snake) and a maximum of ±2.25% against the dollar (the Tunnel). In June 1973 the Snake in the Tunnel became the plain Snake in which the maximum fluctuation against the dollar was abandoned.

The adoption of floating exchange rates stood in marked contrast to the setting-up of the Bretton Woods system. There was no general agreement to adopt floating exchange rates or what rules should govern the conduct of future exchange rate policies. Rather, the move to floating rates was a somewhat disorderly and haphazard product of the breakdown of the fixed exchange rate system.

11.5 Why did the Bretton Woods system break down?

The Bretton Woods System operated with reasonable success and only occasional realignments from 1947 to 1971. Explanations of its breakdown generally concentrate on the problems of liquidity and the lack of an adequate adjustment mechanism.

The liquidity problem

Well before the eventual demise of Bretton Woods, Robert Triffin (1960) had predicted an eventual loss of confidence in the system. Triffin argued that there was an inherent contradiction in the gold–dollar standard. For the Bretton Woods system to function successfully it was essential that confidence was maintained in the US dollar; so long as Central Bank's knew that dollars could be converted into gold at $35 per ounce they would willingly hold dollars in their reserves. Triffin pointed out that as international trade grew, so would the demand for international reserves, namely US dollars. To meet the demand for these reserves the Bretton Woods system depended on the US running deficits, with other countries running surpluses and purchasing dollars to prevent their currencies appreciating. Hence, over time, the stock of US dollar liabilities to the rest of the world would increase and this rate of increase would be higher than the annual addition to the US gold reserves resulting from gold-mining activities. As a result, the ratio of US dollar liabilities to gold held by the US Federal Reserve would deteriorate until eventually the convertibility of dollars into gold at $35 per ounce would become *de facto* impossible.

As it became apparent that the US authorities would not be able to fulfil their convertibility commitment, Triffin predicted that central banks would begin to anticipate a devaluation of the dollar rate against gold. In anticipation of this, central banks would start to convert their reserves into dollars and stop pegging their currencies against the dollar leading to an inevitable breakdown of the system. The 'Triffin dilemma' was that continued USA deficits would undermine the Bretton Woods system, yet if the US took measures to curb its deficits this would lead to a shortage of world reserves which would undermine the growth of world trade and exert deflationary pressures on the world economy.

Table 11.2 shows the decline in the ratio of US reserves relative to its liquid liabilities as predicted by Triffin's analysis. The Bretton Woods system worked well in the 1950s, but the confidence in the system slowly deteriorated in the 1960s as US liquid liabilities began to outstrip US reserves; the deterioration is particularly marked from 1968 to 1972 corresponding to the collapse of the system.

Table 11.2 Ratio of US reserves to liquid liabilities

1950	2.73	1964	0.58
1952	2.38	1966	0.50
1954	1.84	1968	0.41
1956	1.59	1970	0.31
1958	1.34	1972	0.16
1960	0.92	1974	0.14
1962	0.71	1976	0.22

Source: Milner and Greenaway (1979), p. 271

Box 11.1

The creation of special drawing rights

Although the international monetary system was under no real strain around the mid-1960s, there was a feeling that the growth of international reserves was inadequate. This led to fears that the growth of world trade and with it economic growth would be unnecessarily constrained. In addition, the mechanism for increasing reserves was regarded as being too dependent upon the USA running balance of payments deficits which, as Triffin's analysis had shown, could eventually undermine the whole system. These factors led to a discussion among IMF members over how to supplement the stock of international reserves.

The result of these deliberations was the First Amendment of the IMF Articles of Agreement in 1967, which empowered the Fund to create a Special Drawing Account to supplement its quota system which operates under its General Account. Under the scheme a new reserve asset was to be created by the Fund called the Special Drawing Right (SDR). Unlike quotas which are backed by the deposits of Fund members, the SDR's value as a reserve asset rests on it being regarded as an acceptable means of exchange between central banks and the Fund.

Under the SDR scheme, each member of the Fund is allocated a specified annual amount of SDRs in proportion to their quota with the Fund. The cumulative total holdings of SDRs allocated to a country is known as its 'net cumulative allocation'. The value of an SDR was originally set at 1/35th of an ounce of gold, which was equivalent to $1. A country can draw upon its SDR allocation whenever it is experiencing balance of payments difficulties or needs to supplement its reserves. In contrast to quota drawings, SDR drawings do not require consultation with the Fund, do not have conditionality attached and are not subject to repayment. Since SDR drawings are not subject to repayment they constitute a net addition to global reserves. However, over a five-year period a member has to maintain its SDR balance at an average of 30% of its net cumulative allocation (reduced to 15% in 1979).

A country that draws upon its SDR allocation can exchange the SDRs with foreign authorities for their currencies thereby increasing its reserves. All members of the Fund are obliged to accept SDRs in exchange for their national currency up to three times its net cumulative allocation. Countries drawing SDRs have to pay interest while countries in receipt of SDRs receive interest.

An increase in SDR allocations requires the consent of 80% of IMF votes. The first planned allocation of SDRs for the period 1970–72 was $9.5 billion. In the event, these allocations proved very ill-timed because they coincided with a massive surge in international liquidity resulting from massive purchases of dollars in the final years of the Bretton Woods system.

In July 1976 the value of the SDR was changed from $1 to a weighted basket of 16 currencies, and in January 1981 the SDR value was redefined as a weighted basket of five currencies; these currencies being the US dollar, the deutschmark, yen, French franc and pound sterling. The introduction of the euro led to it being redefined as a basket of just four currencies in January 2001, the weights were the dollar (45%), euro (29%), yen (15%) and pound sterling (11%). The role of the SDR in the international financial system is fully covered in Clark and Polak (2004).

An alternative interpretation of the demise of Bretton Woods

Although the Triffin dilemma at first sight seems to fit the facts quite well and is commonly held as the major cause of the breakdown of the Bretton Woods system, Jurg Niehans (1984) and Paul De Grauwe (1989) have suggested a somewhat different interpretation of events. Their interpretation is based upon an application of what is known as Greshams Law. Thomas Gresham (1529–79) argued that when there is a discrepancy between the official rate of exchange between two assets and their private market rate of exchange, the asset that is undervalued at the official rate will disappear from circulation, while the asset that is overvalued will continue in circulation. When applied to the monetary field this means that 'bad money drives out good money'.

Greshams Law can equally provide an insight into the collapse of the Bretton Woods system. In this case, the two assets to be considered are gold and the dollar. Under the Bretton Woods system the official rate of exchange of the these two assets was set at $35 pcr troy ounce. The US authorities were committed to buy and sell gold with foreign monetary authorities at this price. With US prices increasing by some 40% between 1959 and 1969, the price of gold should, *ceteris paribus*, have risen by a similar amount. Indeed, as we have seen in the private market there was a persistent upward pressure on the price of gold leading to the setting-up of the gold pool. However, these gold sales became so significant the loss of gold led central banks to disband the gold pool in 1968. A two-tier market for gold led to the private market price of gold rising above the official rate.

Once the official price of gold became undervalued compared to the private rate, central banks could easily have caused a major run on the dollar by converting their dollar reserves into gold and then sold the gold on the private market at a profit. In a bid to preserve the fixed exchange rate system in 1967, the USA secured an agreement from foreign central banks not to convert their dollar reserves into gold or to sell gold to private markets. In effect, the dollar was *de facto* no longer convertible into gold. In the end, following a further deterioration of the US balance of payments in 1970 and 1971, President Nixon announced the *de jure* suspension of dollar convertibility into gold. Dollars had driven out gold in accordance with Gresham's Law.

Lack of an adjustment mechanism

The Bretton Woods system permitted a realignment of exchange rate parities as a last resort in case of 'fundamental disequilibrium' of a member's balance of payments. In practice, however, countries proved extremely reluctant to either devalue or revalue their currencies or undertake other economic policy measures required to ensure sustainable balance of payments positions. The fact that 'fundamental disequilibrium' was not defined did not help.

The USA could not devalue the dollar in terms of gold since this would undermine confidence in the whole system. In addition, a dollar devaluation against gold did not improve US competitiveness if other countries maintained their exchange rate parities against the dollar. As such, the USA was expected to pursue appropriate deflationary policies at home to keep the size of its balance of payments deficit under control. In practice, the USA was extremely reluctant to deflate its economy to regulate its deficit. Indeed, from the mid-1960s President Johnson financed US involvement in Vietnam and a series of domestic social programmes through inflationary money supply increases rather than through higher taxation. The expansionary US monetary policy inevitably resulted in higher US inflation and a significant widening of its balance of payments deficits.

Other countries suffering persistent current account deficits could have resorted to devaluation. In practice, deficit countries proved extremely reluctant to devalue their currencies because such action was viewed as a sign of governmental and national weakness. The sense of national crisis that accompanied the UK labour government's devaluation of sterling in 1967 is an example of this phenomenon. The deficit countries were equally reluctant to adopt deflationary policies which could cure the deficits since most had committed themselves to the objective of achieving full employment. With the deficit countries reluctant to adjust, it was then necessary that surplus countries take action to reduce their surpluses.

The surplus countries included Germany, Japan and Switzerland, but they proved as reluctant to revalue their currencies as the deficit countries were to devalue. This was because the undervaluation of their currencies had enabled them to experience strong export growth and biased their economies towards the production of tradable goods. They believed that to revalue their currencies would risk ending export growth and lead unemployment in their economies as their tradables industries would be forced to contract. In addition, they were not prepared to reflate their economies as a means of reducing their surpluses because of they feared the inflationary consequences.

The recognition that in a fixed exchange rate regime the pressure was normally on debtors to undertake economic adjustment because of the fall in their reserves required to defend the exchange rate had led to the inclusion of a 'scarce currency clause' in the IMF articles. This permitted debtor countries to adopt penal measures against persistent surplus countries, but it was never invoked.

With neither deficit or surplus countries being prepared to adjust their economies or exchange rates the question of how to maintain fixed exchange rate parities in the face of persistent balance of payment imbalances required an answer. In a bid to prevent exchange rate realignments, the surplus countries supplied the deficit countries central banks with reserves on a credit basis to enable them to prevent devaluations of their currencies. Packages were arranged to support the Italian lira in 1964 and sterling in 1965. In retrospect, it is clear that such packages were only delaying the day when exchange rate parities would have to be realigned and constituted no more than a papering over the cracks.

The seigniorage problem

The pivotal role of the dollar meant that the USA was the major source of international liquidity under the Bretton Woods system. To acquire reserves the rest of the world had to run balance of payments surpluses while the USA ran deficits. This meant that the rest of the world had to consume less than it was producing, while the USA had the privilege of being able to consume more than it was producing. President Charles de Gaulle of France argued that the system conferred an 'exorbitant privilege' on the USA, the USA being able to gain productive long-term assets from its overseas investments in exchange for short-term dollar liabilities. Dollars treasury bonds accumulated by the rest of the world yielded relatively low rates of interest and their purchasing power was eroded by US inflation. In effect, the USA was able to borrow at very low real rates of interest. The actual methodology to calculate the value of such 'seigniorage' benefits has been an area of controversy. There was resentment on the part of some deficit countries (for example Italy) that they had to adopt deflationary policies to correct their balance of payments deficits, while because of the reserve currency status of the dollar the USA was under no corresponding pressure to correct its deficits. The perceived seigniorage benefits conferred to the USA, while not one of the major reasons for the breakdown of the Bretton Woods scheme, did, however, when the system was under strain weaken the resolve to save the system.

11.6 The post-Bretton Woods era

The first oil shock and its aftermath

The return to floating exchange rates was initially regarded by central bankers as only a temporary development until a new monetary order could be established. In the event, any hopes of a return to fixed parities were overtaken by events. As a result of the Arab–Israeli conflict at the end of 1973, the Oil Petroleum Exporting Countries (OPEC) quadrupled the price of oil which had a huge impact on the world economy and effectively ended any hopes of restoring a fixed exchange rate system. The huge oil price rise meant a significant deterioration of the oil importing countries' terms of trade (average price of exports/average price of imports) with the OPEC countries, as shown in **Table 11.3**, and a with it significant deficits in their current accounts as shown in **Table 11.4**.

Non-oil exporting less-developed countries were particularly hard hit both by the rise in the price of their oil imports and by the recession in the industrialized countries which reduced their export earnings. As a result the LDCs as a group experienced massive current account deficits which rose from $8.7 billion in 1973 to $51.3 billion in 1975. In order to assist them, the IMF set up an 'oil facility' which borrowed funds from the surplus OPEC countries for lending to the LDCs.

The impact of the oil shock was far from uniform, as some countries were more dependent than others on oil imports. For example, Japan as a major oil importer

Table 11.3 The real price of OPEC crude oil

1973	1974	1975	1976	1977	1978	1979	1980
100	226	224	241	239	213	280	402

Note: Index of OPEC oil prices, deflated by index of prices of exported manufactured goods of the major industrial countries.
Source: Adapted from Bank of England Quarterly Bulletin, Dec. 1980, p. 404.

Table 11.4 Global current account balances, 1973–80 ($ billions)

	1973	1974	1975	1976	1977	1978	1979	1980
Industrial countries	11.3	−9.6	19.4	−0.5	−4.6	30.8	−7.8	−44.1
OPEC	6.2	66.7	35.0	40.0	31.1	3.3	68.4	112.2
LDCs	−8.7	−42.9	−51.3	−32.9	−28.6	−37.5	−57.6	−82.1

Sources: IMF Annual Reports, various issues.

suffered greatly from the shock as its current account surplus of $100m in 1973 became a deficit of $4,500 million in 1974; the UK deficit widened from $1,200 million in 1973 to $7,800 million in 1974.

Due to its differential impact and the different policy responses adopted by governments to deal with the shock there were marked divergences in inflation rates. Italy and Britain both keen to avoid recessions adopted expansionary macroeconomic policies which, superimposed upon the inflationary impact of the oil shock, led to rapid inflation and a significant worsening in their current accounts (see **Tables 11.4** and **11.5**);

Table 11.5 Current account balances of the major industrialized countries, 1972–2006 (percentage of GDP)

	United States	Canada	Japan	United Kingdom	Germany	Italy	France
1972	−0.5	−0.3	2.2	0.3	0.5	1.5	0.1
1973	0.5	0.2	0	−1.3	1.5	−1.5	0.6
1974	0.1	−0.9	−1.0	−3.8	2.8	−4.3	−1.4
1975	1.1	−2.7	−0.1	−1.4	1.0	−0.3	0.8
1976	0.2	−2.1	0.7	−0.8	0.8	−1.3	−1.0
1977	−0.7	−2.0	1.6	−0.1	0.8	1.0	−0.1
1978	−0.7	−2.0	1.7	0.7	1.4	2.1	1.4
1979	0	−1.8	−0.9	−0.2	−0.7	1.6	0.9
1980	0.1	−0.4	−1.0	1.2	−1.6	−2.3	−0.6
1981	0.2	−1.7	0.4	2.6	−0.6	−2.4	−0.8
1982	−0.4	0.8	0.6	1.7	0.8	−1.7	−2.2
1983	−1.3	−0.4	1.8	1.2	0.8	0.2	−0.9
1984	−2.6	−0.2	2.8	0.5	1.7	−0.7	−0.1
1985	−3.0	−1.3	3.6	0.6	2.8	−0.9	−0.1
1986	−3.4	−2.8	4.3	−0.2	4.6	0.3	0.3
1987	−3.5	−2.8	3.6	−1.1	4.2	−0.3	−0.5
1988	−2.5	−3.5	2.7	−3.5	4.2	−0.8	−0.5
1989	−1.9	−4.1	2.0	−4.3	4.8	−1.4	−0.5
1990	−1.4	−3.8	1.5	−3.4	3.3	−1.6	−0.8
1991	0.1	−3.7	2.0	−1.8	−1.2	−2.0	−0.4
1992	−0.8	−3.6	2.9	−2.1	−1.0	−2.3	0.4
1993	−1.2	−3.9	3.0	−1.9	−0.7	0.8	0.8
1994	−1.7	−2.3	2.7	−1.0	−1.4	1.2	0.5
1995	−1.5	−0.8	2.1	−1.3	−1.1	2.3	0.7
1996	−1.5	0.5	1.4	−0.9	−0.6	3.2	1.3
1997	−1.6	−1.3	2.3	−0.1	−0.4	2.8	2.7
1998	−2.4	−1.2	3.0	−0.5	−0.6	1.9	2.7
1999	−3.2	0.3	2.6	−2.7	−1.1	0.7	2.9
2000	−4.2	2.7	2.5	−2.5	−1.4	−0.6	1.4
2001	−3.8	2.3	2.2	−2.3	0.1	−0.1	1.7
2002	−4.5	2.0	2.8	−1.7	2.1	−0.8	1.0
2003	−4.8	2.0	3.1	−1.9	2.3	−1.4	0.4
2004	−5.7	3.4	3.5	−2.2	3.3	−0.5	0.2
2005	−6.2	3.9	3.5	−2.4	3.9	−1.6	0.2
2006	−6.4	4.3	3.7	−2.2	4.7	−1.9	0.6

Note: Figures for 2005 and 2006 are forecasts.
Source: OECD *World Economic Outlook*.

Table 11.6 Inflation rates in the major industrialized countries, 1972–2006 (percentage change from previous year)

	United States	Canada	Japan	United Kingdom	Germany	Italy	France
1972	3.9	4.2	5.6	6.5	5.7	6.4	6.3
1973	6.1	6.4	10.7	8.6	6.3	13.8	7.4
1974	10.5	10.5	21.2	16.9	7.0	21.3	14.8
1975	8.1	10.6	11.3	23.7	6.2	16.6	11.8
1976	5.8	7.3	9.2	15.8	4.2	17.7	9.9
1977	6.6	7.4	7.2	14.8	3.6	17.6	9.4
1978	7.1	7.6	4.5	9.1	2.7	13.1	9.1
1979	9.2	8.5	3.6	13.6	3.9	14.5	10.8
1980	10.9	10.0	7.5	16.2	5.8	20.6	13.3
1981	8.9	11.2	4.6	11.2	6.2	18.1	13.0
1982	5.8	10.2	2.7	8.7	5.1	17.0	11.5
1983	4.6	6.3	2.1	4.8	3.2	14.7	9.7
1984	3.8	3.9	2.6	5.0	2.5	11.9	7.7
1985	3.7	3.7	2.3	5.3	1.8	9.3	5.8
1986	2.8	3.8	0.7	4.0	−0.6	6.3	2.7
1987	3.8	4.0	0.5	4.3	0.5	5.4	3.2
1988	4.2	3.8	0.5	5.0	1.3	5.9	2.7
1989	4.9	4.7	2.1	5.9	2.9	6.6	3.4
1990	5.1	4.3	2.6	5.5	2.7	6.3	2.8
1991	4.2	5.6	3.2	7.5	4.1	6.2	3.4
1992	3.0	1.5	1.7	4.2	5.1	5.0	2.5
1993	3.0	1.9	1.3	2.5	4.4	4.5	2.2
1994	2.6	0.2	0.7	2.0	2.7	4.2	1.7
1995	2.8	2.2	−0.1	2.7	1.7	5.4	1.8
1996	2.9	1.6	0.1	2.5	1.2	4.0	2.1
1997	2.3	1.6	1.7	1.8	1.5	1.9	1.3
1998	1.5	1.0	0.7	1.6	0.6	2.0	0.7
1999	2.2	1.7	−0.3	1.3	0.6	1.7	0.6
2000	3.4	2.7	−0.7	0.8	1.4	2.6	1.8
2001	2.8	2.5	−0.7	1.2	1.9	2.3	1.8
2002	1.6	2.2	−0.9	1.3	1.3	2.6	1.9
2003	2.3	2.8	−0.3	1.4	1.0	2.8	2.2
2004	2.6	1.9	−0.1	1.3	1.7	2.1	2.3
2005	2.4	2.0	0.1	1.7	1.3	2.5	1.8
2006	2.1	1.8	0.6	2.1	0.6	2.2	1.8

Notes: The above inflation rates are based on private consumption deflators. The methodology for calculating inflation has changed substantially in recent years. For example changes in US methodology have lowered US reported inflation significantly, and for this reason the data reported for all countries for 1991 onwards differ from the methodology for the 1972–90 period. Figures for 2005 and 2006 are forecast values.
Source: OECD *Economic Outlook*.

simultaneously there was a sharp rise in unemployment and the combination of rising inflation (**Table 11.6**) and rising unemployment gave rise to the term stagflation. Other countries such as Germany and Japan, who were much more concerned to control their inflation rates, adopted tight macroeconomic policies. Apart from its effect on current account balances the oil shock plunged the world

Table 11.7 Growth rates of real GDP in the major industrialized countries, 1972–2006 (percentage change from previous period)

	United States	Canada	Japan	United Kingdom	Germany	Italy	France
1972	5.0	5.7	8.5	3.5	4.2	2.7	4.4
1973	5.2	7.7	7.9	7.1	4.7	7.1	5.4
1974	−0.5	4.4	−1.4	−1.5	0.2	5.4	3.1
1975	−1.3	2.6	2.7	−0.7	−1.4	−2.7	−0.3
1976	4.9	6.2	4.8	2.7	5.6	6.6	4.2
1977	4.7	3.6	5.3	2.3	2.7	3.4	3.2
1978	5.3	5.6	5.2	3.6	3.3	3.7	3.4
1979	2.5	3.6	5.3	2.8	4.0	6.0	3.2
1980	−0.3	1.5	2.8	−2.2	1.0	3.5	1.6
1981	2.5	3.7	3.2	−1.3	0.1	0.5	1.2
1982	−2.1	−3.2	3.1	1.7	−0.9	0.5	2.5
1983	4.0	3.2	2.3	3.7	1.8	1.2	0.7
1984	6.8	6.3	3.9	2.4	2.8	2.6	1.3
1985	3.7	4.8	4.4	3.5	2.0	2.8	1.9
1986	3.0	3.3	2.9	4.4	2.3	2.8	2.5
1987	2.9	4.2	4.2	4.8	1.5	3.1	2.3
1988	3.8	5.0	6.2	5.0	3.7	3.9	4.5
1989	3.4	2.4	4.8	2.2	3.6	2.9	4.3
1990	2.5	−0.2	5.1	0.4	5.7	2.2	2.5
1991	−0.2	−2.1	3.4	−1.4	5.1	1.4	1.0
1992	3.3	0.9	1.0	0.2	1.8	0.7	1.3
1993	2.7	2.3	0.2	2.3	−1.1	−0.9	−0.9
1994	4.0	4.8	1.1	4.4	2.4	2.3	1.9
1995	2.5	2.8	1.9	2.9	1.8	3.0	1.8
1996	3.7	1.6	3.4	2.8	0.8	1.0	1.0
1997	4.5	4.2	1.9	3.3	1.5	2.0	1.9
1998	4.2	4.1	−1.1	3.1	1.7	1.7	3.6
1999	4.4	5.5	0.1	2.9	1.9	1.7	3.2
2000	3.7	5.2	2.8	3.9	3.1	3.2	4.2
2001	0.8	1.8	0.4	2.3	1.0	1.7	2.1
2002	1.9	3.4	−0.3	1.8	0.1	0.4	1.1
2003	3.0	2.0	2.5	2.2	−0.1	0.4	0.5
2004	4.4	3.0	4.0	3.2	1.2	1.3	2.1
2005	3.3	3.3	2.1	2.6	1.4	1.7	2.0
2006	3.6	3.1	2.3	2.4	2.3	2.1	2.3

Note: Figures for 2005 and 2006 are forecasts.
Source: OECD *Economic Outlook*.

into recession in 1974–75 with the USA, Japan, UK and Germany all experiencing negative real growth rates (**Table 11.7**) having previously experienced very high growth rates in 1973. There was also a pronounced rise in unemployment levels in many countries (see **Table 11.8**).

Table 11.8 Standardized unemployment rates in the major industrialized countries (percentage of civilian labour force)

	United States	Canada	Japan	United Kingdom	Germany	Italy	France
1972	5.5	6.2	1.4	4.0	0.8	6.3	2.8
1973	4.8	5.5	1.3	3.0	0.8	6.2	2.7
1974	5.5	5.3	1.4	2.9	1.6	5.3	2.8
1975	8.3	6.9	1.9	4.3	3.6	5.8	4.0
1976	7.6	7.1	2.0	5.6	3.7	6.6	4.4
1977	6.9	8.0	2.0	6.0	3.6	7.0	4.9
1978	6.0	8.3	2.2	5.9	3.5	7.1	5.2
1979	5.8	7.4	2.1	5.0	3.2	7.6	5.9
1980	7.0	7.5	2.0	6.4	2.9	7.5	6.3
1981	7.6	7.6	2.2	8.3	4.5	6.3	7.4
1982	9.7	11.0	2.3	9.7	6.4	6.9	8.0
1983	9.6	11.9	2.7	10.5	7.9	7.7	8.3
1984	7.5	11.3	2.7	10.7	7.9	8.5	9.7
1985	7.2	10.5	2.6	11.2	7.2	8.1	9.7
1986	7.0	9.6	2.8	11.2	6.5	8.9	9.8
1987	6.2	8.8	2.8	10.3	6.3	9.6	9.9
1988	5.5	7.8	2.5	8.5	6.2	9.7	9.4
1989	5.3	7.5	2.3	7.1	5.6	9.7	8.9
1990	5.6	8.1	2.1	6.9	4.8	8.9	8.5
1991	6.8	10.3	2.1	8.6	4.2	8.5	9.0
1992	7.5	11.2	2.2	9.8	6.4	8.7	9.9
1993	6.9	11.4	2.5	10.0	7.7	10.1	11.1
1994	6.1	10.4	2.9	9.2	8.2	11.0	11.7
1995	5.6	9.4	3.1	8.5	8.0	11.5	11.1
1996	5.4	9.6	3.4	8.0	8.7	11.5	11.6
1997	4.9	9.1	3.4	6.9	9.7	11.6	11.5
1998	4.5	8.3	4.1	6.2	9.1	11.7	11.1
1999	4.2	7.6	4.7	5.9	8.4	11.3	10.5
2000	4.0	6.8	4.7	5.4	7.8	10.4	9.1
2001	4.7	7.2	5.0	5.0	7.8	9.4	8.4
2002	5.8	7.7	5.4	5.1	8.7	9.0	8.9
2003	6.0	7.6	5.3	5.0	9.6	8.6	9.4

Source: OECD *Economic Outlook*.

11.7 The Jamaica Conference of 1976

In November 1975 a meeting of the major industrial nations at Rambouillet agreed to amend the Articles of Agreement of the IMF to legitimize the floating exchange rate regime. The details of the Second Amendment were worked out at the IMF annual conference held at Kingston, Jamaica, in January 1976. At Kingston the members of the Fund formally legitimized the new floating exchange rate system. In addition to abolishing the official price of gold, the conference aimed at increasing the importance of SDRs (see **Box 11.1**) in international reserves, and there was a declaration that the SDR should become the 'principal reserve asset'.

The Second Amendment

The Second Amendment of the IMF's Articles which came into effect in April 1978 formally gave national authorities a large degree of discretion in selecting their exchange rate arrangements. It also urged the IMF to adopt a policy of 'firm surveillance' over its members' exchange rate policies.

Article IV of the Second Amendment defined the obligations and responsibilities of Fund members. Each member was obliged to notify the Fund of its exchange rate arrangement, but Fund members were basically free to do as they wished – peg to the SDR or another currency, pursue cooperative arrangements with other members, or adopt other exchange rate arrangements of their choice! About the only thing members could not do was to peg their currency to gold.

In addition to defining what members of the Fund could do, the amendment also defined the role of the IMF as being to oversee the international monetary system to ensure its effective operation. In particular, the Fund was expected to:

> . . . exercise firm surveillance over the exchange rate policies of members, and shall adopt specific principles for the guidance of all members with respect to those policies.

Member countries are obliged to supply the Fund with information necessary for surveillance and when requested consult with the Fund over its exchange rate policy. The initial guidelines drawn up by the Fund were summarized by three principles:

> A) A member shall avoid manipulating exchange rates or the international monetary system in order to prevent effective balance of payments adjustment or to gain an unfair competitive advantage over other members.
> B) A member should intervene in the exchange market if necessary to counter disorderly conditions which may be characterised *inter alia* by disruptive short-term movements in the exchange value of its currency.
> C) Members should take into account in their intervention policies the interests of other members, including those of countries in whose currencies they intervene.

Indications of attempts to maintain unrealistic exchange rates include sustained one-way reserve movements, the introduction of trade and/or capital controls and large-scale official borrowing. However, the IMF was not empowered to penalize governments that chose to ignore its guidelines. All in all the Second Amendment was merely a formal recognition of the end of the Bretton Woods system.

11.8 The Snake and the EMS

The member countries of the European Economic Community (EEC) had long been concerned that their large degree of trading links with one another could be threatened by exchange rate instability. This, coupled with the longer-term aspiration for a fully fledged economic and monetary union between the EEC countries, led to the setting up of the Snake in 1972 which had a chequered history and was replaced by the EMS which commenced operations in 1979. The operation of the Snake and EMS is dealt with more extensively in Chapter 16. What is important in the scheme of international monetary relations is that both the arrangements involved a zone of exchange rate stability between the exchange rates of the European currencies reflected in large part a dissatisfaction with allowing exchange rates to be determined by the free market.

11.9 The second oil shock

Towards the end of 1978 the Iranian revolution disrupted its oil exports and led to a further hike in OPEC oil prices from $13 a barrel in mid-1978 to $32 a barrel in mid-1980. Although this hike was not as great as in the case of the first oil price shock, the recession that followed in the industrialized nations was far more pronounced. This was mainly because, on the basis of experience from the earlier shock, governments were keen to minimize the inflationary consequences, and as a result authorities of the industrialized countries adopted restrictive policy responses. These policies led to a rise of world interest rates and major recessions in the years 1980–81, particularly in the USA and the UK. Nonetheless, the recessions meant that the adjustment of the balance of payments deficits caused by the shock was quicker than that following the first oil shock. The OPEC surplus in 1980 of $112 billion was turned into a deficit by 1982.

11.10 The dazzling dollar, 1980–85

The period January 1980 to May 1985 witnessed a relentless substantial appreciation of the US dollar; the dollar nominal effective exchange rate appreciated by around 50% and even more in real terms (see **Figure 11.1**). One of the major reasons advanced for the appreciation was the divergent macroeconomic policy stances pursued by the USA, Europe and Japan. US authorities operated a tight monetary policy but had a rather relaxed fiscal policy, with the US budget deficit rising from $16 billion in 1979 to $204 billion in 1986. This stood in contrast to the tight monetary and fiscal policy operated by the Europeans. As US real interest rates rose relative to rates in Europe, funds were attracted into the USA to finance its growing current account deficit. The US administration argued that the appreciation of the dollar reflected the strength of the US economy and that it was not a policy problem.

However, as the dollar appreciation continued it started to provoke a great deal of concern. A squeeze on US export and import-competing industries contributed to a rapidly deteriorating balance of payments which in turn led to persistent calls in Congress for protectionist measures to be adopted against trading partners, especially Japan. Although the Europeans and Japanese were benefiting from increased exports to the USA, they were concerned about the mounting threat of US protectionism. The Europeans and Japanese viewed the US budget deficit as the principal cause of the US current account deficit and argued that the deficit could only be remedied by policies designed to reduce the US budget deficit. The increasing concern about the US economy and the strength of the dollar contributed to in large part to the issuing of the Plaza Accord.

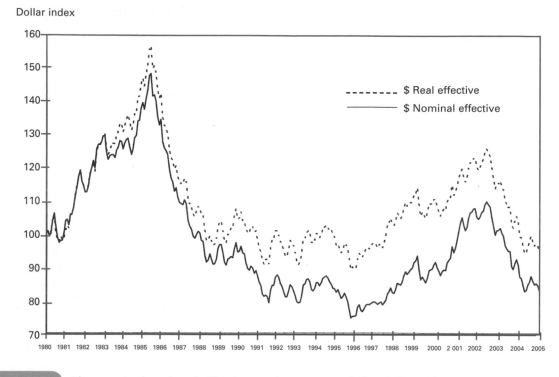

Dollar index

Figure 11.1 The nominal and real effective exchange rate of the dollar, 1980–2005

11.11 From Plaza to Louvre and beyond

In September 1985, finance ministers and central bank governors from the so-called G-5 countries (France, West Germany, United States, United Kingdom and Japan) met at the Plaza hotel and issued a communique known as the Plaza Accord. The statement said that the exchange rate of the dollar did not accurately reflect changes in the economic fundamentals, notably the US pledge to reduce its budget deficit and measures to stimulate demand in Japan. A further depreciation of the dollar was considered desirable and, importantly, there was a commitment to 'cooperate more closely to encourage this when to do so would be helpful'. This was followed by purchases of deutschmark and yen. The Plaza Accord was a tangible sign of growing dissatisfaction with floating exchange rates. Following the Plaza Accord the dollar depreciated throughout 1986, although the extent to which the depreciation can be attributed to the Plaza Accord is a matter of conjecture, especially as the dollar had begun to depreciate prior to the Plaza meeting. The depreciation of the dollar was so substantial that the concern by early 1987 switched to stemming the dollar decline.

At a G-7 meeting held at Paris in February 1987, the finance ministers issued what is known as the Louvre Accord. They made it known that they felt that the dollar had depreciated far enough and that exchange rates were 'broadly consistent with underlying economic fundamentals'. Furthermore, there was agreement to 'cooperate closely to foster exchange rates around current levels'. The Accord was backed up by an unpublished agreement between the parties that it is believed was aimed to keep the dollar within a 5% target band against the deutschmark and the yen.

Exchange rates remained fairly stable following the Louvre Accord, but pressure for a further depreciation of the dollar led to large-scale purchases of dollars by the Japanese. The dollar remained stable until October 1987 when, following the collapse of stockmarkets around the world, it came under renewed pressure. The stockmarket collapse led to fears that it would be followed by a major worldwide recession as had happened following the stockmarket collapse in 1929. It was feared that the reduced wealth and US plans to reduce its budget deficit would lead to a cut in expenditure that could herald a worldwide recession. To reduce the risk of recession there was a significant loosening of monetary policy around the world, with central banks reducing interest rates. Only in January 1988 with signs that the US trade deficit had started to bottom-out did the dollar begin to recover.

11.12 Currency turmoil and crises post-1990

The significant loosening of monetary policy following the stockmarket collapse of 1987 eventually led to renewed pressure on world inflation, which in turn required a series of interest rate rises to bring it under control. In turn the interest rate rises led to recessions for the US and UK economies in 1991. The early 1990s also witnessed unprecedented currency turmoil leading the Bank of International Settlements to state in its 1994 Annual Report that:

> Technology, innovation, free capital mobility and investors' desire for international portfolio diversification have by now all combined to increase vastly the potential for shifting large amounts of financial capital around the world, and across currencies, at great speed . . . it is probably no exaggeration to say that the period from late 1991 to early 1993 witnessed the most serious and widespread foreign exchange market crisis since the breakdown of the Bretton Woods system twenty years ago.

The origins of the currency turmoil dated back to the collapse of the Berlin Wall in November 1989 and the subsequent reunification of East and West Germany, followed by a decision to allow East German ostmarks to be converted into deutschmarks at the very generous exchange rate parity of 1 ostmark to 1 deutschmark. This led to a near-30% increase in the German money supply heightening inflationary fears. In addition, to pay for massive fiscal transfers to prop up an ailing East German economy, the German authorities became major issuers of long-term bonds pushing up German interest rates significantly. This meant that other countries in Europe that had currencies pegged to the deutschmark in the Exchange Rate Mechanism (ERM) were forced to raise their rates.

In June 1992, Danish voters narrowly rejected the Maastricht Treaty, European legislation concerned with creating a monetary union in Europe. This led to the emergence of exchange rate tensions within the ERM, and particularly vulnerable to speculative attack were the Italian lira, due to question marks over the sustainability of its budget deficit, and the pound sterling that has joined the system in May 1990 but was increasingly perceived as overvalued at its central parity of 2.95DM/£1. At the end of August 1992, opinion polls indicated a possible French rejection of the Maastricht Treaty and the Italian lira fell towards its floor in the ERM. In early September the

Italians raised their interest rates sharply to defend the lira while the UK authorities announced massive borrowing equivalent to 20 billion deutschmarks to bolster the ability of the Bank of England to defend sterling.

Following a speculative attack, the Finnish were forced to float the markka on 8 September, and Swedish interest rates were raised to defend the krone. On 14 September the Italian lira was devalued by 7% in the face of massive speculative pressure. Encouraged by these successes, speculators turned their attention on the pound sterling and, despite massive intervention by the Bank of England and a 5% rise in interest rates in a single day, the UK authorities were forced to suspend sterling's membership of the ERM on 16 September.

On 17 September further speculation against the Italian lira led to its suspension from the ERM and a devaluation of the Spanish peseta by 5%. The French franc, Danish krone and Irish punt were successfully defended, and following a joint statement by the French and German authorities that 'no change in the central rate is justified', several weeks of calm returned. However, on 19 November the Swedish authorities were forced to abandon the Kronor peg to the European Currency Unit (ECU). This in turn led to speculative attacks against the Portuguese escudo and Spanish peseta which were both devalued by 6% on 22 November. Speculative pressures continued, and on 10 December the Norwegian authorities ended their peg to the ECU. However, speculative attacks against the French franc were successfully resisted by a combination of French interest rate rises combined with a cut in German interest rates and strong support by the German and French authorities for the franc–deutschmark parity.

The Irish punt was finally devalued by 10% on 30 January 1993, and in May 1993 further speculation led to devaluations of the escudo by 6.5% and the Spanish peseta by 8%. Further speculative attacks were mounted against the French franc, reaching unprecedented levels when on 29 July Germany failed to reduce its key discount rate despite market expectations of a 50 basis point cut. This led to massive selling of most ERM currencies against the deutschmark on 30 July, and left five currencies at the bottom of their ERM band. Over the weekend of 31 July and 1 August, central bank governors met and decided that the only way to save the system from complete collapse was to widen the bands in the ERM from ± 2.25% to a much wider ± 15%. The last-minute widening reduced speculative pressures within the system and monetary tensions eased, allowing German and French interest rates to fall, and 1993 witnessed a spectacular bull market for bonds and equities which came to an abrupt end in 1994 when the dollar hit new lows against the yen and the Federal Reserve again raised interest rates.

The Mexicican 'Tequila crisis' of 1994–95

At the end of 1991 the Mexican government announced a change in its exchange rate such that the Mexican peso's permissible band of fluctuation against the US dollar was widened. Despite this, the Mexican peso remained very strong against the US dollar, trading for much of the period 1992/93 at its appreciation limit against the dollar. The strength of the peso was because the Mexican government had privatized and deregulated its banking system, combined with opening-up its capital account, the perceived success of the Brady Plan in restructuring Mexico's debt, and Mexico joining the North American Free Trade Area (NAFTA) in 1993. However, starting in early 1994 things changed; there was civil unrest with an armed rebellion in the southern state of

Chiapas in January 1994, the assassination of the ruling party's presidential candidate ahead of a presidential election, and a perceived increase in the risk of devaluation, in part because the previous appreciation of the peso had led to a very large current account deficit of 8% of GDP. In addition to the internal factors, rises in US interest rates started a reversal of the capital inflows Mexico had been experiencing. There was a significant fall in the foreign exchange reserves of the central bank throughout the year as foreign exchange market participants and local residents began to anticipate a devaluation. The speculative attack reached fever pitch after the election of a new President at the start of December, and by mid-December the foreign exchange reserves were virtually wiped out. On 20 December the Mexican government announced a devaluation of the peso from 3.50 pesos to 4.025 pesos per dollar, some 15% below its previously announced lower limit. This set off a further speculative attack against the peso such that it was forced to float, which then led to panic on the part of foreign investors and the peso fell dramatically to 7 pesos per dollar by March 1995 and to 7.7 pesos per dollar by the end of 1995.

The crisis put the economy on the brink of default on its external debt; fear of this and the possible implications led the US Treasury, in conjunction with the IMF, to arrange an emergency $48 billion rescue package. The rescue package meant that the country avoided an economic catastrophe, but nonetheless rises in interest rates and fiscal cutback meant that output fell by 6.6% in 1995, unemployment doubled and inflation rose from 6.9% in 1994 to 35% in 1995. The Mexican crisis not only adversely affected the Mexican economy, but also led to significant falls in many other developing countries' stockmarkets and currencies, and this process of contagion from the Mexican markets to other developing countries gave rise to the so-called 'Tequila effect'. Fortunately, the economic crisis was relatively short-lived and in 1996 the Mexican economy rebounded strongly.

The 1997–98 Asian crisis

Another period of almost unprecedented financial turmoil began on 2 July 1997, following the devaluation of the Thai baht. The Asian economies had during the 1990s been viewed as highly successful fast-growing economies, and they were extremely successful in attracting international capital inflows. Terms like the 'Asian miracle' had become part of the international lexicon. However, the international capital inflows had contributed to property and stockmarket bubbles in many of the economies and the fast growth had disguised structural flaws in their financial systems. When the bubbles began to burst there was a rush on the part of international investors to exit the region and the capital inflows abruptly became substantial capital outflows. The result was a substantial fall in property values, stockmarket indices and in the value of many of the currencies. The turmoil went on from July 1997 through to the end of 1998, by which time the stockmarkets and currencies began to recover. The Asian crisis is more comprehensively covered in Chapter 17.

The 1998 Russian crisis

Although the Russia economy weathered the Asian financial crisis quite well, the Russian economy was nonetheless extremely weak. The government was running a large fiscal deficit which was financed partly by rouble debt but also in large part by issuing debt in US dollars with an ever-rising rate of interest. By July 1998, the Russian government was having increasing trouble financing its fiscal deficits as foreign investors became increasingly worried about the prospects for repayment. Concern about the fate of the Russian economy led to an agreement between Russia and the IMF for a loan of $23 billion. However, after an initial tranche of the loan of $5 billion was made, the Russian government decided to renege on the conditions attached to the loan. The rouble which had been pegged to the US dollar started to come under severe speculative attack; in particular, many wealthy Russians anticipating a devaluation sold domestic assets such a shares and bonds leading a collapse in their prices and sold the roubles raised to acquire US dollars. In a bid to salvage the situation, on 17 August 1998 Russia unilaterally announced a restructuring of its rouble-denominated debt and a moratorium on its foreign debt obligations combined with a floating of the rouble. The Russian restructuring effectively wiped out most of its rouble-denominated debt and caused panic on the part of international investors about the implications of the moratorium for foreign debt repayment. A Russian request for the next instalment on its loan was turned down by the IMF since the government had reneged on its promised fiscal reforms. The refusal of the IMF to grant the next instalment came as a major shock to foreign holders of Russian debt that had assumed that Russia was 'too important to fail' and would be bailed out because of its political and strategic importance. The result of the effective Russian default led international investors to reassess the risks of investing in emerging markets more generally, and there were significant declines in both emerging and global stockmarkets. This was particularly the case because the Russian crisis coincided with the collapse of the investment fund Long-Term Capital Management on 23 September 1998 (see later).

The 1999 Brazilian crisis

The Russian crisis had a direct impact on Brazil. Similarities between Russia and Brazil had been noted by speculators, in particular, like Russia, it had huge public-sector deficits combined with a large external debt. Following the Russian default, the Brazilian real had been under increasing speculative attack and in a bid to forestall a crisis the IMF arranged a $40 billion loan in December 1998. The aim of the emergency loan was to calms investors' fears and give Brazil time to implement a fiscal reform package. However, speculators remained unconvinced and speculative pressures continued until in January 1999 the Brazilian government announced an 8% devaluation of the real. The devaluation, however, proved insufficient and the real was forced to float and quickly fell some 40% against the US dollar. The Brazilian economy moved into a sharp recession with output falling some 6.1% in 1999. While the Brazilian economy did make some recovery in 2000 and 2001, it was adversely affected by the Argentinean crisis of 2001–02 with output falling 8.9% in 2002 and 7.6% in 2003.

The Long-Term Capital Management crisis

Long-Term Capital Management (LTCM) was a hedge fund founded in 1994 which had two Nobel Prize-winners in economics among its partners, Myron Scholes and Merton Miller. The fund took what were regarded as low-risk speculative positions in government and corporate bonds based on interest rate spreads. It took speculative positions when interest rate spreads in the markets were unusually high, predicting that they would fall. The trouble was that its positions were highly leveraged, and on a capital base of some $5 billion it had positions in the markets totalling around $1.3 trillion and loans totalling over $200 billion. When the Russians announced a default on their debt this had the effect of widening the interest rate spreads in the financial markets and there was a 'flight to quality' in international financial markets. The result was that LTCM's capital base was quickly eroded, and once word got out in the markets that it was in trouble, its positions worsened even further. The Federal Reserve, concerned that a failure of LTCM could create a global financial panic, organized a rescue involving a consortium of 14 American and European financial institutions that themselves would have been in trouble if LTCM had to liquidate its positions at the then prevailing market prices. They agreed to inject some $4 billion of capital in return for effective control of LTCM. The capital injection meant LTCM was able to liquidate its positions in a controlled manner, and although the announcement of the rescue package itself frightened the financial markets a global financial disaster was averted. Nonetheless, there were severe falls in stockmarkets and corporate bond markets for quite some time due to a combination of the Russian crisis and LTCM's problems.

The Turkish crisis of 2001

The start of the new century did not lead to an ending of the currency turmoil. The Turkish economy and its macroeconomic management has been a problem for many decades and it has resorted to IMF loan packages on many occasions. In January 2000, Turkey arranged a further $8 billion loan from the IMF and committed itself to major economic reform and the lowering of its inflation rate (then standing at close to 100% per annum). The economic reform package included restructuring of its banking system and improving its regulation, a privatization programme, a cut in subsidies and a reduction in its fiscal deficit. In addition, in a bid to bring down its inflation rate it adopted a crawling peg arrangement for its currency against a basket of the euro and US dollar. The loan and adoption of the new programme was initially well-received and there were large capital inflows into the country with strong economic growth. However, by November there were signs of problems, the fiscal deficit remained large and the current account deficit had widened to 5% of GDP and foreign investors began to worry about the possibility of a devaluation. Fears were heightened in December following the arrests of some well-known bankers. Overnight interest rates were raised to an annualized 800% in early January 2001 in a bid to reduce the speculative pressures, and a new IMF loan of $7.5 billion was announced. While this brought a transitory calm, political infighting between the President and the Prime Minister over the pace and scale of economic reforms led to a further speculative attack against the Turkish lira in February 2001. Despite a further huge rise in overnight interest rates to as high as an annualized 4,000% on 21 February, and large-scale intervention in the foreign exchange market, the speculative attack proved successful and on 22 February the authorities gave up the lira peg and announced a move to a floating exchange rate within two days the lira fell some from 687,200 to 900,000 per dollar, then to 1,300,000 by 11 April 2001 and 1,600,000 by 30 October 2001. The country went into a major recession and by May 2001 found itself arranging yet another loan from the IMF!

The Argentinian default of 2002

In 1991 Argentina commenced a currency board arrangement (see **Box 11.2**) that pegged the peso to the US dollar at one peso per US dollar. The arrangement initially seemed to work quite well. Argentina experienced strong economic growth and was successful in bringing down its inflation rate from over 100% in 1991 to below 1% in the years 1996 to 1998 inclusive. While the currency board arrangement was extremely successful in helping bring down Argentina's inflation rate, it also meant that the peso itself was one-for-one linked to movements of the US dollar against other currencies. The Brazilian devaluation of 1999 had already meant a recession in the Argentinian economy, but the strength of the US dollar during 1999 and 2001 meant that Argentina became increasingly uncompetitive as reflected in real GDP falls of 3.4% in 1999, 0.8% in 2000 and 4.4% in 2001, and large current account deficits. By the end of 2001 its real trade-weighted exchange rate was some 20% above its level in 1991. In addition, the recession contributed to a worsening of Argentina's fiscal position. Following the election of a new government in 1999 there were increasing concerns about the sustainability of the peso–dollar parity, and during 2001 Argentina's interest rates began to rise. In a bid to stop the pressure on the peso the government reached an agreement with the IMF for a $14 billion loan. However, the respite was short-lived as Argentina failed to reduce its fiscal deficits. Domestic residents increasingly began to question the sustainability of the peg and attempted to withdraw pesos so that they could convert them into dollars. In a bid to stop deposit withdrawls the government temporarily closed the banks in November and announced heavy restrictions on withdrawls when they reopened. All this just increased the speculative pressures on the peso, and in late December the government announced a default on its foreign debts. In January 2002 the peso was devalued to 1.40 pesos per dollar, but speculative pressures continued and the peso was forced to float and quickly fell to 4 pesos per dollar. In 2002 there was a severe fall in GDP of 10.9% and a steep rise in unemployment. Despite an economic recovery in 2003 and 2004, in early 2005 the Argentinian government was taking a tough stance in negotiations with its creditors affected by its debt default, offering them roughly 30 cents on the dollar on the defaulted debt.

Unlike many of the other crises, the Argentinian crisis had been largely foreseen by foreign investors and banks that had accordingly reduced their exposure to the country, and so it was mostly domestic banks that incurred large losses due to a mismatch between their dollar liabilities and dollar assets, and a number of banks were closed. Although there was no initial impact on other countries in the region, the Uruguay economy was adversely affected by the loss of Argentinean tourism and business and repatriation of funds by Argentinian residents from Uruguayan accounts, and in June, following a large fall in its foreign exchange reserves, the Uruguay government announced that its peso would float and within two weeks its currency fell by 50%. A run on bank deposits in Uruguay by nervous investors (who had probably learnt from the Argentinian experience!) led to a four-day closure of its banks which were reopened only when an emergency loan had been arranged with the United States. Brazil also got temporarily caught up in the fallout from the Argentinian default, and in July 2002 foreign investors concerned about its external debt pulled funds out of the country and the real fell by some 20%. A crisis was averted and the real stabilized when the IMF arranged an additional $30 billion loan package.

Yen/$

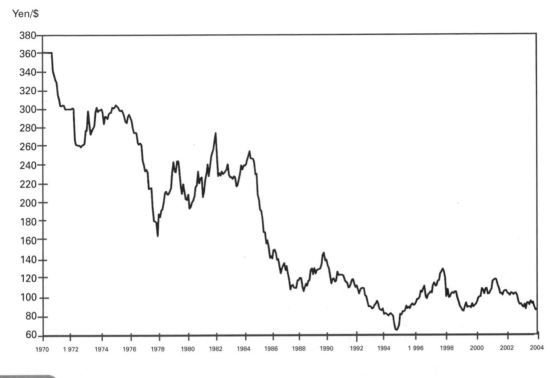

Figure 11.2 The yen–dollar exchange rate, 1970–2005

Dollar turbulence

The dollar itself has not been immune to currency turbulence; between January and mid-April 1995 the dollar depreciated from 100 yen/$1 to a mere 80 yen/$1 and from DM1.56/$1 to DM1.35/$1. However, during August and September 1995 the dollar depreciation was reversed, in part due to intervention by the central banks of Germany, Japan and the USA. The subsequent reversal in the dollar's fortunes was reflected by the fact that in October 1997 it was trading at 120 yen/$1. The moves of the US dollar against the Japanese yen are shown in **Figure 11.2**.

Box 11.2

'Hard pegs': currency boards versus dollarization

As we shall see in section 11.13, some economists feel that with today's highly mobile capital any country that has a merely 'fixed but adjustable exchange rate' regime will be vulnerable to periodic speculative attacks. The choice of exchange rate regime for a developing or emerging market economy is to either allow the exchange rate to float freely or opt for a 'hard peg' of a currency board, or even more strongly give up its currency altogether and adopt a foreign currency – a process referred to as 'dollarization'. The two regimes have become much more relevant in recent years, Argentina enacted a currency board arrangement in 1991, Hong Kong has had a currency board arrangement since 1983, and Estonia (1992) and Lithuania (1994) →

➜

who had no track record of monetary policy management established currency boards following the break-up of the Soviet Union, to be followed by Bulgaria (1997) and Bosnia (1998). In the cases of Estonia and Lithuania the currency boards are now based on parities against the euro. Other countries have gone further and given up their own money and adopted the US dollar as their local currency; Panama, Micronesia and the Marshall Islands currently use the dollar as their currency. In September 2000 Ecuador dollarized is economy, followed by El Salvador at the beginning of 2001 so ending its fixed exchange rate between the colon and the dollar. Indeed, in crises-prone countries such as Mexico, Brazil, Argentina and even Russia and Indonesia there have been debates about adopting the US dollar as their currency.

Under a currency board arrangement the local currency is fixed to a foreign currency (say the US dollar) at a given parity (one for one in the case of the peso and 7.74 Hong Kong dollars per US dollar in the case of Hong Kong), and the local currency is 100% backed by central bank holdings of the foreign currency. The central bank can only increase the domestic money supply if it has an equivalent increase in its holdings of foreign currency assets. The central bank is forbidden to hold domestic currency-denominated assets and is unable therefore to monetarize any fiscal deficits by purchasing local government bonds. The central bank in effect becomes a 'vending machine' exchanging at the announced parity of the local currency for the US dollar whenever required by economic agents. The primary aim of a currency board is to instil confidence in the local currency by providing an anchor for inflation expectations, since private agents know that the central bank is forbidden to monetarize fiscal deficits or print excessive amounts of money. It is also hoped that the government will be forced to be disciplined in the conduct of its fiscal policy since it knows that it will not be able to 'borrow' by selling bonds to the central bank. A currency board should help to regulate the country's balance of payments position; if the country is running a combined current and capital account in surplus, then the foreign exchange reserves of the central bank will increase enabling it to expand the money supply which will in time reduce the surplus. Conversely, if the combined current and capital account are in deficit, then the foreign exchange reserves of the central bank will fall reducing the money supply which will in time reduce the deficit. Finally, the system should prove resilient to speculative attacks since the central bank cannot run out of reserves as the domestic money supply is fully backed by central bank holdings of the domestic currency.

There are, however, some problems with a currency board arrangement. Since a currency board cannot acquire domestic securities it is unable to lend to domestic banks in times of financial crisis. This was clearly shown in the case of Argentina when the public attempted to withdraw deposits from the banking system, and the central bank was not in a position to provide the banks with the necessary liquidity meaning that the banks were closed and restrictions had to be placed on deposit withdrawals. Also, by ruling out the possibility of a surprise devaluation or the ability to finance larger fiscal deficits, the central bank is in no position to help the economy out of recession. Furthermore, as the case of Argentina showed, if the dollar appreciates strongly then this will undermine the competitiveness of the local economy especially if other regional competitors have devalued their currencies. A final problem with a currency board arrangement is that it may be difficult to convince financial markets and private agents that the situation will never be reversed and that the peg will not be changed. This was clearly the case in Argentina, as when both financial markets and local residents foresaw an end to the peg, there was a steep rise in interest rates to compensate for the risk of devaluation and a rush to withdraw deposits and large-scale capital flight into US dollars.

➜

→
  Given that a currency board may not be a sufficiently hard regime in convincing financial markets and economic agents that the peg will not be ended, some have argued in favour of dollarization which means withdrawing the local currency from circulation. Dollarization is seen as having a key advantage over a currency board system in that by ending the risk of a devaluation, it will ensure the country is not subjected to a speculative attack such as that which ended the Argentinean board and which caused enormous problems for the Hong Kong Monetary Authority during the Asian crisis. By ending the risk of a devaluation, local interest rates will no longer contain a devaluation premium. Another advantage is that there are savings in administrative and transaction costs of having to convert the local currency into dollars for trade and financial purposes. However, even complete dollarization is not without its problems. Firstly, under a currency board the government holds dollar bills and bonds which earn it a rate of interest from the US Treasury; if it moves from a currency board to dollarization, it sells the US bonds it holds as foreign exchange reserves and uses the dollars raised to replace the local currency. It therefore foregoes the rate of interest held on US dollar bonds and hands over the seigniorage benefit of issuing its own currency to the US government. Another problem which it shares with a currency board is that by giving up its monetary autonomy, the US Federal Reserve sets its monetary policy and interest rates according to economic conditions in the United States, hence a dollarized economy faces the risk of rising interest rates when its economy may be in recession. Another problem is that although the risk of devaluation may be reduced, since government debt will subsequently be issued in dollars, which the local government can no longer print, then the country will be still be subject to a possible financial crisis and rising interest rates on its debt should economic agents fear out-of-control public finances and a risk of default. Also, should the economy be hit by a major economic shock requiring a devaluation of its currency, then by being dollarized it will not have available to it the depreciation/devaluation option. Finally, the country's international competitiveness will be subject to the vagaries of the ups and downs of the US dollar. Those interested in exploring this issue further are advised to read Altig and Humpage (1999) and Berg and Borenstein (2000).

11.13 The present exchange rate system

The present exchange rate system permits countries to adopt whatever exchange rate policy they wish providing that they do not peg their currencies to the value of gold. In practice, there exists a wide range of exchange rate polices from completely free-floating to various pegging arrangements including currency boards. **Table 11.9** shows the exchange rate arrangements of Fund members as at 30 June 2004.

11.14 The bipolar view of the international monetary system: which exchange rate regime is best?

Following the series of exchange rate crises, particularly the speculative attack on the ERM countries in the early 1990s and the Mexican speculative attack of 1994–95, a number of well-known academics suggested that there was no room for a halfway house in a world of high capital mobility, and that there was little scope for currencies to be in a pegged but adjustable arrangement. The international monetary system

Table 11.9 Exchange rate arrangements, 30 June 2004

Exchange rate arrangements with no separate legal tender				
		CFA franc zone		
Another currency as legal tender	*ECCU*	*WAEMU*	*CAEMU*	*Euro Area*
Ecuador	Antigua and Barbuda	Benin	Cameroon	Austria
El Salvador	Dominica	Burkina Faso	Central African	Belgium
Kiribati	Grenada	Côte d'Ivoire	Rep. Chad	Finland
Marshall Islands	St Kitts and Nevis	Guinea-Bissau	Congo	France
Micronesia	St. Lucia	Mali	Rep of Equatorial Guinea	Germany
Palau	St Vincent and the Grenadines	Niger	Gabon	Greece
Panama		Senegal		Ireland
San Marino		Togo		Italy
Timor-Leste				Luxembourg
				Netherlands
				Portugal
				Spain

Currency board arrangements
Bosnia and Herzegovina
Brunei Darussalam
Bulgaria
China-Hong Kong SAR
Djibouti
Estonia
Lithuania

Other conventional fixed-peg arrangements		
Against a single currency		*Against a composite*
Aruba	Maldives	Botswana
Bahamas	Namibia	Fiji
Bahrain	Nepal	Latvia
Barbados	Netherlands Antilles	Libyan Arab Jamahiriya
Belize	Oman	Malta
Bhutan	Qatar	Morocco
Cape Verde	Saudi Arabia	Samoa
China, P.R. of	Seychelles	Vanuatu
Comoros	Suriname	
Eritrea	Swaziland	
Guinea	Syrian Arab Rep.	
Iraq	Turkmenistan	
Jordan	Ukraine	
Kuwait	United Arab Emirates	
Lebanon	Venezuela	
Lesotho	Bolivariana de	
Macedonia, FYR	Zimbabwe	

Pegged exchange rates within horizontal bands	
Within a cooperative arrangement	*Other band arrangements*
Denmark	Cyprus
Slovenia	Hungary
	Tonga

Table 11.9 cont.	Crawling pegs		

Bolivia
Costa Rica
Honduras
Nicaragua
Solomon Islands
Tunisia

Exchange rates within crawling bands			

Belarus
Romania

Managed floating with no predetermined path for the exchange rate			
Afghanistan	Gambia	Lao PDR	Rwanda
Algeria	Ghana	Mauritius	Serbia and Montenegro
Angola	Georgia	Mauritania	São Tomé and Príncipe
Argentina	Guyan	Moldova	Slovak Rep.
Azerbaijan	Haiti	Mongoloia	Singapore
Bangladesh	Indonesia	Mozambique	Sudan
Burundi	India	Myanmar	Tajikistan
Cambodia	Iran	Nigeria	Thailand
Croatia	Jamaica	Pakistan	Trinidad and Tobago
Czech Rep.	Kazakhstan	Paraguay	Uzbekistan
Egypt	Kenya	Peru	Vietnam
Ethiopia	Kyrgyz Rep.	Russian Federation	Zambia

Independently floating			
Albania	Guatemala	New Zealand	Switzerland
Armenia	Iceland	Norway	Sri Lanka
Australia	Israel	Papua New Guinea	Tanzania
Brazil	Japan	Philippines	Turkey
Canada	Korea	Poland	Uganda
Chile	Liberia	Sierra Leone	United Kingdom
Colombia	Madagascar	Somalia	United States
Congo	Malawi	South Africa	Uruguay
Dominican Rep.	Mexico	Sweden	Yemen

ECCU = Eastern Caribbean Currency Union; WAEMU = West African Economic and Monetary Union; CAEMU = Central African Economic and Monetary Union.
Source: IMF.

would increasingly become a bipolar world where countries either opted for a 'hard peg' such as a currency board or a monetary union at one extreme, or fully floating at the other extreme. For example, Eichengreen (1994 pp. 4–5) argued that countries 'will be forced to choose between floating exchange rates on the one hand and monetary unification on the other'. Similarly, Obstfeld and Rogoff (1995 pp. 74) argued that for countries with an open capital account, 'there is little, if any, comfortable middle ground between floating rates and the adoption of a common currency'. In more recent papers, Summers (2000, p. 8) argues that for economies with access to international capital markets, 'the choice of appropriate exchange rate regime . . . increasingly means a move away from the middle ground of pegged but adjustable fixed exchange rates towards the two corner regimes'. Finally, Fischer (2001 p. 22) looking at the IMF classification of exchange rate arrangements argues that, 'in the last decade, there has been a hollowing out of the middle of the distribution of exchange rate regimes in a bipolar direction, with the share of both hard pegs and floating gaining at the expense of soft pegs'. Nonetheless, the bipolar view of the international monetary system has been recently challenged on an empirical basis by Rogoff *et al.* (2003), who following an extensive empirical study of the issue find:

> no support for the popular bipolar view that countries will tend over time to move to the polar extremes of free float or rigid peg. Rather, intermediate regimes have shown remarkable durability. The analysis suggests that as economies mature, the value of exchange rate flexibility rises. For countries at a relatively early stage of financial development and integration, fixed or relatively rigid regimes appear to offer some anti-inflation credibility gain without compromising growth objectives. As countries develop economically and institutionally, there appear to be consider-able benefits to more flexible regimes. For developed countries that are not in a currency union, relatively flexible exchange rate regimes appear to offer higher growth without any cost in credibility. (Rogoff *et al.* 2003, p. 1)

An interesting point made in the Rogoff *et al.* study is that fixed or relatively rigid exchange rate systems do not seem to cause particular harm to the economic growth rates of developing economies with limited financial market development. Indeed, they can provide a useful anchor for gaining anti–inflation credibility, provided the country pursues a reasonable monetary policy. However, as the country develops economically and institutionally to become an emerging market economy, there are 'considerable' gains to be had from adopting a more flexible exchange rate regime; while for devel-oped countries that are not part of a currency union, flexible exchange rates seem to promote higher growth without loss of inflation credibility provided they are accompa-nied by an appropriate institutional framework such as an independent central bank. An important point made by Rogoff *et al.* and Levy-Yeyati and Sturzenegger (2003) is that it is important to distinguish between the *de jure* exchange rate regime of a country and its *de facto* regime. Many developing countries that claim to be free-floating in fact intervene quite extensively in the foreign exchange market. Indeed, this is also true of some developed nations such as Japan, although the yen was supposed to be floating during the period 2001 to 2004, it is estimated that the Bank of Japan purchased around $700 billion US dollars in the foreign exchange market! Rogoff *et al.* show that while floating exchange rates using the *de jure* classification have become more commonplace, it is not true if one uses a *de facto* classification system.

One, of course, has to be quite careful in interpreting the results of economic performance under different exchange rate regimes. For example, the Argentinian peso was classified as a 'hard-peg' currency following its adoption of a currency board *vis-à-vis* the US dollar, but of course the peso freely floated against other currencies with whom it traded (and which were not pegged to the dollar) since the US dollar is a freely floating currency. In addition, when the peso peg was ended in 2002, it coin-cided with a major recession in the country that it would be unfair to attribute to its floating. In Europe in the early 1980s, although many currencies were classified as belonging to the fixed exchange rate system of the EMS, there were such frequent realignments for some currencies such as the Italian lira and French franc that they might as well have been classified as managed-floating! An attempt to adopt a more useful *de facto* exchange rate regime classification is made in Reinhart and Rogoff

(2004) who, using five-year time horizons, distinguish between five coarse types of exchange rate regime: fixed, limited flexibility, managed floating, freely floating, and freely falling. Far from finding a move to a bipolar world, Rogoff *et al.* (2003), looking at the period 1973–99, found that only 20% of regimes were pure floats, 60% were intermediate or pegged regimes, and 20% were freely falling. They argue that the *de jure* classification system substantially overstates the existence of feely floating or hard-peg currencies compared to reality (2003, p. 13):

> While *de jure* intermediate regimes rose from around 10 percent of all exchange rate regimes in the mid-70s to about a quarter in the late 1990s, the proportion of *de facto* regimes with an intermediate degree of flexibility has remained at about one half since the mid 1970s. Within intermediate regimes, however, managed floats have become more prevalent in emerging markets over the past decade, while other developing countries have tended to move in the opposite direction toward more limited flexibility.

While some countries like Argentina and Malaysia moved to hard pegs in the 1990s, and others such as Indonesia, Korea and South Africa moved to floating, there were many other countries that moved away from the bipolar view (using the *de facto* system) to intermediate regimes such Brazil, Peru, Poland, Russia and Venezuela.

The question of which regime is best for economic performance remains a controversial and unresolved issue. Ghosh *et al.* (2003) find that inflation is significantly lower under fixed exchange rate regimes than in intermediate or freely-floating regimes, in part due to a credibility effect and in part due to a discipline effect. However, they do not find evidence of a link between the choice of exchange rate regime and economic growth. By contrast, Levy-Yeyati and Strurzenegger (2003) find evidence that flexible exchange rates seem to be associated with higher growth in developing countries and emerging market economies, although no such link is found for developed industrial countries. Indeed, Levy-Yeyati and Strurzenegger (2003, p. 1178) find that in aggregate 'fixers grow on average 0.78% less than floaters. This suggests that, everything else equal, a country that systematically opted to float its exchange rate after the demise of Bretton Woods would have ended up in 2000 with an output 22% larger than one that chose to fix.' Both papers also find some evidence that fixed exchange rate regimes seem to be associated with higher output volatility. Rogoff *et al.* using a sample of 158 countries for the period 1970–99 examine *de facto* exchange rate regimes against four criteria: inflation, economic growth, variability of growth and the occurrence of crises. A summary of their aggregate results is reported in **Table 11.10.**

A look at the aggregate figures seems to suggest that on the inflation rate score freely floating countries do quite well, but this excludes countries whose currencies are freely falling (inflation rates over 40%) which are normally classified as floating currencies! On economic growth there is relatively little difference between the first four regimes, with a slightly better performance of fixed or limited flexibility regimes but this may be at the cost of greater variability of output compared to floating. Finally, the probability of a crisis does not appear to differ greatly between regimes, although limited flexibility does not fare very well. In the latter case, however, one has to be careful because the aggregate figures are a combination of advanced, emerging and developing countries and hide quite big variations between these groups. In

Table 11.10 Economic performance of different exchange rate regimes

	Peg	Limited flexibility	Managed floating	Freely floating	Freely falling
Inflation	17.1	11.1	14.2	9.9	391.7
	(6.5)	(8.3)	(10.8)	(4.8)	(57)
Real GDP growth	2.1	2.4	1.7	1.8	−1.3
per capita	(2.2)	(2.6)	(2.0)	(2.0)	−(0.6)
Growth volatility	3.7	2.8	3.5	2.7	4.7
	(2.4)	(1.8)	(2.3)	(1.3)	(3.7)
Balance of payments/ currency crisis probability	4.1%	4.1%	9.2%	4.6%	not reported

Notes: (a) The probability of a crisis is calculated by dividing the number of occurrences of a crisis under a particular regime by the total number of regime years. Each crisis is counted only once and hence, if it persists over multiple years, the subsequent years are not taken into account in the calculation. Additionally, the years an exchange rate regime transition takes place (i.e. the year preceding, the year during, and the year following the transition) are excluded from the computation. A crisis is considered as having occurred when the weighted average of one-month changes in the exchange rate and reserves is more than three (country-specific) standard deviations above the country average. (b) Since the samples include many countries some of which exhibit very high volatility of growth, such as transition economies, countries facing war etc. it, may be more appropriate to look at median values rather than mean values. The median values are in parentheses.
Source: Rogoff *et al.* (2003), various tables.

particular, Rogoff *et al.* find that emerging market economies are far less exposed to risk of a banking and/or balance of payments crisis when they have a floating exchange rate regime than when they have a fixed exchange rate regime. For example, they have a 7.7% probability of a twin crisis of balance of payments (currency) and banking crisis with a peg, and only 1.8% probability with limited flexibility. This latter fact may be particularly pertinent to the choice of exchange rate regime for an emerging market economy, since Kaminsky and Reinhart (1999) argue that twin crises have particularly high costs. In such economies, such crises usually commence with the onset of domestic financial distress, which accelerates when a currency crisis then also sets in, leading to a 'vicious cycle'. The costs of such crises are high both in terms of the ultimate bailout costs to recapitalize the banking system, and in terms of foreign exchange reserve losses.

While there are an increasing number of studies looking at the association between exchange rate regime and economic performance, the results must be treated with a high degree of caution. In particular, the methodology employed and classification system used can vary quite a lot in the studies. Also, association does not imply causation and there may be many other reasons for the divergences in performance particularly as between developed and emerging and developing countries. Developed countries usually have more stable and better developed institutional frameworks, stronger financial systems and better access to international capital markets which make them better able to cope with economic shocks whatever exchange rate regime they choose. By contrast, emerging market economies may be particularly vulnerable to economic shocks since their financial systems and institutional frameworks are less-developed and their access to capital markets more constrained in times of economic distress.

11.15 Reform of the international monetary system

The present international monetary system has been called a 'non-system' as there are is no clear set of exchange rate arrangements among the major international currencies (the dollar, yen, euro and sterling), and as **Table 11.9** shows a whole host of exchange rate regimes coexist between currencies. The large and dramatic currency swings between the major currencies, particularly between the dollar and other currencies (see Chapter 6 for plots), have led to a variety of proposals to reform the system. All the proposals are based upon the view that it is desirable to limit the exchange rate swings between the major currencies, but the proposals differ over the best method to achieve this. Three of the best-known proposals to bring some stability to the international monetary system have been made John Williamson, Ronald McKinnon and James Tobin and are worthy of some consideration. At the end, we also consider a more recent and more radical set of proposals that focus on the recent crises and the perpetual problem of sovereign market debt under the grand title of 'Reform of the International Financial Architecture'.

11.16 The Williamson target zone proposal

In a number of papers, John Williamson in conjunction with other authors (1985, 1987, 1988) has proposed that the exchange rate between the major international currencies should be managed within a target zone system. For each of the major currencies Williamson has suggested a method to calculate the currency's 'Fundamental Equilibrium Effective Exchange Rate' (FEEER). Broadly speaking the FEEER is a real effective exchange rate that is consistent with a sustainable current account position. The calculated FEEER would be periodically adjusted as the economic fundamentals change (for example relative inflation rates), and should not therefore be confused with a fixed central rate. A country's exchange rate would then be allowed to fluctuate within a system of 'soft-edged bands' of ± 10% either side of the FEEER. The idea of soft bands is that the authorities will not necessarily be committed to buy or sell the currency if it reaches the upper or lower limit of its band. This, it is argued, will prevent creating a one-way bet for speculators who insist on selling a weak currency at the lower limit of its band knowing that the authorities will be obliged to purchase the currency at what will prove to be a high rate once the currency is forced out of its band.

According to Williamson, the target zone proposal would have helped prevent the dramatic real appreciation of the dollar during 1980–85 because the USA would not have been able to pursue such an expansionary fiscal policy over that period. Furthermore, Williamson and Miller (1987) argue that the target zone proposal can help rule out the possibility of self-fulfilling and destabilizing foreign exchange speculation. There has been criticism of the methodology used to calculate FEEERs, and that the bands and adjustments of FEEERS will fail to rule out major exchange rate swings. For an extensive review and critique of many issues raised by target zones the reader is referred to Frenkel and Goldstein (1986).

11.17 The McKinnon global monetary target proposal

Ronald McKinnon (1982, 1984a and 1984b) has argued that much exchange rate volatility is due to the process of currency substitution. McKinnon argues that in a world in which there are few capital controls, multinational corporations and international investors like to hold a portfolio of various national currencies. He argues that demand to hold a portfolio of national currencies is quite stable but that the composition of the total portfolio can be highly volatile. This means that rigid control of the supply of the individual national currencies in the portfolio is inappropriate. He suggests 'that the Friedman rule for smooth monetary growth should be shifted from a national to a carefully defined international level'. For example, if there is a switch in portfolios away from the US dollar to hold the euro, and national money supplies are unchanged, there will be a depreciation of the dollar and appreciation of the euro. In turn, this will exert effects on the real economies of the two economies.

McKinnon argues that these disruptive real exchange rate changes can be avoided if the European (German) and US authorities peg their exchange rate by contracting the US money supply (thereby eliminating the excess supply of dollars) and expanding the European money supply (thereby eliminating the excess demand for euros). Such a result would happen if the US and European authorities pursued policies of non-sterilized intervention in the foreign exchange market, purchasing the excess dollars with euros. This policy, while leading to changes in national money stocks, would leave the global money supply and exchange rates unchanged and leave the two economies unaffected by the process of currency substitution.

The McKinnon argument that currency substitution is a widespread phenomenon and therefore a major cause of exchange rate volatility has been widely challenged (for example Dornbusch, 1983). It is more likely that the major source of financial portfolio shifts is not between domestic and foreign currencies but between domestic and foreign bonds. As it happens, the appropriate response to deal with such switches is sterilized intervention to peg the exchange rate. For example, if there is a decrease in the demand for US bonds and increase in the demand for European bonds. The appropriate response of the US authorities to this would be to sell European bonds and purchase the excess supply of US bonds, this would leave interest rates and exchange rates unchanged.

There are numerous problems with the McKinnon proposal. Many economists dispute his suggestion that currency substitution is a major force in exchange rate movements. Also, by fixing the nominal exchange rate at some PPP level the proposal does not allow for the possibility of real exchange rate changes which some economists believe have been a major force behind large exchange rate swings. As we saw in Chapter 6, if Japanese tradables productivity growth is higher than US tradables growth, then over time there needs to be a real appreciation of the yen against the dollar. If not, the yen will become undervalued in relation to the dollar and this could lead to serious trade frictions.

11.18 The Tobin foreign exchange tax proposal

James Tobin (1978) has argued that much of the disruptive exchange rate movements witnessed under floating regimes have been caused by destabilizing short-term capital flows. He argues that the highly integrated world capital markets leave very little room for national authorities to pursue independent monetary polices:

> National economies and national governments are not capable of adjusting to massive movements of funds across the foreign exchanges, without real hardship

and without significant sacrifice of the objectives of national economic policy with respect to employment, output, and inflation. Specifically, the mobility of financial capital limits viable differences among national interest rates and this severely restricts the ability of central banks and governments to pursue monetary and fiscal policies appropriate to their national economies. (1978, p. 154)

Specifically, a raising of the domestic interest rate can cause a sharp real appreciation while a lowering of interest rates can lead to a sharp real depreciation. To reduce these effects, Tobin suggests that a tax be imposed on all foreign exchange transactions, 'to throw some sand in the wheels of our excessively efficient international money markets' (p. 154). The tax would reduce the incentives for speculators to suddenly flood money into and out of a currency in response to small interest rate changes. Tobin argued that a small tax of say 1% would especially hit short-term capital movements but not greatly interfere with longer-term capital movements. This would restore some autonomy to domestic monetary authorities.

Tobin acknowledges that in order to be effective and avoid evasion, the tax would have to be applied to all foreign exchange transactions and not merely to capital transactions. He acknowledges that there would be a curtailing effect on international trade but argues that the reduced exchange rate movements and extra degree of national monetary autonomy would be worthwhile.

Tobin's proposal differs significantly from those of Williamson and McKinnon because his proposal is motivated by the belief that the exchange rate regime is not the major problem; rather he traces the problem to excessive capital movements. He displays considerable scepticism over the rationality of foreign exchange market speculation and argues that unlike irrational speculation in innocuous markets likes rare coins, such speculation in the foreign exchange market has very harmful effects.

There have been numerous criticisms levelled against Tobin's proposal. Clearly not all short-term capital movements are undesirable, and the tax would prevent some stabilizing movements. For instance, to the extent that the tax was effective it would reduce the depth and breadth of markets, and this reduction in liquidity could well make the markets more volatile rather than less volatile. Furthermore, some argue that in order to be effective the tax would have to be set at a level that would have a significant curtailing effect on international trade. Another problem is that with today's modern financial markets it is likely that the tax would be easily circumvented as financial innovation would lead to a replication of speculative positions through synthetic instruments that were unaffected by the tax. As for the extra degree of national monetary autonomy that the policy may give, it is not clear that this would be wisely used. It is argued that it is precisely the threat of sudden exchange rate movements that imposes a degree of discipline on national authorities' conduct of economic policies, as Haggard and Maxfield (1996, p. 36) put it 'increased financial integration holds governments hostage to foreign exchange and capital markets, forcing greater fiscal and monetary discipline than they might otherwise choose'. Finally, in a bid to avoid the tax there could a greater use of barter trade which is notoriously inefficient.

11.19 Reform of the international financial architecture

The aim of the debate on reform of the international financial architecture has been about reducing the frequency of crises and also the costs, both financial and economic, when they do occur. The origins of this debate follow on from a study commissioned by the Group of 10 industrialized nations, to see what lessons could be distilled from the Mexican 1994–95 crisis. The report was chaired by Jean-Jacques Rey from Belgium and has become known as the Rey Report (1996). The Rey Report was particularly concerned about the problem of moral hazard and the fact that automatic recourse to large-scale official financing was bailing out imprudent borrowers and lenders alike:

> [N]either debtor countries nor their creditors should expect to be insulated from adverse financial consequences by the provision of large-scale official financing in the event of a crisis. Markets are equipped, or should be equipped, to assess the risks involved in lending to sovereign borrowers and to set the prices and other terms of the instruments accordingly. (Rey Report, 1996)

The series of crises that have afflicted developing and emerging market economies in the past 20 years, and particularly following the Asian financial crisis, has stimulated a more intense debate about whether there are fundamental flaws in the international monetary system that need addressing. In particular, as we shall see in Chapter 17, the Asian financial crisis affected a number of countries which looked to be in good shape on the basis of their macroeconomic fundamentals. None of the countries were running excessive budget deficits, inflation rates were under control and none were engaging in overly expansionary monetary policies. Although there were current account imbalances they hardly seemed to merit the kind of crisis that subsequently occurred. In retrospect, it seems that the crisis that afflicted these economies was not because of national policy mismanagement of these economies, but rather possibly something to do with fundamental flaws in the current international financial system. In addition, international policy-makers were disturbed by the way in which an apparently innocuous devaluation of the Thai baht could have such a contagious effect on so many other countries. The term economic contagion captures the idea that an adverse economic event in one country could quickly spread and infect (that is provoke a crisis) in otherwise healthy looking economies. Another element of the international system has been the large amount of sovereign debt that has made countries vulnerable to speculative attacks. In a speech in at the end of 2001 Anne Krueger, Deputy Managing Director of the IMF, put it this way:

> We lack incentives to help countries with unsustainable debts resolve them promptly and in an orderly way. At present the only available mechanism requires the international community to bail out the private creditors. It is high time this hole was filled.

We cannot go into great detail on all the various proposals for reform that have been put forward or the criticisms and merits of them here, the interested reader is referred to Rogoff (1999) and Frankel (1999), but it is clear that there are a number elements that those arguing for reform are concerned about. It should also be remembered that there are those that argue that the present system is not really in need of much reform. Instead they argue that prevention is better than the cure, and there would be less likelihood of crises if the banking and financial systems in developing and emerging market economies were improved. In particular, there should be more transparency in the provision of information, better banking systems operating with proper risk-return criteria, combined with better regulation and supervision and improved corporate governance of the companies to which they lend. These should be coupled with sounder rules for public finances and independent central banks mandated to seek price stability, and so forth.

There is an intense debate about the role of the IMF in the international monetary system. At one extreme some would like to see it abolished since its very existence encourages some reckless behaviour on the part of borrowers and lenders of funds, who factor in the likelihood of an IMF rescue package should things go wrong. In other words, the IMF itself introduces moral hazard (see **Box 17.1** for more details) into international capital markets making crises more likely to occur than if the IMF did not exist. At the other extreme, there are those that argue that the IMF lacks the necessary funds to do its job properly, it is forced to require overly burdensome adjustment on the part of crisis-afflicted nations since it simply does not have sufficient funds to grant them what they need to mitigate the crises they confront. Others argue that the IMF needs to redefine its role and show greater variety in its programmes than the standard deflationary package that it normally requires a country to follow. In particular, some critics whilst acknowledging that the IMF has a valid role to play when crises occur, argue that it should restrict itself primarily to financial issues and keep out of areas such as structural reform requiring bank closures and privatization. It should also consider the social impact of its programmes; for example, the likely impact of its proposed programme on unemployment rates and economic growth.

Another element of the international financial system that may not be reformable but might be made less significant for developing and emerging market economies, is the free movement of international capital. Some well-known economists such as Jagdish Bhagwati (1998), Paul Krugman (1998) and Dani Rodrik (1998) have argued that the current IMF rules that require members to seek the ultimate goal of capital-account convertibility should be relaxed – developing and emerging market economies should be permitted to use capital controls so that they can regain some monetary and macroeconomic independence. Bhagwati is very critical of both the US Treasury and the IMF for rushing too many developing and emerging market economies into relaxing their capital controls without sufficient consideration of whether their domestic banking and financial systems were sufficiently strong and well-regulated to cope with the capital inflows and outflows to which they would be exposed.

New international lender of the last resort facilities – some authors such as Mishkin (1994) and Fischer (1999) argue that there needs to be a new international agency with credit lines ready to make emergency loans to countries being subjected to 'unwarranted' speculative attacks. The mere knowledge that such an agency exists would make speculators wary of taking on currencies where the fundamentals were relatively sound but which are vulnerable to a speculative attack because, for instance, they posses a low level of foreign exchange reserves or are stuck in a recession. Others are worried that such lender-of-last-resort facilities would merely exacerbate the problem of moral hazard and that the G-7 countries and the IMF countries already effectively provide such a facility.

The problem of the large overhang of sovereign debt has been a recurrent theme in many of the recent crises. Some argue that certain countries have such high levels of external debt that they are effectively bankrupt or placed in a position where economic growth is severely constrained for the foreseeable future by the need to make debt repayments at the expense of living standards and investment in the country's future.

It is argued that there may need to be an international bankruptcy court along the lines proposed by Sachs (1995) where nation states with excessive debt levels could go to seek some sort of protection from their creditors, akin to the use of Chapter 11 bankruptcy provisions that corporations frequently use in the United States, or Chapter 9 provisions which cover bankrupt local and state governments. The court would be able to grant the debtor nation a right to suspend payments to creditors and possibly mandate an orderly restructuring package and even debt relief. Such a court would need to be invested with powers that would be enforceable and possibly override conflicting national laws and existing debt clauses. Chapter 11 provisions apply to corporations and gives the court extensive powers including the ability to fire the existing board of directors, which is hardly going to be allowed at the country level! Not everyone agrees that such a court would be a good idea; some argue it would inevitably become 'a friend' of either the debtors or the creditors. Others argue that such a court is unnecessary and it should be left to the markets to insert innovative clauses into debt securities issued by debtor nations making it more transparent and automatic what should happen in the event of a declared default; this way investors in such bonds would have clearer evaluation of the risks they face and less room to complain should a default be declared.

While there are numerous proposals for reform of the international financial system, it is quite clear that there is no consensus concerning the best way to progress forward. As Eichengreen (1999) notes, some of the grander schemes, are 'politically unrealistic, technically infeasible, or unlikely to yield significant improvements in the way crises are prevented, anticipated or managed'. The differing proposals reflect differing views on what are the problems of the current system and even when commentators agree on the identification of a problem there is not necessarily an agreement on the best way to solve the problem. Often the views are diametrically opposite, some argue for floating exchange rates while others argue that fixed rates are best, some argue for an international lender of the last resort while others oppose it on the grounds that it will add to the problem of moral hazard.

11.20 Conclusions

Since the Second World War the international monetary system has moved from the Bretton Woods system which represented a cooperative venture between the major industrialized countries with the dollar at the heart of the system into a far more diversified system. To some extent this reflects the fact that the world economic system has evolved from one which was dominated by the US economy to one in which economic power is increasingly shared between an integrated Europe, Japan and the USA and other emerging regions such as Southeast Asia and Latin America. The Bretton Woods system was designed for a world economy that was dominated by the United States. While the dollar still remains the major reserve currency and this role has to date only been infringed upon at the margins by the SDR, there is no doubt that the new European currency, the euro, will over time impinge upon the dollar's dominance and the international monetary system is likely to look very different in 20 years' time.

A greater sharing of economic power has been accompanied by a larger degree of interdependence between economies with respect to both trade and capital flows, and the international monetary system has been constantly evolving to cope with these changes. The move to floating exchange rates was partly motivated by a desire to provide countries with an extra degree of independence in an increasingly interdependent world. However, the policy divergences and real exchange rate changes throughout the 1980s and 1990s and early part of this century have amply demonstrated that floating exchange rates do not provide an escape from this interdependence. The currency turmoil in the 1990s and the post 2000 crises and the dramatic movements between the dollar and euro have demonstrated that a stable international monetary system has yet to emerge. This recognition has led to increased discussion among policy-makers about policy coordination, and economists have become increasingly interested in the empirical performance of different exchange rate regimes. At times, such as indicated by the Plaza and Louvre Accords, this discussion has led to concerted action. Dissatisfaction with the present system, particularly with the large real exchange rate changes that have occurred, has led to a variety of differing proposals which all seem to have the motivation to limit by one means or another the substantial real exchange rate changes that have occurred. Many of the recent crises have been concentrated in developing and emerging market economies and there is an intense debate about what is the best exchange rate regime that such countries should adopt.

There have recently been a number of empirical studies looking at the choice of exchange rate regime on macroeconomic performance, and while the results are somewhat unclear and need to be interpreted with caution, it does seem to be the case that fixed exchange rates may well be more appropriate regimes for developing countries with limited access to international markets and who lack stable institutional structures and developed financial markets. While for developed nations which have ready access to international capital markets and stable institutional frameworks and relatively well-developed financial institutions/markets, the choice of exchange rate regime does not matter so much. More interestingly, the recent research tentatively suggests that the choice of exchange rate regime may well be more critical for emerging market economies that are developing their institutional infrastructures, financial institutions and markets and that have significant but volatile access to international capital markets. The evidence, although not clear-cut, suggests that as they develop, emerging market economies may well benefit in the way of improved economic performance and reduced risk of a crisis by increasing the degree of flexibility accorded to the exchange rate.

Further reading

Altig, D.E. and Humpage, O.F. (1999) 'Dollarization and Monetary Sovereignty', Federal Reserve Bank of Cleveland, Economic Commentary.

Argy, V. (1981) *The Postwar International Money Crisis: An Analysis* (London: George Allen & Unwin).

Berg, A. and Borenstein, E. (2000) 'The Pros and Cons of Full Dollarization', IMF Working Paper no. 00/50, Washington.

Bhagwati, J. (1998) 'The Capital Myth: The Difference Between Trade in Widgets and Trade in Dollars', *Foreign Affairs*, vol. 77, pp. 7–12.

Bordo, M.D and Eichengreen, B. (eds) (1993) *A Retrospective on the Bretton Woods System: Lessons for International Monetary Reform* (Chicago: University of Chicago Press).

Clark, P. and Polak, J. (2004) 'International Liquidity and the Role of the SDR', IMF Staff Papers, vol. 51, no. 1, pp. 49–71.

Corden, W.M. (1981) *Inflation, Exchange Rates and the World Economy* (Oxford: Clarendon).

De Grauwe, P. (1989) *International Money* (Oxford: Clarendon Press).

Dornbusch, (1983) 'Flexible Exchange Rates and Interdependence', *IMF Staff Papers*, vol. 30, pp. 3–30.

Dunn, R. (1983) 'The Many Disappointments of Flexible Exchange Rates', *Princeton Essays in International Finance*, no. 154.

Edison, H.J., Miller, M.H. and Williamson, J. (1987) 'On Evaluating and Extending the Target Zone Proposal'. *Journal of Policy Modelling*, vol. 9, pp. 199–227.

Eichengreen, B. (1994) *International Monetary Arrangements for the 21st Century* (Washington: Brookings Institution).

Eichengreen, B. (1999) *Toward a New International Financial Architecture* (Washington: Institute for International Economics).

Fischer, S. (1999) 'On the Need for an International Lender of Last Resort', International Monetary Fund, speech (www.IMF.org.).

Fischer, S. (2001) 'Exchange Rate Regimes: Is the Bipolar View Correct?', *Journal of Economic Perspectives*, vol. 15, no. 2 (Spring), pp. 3–24.

Frankel, J.A. (1985) 'The Dazzling Dollar', *Brookings Papers on Economic Activity*, vol. 1, pp. 199–217.

Frankel, J.A. (1999) 'No Single Currency Regime Is Right for All Countries at All Times', Princeton Essays in International Finance no. 215, Princeton.

Frenkel, J.A. and Goldstein, M. (1986) 'A Guide to Target Zones', *IMF Staff Papers*, vol. 33, pp. 623–73.

Ghosh, A.R., Gulde, A. and Wolf, H.C. (2003) *Exchange Rate Regimes: Choices and Consequences* (Cambridge Mass.: MIT Press).

Haggard, S. and Maxfield, S. (1996) 'The Political Economy of Financial Internationalization in the Developing World', *International Organisation*, vol. 50, pp. 35–68.

Kaminsky, G. and Reinhart, C. (1999) 'The Twin Crises: The Causes of Banking and Balance of Payments Problems', *American Economic Review*, vol. 89, pp. 473–500.

Kenen, P.B., Padadia, F. and Saccomanni, F. (eds) (1994) *The International Monetary System*, (Cambridge: Cambridge University Press).

Krugman, P. (1998). 'Saving Asia: It's Time to Get Radical', *Fortune*, September 7, pp. 74–80.

Levy-Yeyati, E. and Sturzenegger, F. (2002) 'Classifying Exchange Rate Regimes: Deeds versus Words', Universidad Torcuato Di Tella.

Levy-Yeyati, E. and Sturzenegger, F. (2003) 'To Float or to Fix: Evidence on the Impact of Exchange Rate Regimes on Growth', *American Economic Review*, vol. 9, no. 4. pp. 1173–93.

McKinnon, R.I. (1981) 'The Exchange Rate and Macroeconomic Policy: Changing Postwar Perceptions', *Journal of Economic Literature*, vol. 19, pp. 531–57.

McKinnon, R.I. (1982) 'Currency Substitution and Instability in the World Dollar Standard', *American Economic Review*, vol. 72, pp. 320–33.

McKinnon, R.I. (1984) *An International Standard for Monetary Stabilization*, Institute for International Economics, Policy Analyses no. 8. (Cambridge, Mass.: MIT Press).

McKinnon, R.I. (1988) 'Monetary and Exchange Rate Policies for International Financial Stability: A Proposal', *Journal of Economic Perspectives*, vol. 2, pp. 83–103.

Miller, M. and Williamson, J. (1987) 'The International Monetary System: An Analysis of Alternative Regimes', *European Economic Review*, vol. 32, pp. 1031–48.

Milner, C. and Greenaway, D. (1979) *An Introduction to International Economics* (London: Longman).

Mishkin, F. (1994). 'Preventing Financial Crises: An International Perspective', National Bureau of Economic Research Working Paper no. 4636.

Niehans, J. (1984) *International Monetary Economics*, (Oxford: Philip Allan).

Nurkse, R. (1944) *International Currency Experience* (New York: League of Nations).

Obstfeld, M. and Rogoff, K. (1995) 'Exchange Rate Dynamics Redux', *Journal of Political Economy*, vol. 103, pp. 624–60.

Reinhart, C. and Rogoff, K. (2004) 'The Modern History of Exchange Rate Arrangements: A Reinterpretation', *Quarterly Journal of Economics*, vol. 113, pp. 1–48.

Rey (G-10) Report (1996) 'The Resolution of Sovereign Liquidity Crises', International Monetary Fund, Washington.

Rodrik, D. (1998) 'Who Needs Capital-Account Convertibility?', in F. Stanley *et al.* (eds), *Should the IMF Pursue Capital-Account Convertibility?* Essays in International Finance No. 207, International Finance Section, Department of Economics, Princeton University.

Rogoff, K. (1999) 'International Financial Institutions for Reducing Global Financial Instability', *Journal of Economic Perspectives*, vol. 13, no. 4, pp. 21–42.

Rogoff, K., Husain, A.M., Mody, A., Brooks, R. and Oomes, N. (2003) 'Evolution and Performance of Exchange Rate Regimes', IMF Working Paper WP/03/243, Washington.

Sachs, J. (1995) 'Do we Need an International Lender of Last Resort?', The Frank D. Graham Memorial Lecture delivered at Princeton University.

Scammell, W.M. (1987) *The Stability of the International Monetary System* (London: Palgrave: Macmillan).

Solomon, R. (1982) *The International Monetary System, 1945–81* (New York: Harper & Row).

Summers, L.H. (2000) 'International Financial Crises: Causes, Prevention, and Cures', *American Economic Review*, Papers and Proceedings, vol. 90, no. 2, pp. 1–16.

Tew, B. (1988) *The Evolution of the International Monetary System 1948–88* (London: Hutchinson).

Tobin, J. (1978) 'A Proposal for International Monetary Reform', *Eastern Economic Journal*, vol. 4, pp. 153–9; reprinted in J. Tobin (1982) *Essays in Economics* (Cambridge, Mass.: MIT Press).

Triffin, R. (1960) *Gold and the Dollar Crisis* (New Haven, Conn.: Yale University Press).

Willet, T. (2000) 'International Financial Markets as Sources of Crises or Discipline: The too Much too Late Hypothesis', *Princeton Essays in International Finance*, no. 218.

Williamson, J. (1977) *The Failure of World Monetary Reform* (Sunbury: Nelson).

Williamson, J. (1983) *The Exchange Rate System*, Institute for International Economics, Policy Analyses no. 5 (Cambridge Mass.: MIT Press).

12

The Eurocurrency and Eurobond Markets

12.1 Introduction

In this chapter we take a detailed look at two important markets that exert a great deal of influence on the international financial system, the Eurocurrency market and the Eurobond market. Eurocurrency markets are defined as banking markets which involve short-term borrowing and lending conducted outside of the legal jurisdiction of the authorities of the currency that is used. For example, Eurodollar deposits are dollar deposits held in London and Paris. The Eurocurrency market has two sides to it; the receipt of deposits and the loaning out of those deposits. By far the most important

Table 12.1 The gross size of the Eurocurrency market in selected years

Year	US$ billions	Year	US$ billions
1963	12.4	1984	2,153.2
1964	14.9	1986	3,221.1
1966	26.5	1988	4,511.3
1968	46.4	1990	6,253.8
1970	93.2	1992	6,197.7
1972	149.9	1994	7,116.7
1974	248.0	1996	8,309.2
1976	341.7	1998	9,898.6
1978	549.6	2000	10,765.2
1980	1,011.7	2002	13,375.0
1982	1,514.7	2003	15,928.9

Source: Bank for International Settlements.

Eurocurrency is the Eurodollar which currently accounts for approximately 60–65% of all Eurocurrency activity, followed by the Euroeuro, Eurofrancs (Swiss), Eurosterling and Euroyen. The use of the prefix Euro is somewhat misleading because dollar deposits held by banks in Hong Kong or Tokyo are equally outside the legal jurisdiction of the US authorities and also constitute Eurodollar deposits. This more widespread geographical base means that Euromarkets are often referred to as 'offshore' markets.

Since the 1960s there has been an astonishing rate of growth of the Eurocurrency market (see **Table 12.1**). In 1963 the gross total value of Eurobank assets (a similar figure applies to deposit liabilities) was approximately $12.4 billion, but by the end of 2003 the Eurodollar market stood at $15,929 billion, works out at an average growth rate of 19.6% per annum over the 40 years! Measuring the actual size of the Eurocurrency market presents some difficulty because a distinction needs to be made between the gross and net size of the Eurocurrency market. The gross measure includes both non-Eurobank and interbank deposits, while the net measure excludes interbank deposits. The gross measure gives an idea about the overall activity in the Euromarkets while the net measure gives a better indication concerning the ability of the Eurobanking system to create credit.

The Eurocurrency market is part of the international money market since it involves lending and borrowing for a period of less than a year. By contrast, the Eurobond market is part of the international capital market and involves lending and borrowing for a periods of more than a year. A Eurobond is a bond that is sold by a government, institution or company in a currency that is different from the country where the bond is issued. For example, a dollar bond sold in London is a dollar Eurobond and a sterling bond sold in Germany is a sterling Eurobond. Both the Eurocurrency and Eurobond markets are in many ways a phenomenon of the increasingly open world trading system. There is no reason why borrowing and lending in a given currency needs be carried out exclusively in the particular country that issues the currency.

In this chapter, we deal with the origins and reasons for the subsequent rapid growth of Eurocurrency and Eurobond markets over the last three decades. We also examine the basic functioning of these markets and their economic impact. Firstly we look at the Eurocurrency markets and then look at the Eurobond markets.

12.2 Participants in the Eurocurrency and Eurobond markets

Before looking at the Eurocurrency and Eurobond markets it is worth examining the participants that use these markets and their motivations. The are numerous participants in the international money and capital markets, including national governments, local authorities, financial institutions such as banks, multinational firms, companies and international institutions such as the International Monetary Fund, World Bank and European Investment Bank as well as private investors. Most industrialized countries' participants act both lenders and borrowers of funds, while many developing countries use the markets almost exclusively for borrowing purposes. The various types of capital flows between economic agents of different countries are motivated by various factors; these include:

1   Trade financing motive – much trade is financed by borrowing on the international money and capital markets.
2   Borrowing/lending motive – many capital flows are simply motivated by the desire of savers to get the best possible return on their money, while borrowers are merely seeking to obtain the lowest possible interest rate.
3   Speculative motive – much borrowing or lending is due to the taking of speculative positions based on profiting from prospective interest rate and exchange rate changes.
4   Hedging motive – much borrowing and lending is motivated by a desire to hedge positions; that is, to avoid losses resulting from prospective interest rate and exchange rate changes.
5   Capital flight motive – many movements of capital are motivated by a desire to protect investors funds from penal taxation, possible seizure by the domestic government or to escape potential restrictions being imposed on convertibility or to avoid political risk.

12.3 The origins and development of the Eurocurrency market

The origins of the Eurocurrency market can be traced back to 1957. The Russians having acquired US dollars through their exports of raw materials were, given the strong anti-communist sentiment prevailing in the USA and the 'cold war', reluctant to hold these funds with US banks. Instead, they were held in an account with a French bank in Paris, the cable address of which was EURO-BANK. Also in 1957, the Bank of England introduced restrictions on UK banks' ability to lend sterling to foreigners and foreigners' ability to borrow sterling. This induced UK banks to turn to the US dollar as a means of retaining London's leading role in the financing of world trade. In 1958 the abolition of the European Payments Union and restoration of convertibility of European currencies meant that European banks could now hold US dollars without being forced to convert these dollar holdings with their central banks for domestic currencies.

An important impetus for the rapid growth of the Eurodollar market came from the increased regulation of domestic banking activities by the US authorities. Three measures were of particular note in this respect. In 1963 the US government introduced Regulation Q which imposed a 5.25% ceiling on the rate of interest that US banks could pay on savings and time-deposit accounts (the idea being to prevent US banks pushing up interest rates in a competition for depositors' funds, which might then lead to risky lending policies). Since the regulation did not apply to offshore banks this encouraged many US banks to set up subsidiaries abroad in centres such as London. In the same year, the US authorities concerned about the impact of capital outflows on the US balance of payments introduced the Interest Equalization Tax (IET). The IET raised the cost to foreigners of borrowing dollars in New York but this then led them to borrow funds on the Eurodollar market (the IET was abolished in 1974). A further measure that restricted lending to foreigners by US banks was the Voluntary Foreign Credit Restraint Guidelines which were issued in 1965 and made compulsory in 1968.

This increased regulation of US domestic banks gave a boost to the development of Eurobanking activities to circumvent the effects of these controls. Many US banks decided to set up foreign branches and subsidiaries to escape the banking regulations. Indeed, since US banking law severely restricted US banks ability to operate in more than one state setting up subsidiaries abroad was an important means of expansion for many US banks. More importantly, the regulations conferred a competitive edge to Eurobanks which were not subject to such regulations.

Following the hike in oil prices in 1973/74, the Oil Petroleum Export Countries (OPEC) deposited large amounts of surplus dollars on the Euromarkets. The Eurobanks then on-lent much of the funds to oil-importing countries that faced balance of payments problems. As such the Eurobanks played an important intermediary role in recycling funds from the surplus OPEC countries to the deficit oil importing countries. A similar role was performed by the Eurobanks following the second oil price shock at the end of 1978 though on a lesser scale. The large majority of loans made by the Eurobanks to the developing countries in the 1970s and early 1980s were made by syndicates of Eurobanks. A syndicate is normally led by a lead or managing bank with other banks that wish to participate in a loan contributing its funding. Such syndicated loans are useful from the perspective of individual Eurobanks because they reduce the exposure of a Eurobank to a given borrower, and by participating in a wide range of syndicated loans a Eurobank can diversify and reduce its loan risks far more than by engaging in a limited number of large individual loans.

A final factor behind the growth of Eurobanking activity has been the rapid growth of world trade, which means that more companies have excess working balances in a foreign currency on which they seek high rates of return, while others require short-term borrowing facilities at competitive rates of interest.

In December 1981 the Federal Reserve, recognizing that many US Banks had set up offshore branches to avoid US regulations in exotic locations such as the Bahamas and Cayman Islands, decided to legalize so-called International Banking Facilities (IBFs). IBFs essentially permit US banks to conduct Eurobanking business free of US regulations in the United States by maintaining a separate set of books for this business. IBFs are not subject to reserve requirements, interest rate regulations or deposit insurance premiums, but they can only accept deposits and make loans to non-US residents. In addition, IBF business is maintained on a separate book to the parent bank. IBFs have proved to be popular since their inception and much business that was previously carried out in offshore offices has been relocated back to the USA. Following the success of IBFs, in 1986 the Japanese government permitted the setting-up of a Japanese Onshore Market (JOM) which likewise permits Japanese banks to take on Euroyen deposits in Tokyo provided these are not onlent to domestic Japanese residents.

12.4 The characteristics of the Eurodollar market

The major centres for Eurobank activity are London, Paris, New York, Tokyo and Luxembourg. Offshore banking centres in Bahrain, Bahamas, the Cayman Islands, Hong Kong, Panama, Netherlands Antilles and Singapore account for most of the remaining business.

Eurobanks are generally free of government regulation, and more specifically they do not face compulsory reserve requirements, interest ceilings or deposit insurance. The main users of the Eurocurrency market facilities are the Eurobanks themselves, non-Eurobank financial institutions, multinational corporations, international institutions and central and local government. Multinationals are attracted by the relatively high interest rates paid on their surplus corporate funds and the competitive borrowing rates. International organizations such as the World Bank frequently borrow funds from Eurobanks for lending to developing countries. A large proportion of Eurocurrency transactions are between Eurobanks themselves, those with surplus funds loaning to Eurobanks that have lending possibilities but are short of funds.

The pivotal rate of interest for the Eurocurrency markets is the London Inter-Bank Offer Rate (LIBOR), which is the rate of interest that London clearing banks will charge for loans between themselves on the London interbank market. Non-bank borrowers then pay a spread above LIBOR depending on their credit rating and the lending bank's transaction costs; non-bank depositors typically receive a rate of interest on their deposits below LIBOR. In the early days of the Euromarket, the interest paid on deposits and charged for loans was usually fixed for the whole period of the deposit or loan. Increasingly, however, floating interest rates based on LIBOR have become the norm for medium to long-term (above six months) deposits and loans. With floating rates, the interest charged on a medium to long-term loan is adjusted every three or six months to stay a fixed spread above LIBOR. In effect, many long-term loans are a succession of short-term loans that are automatically 'rolled over', but at interest rates that vary in line with changes in LIBOR. There are usually penalties to be paid if deposits are withdrawn before maturity.

One of the interesting characteristics of the structure of Eurobanks assets (loans) and liabilities (deposits) is that they are predominately of a short-term nature with some deposits being as short as one day (overnight deposit) and the vast majority under six months. Furthermore, there is a close matching of the maturity structure of deposits and liabilities, typically if money is taken in for three (six) months then it will be loaned out for three (six) months. This is because Eurobanks have to be wary of sudden large withdrawals of short-term funds. Another motivation behind the close matching of assets and liabilities is that it reduces the risks to the banks due to interest fluctuations. Consider a simple example of the risk involved when liabilities and assets are not matched. In the case where a Eurobank receives a $1 million three-month deposit on which it has to pay 7.5% interest and it loans out the funds at 8% for six months, if at the end of three months a rise in deposit interest rates means that it has to pay 9% to retain the deposit it would effectively be losing money on the remaining three months on the outstanding loan. This would not be the case if the loan was renewable at three months since it could then raise the interest charged on the loan for its remaining three months to, say, 9.5%. This close matching of assets and liabilities stands in contrast to the balance sheets of domestic banks which usually accept short-term demand and time deposits and then engage in medium to long-term lending. It should be noted that since 1982 the existence of Eurodollar futures markets in Chicago, New York and London has enabled Eurobanks to protect themselves against interest fluctuations without matching their assets and liabilities.

12.5 The competitive advantage of Eurobanks

The main reason for the continuing success of Eurobanking despite the relaxation of regulation on US banks is that they are able to offer higher deposit rates and lower loan rates than US banks. It is this competitive edge which is the fundamental reason for their continued popularity and growth. The competitive advantage of Eurobanks is illustrated in **Figure 12.1**.

The Eurobanks are generally able to pay a higher rate on deposits and charge a lower rate for loans than US banks can for similar facilities. This implies that the interest rate spread, that is the difference between the rate paid on deposits and charged for loans, is lower for the Eurobanks than US banks. The lower Euro-interest spread can be accounted for by a number of factors:

1   Eurobanks, unlike domestic banks, are free of regulatory control and in particular they are not required to hold reserve assets. This gives them a competitive advantage over domestic banks which are required to hold part of their assets in zero or low-interest liquid assets to meet official reserve requirements. Since Eurobanks are not subject to reserve requirements they are able to hold less money in the form of low-interest reserves enabling them to pay a higher interest rate on deposits and charge a lower rate on loans. For example, up until 1990 the Federal Reserve imposed a 3% reserve requirement on US banks so that for every $100 taken in only $97 could be lent out, on an interest rate of 10% this amounts to the need to charge 10.31% to cover the cost of the reserves.
2   Eurobanks benefit from economies of scale, the average size of Eurobanks deposit and loans (hundreds of thousands and usually millions of dollars) is considerably greater than those of domestic banks (usually tens, hundreds and thousands of

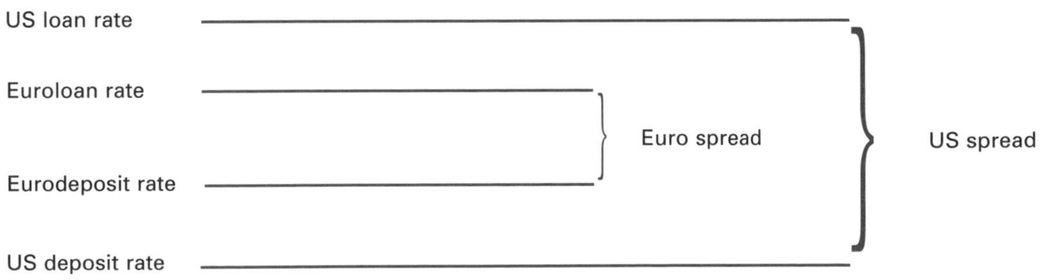

US loan rate

Euroloan rate

Euro spread   US spread

Eurodeposit rate

US deposit rate

Figure 12.1   Comparison of US certificate of deposit and Eurodollar interest spreads

dollars). This means the average operating cost associated with each dollar deposit and loan transaction is much lower for Eurobanks.

3   Eurobanks avoid much of the personnel, administration costs and delays associated with complying with domestic banking regulations. Eurobanks do not have to maintain a large branch network for their business whereas domestic banking activity usually requires the maintenance an extensive branch network. In addition, domestic banks need extensive internal control mechanisms and large costly legal departments whereas Eurobanks have far less need for these.

4   The Eurobanking business is highly competitive internationally with relatively easy entrance requirements as compared to domestic banking activity, this encourages greater efficiency and more competitive pricing on the part of Eurobanks.

5   Eurobanks do not have to pay deposit insurance whereas US banks have to insure their deposit base with the Federal Deposit Insurance Corporation (FDIC).

6   Eurobank lending is almost exclusively to high-quality customers with a virtually negligible default rate, which contrasts with the relatively high default rates faced by domestic banks that have to charge an appropriate default risk premium in the way of higher lending rates and lower deposit rates of interest.

12.6 The coexistence of domestic and Eurobanking

Since Eurobanks generally pay higher interest rates on deposits and charge lower interest rates on loans than US-based banks, then it is natural to ask why all borrowing and lending is not carried out via Eurobanks? The answer lies in the transaction costs for the parties involved. It usually pays a US firm to go to its local US bank for a loan because the local bank will have a record and understanding of the business and will be able to assess more easily the risk of lending to the business, secure collateral and monitor the progress of the loan. If the firm were to go to a Eurobank it could prove expensive to convince the Eurobank that it is creditworthy and that the project is soundly based. Similarly, except for substantial sums of money it is not usually worth individuals and small enterprises holding a Eurodeposit as they rarely have sufficient surplus funds to be of interest to the Eurobanks, and most private agents prefer the use of other bank facilities such as cheque accounts, easy access to funds and the like which are not offered by the Eurobanks.

12.7 The creation of Eurodollar deposits and loans

Eurobanks are basically financial intermediaries whose function is channelling funds from a non-bank lender to a non-bank borrower. Between the deposit and the lending there may be a series of interbank transactions. To enhance the understanding of Eurocurrency markets we consider a hypothetical example of how Eurocurrency deposits and loans are created. Assume that a US multinational SUPER Corp starts off the process by transferring $50 million from its US bank account into a Eurodollar deposit account with EUROBANK A. EUROBANK A may not have an immediate use for these funds but EUROBANK B has a client MINI Corp who wishes to borrow $50 million but EUROBANK B is short of the necessary funds. In this instance, EUROBANK B borrows the $50 million from EUROBANK A at $LIBOR and then loans the funds to an ultimate borrower MINI Corp. A summary of these transactions is shown in **Figure 12.2**.

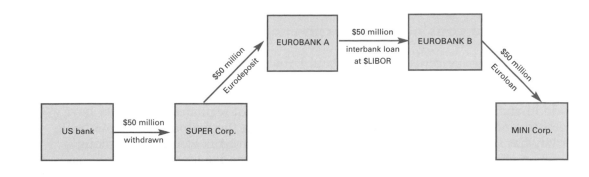

Figure 12.2 The creation of Eurobanking activity

From these transactions we can see what has basically occurred: SUPER Corp has switched a dollar deposit from a US bank to EUROBANK A; EUROBANK A has a new deposit liability to SUPER Corp but also now holds increased funds which it can utilize for lending purposes. As far as the US banking system is concerned, the amount of deposits held by the non-bank public has fallen; however, these funds have been switched into the Eurobanking arena. The transfer of funds from EUROBANK A to EUROBANK B constitutes an interbank transaction, the effect of which is to raise the total of Eurodollar deposits from $50 million to $100 million. We can now distinguish between the effect on the net size of the Eurodollar market – the original $50 million deposit and the gross size of $100 million which includes the interbank transaction. With the loan to MINI Corp the funds that were initially deposited by SUPER Corp have been given an ultimate use.

The Eurobanks are in effect acting as financial intermediaries ensuring that surplus funds from one organization (SUPER Corp) are transferred to other organizations with borrowing requirements (MINI Corp). When MINI Corp starts to spend money, then the dollars have ultimately been derived from the US banking system not from the Eurobanks. Only the US banking system creates dollars, the Eurobanks create deposits which are not a means of payment. Eurobanks are essentially financial intermediaries, they accept deposits and then loan out these funds.

The real question which now arises is what MINI Corp does with its borrowed funds. If it were to just redeposit them with another Eurobank then the whole process could be restarted; however, this is most unlikely to be the case. More likely, MINI Corp will use the funds to pay various bills due or finance a project, and only a small fraction of its $50 million (for example $1 million to $5 million) will eventually end back in the Eurobanking system which can then be used to create further credit.

This is a highly simplified example of the way the Eurobanking system creates credit. There are some obvious limits to the amount of credit created by the Eurobanking system. In the first instance, EUROBANK A and EUROBANK B are unlikely to lend out instantly all the deposits they receive and then MINI Corp is likely to redeposit only a fraction of its money with the Eurobanking system. It is quite likely that most of the money received by MINI Corp will eventually be reinjected into the American economy and thereby returned to the US banking system, from which there may be some limited leakage back to the Eurocurrency markets.

12.8 The pros and cons of the Eurocurrency markets

One of the major concerns expressed about Eurocurrency markets is that they have enormous amounts of funds and the potential to create credit and yet remain unregulated. Some argue that Eurobanking activity is a ticking time-bomb underneath the world financial system. The fact that Eurobanks are not regulated and do not have access to lender-of-last-resort facilities, combined with the high degree of interbank activity has led to concerns that the failure of one Eurobank would have serious knock-on effects on other Eurobanks and in so doing endanger the entire international financial system.

Another concern expressed about the Euromoney markets is about their potential impact on inflation. The rapid growth of the Eurocurrency markets in the 1960s and 1970s coincided with a pronounced rise in the inflation rates of the industrialized nations. Some policy-makers and economists argued that Eurocurrency market growth was partly responsible for this. The basis of the argument was that the growth of Eurocurrency markets with no reserve requirements had an expansionary effect on national money supplies and thereby helped to fuel inflation rates. For example, Friedman (1969) and Mayer (1970) made initial estimates which suggested that Euromarkets had a very expansionary effect on money supplies because of their low reserve ratios. However, Klopstock (1968) noted that Eurobanks have very low redeposit ratios which considerably reduced their ability to create credit. Furthermore, McKinnon (1977) makes the important point that what is important in deciding whether Eurobanks are responsible for credit creation is their net addition to the supply of dollars, that is, the addition to the global supply of dollars as compared to the supply of dollars in their absence. On this basis he finds little evidence to support the view that the Eurocurrency markets have led to a massive expansion of global money supplies. Other authors, such as Dufey and Giddy (1978), have argued that the Eurodollar market is essentially a substitute for the domestic dollar market on both the deposit and loan side. In the first instance, the deposits they attract are essentially taken away from the US banking system, while the loans that they make are likewise substitutes for loans by US banks. This being the case, the idea of a separate Eurodollar multiplier is not a particularly relevant concept.

Hogan and Pearce (1982) have objected to the Euromoney markets on other grounds, in particular they are very concerned about the fact that Euromarkets enable deficit countries to finance their deficits with relative ease. They argue that the rapid growth of Eurocurrency markets is due to one set of countries being in persistent balance of payments surplus and another group in persistent deficit. The Euromarkets are viewed as recycling funds from the surplus countries to the deficit countries; and if the recycling goes on for a number of years the outstanding loans to deficit countries will grow and grow. Hogan and Pearce are very concerned about the fact that Euromarkets enable deficit countries to finance their deficits with relative ease and believe that Euromarkets encourage excessive borrowing. Further, deficit countries can avoid the need to pursue prudent macroeconomic policies. Hogan and Pearce argue that there are a number of dangers that could hit the Eurobanking system. The deficit countries that have over-borrowed might not wish to repay, which in turn might provoke a crisis of confidence in the Eurobanking system. Another problem might be that depositors with funds in the Eurobanking system could get concerned at the growing size of Eurobanks exposure to the deficit countries and this could lead them to withdraw their dollars deposits from the Eurobanks which in turn could lead to a problem for the deficit countries that are unable to roll over their loans. Hogan and Pearce are so concerned about the build-up of debt possibilities that they advocate Euromarkets' 'immediate death should be engineered with a maximum of speed and minimum of fuss' (pp. 127–8).

It cannot be denied that in the 1970s there was a great deal of recycling of petro dollars by Eurobanks to a number of Latin American countries which had received much of the dollar surpluses of the Oil Petroleum Exporting Countries to finance their deficits. However, a great deal of the financing of these deficits was also carried out by US domestic banks. The fact that much of this lending eventually proved to be unwise (see Chapter 15) is not just a judgement against much Eurobank lending, but also against the lending policies of many domestic US banks. Also, it is not so clear that Eurobanks are doing any harm. It must be emphasized that Eurobanks ultimately act as intermediaries for the recycling of funds because they are the most efficient institutions for doing this. If they had not been in existence then petrodollar recycling would most probably have still taken place, only less efficiently so by the US banking system.

Other authors have argued that Eurobanks have enabled speculators to easily raise funds to mount speculative attacks on currencies and in so doing increased currency volatility in general. Against this, it could be argued that the fact that there are enormous sums of speculative balances on the Euromarkets acts as an important discipline of government macroeconomic policies and in so doing leads to more stable macroeconomic policies and exchange rates.

Despite these concerns, it must be remembered that the Eurocurrency markets have increased the range of facilities available to both borrowers and lenders. In addition, they do so at very competitive rates of interest. They have not only facilitated financial transfers between private economic agents, but also between countries enabling countries to finance current account deficits with somewhat greater ease than before the Euromarkets existed.

12.9 Euromarkets and government regulation and policy

While domestic banking has remained subject to various regulatory requirements this is not the case with Euromarkets. Examples of two of the most commonly used regulations governing domestic banking activities are reserve requirements imposed by the authorities to limit domestic banks ability to create credit and deposit insurance designed to protect depositors should a bank become insolvent.

The lack of regulation governing Eurobanks has often led to calls for some degree of international regulation of their activities. In particular, given the amount of inter-bank lending on the Euromarkets there has always been a fear that were one Eurobank to fail this could trigger the failure of many Eurobanks. This being the case, the need for effective regulation has been regarded as important in ensuring that Eurobanks conduct their business in a sound manner. However, effective regulation of Eurobanks is fraught with problems. Say the US authorities were to regulate US Eurobanks, all this would be likely to do is to shift Eurobanking activities to non-US Eurobanks. Similarly, if regulation is exercised by a particular Eurobanking centre such as London, then all this would be likely to do is to shift Eurobanking business to other non-regulated centres. Unilateral regulation by one particular government or Eurobanking centre is unlikely to lead to greater regulation of Eurobanking activity because it would most probably just result in a shift of Eurobanking business to other unregulated Eurobanks and centres.

It would seem that effective regulation of Eurobanking activities would require multilateral regulation and guidelines. However, given the high degree of competition for Eurobanking business such multilateral cooperation is unlikely to be forthcoming. The very fact that Eurobanks have managed to grow rapidly because of the lack of regulation of their activities has probably had the effect of reducing the degree of regulation covering domestic banking activity. Once a regulation is applied to a domestic banking activity, it is often the case that the business is diverted to the Eurobanks where it is free of the constraint. Furthermore, the desire to bring some Eurobank business back to the domestic banking arena has often acted as a stimulus to the relaxation of domestic regulations.

12.10 The international capital market and the Eurobond market

The international capital market is a longer-term market than the Eurocurrency market, in which borrowers and lenders of funds from different countries are brought together to exchange funds. The international capital market is made up of three markets: (1) the domestic bond market, (2) the foreign bond market and (3) the Eurobond market. A domestic bond is a bond issued in the currency of the country of issue by a domestic entity; for example, a US dollar Treasury bond issued by the US Treasury or a dollar Corporate bond issued by a US corporation in the United States. A foreign bond is a bond issued by a foreign entity in the domestic currency of the country of issue – an example of this would be a British company that issues a dollar bond in the US market, such a foreign bond is known as a yankee, and other foreign bonds have names symbolizing the country whose currency is being borrowed such as Bulldogs for sterling bonds, Samurais for yen bonds and Matadors for Spanish euro-denominated bonds. A Eurobond is a bond that is sold by a government, institution or company in a currency different from the country where the bond is issued. For example, a dollar bond sold in London is a dollar Eurobond, and a sterling bond sold Germany is a sterling Eurobond.

Since the early 1960s, the international capital market has grown at an astonishing pace both in terms of the funds transferred and the number of participants in the market. The Eurobond market has grown from its origins in the mid-1960s to such an extent that the outstanding value of dollar Eurobonds issued significantly exceeds the issue of domestic US corporate bonds. These days there is no need for securities markets to be restricted to national boundaries. Economic agents may seek to raise funds in either the domestic or a foreign currency and in seeking to raise the funds at the cheapest possible cost they may seek the assistance of foreign financial institutions and foreign financial centres who in turn can attract both domestic and foreign investors. In the following section, we pay particular attention to the Eurobond market which has become a particularly significant source of funds.

12.11 The origins and development of the Eurobond market

The first Eurobond was issued in 1963 and since then the market has grown enormously, particularly during the 1980s and 1990s. The Eurobond market dates back to the imposition of the Interest Equalization Tax by the US authorities on US citizens that held dollar bonds issued by foreign entities in the United States. The US authorities imposed the tax because of concern about the long-term outflow of capital on the US balance of payments. By reducing the attractiveness to US investors of investing in foreign bonds, the tax provided a stimulus for foreign entities to issue US dollar bonds outside of the United States. A further incentive for the development of the Eurobond market was that the US authorities also imposed withholding taxes on foreign citizens that held US bonds, and this meant that foreign citizens had a clear incentive to hold Eurobonds that were not subject to taxation by the US authorities.

Although the IET was abolished in 1974 and withholding taxes removed in 1984, the Eurobond market continued to prosper. The Eurobond market growth in the 1980s was partly stimulated by the fact that corporations found banks increasingly reluctant to lend funds due to problems stemming from the third world debt crisis (see Chapter 15). Furthermore, many corporations realized that they could exploit their credit ratings which were often as good if not better than some of the banks that they had traditionally borrowed funds from, especially as they increasingly deemed the rates of interest and security requirement of banks to be excessive. In addition, many corporations found that banks were reluctant to lend at fixed rates of interest at the longer time horizons that corporations were interested in. The major advantage of a Eurobond issue over domestic and foreign bond issues is that there are less stringent regulatory and disclosure requirements on the corporate issuer and a greater variety or different bond types can be issued. In sum, the Eurobond market generally means lower cost finance for well known companies than borrowing directly from banks or the domestic bond market.

12.12 Typical features of a Eurobond

Dollar-denominated Eurobonds have traditionally been the most popular form of issue, although the dollar predominance is less than in the Eurocurrency loans market. In recent years, however, the euro has been very popular as shown in **Table 12.2**. The main reason for this is that many corporations have been keen to attract savings from countries with high savings ratios, especially Japan and Germany, whose investors tend to be more keen to buy Eurobonds which are denominated in their local currency.

Table 12.2 International bond issues by currency

Currency	Rank	2004 Total raised (in billions)	Number of issues
Euro	1	$842	2,259
US dollar	2	$434	1,405
Yen	3	¥2,481	667
Sterling	4	$34	132

Source: Dealogic.

Most (approximately 75%) Eurobond issues are undertaken by very highly rated instituting with AAA and AA credit ratings. The market is used extensively by governments, international organizations such the World Bank, the European Investment Bank and multinational corporations. Some issuers use the market to raise funds in currencies they do not wish to ultimately hold but as part of a Swap deal (see Chapter 13). The yield at which a borrower obtains funds will depend on market conditions and the credit rating of the issuer, with governments typically being able to raise funds at a lower cost than corporations with an equivalent credit rating.

Eurobonds come in a variety of forms, and the most common type are known as **straights** which pay fixed rates of interest with repayment of principal upon maturity. Increasingly popular are **floating-rate notes** which are Eurobonds on which the interest rate is adjusted every three to six months in line with changes in a key interest rate such as LIBOR. Floating-rate issues are especially popular with banks that wish to invest surplus funds, since the floating rate of interest means that the capital value of the bond is largely unaffected by interest rate movements. A convertible bond gives the owner the right to convert the bond into ordinary shares in the issuing company at a predetermined price sometime in the future. Convertible bonds usually pay a below-market rate of interest with holders attracted by the potential gain on the possibility of a share price conversion. Some Eurobonds have a warrant attached that gives the holder the right to buy shares in the company at a predetermined price in the future; the warrants can be detached from the bond and traded separately.

The Eurobond market is primarily a medium-term borrowing market with the vast majority of issues (approximately 80%) being for under 10 years with many typically for five to seven years, which contrasts with the domestic bond market which is generally speaking a longer-term market with most borrowing ranging from 10 to 30 years. Most Eurobonds are issued at fixed rates of interest and others are issued at floating rates of interest or equity related. Many issues are sold at short notice to take advantage of what are perceived to be favourable market conditions. **Table 12.3** summarizes the typical features of a dollar Eurobond issue.

The bearer form of most Eurobond issues is a particular attraction for international investors that like to avoid open registration of their ownership (although they are legally obliged to reveal coupon earnings to their tax authorities this may not always happen!). Another attraction of Eurobond issues for investors is that they are free of withholding taxes and this means that investors can save on paperwork when seeking to avoid double taxation on their interest income. The typical Eurobond investor has been characterized as a 'Belgian dentist', an investor that wishes to earn a little bit more interest than is available on government bonds but who also wants a very safe investment and is hence attracted by the high credit rating of most Eurobond issuers.

12.13 Control and regulation of the Eurobond market

Eurobonds are generally exempt from the rules and regulations that govern the issue of foreign bonds in a country; for example, the need to issue very detailed prospectuses and withholding taxes (taxes on non-residents which are deducted at source). However, Eurobond issues and trading do have to meet certain regulatory requirements and a self-regulatory body known as the International Securities Market Association sets rules and standards.

Table 12.3 Features of a typical dollar Eurobond issue

Amount:	$100 million – $2,000 million.
Issuers:	Governments, international organizations; for example the World Bank, the European Investment Bank, banks/financial institutions and major corporations with AAA and AA credit ratings accounting for approximately 75% of all corporate issues.
Maturity:	Normally 10 years or less. Most issues being in the 4–7 year range.
Principal:	Typically repayable in full upon maturity ('bullet form'). Occasionally some issues have the principal repayable in stages over the life of the bond and sometimes the principal repayable linked to movements in a market index such as the Nikkei or Standard & Poor 500.
Coupon:	Payable annually. Vast majority are 'straights'; that is, at a fixed coupon. pproximately a quarter of issues are at a variable coupon linked to a spread over LIBOR (or some other benchmark) known as floating rate notes.
Yield:	Spread over US Treasury bonds depends on credit rating. AAA governments around 10–20 basis points AAA corporates around 20–40 basis points AA governments around 30–50 basis points AA corporates around 40–80 basis points A governments around 50–100 basis points A Corporates around 80–110 basis points BBB around 120+ basis points The above margins are only indicative and they can quite easily change substantially depending on market conditions and the date to maturity.
Security:	Usually senior unsecured debt (that is, high priority in case of closure of the business). In some instances, the bond is backed by letter of credit or other collateral such as outstanding company assets.
Form:	Bearer form. Holder is deemed to be owner and the anonymity is one of the attractions to investors.
Tax status:	The bonds are issued free of withholding taxes.
Listing:	London or Luxembourg.
Denominations:	$1,000; $5,000; $10,000
Special features:	Many bonds have call-back features typically after 5 years; some have warrants attached and others can be converted into equity at a predetermined price.

Despite the fact that the Eurobond market is by definition outside the legal jurisdiction of the country of the currency of issue, this does not mean that the national authorities of the currency in question are unable to exert significant influence on the Eurobond market. National governments have always exerted control on national capital markets for a number of reasons; the most important is that they are usually huge borrowers themselves, they are also keen to encourage scarce domestic capital to be invested in domestic bond issues and they are also concerned about possible tax avoidance and impact of outflows of capital on the value of their currency. Governments still have a number of means of controlling the issue of Eurobonds in their national currencies. Firstly, most clearance of funds raised in Eurobond issues is done through the clearing system of the domestic banking system of the currency in question giving the central bank of that currency the ability to prohibit issues if it so wishes. Secondly, governments can exert pressure on both domestic investment banks and foreign investment banks not to participate in Eurobond issues with the implicit threat of losing government business and ultimately their licence to operate in their country. The Swiss authorities have effectively prevented Eurobond issues in Swiss francs, requiring all Swiss franc issues to be done in Switzerland, and the Japanese have managed to exert strong control over Eurobond issues in yen.

The US authorities have generally had a concerned but tolerant attitude to the Eurobond market. The main concern has been that because Eurobonds are issued in bearer form then the possibility of tax avoidance is high. Another concern is that the US government is itself a large borrower of funds and to some extent finds itself in competition with the attractive rates of interest offered on dollar Eurobonds. The US authorities also claim that they wish to protect US investors from investment risk due to the looser regulatory and disclosure requirements. For these reasons, the US authorities prohibit the sale of Eurobonds by investment banks to US citizens, with the Stock Exchange Commission requiring US investment banks to take measures 'reasonably designed to preclude distribution or redistribution of the securities, within, or to nationals of, the United States'. However, there is currently no law preventing US citizens purchasing Eurobonds on their own initiative, although they would clearly be expected to reveal any coupon earnings in their tax declaration. The private placements rule 144A permits sophisticated US financial institutions to hold Eurobonds in their investment portfolio so long as they are clearly held for investment purposes.

12.14 The management of a Eurobond issue

A typical Eurobond issue involves the formation of three groups: (i) the management group, (ii) the underwriting syndicate and (iii) the selling group. The issue is handled on behalf of a client by a lead or managing bank, and where the deal involves a particularly large sum of money other co-managers may be appointed. The lead manager and co-managers together form the management group. The borrower and the lead bank will have initial discussions concerning the currency of issue, the amount and terms at which the borrower would like to raise funds. The next stage involves appointing an underwriting syndicate of typically between 10 to 200 banks/securities houses to underwrite the issue so that the issuer is guaranteed the funds. The underwriting group which also includes the banks from the management group also has the task of assisting in the placing the issue with Eurobond investors. A final group, which comprises the management group and the underwriting syndicate plus other selected banks form the selling group whose task is to place the issue with Eurobond investors.

A typical Eurobond issue is partly placed with institutional investors and partly with private investors, with the latter usually accounting for around a half of the value of the issue. A few weeks or sometimes days prior to an issue being placed on the market a 'red herring' prospectus is issued which sets out the likely features of the bond and is used by the selling group to canvass interest in the issue. In some cases, the bond trades in a 'grey market' which is a short-term forward market which gives prospective investors an opportunity to see the likely trading range for the market price of the issue. The selling group on the basis of feedback from potential investors will return to the issuer to 'fine-tune' the issue adjusting the final terms so as meet some of the prospective investors' demands. Once the terms of the issue are finalized, the selling group will commit itself to buying the entire issue at a discount to the offer price and a final prospectus is printed and distributed to potential investors.

Competition between members of the selling group is fierce and it may well be the case that different investors are able to buy the bonds at different prices, often at a discount to the offer price stated in the prospectus. The lead manager is expected to ensure, using their own funds if necessary, an orderly primary and secondary market in the issue and failure to do so would adversely affect their reputation in the Eurobond market. Unlike domestic bond markets, the secondary market in Eurobonds is relatively 'thin' and most Eurobond investors tend to hold the issue right through to maturity. Nonetheless, for some of the very large issues with well-known issuers, the secondary market can be reasonably active and Eurobond market-makers quote bid-offer prices. The bid–offer spread in the Eurobond market can typically range from 50 to 75 basis points, which contrasts to the spread for US Treasury bonds which, because of the greater liquidity, is typically less than 10 basis points.

The lead bank and the underwriting syndicate charge the client for both managing, placing and underwriting the issue. On occasions, the underwriting syndicate will actually purchase part or all of the issue and then hopefully place it with clients at a higher price and thus make a profit. A typical fee structure involves 20% of fees going to the management group, 20% to the underwriting group and 60% to the selling group. The fees and precise proportions between the groups are variable depending upon how complex the issue is, the credit rating of the issuer and how easy the issue is to place with investors. The total fee as a percentage of the value of the issue is usually in the range of 0.5 to 2% depending upon the complexity and degree of difficulty of placing the issue. Competition for Eurobond business is extremely fierce, particularly as banks are keen to appear highly placed in the Eurobond league tables such as **Table 12.4**. In some Eurobond issues the management group may even confine all three tasks to itself so as to maximize its fee earnings.

Table 12.4   Top international bond lead managers, 2004

Manager	Rank	Amount $ billion	% Share	Issues
Deutsche Bank	1	126.90	8.57	683
Citigroup	2	117.48	7.94	374
CSFB	3	94.72	6.40	408
Merrill Lynch	4	93.87	6.34	247
Morgan Stanley	5	93.83	6.34	483
Barclays Capital	6	87.55	5.91	461
JP Morgan	7	84.55	5.71	310
UBS	8	77.01	5.20	507
Lehman Brothers	9	70.40	4.76	361
HSBC	10	63.68	4.30	346
Industry totals		1480.9	100	5,310

Source: Dealogic, 12 months to 9 August 2004.

12.15 Innovations in the Eurobond market

The first Eurobond issues were in the form of 'straights', that is borrowing at a fixed rate of interest, but the Eurobond market has since developed so that many Eurobond issues now have innovative features. These days a good proportion (around a quarter) of Eurobond issues are floating-rate notes, and another major innovation is that many recent Eurobond issues are denominated in the euro.

Other innovations include the issue of convertible Eurobonds whereby the investor has the right to convert the bond into shares in the company at a predetermined price. Some Eurobonds are issued with warrants attached which can be traded separately giving the holder the right to buy shares at a predetermined price. Many Eurobond issues also have a 'call-back' feature which enables the issuer to buy back the issue should it wish to do so (a particularly useful feature the borrower's cash flow turns out to be better than expected or if interest rates decline sufficiently). More recently, in some Eurobond issues the principal to be returned to the investor is linked to movements in a broad equity market index such as the Nikkei 225. Another recent innovation is asset-backed Eurobonds; with these, illiquid assets such as the outstanding loans of a bank are sold in the form of a Eurobond promising to pay a given coupon based on the income from the outstanding loans. Such bonds can still have a AAA rating because the bond will typically be over-collaterized, that is, backed up by loans with a face value considerably higher than that of the bond so even if allowance is made for default on some of the outstanding loans the Eurobond investor can expect to receive full payment.

In recent years, the Eurobond market has been opened up to governments from so-called emerging markets such as Argentina, Mexico, Venezuela, South Africa, China, Poland and South Korea. Some of the high-risk countries such as Brazil and Mexico may at times need to pay 500 basis points or more above the equivalent US Treasury bond rates, while other emerging countries such as China, Poland and South Africa can get away with borrowing at a spread of 150 basis points or less. In many ways the Eurobond market has the potential to provide a valuable source of funding for emerging-market governments, although such borrowers are of a higher risk than traditional Eurobond borrowers.

All of these innovative features, as well as the fact that interest is paid once a year and the lower liquidity of Eurobonds compared to Treasury bonds make it quite difficult to compare the yields on Eurobonds with standard Treasury and Corporate bonds. Nonetheless, a typical Eurobond offers a premium over the standard Treasury bond of between 30 to 150 basis points depending on the credit rating of the issuer. More importantly, from the viewpoint of the issuer the typical costs savings of a Eurobond issue compared to a domestic bond issue can range from 25 to 200 basis points.

12.16 Conclusions

The growth of parallel money markets such as the Eurocurrency markets has made the process of monetary control more difficult for central banks, in stark contrast to the days when they themselves were the main source of liquidity for banks short of funds. Up to the early 1960s any shortage of liquidity by banks would have led to heavy calls for funds in the money market, and the central bank could then charge a high rate of interest in its capacity of lender of last resort. These days, if banks are short of funds they have plenty of alternatives other than the central bank, such as the interbank market and the Euro-currency markets. This diminishing importance of the central bank is reflected in the fact that financial institutions increasingly use LIBOR as the key reference rate of interest, rather than Treasury Bill rates or central-bank lending rates.

Nonetheless, central banks still maintain a very high degree of influence over short-term interest rates through open market operations. Indeed, if a central bank decides to create a general shortage of funds through large Treasury bill sales this is bound to eventually filter through to the other markets. The rates of interest in the Eurocurrency and offshore markets are ultimately linked to the domestic markets of the relevant Eurocurrency. For example, if the US Federal Reserve sells Treasury bills, short-term interest rates rise in the USA, then Eurobanks will find that they need to raise their Eurodollar interest rates in order to prevent a seepage of funds back to the US market. Conversely, if the Federal reserve conducts an expansionary open market operation, it purchases Treasury bills so lowering the US interest rate, there will then be a seepage of funds into the Euromarkets and Eurobanks will find they are able to raise dollar funds at a lower cost so lowering the Eurodollar rates.

The growth of Eurobanking activity has been blamed for many things, ranging from the breakdown of the Bretton Woods system, to the rise in worldwide inflation and the third-world debt crisis (see Chapter 15). In reality, the Eurobanks provide services that are clearly in demand as is verified by their rapid growth. In particular, their competitive deposit and lending rates prove to be attractive for both investors and borrowers of funds.

Eurobanks have been largely responsible for the increased degree of financial integration between economies and they perform a particularly important role in recycling funds from surplus to deficit companies and countries. While this increased financial integration has made monetary control more difficult for domestic authorities, it must be concluded that the Euromarkets themselves have not had a significant inflationary impact upon the world economy. Although a switch from domestic to Eurodeposits may free some reserves for additional lending, the overall effect on liquidity is not particularly significant and is not necessarily undesirable.

In the end, it is clear that Eurobanks have not had a harmful effect on the way economies work, and their overall macroeconomic importance has frequently been exaggerated. Many of the transactions carried out by Eurobanks would be undertaken in their absence by domestic banks only less efficiently so. Eurobanks have expanded rapidly partly because the demand for their services has expanded with the increased degree of trade among nations. Much of this business has ultimately gone to Eurobanks rather than domestic banks because they have a competitive advantage in the provision of the requisite banking services.

The Eurobond market is constantly evolving and innovating to meet the changing preferences of both borrowers and investors of funds. Today Eurobonds come in a huge variety of different forms varying in the credit rating of the issuer, the maturity of the issue, the liquidity of the secondary market, the currency of denomination, whether of a fixed or variable rates and in specific features. This makes comparing different Eurobonds a complex issue. The bond market is constantly evolving and innovating to meet the changing preferences of both borrowers and investors of funds. These days, with the abolition of exchange rate controls the domestic capital market is in fierce competition with other markets such as the Eurobond market to attract scarce international capital. The Eurobond market has the advantage of lower regulatory requirements which reduces borrowing costs for issuers and allows for more innovative features to be introduced compared with a domestic bond issue.

Further reading

Duffey, G. and Giddy, I. (1978) *The International Money Market* (Englewood Cliffs, New Jersey: Prentice-Hall).

Einzig, P.A. (1973) *The Eurodollar System* (New York: St Martin's Press).

Friedman, M. (1969) 'The Eurodollar Market: Some First Principles', *Morgan Guaranty Survey*, October, pp. 4–14.

Hewson, J. (1975) *Liquidity Creation and Distribution in the Euro-Currency Markets* (Cambridge, Mass.: Lexington books).

Hewson, J. and Sakakibara, E. (1974) 'The Eurodollar Multiplier: A Portfolio Approach', *IMF Staff Papers*, vol. 21, pp. 307–28.

Hewson, J. and Sakakibara, E. (1976) 'A General Equilibrium Approach to the Euro-Dollar Market', *Journal of Money Credit and Banking*, vol. 8, pp. 297–323.

Hogan, W.P. and Pearce, I.F. (1982) *The Incredible Eurodollar* (London: George Allen & Unwin).

Klopstock, F. (1968) 'The Euro–dollar Market: Some Unresolved Issues', *Princeton Essays in International Finance*, Princeton, no. 65.

Klopstock, F. (1970) 'Money Creation in the Euro–dollar Market: Some Unresolved Issues', *Federal Reserve Bank of New York Monthly Review*, January, pp. 12–5.

Mayer, H.W. (1970) Some Theoretical Problems Relating to the Eurodollar Market', Princeton Essays in International Finance, Princeton, no. 125.

McKinnon, R.I. (1977) 'The Eurocurrency Market', *Princeton Essays in International Finance*, Princeton, no. 125.

McKinnon, R.I. (1979) *Money in International Exchange* (Oxford: Oxford University Press).

Niehans, J. and Hewson, J. (1976) 'The Eurodollar Market and Monetary Theory', *Journal of Money Credit and Banking*, vol. 8, pp. 1–27.

Swoboda, A.K. (1968) 'The Eurodollar Market: An Interpretation', *Princeton Essays in International Finance*, Princeton, no. 64.

13

Currency Derivatives: Futures, Options and Swaps

13.1 Introduction

Since the early 1970s there has been an enormous growth in the use of what is known as derivative instruments. In this chapter we look at three types of derivative contracts: futures, options and swaps. The aim of the chapter is to introduce the reader to the basic features. In particular, we emphasize how the contracts can be used for both speculative and hedging purposes and the advantages and disadvantages of the various contracts. We also look at basic formulae governing the appropriate pricing of futures and options contracts.

Standardized financial futures and options contracts are traded on organized exchanges. They were first traded on the Chicago Board Options Exchange (CBOE) in the early 1970s, and in 1982 London opened the London International Financial Futures Exchange (LIFFE) which in 2001 was merged with the Amsterdam, Paris and Belgium Exchanges to create Euronext.LIFFE. Since then Euronext has also merged with the Lisbon Stock Exchange. A significant amount of trading in foreign currency options is done outside of the major exchanges in what is known as the 'Over-the-Counter' market (OTC) in which banks and other financial institutions design contracts tailor-made to meet the specific needs of their corporate clients. The swaps market is an over-the-counter (OTC) market with swaps between two parties being arranged on tailor-made basis.

13.2 The growth of derivative markets

The phenomenal growth of trading in these derivative instruments has been one of the most important developments in international financial markets over the last three decades. The 1980s witnessed an astonishing growth of futures and options markets and this trend has continued into the 1990s as shown in **Table 13.1**.

There are numerous reasons for the rapid growth of futures and options markets, which include:

Table 13.1 The growth of exchange-traded futures and options contracts

Turnover of futures contracts traded on international exchanges
(Numbers of contracts in millions)

Instruments	1990	1995	2000	2003
Interest rate	219.1	561.0	781.2	1576.8
Currency	29.7	99.6	43.6	58.7
Equity index	39.4	114.8	225.2	725.7
All markets	288.2	775.4	1050	2361.2

Turnover of options traded on international exchanges
(Numbers of contracts in millions)

Instruments	1990	1995	2000	2003
Interest rate	52.0	225.5	107.6	302.2
Currency	18.9	23.3	7.1	14.3
Equity index	119.1	187.3	481.4	3233.9
All markets	190.0	436.1	596.1	3550.4

Source: Bank for International Settlements.

1   The volatility of foreign exchange markets following the collapse of the Bretton Woods system of fixed exchange rates (see Chapter 11), combined with the fact that greater freedom of movement of capital internationally has created a large demand on the part of companies, investors, fund managers and the like for a means to cope with the greater volatility and risk.

2   Futures and options markets enable traders to take speculative positions on price movements for a low initial cash payment, known as the initial margin.

3   Futures and options contracts enable traders to take short positions, that is sell (or have the right to sell) something they do not own with considerable ease. This means that taking a position on a currency depreciation is made as easy as taking a position on currency appreciation.

4   Unlike forward contracts where there is a degree of counterparty risk, all futures and options contracts are guaranteed by the exchange on which they are traded.

13.3 Exchange-traded futures and options contracts

Exchange-traded currency futures and options contracts were traditionally sold in a central exchange by an open outcry system. Under this system, traders congregate around a 'pit' on the trading floor of the exchange and contracts are bought and sold at prices within hearing distance of all other traders. Once a contract price is agreed, the traders fill out trading slips which are then matched by the exchange clearing house. Once the clearing house confirms the deal, a futures or options contract is in existence and the contract is guaranteed by the exchange. This means that if one of the parties fails to fulfil its obligations, then the exchange will assume the defaulting parties obligations. Effectively the exchange removes counterparty risk; the only credit risk involved is that of the exchange. These days, however, most exchanges are switching to computer-based trading systems.

One of the major advantages of exchange-traded futures and options contracts is that the exchange guarantees every contract, thus relieving the gaining party of a futures or options contract the risk of default by the losing party and relieving the need to evaluate the creditworthiness of the counterparty. To limit its exposure, exchange regulations require that each counterparty to a futures contract and the seller (writer) of an option contract makes an initial deposit with the exchange known as the 'initial margin' (this is usually between 2 to 10% of the value of the contract). Once the contract involves a party making a loss greater than the initial margin, further deposits are required on a daily basis from the losing party known as 'variation margin' to reflect the potential loss associated with the contract. The 'marking to market', that is calculation of variation margins, is carried out at the end of each day on the basis of the settlements price (usually the closing price). The other party has its profit position credited to its margin account. Since all potential losses have to be paid for on a daily basis this limits the exposure of the exchange. In the rare event that a trader were to fail to settle a margin payment, the exchange has the right to close the traders position by taking an offsetting contract limiting its potential exposure to that trader's position. A further means by which the exchange limits its exposure is that dealing is restricted to members of the exchange who are usually representatives of well-established financial institutions. The exchange also protects itself by careful selection of authorized traders and by imposing high membership requirements and standards. The exchange also constantly monitors members' positions. In addition, an exchange will maintain a large clearing fund to meet unforeseen circumstances.

13.4 Currency futures and currency forwards

A currency futures contract is an agreement between two counterparties to exchange a specified amount of two currencies at a given date in the future at a predetermined exchange rate. As such, they are basically standardized forward contracts that we examined in Chapter 1. For example, a currency futures contract may specify €125,000 per contract is being bought or sold. With a forward contract, the amount to be exchanged is negotiable between the two parties; for example, the two parties can agree to buy/sell say €122,000 forward.

Table 13.2 shows the dollar–euro (€125,000) contract offered by the Chicago Mercantile Exchange (CME). The CME also offers a number of currency contracts including dollar–Australian dollar (A$100,000), dollar–Canadian dollar (C$100,000), dollar–Mexican peso(500,000 peso), dollar–sterling (£62,500) and dollar–yen (¥12.5 million). The contract specifies the amount of currency to be exchanged, the Exchange on which the contract is traded, the delivery date and the process for delivery.

One party agrees to sell the currency (go short) and the other party agrees to purchase the currency (go long). Despite their high degree of similarity there are some practical differences between currency forward and futures contracts, and Table 13.3 summarizes these between currency forwards and currency futures contracts.

The main differences are:

1   A currency futures contract is a standardized notional agreement between two counterparties to exchange a specified amount of a currency at a fixed future date for a predetermined amount. A forward contract is the amount of currency to be exchanged determined by the mutual agreement of the two parties.
2   Futures contracts are traded on an exchange while forward contracts are over-the-counter instruments with the exchange being made directly between two parties.
3   Futures contracts are guaranteed by the exchange whereas forward contracts are not. The fact that futures contracts are guaranteed by the exchange on which they are traded removes the counterparty risk inherent in forward contracts. With a forward contract each counterparty needs to carefully consider what will happen if

Table 13.2 Dollar per euro futures contracts (CME), €125,000

	Open	Sett. price	Change	High	Low	Est. vol	Open int.
March	1.3472	1.3376	−0.0114	1.3504	1.3355	83,041	146,886
June	1.3433	1.3399	−0.0113	1.3524	1.3390	91	1,461

Source: *Financial Times*, 5 January 2005.

Table 13.3   Similarities and differences between currency forwards and futures

Forwards	Futures
An agreement to exchange currencies sometime in the future	An agreement to exchange currencies sometime in the future
Larger range of delivery dates	Limited range of delivery dates
Amount to be exchanged is negotiable	Contracts are for standardized amounts
Each party faces some counterparty risk	Contracts are guaranteed by the futures exchange
No margin is required	Initial margin required; variation margin may be called for
Obligation cannot be easily sold onto a third party	Obligation can be easily sold on to a third party
Buying and selling via screen-based market	Buying and selling a mix of pit open outcry and screen based trading
Usual contract size of at least $5 million	Smaller contract sizes usually around $50,000–$100,000
Covers over 50 currencies	Covers only major currencies
Profit/loss only realizable on maturity of contract	Profit/loss can be realized prior to maturity
Contract is completed by the annual delivery of the underlying security	In around 99% of cases there is no actual delivery since traders enter into reversal trades

the other party is incapable of seeing through their commitment which may involve quite substantial losses. This credit risk tends to limit the forward market to only very high-grade financial and commercial institutions.

4   Futures contracts are generally regarded as having greater liquidity than forward contracts. Their standardized nature means that futures contracts can easily be sold to another party at any time up until maturity at the prevailing futures price with the trader being credited with a profit or loss. Since forward contract obligations cannot be transferred to a third party they are relatively illiquid assets. The only way for a trader to get out of a forward contract is to take out a new offsetting forward position. For example, if a trader is committed to buying £1 million of sterling forward at $1.90/£1, then the only way out of the forward contract is to take out another forward contract to sell £1 million sterling with another party. There are two problems with this: (i) the trader is now exposed to two counterparties (doubling the counterparty risk), and (ii) the maturity date of the second forward contract may not be perfectly matched with that of the first forward contract. For example if the original forward contract is for 90 days and if 20 days later he tries to take an offsetting position, the nearest available forward contract is 60 days leaving 10 days of open exposure.

Open interest and reversing trades

Two important but linked terms that crop up in connection with futures trades are the open interest in a contract and the concept of reversing trades. Open interest is the outstanding number of contracts obligated for delivery. Consider four traders A, B, C and D, none of whom has any current position in a futures contract. If trader A takes a long position in a new contract with trader B taking a short position, then the open interest rises by one contract. Similarly, if trader C takes a long position in a futures contract with trader D taking the short position, then open interest rises by a further one contract.

The commodity or financial asset to be delivered in fulfilment of the contract is known as the **underlying**. For most futures contracts, especially those that involve physical commodities such as gold, cotton and so on, the physical delivery of the commodity would be a cumbersome process. To avoid getting involved in the actual delivery process most traders will therefore enter into what is known as a **reversing trade** prior to the maturity of the contract. That is, they will liquidate their position at the clearing house so that they neither have to actually deliver or actually receive the underlying. In our example, traders A and C are committed to buying the underlying upon expiry while traders B and D are committed to delivering the underlying currency upon expiry. Trader A may not actually wish to receive the underlying currency and trader D may not wish to actually deliver the underlying currency. Hence, at some date prior to expiry trader A and trader D may take out reversing trades to liquidate their positions. Trader A will take out a contract to sell the underlying (at the then prevailing market price). As far as the clearing house is concerned trader A will have no net position in the futures market since it has an identical futures contract to both receive and deliver the underlying currency. If trader A sold his contract to a new party E then the open interest would have been left unaffected by A's trade. If, however, trader A had sold his position to trader D who was also undertaking a reversing trade, then open interest would have declined by one since both A and D have effectively negated their positions with the clearing house.

Figure 13.1 shows the typical profile of open interest on futures contracts from the day trading in the contract is started (contract originates) to the time that the contract expires.

Each contract starts with zero open interest and during the early days of the opening of a futures contract open interest in the contract slowly builds up as the number of new contracts increases. However, eventually open interest in the contract peaks. Thereafter, as the expiry date of the contract nears, the number of traders involved in reversing trades increases so that open interest rapidly declines until the expiry date when open interest falls to zero.

13.5 The use of currency futures for hedging purposes

Currency futures can be used both for managing risks and assuming speculative positions. Let us consider a simple example of how a currency futures contract can be used for hedging purposes.

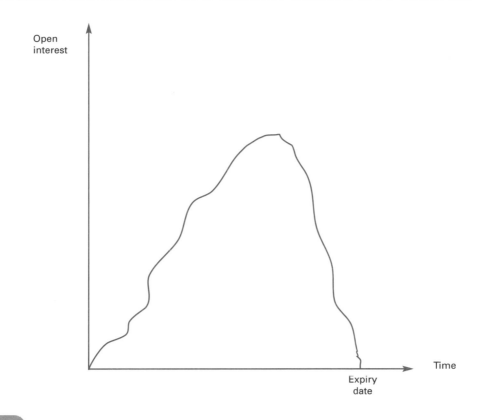

Figure 13.1 Typical open interest profile

Numerical Example

A currency futures contract used for hedging
Suppose a UK exporter has made export sales to the United States and in six months' time is due to receive $1.9 million. The firm wishes to protect itself and ensure that the sale is profitable when translated back into UK pounds. The firm is able to obtain a six-month futures quotation of $1.90/£1, and because US and UK interest rates at the six-month time horizon are assumed to be equal the spot rate is also $1.90/£1. The exporter is concerned that the pound will appreciate over the next six months to say $2/£1 and wishes to protect himself against the possible adverse currency movement (which would mean his $1.9 million would only be worth £950,000). The trader could take out 16 contracts to buy £62,500 at $1.90/£1 and therefore be guaranteed £1,000,000 with the $1,900,000.

Suppose that in six months' time when in receipt of the $1.9 million the trader has been proved right and the dollar sterling parity is $2/£1, and because on expiry the futures price is equal to the then prevailing spot price the futures contract is also valued at $2/£1. In these circumstances, the trader will now be in a position to close his futures contract by selling 16 sterling contracts at $2/£1. The trader has therefore closed out his futures contract position at a profit of 10 cents (buying pounds at $1.90 and selling them at $2.00), his profit from the futures contract is ($0.10 × 62,500 × 16 = $100,000). The hedger therefore has a total of $1,900,000 which can be converted at $2/£1 in which to give £950,000 and $100,000 profit from the futures contract which can be converted spot at $2//£1 to yield £50,000 and so he obtains a guaranteed £1 million.

Suppose that in six months' time when in receipt of the $1,900,000 the trader has been proved wrong and the dollar–sterling parity is $1.80/£1, and since futures prices equal spot prices on expiration the futures contract is also valued at $1.80/£1. In these circumstances the trader will now be in a position to close his futures contract by selling 16 sterling contracts at $1.80/£1. The trader has therefore closed out his futures contract position at a loss of 10 cents (buying pounds at $1.90/£1 and selling them at $1.80/£1) so his loss from the futures contract is ($0.10 × 62,500 × 16 = –$100,000). The hedger therefore has a total of $1,800,000 left to be converted at $1.80/£1 in the spot market and so he obtains a guaranteed £1 million. Either way, whatever the dollar–sterling parity turns out to be, the futures market has been successfully used for hedging purposes. Indeed, in this example the hedger has achieved a perfect hedge.

In the numerical example above that we have used, the spot and forward rates move exactly in tandem, and to the extent that they do not there is still some residual risk for an investor. For example, when the spot rate moves from $1.90/£1 to $2.00/£1, if the futures rate only moved from $1.90/£1 to $1.98/£1 then the profit on closing out the futures contract would only have been eight cents so yielding $0.08 × 62,500 × 16 = $80,000 in profit from the futures contract. This would give him $1,980,000 which could be converted at $2/£1 yielding £990,000 which is £10,000 short of a perfect hedge. The risk of an adverse change in the spread between the spot and futures rate is known as basis risk. Basis risk is usually considered to be a relatively minor risk compared to having an open (unhedged) position.

Another way in which futures contracts may not provide a perfect hedge is due to the fact that they come in standardized amounts. In the example, we have considered the $1.9 million conveniently purchases exactly 16 sterling contracts at $1.90/£1 (since £1,000,000/£62,500 = 16). If the firm was expecting to receive $1,950,000, then at $1.90/£1 it could purchase 16 contracts corresponding to $1,900,000 (16 × 62,500 × 1.9) = £1,000,000 but there would be a residual of $50,000 that would be unhedged.

13.6 The symmetry of profit/losses on futures/forward positions

An important point about currency futures and forward contracts is that the gains or losses of the two parties engaged in the contract are symmetrical around the difference between the spot price on expiry of the contact and the futures price at which the contract was taken out. This is illustrated in **Figure 13.2**.

In the figure it is assumed that a one-year futures contract is taken out on sterling at a price of $1.90/£1; that is, one party has agreed to buy sterling at $1.90/£1 while the other has agreed to sell sterling at $1.90/£1. On the horizontal axes we have the future spot price of sterling in one year's time. If the spot price of sterling in one year's time is above $1.90/£1 the buyer of the sterling future will have a profit of one cent for every one cent that the future spot price is above $1.90/£1. For example, if the spot price of sterling on maturity is $2.10/£1 then he makes 20 cents per £1 purchased since he buys the sterling at $1.90/£1 in fulfilment of the futures contract and can sell each £1 spot for $2.10/£1. If, however, the future spot price is only

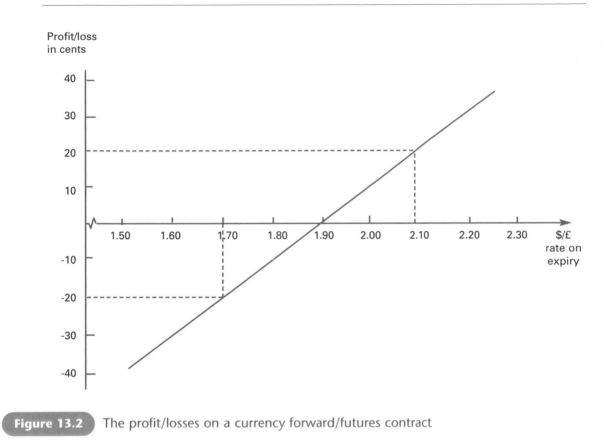

Profit/loss
in cents

Figure 13.2 The profit/losses on a currency forward/futures contract

$1.70/£1 in one year's time he must pay $1.90/£1 to obtain sterling and can only sell the sterling at $1.70/£1 so incurring a loss of 20 cents. The gain (or loss) of the buyer of the sterling futures contract is mirrored by the corresponding loss (or gain) to the seller of the sterling future. One party to a futures/forward contract is always likely to lose in the sense that the future spot price will generally be different than the price agreed in the futures/forward contact.

13.7 The pricing of currency futures

Since currency futures are very similar to currency forward contracts, it is not surprising that the covered interest parity (CIP) formula is crucial to the determination of currency futures prices. The main difference is that for currency futures they have to be marked to market every day and this needs to be taken into account when applying the covered interest parity formula. The appropriate futures price for a dollar per pound parity is given by equation (13.1) or equivalently equation (13.2):

$$F = S \times \frac{1 + (r_{us} \times T)}{1 + (r_{uk} \times T)} \tag{13.1}$$

or

$$F = S e^{(r_{us}-r_{uk})T} \qquad\qquad (13.2)$$

where F is the futures price in dollars per pound, S is the spot exchange rate in dollars per pound, e is the natural number 2.71828, r_{us} is the US interest rate, r_{uk} is the UK interest rate, and T is the time left to maturity of the contract expressed as a fraction of a year.

Numerical Example

The US interest rates is 5% and the UK interest rate is 8%. The spot dollar sterling rate is $1.90/£1. The price of a six-month (180 days) sterling futures contract which is 100 days into the contract has 80 days to maturity which means that $T = (180 - 100)/360 = 0.2222$, and the relevant futures price is therefore:

$$F = \$1.90 \times \frac{[1 + (0.05 \times 0.2222)]}{1 + (0.08 \times 0.2222)}$$

$$= \$1.90 \times \frac{1.01111}{1.01778}$$

$$= \$1.8876/£1$$

or

$$F = S e^{(r_{us}-r_{uk})T}$$
$$= \$1.90 \times 2.71828^{(0.05-0.08)0.2222}$$
$$= \$1.8876/£1$$

Notice, that the pound is at a discount on the futures market, because the holder of sterling benefits from a higher interest rate. To compensate for the lower interest on holding dollars, · the dollar is a forward premium enabling dollar holdings to be converted back into sterling at a favourable rate in the future. If an investor had £1,000 he could hold it in the UK and earn 8% for 80 days so that becomes £1,017.75. Alternatively, he could sell pounds spot at $1.90/£1 obtaining $1,900 knowing that earning 5% over 80 days this will become $1,921.11, and simultaneously take out a futures (forward) contract to sell $1,921.11 at $1.8876/£1 which works out at £1017.75. In other words, the price of the futures contract ensures that there are no arbitrage profits to be made.

13.8 Currency options

Currency options were first traded on the Philadelphia Exchange in the early 1980s, but since then they have become increasingly popular instruments on other exchanges such as London, Paris and Singapore. In this and the following sections we explain what a currency option contract is and we consider how a currency options contract can be used for both speculative and hedging purposes. We also discuss the economic role that option contracts can fulfil and emphasize the differences between futures and options contracts.

A currency option is a contract that gives the purchaser the right but not the obligation to buy or sell a currency at a predetermined price sometime in the future. The currency in which the option is granted is known as the **underlying currency**. The currency to be exchanged for the underlying currency is known as the **counter currency**, if the contract specifies the right to buy £62,500 at $1.90/£1 then the pound is the underlying currency and the dollar is the counter currency. An option contract involves two parties, the **writer** who sells the option and the **holder** who purchases the option. The holder of an option contract has the right but not the obligation to either buy or sell the underlying currency at a predetermined exchange rate in the future. If the option contract gives the holder the right to purchase the underlying currency at a predetermined price from the other party the contact is known as a **call option**. If the option's contract gives the owner the right to sell the underlying currency at a predetermined exchange rate from the other party the contact is known as a **put option**. An option contract that can be exercised any time up until its maturity date is known as an **American option** while an option that can only be exercised on the expiration date is known as a **European option**. The price at which the underlying currency can be bought or sold is known as the **strike price** (or **exercise price**). The date at which the contract expires is known as the **expiry date** or **maturity date**.

The price paid by the holder to the writer for an option is known as the **option premium**. **Table 13.4** shows various call and put option premiums quoted on the Chicago Mercantile Exchange for the dollar–euro exchange rate as at 5 January 2005. The options traded on this market are American options and can be exercised at any time to maturity.

The table shows the premium measured in US cents for traded currency options of the dollar against the euro; the spot exchange rate of the dollar against the euro at the close of business on 4 January 2005 was $1.3293/€1. A trader can buy a call option (that is, right to buy euros) at a strike of $1.3200/€1 expiring in March 2005 for 4.00

Table 13.4 Chicago Mercantile Exchange dollar per euro option contract size €125,000 ($12.50 per tick)

Strike price ($/€)	Calls			Puts		
	Jan.	Feb.	Mar.	Jan.	Feb.	Mar.
1.3200	2.96	3.50	4.00	0.15	0.89	1.44
1.3300	1.06	2.79	3.35	0.36	1.19	1.83
1.3400	0.60	1.51	2.13	0.78	1.76	2.32
1.3500	0.25	1.14	1.69	1.47	2.33	2.92

Previous day's volume: calls 6,094; puts 16,026; open interest 64,441

Note: Spot exchange rate was $1.3293/€1.
Source: *Financial Times*, 5 January 2005.

US cents per euro. For February 2005 the same strike price can be bought for 3.50 US cents per euro. Similarly, a put option (right to sell euros) for $1.3200/€1 expiring in March 2005 can be bought for 1.44 US cents per euro.

Numerical Example

Profit/loss profiles for a currency call option
The profit and loss profiles for a contract on a March 2005 call will depend upon the actual exchange rate prevailing in March 2005. Let us first consider the profit profile for such a call at a strike price of $1.3200/€1. If the future spot exchange rate is less than $1.3200/€1, then it does not pay the holder of the option to exercise his option as it is cheaper to buy euros in the spot market and he will lose the premium paid of 4.00 cents per euro (that is, $5,000 in total). If the future spot exchange rate is between $1.3200/€1 and $1.3600/€1 it will pay the holder of the option to exercise the option although a loss will be made of the future spot price less the strike price and option premium. If the future spot price is above $1.3600/€1, the call option will make a profit. The writer of the option makes a profit or loss that is the mirror image of the profit and loss profile of the holder. The profit and loss profile for various exchange rates in March 2005 is illustrated in **Table 13.5**. The profit/loss per contract is found by multiplying the profit or loss per euro by the contract size of €125,000.

Table 13.5 The profit/loss on a March call for different spot exchange rates on expiry of the contract

Details of contract
Call option price 4.00 cents
Strike price $1.32/€1
Expiration   March
Value of contract €125,000
Total premium per contract $5,000

Possible values of spot exchange rate on expiry	Profit/loss on long call i.e. holder per € in cents	Profit/loss on short call i.e. writer per € in cents	Profit/loss on long call i.e. holder per contract	profit/loss on short call i.e. writer per contract
1.15	−4.00	+4.00	−$5,000	+$5,000
1.20	−4.00	+4.00	−$5,000	+$5,000
1.25	−4.00	+4.00	−$5,000	+$5,000
1.30	−4.00	+4.00	−$5,000	+$5,000
1.31	−4.00	+4.00	−$5,000	+$5,000
1.32	−4.00	+4.00	−$5,000	+$5,000
1.33	−3.00	+3.00	−$3,750	+$3,750
1.34	−2.00	+2.00	−$2,500	+$2,500
1.35	−1.00	+1.00	−$1,250	+$1,250
1.36	0	0	$0	+$0
1.37	1.00	−1.00	+$1,250	−$1,250
1.38	2.00	−2.00	+$2,500	−$2,500
1.39	3.00	−3.00	+$3,750	−$3,750
1.40	4.00	−4.00	+$5,000	−$5,000
1.45	9.00	−9.00	+$11,250	−$11,250
1.50	14.00	−14.00	+$17,500	−$17,500
1.55	19.00	−19.00	+$23,750	−$23,750

We now proceed to examine with the aid of a couple of examples how the use of options contracts contrasts with using futures contracts for hedging and speculative purposes.

13.9 ▸ A currency option versus a forward contract for hedging

In January a US company orders £1 million of goods from a British company which will be delivered in six months' time. Upon delivery the goods must be paid for in cash. The pound has been weak against the dollar and has depreciated from $2.00/£1 to $1.80/£1 over the last year. The company feels that the pound is likely to bounce back (that is, appreciate) and so wishes to protect itself from any rise in the pound. The firm, however, would like to take advantage of any further appreciation of the US dollar should it occur. The spot rate of the pound is $1.80/£1 while the forward/futures rate is $1.75/£1. Alternatively, the company can buy a six-month call option to buy sterling at $1.75/£1 for 8 cents per pound.

Table 13.6 compares the costs of obtaining the £1 million using an options contract versus a forward contract. A forward contract will mean he has to give $1,750,000 regardless of the exchange rate in six months' time. The call option will be exercised so long as the dollar/pound is above $1.75/£1 in six months' time. The table also looks at what would happen if the position is left unhedged and he simply purchases the £1 million spot in six months at whatever the exchange rate then happens to be.

With the options contract, the position can be hedged for a premium of $80,000 which will give the holder the right to buy £1 million at a rate of $1.75/£1. If the dollar–pound parity is above $1.75/£1, then the option will be exercised and the US company will have to pay only $1,750,000 to obtain £1,000,000 which, given that the option has cost $80,000, gives a total cost of $1,830,000. If the dollar–pound rate is below $1.75/$1, then the option contract will not be exercised and the US firm will instead take advantage of the strong dollar to buy pounds spot at the prevailing rate; for example, if the rate is $1.50/£1 then the firm will obtain £1,000,000 for $1,500,000 which given that the option has expired worthless implies a total cost of $1,580,000. An alternative means of hedging would be for the firm to take out a six-month forward contract to buy £1 million pounds at $1.75/£1, which means the firm is guaranteed to obtain the required sterling for $1,750,000 no matter what the spot rate is six months hence. Finally, with an unhedged position the firm will have to pay whatever the spot exchange rate is six months hence.

Overall, **Table 13.6** shows very clearly the advantages and disadvantages of hedging using an option or futures contract. The option contract enables the firm to fix a maximum payable price but also take advantage of a favourable movement in the exchange rate. The forward rate provides the firm with full certainty over the future cost of obtaining £1 million but, unlike the option contract, does not permit the firm to take advantage of a favourable movement in the exchange rate. Both futures and options contracts help reduce the risk to the firm as compared to taking an unhedged position.

Table 13.6 Comparison of hedging using futures and options

Spot exchange rate on expiry of the futures or options contract	Cost with option contract	Cost with forward contract	Cost if buys spot contract
2.00	$1,830,000	$1,750,000	$2,000,000
1.95	$1,830,000	$1,750,000	$1,950,000
1.90	$1,830,000	$1,750,000	$1,900,000
1.85	$1,830,000	$1,750,000	$1,850,000
1.84	$1,830,000	$1,750,000	$1,840,000
1.83	$1,830,000	$1,750,000	$1,830,000
1.82	$1,830,000	$1,750,000	$1,820,000
1.81	$1,830,000	$1,750,000	$1,810,000
1.80	$1,830,000	$1,750,000	$1,800,000
1.79	$1,830,000	$1,750,000	$1,790,000
1.78	$1,830,000	$1,750,000	$1,780,000
1.77	$1,830,000	$1,750,000	$1,770,000
1.76	$1,830,000	$1,750,000	$1,760,000
1.75	$1.830,000	$1,750,000	$1,750,000
1.74	$1,820,000	$1,750,000	$1,740,000
1.73	$1,810,000	$1,750,000	$1,730,000
1.72	$1,800,000	$1,750,000	$1,720,000
1.71	$1,790,000	$1,750,000	$1,710,000
1.70	$1,780,000	$1,750,000	$1,700,000
1.69	$1,770,000	$1,750,000	$1,690,000
1.68	$1,760,000	$1,750,000	$1,680,000
1.67	$1,750,000	$1,750,000	$1,670,000
1.66	$1,740,000	$1,750,000	$1,660,000
1.65	$1,730,000	$1,750,000	$1,650,000
1.60	$1,680,000	$1,750,000	$1,600,000
1.55	$1,630,000	$1,750,000	$1,550,000
1.50	$1,580,000	$1,750,000	$1,500,000
1.40	$1,480,000	$1,750,000	$1,400,000

13.10 A currency option versus a forward for speculating

The spot rate of exchange is $1.80/£1, while a year ago the rate was $2.00/£1. A specu-lator feels that sterling is likely to appreciate to say $2.00/£1. He has two speculative choices (i) take out a forward contract to buy sterling at $1.75/£1, or (ii) buy a call option on sterling giving him the right to buy at $1.75/£1, the premium of the call being 8 cents. The profit and loss profile of an $80,000 open position in options versus the forward contract is shown in **Table 13.7**.

In the table a speculator is assumed to have $80,000 available for speculative purposes and he feels that the pound is likely to appreciate from $1.80/£1 to $2.00/£1. He could choose between taking out a forward contract at $1.75/£1 to buy $80,000 of sterling, that is £45,714.28, or buy an option to purchase 1 million pounds at $1.75/£1 for 8 cents per £1. Let us first consider the options contract. An $80,000 investment gives the right to purchase £1,000,000 worth of sterling at the rate

Table 13.7 A currency option versus a currency forward for speculation

| Spot exchange rate 1 year hence | Per £1 option | Per £1 forward | $80,000 open position | |
			Option	Forward
2.20	+0.37	+0.45	+$370,000	+$20,571.43
2.10	+0.27	+0.35	+$270,000	+$16,000.00
2.00	+0.17	+0.25	+$170,000	+$11,428.57
1.90	+0.07	+0.15	+$70,000	+$6,857.14
1.85	+0.02	+0.10	+$20,000	+$4,571.43
1.84	+0.01	+0.09	+$10,000	+$4,114.29
1.83	0	+0.08	$0	+$3,657.14
1.82	−0.01	+0.07	−$10,000	+$3,200.00
1.81	−0.02	+0.06	−$20,000	+$2,742.86
1.80	−0.03	+0.05	−$30,000	+$2,285.71
1.79	−0.04	+0.04	−$40,000	+$1,828.57
1.78	−0.05	+0.03	−$50,000	+$1,371.43
1.77	−0.06	+0.02	−$60,000	+$914.29
1.76	−0.07	+0.01	−$70,000	+$457.14
1.75	−0.08	0	−$80,000	$0
1.74	−0.08	−0.01	−$80,000	−$457.14
1.73	−0.08	−0.02	−$80,000	−$914.29
1.72	−0.08	−0.03	−$80,000	−$1,371.43
1.71	−0.08	−0.04	−$80,000	−$1,828.57
1.70	−0.08	−0.05	−$80,000	−$2,285.71
1.69	−0.08	−0.06	−$80,000	−$2,742.86
1.68	−0.08	−0.07	−$80,000	−$3,200.00
1.67	−0.08	−0.08	−$80,000	−$3,657.14
1.66	−0.08	−0.09	−$80,000	−$4,114.29
1.65	−0.08	−0.10	−$80,000	−$4,571.43
1.60	−0.08	−0.15	−$80,000	−$6,857.14
1.50	−0.08	−0.25	−$80,000	−$11,428.57
1.40	−0.08	−0.35	−$80,000	−$16,000.00
1.30	−0.08	−0.45	−$80,000	−$20,571.43

$1.75/£1; that is, $1,750,0000, at a premium of 8 cents per pound. If the spot rate in six months' time is above $1.75/£1 then the option will be exercised. Say the specula-tor is correct and the spot exchange rate on expiry of the contract is $2.00/£1, then the speculator will buy £1,000,000 at $1.75 for a total cost of $1,750,000 and immedi-ately convert the £1,000,000 back at $2.00/£1 to receive $2,000,000, so leaving a profit of $2,000,000 − $1,750,000 − $80,000 (the option premium paid) = $170,000. So long as the future spot rate is above $1.83/£1 so that the 8 cents cost of the option premium is covered, then the option can be profitably exercised. Between $1.75 and $1.83 the option will still be exercised but an overall loss made. If the rate is below $1.75 then the option will not be exercised and the speculator will lose the entire $80,000 premium!

As an alternative to the options contract, the speculator could take an $80,000 position in the forward market, that is contract to buy $80,000/1.75 = £45,714.28 forward. If the speculator is proved right, and the future spot rate turns out to be $2.00/£1, then on delivery of the forward contract he will give $80,000 and receive £45,714.28; he can then immediately sell the £45,714.28 at $2.00/£1 and receive back $91,428.56 implying a profit of $91,428.56 – $80,000 = $11,428.56. For each one cent the spot rate in one year's time is above $1.75 he makes a profit of $457.14, and for each cent the rate is below $1.75 he makes a loss of $457.14. For instance, if the future spot rate is $1.60/£1 then on delivery of the forward contract he will give $80,000 and receive £45,714.28 which he can then immediately sell at $1.60/£1 and receive back $73,142.84, implying a loss of $73,142.84 – $80,000 = –$6,857.16.

We can see from this example that an option contract offers a very different risk–return profile for speculative purposes than that offered by the forward/futures contract. The option contract offers an asymmetric profit and loss profile; on the one hand, it offers potentially huge gains but the speculator runs the risk of losing all his $80,000. The forward market offers a symmetric and far less dramatic speculative profit/loss profile.

Options contracts can also provide extremely attractive and at times spectacular speculative returns compared to taking speculative positions in the cash or forward market. However, against this, it must be borne in mind that many options contracts lapse without being exercised and the speculator thereby risks losing all of the option premium paid. Also, as we shall see in section 13.15, the more likely an option is to be exercised the higher will be its premium and the lower the consequent profit profile. One of the features that makes options so attractive is their asymmetrical profit/loss profile which means that holders can combine limited downside losses (the premium paid) with unlimited upside potential profit, this contrasts with the symmetric profit/loss profile offered by futures/forward contracts. Writing options is a far riskier business since the potential profit is limited to the option premium while the potential losses can be very high relative to the premium received.

The role of option contracts

Option contracts provide a cheap and flexible way for economic agents to control some significant risks and to take on highly leveraged speculative financial positions. In other words, options enable risks to be transferred from one party that wishes to reduce its risk exposure, to another party that is willing to take on that risk for a premium. Like other financial instruments options attract hedgers, speculators and arbitrageurs. Hedgers' basic motivation in dealing with options is to control their risk exposure. By contrast, speculators' motivation for dealing in options is the hope of making profits by taking a risk position.

Differences between options and futures contracts

Options and futures contracts are both examples of derivative instruments in that their price is derived in relation to the spot price and they can also both be used for hedging and speculative purposes; however, there are some significant differences in the two contracts. With an option contract the buyer of the option is not obliged to transact, whereas both parties to a futures contract are obliged to transact. The other major difference lies as our examples illustrate in the risk–return characteristics of the contract. With a futures contract, for every cent the future spot price is above the futures rate on expiry of the contract, the buyer makes a cent and the seller loses a cent on the contract. This is not the case with an options contract; the maximum loss of the option holder is limited to the premium paid for the option, which is the maximum possible gain for the option writer. However, there is unlimited potential profit for an option holder and likewise unlimited potential loss for the writer. This fundamental difference in the risk/return characteristics of futures and options is very important, futures may be useful instruments for hedging against symmetric risks, while options can prove useful for hedging against asymmetric risks.

13.11 The pricing of currency options

In this section, we look at the more complex question of option pricing. In particular, we examine the factors that determine the price of a currency call option. We first look at these factors from an intuitive stance and then proceed to analyse the famous currency option pricing formula which was put forward in a paper by Garman and Kohlhagen (1983) which built upon the path-breaking option pricing formula for shares devised by Black and Scholes (1973).

The principles of option pricing

When considering the price of a currency option we need to bear in mind exactly what the buyer of an option is purchasing. An option offers the purchaser limited downside loss as given by the option premium paid, combined with unlimited upside potential profit. An option that has no chance of ever being exercised would be worthless; however, if an option has a high probability of being exercised then one should expect to pay more for it. A fundamental principle underlying the pricing of an option is that the greater the probability of an option being exercised the higher will be its premium. The other key factor that is crucial is the expected profit if the option were to be exercised.

Bearing these basic principles in mind, let us consider conceptually the factors that are likely to influence the price of a European currency call option using the dollar–pound parity. Payment for a European call option on sterling gives the buyer the right to buy sterling at a predetermined rate at a given date in the future. There are six crucial factors that determine the likelihood of a currency call option being exercised, and that hence influence the price to be paid for the call option:

1   The **spot exchange rate** – the higher spot price of sterling (dollars per pound) the more likely the option is to be exercised for any given strike price and consequently the higher the price of a call option.
2   The **strike price** – the higher the strike price of a call option on sterling (dollars per pound) the less likely it is that it will be exercised for a given spot rate and hence the lower its price.
3   The **time left to expiry** – the longer the time left to expiry then the more the chance of the option being exercised and hence the higher its price.
4   The **volatility** – the more volatile the dollar–sterling parity the more likely that its price at the time of expiry will exceed the strike price and hence the higher the price of the option.

Table 13.8 Table of factors affecting a currency call option's premium

Factor – a rise in:	European call
Spot price	+
Strike price	–
Time to expiry	+
Volatility	+
Domestic interest rate	–
Foreign interest rate	+

5   The **underlying currency (£) interest rate** – the purchaser of a sterling option is paying the issuer dollar cash for an option that can be exercised to buy a given amount of sterling in the future. The option holder pays the premium in dollars, foregoing the US interest rate on the dollar option premium but in return is acquiring a right to obtain sterling in the future rather than spot. A rise in the UK interest rate makes holding sterling today more attractive and therefore the call option less attractive since one is foregoing more sterling interest. For this reason, other things being equal, a call option premium on sterling needs to lower the higher the UK interest rate.

6   The **counter currency ($) interest rate** – the purchaser of a sterling option is paying the issuer dollar cash for an option who can be exercised to buy a given amount of sterling in the future. The option holder that pays the premium in dollars is able to keep far more of his funds in dollars than if he had to buy the pounds spot for a relatively small dollar premium. Hence, a rise in the US interest rate makes the call option more attractive. For this reason, other things being equal, the premium for a call option on sterling needs to increase as the US interest rate rises.

Table 13.8 summarizes the relationship between each of these six determinants of a currency call option.

13.12 Intrinsic value and time value

An option premium is made up of two components, the **intrinsic value** and the **time value**. The intrinsic value is the gain that would be realized if an option was exercised immediately, which for a currency call option, is simply the currency spot rate less the strike price of the underlying currency. For a put option it is the strike price less the spot price of the underlying currency.

  Intrinsic value for a call option = spot price – strike price
  Intrinsic value for a put option = strike price – spot price

If an intrinsic value for an option exists, then the option is said to be 'in-the-money'. For a call option, if the strike price is below the cash price it will have an intrinsic value and is therefore in-the-money. If the strike price is above the cash price the call option will have zero intrinsic value and is said to be 'out-of-the-money'. If the strike

Table 13.9 In-the-money, at-the-money and out-of-the-money

	Call	Put
In-the-money	Spot rate above strike price	Spot rate below strike price
At-the-money	Spot rate equals strike price	Spot rate equals strike price
Out-of-the-money	Spot rate below strike price	Spot rate above strike price

price is equal to the spot price the asset is **'at-the-money'** with zero intrinsic value. **Table 13.9** summarizes the various possible states for both call and put option contracts. The intrinsic value reflects the price that would be received, if the option were 'locked in' today at the current market price. The intrinsic value of an option is either positive or zero.

The **time value** of an option is the option premium less the intrinsic value, and reflects the fact that an option may have more ultimate value than its intrinsic value.

Time value = option premium – intrinsic value

An option buyer, even if the option is out-of-the-money, will still have some hope that at some time prior to expiry changes in the spot price will move the option into the money or further increase the value of the option if it is already in-the-money. This prospect gives an option a value greater than its intrinsic value.

Numerical Example

Intrinsic and time value

Example 1
Consider a call option valued at 9 cents to buy sterling at $1.75/£1 and the spot price of sterling is $1.80/£1. The option is in-the-money to the tune of 5 cents and so has an intrinsic value of 5 cents; the other 4 cents represents the time value.

Example 2
Consider a call option valued at 3 cents to buy sterling at $1.75/£1 and the spot price of sterling is $1.65/£1. The option is out-of-the-money to the tune of 10 cents and so has no intrinsic value; the whole value of the option, that is 3 cents, is time value.

13.13 The distribution of the option premium between time and intrinsic value

One of the crucial assumptions underlying the theory of currency option pricing is that the natural logarithm of the spot exchange rate is normally distributed; that is, it follows a log-normal distribution. A variable that has a log-normal distribution can have any value between zero and infinity as shown in **Figure 13.3**.

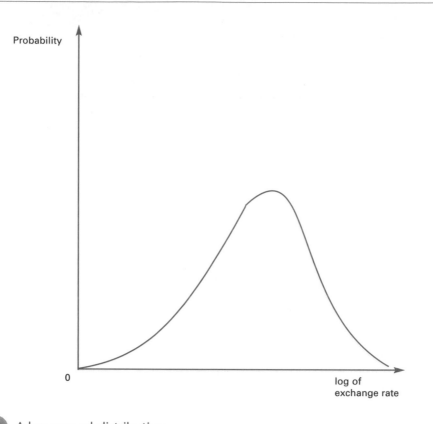

 Figure 13.3   A log-normal distribution

The time value for a given expiry date will get closer to zero the more in-the-money or out-of-the-money the contract is. This idea is illustrated in **Figures 13.4** that shows the various probability factors behind the intrinsic and time-value components of an option. There is a log-normal distribution around the spot price such that the spot price may go up or down by a given amount with equal probability; however, the larger the move in any direction the smaller the probability.

Figure 13.4a shows a deep in-the-money option, with the spot rate S exceeding the exercise rate X. This option has a roughly 50% chance of appreciating (rising) further giving good upside potential; however, there is also a lot of intrinsic value that could easily be reduced or even lost entirely if the exchange rate of the underlying currency were to depreciate (fall), which means that the time value is given by the potential upside area minus the potential loss of the intrinsic value which is quite high, leaving a small amount of time value.

Figure 13.4b shows a slightly in-the-money option, with the spot rate exceeding the exercise rate. The underlying currency option has a roughly 50% chance of appreciating (rising) further giving good upside potential; however, there is a lower intrinsic value that could be wiped out or reduced than in case of **Figure 13.4a**, so the time value which is given by the potential upside area minus the potential loss of the intrinsic value is higher due to the lower intrinsic value.

Figure 13.4c shows an at-the-money option, with the spot rate equal to the exercise rate. The time value of the option is at its maximum reflecting that any appreciation

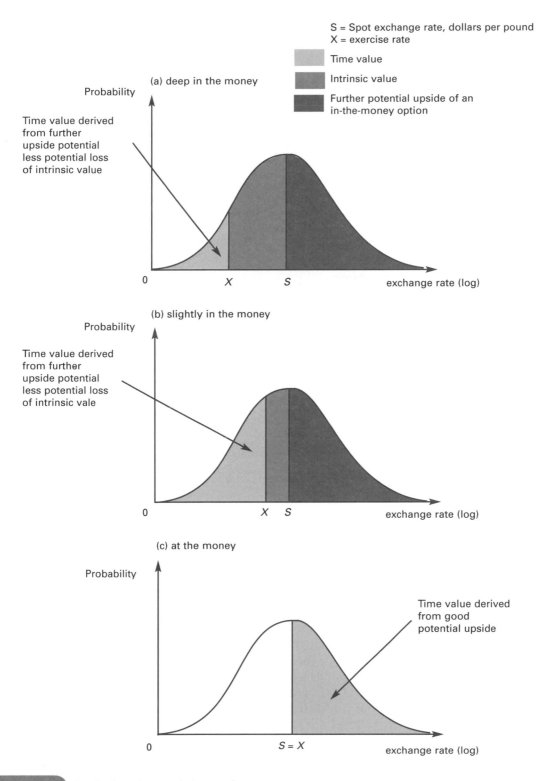

S = Spot exchange rate, dollars per pound
X = exercise rate

Time value

Intrinsic value

Further potential upside of an
in-the-money option

(a) deep in the money

Probability

Time value derived
from further
upside potential
less potential loss
of intrinsic value

0   X   S   exchange rate (log)

(b) slightly in the money

Probability

Time value derived
from further
upside potential
less potential loss
of intrinsic vale

0   X S   exchange rate (log)

(c) at the money

Probability

Time value derived
from good
potential upside

0   S = X   exchange rate (log)

 Figure 13.4 Intrinsic value and time value

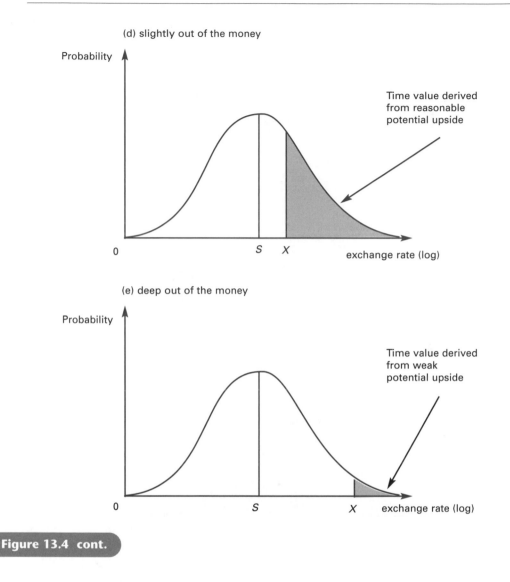

Figure 13.4 cont.

(rise) of the underlying currency will place the option in-the-money, while there is no intrinsic value to be lost.

Figure 13.4d shows a slightly out-of-the-money option, with the spot rate slightly below the exercise rate. The option has no intrinsic value but there is a good chance, although less than in **Figure 13.4c**, that the spot rate may appreciate and so exceed the exercise rate prior to maturity. For this reason, the option will have a lower time value than in **Figure 13.4c** other things being equal.

Figure 13.4e shows a deep out-of-the-money option, with the spot rate well below the exercise rate. The option has no intrinsic value and there is only a relatively small chance that the spot rate will appreciate sufficiently to exceed the exercise rate prior to maturity. For this reason, the option has only a small time value which is lower than in the case of **Figure 13.4d**, other things being equal.

An important point shown by **Figure 13.4** is that the value of the option falls, other things being equal (that is for a given exercise price, volatility, risk-free rate of

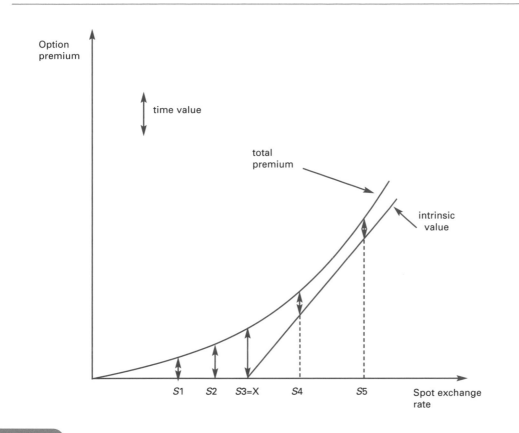

Figure 13.5 The distribution of a call premium between time and intrinsic value

interest and term to maturity), as we move from **a** to **e** since the probability of the option being exercised, that is the area to the right of the exercise rate, decreases.

Figure 13.5 shows the distribution of the total option premium between time value and intrinsic value for a variety of spot exchange rates ($S1$, $S2$, $S3$, $S4$ and $S5$), other things being equal and a given strike price (X). A deep out-of-the-money option with price $S1$ has zero intrinsic value and a small amount of time value. If the spot exchange rate were higher at $S2$ so that the option is only slightly out-of-the-money, the option premium has zero intrinsic value but more time value reflecting the greater probability of being exercised than at $S1$. When the spot price $S3$ is equal to the exercise price, that is the contract is at-the-money, the entire premium is made of the time value which is at its maximum. Above the exercise price, the option premium starts to have a positive intrinsic component which increases by 1 unit for each 1 unit the spot price exceeds the exercise price; however, time value starts to fall because although there is further upside potential there is the risk that some (or all) intrinsic value can be lost, so at $S4$ time value is smaller than at $S3$ although the total option premium is higher. At the spot price $S5$ the option is deep-in-the-money with a large component of intrinsic value and continued upside potential and only a slight risk that the option will end up worthless, and this is reflected in a small amount of time value. The lesson is that the more in-the-money the contract, the greater the probability that the option holder will be able to exercise the contract and therefore the lower the time value on

Table 13.10   Intrinsic value and time value

Deep out-of-the-money (**Figure 13.4a**)	Zero	Low	Small upside potential
Slightly out-of-the-money (**Figure 13.4b**)	Zero	High	High upside potential high downside protection
At-the-money (**Figure 13.4c**)	Zero	Maximum	Maximum upside potential Maximum downside protection
Slightly in-the-money (**Figure 13.4d**)	$S - X$	High	High downside protection High upside potential
Deep in-the-money (**Figure 13.4e**)	$S - X$	Low	Small downside protection

Note: S = cash or spot price of the underlying asset and X is the exercise price of the call option.

the contract. Similarly, the more out-of-the-money the contract, the greater the probability that the contract will not be exercised and therefore the lower its time value. **Table 13.10** summarizes the division of the option premium between intrinsic and time value for various option statuses and the reason for the time value.

13.14 The Garman and Kohlhagen option-pricing formula

In this section we outline the Garman and Kohlhagen (1983) formula for the pricing of currency options. The formula applies to European currency options, and for the purpose of our analysis we will deal with the pricing of a call option; we make the following assumptions:

1   The option is a European option; that is, it cannot be exercised prior to maturity.
2   The underlying currency interest rate (r_{uk}) and counter-currency interest rates (r_{us}) are fixed during the life of the option.
3   The foreign exchange markets are perfectly efficient with zero transactions costs, no bid–ask spread and no taxes.
4   The exchange rate is log normally distributed, with a constant mean and standard deviation.
5   It is possible to short sell the currency and utilize the proceeds obtained without restriction.
6   The spot rate of the currency moves in a continuous fashion.

The Garman and Kohlhagen formula for the pricing of a call option is given by the formula:

$$C = Se^{-r_{uk}T} N(d1) - Xe^{-r_{us}T} N(d2) \tag{13.3}$$

The $d1$ and $d2$ terms are given by:

$$d1 = \frac{(r_{us} - r_{uk} + \sigma^2/2)T}{\sigma\sqrt{T}}$$ (13.4)

and

$$d2 = d1 - \sigma\sqrt{T}$$ (13.5)

where C is the call premium (measured in cents), S is the spot exchange rate (measured in dollars per pound), X is the exercise price (measured in dollars per pound), e is the natural number 2.7182, r_{us} is the risk-free interest rate of the United States, r_{uk} is the risk-free interest in the United Kingdom, T is the time left to maturity expressed as a fraction of a year, σ^2 is the variance of the spot rate on an annual basis, and σ is the standard deviation of the spot rate on an annual basis

The essential meaning of equation (13.3) is that the value of the call today is the present value of the expected value of the option upon expiry. The expected value involves use of the cumulative normal distribution tables; essentially $Se^{-r_{uk}T} N(d1)$ is the expected present value of the spot rate upon expiry (using the underlying currency interest rate). While the term $Xe^{-r_{us}T} N(d2)$ is the present value of the strike price on expiry (using the counter currency interest rate).

Interpretation of the $N(d1)$ and $N(d2)$ terms

The $N(d1)$ and $N(d2)$ terms involving the cumulative probability function are the terms which take into account the risk of the option being exercised. The $N(d1)$ term reflects the cumulative probability relating to the spot exchange rate, and its value shows the amount by which the option premium increases for each 1 cent rise in the dollar–pound exchange rate. The value of $N(d1)$ lies between 0 and 1. If the spot rate is deeply out-of-the-money (e.g. **Figure 13.4e**) then a 1 cent appreciation of the pound will have little effect on the call premium since it remains unlikely the option will be exercised, so that $N(d1)$ will be low, for example 0.2. If the option is currently at-the-money, then there is a 50% chance it will end up in-the-money and a 50% chance it will end up out-of-the-money so that $N(d1)$ will be 0.5 (**Figure 13.4c**); that is, if the pound appreciates by 1 cent, then the call premium will rise by 0.5 cents. If the option is already deep in-the-money, each 1 cent appreciation in the pound will be increasingly reflected in the call premium on the pound so that $N(d1)$ will get closer to 1 (**Figure 13.4a**), for example 0.9. The greater the spot appreciation of the pound in relation to the exercise rate, the higher the value of $N(d1)$.

The $N(d2)$ term reflects the cumulative probability relating to the exercise rate; that is, $N(d2)$ is the probability that the call option will actually be exercised, and is represented by the area to the right of the exercise rate in **Figures 13.4a** to **13.4e**. If $N(d2)$ is 0.60 then there is a 60% chance that the option will be exercised. The value of $N(d1)$ is always greater than $N(d2)$ except in the limiting case where the option is certain to be exercised, in which case $N(d1) = N(d2)=1$.

13.15 A numerical example of the Garman–Kohlhagen formula

Let us consider the dollar premium that is payable for a currency call option on sterling. Assume that the current spot rate is \$1.80/£1 and an investor buys a call option to purchase sterling at a strike price of $1.75/£1. The US interest rate is 6% and the UK interest rate is 9%, and the standard deviation (σ) is 20% (expressed as 0.20 in formula). The option has 180 days to expiry, so that:

$S = \$1.80/£1$
$X = \$1.75/£1$
$r_{us} = 0.06$
$r_{uk} = 0.09$
$T = 0.5$ (approx)
$\sigma = 0.20$ (20%) so that $\sigma^2 = 0.04$

We first calculate the value of $d1$:

$$d1 = \frac{1n(S/X) + [r_{us} - r_{uk} + \sigma^2/2]T}{\sigma\sqrt{T}} \tag{13.4}$$

that is:

$$d1 = \frac{[1n(1.80/1.75) + (0.06 - 0.09 + 0.2^2/2]0.5}{0.2\sqrt{0.5}} = 0.16$$

From the cumulative normal distribution of **Table 13.14**, supplied in the Appendix at the end of this chapter, we find:

$N(d1) = N(0.16) = 0.5636$

Note that if the value we find for $N(d1)$ or $N(d2)$ is negative, then when we look up the value in **Table 13.14** we must subtract the value we find in the table from 1. For example, in the table we need to look up the value $N(d1)= -0.035$ (this is the value we would get if the strike price was $1.80 instead of $1.75). First, we look up 0.035 in the table which gives 0.5140 (mid-way between 0.5120 and 0.5160); we then subtract this so that $N(d1)=N(-0.035)$ is given by $1 - 0.5140 = 0.486$. For positive values of $N(d1)$ and $N(d2)$ we just use the value listed in the table.

We next calculate the value of $d2$ repeating equation (13.5):

$$d2 = d1 - \sigma\sqrt{T} \tag{13.5}$$

that is,

$$d2 = 0.16 - 0.2\sqrt{0.5} = 0.02$$

From the cumulative normal distribution table supplied at the end of the chapter we find:

$N(d2) = N(0.02) = 0.508$

With these calculations we are now in a position to calculate the price of the option:

Table 13.11   The Values of $N(d1)$ and $N(d2)$ for different spot exchange rates

Spot exchange rate ($/£)	d1	N(d1)	d2	N(d2)	Call premium in cents
$1.65/£1	−0.45	0.3264	−0.59	0.2776	4.34
$1.70/£1	−0.24	0.4052	−0.38	0.3520	6.07
$1.75/£1	−0.04	0.4840	−0.18	0.4286	8.18
$1.80/£1	0.16	0.5636	0.02	0.5080	10.71
$1.85/£1	0.36	0.6406	0.22	0.5871	13.59

Note: T = 6 months (0.5 in formula), r_{uk} = 9% (0.09 in formula), r_{us} = 6% (0.06 in formula), standard deviation = 20%(0.2), and strike price = $1.75/£1.

$$C = Se^{-r_{uk}T} N(d1) - Xe^{-r_{us}T} N(d2)$$

Substituting the appropriate values yields:

$$C = 1.80 \times 2.7182^{-0.09(0.5)} \times 0.5636 - 1.75 \times 2.7182^{-0.06(0.5)} (0.508)$$
$$= 0.1071, \text{ that is } 10.71 \text{ cents}$$

Since the spot rate $1.80/£1 exceeds the strike price $1.75/£1, then of the 10.71 premium 5 cents is intrinsic value and 5.71 cents is time value. The above calculations are based upon a spot exchange rate of $1.80/£1 and a strike price of $1.75/£1. **Table 13.11** shows how the values of $N(d1)$ and $N(d2)$ change as the value of the current share price changes, and the resulting call price in pence.

The intrinsic value of an option is easily calculated as is the time left to expiration. The underlying and counter-currency risk-free interest rates are all measurable, and the most contentious thing to measure is volatility. Ideally, the efficient pricing of options requires a measurement of volatility likely to occur in the future. **Historical volatility** may be a useful measure for this purpose, but it could prove to be defective as the past is not necessarily a good guide to the future. In addition, an appropriate measure of historical volatility is still needed; should it be based on the last month's exchange rate volatility, the last three months, the last six months or last year? Another problem with historical volatility is that it usually fails to pick up the possibility of large discrete shifts. **Expected volatility** will differ from one market participant to another, and therefore the view of the appropriate market price of an option will vary between market participants. **Implied volatility** is the volatility implicit in the current option price, found by taking the current price of the option and finding a volatility that when plugged into the option pricing formula gives the current market price of the option (this is easily calculated by today's spreadsheets).

13.16 Problems with the currency option-pricing formula

The formula we have looked at is only applicable to European options, American options are usually priced slightly higher than European options because of the extra advantage that they give to the holder of being able to exercise the option at any date prior to maturity. Another problem is that the formula assumes that the log of the exchange rate follows a log-normal distribution. In the real world exchange rate distributions tend to be leptokurtic, that is to have fatter tails than a normal distribution, meaning that there are better chances of an option being exercised than suggested by the standard currency option pricing formula. Hence, real-world option premiums tend to exceed the theoretical price derived from the Garman–Kohlhagen formula.

13.17 The over-the-counter market in options

Major international banks have for many years marketed the advantages and flexibility of currency options to their multinational corporate and other clients. Since multinational corporations have varied demands, not all of which can be matched by exchanges, banks have found it worthwhile to offer tailor-made options contracts to meet the specific needs of their clients. This tailor-made market which allows for negotiation of the terms of the contract between the writer and holder of an option is known as the over-the-counter market (OTC). The OTC market is dominated by major banks and securities houses, which contrasts with the standardized contracts on offer at various exchanges. The major advantage of the OTC market is that a client's specific needs with regard to the size, exercise price and expiry date of the contract can be met. However, there are also a number of disadvantages of the OTC market: (i) the relatively small number of buyers and sellers means that the contract could be mispriced, (ii) the lack of standardization of the contracts in the OTC market means that the secondary market for OTC contracts is severely limited, so OTC instruments lack the liquidity that is a vital part of exchange-traded options, and (iii) the holder of the option runs the risk of default on the part of the writer whereas exchange-traded options are guaranteed by the exchange. For this reason, only high-quality financial institutions tend to be involved in the OTC market.

13.18 The swaps market

A swap is an agreement between two parties to exchange two differing forms of payment obligations, and there are basically two types of swaps: (i) interest rate swaps and (ii) currency swaps. In an interest rate swap, the exchange involves payments denominated in the same currency, while in a currency swap the exchange involves two different currencies.

The first well-documented currency swap involved the World Bank and International Business Machines (IBM) in 1981, whereby the World Bank committed itself to financing some of IBM's deutschmark/Swiss franc debt in return for a commitment by IBM to finance some of the World Bank's dollar debt. Since the early 1980s there has been an enormous growth in the swap market, **Table 13.12** shows the value of currency swaps for the period 1998–2003.

Like many other financial instruments, swap agreements are used to manage risk exposure; however, as we shall see, one of the main reasons for the rapid growth of the swap market has been that they enable parties to raise funds more cheaply than would otherwise be the case. The swap market is used extensively by major corporations, international financial institutions and governments and is an important part of the international bond market. The swap market is currently organized by the

Table 13.12 Currency composition of notional principal value of outstanding currency swaps (US$ billions)

	1998	1999	2000	2001	2002	2003
US dollar	15810	12834	14073	15410	16500	21429
Japanese yen	5319	4236	4254	4178	4791	5500
Euro	na	4667	5981	6368	7818	10145
Pound sterling	2612	2242	2391	2315	2462	4286
Other	12261	4709	3993	5255	5349	7608
Gross total	36,002	28,688	31,322	33,496	36,920	48,968
Net total	18,001	14,344	15,666	16,748	18,460	24,484

Notes: (1) Figures for currency swaps are gross and have not been adjusted for double counting as each currency swap involves two currencies. To obtain the net figure the quoted currency swap figures need to be halved. (2) The notional principal amount while giving an idea of market size, should not be viewed as the amount potentially at risk, since it is the interruption of the cash flows between parties to a swap agreement that is at risk and this is a very small fraction of the above figures.
Source: Bank for International Settlements.

International Swap Dealers Association (ISDA) which since 1985 has been responsible for standardizing documentation and dealing terms in the swap market.

13.19 Potential currency swap scenarios

We shall first consider a few scenarios where companies might use in the currency swap market.

Scenario 1: reducing the cost of raising finance

A currency swap might prove attractive for two companies that have differing abilities to raise funds in different markets. A Chinese company might wish to raise dollar funds at a floating rate of interest, while a US company might wish to raise yen at a fixed rate of interest. It might be the case that Japanese investors are not too keen on US companies but are keen to invest in Chinese companies, while US investors are not too keen to lend to Chinese companies. In such circumstances, there may be a swap opportunity with the Chinese company raising yen funds at a fixed rate of interest, while the US company raises dollar funds at a floating rate of interest, the companies then swap the funds raised and the corresponding obligations. The net result is then that the Chinese company gets the dollar funds it needs at a fixed rate of interest cheaper than it could have raised the funds itself, while the US company would get the fixed rate yen funds at cheaper cost than if it had raised the funds itself.

Scenario 2: changing debt structures on a balance sheet

Company A has a lot of dollar-denominated debt on the liability side of its balance sheet and would like to switch some of this into sterling debt. Meanwhile company B has a lot of sterling debt on its books and would like to switch some of this into dollar debt. Rather than each company go through the costly process of buying back its debt and then issuing new debt in its preferred currency, the companies could negotiate a swap agreement whereby they exchange their debt and the corresponding obligations. In the end, company A finances part of company B's sterling debt while company B finances part of company A's dollar debt.

Having looked at some potential Swap scenarios, we now proceed to examine some specific numerical examples of Swaps. To concentrate on the basic issues we shall ignore charges by an intermediary for arranging the Swap.

13.20 A currency swap agreement

In a currency swap, differing currencies are involved. Consider the following scenario of two companies, one a British company wishing to raise $180 million for 10 years at a floating rate of interest for investment in the United States, the other a German company that wishes to raise £100 million for 10 years at a fixed rate of interest for investment in the United Kingdom. We assume that the spot exchange rate is $1.80/£1.

The UK company can borrow $180 million at a floating rate of interest but is advised that it will have to pay dollar London Interbank Offer Rate (LIBOR) + 0.75%, its repayments being adjusted annually in line with changes in LIBOR. The German company could borrow £100 million of funds directly at a fixed rate of interest of 8.50%. A swap dealer that has both these clients on its books may spot a swap opportunity. The dealer knows that market conditions would permit the UK company to borrow £100 million on the London market at a fixed rate of interest of 8%, while a current US investment bias for German companies would enable the German company to borrow $180 million at LIBOR + 0.25%. The borrowing opportunities open to the two companies are shown in **Table 13.13**.

If they were to exchange debt obligations, the UK company would be able to gain dollar finance at LIBOR + 0.25% saving 50 basis points, while the German company would be able to gain sterling finance at 8% saving 50 basis points. The mechanics of the currency swap can be summarized using Swap boxes as in **Figure 13.6**.

The figure first indicates the position of each company without a swap, the UK company would raise $180 million in the USA at a floating rate of interest 75 basis points over LIBOR. The German company would raise £100 million at a fixed rate of interest of 8.5%. As a prelude to the swap, since the UK company can raise sterling fixed rate funds in the UK market cheaper than the German company, it will issue £100 million at a fixed rate of interest of 8% (straight arrow for fixed), while the German company will raise $180 million in the USA at a floating rate of interest of LIBOR + 0.25% (squiggly arrow for floating). We then have the initial exchange of

Table 13.13   A currency swap

	UK sterling fixed rate	US dollar floating rate
British company	8%	LIBOR + 0.75%
German company	8.5%	LIBOR + 0.25%

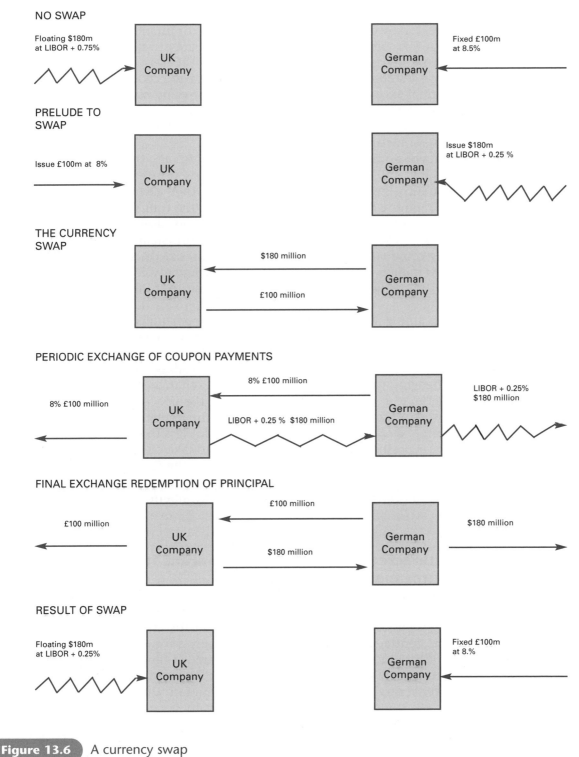

NO SWAP

Floating $180m
at LIBOR + 0.75%

UK Company

German Company

Fixed £100m
at 8.5%

PRELUDE TO SWAP

Issue £100m at 8%

UK Company

German Company

Issue $180m
at LIBOR + 0.25 %

THE CURRENCY SWAP

UK Company

$180 million

£100 million

German Company

PERIODIC EXCHANGE OF COUPON PAYMENTS

8% £100 million

UK Company

8% £100 million

LIBOR + 0.25 % $180 million

German Company

LIBOR + 0.25%
$180 million

FINAL EXCHANGE REDEMPTION OF PRINCIPAL

£100 million

UK Company

£100 million

$180 million

German Company

$180 million

RESULT OF SWAP

Floating $180m
at LIBOR + 0.25%

UK Company

German Company

Fixed £100m
at 8.%

Figure 13.6 A currency swap

principal, the UK company gives the German company the £100 million while the German company gives the UK company the $180 million it requires (a fair exchange at the $1.80/£1 parity). Next we have the periodic exchange of interest payments by the two companies, the UK company pays dollar LIBOR + 0.25% to the German company which is used to repay holders of its bonds, while the German company pays the UK company 8% sterling which is used to pay its bond holders. Finally after 10 years we have the final exchange of principal, the UK company pays the German company $180 million so that it can pay back its US bond holders upon maturity, while the German company will pay the UK company £100 million so that it can pay its UK bond holders upon maturity.

In effect the currency swap has enabled the UK company to raise the $180 million it required at dollar LIBOR + 0.25%, thus saving itself 50 basis points (or $900,000 per year) over what it would cost to raise the funds itself in the USA. The German company manages to raise the £100 million it requires at 8.0%, thus saving itself 0.5% (or £500,000 per year) over what it would cost to raise the funds itself in the United Kingdom. Strictly speaking the initial and final exchange of principal is unnecessary since the UK company could convert the £100 million it raises at the spot rate of $1.80/£1 into the $180 million it needs, and the German company convert the $180 million it raises into £100 million. The main feature of the swap is the interest rate exchange.

Effectively the swap arrangement exploits an arbitrage opportunity enabling the UK company to obtain US funds at the same rate as the German company, and the German company the opportunity to raise funds at a similar cost to the UK company. Prior to the development of swap markets such arbitrage opportunities were undertaken by hedging the position in the forward exchange market. The UK company would raise funds at floating rates of interest in the UK convert these into dollars and then use the forward exchange rate to hedge the foreign exchange risk. However, most forward markets for foreign exchange are for less than two years. In order to hedge a 10-year position each party would have to take out an annual forward contract for each of the next 10 years. Furthermore, the forward rate contracts is takes out may still not be ideal if the forward rate is moving against the company. With the swap agreement each party is achieving a perfect 10-year hedge in one contract.

13.21 Distinguishing characteristics of the swap market from the forward and futures markets

A swap agreement is basically the same as a forward/futures contract in that both parties are committing themselves to a stream of future obligations just as participants do in a forward/futures contract. Although a swap is basically a forward contract, there are nonetheless significant differences between exchange-traded futures contracts and the obligations entered into in a swap contract. The most obvious difference is that exchange-traded futures contracts are of a much shorter duration than the vast majority of swap contracts. While most futures contracts are usually for a year or less, most swap contracts cover periods ranging from 5 to 20 years and possibly longer. This factor is particularly important in explaining the popularity of swap contracts to business; swaps offer hedging possibilities that meet the longer time frame within which many businesses have debt obligations.

Futures contracts are also highly standardized contracts that may not meet the specific needs of a firm because of their limited time horizon and few fixed expiry dates each year. By contrast, with a swap agreement a party is able to obtain a highly specific agreement with a time horizon and payment schedule matched closely to its needs.

Another significant difference between futures and swaps is that futures contracts are highly regulated contracts that come under the control of the relevant futures exchange. A significant advantage of futures contracts is that the exchange will guarantee the obligations should one of the parties default on its obligations. By contrast, the swap market is less regulated and unless the counterparties ensure the agreement is underwritten by a third party there is the risk that one of the parties will not fulfil its obligations.

A significant advantage of futures contacts over swaps are that there is an active secondary market in futures contracts, so that obligations can be easily be terminated by selling the contract to another party. By contrast, swap agreements because of their non-standardized nature have a far less active secondary market, and a swap agreement can only be cancelled with the consent of both parties. A party that wishes to end its swap obligations will either have to enter a swap buy-back, a swap sale, or swap reversal with another counterparty that reverses (as closely as is possible) the cash flows inherent in its original swap agreement.

13.22 Conclusions

In recent years currency derivatives have become one of the most important tools for risk management. Properly used they can be useful tools to reduce the foreign exchange risk and offer an attractive alternative to the traditional forward market. Futures contracts are basically very similar instruments to forward contracts but have some distinguishing features which can give them an edge over the use of forward contracts in many circumstances. The key to the successful use of currency futures contracts for hedging purposes is that the adverse implications of any change in the spot market is offset by a profit from an appropriate futures contract. A currency futures contract enables a firm to hedge against exchange rate risk by buying (selling) a futures contract at a guaranteed exchange rate in the future regardless of what the corresponding future spot exchange rate turns out to be. The present range of currency futures contracts means that the exchange rate risk facing companies and fund managers of adverse movements in currencies can generally be considerably reduced or even eliminated, at least up to the 12-month horizon. In addition to hedging, futures contracts are useful instruments for taking speculative positions. For example, if a speculator feels that a currency is likely depreciate compared to the futures rate it is remarkably easy to take out a short position. The low margin requirements also make speculation relatively easy.

Option contracts offer a different payoff profile to futures contracts and as such provide a very useful hedging/speculative alternative to forward and futures contracts. The options market is now established as one of the most important growth areas of financial markets. Currency options can help investors to hedge positions at relatively low cost and may prove more suited to hedgers needs than futures contracts. While buying a futures contract guarantees the price to be paid in the future regardless of what the corresponding future spot price turns out to be, hedging with a futures contract means that the investor also gives up the opportunity to benefit from a favourable price movement. It is here that options contract can provide an important alternative because by hedging with an options contract the hedger can ensure a maximum price to be paid in the future and yet still be able to take advantage of a favourable exchange rate movement. Properly used, options contracts are extremely useful hedging tools. The symmetric risks involved in forwards and futures contracts contrasts with the asymmetric risks of options contracts. For this reason, options tend to be more costly hedging instruments to purchase; to induce a party to write an option the purchaser must be prepared to pay a fee that reflects the increased exposure to the writer.

Another attractive feature of options is that they can be combined with other options, futures and spot positions to devise numerous innovative speculative and hedging strategies. Overall, therefore, option contracts enable investors, hedgers and speculators to take positions more akin to their risk–return preferences.

Swap contracts can enable firms to obtain long-term finance at a lower cost than would otherwise be the case and can also be used to hedge longer-term currency risk at time horizons greater than available by the use of traditional forward markets. The swap market has grown enormously since the first swaps took place in the early 1980s, so that in 2003 the outstanding gross notional principal amount of currency swaps was estimated to be around $48,000 billion. The market has matured so much that the potential gains to be had from swaps has fallen from around 50 basis points to more like 5 to 10 basis points. The development of the swap market has been one of the most significant developments in the bond market since it has enabled firms to obtain lower-cost financing and also to hedge risks at far longer-term horizons than is possible with futures and options.

Arranging swaps and even becoming a counterparty to swap arrangements has generated a source of fee income for banks but has also meant that they have had to adopt new risk-management techniques and procedures. Underwriting a swap deal involves some 'off-balance-sheet' exposure for a bank should one of the counterparties default on its obligations. Hence, a bank needs to keep a careful eye on its potential swap exposures and the creditworthiness of the parties with whom it deals.

It should also be remembered that the Swap contracts examined in this chapter have been major simplifications of actual swaps carried out in the real world. In practice, Swap agreements involve more complexity in that the two swap parties may wish to exchange different notional principal amounts, have different payment dates, and in the case of currency swaps an intermediary has to take into account different interest rate conventions, such as different day counts used in different countries.

Appendix

Table 13.14 The cumulative standard normal distribution

	.00	.01	.02	.03	.04	.05	.06	.07	.08	.09
0.0	.5000	.5040	.5080	.5120	.5160	.5199	.5239	.5279	.5319	.5359
0.1	.5398	.5438	.5478	.5517	.5557	.5596	.5636	.5675	.5714	.5753
0.2	.5793	.5832	.5871	.5910	.5948	.5987	.6026	.6064	.6103	.6141
0.3	.6179	.6217	.6255	.6293	.6331	.6368	.6406	.6443	.6480	.6517
0.4	.6554	.6591	.6628	.6664	.6700	.6736	.6772	.6808	.6844	.6879
0.5	.6915	.6950	.6985	.7019	.7054	.7088	.7122	.7157	.7190	.7224
0.6	.7257	.7291	.7324	.7257	.7389	.7422	.7454	.7486	.7517	.7549
0.7	.7580	.7611	.7642	.7673	.7704	.7734	.7764	.7794	.7823	.7852
0.8	.7881	.7910	.7939	.7967	.7995	.8023	.8051	.8078	.8106	.8133
0.9	.8159	.8186	.8212	.8238	.8264	.8289	.8315	.8340	.8365	.8389
1.0	.8413	.8438	.8461	.8495	.8508	.8531	.8554	.8577	.8599	.8621
1.1	.8643	.8665	.8686	.8708	.8729	.8749	.8770	.8790	.8810	.8830
1.2	.8849	.8869	.8888	.8907	.8925	.8944	.8962	.8980	.8997	.9015
1.3	.9032	.9049	.9066	.9082	.9099	.9115	.9131	.9147	.9162	.9177
1.4	.9192	.9207	.9222	.9236	.9251	.9265	.9279	.9292	.9306	.9319
1.5	.9332	.9345	.9357	.9370	.9382	.9394	.9406	.9418	.9429	.9441
1.6	.9452	.9463	.9474	.9484	.9495	.9505	.9515	.9525	.9535	.9545
1.7	.9554	.9564	.9573	.9582	.9591	.9599	.9608	.9616	.9625	.9633
1.8	.9641	.9649	.9656	.9664	.9671	.9678	.9686	.9693	.9699	.9706
1.9	.9713	.9719	.9726	.9732	.9738	.9744	.9750	.9756	.9761	.9767
2.0	.9772	.9778	.9783	.9788	.9793	.9798	.9803	.9808	.9812	.9817
2.1	.9821	.9826	.9830	.9834	.9838	.9842	.9846	.9850	.9854	.9857
2.2	.9861	.9864	.9868	.9871	.9875	.9878	.9881	.9884	.9887	.9890
2.3	.9893	.9896	.9898	.9901	.9904	.9906	.9909	.9911	.9913	.9916
2.4	.9918	.9920	.9922	.9925	.9927	.9929	.9931	.9932	.9934	.9936
2.5	.9938	.9940	.9941	.9943	.9945	.9946	.9948	.9949	.9951	.9952
2.6	.9953	.9955	.9956	.9957	.9959	.9960	.9961	.9962	.9963	.9964
2.7	.9965	.9966	.9967	.9968	.9969	.9970	.9971	.9972	.9973	.9974
2.8	.9974	.9975	.9976	.9977	.9977	.9978	.9979	.9979	.9980	.9981
2.9	.9981	.9982	.9982	.9983	.9984	.9984	.9985	.9985	.9986	.9986
3.0	.9987	.9987	.9987	.9988	.9988	.9989	.9989	.9989	.9990	.9990
3.1	.9990	.9991	.9991	.9991	.9992	.9992	.9992	.9992	.9993	.9993
3.2	.9993	.9993	.9994	.9994	.9994	.9994	.9994	.9995	.9995	.9995
3.3	.9995	.9995	.9995	.9996	.9996	.9996	.9996	.9996	.9996	.9997
3.4	.9997	.9997	.9997	.9997	.9997	.9997	.9997	.9997	.9997	.9998

Further reading

Black, F. and Scholes, M. (1973) 'The Pricing of Corporate Liabilities', *Journal of Political Economy*, vol. 81, pp. 637–54.

Garman, M.B. and Kohlhagen, S.W. (1983) ' Foreign Currency Option Values', *Journal of International Money and Finance*, vol. 2, pp. 231–37.

Hull, J.C. (2003) *Options, Futures and Other Derivatives* (New York: Prentice Hall).

Kolb, R.W. (2002) *Futures, Options and Swaps* (Oxford: Basil Blackwell).

Pilbeam, K.S. (2005) *Finance and Financial Markets* (Basingstoke: Palgrave Macmillan).

14

International Macroeconomic Policy Coordination

14.1 Introduction

For the majority of this text, we have confined our analysis to the study of a small open economy. By definition the policy measures taken by such an economy have no significant impact upon its trading partners. The small economy assumption is useful in that it makes it plausible to ignore possible reactions to its policies from trading partners. In the real world, however, the actions taken by one country will often have significant effects upon their trading partners. This means that the countries are interdependent and policy measures adopted by one of the economies may provoke a reaction from its trading partners that can reinforce, weaken or even offset its policy. Where such interdependence exists it is frequently argued that countries should consider coordinating their macroeconomic policies to avert the possibility of conflict and improve their positions as compared to pursuing unilateral policies.

In this chapter, we shall look at some of the major issues raised by the topic of international macroeconomic policy coordination. These issues include: What is meant by coordination of economic policies? Why does the need for international policy coordination arise? Is coordination always superior to non-coordination? What are the obstacles that prevent greater international coordination?

14.2 What is meant by international policy coordination?

International policy coordination is a very loose term and is sometimes used inter-changeably with the word cooperation, and the proper distinction between the two terms is not clearly defined in the literature. Perhaps the most useful distinction is that made by Henry Wallich:

> 'Cooperation' falls well short of 'coordination', a concept which implies a signifi-cant modification of national policies in recognition of international economic interdependence . . . But 'cooperation' is more than 'consultation', which may mean little more than that other interested parties will be kept informed. (1984, p. 85)

Notwithstanding this distinction, we shall use the term coordination throughout this chapter although the lower levels of coordination such as the exchange of informa-tion might be considered more appropriately as examples of cooperation.

International policy coordination is primarily about some form of cooperative rela-tionship between the policy-makers/authorities of two or more nations. Thus, interna-tional policy coordination does not *per se* directly involve the private sector. As we shall see, this latter point is important because an arrangement made between national authorities might be undermined by a suspicious private sector. To provide an operational framework for the discussion we shall distinguish between a hierarchy of three types of coordination: the exchange of information; the acceptance of mutu-ally consistent policies; and joint action.

The exchange of information

A minimal type of coordination is the exchange of information between the authori-ties of two or more countries. This exchange may be on a limited or quite considerable scale. The type of information that might be exchanged includes the authorities' views about the appropriate value of the exchange rate, the present and future course of their domestic macroeconomic policies and intentions with regard to future exchange market intervention, economic forecasts and principal objectives of economic policies, and so on. The exchange of information will not by itself lead to agreement on what are the appropriate macroeconomic polices, let alone joint action. As such, it repre-sents a minimal level of coordination. What it is likely to lead to is a better under-standing of how conflict can be averted and where the greatest uncertainty lies.

Mutually consistent policies

The exchange of information may provide the basis for more active coordination in that the countries concerned accept either formally of informally to adopt consistent macroeconomic policy stances. Each country takes into account the aims and policies of other countries when formulating its own policy stance. Coordination at this level means the authorities pursue mutually compatible target values and adjust the selection of policy instruments, their magnitude and timing to avoid conflict with other countries. Such coordination requires an exchange of information with other countries and that account be taken of the policies and objectives being pursued in those other countries.

Joint action

Having exchanged information and agreed on mutually consistent target values for the objectives of economic policy, the authorities of the two economies could go one step further and agree on joint action to achieve desired targets. For example, if a certain value of the real exchange rate is required to achieve these objectives, joint action would mean that the two authorities act together to manipulate the exchange rate in the desired direction. Joint action means not only an agreement on the appropriate exchange rate value, but also concerted action to achieve that rate. As we shall see, much of the recent literature on macroeconomic policy coordination has focused mainly on two types of joint action. One is when fiscal and monetary policies are adjusted to maximize joint welfare, the other is when the exchange rate is jointly targeted. Some proposals for policy coordination combine fiscal and monetary policies with some form of exchange rate targeting.

14.3 Why does the need for international policy coordination arise?

Coordination of macroeconomic and exchange rate policies would not be necessary if exchange rate changes truly insulated one country from another, as advocates of floating exchange rates had presupposed. In such circumstances, one economy would not be affected by the policy mix pursued in other economies. Experience with floating exchange rates has amply demonstrated that such independence does not exist. In particular, the phenomenon of exchange rate 'overshooting' (see Chapter 7) means that the monetary policy pursued in one country will have spillover effects on its trading partners. An initial money expansion will lead to a depreciation of the expanding country's real exchange rate conferring it a competitive advantage. However, the real exchange rate of its trading partners will have appreciated reducing their exports and thereby their income and employment levels.

Economic policy coordination is only necessary if economic policies themselves have effects upon the real economy. If monetary and fiscal policies have no effect on employment and output levels as some theorists argue, then there would be no benefits to be derived from international coordination of such policies. As Alfred Steinherr puts it:

> In a world where markets for all possible trades exists ('completeness of markets'), where all markets, including the labour market, are competitive and all prices fully flexible, where all agents are rational and adjustment costs of pricing and input decisions negligible there is no need for adjustment policies, and therefore no need for co-ordination. Each economy would then adjust instantaneously to any surprises ('shocks') and operate at its natural employment level and there would be no overshooting of the exchange rate. Thus the need for policy coordination may

from this angle be regarded as due to market imperfections. According to this view reduction of imperfections would reduce the need for policy intervention and coordination, and act as a substitute for coordination. Needless to say, not all imperfections can be eliminated in the real world. As a consequence policies can potentially improve the market outcome and, in interdependent economies produce spillover effects. (1984, p. 77)

Frenkel (1983) points out that spillover effects that give rise to the need for coordination are the result of two important linkages between the domestic economy and the rest of the world. In the first instance, countries are connected via trade flows, the exports of one country are the imports of another and vice versa. Changes in these volumes will affect the national incomes of the countries concerned and with it employment levels. The second vital linkage is that provided by international capital movements; these permit the transmission of economic disturbances from one economy to another by freeing an economy from the need to keep its current account in balance. In this way, policies that influence the current account position of a country will have spillover effects on its trading partners' current account positions. Capital movements also have the effect of tying international interest rate differentials and expected exchange rate changes via the uncovered interest parity condition. As such, policies that influence the domestic interest rate will have effects on trading partners via induced changes in the real exchange rate.

In effect, the need for coordination is derived from spillover effects associated with interdependence. Cooper (1985) defines structural interdependence as a situation whereby the structures of two or more economies are such that economic events in one significantly influence economic events in the others. Hence, if economic policies adopted in one country affect its real economy then they will also have spillover effects on other countries. In such circumstances, the optimal course of action for one country will depend upon the course of action taken by other countries. Interdependence means that a country cannot achieve its objectives without these being mutually consistent with those pursued by other countries. Furthermore, the resulting policy interdependence means that a country has to take into account the policies of other countries. This implies the need for a certain degree of international policy coordination if countries wish to achieve their objectives. The need is especially acute where the trade and capital linkages are high such as that which exists between the European Union member states.

As an illustration of the interdependence between economies, **Table 14.1** presents the results of the effects of monetary and fiscal expansion by the USA and non-US OECD countries according to a variety of well-known models of the international economy (this approach is further discussed later in the chapter in section 14.8).

14.4 The benefits from international policy coordination

When one talks about the benefits to be derived from international policy coordination these will be dependent upon the type and degree of coordination undertaken. In general, terms coordination is a means of preserving and improving the benefits associated with increased interdependence such as the gains from trade and access to international capital markets. In this section, we examine from a theoretical viewpoint the potential benefits from coordination.

Table 14.1 Simulation effects of monetary and fiscal policy changes[1]

International model	Monetary expansion[2]								Fiscal expansion[3]							
	In USA				In non-US OECD				In USA				In non-US OECD			
	GNP effect (in per cent)		CA effect ($billions)		GNP effect (in per cent)		CA effect ($billions)		GNP effect (in per cent)		CA effect ($billions)		GNP effect (in per cent)		CA effect ($billions)	
	D	F	D	F	D	F	D	F	D	F	D	F	D	F	D	F
MCM	+1.5	−0.7	−3.1	−3.5	+1.5	0	+3.5	+0.1	+1.8	+0.7	−16.5	+8.9	+1.4	+0.5	−7.2	+7.9
EEC	+1.0	+0.2	−2.8	+1.2	+0.8	+0.1	−5.2	+1.9	+1.2	+0.3	−11.6	+6.6	+1.3	+0.2	−9.3	+3.0
EPA	+1.2	−0.4	−1.6	−10.1	0	0	−0.1	+0.1	+1.7	+0.9	−20.5	+9.3	+2.3	+0.3	−13.1	+4.7
LINK	+1.0	−0.1	−5.9	+1.5	+0.8	+0.1	−1.4	+3.5	+1.2	+0.1	−6.4	+1.9	+1.2	+0.2	−6.1	+6.3
LIVERPOOL	+0.1	0	−13.0	+0.1	+0.4	+1.6	+7.1	−8.2	+0.6	0	−7.0	+3.4	+0.3	−0.5	−17.2	+11.9
MSG	+0.3	+0.4	+2.6	−4.4	+0.2	+0.3	−15.9	+12.0	+0.9	+0.3	−21.6	+22.7	+1.1	+0.4	−5.3	+10.5
MINIMOD	+1.0	−0.2	+2.8	−4.7	+0.8	−0.3	+3.6	−1.4	+1.0	+0.3	−8.5	+5.5	+1.6	+0.1	−2.2	+3.2
VAR	+3.0	+0.4	+4.9	+5.1	+0.7	+1.2	+5.2	−10.0	+0.4	0	−0.5	−0.2	+0.5	+0.3	+1.7	−2.6
OECD	+1.6	+0.3	−8.4	+3.1	+0.8	+0.1	−1.6	+2.3	+1.1	+0.4	−14.2	+11.4	+1.5	+0.1	−6.9	+3.3
Taylor	+0.6	−0.2	–	–	+0.8	−0.1	–	–	+0.6	+0.4	–	–	+1.6	+0.6	–	–
Wharton	+0.7	+0.4	−5.1	+5.3	+0.2	0	+2.6	+0.5	+1.4	+0.2	−15.4	+5.3	+3.2	0	−5.5	+4.7
DRI	+1.8	−0.6	−1.4	+14.5	–	–	–	–	+2.1	+0.7	−22.0	+0.8	–	–	–	–
Average[4]	+1.2	0	−2.8	+0.7	+0.6	+0.3	−0.2	+0.1	+1.2	+0.4	−13.1	+6.9	+1.5	+0.2	−7.1	+5.3

Notes: [1]Effects on gross national product (GNP) and current account (CA) of respective domestic (D) and foreign economies (F); [2]increase in the money supply of 4% phased in over 4 quarters; [3]increase in government expenditure equal to 1% of GNP; [4]average of the reporting models.
MCM = Federal Reserve Board; EEC = European Commission; EPA = Japanese Economic Planning Agency; LINK = Project Link; Liverpool = Patrick Minford; MSG = McKibbin-Sachs; MINIMOD = Haas-Masson (IMF); VAR = Sims-Litterman; OECD = Interlink; Taylor = Stanford; Wharton; DRI = Data Resources.
Source: Frankel and Rockett (1988).

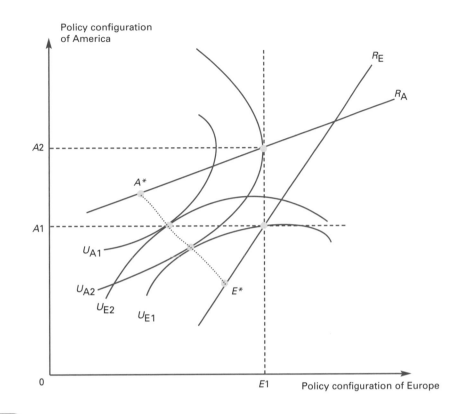

Figure 14.1 The derivation of the Hamada diagram

The potential gains from coordination of macroeconomic policies internationally have been conceptually illustrated by Hamada (1974, 1976 and 1985) using what has become known as the Hamada diagram. The principles underlying the derivation of the Hamada diagram for the hypothetical case of Europe and America are shown in **Figure 14.1**.

In the Hamada diagram, the macro policy configuration of Europe is shown on the horizontal axis, while the macro policy configuration of America is shown on the vertical axis. For instance, as we move along the horizontal axis the macro policy stance of Europe may be more expansionary, and likewise as we move up the vertical axis for America. Because the two countries are interdependent the optimal policy stance for Europe is dependent upon the policy stance taken by the America, and vice versa.

Conceptually, there must be a point on the diagram for Europe that gives a combination of its own policy stance and that of America which it prefers to all other possible policy combinations. This point of bliss for Europe is given by point E*. Likewise, for America there must be a combination of its own policy and that of Europe that it prefers to all other policy combinations and this is given by point A*.

For both Europe and America we can draw sets of elliptically shaped indifference curves U_E and U_A that denote combinations of European and American policies that yield the same level of utility. From the viewpoint of Europe, the closer the policy configuration of the two economies puts it on a utility curve U_E to point E* the better off it is. Hence, a combined policy configuration that puts it on utility curve U_{E1} is preferred to U_{E2}. Similarly, from the viewpoint of America, the closer the policy configuration of the two countries put it on a utility curve to point A^*, the better off it is. A combined policy configuration that puts it on utility curve U_{A1} is preferred to U_{A2}. In the special case, where the two countries are totally independent the utility curves for Europe are vertical straight lines and the utility curves for America are horizontal straight lines. Each country could then achieve its optimal level of welfare merely by adjusting its own policy instruments regardless of the policy pursued by the other country.

The problem for each economy is to determine its optimal policy stance for any given policy stance of the other, this yields a policy reaction schedule for each economy. The policy reaction schedule for Europe is found by taking a given policy stance of America and finding a utility curve U_E which is tangential to it; this is the utility closest to point E^*, which means Europe adopts policy stance $E1$ when the USA is pursuing policy $A1$. One can find various other optimal policy stances of Europe given a different policy stance by America, and by joining the points together gives the policy reaction function of Europe as R_E. Similarly, the policy reaction schedule for America is found by taking a given policy stance of Europe such as $E1$ and finding a utility curve U_{A2} which is tangential to a vertical line from $E1$. This is the utility curve closest to point A^* which means America's best policy stance is $A2$. In a like manner, one can find various other optimal policy stances of America given a different policy stance by Europe and joining the points together gives the policy reaction function of America as R_A.

The locus of points passing between E^* and A^*, where the utility curves U_E and U_A are tangential to one another is known as the pareto contract curve. Since the indifference curves are tangential to one another along the contract curve this indicates that one country can be made better off only by making the other country worse off. In the region of the contract curve between E^* and A^* the closer we are to point E^* (the further from point A^*) the better off is Europe and the worse off is America. Conversely, the closer we are to point A^* (the further from point E^*) the better off is America and the worse off is Europe. Note that the utility curves are drawn as oval-shaped ellipses, with the level of utility falling the further an oval-shaped curve is from the country's preferred point.

We can now use the Hamada diagram to illustrate the potential gains from the coordination of macro policies between the two economies. This is illustrated in **Figure 14.2**.

To establish potential gains from international macro policy coordination it is necessary to compare the possible situation under coordination *vis-à-vis* a scenario of non-coordination. The problem is that there is a range of possible coordination scenarios, and likewise one could envisage a range of non-coordination scenarios. **Figure 14.2** compares possible coordination scenarios with two popular non-coordination scenarios known as Nash and Stackleberg equilibriums.

In the Nash non-cooperative scenario each economy takes the policy stance of its partner economy as beyond its influence and adopts its optimal isolationist policy in this belief. If Europe pursues policy $E1$ the optimal policy for America is $A1$, but given the USA pursues $A1$ the optimal policy for Europe is $E2$, given Europe pursues $E2$ the optimal policy for America is $A2$, and so on. The economies continue to interact in this manner despite the fact that each economy's policy strategy choice does influence the choice of the other. A Nash equilibrium is finally reached when there is no incentive

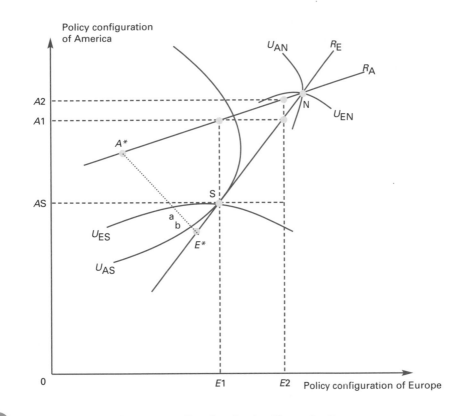

Policy configuration of America

Figure 14.2 Coordination and non-coordination in the Hamada diagram

for either economy to change its policy stance, taking the other's policy as given. In the Hamada diagram the Nash equilibrium is given by point N where the two reaction schedules intersect. At point N there is no incentive for either economy to change its policies. America is on utility curve U_{AN} while Europe is on utility curve U_{EN}.

With the Stackleberg scenario, one of the two countries (the leader) is assumed to be more intelligent than in the Nash scenario and realizes that its policy stance influences the choice of the other country, while the other (the follower) ignores the influence of its policy stance on the leader. Consequently, the leader anticipates possible rational reactions of the follower when making its policy choice. In **Figure 14.2** we assume that America is the leader and this leads to a Stackleberg equilibrium at point S. At point S there is a utility curve U_{AS} just tangential to Europe's reaction schedule R_E. This is the closest indifference curve to point A^* that America can reach knowing the whole range of possible reactions of Europe. With America pursuing Stackleberg policy AS the best policy for Europe is $E1$.

When comparing the Nash and Stackleberg non-cooperative equilibriums the Stackleberg solution is certainly superior for the leader compared to the Nash solution, and may or may not prove superior to the Nash solution for the follower. However, both the non-cooperative scenarios are pareto-inefficient since they do not lie on the contract curve $E^* A^*$. In theory, both economies could agree to adopt policy combinations that make them both better-off compared to either the Nash or Stackleberg non-cooperative scenarios. For example, between the portion ab on the contract curve A^*E^*

both countries would be on higher utility curves compared to the Stackleberg scenario. Hence, with coordination of economic policies the level of welfare both economies can be raised as compared to non-coordination. If the economies agree to coordinate to get onto the contract curve, the precise position they get to depends upon their relative bargaining strengths. The stronger the relative bargaining power of Europe the closer the position on the contract curve will be to point E^*, while the stronger the bargaining position of America the closer the solution on the contract curve will be to A^*.

In passing, we note that if both countries were to try to become a Stackleberg leader a situation known as 'Stackleberg warfare' would break out; this has no equilibrium solution because the assumptions each country makes are mutually inconsistent. Another important point made by Currie (1990) is that international macroeconomic policy does not require that the two countries' governments have the same objectives or even the same set of preferencees. Indeed, this point is illustrated in the Hamada diagram where the two countries' governments have different points of bliss.

14.5 A game theory demonstration of the gains from coordination

The Stackleberg and Nash solutions illustrated by the Hamada diagram are demonstrations of the results of traditional game theory. Simple game theory is usually presented as a pay-off matrix, an example of which is set out in **Figure 14.3**.

The figure illustrates depicts what is known in game theory as a pay-off matrix. We assume that the pay-off to each economy is measured by a 'misery index', which is simply the sum of an economy's inflation and unemployment rates. For simplicity of exposition we shall assume that policy-makers regard an additional 1% of inflation to be equally as bad as an additional 1% of unemployment. This being the case, the aim of economic policy will be to minimize an economy's misery index. The first figure of each of the two figures separated by a comma is the misery index (pay-off) of Europe, while the second is the pay-off of America. For example, if Europe pursues policy 1 and America pursues policy 4, the result will be a misery index of 7 for Europe and 15 for America. Similarly, if Europe pursues policy 2 while America pursues policy 3, the pay-off will be a misery index of 15 for Europe and 6 for America.

Using the pay-off matrix it is straightforward to illustrate the potential gains from coordination of policies. Suppose that each economy seeks to minimize its misery index but chooses its policy package in isolation without any coordination. When

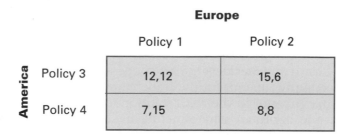

Figure 14.3 A game theory pay-off matrix demonstration of the gains from coordination

deciding whether or not to pursue policy 1 or policy 2, Europe does not know what policy will be chosen by America. Hence, the authorities of Europe will consider the consequences for if America pursues either policy 3 or policy 4. If America were to pursue policy 3, the best policy for Europe is policy 1 which gives it a misery index of 12 compared to 15 if it pursued policy 2. If America were to pursue policy 4, the best policy for Europe is again policy 1 which gives it a misery index of 7 compared to a misery index of 8 were it to employ policy 2. Hence, no matter what policy is chosen by America the best isolationist policy for Europe is to pursue policy 1. An analogous set of reasoning applies to the policy choice of America. If Europe pursues policy 1, the best policy for America is policy 3 giving a misery index of 12 compared to 15 if it pursues policy 4. Likewise, if Europe pursues policy 2 the best policy for America is again policy 3 which gives misery index of 6 as opposed to 8 if it pursues policy 4. Hence, no matter what policy is chosen by Europe the best isolationist policy for America to pursue is policy 3.

The result of each making its policy decisions in isolation is that Europe pursues policy 1 while America pursues policy 3. The resulting misery index for both economies is 12. This non-cooperation scenario is worse for both economies than if they were to engage in cooperation. By cooperation Europe could agree to pursue policy 2 and America agree to pursue policy 4. This policy configuration gives both countries a misery index of only 8, which is superior to the 12 of acting in isolation.

One of the problems for such cooperative agreements is that once there is an agreement there may be incentives for one or more parties to renege on the agreement. Suppose Europe and America agree to cooperate and pursue policies 2 and 4 respectively. If Europe is sure that America will adopt the agreed policy 4 then the best policy for Europe to pursue is not policy 2 to which it agreed, but rather policy 1. Similarly, if America is sure that Europe will pursue policy 2 then the best policy for it to pursue is policy 3 rather than policy 4. Hence, it is possible that cooperative agreements will be undermined at times by reneging by one or more parties to the agreement. As such, there may need to be stiff penalties against parties that renege and a monitoring system designed to spot any reneging country.

14.6 Other potential benefits from coordination

The Hamada diagram and pay-off matrix illustrations provide simple demonstrations of the potential gains to be had from international policy coordination. However, the analysis is simple in that each country is assumed to know the range of potential policies that the other country could pursue and can also calculate the consequences of various policy combinations on its own welfare. In the real world we can expect some gains from coordination that are not well-illustrated by traditional game theory, these include:

- **Reduction of uncertainty.** One of the major benefits to be expected from cooperation is that it should help reduce the uncertainty element associated with the implementation of policy. When economies are interdependent, the course of action that a country should take will be difficult to decide in isolation because the optimal policy will depend upon the policy actions of others. In the real world a country rarely knows the course of action that will be taken by other economies and their probable reactions to changes in its own policy stance. Coordination has the potential to reduce the possibility of serious conflict. An exchange of information improves the information set available to the authorities enabling them to pursue superior policies than could be pursued without such information. In the absence of an information exchange, there may be serious shortcomings in policy design, particularly with regard to miscalculation about the reactions of foreign authorities. Such errors could prove very costly in today's interdependent economies. Furthermore, the reduced possibility of conflict will improve the environment in which international trade is conducted.

- **Coordination may avoid excessive deflation.** Oudiz and Sachs (1985) point out that coordination may prove crucial to improving welfare when the foreign exchange market is forward-looking. One way that authorities may be tempted to control inflation in isolation is to announce today that money supply growth will be lower in the future. If such an announcement is believed, the authorities of that country will benefit from an immediate real appreciation of their currency reducing present inflation. The other country, however, will experience a real depreciation of its currency giving a boost to its inflation rate. In the absence of coordination both countries may be tempted to engage in competitive announcements of intentions to control future monetary growth. Only a coordination agreement between the two countries to avoid such a competitive manipulation of the exchange rate can remove the danger of excessive deflation.

14.7 The potential for coordination to make countries worse off

There is an intuitive inclination to believe that international policy cooperation must improve the welfare of each of the countries involved and thereby global welfare as compared to non-coordination scenarios. This intuition runs as follows: since at worst countries could cooperatively agree to pursue similar policies as in a non-coordination scenario, then the policies they choose under coordination must be superior or they would have pursued the non-cooperative policies. However, the literature has shown that this is not necessarily the case. There are three instances in which coordination between two or more countries may make the participating countries worse off rather than better off. One involves an unfavourable reaction by private agents to coordination between authorities; another involves an unfavourable reaction by third countries to coordination between a sub-set of countries. A final instance involves coordination making countries worse off because the policies pursued are based on the wrong economic model.

The reaction of private agents

Kenneth Rogoff (1985) pointed out that coordination between national authorities is only potentially superior to non-coordination because it is necessary to take into account the reaction of the private sector. The basic argument put forward by Rogoff is that the behaviour of private agents cannot be considered by the authorities as indifferent to any arrangements that they come to with trading partners. Rogoff argues that an adverse reaction by private agents to a cooperative arrangement between national authorities can make things worse rather than better.

Specifically, Rogoff considers the case where national authorities seek to raise the level of employment in their economies in a model in which there is exchange rate overshooting. Acting in isolation, each country resists the temptation to inflate because they realize that this will lead to a real depreciation of their currencies which will raise import costs and lead to a quick upward adjustment to domestic wages and prices. If, however, the central banks come to an agreement to inflate together to raise employment levels, they can overcome the fear a depreciation of their real exchange rate. This means that with coordination the incentives to inflate are greater. Rogoff argues that rational private agents will take this additional inflation risk into account when setting their wage contracts and raise their wage demands accordingly. In such circumstances, the authorities may face a higher average inflation rate in a coordination regime than acting in isolation.

The possibility that coordination between authorities may lead to a deterioration in global welfare stems from a credibility problem *vis-à-vis* the private sector. Rogoff suggests that one way to remove this adverse risk of policy coordination is for the coordinating governments to make institutional changes to improve their credibility, such as making their central banks independent with a statute committing them to price stability (low inflation). This would then remove private agents' mistrust of the authorities enabling them to coordinate to improve their economic welfare.

The reaction of third countries

It is conceivable that cooperation between two or more countries that would ordinarily raise their joint welfare could provoke an adverse reaction by third countries. If an adverse reaction by third countries has a significant negative impact on the coordinating countries then its is possible that the cooperating countries end up worse off. For example, Europe and America might decide to deflate their economies in their joint interest, but because of the adverse effects for Japanese exports this may lead Japan to deflate its economy which then exacerbates the recession in America and Europe above what they anticipated, making them worse-off than if they had not agreed to joint deflation.

Cooperation based on the wrong model

Frankel and Rockett (1988) argue that cooperation may prove inferior to non-cooperation due to the presence of uncertainty over the true economic model. In a world of uncertainty, the structural parameters and linkages between economies as well as the relationship between instruments and targets are not known for sure. Given this, it is possible that if countries agree to coordinate their monetary and fiscal policies based on particular models of their economies and the model(s) used turn out to be the wrong model(s) the agreed cooperative policies may be seriously defective and make one or both countries worse-off as compared to non-coordination. The results of the Frankel and Rockett study are considered more fully in the following section.

14.8 Estimates of the benefits and losses from international policy coordination

While it is practically impossible to measure the benefits or losses from international policy coordination in the real world, because of the perennial problem of estimating what would have happened in the absence of coordination, this has not prevented a number of researchers using economic models to make simulation estimates of the potential gains/losses associated with international macroeconomic policy coordination. One of the most interesting studies is that carried out by Frankel and Rockett (1988).

To estimate the potential benefits from international policy coordination Frankel and Rockett used 10 different economic models, as listed in **Table 14.1**. These models are representative of a variety of economic methodologies ranging from detailed large-scale structural models to more reduced-form models of economies. The models reflect a spectrum of Keynesian, monetarist and neoclassical schools of economic thought.

The basic methodology used by Frankel and Rockett is as follows: each government is assumed to believe that one of the 10 models is the correct economic model and may or may not be correct in that assumption. For example, two possible scenarios are that the US may believe in the MCM model, while Europe may believe in the OECD model, or the US believes in the OECD model while Europe believes in the EEC model. In some cases, the two countries may believe in the same model. Each country agrees to coordinate with the other country to maximize their perceived joint welfare as compared to the perceived Nash non-cooperative outcome. In total there are 100 coordination scenarios to examine, because for each of the 10 models that the USA might believe in, there are 10 alternative models that the Europeans could use.

For each of the 100 scenarios Frankel and Rockett examine the welfare effects for both the USA and Europe of the coordination scenario as compared to the Nash non-cooperation scenario. To measure the potential welfare gain or loss to each country from coordination under the various scenarios it is necessary to know what the true model is. For each of the 100 scenarios, Frankel and Rockett examine the welfare gains/losses to the USA and Europe by assuming in turn that each of the 10 models is true. For example, in the scenario where the USA believes in the MCM model and Europe believes in the OECD model, the potential gains/losses in welfare to each of the two parties are examined by assuming that in turn the MCM model is true, then the EEC model is true then the EPA model is true, and so on. This means that there are 100 times 10, that is 1,000 possible welfare gain/loss scenarios for each country to examine.

Frankel and Rockett discover that out of the 1,000 possible combinations of coordination between the two economies, US welfare was improved in 546 cases, while it ended up worse-off in 321 cases and its welfare was unchanged in 133 cases. Europe's welfare was improved in 539 cases while it ended up worse-off in 327 cases and its welfare was unchanged in 134 cases. Hence, although on balance a country is likely to gain from coordination, there remains a very significant chance (approximately 32%) that it will end up worse-off as a result of coordination because coordination has been based upon the wrong economic model. Even these results are slightly biased in favour of coordination because in instances where at least one of the countries is using the correct model, coordination is bound to be beneficial to that country or it would not have agreed to coordinate. By excluding such cases there are 810 combinations where neither country is correct. In these cases, the USA has gains in 419 cases, losses in 286 cases and no effect in 105. For Europe there are gains in 408 cases, losses in 298 and no effect in 104.

Frankel and Rockett recognize that the above methodology may underestimate the case for coordination because policy-makers do not explicitly take into account the possibility that the model they utilize may be invalid. If policy-makers take into account the presence of model uncertainty, then the probability of success from coordination is significantly raised; a result that is confirmed by Ghosh and Masson (1988). Holtham and Hughes-Hallett (1987) show that by eliminating instances where one of the countries expects the other countries to be worse-off according to its model considerably enhances the probability of coordination raising the welfare of the countries concerned. They argue that in practice governments will wish to avoid circumstances where they benefit and the other country is made worse-off (so called 'weak bargains') from coordination because this would encourage the other country to renege and jeopardize future coordination between the countries.

With regard to the magnitude of gains from international policy coordination, a number of authors such as Oudiz and Sachs (1984), Oudiz and Sachs (1985) and Frankel and Rockett (1988) have shown that the potential welfare gains from macroeconomic coordination are not very high, even under conditions very favourable to coordination. These conditions are that both countries use the same model and that model is in fact the true model; in such circumstances cooperation must leave both parties better-off or they would not cooperate. Oudiz and Sachs (1985) calculate that even in the case where the USA, Japan and West Germany coordinated their fiscal and monetary polices perfectly for the mid-1970s the gains from coordination were less than 0.5% of GNP for each country. Marcus Miller and Mark Salmon (1985) argue that in the long run there are no gains from international coordination, since in each country the equilibrium level of output is determined by a vertical Phillips curve and floating exchange rates permit the desired level of inflation to be achieved without the need for international policy coordination. They conclude that; 'What gains there may be from coordination must come therefore, in choosing the path towards equilibrium and not in the final equilibrium.'

Although the gains from international coordination seem to be relatively small, using a somewhat different methodology can substantially raise the gains from coordination. McKibben and Sachs (1991) find that monetary policy coordination brings about relatively insignificant gains but a combination of both monetary and fiscal coordination leads to more significant gains. Often coordination is brought about because economies are afflicted by common shocks. Currie, Levine and Vidalis (1987) find that while the gains from cooperation are small in the case of transitory shocks, the estimated gains rise steeply as the persistence of a shock increases. In a similar vein, Holtham and Hughes-Hallett (1987) find that the gains from international coordination in the face of permanent shocks can amount to 4–6% of GDP.

More recently there has been an interest in using the new open-economy macroeconomic (NOEM) models, which are based upon microeconomic foundations and monopolistic competition with explicit consumer utility functions to analyse the potential gains to be had from monetary cooperation (see **Box 7.2**). Results obtained from these models are very sensitive to the parameter values assumed and particular model specification employed. In an early analysis of the issues, Obstfeld and Rogoff (2002) found the gains from monetary policy coordination to be negligible. However, in a recent paper Tchakarov (2004) finds that the gains from international monetary policy coordination can be as high as 2.2% of steady-state consumption when different plausible parameter values to those employed by Obstfeld and Rogoff (2002) are used. It seems that the NOEM models are unable to resolve the controversy about the potential benefits from international policy coordination!

Before concluding this section, it is worth remembering that even if the true model were employed by coordinating countries, the rules required to achieve fully optimal policy coordination are likely to prove to be extremely complex, too complex to be implemented in practice. Given this, estimates of the gains from fully optimal coordination even though not particularly pronounced probably need to treated as generous estimates of the real-world benefits from coordination. This critique is particularly applicable to the NOEM models which require an implausible amount of computational ability on the part of economic agents and policy-makers.

14.9 Problems and obstacles to international policy coordination

The previous section showed that international policy coordination may have a role in raising global welfare even though the precise gains will be difficult to quantify. Indeed, there are plenty of real-world examples of countries involving themselves in some form of international coordination, membership of the Bretton Woods system, the EMS, European Monetary Union and the IMF and OECD are all examples of differing types of international macroeconomic cooperation and coordination. However, casual observation suggests that the degree of observed international policy coordination falls far short of the degree of interdependence between economies. For this reason, we need to consider some of the major obstacles that inhibit greater international macroeconomic policy coordination.

Negotiation and reduced flexibility costs

Once a country decides to try and improve its welfare by engaging in international policy coordination, an obstacle to it actually achieving a successful coordination package is the negotiation process. Reaching agreement on a successful international macroeconomic policy stance can prove extremely difficult and complex and this complexity will increase exponentially with the number of targets, instruments and countries involved in the process. In addition it is difficult for many governments to precommit themselves in areas such as fiscal policy. This being the case, international macroeconomic policy coordination is more likely to yield results when the number of countries is small and objectives are limited. Once a coordination package is agreed upon, it is likely that policy-makers will find that they have less flexibility and there will be delays when implementing their policies as they have to obtain agreement from other countries when altering their policies.

Disagreement over appropriate macroeconomic policies

One of the major obstacles to greater coordination is not so much a ignorance on the part of policy-makers to the potential benefits to be derived, but rather disagreement over how to realize them. The debate in macroeconomics over the role, impact and effectiveness of fiscal and monetary policies and major international policy issues such as the desirability of fixed and floating exchange rates is far from settled as a reading of this book reveals! This disagreement is not restricted to the quantitative effects of given policy mixtures but often concerns the qualitative aspects. Uncertainty also exists over the appropriate instrument to employ to achieve a given policy objective. This uncertainty over means–ends relationships leaves enormous scope for disagreement between countries that share similar objectives. As Ralph Bryant puts it:

In real-life discussions among national governments, the most fundamental obstacle to more cooperation is not lack of awareness of the potential gains from coordination. Nor is it merely lack of political will. To be sure, both those lacunae are important . . . Yet a still more important obstacle is the tremendous uncertainty about the magnitudes, and even the signs, of cross-border transmissions of economic forces. (1985, p. 216)

The point is that theoreticians that analyse the benefits to be derived from coordination using a game theoretic approach in which the pay-off matrix is known simplify the obstacles to agreement between policy-makers who don't know the pay-off matrix or the best policies to pursue to reap gains from coordination.

Indeed, this lack of agreement over the best policy exists just as much within as between countries. Such disagreement extends to differences of view over the current state of the economy and what are the appropriate priorities for the economy.

Not all countries gain from coordination

If the pay-off matrix is known and means–end relationships are fairly clear, it may be possible for policy-makers to improve their joint welfare by cooperation. However, designing a cooperative policy that maximizes joint welfare does not necessarily mean that each individual country which is party to the agreement necessarily gains; it may be the case that some countries are made worse-off when designing a cooperative agreement. In such circumstances, to make it worthwhile for loser countries to engage in policy cooperation it is necessary for some form of compensation to be paid. This is especially the case if the loser countries are the ones that have to make the biggest policy adjustments (from which other countries gain). In the real world, examples of compensation for countries that undertake macroeconomic policies that are beneficial to the rest of the world but harmful to themselves are difficult to cite. In practice, this means that cooperative agreements may be restricted to instances where all countries are made better-off which would accordingly reduce the potential gains from coordination.

Reneging and the problem of time consistency

Another potential problem with policy coordination is derived by using dynamic game theory, and this highlights the problem of time consistency (see Kyland and Prescott 1977). A policy is said to be time inconsistent if there is an incentive to depart from the policy at any time now or in the future. A time-inconsistent coordination arrangement would imply that there are incentives for one or more of the countries that are party to a coordination package to renege, either in the present or sometime in the future. Using advanced game theory, Currie and Levine (1985) have shown that the problem of time consistency can pose a major threat to coordination. The reason is that a country which reneges on a time inconsistent cooperative agreement may retain an advantage in the long run. Moreover, the threat of retaliation by a partner country may not be credible because such retaliation would make the retaliating country worse off. An associated problem is that making a cooperative agreement time consistent may lead to markedly inferior outcomes compared to a time-inconsistent fully optimal cooperative policy. While this may provide a strong incentive for far-sighted governments not to succumb to the temptation of reneging,

Currie and Levine suggest the need for innovative punishment clauses as part of cooperative agreements to overcome the threat of countries reneging.

In practice, governments may be very reluctant to renege on coordination agreements and would only rationally do so if the perceived benefits of reneging exceed the perceived costs. By breaking a cooperative agreement the authorities may face penalties from other countries and be excluded from future participation in cooperative agreements. Currie, Levine and Vidalis (1987) argue that in practice these costs will comfortably exceed the benefits, making reneging a fairly rare phenomenon. In a similar vein, Hughes Hallet (1986) argues that the risks and associated costs of retaliation against cheating parties are relatively high, while the gains from a successful cheat are relatively low making cheating a risky strategy with a negative expected outcome.

14.10 Conclusions

International policy coordination is a very complex issue, posing new issues for policy-makers that do not arise if they pursue policies in isolation. These issues are so complex that we should not expect coordination to yield globally optimal solutions. In practice, coordination is likely to remain restricted to certain domains such as the exchange of information, exchange rate policy and monetary policy where means–ends relationships are reasonably clear (avoidance of conflicting policies, preservation of trade flows and inflation control) and the potential gains from coordination greatest. However, Europe is currently engaged on an attempt to coordinate its fiscal policy rules in the form of the Stability and Growth Pact which restricts the size of budget deficits in the Eurozone area to less than 3% of GDP, already this cooperative agreement has come under severe stress (see Chapter 15) with two of the key countries France and Germany exceeding the prescribed deficits.

It is noticeable that cooperation has proved easier in the trade arena with such arrangements as the General Agreement on Trade and Tariffs (now the World Trade Organization) and the European Union. There is a large consensus in the trade literature that increased trade is beneficial for all countries, which contrasts with the lack of agreement in the international macroeconomic sphere with arguments over the merits of fixed, floating and managed exchange rates and controversy over the role and effectiveness of fiscal and monetary policy in influencing economic activity.

While uncertainty can prove to be a major obstacle to greater international coordination, this should not be overstated. Uncertainty can at times prove to be an incentive to international coordination; the exchange of information motivated by the desire to avoid policy conflict is one of the most common types of coordination that actually takes place in the real world. In addition, countries have been sufficiently uncertain about the relative merits of over and undervalued exchange rates that they have not become involved in competitive exchange rate manipulations. An overvalued exchange rate in relation to PPP has been viewed as advantageous in the fight against inflation, while an undervalued rate is viewed as useful in giving a boost to exports and employment. This uncertainty may account for the lack of 'exchange rate wars' experienced under floating rates despite the major real exchange rate changes that have occurred.

The move from fixed to floating exchange rates has coincided with a decline in the relative economic influence of the United States. The Bretton Woods system has been analysed as a situation where the USA was the leader and Europe and Japan were followers, as in a Stackleberg scenario. Since the adoption of floating exchange rates the relative economic dominance of the USA has declined while the economic importance of Europe and Japan has risen, such that the Stackleberg scenario is no longer an adequate characterization. In such a tripolar world the dangers of a Nash-type scenario are ever-present, especially given the extra degree of freedom associated with floating exchange rates.

A useful distinction can be made between global and sub-global coordination. Global coordination involves countries from different regions of the world that have a significant impact on the global economy. The three countries that qualify in this category are the United States, Japan and Germany. Sub-global coordination refers to coordination between countries which are not necessarily important at the global level but that have a high degree of structural interdependence with one another. The Bretton Woods system represented an example of global coordination, whereas the European Monetary System and its replacement by the European Monetary Union represents an example of sub-global coordination. The move from a US-dominated world to a tripolar one has to date increased the importance of sub-global coordination relative to global coordination, though there is no obvious reason for this.

The theoretical and simulation literature has served as a warning that policy-makers should not expect substantial gains from the coordination of economic policies internationally. Although this message may sound pessimistic, in many ways it is a reflection of the increasing scepticism concerning the ability of governments influence the real economy in a desirable and predictable fashion via manipulation of fiscal and monetary policies even in a closed economy framework.

Further reading

Artis, M. and Ostry, S. (1986) *International Economic Policy Coordination*, Chatham House Papers no. 30 (London: Routledge & Kegan Paul).

Bryant, R.C., Currie, D.A., Frenkel, J.A., Masson, P.R. and Portes, R. (eds) (1989) *Macroeconomic Policies in an Interdependent World* (Washington: IMF).

Cooper, R.N. (1985) 'Economic Interdependence and Coordination of Economic Policies', in R.W. Jones and P. B. Kenen *Handbook of International Economics*, Vol. II (Amsterdam: Elsevier).

Currie, D. (1990) 'International Policy Coordination', in D.T. Llewellyn and C. Milner (eds), *Current Issues in International Monetary Economics* (London: Pilgrave Macmillan).

Currie, D.A., Holtham, G. and Hughes Hallett, A. (1989) 'The Theory and Practice of International Policy Coordination: Does Coordination Pay?', in R.C. Bryant, D.A. Currie, J.A. Frenkel, P.R. Masson and R. Portes (eds), *Macroeconomic Policies in an Interdependent World* (Washington: IMF).

Currie, D.A., Levine, P. and Vidalis, N. (1987).'International Cooperation and Reputation in an Empirical Two-Bloc Model', in R. Bryant and R. Portes (eds), *Global Macroeconomics: Policy Conflict and Cooperation* (London: Palgrave Macmillan).

Frankel, J.A and Rockett, K.E. (1988) 'International Policy Coordination When Policymakers Do Not Agree on the True Model', *American Economic Review*, vol. 78, no. 3, pp. 318–340.

Frenkel, J.A. (1983) 'Monetary Policy: Domestic Targets and International Constraints', *American Economic Review Papers and Proceedings*, pp. 48–53.

Ghosh, A.R. and Masson, P. (1988) 'International Policy Coordination in a World with Model Uncertainty', *IMF Staff Papers*, vol. 35, pp. 230–58.

Group of 30 (1988) *International Policy Coordination*, London.

Hamada, K. (1974) 'Alternative Exchange Rate Systems and the Interdependence of Monetary Policies', in R.A. Aliber (ed.), *National Monetary Policies and the International Financial System* (Chicago: University of Chicago Press).

Hamada, K. (1976) 'A Strategic Analysis of Monetary Interdependence', *Journal of Political Economy*, vol. 84, pp. 677–700.

Hamada, K. (1985) *The Political Economy of International Monetary Interdependence* (Cambridge, Mass.: MIT Press).

Holtham, G. and Hughes-Hallett, A. (1987) 'International Policy Cooperation and Model Uncertainty', in R. Bryant and R. Portes (eds), *Global Macroeconomics: Policy Conflict and Cooperation* (London: Macmillan).

Hughes Hallet, A. (1986) 'International Policy Design and the Sustainability of Policy Bargains', *Journal of Economic Dynamics and Control*, vol. 10, pp. 467–94.

Kyland, F.E. and Prescott, E.C. (1977) 'Rules Rather than Discretion the Inconsistency of Optimal Plans', *Journal of Political Economy*, vol. 85,pp. 473–91.

McKibben, W.J. and Sachs, J. (1991) *Global Linkages, Macroeconomic Interdependence and Cooperation in the World Economy* (Washington: Brookings Institute).

Miller, M. and Salmon, M. (1985) 'Policy Coordination and Dynamic Games', in W.H. Buiter and R.C. Marston (eds), *International Economic Policy Coordination* (Cambridge: Cambridge University Press).

Obstfeld, M. and Rogoff, K. (2002) 'Global Implications of Self-oriented National Rules', *Quarterly Journal of Economics*, vol. 117, pp. 503–35.

Oudiz, G. and Sachs, J. (1984) 'Macroeconomic Policy Coordination Among the Industrialized Economies', *Brookings Papers on Economic Activity*, vol. 1, pp. 1–64.

Oudiz, G. and Sachs, J. (1985) 'International Policy Coordination in Dynamic Macroeconomic Models', in W.H. Buiter and R.C. Marston (eds), *International Economic Policy Coordination* (Cambridge: Cambridge University Press).

Rogoff, K. (1985) 'Can International Monetary Policy Cooperation be Counterproductive?', *Journal of International Economics*, vol. 18, pp. 199–217.

Steinherr, A. (1984) 'Convergence and Coordination of Macroeconomic Policies: The Basic Issues', *European Economy*, pp. 69–110.

Tchakarov, I. (2004) 'The Gains from International Monetary Cooperation Revisited', IMF Working Paper WP 04/01, Washington.

Wallich, H.C. (1984) 'Institutional Cooperation in the World Economy', in J.A. Frenkel and M.L. Mussa (eds), *The World Economic System: Performance and Prospects*, (Cambridge, Mass.: Dover).

15

The International Debt Crisis

15.1 Introduction

On 12 August 1982, the Mexican government announced that it could not meet its forthcoming debt repayments on its $80 billion of outstanding debt to international banks. This was the first sign of the international debt crisis. Soon after the Mexican announcement a number of other developing countries announced that they too were facing severe difficulty in meeting forthcoming repayments. Throughout the 1980s and 1990s and the early part of the new century the problems faced by the developing countries in servicing their debts has been one of the major international policy issues, and granting of debt relief has recently also become a major policy issue.

The debt crisis encompassed a wide set of countries from low-income developing nations to middle-income countries. In this chapter, we concentrate primarily upon four countries that were classified by the World Bank in its 1994 *World Debt Tables* as severely indebted middle-income countries (SIMICs), that is Argentina, Brazil, Mexico and Venezuela. In its 2004 *Global Development Finance Report* the World Bank classification of a SIMIC is that the country must be a middle-income country (an annual income of between $736 and $9,075 per capita) and have one of two key ratios above certain critical levels. These ratios are the present value of debt to gross national income (GNI) (80%) and the present value of debt to exports of goods and services (220%). Other than the SIMICs there is a group classified moderately indebted middle-income countries (MIMICs), a group classified as severely indebted low-income countries (SILICs), and a group of moderately indebted low-income countries (MILICs) and less-indebted middle-income countries (LIMICS). As we shall see, in 2002 only Argentina and Brazil of the four countries we examine remained classified as SIMICs with Mexico and Venezuela having shown a marked improvement resulting in them being listed as LIMICs.

Although they were both severely indebted, there are considerable contrasts between the SIMICs and the SILICs. The 15 SIMICs identified by the World Bank in 1994 were especially concentrated in Latin America, and in 1994 their combined external debt amounted to $587.4 billion the majority of which was owed to private sources made up primarily of commercial banks. By contrast, the majority of the 35 SILICs identified by the World Bank in 1994 were to be found in sub-Saharan Africa, and in 1994 their combined external debt amounted to $223.6 billion with the vast majority owed to governments and official agencies and the remainder to private sources.

The international debt crisis raised many questions. How did the crisis come about? Why did international banks lend so much money to these countries? Why did the indebted countries not go into outright default? How was the debt crisis managed? How successful has the management of the crisis been? What lessons can be learned from the crisis? In this chapter we examine possible answers to these questions. We pay special attention to the debt problems of the four major debtors located in Latin America – Mexico, Argentina, Brazil and Venezuela. The concentration of commercial bank loans in these four economies led to fears that if any of them defaulted, this would undermine the banks that lent to them, especially the US banks that had massive exposures, and threaten an international financial crisis. The resulting knock-on effects would push the world into a major economic recession.

15.2 The low and middle-income developing countries

The developing countries are traditionally distinguished from the developed economies by their lower per capita GNP. However, developed and developing countries are far from homogenous groups. Low-income developing countries can be placed into two categories:

- **Low-income developing countries** – typically with incomes of less than $735 per capita at 2002 prices, and these include most of sub-Saharan Africa.

- **Middle-income developing countries** – this group comprises a very wide range of countries with incomes in the region of more than $725 per capita and less than

$9,055 per capita at 2002 prices. Some of this group can be classified as low-middle-income countries, which includes most countries in Latin America with per capita incomes in 2003 being Argentina ($3,000), Brazil ($2,700), Mexico ($6,100) and Venezuela ($3,300), and many richer African countries.

15.3 Characteristics of typical middle-income developing countries

Since the debt crisis has been predominately confined to developing countries, especially those in the low-middle-income group, some discussion of the main features of such middle-income developing countries is necessary. Although it is difficult to generalize, the following represents a list of the main differences between developed and middle-income less-developed economies:

- **Financial markets**. The financial markets in developing countries tend to have a relatively limited range of investment opportunities for savers and are normally subject to a high degree of government control. Unlike developed countries that tend to have well-developed stockmarkets, developing countries' stockmarkets can be fairly rudimentary in nature and companies have traditionally been heavily reliant on banks for funding. Banks are usually either state-owned or subject to heavy government control aimed at maintaining low real interest rates designed to stimulate investment. A major problem that results from these low real interest rate policies is that it tends to further discourage saving which is already low because of low income levels. Low savings combined with low real interest rates lead to an excess demand for funds requiring credit rationing. Under credit rationing the decisions as to which industries can borrow and how much is largely determined by the government of the day. In addition, the low interest rates stimulate expenditure on imports contributing to balance of payments problems.
- **Exchange rate pegging and exchange controls**. The exchange rates of developing countries are frequently pegged to the US dollar, the euro or a mixture of currencies often on a 'crawling-peg' basis. Since developing countries tend to have relatively high inflation rates, pegging their currencies against foreign currencies which have lower inflation rates would be impractical as they would quickly lose competitiveness. For this reason, they frequently devalue the central rate against the currencies to which they are pegged. One of the problems with such crawling peg arrangements is that if the currency to which they are pegged appreciates, such as the strong dollar appreciation between 1980 and 1985, this can prove to be disastrous for the developing countries' exports. For this reason, some developing countries prefer to peg to a basket of currencies such as the SDR, that will tend not to appreciate or depreciate as much as an individual currency.

  In addition to pegging their exchange rates, many developing countries make extensive use of capital controls, with the central bank applying various restrictions on the purchase and sale of foreign currencies. These restrictions serve several purposes as far as the developing countries' governments are concerned. By restricting the ability of their residents to invest their savings abroad, the controls enable the government to borrow funds from its residents at a lower rate of interest than would otherwise be the case. Controls are usually heavily biased against capital outflows, restricting sales of the home currency and reducing the strain on foreign currency reserves which would otherwise be required to defend a pegged exchange rate.

The exchange controls normally require that home residents obtain government permission to purchase foreign currencies. Often the authorities combine the controls with multiple exchange rate systems, which means that the authorities may offer a different rate of exchange depending upon the nature of the particular transaction. For instance, if the foreign currency is required to pay for imports of capital equipment or essential items, the authorities will usually offer a more favourable rate of exchange than if it is required to pay for the import of luxury consumption goods. This is because capital imports and cheap prices for essentials are considered more favourable to economic development.

- **Low degree of diversification**. The output of less-developed economies is usually far less diversified than that of developed countries. Agricultural output can represent a fairly high proportion of GDP and usually their exports are made up of relatively few commodities, such as raw materials and agricultural goods. This means their economic performance can be subject to a wide degree of fluctuation due to bad harvests or changes in the value of their principal exports. The prices of primary products produced and exported by developing countries tend to fluctuate far more than the manufactured products of developed economies. This price variability means that the incomes and trade performances of developing countries can be subject to large year-to-year fluctuations. Recessions in industrialized countries are especially harmful to developing countries as they experience both a fall in the price of their primary products and a decline in their export volumes meaning large reductions in their export revenues.

- **Inflationary environment**. The developing countries tend to have persistent problems with controlling their inflation rates. Government budget deficits are frequently financed by the government resorting to money-creation, partly because the financial markets are too rudimentary to raise the required borrowing from domestic sources and partly governments find taxing their citizens to be politically unpopular and often easily evaded. The resulting inflation reduces the real value of money held by domestic residents constituting an 'inflation tax' and reduces the real value of outstanding government debt.

To protect workers' wages from the effects of the inflationary environment there can be a high degree of wage indexation so that wages rise in line with prices. Wage indexation makes it very difficult for the authorities to bring inflation under control because at the same time the authorities take measures to slow down future inflation, wages are being adjusted upwards on the basis of previous inflation. Indexation also means that real wages are difficult to reduce should an economic shock such as a deterioration in the country's terms of trade require such a fall. Consequently, such shocks normally lead to increased unemployment. A rapidly growing workforce leads to a continuous upward pressure on government expenditure to provide employment in state enterprises.

15.4 The economics of developing country borrowing

A key question relating to the debt problem is why were the middle-income developing countries eager to borrow and the commercial banks so willing to supply the funds in the first place? From the perspective of the developing countries, their combinations of low incomes and poorly developed capital markets mean that there is insufficient domestic savings to provide the finance for domestic investment. Their relatively low capital stock means that there are plenty of opportunities for profitable investment, and low capital to labour ratio means that the marginal productivity of capital is high. By borrowing funds from abroad they can raise domestic investment above domestic savings which in turn leads to a higher rate of economic growth than in the absence of such borrowing. The fact that investment then exceeds domestic savings implies that the country is running a current account deficit the counterpart of which is the capital inflow on the capital account. Later on, the developing country will have to repay the principal and interest on the loans extended to it. The hope is that the state of the economy will be such that repayments should present no problems.

As for the developed economies, their relatively high incomes and sophisticated financial markets lead to relatively high savings ratios, while their relatively high capital to labour ratios means that the marginal productivity of capital is relatively low restricting the amount profitable investment opportunities. This means that there is an excess of savings looking for appropriate investment opportunities, which exist in abundance in developing countries who in turn lack the required funds. Hence, there is the potential for profitable exchange between the developed and developing countries. The developing countries can utilize the excess savings of the developed countries for investment while the lending developed countries have higher prospective returns from investing in the developing countries than domestic investments.

15.5 Different types of capital inflows into developing countries

There are a variety of means available for developing countries to attract capital inflows from the developed economies to finance new investment.

- **Bond finance.** The developing countries' governments can issue bonds to foreign investors with a guaranteed rate of interest depending upon the maturity date of the bond and whether or not it is denominated in the domestic or foreign currency. If the bond is issued in the domestic currency it is subject to 'inflation risk' because there is a danger that higher than expected inflation in the issuing country could undermine the real redemption value of the bond. Alternatively, if the bond is issued in a foreign currency it is subject to 'default risk' which is the danger that the developing country will not be able to redeem the bond.
- **Bank loans.** The developing countries can borrow money from the commercial banks of the developed countries. Such loans are usually made either at fixed or floating rates of interest and may be of a short or long-term nature. During the 1970s and 1980s this was the major source of finance for the Latin American countries. The loans extended were predominately 'syndicated loans'; that is, loans made by syndicates of international banks. These loans were generally made in US dollars at floating rates of interest, such that the repayments could be adjusted upwards or downwards in line with changes in international interest rates. The key rate of interest for such loans being the dollar London Inter-Bank Offer Rate ($LIBOR), the rate of interest at which banks in London lend dollars to one another. Loans to developing countries are normally expressed as a margin over dollar LIBOR.

- **Foreign direct investment (FDI).** Another means by which the developing countries can raise foreign finance is by attracting direct foreign investment into the country. Such investment can take many forms, it could involve a foreign multinational acquiring equity in a domestically owned business, a multinational expanding an existing subsidiary, or foreign investors setting up a completely new enterprise in the developing country. Such direct investment is a popular method of multinationals investing in developing countries since it gives them both ownership and control over the businesses that they set up and acquire. In addition, it is regarded as a qualitatively different type of capital inflow representing a long term investment and a vote of confidence in the developing country.
- **Official finance.** In addition to private sources of foreign investment, the developing countries are also able to raise money for developmental purposes directly from foreign governments and international institutions. Loans from foreign governments are often made at below market rates of interest to developing countries as part of their foreign-aid programmes, while loans from the World Bank come at favourable rates of interest because the World Bank has a top credit rating which enables it to raise large sums of capital from private markets at a lower rate of interest than is possible for an individual developing country.

Overall, a clear distinction needs to be made between debt finance and equity finance. Debt finance of which bond, bank and official finance are examples, requires the debtor to repay the principal and the rate of interest attached to the loan whatever the economic situation in the debtor nation. If the country faces a worsening of its economic circumstances, it must repay the principal and interest on its outstanding debt regardless. This contrasts with equity finance whereby the foreign investors either own shares or have direct control of developing countries' companies. In these cases, the repayment for their investment is in the form of profits and dividend and changes in the value of the companies is directly related to the performance of the companies and the developing country concerned. If the developing country faces adverse economic conditions this will lead to less repayments to foreigners in the form of reduced profits and dividends, and conversely economic prosperity in the developing will lead to larger profits and dividend payments to foreign investors.

15.6 Measures of indebtedness

When deciding whether to extend a new loan or to make provisions against existing loans or even whether to write off parts of their outstanding loans, private banks will want to know the probability of the existing debt or new loan being repaid. This will enable them to balance the risk and return elements of the loan. The problem is that there is no unique indicator or measure of the burden imposed on a country by its external indebtedness. In order to assess the risks, banks will have to arrive at a view of the economic and political state of a country. In arriving at their decision on risks, banks rely on a range of indicators many of which are reported by the World Bank in its *Global Development Finance Report*. Some of the most popular statistics employed to assess country risk are:

- **External debt as a percentage of exports of goods and services.** This expresses the country's external debt both private, public and publicly guaranteed as a ratio

---

Box 15.1

Some debt terminology

Within the context of the international debt crisis, many terms are frequently employed and for this reason are worth defining:

- **Public and publicly guaranteed debt**. Most of the loans made to developing countries are made either directly to the developing country government or to state-owned enterprises, and such debt is known as public debt. Foreign loans to developing countries are frequently made to the private sector, but because such lending is regarded as highly risky, it is usually necessary for the developing country government to guarantee to fulfil the loan contract in the case of non-payment by the private borrower; this type of obligation is known as publicly guaranteed debt. The presence of exchange controls in many developing countries means that the developing countries' governments usually get involved in loan agreements between foreign and domestic residents.
- **Total external debt**. This is the sum of private non-guaranteed debt and public and publicly guaranteed debt.
- **Debt service**. This is the sum of principal and interest rate repayments that a country has to make during a given time period.
- **Default**. A developing country is said to be in default when it fails to make the repayments of principal and/or interest specified in its loan contract and has no intention of repaying in the future.
- **Moratorium**. A developing country announces its refusal to make the payments of principal and/or interest specified in its loan contract until it can come to an agreement over future repayments with its creditors. A moratorium differs from default in that the debtor has the intention to continue repayments later on provided it can reach suitable repayment arrangements with its creditors.
- **Debt rescheduling**. This occurs when all or part of the repayments of principal and/or interest due on outstanding debt are postponed to some date in the future. Importantly, when debt is rescheduled interest is payable on the postponed repayments.
- **Debt provisioning**. This is the term used when banks decide to set aside funds into their reserves to cushion themselves against the costs of a debtor nation defaulting on part of its obligations. The provisioning does not alter the contractual obligations of the debtor to repay its borrowing.
- **Debt forgiveness**. This occurs when the creditor writes off part or all of the principal and/or interest payable on an outstanding loan. Debt forgiveness thereby reduces the contractual obligations of the debtor.

---

of its export earnings. The idea is that the export earnings are the means by which the country earns foreign currency to pay off its debt. Problems with this ratio are that exports may be subject to a high degree of fluctuation from year to year and there are alternative measures a country can employ to pay off its external debt other than increasing its export revenues; for example, cutting down import expenditure or running down its foreign exchange reserves.
- **Reserves as a percentage of total external debt**. This is a measure showing the reserves that the central bank of the debtor nation could in theory use to pay off its external debt.

- **External debt as a percentage of gross national income**. This is a measure that gives an idea of the total debt burden in relation to the GNI of the country. However, it says nothing about the annual burden imposed on the country, the amount of repayments falling due or which section of the community the burden will fall upon.
- **Total debt service as a percentage of exports of goods and services**. This measures the public and publicly guaranteed principal and interest repayments that the country has to make as a percentage of it exports of goods and services. It gives an indication of the annual burden facing a debtor in relation to its export earnings. The major problem is the effects of variations in export earnings and this measure only gives the burden for the particular year under consideration.
- **Total debt service as a percentage of gross national income**. This figure measures the public and publicly guaranteed principal and interest repayments that the country has to make as a percentage of its GNI.

Of course, other statistics such as the evolution of the current account, unemployment rates and the rate of growth of GDP are usually taken into account when assessing the risk of lending to a given country. Other non-economic variables which rely upon judgement are also used, including the likelihood of internal conflict, degree of religious conflict, wealth disparity measures and so forth. It is apparent that no individual indicator can provide an adequate measure of the complexity of a country's debt problem, and for this reason the various debt measures are usually weighted to provide a formal index measure of the probability of default. Nonetheless, there is plenty of scope for assessments to differ depending upon the list of variables chosen and then the weight attached to each measure.

Even when used in combination, the various measures do not necessarily provide an accurate picture of the creditworthiness of different countries. They neglect factors such as the differing degrees of vulnerability to external shocks, differing capacities to increase export earnings and differing future economic prospects of the economies. In addition, there may be a difference between the ability of a country to service its external obligations and its willingness to do so, although the two are usually positively correlated. An understanding of country-risk assessment is an essential background to the study of the debt crisis because part of the blame for the crisis is attributable to the inadequacies of the measures used by the banks when extending loans to the debtor nations in the first instance.

15.7 Background and origins of the debt crisis

Although the debt crisis flared up in the early 1980s, the developing countries had previously defaulted on loan repayments in the 1930s. Bolivia had defaulted in 1931 and was followed by most other Latin American countries during the next three years. The effect of these defaults was to make developed countries extremely wary of lending to the developing countries on other than a short-term basis right up to the 1970s. Nevertheless, a great deal of direct investment in developing countries took place in the 1950s and 1960s, especially with a view to exploiting their raw material resources which were a necessary base for reconstruction and economic growth in the developed countries. The main threat posed to such investment was that of excessive taxation or even nationalization by the developing country concerned.

The origins of the debt crisis date back to the oil price shock following the Egypt–Israel war of October 1973. The quadrupling of the oil price was particularly harmful to the non-oil-producing developing countries, who experienced an enormous increase in their import expenditure, and on top of this the resulting recession in developed countries severely curtailed their export earnings. As a result of this the current account deficits of the developing countries rose from $8.7 billion in 1973 to $42.9 billion in 1974 and $51.3 billion in 1975. The terms of trade index of oil-importing developing countries deteriorated substantially between 1973 to 1975 from 100 to 40, this meant that in 1975 they needed two and a half times of export volumes for every unit of imports than they had in 1973.

While the oil price rise put the developing countries' and developed countries' current accounts into heavy deficit, the counterpart of this was that the OPEC members experienced a massive increase in their current account surplus which rose from $6.2 billion in 1973 to $66.7 billion in 1974. The absorptive capacity of the OPEC economies was such that this enormous increase in their incomes could not all be spent on increased imports of investment and consumption goods. In consequence, they placed much of the so-called 'petrodollars' on the London and New York money markets. OPEC members preferred to deposit their money with developed countries' financial centres rather than lend directly to oil-importing developing countries because they offered a security and range of investment opportunities for their funds that the developing countries could not compete with.

The enormous funds received by London and US banks raised the issue of how the banks could profitably utilize the money. The rise in inflation resulting from the oil shocks meant that real interest rates in industrialized countries were either low or even negative. By contrast, developing governments were keen to avoid having to adopt deflationary measures to control their current account deficits; instead they sought to borrow funds to finance the deficits. The alternative of an IMF adjustment package that would have severely curtailed economic growth was not considered particularly appealing.

The view prevalent among the international banking community that Latin America was set for high rates of economic growth, led to a 'recycling' of the petrodollars in the form of massive lending to the developing countries. Most of the loans made to the developing countries were made in dollars by syndicates of international banks with floating rates of interest based upon a margin over dollar LIBOR. Banks preferred to lend at floating rates of interest because the rates they paid on their deposits were variable; they were keen to protect themselves should the rates of interest they had to pay on deposits rise. The other side of the coin was that it left the developing countries exposed to the risk of a sudden rise in world interest rates. Since the vast majority of developing countries' borrowing was public or publicly guaranteed, the banks regarded the risk of any default on the debt as being negligible. It is of note that, at the time, the recycling was highly praised by governments and international institutions although the IMF was more cautious.

15.8 The emergence of the debt crisis

Although developing countries' indebtedness rose substantially from $130 billion in 1973 to $336 billion in 1978, the developing countries were experiencing healthy rates of economic growth and not having any particular difficulties in servicing their debts. However, a number of unfavourable factors led to a rapid deterioration of their indebtedness and ability to service their repayments over the following four years.

In 1979 the OPEC cartel more than doubled the price of oil from $13 per barrel to $32 per barrel. Industrialized countries' response to this second oil shock was more uniform than that following the first oil shock; they were determined to reduce the inflationary consequences even if this meant an increase in their unemployment levels. At the end of 1979 the US authorities adopted a tight monetary policy designed to control its inflation rate, with the UK, Germany, France, Italy and Japan adopting similarly tough policies. By contrast, the developing countries preferred to borrow further funds and their outstanding debt nearly doubled from $336 billion in 1978 to $662 billion in 1982. Cline (1984) has estimated that higher oil prices accounted for some $260 billion increase in non-oil-producing less-developed country (LDC) debt.

In addition to increasing indebtedness, there was a substantial rise in interest rates due to a rapid rise in the US budget deficit, with the dollar LIBOR interest rate rising from 9.5% to 16.6% between mid-1978 and mid-1981. The rise in interest rates was one of the major factors contributing to the severe world recession of 1981 to 1983. In turn, the recession had a devastating effect on the developing countries because it both dramatically reduced their export volumes and reduced the price of their exports, leading to a substantial fall in their export earnings. In addition, the recession induced the developed economies to adopt a more protectionist stance *vis-à-vis* imported goods which further squeezed developing countries' export earnings. **Table 15.1** shows the evolution of the current accounts of the big four debtor nations.

The high US interest rates and borrowing had two other effects. First, bankers were less willing to lend to the developing countries because of the increased attraction of lending the money to the USA. Second, the high interest rates contributed to a rapid real appreciation of the US dollar which in turn meant an increase in the real value of developing countries' debt-service repayments.

The result of all these factors was that in 1982 most developing countries, particularly in Latin America, found themselves both with record levels of indebtedness and debt-service repayments, while their ability to raise revenues to finance the repayments had greatly diminished. Much of the borrowing they had undertaken had not been

Table 15.1 Current account balance of the big four debtors, 1972–82 (percentage of GDP)

Year	Argentina	Brazil	Mexico	Venezuela
1972	−0.5	−2.9	−2.0	−0.7
1973	1.0	−2.7	−2.6	5.2
1974	0.1	−7.3	−4.0	22.0
1975	−3.3	−5.7	−4.6	7.9
1976	1.2	−4.3	−3.8	0.8
1977	2.2	−2.9	−2.3	−8.8
1978	2.8	−3.5	−3.1	−14.6
1979	−0.5	−4.7	−4.1	0.7
1980	−3.1	−5.3	−4.0	8.0
1981	−3.8	−4.4	−5.8	6.0
1982	−4.1	−6.1	−3.7	−6.3

Source: IMF, *International Financial Statistics.*

profitably used for investment purposes but merely wasted on inefficient state enterprises and maintaining artificially high consumption levels. Although we concentrate primarily on the external factors behind the debt crisis there is no doubt that domestic economic policy mismanagement played a major part in the debtors problems.

15.9 The Mexican moratorium

The debt crisis began with the Mexican moratorium which was announced on 12 August 1982. In the early 1980s the Mexican economy was facing a mixture of external and internal problems. Since the mid-1970s Mexico had been a major oil exporter and for this reason was a beneficiary of the rise in oil prices resulting from the 1973–74 and 1979 oil shocks. As the Mexican state both owned and controlled the oil industry, the revenues from oil sales accrued directly to the government. International bankers particularly in the USA looking at Mexican oil reserves viewed Mexico as a very safe place to lend money. Given its high oil revenues the Mexican government was keen to adopt a programme of increased public expenditure for improving Mexico's infrastructure and a variety of social programmes. The result was that the government ran a huge fiscal deficit which led to high economic growth. Overall, Mexico experienced a prosperous decade in the 1970s.

Following the second oil shock some major problems began to confront the Mexican economy. In the aftermath of the first oil shock the industrialized countries had taken measures to reduce their dependence on imported oil so that their response to the rise in oil prices following the 1979 price shock was more elastic than was the case in 1974. In addition, the major worldwide recession led to a further decline in the demand for oil. Mexico's relatively high inflation rate (27% in 1981) made the peso which was pegged to the US dollar increasingly overvalued. The peso overvaluation, combined with the authorities fiscal deficit (some 16.2% of GDP in 1982) and the decline in oil export revenues meant that Mexico's current account moved into a large deficit (12.5% of GDP in 1981 and 6.2% of GDP in 1982).

The Mexican economy's problems, especially the widely perceived view that its currency was overvalued, had for some time led to speculation that the peso would be devalued. Speculation against the peso meant large capital outflows and a fall in the reserve holdings of Banco de Mexico's (Mexico's central bank) reserves. In a bid to reduce the current account deficit the peso was devalued in February 1982, but the government failed to adopt other measures to control the deficit such as reducing its fiscal deficit and monetary growth rate. In such circumstances, the main effect of the devaluation was to give an additional boost to Mexico's inflation rate. The deteriorating position of Mexico's economy and the lack of confidence in its government's resolve to reduce its budget deficit made international bankers increasingly reluctant to extend further new loans Mexico.

Mexico's ever-increasing debt repayments, while its ability to service them was being undermined by its reduced export earnings, led to further speculation against the peso and a run on the Banco de Mexico's reserves. To stop a crisis developing, on 12 August 1982 the Mexican government announced a moratorium on its debt repayments until a satisfactory arrangement could be drawn up with its creditors. Mexico requested further new loans from foreign governments and a rescheduling of its principal repayments which were falling due. In addition, Mexico made a request for loans from the IMF in return for the adoption of an IMF-sponsored stabilization programme.

15.10 The dimensions of the debt crisis

As a result of the Mexican moratorium international banks began to realize that many other countries were facing similar difficulties in servicing their debt; **Table 15.2** shows the rapid growth of external debt for the big four debtors.

The real fear of both the banks and the authorities in the industrialized countries was that if Mexico went into default they would be quickly followed by other major debtors. Many US banks had more loans outstanding in Latin America than the value of their equity, as shown in **Table 15.3**, and a default by any of the big four debtor nations could easily have set off a chain reaction of banking failures and provoked a collapse of the banking systems in the developed countries. Not surprisingly, both the banks and authorities of the industrialized countries were determined to avert such a scenario.

Precisely how the banks got so heavily exposed with their developing country lending is not easy to explain (see Nunnenkemp, 1986, Chapter 7 for an extended discussion). In retrospect there were clear flaws in their credit-rating procedures and they got somewhat carried away with syndicated loans. As Graham Bird explains, the most simple and convincing explanation was that the banks made major mistakes:

> Certainly, looking back at the 1970s, it appears now that the banks overlent. With the benefit of hindsight, such overlending can be explained in a number of ways. With little recent evidence of country default, the banks probably underestimated the risks of lending. They probably lacked the information necessary to calculate such risks and they may have miscalculated the impact of world recession and rising interest rates on the position of the debtors. Beyond this, a belief that short term lending would enable them to extricate themselves if necessary and a confidence

Table 15.2 Total external debt of big 4 debtors, 1970–2002 (US $ millions)

Year	Argentina	Brazil	Mexico	Venezuela
1970	5,801	5,734	6,969	1,422
1972	6,028	10,165	7,028	1,712
1974	6,789	19,416	11,946	1,784
1976	8,258	29,031	20,520	3,311
1978	13,276	53,614	35,732	16,568
1980	27,157	70,838	57,378	29,310
1982	43,634	92,221	86,019	32,094
1984	48,857	105,015	94,822	36,881
1986	52,450	113,043	100,872	34,637
1988	58,741	119,344	99,213	34,738
1990	62,257	121,465	104,449	33,170
1992	65,397	130,547	112,227	37,848
1994	70,566	151,104	128,302	36,850
1996	81,588	181,322	156,255	34,490
1998	141,549	241,010	158,874	37,752
2000	145,879	238,793	150,313	38,152
2002	132,314	227,932	141,264	32,563

Source: World Bank, Global Development Finance (formerly World Debt Tables).

Table 15.3 US banks' exposure to five Latin American countries in 1982 (loan exposure as a percentage of bank capital)

Manufacturers Hanover	262.8
Crocker National	196.0
Citibank	174.5
Chemical	169.7
Bank of America	158.2
Chase Manhattan	154.0
Bankers Trust	141.2
Morgan Guaranty	140.7

Note: The five countries are Argentina, Brazil, Mexico, Chile and Venezuela.
Source: Nunnenkamp (1986), p. 102.

generated by the fact that other banks were also lending, as well as a belief that banks would not be allowed to go bust by national and international regulatory authorities, all had the effect of reducing their perceived risks. (1989, p. 17)

15.11 A supply and demand framework for analysing the debt crisis

Modelling the debt crisis is an extremely complex task because so many variables influence lending and borrowing decisions. Nevertheless, the explosion of new lending up to 1981 and the fall off after 1982 can be very approximately modelled using a supply and demand for new loans framework as illustrated in **Figure 15.1**. When

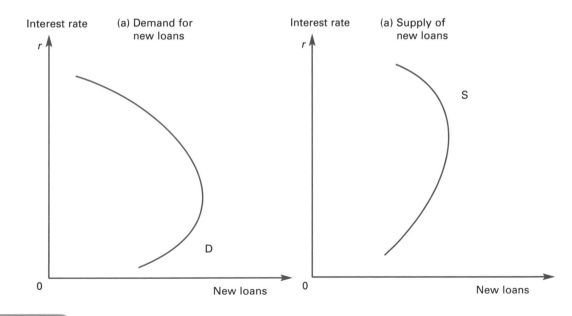

Figure 15.1 Supply and demand schedules for new loans

determining the slope of the supply and demand schedules for new loans problems are encountered because of the need to distinguish the effects of interest rate changes on the stock of outstanding debt. The demand for new loans comes from the debtor nation and is assumed to be inversely related to the rate of interest, as a lower rate of interest makes borrowing more attractive to debtor nations. However, it can be argued that lower interest rate payments, by reducing the debt-service payments on existing debt that a debtor has to make, may actually lead to a fall in its demand for new loans. If this latter effect is strong this may mean an upward-sloping demand schedule.

The supply of loans schedule is given by S and has been drawn positively-sloped initially but backward-sloping once interest rates rise to a certain level. The problem facing the banks is that new lending in the current period will decrease the incentives for debtors to default today while increasing the potential and incentives for the debtor to default in future periods. Hence, the banks will only be prepared to supply new loans in the current period if there is a sufficient rise in the interest rate to compensate. However, beyond a certain rate of interest there is a danger that debtors may be encouraged to default and for this reason, above this interest rate, the banks may be less willing to make new loans leading to a backward-sloping supply of new loans schedule.

For the purposes of our basic analysis, we shall assume that the supply and demand schedules have their conventional slopes. **Figure 15.2** illustrates the supply and demand for loans situation in 1973–1982 and 1983–94. In **Figure 15.2(a)** the supply and demand situation just prior to the first oil shock is represented by S1 and D1 with the corresponding new loans being L1. The OPEC oil shock affected both the supply and demand for funds. To finance their current account deficits there was an increase in demand for new loans represented by a rightward shift of the demand schedule from D1 to D2. The OPEC producers deposited their money balances on the international

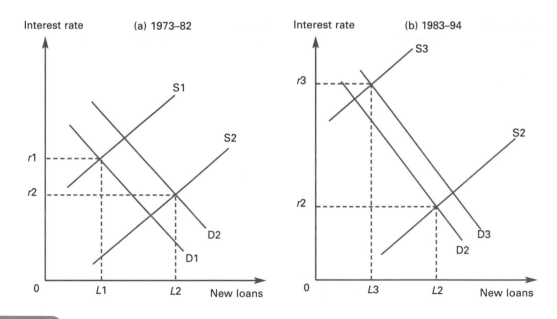

Figure 15.2 The supply and demand for new loans, 1973–94

money markets which greatly increased the supply of funds available for lending to the developing countries, and this is represented by a rightward shift of the supply of loans schedule to S2. In **Figure 15.2(a)** the shift of the supply schedule is assumed to be greater than the shift of the demand schedule so that the interest rate falls. Overall lending increases from $L1$ per annum to $L2$ while the interest rates remained fairly low.

The situation changed somewhat in 1982 and right up to 1994. While the demand for funds may still have been increasing from D2 to D3, there was a large leftward shift of the supply of funds from S2 to S3. This shift can largely be explained by the dramatic change in the perceived risks of lending to the debtor countries resulting from the Mexican moratorium. Another factor accounting for the supply shift was the increasing attractiveness of lending funds to countries like the United States due to the need to finance its increasing budget and current account deficit. As a result the interest rates charged rose while the volume of new lending declined.

15.12 The economics of default

Once the enormity of the debt crisis emerged the main aim of the commercial banks and authorities of the industrialized nations was to avoid one of the major debtor nations declaring default on its debt obligations. Much of the handling of the debt crisis since 1982 can be viewed as the authorities and commercial banks of developed countries adopting strategies designed to avert such a default, while at the same time attempting to minimize the financial losses for the banks involved. Since most of the loans taken out by the developing countries were government or publicly-guaranteed, any default would represent a sovereign default; the most important point about this type of default is that there are no legal remedies available for the creditors to retrieve their money. Nevertheless, debtor nations are normally very reluctant to default on their loans because the savings in the way of repayments are usually less than the perceived costs of declaring default. We now proceed to examine these potential costs of default.

The costs of sovereign default

Since a debtor government cannot be legally brought to account for a failure to repay its external debts, there must be some perceived costs associated with sovereign default that make countries reluctant to declare default. The three most commonly cited costs of declaring default are:

- **Exclusion from future borrowing.** A country that declares default on its external obligations is likely to be excluded from the possibility of future external borrowing. Those foreign creditors that lose from the default will not be prepared to lend further funds, while prospective lenders will view lending to the country as especially risky. In addition, creditor governments could prevent the IMF and World Bank making further funds available to the defaulting nation. Unable to attract foreign funds for investment purposes, the defaulting nation will be constrained to finance its domestic investment from its relatively low domestic savings which will limit its economic growth. In addition, the country will not be able to smooth out the costs associated with adverse economic shocks by borrowing on world capital markets.

- **Reduced gains from trade**. One of the major costs associated with default would be that the defaulting country would face the increased possibility of protectionist trade measures being adopted against it. There would be a risk that its exports could be subject to seizure when passing through international borders. Gaining trade credit to finance imports will prove difficult in the light of its default, and hence default is likely to result in a substantial reduction of the defaulting country's volume of trade and with it major welfare losses.
- **Seizure of overseas assets**. Although creditors of the defaulting country would be unable to take the debtor governments to court, they might be able to persuade their governments to freeze or seize assets of the defaulting nation held in the creditor's legal jurisdiction. Many developing countries' governments hold large proportions of their gold and foreign exchange reserves with central banks of the developed nations and they would be worried about the freezing of those assets if they were to default on loans extended by official creditors.

The perceived costs of default are especially worrisome for developing countries' governments because they are very difficult to quantify and plagued by uncertainty. A debtor government can only guess the extent and duration for which its trade volumes and borrowing capacity would be undermined. The costs of an individual debtor going into default while other debtors do not are likely to be particularly high, especially as creditors would want to demonstrate to other debtors that default is a costly option. If all major debtors were to declare default, the creditor nations would have considerably less scope to adopt penalties. This being the case, the creditor nations would have incentives to avoid the formation of debtors' cartels.

The benefits of default

The benefit from the debtor nation's viewpoint of defaulting is that it saves both the repayment of principal due and the interest due on his outstanding debt. Such a sum represents the debt-service repayment:

$$DS = P + r D \tag{15.1}$$

where DS is debt-service repayment, P is principal and interest due, r is the rate of interest and D is the stock of debt remaining. Equation (15.1) says that the debt service to be paid is the principal and interest due plus the interest payment on the stock of outstanding debt.

Although the debt-service ratio represents the payments that the debtor will be expected to make, it does not represent the net repayment, The net repayment is the debt service less net new loans received, which is known as the net resource transfer (*NRT*) from the debtor to the creditor nations.

$$NRT = P + r D - L = DS - L \tag{15.2}$$

where L is the net new loans received by the debtor.

The net resource transfer in this simple model can be thought of as the net saving or benefit from defaulting on the debt. Let us assume that the perceived costs of default are some constant value C. This being the case, the country will not default so long as the net resource transfer is less than the perceived costs of default. A country will not default on it debt provided:

$$NRT = P + r\,D - L < C \qquad (15.3)$$

while a country will default on its debt if:

$$NRT = P + r\,D - L > C \qquad (15.4)$$

Notice that according to equation (15.4) that since the costs of default are positive, a debtor will only consider default if the net resource transfer from the developing countries to its creditors is positive. In other words, the debtor's debt-service payments exceed the new loans that it receives implying a positive benefit from default that exceeds the positive costs of defaulting.

Equations (15.3) and (15.4) are very important in understanding the various strategies adopted by banks to encourage the debtor nations not to default. To avoid default the banks must keep the benefits of default lower than the costs of default, and this can be done by either raising the perceived costs of default or reducing the costs of servicing the debt. Commercial banks can persuade debtors not to default by a variety of mechanisms. They can reduce the principal repayments due by restructuring debt repayments over longer time horizons, they could reduce the interest rate repayments due on the stock of outstanding debt, reduce the stock of debt outstanding or engage in new lending. All these methods of reducing the perceived benefits from defaulting have cropped up in one form or another in the management of the debt crisis since its emergence in 1982.

15.13 The role and viewpoints of the actors in the debt crisis

There were very divergent views on the nature and extent of the debt crisis and these differences led to differing perspectives on how to best manage the crisis. These viewpoints were partly coloured by the differing interests of the four major actors involved, that is the international banks that lent the funds, the authorities of the developed nations, international institutions notably the World Bank and the IMF, and the debtor nations. We shall briefly overview their perspectives and roles in the crisis, although we need to be wary of treating these actors as homogenous groups. For example, the international banks that lent the money had differing degrees of exposure, faced differing regulatory and tax regimes and often had diverse views on the appropriate policy response. Likewise, the debtor nations had differing degrees of indebtedness, differing repayment burdens and prospects with regard to debt repayment. As for the national authorities, their economies had varying degrees of trading links and different historical and strategic relationships with the debtors.

The commercial banks

The immediate reaction of international banks to the emergence of the debt problem was to view it as primarily a 'liquidity crisis'. Bankers believed that high interest rates and a large amount of principal repayments falling due combined with adverse economic conditions had meant that the debtor nations were finding themselves in only short-term difficulties. To support this viewpoint it was argued that the debt profile of the debtors was primarily of a short-term horizon and that nations do not go bankrupt. As such, the banks early on sought solutions based upon restructuring debtors' repayments to give the debtors more time to pay. Banks initially preferred rescheduling debt repayments and at the same time sought to ensure that additional interest was paid on the postponed principal repayments. Following the onset of the crisis the banks were very reluctant to extend new funds to the debtors given the precarious position of their outstanding loans; many bankers took the view that extending new loans to the debtors was 'throwing good money after bad'. Despite this, the banks realized that without new loans the incentives for the debtors to default would rise and so some further lending was an essential part of restructuring packages designed to avert default.

Bankers were opposed to granting any debt forgiveness for a number of reasons. They argued that granting debt forgiveness to one country would lead other debtors to seek similar relief. Also debt relief might discourage the debtors from taking the measures necessary to improve their economic performance to ensure they qualify for debt relief. In addition, bankers argued that granting a country a degree of debt relief would brand it as uncreditworthy so that new loans to the country would dry up. In sum, the view of the banking community was that granting debt relief was too costly for banks to contemplate and ultimately harmful to the debtor nations themselves. Banks argued that any new lending to the Latin American countries should be carried out by the national authorities of the industrialized countries and international institutions. The banks were also keen to treat each debtor on a 'case-by-case' approach, motivated not only by a belief that the circumstances facing each debtor were different but also because the different creditor banks had varying degrees of exposure to each debtor making a uniform solution impracticable.

National authorities

The national authorities of the industrialized countries were primarily concerned to avoid a calamitous collapse of their banking systems which could result from a default by one of the major debtors. However, they were also extremely wary of utilizing public funds to ease the debtors' plight. Authorities did not wish to be seen to be 'bailing out' the commercial banks whose lending had gone bad. In addition, any significant assistance would be extremely costly and be at the expense of reduced public expenditure or increased taxes. A general feeling was that further loans by the authorities would not help when the problem of the debtors was having too much debt already. Nevertheless, the authorities (especially the US administration) had strategic and economic interests in Latin American debtors making it impossible for them to be indifferent to the debtors' plight. Rather than get involved in lending new money to the developing countries, most authorities were prepared to allow some tax concessions for provisions banks made against possible losses on their lending to developing countries. In addition, authorities were prepared to increase the amount of capital available to the World Bank and the IMF for lending to developing countries. Channelling funds via these institutions was considered useful because both the World Bank and the IMF could ensure the developing countries undertook appropriate measures to reform their economies and developing countries nearly always ensure repayment of funds to these institutions.

The IMF and the World Bank

The two main international institutions involved in the debt crisis played somewhat differing and at times conflicting roles although in the later stages there was a more coherent policy stance. The World Bank was very much concerned about the sheer size and extent of the debt crisis, and particularly the costs in terms of slower development that debt repayments impose upon the debtor nations. On the other hand, the IMF saw its main role as ensuring that the debtor nations that came to it for assistance adopted the tough economic measures required to improve their longer-term ability to service their debt. Another role played by the IMF was to ensure that creditor banks continued sufficient new lending to the debtor nations to make it worthwhile for the debtor nations to accept an IMF-sponsored adjustment package.

From time to time the two institutions came into conflict over the handling of the debt crisis, the World Bank criticizing the IMF for setting too severe economic adjustment programmes and to some extent taking infringing upon the Bank's traditional domain. Overall, the direct financial impact that the two organizations could make was very much limited by the amount of finance they had available. The World Bank had to be careful not to undermine its AAA credit rating by overextending itself to the SIMICs, while the amount of short-term finance provided by the IMF was quite limited compared to the extent of the debt crisis.

The debtors

The debtors to a large extent viewed the crisis that they found themselves in as not of their making but due to a combination of external factors beyond their control. As such, they felt that the creditor banks should allow some degree of debt-forgiveness in the form of reducing the stock of debt owed by the debtors and/or reduced interest rate repayments below market rates. Surprisingly, attempts to form a debtors' cartel to improve their bargaining positions *vis-à-vis* the creditor banks did not come to anything. This was partly because the debtors had differing debt problems and so were unable to agree on the way they could best be helped, while in addition the debtors were in competition with one another for whatever new lending was available and creditor banks were careful to treat them on a case-by-case basis rather than as a group. The debtors consistently argued their need for some debt forgiveness as an incentive to make economic adjustments in their economies. Without such relief they would have little incentive to adjust as all the improved economic performance would go to creditors to pay off their debts.

15.14 The management of the debt crisis

The debt crisis was managed throughout on a case-by-case basis, with the creditor banks dealing with each debtor nation individually rather than collectively as a group. Banks argued that this was the only realistic option because the problem confronting each of the debtors had its own particular characteristics, requiring its own solutions. Another advantage of this strategy from the viewpoint of the banks is that it helped to prevent the formation of a debtors cartel that would have resulted in an increased bargaining weight of the debtor nations. Despite this, however, there were common characteristics in the treatment extended to the debtors. The management of the debt crisis can be divided up into three distinct phases (1) the crisis-management phase 1982–October 1985, (2) the Baker Plan phase October 1985–March 1989, and (3) the post-Brady Plan phase March 1989–present.

Phase 1: crisis management, 1982–October 1985

Bankers initially perceived the crisis as a temporary 'liquidity' problem rather than as a solvency problem; it was argued that the debtors were facing a temporary financing problem due to the rise in US interest rates and a squeeze on their export earnings. As such, the main strategy was to reschedule the debt repayments falling due to avoid an outright default that would seriously threaten the financial stability of exposed banks and the banking community in general. A number of short-term debt rescheduling packages were arranged, the main features of which included a short-term (two to four years) maturity structure on the rescheduled debt, and interest and fees were chargeable for the rescheduling. An important point about the rescheduling agreements was that the banks only lent money so that the debtor countries could continue to service their debts – so-called 'involuntary lending' – all voluntary lending suddenly ceased.

It is important to note that debt rescheduling packages were not unconditional; the debtor had to accept an IMF adjustment programme as part of a rescheduling package, there being no point in extending new money to the debtors unless there were improved prospects of debt-service repayments being made. An IMF adjustment programme generally has the following features:

1 The setting of tight monetary and fiscal targets designed to squeeze aggregate demand in the debtor economies; the tight fiscal policy being based primarily on reducing government expenditure. The tight monetary policy involves the setting of targets for certain monetary aggregates designed to stabilize inflation.
2 A one-off devaluation of the debtor's real exchange rate to improve the country's international competitiveness.
3 Market-based reforms such as reducing food subsidies that distort the allocation of resources and reduced trade protectionism. The privatization of state-owned industries is generally encouraged since it raises finance and is believed to promote greater efficiency. In the financial sector the removal of interest-rate ceilings resulting in generally higher real rates of return is seen as a better means for allocating scarce capital and promoting domestic savings.

The measures have been aptly summed up as 'devaluation, deflation and deregulation'. Overall, the combination of reduced aggregate demand and improved competitiveness from the devaluation is designed to improve the debtor's current account balance and, thereby, its ability to finance its debt-service commitments. Such measures are often costly in the short term resulting in low and even negative economic growth usually accompanied by increased unemployment and rises in the prices of basic commodities such as food. Not surprisingly, IMF programmes can be very unpopular with the public in the debtor nations as they invariably mean reduced living standards.

Evaluation of the crisis-management phase
The crisis-management phase was almost exclusively about ensuring the financial stability of the banks that had lent to the debtor countries. As such, it was essential

that an outright default by any of the debtors be avoided, as such a default could have seriously endangered confidence in the banking system of the industrialized nations. The problem was that relatively little consideration was given to the needs of the debtor countries and that further debt in the form of 'involuntary' lending was piled upon already heavy debt loads. The initial appraisal of the crisis as a temporary liquidity crisis was also somewhat erroneous; the debt crisis was to prove far more serious and long-lasting. **Table 15.4** shows the evolution of external debt statistics and key ratios over the period 1982–2002.

The debtor countries suffered from an immediate drying-up of new bank lending and any funds extended to them were merely to ensure that they continued to pay their debts. Not surprisingly they suffered greatly during the crisis management phase and this was one of the factors that prompted the Baker Plan.

Phase 2: The Baker Plan phase, October 1985–March 1989

In October 1985 the US Treasury Secretary James Baker announced a major three-year initiative for managing the debt crisis. The Baker Plan was launched against a background of increasing disenchantment on the part of debtor nations over the recessionary impact of adjustment programmes and the drying-up of voluntary bank lending. The Plan endorsed the case-by-case approach to dealing with the debt crisis, that is treating each debtor nation in a manner appropriate to its individual circumstances. Baker envisaged debtor nations 'growing-out' of their debt problems by undertaking market-based structural reforms, including trade liberalization, cuts in government expenditure and relaxation of regulations relating to inward foreign investment. An enhanced role for the IMF and World Bank in promoting economic growth was envisaged via increased and more effective structural adjustment lending, and a target of $20 billion over the next three years was set for new lending by the commercial banks to the 15 major debtor nations; such additional lending by private banks being supported by a $10 billion increase in lending by multilateral development banks (mainly the World Bank and the Inter-American Development Bank).

An evaluation of the Baker Plan

Overall, the implementation of the Baker plan was not considered a success. Voluntary bank lending did not resume on the scale envisaged by the Plan and even official lending fell well-short of its target (see Cline, 1995) with only around $1 billion of the projected $10 billion increase being disbursed. Economic growth in Mexico, Brazil and Argentina stagnated and inflation rocketed (see **Tables 15.5** and **15.6**). Although their current account performance stabilized, their rates of economic growth, levels of investment to GDP and trade volumes exhibited a significant slowdown. Indeed, the overall levels of indebtedness and many of the debt service ratios continued to deteriorate.

The reasons for the failure of the Plan were fairly straightforward – there was little incentive for banks to extend further new loans when the problem of the region was already viewed as one of too much debt. Also, the Plan offered little incentive for the debtors to undertake new investment since any improved economic performance would merely result in increased payments to the creditor banks. As a result of economic hardship many countries were not in full compliance with the existing IMF programmes and were in continual dispute with the IMF over the content of stabilization programmes.

Table 15.4 External debt ratios of the big four debtors, 1982–2002

	Principal ratios (%)										
	1982	1984	1986	1988	1990	1992	1994	1996	1998	2000	2002
Argentina											
EDT/XGS	447.3	493.1	593.3	520.6	414.7	441.3	368.0	338.9	379.4	378.0	415.6
EDT/GNP	83.8	67.5	70.5	48.4	46.0	30.4	27.8	41.8	48.6	52.7	138.4
TDS/XGS	50.0	52.4	76.2	44.5	41.1	32.3	31.8	39.4	57.6	70.9	18.3
INT/XGS	36.7	44.1	48.7	27.5	18.1	18.2	19.6	18.8	24.0	30.1	8.1
INT/GNP	6.9	6.0	5.8	2.6	2.0	1.3	1.5	2.3	3.1	4.2	2.7
Brazil											
EDT/XGS	395.4	347.6	449.8	327.2	334.5	318.4	298.2	303.6	372.8	344.5	304.0
EDT/GNP	36.1	52.6	42.1	37.7	26.0	35.5	27.9	23.8	31.3	40.9	52.5
TDS/XGS	81.3	46.3	46.9	46.3	22.4	20.7	31.8	42.2	79.4	93.5	68.9
INT/XGS	49.2	31.3	31.3	34.7	6.1	9.3	12.9	17.5	23.9	24.6	19.6
INT/GNP	4.5	4.7	2.9	4.0	0.5	1.0	1.2	1.4	2.0	2.9	3.4
Mexico											
EDT/XGS	311.5	291.3	422.7	309.1	238.8	238.6	228.1	135.9	113.8	78.0	75.4
EDT/GNP	52.5	57.1	82.6	59.8	43.8	34.6	35.2	49.1	39.0	26.6	22.6
TDS/XGS	56.8	52.1	54.2	48.2	25.9	44.3	33.9	35.2	20.9	30.5	23.2
INT/XGS	40.4	34.7	35.1	27.1	16.7	16.0	14.2	10.1	7.9	7.3	5.8
INT/GNP	6.8	6.8	6.9	5.2	3.1	2.3	2.2	3.6	2.7	2.5	1.7
Venezuela											
EDT/XGS	159.8	195.6	307.8	273.4	154.5	220.9	198.8	128.4	174.7	101.3	111.2
EDT/GNP	41.4	63.8	58.7	59.4	70.3	64.6	64.0	50.1	40.2	31.8	35.6
TDS/XGS	29.5	25.2	45.3	43.7	23.2	19.4	19.9	18.4	27.9	16.2	25.6
INT/XGS	17.5	15.2	27.4	24.6	24.6	15.1	12.5	8.0	11.4	7.1	7.7
INT/GNP	4.5	5.0	5.2	5.3	6.9	3.7	3.7	3.1	2.6	2.2	2.5

Notes: EDT = total external debt; XGS = exports of goods and services; GNP = gross national product; INT = interest repayments; TDS = total debt service.
Source: World Bank, *Global Development Finance Reports.*

Table 15.5   Inflation rates of the big four debtor countries (% per annum)

Year	Argentina	Brazil	Mexico	Venezuela
1982	164.8	97.8	58.9	9.6
1983	343.8	142.1	101.8	6.3
1984	626.7	197.0	65.5	12.2
1985	672.1	226.9	57.7	11.4
1986	90.1	145.2	86.2	11.5
1987	131.3	229.7	131.8	28.1
1988	343.0	682.3	114.2	29.5
1989	3,079.8	1,286.9	20.0	84.2
1990	2,310.0	2,937.8	26.7	40.8
1991	272.0	440.9	22.6	34.2
1992	24.6	1008.7	15.6	31.4
1993	10.6	2,246.7	9.7	38.1
1994	4.3	2,075.9	6.9	60.1
1995	3.3	66.0	35.0	59.9
1996	0.2	15.8	34.4	99.9
1997	0.5	6.9	20.6	50.0
1998	0.9	3.2	15.9	35.8
1999	−1.2	4.9	16.6	23.6
2000	−0.9	7.0	9.5	16.2
2001	−1.1	6.9	6.4	12.5
2002	25.9	8.5	5.0	22.4
2003	13.4	14.7	4.5	31.1
2004	5.7	7.2	4.9	21.5

Source: IMF, *International Financial Statistics*, 2004 figures are forecasts.

The shift from Baker to Brady

The failure of official agencies to resolve the crisis meant that the banks increasingly sought other means of resolving their difficulties. From the mid-1980s a secondary market for developing country debt emerged on which the creditor banks could sell their outstanding loan assets to third parties (mainly other commercial banks) at a discount to its face value; the size of the secondary market was estimated by the IMF to be approximately $5 billion in 1985 and $30–40 billion in 1988. Part of the secondary market is made up of swaps between banks which enable them to reshuffle their loan exposure portfolios to various countries. The price of secondary debt of the 15 SIMIC (1994 classification) debtor nations plummeted from an average 70 cents to 35 cents per dollar over the period of the Baker Plan, reflecting the increasing probability that a significant proportion of the debt would eventually have to be written off. One of the reasons behind the rising discount was a Brazilian moratorium on its debt repayments announced in February 1987 which increased the perception that the debt crisis would be difficult to resolve without some form of debt reduction. Worsening market valuations made it increasingly untenable for banks not to make provisions against the loans.

Following the Brazilian moratorium, Citicorp – the major US bank – announced in May 1987 that it was setting aside $3 billion to its loan-loss reserves against its lending

Table 15.6 Economic growth of the big four debtor countries (% per annum of GDP)

Year	Argentina	Brazil	Mexico	Venezuela
1973	5.9	13.5	8.4	6.3
1974	5.6	9.7	6.1	6.1
1975	0	4.2	5.6	6.1
1976	−5.3	9.8	4.2	8.8
1977	5.6	4.6	3.4	6.7
1978	−5.3	4.8	8.3	2.1
1979	11.1	7.2	9.2	1.3
1980	1.5	9.1	8.3	−2.0
1981	−5.7	−3.3	7.9	−0.3
1982	−3.1	0.6	−0.6	0.7
1983	4.2	−3.4	−5.3	−5.6
1984	2.0	5.3	3.7	−1.4
1985	−6.9	7.9	2.7	0.2
1986	7.1	7.6	−3.7	6.5
1987	2.6	3.6	1.8	3.6
1988	−1.9	−0.1	1.4	5.8
1989	−6.9	3.3	3.1	−7.8
1990	−1.8	−4.1	3.9	6.9
1991	10.6	0.3	4.2	9.7
1992	9.6	−0.8	3.6	6.1
1993	5.7	4.2	1.9	0.3
1994	5.8	5.8	4.4	−3.0
1995	−2.8	4.2	−6.6	4.0
1996	5.5	2.7	5.1	−0.2
1997	8.1	3.3	6.8	6.4
1998	3.9	0.1	5.0	0.2
1999	−3.4	0.8	3.6	−6.1
2000	−0.8	4.4	6.6	3.2
2001	−4.4	1.3	0	2.8
2002	−10.9	1.9	0.6	−8.9
2003	8.7	0.5	1.3	−7.6
2004	7.6	5.0	3.9	10.6

Source: IMF, *International Financial Statistics.*

to developing countries. Following the Citicorp announcement, provisioning by other banks became inevitable and other major banks both in the USA and Europe announced their own provisioning. Thereafter provisioning became a regular feature in the annual accounts of the major international commercial banks with exposure to the debtor nations. When a bank made provisions it was purely an accounting exercise with the bank putting aside reserves against outstanding loans in low-earning but risk-free assets, the reported profit figures are reduced by the amount of the provisions so lowering dividend payments to bank shareholders. It is important to note that while provisioning prepared the banks for any eventual losses on their outstanding debts, it did not reduce the contractual obligations of the debtors to repay their debt. In other words, provisioning was quite distinct from 'writing off' loans whereby the bank reduces the contractual obligations of the debtor. Nonetheless, provisioning was an important step to clearing the path to some form of debt-forgiveness.

Phase 3: the post-Brady Plan era, 1989–present

A significant reformulation of the strategy for dealing with the debt crisis was signalled by the new US Treasury Secretary Nicholas Brady in March 1989. The case-by-case approach, encouraging debtors to undertake market-based reforms and the adoption of stable macroeconomic policies continued to be viewed as essential components for resolving the debt crisis. However, in addition to emphasizing the need for new bank lending, the Brady Plan also explicitly recognized the contribution that voluntary debt forgiveness could make in resolving the crisis. Brady argued that the path to creditworthiness for many SIMICs required some debt and debt-service reduction on a case-by-case basis. The major innovation of the Brady initiative was its inclusion of official support for debt and debt-service reduction. Both the World Bank and the IMF were asked to set aside funds for this purpose to be targeted at SIMICs with high external debt problems and that were undertaking appropriate adjustment programmes. Subsequently, US Treasury Under-Secretary David Mulford set a target of $70 billion in debt-forgiveness on the $340 billion of debt owed by 39 of the major debtor nations. The IMF and World Bank were earmarked $24 billion of funds that could be used for lending purposes designed to support countries that adopted appropriate economic policies and where a debt and debt-service reduction (DDSR) programme was successfully negotiated.

Under the aegis of the Brady Plan, 25 Debt and Debt Service Reductions (DDSR) agreements were concluded with some 23 countries by December 1995. A summary of the results of various DDSRs between 1988 and 1994 is shown in **Table 15.7**. Between 1989 and 1994 some $370 billion of debt was restructured and $100 billion of debt forgiven in aggregate. Some $224 billion of restructuring was concentrated on the severely indebted countries, with $56 billion forgiven. The DDSRs have been characterised as 'loans for bonds' deals, whereby bank-loan claims were replaced by bond-holding claims. Mexico negotiated a DDSR in March 1990, followed by Venezuela in December 1990, Argentina in April 1993 and Brazil in April 1994. The terms of the individual DDSRs varied but there were common elements:

1   Each creditor bank was offered a menu of policy options to choose from. They could accept a reduction in the principal owed to them, a reduction in the interest payable or a mixture of the two. Alternatively, they could opt to preserve the majority of their existing claims but would then be expected to engage in new lending to the country concerned. In the Mexican deal the reduction on principal was 35% for the 'discount bond' that maintained the market rate of interest at LIBOR + 13/16%; while for the 'par bonds' that maintained their face value, the interest rate was fixed at 6¼%, well below the then prevailing interest rate of 10%. Alternatively, banks that wished to maintain their full claim were expected to provide 'new money' equivalent to 25% of their exposure over three years.

2   Restructured debt normally had a long term to maturity, typically 20 to 30 years, and was usually backed for principal repayment and some interest repayment by a the purchase of zero-coupon US bonds by the debtor nation using a mixture of its own funds and loans from multilateral institutions such as the World Bank and the IMF. In the Mexican deal, in the event that oil prices rose above $14 per barrel

Table 15.7 Debt-restructuring agreements, 1988–94 (US$ millions)

	1988	1989	1990	1991	1992	1993	1994
All developing countries							
Total amount rescheduled	82,813	35,603	78,487	45,235	57,778	64,417	88,928
Debt -forgiveness or reduction	–	–20,450	–32,007	–10,163	–11,359	–8,555	–18,389
Severely indebted middle-income countries							
Total amount rescheduled	58,262	16,111	43,695	17,285	44,564	37,793	64,723
Debt-forgiveness or reduction	–	–9,689	–15,294	–2,706	–6,621	–6,577	–15,236

Source: World Debt Tables, 1996.

(at constant 1989 prices), then bond-holders were entitled to some 'claw back', that is additional payments after seven years.

3   As part of the DDSR the debtor country adopted a medium-term IMF stabilization programme designed to ensure its debt-repayment capacity and a better macroeconomic performance.

An evaluation of the Brady Plan

Authors such as Claessens and Wijnbergen (1993) pronounced the Brady Plan a 'spectacular success'. They view Brady-type deals as having been particularly successful in reducing high and volatile external transfers to more manageable and predictable levels. Cline (1995) also sees the Brady Plan as a success because it achieved significant results at relatively low levels of debt-forgiveness of approximately 15% of the overall debt burden and annual interest savings to the debtor nations of ½ to 1% of their GDP, or around 3% of their export earnings. Cline attributes the success of Brady deals as due to a perception on the part of debtor nations that where was a more equitable sharing of the debt burden between themselves and the creditor banks. Cline argues that a clear distinction needs to be made between the ability to pay on the one hand, and willingness to pay on the other. He argues that debt repayments are usually the lower of these two; throughout the 1980s the willingness to pay was relatively low compared to the ability to pay because the debtors perceived the adjustment packages as placing an unfair burden on themselves and being too biased to the needs of the creditor banks. Brady-type deals and some debt-forgiveness by the banks raised the willingness to pay of many debtors so that payments have become related to the (higher) ability to pay. More recently, Reinhart, Rogoff and Savastano (2003) have coined the phrase 'debt intolerance' to capture the idea that certain countries at certain levels of debt decide to default even though they have the capacity to repay simply because they are not prepared to make the sacrifices necessary to ensure full repayment. It is noticeable that Venezuela, Mexico, Brazil and Argentina have a long history of debt defaults. Part of the problem is that in the short term, governments in these countries like the boost to public and private consumption and investment that capital inflows can bring but they subsequently dislike the debt-servicing payments that follow in the longer run.

Generally speaking, although the Brady Plan was supposed to be a 'voluntary' system there is no doubt that much political pressure was applied to the banks to accept some form of debt-forgiveness either in the form of principal reduction or interest-rate reduction rather than opting to preserve their existing claims and engage in new lending. Indeed, in the Brazilian deal the Brazilian negotiators set an effective limit to the new money option, the Argentinean deal ruled out the new money option completely, and considerable moral suasion was applied to the creditor banks in the Mexican case.

One of the most visible effects of the Brady Plan was that there was a significant return of private capital into each of the big four debtors in the year following the conclusion of a Brady deal. Furthermore, there was a significant increase in the value of secondary market prices on outstanding debt (see **Table 15.8**). The only real black mark against the Brady Plan was that it took approximately five years to achieve the majority of its targets, rather than the three years originally envisaged. Nonetheless, by May 1994 some $60 billion of the target $70 billion of debt had been forgiven, leaving Cline (1995, p. 243) to comment that 'the degree of performance of the plan's original targets can only be judged as remarkable, especially by the standards of most efforts at international economic coordination'.

Table 15.8 Aggregated secondary market prices of debt for the big four debtors (cents per dollar)

Year	Argentina	Brazil	Mexico	Venezuela
1985	65.5	75.0	56.0	74.0
1986	34.9	46.0	50.0	57.0
1987	21.0	40.0	42.8	40.8
1989	28.6	23.1	40.6	37.7
1990	33.0	49.3	53.6	56.1
1991	48.2	30.7	66.1	69.0
1992	63.2	30.4	71.4	58.2
1993	79.2	82.5	89.8	74.1
1994	56.8	57.6	64.3	46.2
1995	68.1	61.8	71.5	56.2
1996	83.7	77.2	86.1	83.0
1997	89.6	81.7	92.0	89.2
1998	86.0	61.5	85.1	63.5
1999	88.7	80.6	91.5	72.8
2000	87.9	83.7	101.0	74.3
2001	29.1	80.7	105.3	69.8

Notes: (a) Aggregate average debt prices based on loan prices, Brady bond prices and bond prices' see source for methodology. (b) The secondary market can at times exhibit quite substantial changes in prices, particularly for countries where the market is rather thin; markets for the above countries debt are fairly well-developed.
Source: Klingen, Weder and Zettlemeyer (2004).

15.15 An overall evaluation of the debt crisis management

An overall evaluation of the management of the debt crisis must to some extent be based upon what the objectives of debt-crisis management have been, Cline (1995) identified three main objectives behind the strategy:

1 Avoidance of a financial crisis and the collapse of the international banking system.
2 Restoration of capital-market access for debtor countries.
3 Minimizing the economic adjustment costs for debtor nations.

With regard to objectives 1 and 2 there is general agreement that the crisis management must be regarded as a success. A major financial crisis for the international banking system was averted and no debtor opted for outright default. The initial crisis management strategy involving concerted 'involuntary' lending prevented an outright default and gave time for banks to build up capital reserves and make loan-loss provisions that ultimately made debt-forgiveness a viable strategy.

It can be questioned whether the initial diagnosis of the crisis as one of illiquidity was correct, and whether insolvency requiring immediate debt-forgiveness would have been more appropriate. Certainly, the failure of the Baker Plan and the success of the Brady Plan is indicative that the debtor countries should have been granted debt-forgiveness at an earlier stage in the crisis. Indeed, David Mulford, the former US

Treasury Under-Secretary who worked extensively on the Brady Plan, has stated that 'In retrospect, Latin America could have suffered less had the international community been prepared earlier to recognise and work with the reality of the markets to resolve the crisis' (*Wall Street Journal*, 21 August 1992). While there is undoubtedly some truth to this, it must also be recognized that the banks were in no real position to consider debt-forgiveness much before the late 1980s following Citicorp's lead in making provisions. In addition, granting debt relief at an early stage may well have increased the eventual write-offs and delayed the adoption of sound macro policies by the debtor nations. In retrospect, the initial diagnosis of illiquidity rather than insolvency was almost certainly correct, in that the total amount of debt-forgiveness eventually granted has been relatively small.

There is some truth to the argument that the majority of the burden was initially placed on the debtor countries and was too biased to the needs of the creditor banks. A fairer sharing of the burden may have been appropriate, especially as the crisis in large part was a reflection of excessive lending by the commercial banks. In the end, however, banks did share a fair degree of the burden by relinquishing approximately one-third of their claims.

The 'quasi voluntary' market-oriented nature of the eventual settlement was an important feature. Had the banks been forced to write down debt, then they would probably have contested such measures in the courts and this would have clouded Latin American access to capital markets for years to come. In the end, the majority of banks voluntarily accepted principal and/or interest rate reduction at a lower rate than they might have expected from the discount on the secondary market price of the debt during the worst days of the crisis. The banks forgave approximately one-third of the money owed, and given that some observers have argued that the debtors had the capacity but were unwilling to pay back all the debt this must be seen as a reasonable sharing of the eventual cost.

Another notable feature of the management of the debt crisis was that the banks were not bailed out at public expense. Although public guarantees exist on some of the Brady exit bonds, the improved economic policies in the debtor nations, lower debt service ratios and their return to capital market access reduced the risk of these guarantees being called upon. What is true is that the share of the official sector in the outstanding debt of the SIMICs increased from 14% in 1982 to around 35% in 1994. However, this mainly reflected the lack of new funds made available by the commercial banks post 1982.

The one area where a question mark hangs over the success of the debt-management strategy is with respect to the third objective. The 10 years following the start of the debt crisis in 1982 have been characterized as a 'lost decade' for Latin America; investment stagnated and per capita incomes in 1992 were lower in each of the big four debtors compared to the 1979–81 average (14.1% in Venezuela, 12.7% in Argentina, 5.7% in Mexico and 2% in Brazil).

The role of the IMF and World Bank in the debt crisis has been criticized as being too biased in favour of the creditors and requiring too heavy an adjustment by the debtors. To some extent this criticism is unfair because the IMF often recommended policy measures that the debtor would have had to undertake anyhow. It merely provided a convenient scapegoat for the debtor government to implement necessary adjustment packages. The IMF and World Bank simply did not have the resources to make more than a marginal impact on debtors' financial positions. Overall, the IMF played a crucial role in coordinating the banks, and its stabilization programmes were an important ingredient in the successful resolution of the crisis.

The case-by-case approach taken to manage the crisis was almost certainly justified. A generalized scheme to settle the debt problem would not have recognized that the economic circumstances and prospects of the debtor nations were immensely varied. Nevertheless, the recognition of the fact that debtors' circumstances differed should also have meant that IMF stabilization programmes exhibited a greater degree of variety than the almost standard package of deflation, devaluation and deregulation. Furthermore, there needed to be a greater recognition that there was a large degree of interdependence among the debtor nations; it was no use encouraging export-led growth by a number of debtors if such measures merely depressed their export prices on world markets leaving their export revenues stagnant. For instance, between 1981–85 Latin American export volumes rose 25% but the deterioration in their terms of trade meant that their export earnings remained stagnant.

15.16 Post-Brady Plan crises in three of the countries

While the Brady Plan was perceived as a great success and as heralding the end of the international debt crisis, this verdict may have been premature. It is certainly the case that the Brady restructuring plan coincided with the ability of the international banking system to write down and restructure much of the debt on their books, and access to international capital markets was also restored many of the debtor nations. However, it is less clear that the problem of debt build-up and debt-service was fully dealt with, as **Table 15.4** shows the level of indebtedness of the big four debtors has continued to rise and their economic growth rates, as shown in **Table 15.6**, remain volatile. Finally, there have been significant post-Brady crises in three of the countries, Mexico in 1994/95, Brazil in 1999, and more recently Argentina declared the largest-ever default on its external debt obligations in January 2002, at the same time it ended its currency-board link to the US dollar (see section 11.12 for details on each of the crises). The Argentinian default in particular means that some of the post-Brady plan evaluations need to be reassessed, and Brazil remains vulnerable and is still classified as a SIMIC. However, the economic situation in Mexico and Venezuela has improived so that they are now classified by the World Bank as less-indebted middle-income countries, a significant improvement on their 1994 classifications.

15.17 Conclusions

The debt crisis arose through a mixture of domestic and external circumstances which varied from debtor to debtor. Nevertheless, the extent and close timing of debtors' problems suggests that common external factors played a significant part in the crisis. It is too simplistic to apportion the crisis solely to excessive borrowing by the debtor nations, since in large part the crisis also reflected excessive lending by the commercial banks.

Although the crisis was in large part due to a combination of events outside the debtor countries' control, up until 1989 most of the adjustment burden for managing the crisis fell heavily on the debtor nations. There is some justification in the criticism that initial management of the crisis was too biased towards the requirements of the creditor banks rather than the needs of the debtor nations. However, following the

Brady Plan the banks did forgive a substantial proportion of the money owed as part of negotiated DDSRs. In the end, debt-forgiveness was crucial in improving the willingness as well as capacity to pay of the debtor nations, particularly as debt reduction was linked to economic reform in the debtor nations. Indeed, debt reduction provided a significant incentive for the debtor nations to undertake economic reform as it guaranteed them a share in any resulting future economic prosperity.

There are numerous lessons to be learnt from the debt crisis and its subsequent management. Most importantly, banks need to be far more discriminating in making sovereign loans in the future and must avoid leaving themselves over-exposed to one particular country or region. Also, when lending funds to governments careful consideration should be given as to whether the loans are being put to productive use by the government concerned or whether the loans are merely being used to finance extravagant social programmes. In addition, banks and creditors need to consider not only a country's capacity to repay loans, but also the likely willingness to repay loans in times of economic difficulty.

Another lesson that emerged is that in times of crisis international organizations such as the IMF and World Bank can play a critically important role in encouraging the adoption of sound macroeconomic policies in debtor countries and in coordinating private-sectors claims. Indeed, many debtor countries have discovered that sound domestic economic policies are ultimately crucial to better economic performance, and by building up confidence can play a critical role in helping a country regain access to international capital markets.

The debt crisis signalled by the Mexican moratorium of 1982 could have resulted in an unprecedented crisis for the industrialized nations' banking systems, but by the early 1990s they were in a position to engage in write-downs and restructuring of debt such that the debt crisis no longer presented a threat to the international financial system. The management of the debt crisis involved a mixture of debt write-off by the banks and economic reform in the debtor nations. The return of capital flows in the form of bond finance, equity investment and foreign direct investment following the conclusion of Brady deals meant that capital-market access for most debtors was restored in just over a decade, which compares very favourably with the four decades of cut-off that followed the Latin American defaults in the 1930s. However, the Argentinean default in 2002, the related problems in Brazil in 1999 and even the Mexican crisis of 1994/95 show that the issue of external debt still represents a threat to the stability of output and economic prospects in Latin America and other countries that have high external debts.

Further reading

Bird, G. (1989) *Commercial Bank Lending and Third World Debt* (London: Palgrave Macmillan).

Claessens, S. and Wijnbergen, S. (1993) 'Interest Rates, Growth and External Debt: The Macroeconomic Impact of Mexico's Brady Deal', World Bank Policy Research Working Papers no. 1147 (Washington: World Bank).

Cline, W. (1984) *International Debt: Systematic Risk and Policy Response* (Cambridge, Mass.: MIT Press).

Cline, W. (1990) 'From Baker to Brady: Managing International Debt', in R. O'Brien and I. Iversen (eds), *Finance and the International Economy* Vol. 3 (Oxford: Oxford University Press).

Cline, W. (1995) *International Debt Reexamined* (London: Longman).

Dornbusch, R. (1985) 'Policy and Performance Links between LDC Debtors and Industrial Countries', *Brooking Papers on Economic Activity*, vol. 2, pp. 303–56.

Griffith-Jones, S. (ed.) (1988) *Managing World Debt* (Hemel-Hempstead: Harvester-Wheatsheaf).

Klingen, C., Weder, B. and Zettelmeyer, J. (2004) 'How Private Creditors Fared in Emerging Market Debt Crises 1970–2000', IMF Working Paper, WP 04/13.

Kuczynski, P. (1988) *Latin American Debt* (Baltimore: Johns Hopkins University Press).

Miller, M. (2002) 'Sovereign Debt Restructuring – New Articles – New Contracts or No Change', International Economic Policy Briefs PB 02-3 (Washington: Institute for International Economics).

Nunnenkamp, P. (1986) *The International Debt Crisis of the Third World* (Brighton: Wheatsheaf Books).

Reinhart, C., Rogoff, K. and Savastano, M. (2003) 'Debt Intolerance', Brookings Papers on Economic Activity, vol. 1, pp. 1–62.

Rey (G-10) Report (1996) *The Resolution of Sovereign Liquidity Crises* (Washington: International Monetary Fund).

Sachs, J. (1984) 'Theoretical Issues in International Borrowing', *Princeton Studies in International Finance*, no. 54.

Sachs, J. (1986) 'Managing the LDC Debt Crisis', *Brookings Papers on Economic Activity*, vol. 2, pp. 397–431.

Sachs, J. and Huizinga, H. (1987) 'US Commercial Banks and the Developing Debt Crisis', *Brookings Papers on Economic Activity*, vol. 2, pp. 555–601.

White, M. (2002) 'Sovereigns in Distress: Do They Need Bankruptcy', *Brookings Papers on Economic Activity*, vol. 1, pp. 1–30.

16

Economic and Monetary Union in Europe

16.1 Introduction

In this chapter, we examine one of the most important economic issues ever tackled by the European Union (EU), namely Economic and Monetary Union (EMU). On 1 January 2002 EMU was finally realized in Europe when 11 founding countries agreed to irrevocably fix their exchange rates with no margin of fluctuation and agreed to replace their national currencies with a new European currency called the euro. As we shall see, as well as agreeing to give up their monetary sovereignty, they also agreed to certain rules which have limited to some extent their freedom with respect to fiscal policy in the form of the 1996 Stability and Growth Pact. Despite its realization, the issue of EMU in Europe still has a great deal of relevance since the United Kingdom, Denmark and Sweden have still not joined. In addition, the European Union was enlarged with 10 new members on 1 May 2004, many of them former Eastern-bloc countries committed in principle to replacing their national currencies with the euro at some point in the future. When joining the EMU countries currently have to accept certain fiscal restraints as outlined in the Stability and Growth Pact and there has been much recent debate about how to reform this pact. Finally, the impact of the monetary union on trade and financial markets and institutions is still very much being felt, and the performance of the European Central Bank and the euro in the foreign exchange markets is closely monitored by financial market participants.

In this chapter, we review the history behind EMU and we spend some time looking at the features and operation of its predecessor, the European Monetary System, which commenced operations in March 1979 and ultimately proved to be the vehicle for achievement of EMU. We describe the EMS and evaluate its performance during its years of operation, including an analysis of the major crises that confronted the system in 1992/93 and the convergence process in the run-up to EMU. We then proceed to look at the economic gains/losses to be expected from EMU including some recent controversial empirical research on the topic. We review the various safeguards that have been put into place to ensure that the euro will be a sound low-inflation currency, with particular focus on the Stability and Growth Pact, and then proceed to look at the arrangements for the management of the euro under the so-called EuroSystem. Finally, we look at some of the issues raised by potential new entrants into the EMU distinguishing between the cases of the United Kingdom and the Accession countries which joined the European Union in 2004.

16.2 The Snake in the Tunnel

Following the collapse of the Bretton Woods System in 1971, there was a great deal of concern at the Community level that if the European Economic Community (EEC) (as it was then called) countries allowed their exchange rates to be determined solely by market forces there might be large and sudden changes in international competitiveness associated with exchange rate movements that could undermine the development of free trade within the Community. Indeed, it was feared that there might even be deliberate competitive depreciations by some countries to gain trading advantage, which could result in trade frictions and the emergence of protectionist pressures within the EEC and possibly threaten the existence of the Community itself. In addition, following the Werner Report of 1972 (see section 16.17) the member countries of the EEC had set a target date for achieving EMU by 1980. As a result of these fears and a desire to introduce a single currency as well as some degree of exchange rate stability, EEC members set up the so-called 'Snake in the Tunnel' which subsequently became the plain 'Snake'.

The Snake system has been characterized as a mini-Bretton Woods, a description that was subsequently applied to the EMS. The Snake in the Tunnel commenced

Table 16.1 Central parity realignments in the Snake

Currency	Mar 1973	Jun 1973	Sep 1973	Nov 1973	Oct 1976	Apr 1977	Aug 1977	Feb 1978	Oct 1978
Belg./Lux. franc					−2.0				+2.0
Deutschmark	+3.0	+5.5							+4.0
Dutch guilder			+5.0		−2.0				+2.0
Swedish krone					−3.0	−6.0			
Danish krone					−6.0	−3.0	−5.0		
Norwegian krone				+5.0	−3.0	−3.0	−5.0	−8.0	

(+) indicates a revaluation; (−) indicates a devaluation.
Source: European Commission.

operations on 24 April 1972 and was made up of the original six EEC members (Belgium, France, Italy, Luxembourg, Netherlands and Germany); on 23 May 1972 the UK and Denmark joined the system and Norway became an associate member. While the member currencies could vary by a maximum of ± 1.125% against each other (the Snake) they could float by ± 2.25% against the US dollar (the Tunnel) as permitted by the Smithsonian agreement (see section 11.4). This smaller margin of fluctuation for the member currencies *vis-à-vis* each other than was permitted against the US dollar gave rise to the term 'Snake in a Tunnel' to describe the system. Indeed, between 1972 and 1976 Belgium and the Netherlands limited the divergence between their currencies to ± 0.75% and this became known as the worm inside the Snake!

The system had a chequered history; the UK abandoned its membership of the system after just six weeks and was followed four days later by Denmark which subsequently rejoined in October 1972. Italy withdrew from the Snake in February 1973 and the tunnel was demolished in March 1973 when the Snake currencies decided on a joint float against the dollar. In April 1973 as part of the Snake system the European Monetary Cooperation Fund (EMCF) was set up to provide credits and support for deficit countries. France left the system in January 1974, rejoined in July 1975 and left again in March 1976. Norway left the system in December 1978. Throughout its life-time the Snake was characterized by a series of devaluations and revaluations which are listed in **Table 16.1**. This coupled with the fact that both Italy and France were out of the system meant that by 1979 the Snake was looking badly mutilated. In the end, the Snake system failed to produce the necessary degree of coordination of economic policies and convergence of economic performance required for its successful operation.

16.3 The background to the European Monetary System

On 17 June 1978, at a conference held in Bremen, six of the community countries committed themselves to the setting-up of the European Monetary System to replace the Snake. The EMS aimed to provide a 'zone of monetary stability' bringing back into the fold countries like Italy and France which had left the Snake. Before looking at the operation of the EMS it is worthwhile reviewing the motivations behind its formation.

Yas-su-Hu (1981) argues that the formation of the EMS has to be seen in a wider context than simply the setting-up of an exchange rate mechanism. He argues that the EMS was based upon a convergence of interests among the EEC countries with regard to a common dollar problem. Under the Bretton Woods system, the dollar was the major international reserve currency, used as a means of settlement between central banks, for exchange market interventions and as a vehicle currency to denominate many international transactions. He argues that the USA was free to run balance of payments deficits to supply the world with the dollars it required. In return for this freedom from balance of payments constraints, the USA was expected to avoid undermining the purchasing power of dollars. When President Nixon suspended dollar convertibility into gold in 1971 the USA had effectively abdicated its responsibility, causing serious economic and financial losses for the Europeans.

The dollar problem had many facets. As the dollar was pegged by foreign central bank purchases of US dollars, this led to a rapid growth in the world money supply and thereby contributed to worldwide inflation. Also, the depreciation of the dollar after suspension of its convertibility meant huge losses for central banks who had purchased dollars under the Bretton Woods system and after the adoption of floating exchange rates as they tried to slow down the appreciation of their currencies against the dollar. In sum, it can be argued that central banks' experience of purchasing and holding US dollars in their reserves had not been a happy one.

Another motivation underlying the Bremen initiative was a desire to provide a stable framework for the conduct of European trade. Since the adoption of floating exchange rates in 1973, there had been very divergent inflation rates, economic growth and balance of payments performances between the EEC economies. European policy-makers were concerned that such divergent economic performances could threaten intra-EEC trade, and it was hoped that stabilizing European currencies would lead to a greater convergence of economic performance and continued growth of European trade.

The EMS commenced operation on 13 March 1979 and, despite much initial scepticism about its survival chances, operated with mixed success for two decades. The EMS consisted of three main features: (1) the Exchange Rate Mechanism (ERM), (2) the European Currency Unit, and (3) financing facilities. A proposed European Monetary Fund was never set up. All members of the EEC joined the EMS, but the UK did not initially participate in the ERM. We now briefly review the three key features as an understanding of these is essential in order to show how EMU was eventually brought about.

16.4 The Exchange Rate Mechanism

The Exchange Rate Mechanism (ERM) consisted of two parts:

1   A grid of bilateral exchange rate bands between each of the member currencies which defined obligatory intervention.
2   An individual band of fluctuation (threshold) for each currency against a European Currency Unit (ECU). The ECU was an artificial currency based upon a calculation of a weighted basket of 12 European currencies. If a currency moved too much against the ECU basket it would lead to the expectation that the authorities of that currency would take policy measures designed to bring it back within its ECU threshold.

Bilateral exchange rate parities and obligatory intervention limits

The bilateral exchange rate aspect of the ERM consisted of a grid of central exchange rates between each pair of currencies in the ERM. Originally each currency could fluctuate a maximum ± 2.25% of its assigned bilateral central rate against another member currency of the ERM. On the setting-up of the system, Italy was allowed to join with a larger band of fluctuation of ± 6%, a similar ± 6% was applied when Spain joined the ERM in June 1989, the UK joined in October 1990, and the Portuguese escudo entered the system in April 1992. However, following an exchange rate crisis on 2 August 1993 there was a widening of permissible fluctuation margins to ± 15% for all currencies. **Table 16.2** shows the central rates of the grid, that also became the fixed bilateral conversion rates between the Euro countries announced on 2 May 1998.

Within the bilateral margins authorities could intervene if they wished but such intervention was not compulsory. **Intra-marginal** intervention was carried out in either EMS or non-EMS currencies (normally the US dollar). Once two currencies reached a bilateral exchange rate margin the authorities of the two currencies were obliged to intervene or take economic policy measures to keep the currencies within their bilateral limits. At the outset of the system, the intention was that obligatory intervention should take place in the relevant EMS currencies rather than in US dollars. For example, if the French franc was at the bottom of its bilateral limit against the deutschmark, the French and/or German authorities would sell deutschmarks and purchase French francs rather than the French use dollars to buy francs. An important feature of the ERM was that any changes in the grid of central rates required 'mutual agreement'. In practice, this meant that parity changes were taken by the finance ministers of the currencies participating in the ERM.

16.5 The European Currency Unit and its role as an indicator of divergence

A key component of the ERM was the ECU which between 1979 and 1999 was a weighted basket of 12 member currencies; the 12 currencies being those of the 12 members prior to the entrance of the three new members. The ECU acted as an 'indicator of divergence' within the ERM. Once a bilateral margin was reached requiring compulsory intervention a question arose as to which authority was responsible for intervention. In the case where the French franc reached its lower bilateral limit against the deutschmark, should the Banque de France use its reserves or raise French interest rates to support the franc, or the Bundesbank sell deutschmarks and accumulate French francs and/or reduce German interest rates?

The ECU was nothing more than a calculation of how a currency was doing against other European currencies. The idea underlying the ECU was that it would single out the currency that was diverging from the average agreed parities before obligatory bilateral exchange rate margins were reached. In effect, the ECU was supposed to act as an alarm bell – once a currency crossed its divergence threshold against the ECU the alarm bell is triggered and the authorities of the diverging currency were expected to take measures to bring its currency back into line. Such action could consist of a change in interest rates and/or in the monetary/fiscal policy pursued by the country. Unlike reaching a bilateral exchange rate limit, triggering the ECU alarm bell did not lead to obligatory intervention, only the expectation of a change in policy stance

Table 16.2 Central rates of the ERM grid in 1998 (bilateral conversion rates announced 2 May 1998)

	DEM 1=	BEF/LUF 100=	ESP 100=	FRF 1=	IEP 1=	ITL 1000=	NLG 1=	ATS 1=	PTE 100=
BEF/LUF	20.6255								
ESP	85.0722	412.462							
FRF	3.35386	16.2608	3.94237						
IEP	0.402676	1.95232	0.473335	0.120063					
ITL	990.2	4799.90	1163.72	295.183	2458.56				
NLG	1.12674	5.46285	1.32445	0.335953	2.79812	1.13812			
ATS	7.03552	34.1108	8.27006	2.09774	17.4719	7.10657	6.24415		
PTE	102.505	496.984	120.492	30.5634	254.560	103.541	90.9753	14.5697	
FIM	3.04001	14.7391	3.57345	0.90642	7.54951	3.07071	2.69806	0.432094	2.96571

Notes:

(a) DEM is deutschmark, BEF/LUF is Belgium/Luxembourg franc, ESP is Spanish peseta, FRF is French franc, IEP is Irish punt, ITL is Italian lira, NLG is Netherlands guilder, ATS is Austrian schilling, PTE is Portuguese escudo, FIM is Finnish markka. (b) It is possible to calculate any permanently fixed bilateral parity from the above gird; for example, Italian lira per French franc is 990.2/3.35386 = 295.183, which is also shown in the grid (FRF 1 = 295.183 ITL).

(*presumption d'action*). Each currency had its own individual divergence threshold against the ECU dependent upon its weight in the ECU; the greater currency's weight, the lower its divergence threshold. The reason for designing the divergence threshold like this was to correct for the fact that currencies with a higher than average weight in the ECU tended to fluctuate less against the ECU than currencies with a lower weight. This is because the higher a currency's weight the more the ECU was made up of that currency and since a currency cannot fluctuate against itself the less likely it is to fluctuate against the ECU. To offset this effect, high-weight currencies were assigned lower divergence thresholds than low-weight currencies. Once a currency deviated too far from its central parity against the ECU then the authorities of that currency were supposed to take measures to bring the currency back into line. For example, once the deutschmark exceeded its divergence threshold against the ECU, the German authorities were expected to take measures to bring the deutschmark back into line. The idea was that this warning bell would lead to action by the responsible country and so avoid reaching obligatory bilateral intervention limits which would provoke speculation about parity changes.

In practice, the divergence indicator did not necessarily work as intended. For example, it was possible for four high-weighted currencies in the ECU basket to appreciate against weaker currencies in the system but keep their same central rate against each other. In such circumstances, they could reach their bilateral parities against the weaker currencies even though they had not reached their divergence thresholds with respect to the ECU.

16.6 Financing facilities and monetary cooperation

Another key feature of the EMS was that each member of the EMS deposited 20% of its gold dollar reserves with the European Monetary Cooperation Fund (EMCF) in exchange for the equivalent value in ECUs; the idea being that authorities use ECUs rather than dollars for their exchange market interventions. Furthermore, since each ECU issued was backed by dollars and gold it was hoped that ECUs would be extensively used for settlements between EEC central banks. The responsibilities of the EMCF were taken over by the European Monetary Institute in January 1994, and by the European System of Central Banks ESCB in 1998.

An important feature of the EMS was that members had access to credit facilities enabling deficit countries to defend their exchange rate parities and manage transitory balance of payments problems. These credit facilities were as follows:

1 **Very short-term financing (VSTF)** – a credit facility which participating central banks granted to one another. Designed predominately to ensure that EMS members who found their currencies under pressure had necessary short-term support to intervene to defend their currency. This credit facility was of unlimited amount with credits and debits denominated in ECUs and the transfers made in the relevant accounts of the EMCF. However, borrowing had to be settled within 45 days with the borrower repaying loans made at relevant money-market interest rates.

2 **Short-term monetary support (STMS)** – the funds available under this credit facility were intended to meet financing needs in instances of temporary balance of payments problems. The system was based upon a system of debtor and creditor

quotas which defined each central bank's borrowing entitlement and financing obligations. Borrowing was for a duration of three months, renewable for a further two periods at the request of the borrowing central bank.

3   **Medium-term financial assistance (MTFA)** – this facility provided credits for participating countries experiencing or seriously threatened with difficulties with their balance of payments over the medium term. Each member had an obligation to grant credit up to a predetermined ceiling, but there was no formal ceiling on the amount of borrowing. Ordinarily no individual country could receive loans of more than 50% of the total committed ceilings. Medium-term loans were for periods of two to five years and conditional upon the borrower taking economic and monetary measures aimed at restoring equilibrium to its balance of payments. The conditionality attached to this facility meant that it was never used!

16.7 An assessment of the European Monetary System

Despite much initial scepticism, many economists were surprised at the resilience and relatively successful operation of the EMS. Against this, however, the system was characterized by periods of turbulence making an overall assessment quite difficult. There are two key areas upon which the EMS has been judged, firstly as a zone of currency stability and secondly as an anti-inflation zone, and we now proceed to look at each of theses issues.

Exchange rate stability in the EMS

In the early days of its operation, some critics of the system viewed the system as a 'mere crawling peg', a fixed exchange rate system with bands in which the central parities are frequently realigned. As **Table 16.3** shows, in the first four years of its operation exchange rate realignments were both frequent and quite substantial. To a large extent, the turbulence of the early years was not surprising given that the second oil shock coincided with the inception of the EMS. However, post-1984 realignments became far less frequent and the realignments much smaller. Indeed, between January 1987 and October 1992 there was 5 1/2 years of stability with only a minor devaluation of the central parity of the lira. Cheung *et al.* (1995) have shown that most realignments in the ERM can be characterized as attempts to restore international competitiveness; that is, move the exchange rate to its PPP level.

Following German reunification and the entrance of the peseta in 1989, the pound in 1990 and the escudo in April 1992, pressures started to build up in the system. In June 1992, a Danish referendum which rejected Danish participation in EMU raised doubts over continued progress towards EMU and concern in the financial markets about the commitment of certain governments towards economic convergence and the maintenance of their exchange rate parities. In particular, strain brought on by German reunification which had led to high German interest rates to finance its growing budget deficit and keep inflationary pressures under control meant that interest rates for other European countries were forced higher in order to maintain their exchange rate parities, since German interest rates effectively placed a floor on other ERM members' interest rates.

With many European economies in recession, speculators became increasingly sceptical about the commitment of governments to defend their exchange rate parities via

Table 16.3 A chronology of developments EMS to EMU

Year	Date	Event
1979	13 Mar.	EMS starts operation (±2.25% for all participants except the Italian lira ±6% band)
	24 Sep.	Deutschmark (+2%), Danish krone (−2.9%)
	30 Nov.	Danish krone (−4.76%)
1981	23 Mar.	Lira (−6%)
	5 Oct.	Deutschmark (+5.5%), guilder (+5.5%), French franc (−3%), lira (−3%)
1982	22 Feb.	Belgian franc (−8.5%), Danish krone (−3%)
	14 Jun.	Deutschmark (+4.25%), guilder (+4.25%), French franc (−5.75%), lira (−2.75%)
1983	21 Mar.	Deutschmark (+5.5%), guilder (3.5%), Danish krone (+2.5%), Belgium franc (+1.5%), French franc (−2.5%), lira (2.5%), punt (−3.5%)
1985	22 Jul.	Belgian franc (+2%), Danish krone (+2%), deutschmark (+2%), Franch franc (+2%), punt (+2%), guilder (+2%), lira (−6%)
1986	7 Apr.	Deutschmark (+3%), guilder (+3%), Belgian franc (+1%), Danish Krone (+1%), French franc (−3%)
	4 Aug.	Punt (−8%)
1987	12 Jan.	Deutschmark (+3%), guilder (+3%), Belgian franc (+2%)
1989	19 Jan.	Peseta enters with ±6% band
1990	8 Jan.	Lira (−3.7%) and adopts ±2.25% band
	8 Oct.	Sterling enters with ±6% band
1992	6 Apr.	Escudo enters with ±6% band
	14 Sep.	Belgian franc (+3.5%), deutschmark (+3.5%), guilder (+3.5%), Danish krone (+3.5%), escudo (+3.5%), French franc (+3.5%), punt (+3.5%), sterling (+3.5%), lira (−3.5%)
	17 Sep.	Sterling and lira suspend membership of ERM, peseta (−5%)
	23 Nov.	Escudo (−6%), peseta (−6%)
1993	1 Feb.	Punt (−10%)
	14 May.	Peseta (−8%), escudo (−6.5%)
	2 Aug.	Widening of margins of fluctuations to ±15% for all ERM currencies, Germany and Netherlands agree to bilaterally maintain their currencies in the ±2.25% band
1995	9 Jan.	Austrian schilling enters with ±15% band
	6 Mar.	Peseta (−7%), escudo (−3.5%)
1996	14 Oct.	Finnish markka enters with ±15% band
	25 Nov.	Italian lira rejoins with ±15% band
1998	16 Mar.	Punt (+3%)
	2 May	Selection of 11 qualifying members for EMU and irrevocable fixing of bilateral exchange rates announced
1999	1 Jan.	EMU came into effect and ERM II starts with Denmark and Greece as members, ±2.25% bands
2001	1 Jan.	Greece enters EMU
2002	1 Jan.	Euro arrives on the streets
2004	28 Jun.	Estonia, Lithuania and Slovenia join ERM II with ±15% bands

Notes: (−) indicates a devaluation, (+) indicates a revaluation.

high interest rates. Doubts about the result of a French referendum on the Maastricht Treaty on 20 September 1992 led to speculative pressure building up on the Italian lira and pound sterling. As a response, both the Italian and British governments issued statements proclaiming they were committed to defend their exchange rate parities. However, due to unprecedented market pressure, the Italians were forced to accept an effective devaluation of the lira of 7% (a combined 3.5% devaluation of the lira and a 3.5% revaluation of all the other ERM currencies). However, this was regarded as insufficient by speculators and on 17 September a further wave of speculative pressure against the lira, pound and peseta led to the suspension of the pound and lira from the ERM, while the peseta was devalued by 5%.

In November 1992 further speculative attacks led to the escudo and peseta being devalued by 6%. Foreign exchange market tensions resurfaced in the first half of 1993 leading to a 10% devaluation of the Irish punt in February 1993 and an 8% devaluation of the peseta and a 6.5% devaluation of the escudo in May 1993. Further exchange rate tensions built up within the system in July 1993, and in a last-minute bid to save the system and remove potential 'one-way bets' the bands were widened from ± 2.25% to ± 15% as from 2 August 1993.

Despite these periodic crises, authors such as Artis and Taylor (1988 and 1994) have shown that both nominal exchange rates and real effective exchange rates had become less volatile for EMS currencies (kroner, Belgian franc, lira, guilder and deutschmark) than for non-EMS currencies (the pound, dollar, yen) since 1979 compared with the first six years of floating. While it is not surprising that nominal exchange rates became more stable, as this is precisely what the ERM is about, the fact that it also holds for real exchange rates is indicative of the fact that as well as providing stability for exchange rates the EMS has also led to a greater convergence of inflation rates.

One of the arguments against adopting exchange rate targets has always been that countries would be forced to adjust domestic monetary policy and interest rates to the needs of maintaining the exchange rate target. Hence, exchange rate stability would be achieved only at the cost of increased domestic instability. Interestingly, Artis and Taylor (1994) found that greater stability of exchange rates was accompanied by increased stability of domestic short-term interest rates for the ERM countries. It seems that countries derived both greater domestic and external financial stability from membership of the ERM. By contrast, Artis and Taylor report that non-ERM countries experienced both greater exchange rate and interest rate volatility post-1982.

Although the EMS resulted in less volatility of real and nominal exchange rates for its members, there is clear evidence of significant changes in the levels of real exchange rates over time, particularly in the 1980s. This is because in the 1980s France, Italy, Denmark and Ireland had higher inflation rates than Germany, and the periodic devaluations of their currencies only partly offset these differentials implying real exchange rate appreciations of their currencies against the deutschmark. In the 1990s, however, French inflation was generally below German inflation leading to much more stability of the real exchange rate.

16.8 The EMS as an anti-inflation zone

In the way of background, before we consider the anti-inflation hypothesis, it was a widely held belief that German inflation had generally been lower than that of other

EU countries because of the independent status of the German Bundesbank. The Bundesbank was given a charter in 1957 that required it to ensure price stability, enabling it to pursue tough monetary policies regardless of political pressures to inflate. Having experienced two periods of hyperinflation in the twentieth century the Germans have a high aversion to inflation. Only in the 1990s were other central banks such as the Banque de France (1993), Banca d'Italia (1992), Bank of Greece (1993), Bank of Portugal (1992), Bank of Spain (1994) and Bank of England (1998) granted similar degrees of independence.

A popular interpretation of the advantages of EMS membership was put forward by Giavazzi and Pagno (1986) and Melitz (1988). According to this interpretation one of the major advantages of ERM membership for relatively high inflation countries such as Italy and France was that participation enabled them to reduce their inflation rates more rapidly, substantially and at lower cost than if they had been non-members. According to this anti-inflation hypothesis, there are two ways that the fight against inflation was assisted by full EMS membership: (i) by giving the authorities an incentive to bring inflation under control, and (ii) by affecting private agents' wage and price behaviour.

With regard to the authorities incentives, both Italy and France (and other members) by making a commitment to peg their nominal exchange rates against the key low-inflation currency in the system – the deutschmark – in effect pledged to bring their inflation rates down to the German level. If their inflation rates remained higher than Germany's then they would be penalized by a loss of international competitiveness. Of course, they could opt for occasional devaluations to maintain their competitiveness, but if France and Italy were to do so too frequently this would signal to economic agents that the authorities were not serious in pursuing anti-inflationary policies. By making a commitment to peg their currencies to the deutschmark the authorities made a visible signal of their commitment to an anti-inflation strategy. So long as they maintained the peg (tying their hands), they gained some of the anti-inflation credibility of the Bundesbank.

The effect of agents' wage and price behaviour is connected with the authorities' incentive/credibility effect. Given that their authorities maintained the peg, economic agents in France and Italy learnt that persisting with high wage and price inflation demands made their economies uncompetitive. This ultimately would lead to job losses and an economic slowdown. Hence, workers had an incentive to lower their wage demands which in turn resulted in lower inflation. In addition, employers would resist excessive wage demands since if they believed that the authorities would maintain the exchange rate peg they would know that the resulting cost-push pressures would undermine their competitiveness in international markets.

Given the anti-inflation incentives for both the authorities and economic agents, it was argued that membership of the ERM assisted in the process of bringing down inflation compared to non-ERM membership. The Italian and French authorities by being members of the ERM were, according to the anti-inflation hypothesis, able to bring down their inflation rates more substantially and more quickly than could have been achieved without membership.

While the anti-inflation hypothesis explained what was in ERM membership for traditionally high-inflation countries, it did not explain German participation in the ERM. Germany had since the Second World War already been a low-inflation country, and the Bundesbank already had anti-inflation credibility. Melitz (1988) argues that the main gain for Germany was that while the nominal exchange rates were fixed and other countries still had relatively high inflation rates, the Germans experienced an improvement in their international competitiveness due to the resulting real depreciation of the deutschmark.

This interpretation of the EMS suggests that all countries got something out of the system, but at a cost. The Italians and French managed to bring down their inflation rates and sustain them at lower rates than had they not joined the system, but at the expense of some loss of international competitiveness. Whereas the Germans probably accepted a marginally higher inflation rate than had they not been EMS members but were compensated by increased international competitiveness. Some empirical evidence on the validity of the anti-inflation hypothesis is presented in **Table 16.4**.

While there is no doubt that average rates of inflation came down in the EMS countries, **Table 16.4** shows that this is not by itself proof of the EMS anti-inflation hypothesis. This is because inflation rates also fell in the non-ERM countries such as the United Kingdom and the United States. In fact, starting from a similar average inflation rate in 1980, the inflation rate in the non-ERM countries was lower than in the ERM countries up to 1985. Only between 1986–91 did the ERM countries have a lower inflation rate; between 1992 and 1998 the non-ERM countries generally had a lower average inflation rate!

There have been several more formal empirical studies of the anti-inflation hypothesis. As is usual in these studies, it is not possible to prove the hypothesis that the EMS has helped to reduce inflation because it is impossible to know what would have happened in the absence of the EMS. The most popular method of seeking supporting evidence for the hypothesis has been to compare the EMS countries' inflation performance with the performance of a group of non-EMS countries as above. Obviously, such a comparison is not conclusive and the results can prove sensitive to which non-EMS countries are chosen for comparison. Urenger *et al.* (1985) undertook an empirical investigation for the EMS countries up until 1984 and found that the EMS had a significant negative effect on EMS inflation rates. However, a study by Susan Collins (1988) which compared seven EMS countries' inflation performance with 15 non-EMS countries, both during the periods 1974–78 and 1979–86, found only limited and inconclusive support for the hypothesis that the inflation rate had come down more significantly for the EMS countries for the whole of the period.

Giavazzi and Giovannini (1988) used a different methodology to test the anti-inflation hypothesis. They exploited the theoretical predictions of what is known as the Lucas critique. In a celebrated paper, Lucas (1976) argued that statistical relationships will change according to the policy regime in force. In the context of the EMS, the change in policy regime represented by the setting-up of the EMS means that the statistical parameters governing wage, price and output behaviour in the countries studied (France, Italy, Denmark and Germany) should have changed given the discipline of the EMS. Giavazzi and Giovannini did not find that the statistical relationships changed significantly if mid-1979 was taken as the starting point. If the starting point was taken from the beginning of 1982, there was some weak evidence of a change in wage and price behaviour, providing some support for the anti-inflation hypothesis. The authors suggest that because of large real depreciation of the lira and franc in 1978, the French and Italian authorities did not have to accept the EMS discipline in the early stages of the system. Furthermore, it took economic agents time to learn the implications of EMS memberships, and the authorities time to earn credibility. Only then did agents revise downwards their wage and price behaviour.

Overall, it appears that one of the reasons for the lack of conclusive support for the

Table 16.4 Inflation in ERM and non-ERM countries

	1980	1981	1982	1983	1984	1985	1986	1987	1988	1989	1990	1991	1992	1993	1994	1995	1996	1997	1998
ERM countries																			
Belgium	6.7	7.1	8.7	7.7	6.3	4.9	1.3	1.6	1.2	3.1	3.4	4.2	2.2	2.5	2.4	1.3	1.8	1.5	0.9
Denmark	12.3	11.7	10.1	6.9	6.3	4.7	3.7	4.0	4.5	4.8	2.6	2.4	2.1	1.3	2.0	2.1	2.1	2.2	1.8
France	13.6	13.4	11.8	9.6	7.4	5.8	2.7	3.1	2.7	3.6	3.4	3.4	2.5	2.2	1.7	1.8	2.1	1.3	0.7
Italy	21.2	19.3	16.4	14.9	10.6	8.6	6.1	4.6	5.0	6.6	6.1	6.2	5.0	4.5	4.2	5.4	4.0	1.9	2.0
Netherlands	6.5	6.7	5.9	2.7	3.3	2.3	0.1	−0.7	0.7	1.1	2.5	3.2	2.8	1.6	2.1	1.4	1.4	1.9	1.8
Germany	5.4	6.3	5.2	3.3	2.4	2.1	−0.1	0.2	1.3	2.8	2.7	4.1	5.1	4.4	2.7	1.7	1.2	1.5	0.6
Average ERM	10.1	10.8	9.7	7.5	6.1	4.7	2.3	2.1	2.6	3.7	3.5	3.9	3.3	2.8	2.5	2.3	2.1	1.7	1.3
Non-ERM countries																			
Austria	6.3	6.8	5.4	3.3	5.7	3.2	1.7	1.4	1.9	2.6	3.3	3.1	3.4	3.2	2.7	1.6	1.8	1.2	0.8
Canada	10.2	12.4	10.8	5.8	4.3	4.0	4.2	4.4	4.0	5.0	4.8	5.6	1.5	1.9	0.2	2.2	1.6	1.6	1.0
Japan	7.8	4.9	2.7	1.9	2.3	2.0	0.6	0.1	0.7	2.3	3.1	3.2	1.7	1.3	0.7	−0.1	0.1	1.7	0.7
Norway	10.9	13.7	11.3	8.4	6.3	5.7	7.2	8.7	6.7	4.6	4.1	3.4	2.3	2.3	1.4	2.4	1.2	2.6	2.3
United Kingdom	18.0	11.9	8.6	4.6	5.0	6.1	3.4	4.1	4.9	7.8	9.5	7.5	4.2	2.5	2.0	2.7	2.5	1.8	1.6
United States	13.5	10.3	6.1	3.2	4.3	3.5	1.9	3.7	4.1	4.8	5.4	4.2	3.0	3.0	2.6	2.8	2.9	2.3	1.5
Average non-ERM	11.1	10.0	7.5	4.5	4.7	4.1	3.2	3.7	3.7	4.5	5.0	4.5	2.7	2.4	1.1	1.9	1.7	1.9	1.3

Note: (a) The above inflation rates are based on consumer price indices. (b) The UK is included as a 'non-member' although it was a member between October 1990 and September 1992. Austria is also included as a non-member although it joined the system in January 1995.

Source: OECD *World Economic Outlook.*

anti-inflation hypothesis is that for the first three years of its operation it is a seriously defective description of the EMS. The differential effects of the second oil shock made authorities very reluctant to accept the discipline of the system, as is amply illustrated by the frequent realignments and the French dash for growth in 1981. It seems that only after 1982 did policy-makers in France, Denmark, Belgium and Italy decide to subject their economies to disinflationary policies. For instance, the French government adopted an austerity package in March 1983 and the Italian authorities repealed wage indexation laws in 1984. The resulting disinflation led to both a rapid decline in EMS inflation rates and a greater degree of convergence as compared to the group of non-EMS currencies.

16.9 Intervention policy in the EMS

Although the EMS was supposed to result in more symmetry with regard to intervention through the mechanism of the ECU divergence indicator, in practice the indicator did not work particularly well. A study of intervention within the EMS by Mastropasqua and Rinaldi (1988) showed some interesting asymmetries and contrasts with respect to intervention behaviour.

The Bundesbank was generally very active with regard to non-obligatory **intra-marginal intervention**. At times, however, particularly when the system was on the verge of realignments (such as in January 1987 and the 1992/93 crises) it was prepared to engage in heavy obligatory **marginal intervention**. The Bundesbank was far more active with regard to the dollar exchange rate; it was a large seller of dollars when the dollar was appreciating during 1980–85 and a large purchaser when the dollar subsequently fell. The other ERM countries were far more active with regard to intra-marginal intervention and keeping their currencies in line with the deutschmark. Increasingly they used deutschmarks in preference to dollars for such intra-marginal intervention.

The other interesting finding was that the Bundesbank typically sterilized its interventions so that they did not affect the German monetary base. That is, purchases or sales of foreign currency that increased or decreased the German money supply were typically offset by sales or purchases of domestic bonds so as to neutralize the effect on the German monetary base. The other EMS countries normally only engaged in partial sterilization (30–40%) so that purchases or sales of foreign currency resulted in expansion and contraction of their domestic money supplies.

The overall picture that emerges is that the Bundesbank managed the external exchange rate of the ERM currencies against the dollar, while the rest of the ERM members took responsibility for ensuring that they keep their exchange rates in line with the deutschmark managing the internal parities. In addition, the Bundesbank by pursuing a sterilization policy generally did not allow its exchange rate policy to influence its money supply and its primary objective of domestic price stability. On the other hand, other ERM countries accepted the discipline of the system, by purchasing their currencies when they were weak to keep them in line with the deutschmark and permitting this intervention to result in a contraction in their money supplies.

Nevertheless, Mastropasqua and Rinaldi (1988) emphasized that intervention was only one of the means by which countries maintained their peg to the deutschmark. The most obvious means was to raise their domestic interest rates when their currencies were under pressure and lower them when the pressure receded. Here, again, there was ample evidence that countries other than Germany undertook most of the adjustment burden, the Bundesbank proving very reluctant to reduce interest rates when the deutschmark was strong. In practice, far from being a symmetrical system it appears that weak currency members accepted the discipline of the EMS both with respect to their intervention and domestic economic policies and were prepared to accept the deflationary consequences necessary to maintain their exchange rate. In the early years of the system some of the countries found the discipline too much and realigned their currencies. .

16.10 The economic performance of ERM and non-ERM countries

While there is reasonable agreement that the EMS succeeded in its aim of becoming 'a zone of currency stability', especially in comparison to currencies that have been left to float such as the dollar, yen and sterling, there is considerable disagreement over the benefits or otherwise of full EMS membership. Even if membership of the ERM helped in the fight against inflation, this may have been at the expense of countries having to adopt deflationary policies leading to lower economic growth and higher unemployment than non-members. **Table 16.5** shows that economic growth was generally lower for the ERM countries, and it can also be shown that unemployment rates were generally higher for the ERM countries as compared to the non-ERM countries.

Having completed a review of the EMS we now proceed to look in detail at the topic of Economic and Monetary Union.

16.11 What is meant by economic and monetary union?

There are two main components to an economic and monetary union between two or more countries; an exchange rate union and complete capital market integration. By an exchange rate union we mean that the countries agree to the permanent fixing of their exchange rates with no margin of fluctuation. For all intents and purposes this is equivalent to the creation of a single currency. Indeed, the creation of a single currency is the logical outcome of such a situation emphasizing the permanency of the arrangement. The second component of a monetary union is complete capital market integration, which means that all obstacles to the free movement of financial capital between the union members are removed. Furthermore, capital market integration also requires that equal treatment afforded to financial capital throughout the members of the union.

While permanently fixed exchange rates and complete capital market integration are explicit requirements for monetary union, these in turn involve some implicit requirements. One is that the members of the union harmonize their monetary policies. Differential monetary growth rates once productivity differentials have been allowed for would lead to differing inflation rates, which would threaten parity changes undermining the requirement of permanently fixed exchange rates. When a single currency is brought into circulation, it requires a union central bank to control its supply and manage the exchange rate of the currency against third country currencies. Such a central bank needs to be invested with a pool of foreign exchange reserves for this purpose.

Hence, a monetary union differs from a fixed exchange rate system in several

Table 16.5 Economic growth in ERM and non-ERM countries

	1980	1981	1982	1983	1984	1985	1986	1987	1988	1989	1990	1991	1992	1993	1994	1995	1996	1997	1998
ERM countries																			
Belgium	2.9	-0.3	1.1	2.0	1.4	2.5	1.2	1.7	4.1	3.8	4.2	1.8	1.3	-0.7	3.3	2.3	0.8	3.8	2.1
Denmark	-0.4	-0.9	3.0	2.5	4.4	4.3	3.6	0.3	1.2	0.6	1.4	1.1	0.6	0	5.5	2.8	2.5	3.0	2.5
France	1.6	1.2	2.5	0.7	1.3	1.9	2.5	2.3	4.5	4.3	2.5	1.0	1.3	-0.9	1.9	1.8	1.0	1.9	3.6
Italy	3.5	0.5	0.5	1.2	2.6	2.8	2.8	3.1	3.9	2.9	2.2	1.4	0.7	-0.9	2.3	3.0	1.0	2.0	1.7
Netherlands	1.2	-0.5	-1.2	1.7	3.3	3.1	2.8	1.4	2.6	4.7	4.1	2.4	1.5	0.7	2.9	3.0	3.0	3.8	4.3
Germany	1.0	1.0	-0.9	1.8	2.8	2.0	2.3	1.5	3.7	3.6	5.7	5.1	1.8	-1.1	2.4	1.8	0.8	1.5	1.7
Average ERM	1.6	0	0.8	1.7	2.6	2.8	2.5	1.7	3.3	3.3	3.4	2.1	1.2	-0.5	3.1	2.5	1.5	2.7	2.7
Non-ERM countries																			
Austria	2.9	-0.3	1.1	2.0	1.4	2.5	1.2	1.7	4.1	3.8	4.2	3.6	2.4	0.3	2.7	1.9	2.6	1.8	3.6
Canada	1.5	3.7	-3.2	3.2	6.3	4.8	3.3	4.2	5.0	2.4	-0.2	-2.1	0.9	2.3	4.8	2.8	1.6	4.2	4.1
Japan	2.8	3.2	3.1	2.3	3.9	4.4	2.9	4.2	6.2	4.8	5.1	3.4	1.0	0.2	1.1	1.9	3.4	1.9	-1.1
Norway	4.2	0.9	0.3	4.6	5.7	5.3	4.2	2.0	-0.5	0.9	1.9	3.6	3.3	2.7	5.3	4.4	5.3	5.2	2.6
United Kingdom	-2.2	-1.3	1.7	3.7	2.4	3.5	4.4	4.8	5.0	2.2	0.4	-1.4	0.2	2.3	4.4	2.9	2.8	3.3	3.1
United States	-0.3	2.5	-2.1	4.0	6.8	3.7	3.0	2.9	3.8	3.4	1.3	-0.2	3.3	2.7	4.0	2.5	3.7	4.5	4.2
Average non-ERM	1.5	1.5	0.2	3.3	4.4	4.0	3.2	3.3	3.9	2.9	2.1	1.2	1.9	1.8	3.7	2.7	3.2	3.5	2.8

Source: OECD *World Economic Outlook.*

fundamental respects. A monetary union is a permanent commitment to peg the exchange rate logically leading to the creation of a single currency. Fixed exchange systems allow for occasional realignments and usually permit margins of fluctuation around a central rate. A monetary union requires a well-developed institutional framework such as a single union central bank. Finally, within a monetary union financial capital must be allowed to move freely between the members of the union. This contrasts with the experience of some fixed exchange rate regimes whereby exchange rate parities are often defended only by resort to capital controls.

16.12 Benefits of economic and monetary union

The benefits and costs associated with the introduction of a single European currency – the euro – legal tender throughout the EU members of the currency union, are a mixture of political, social and economic benefits.

Stimulus to intra-EU trade

The underlying rationale of the European Union is that the removal of barriers to trade by increasing the volume of intra-EU trade will lead to a corresponding rise in the economic prosperity of its members. To maximize the trade flows between the EU member states and achieve a truly single market, it is argued that there needs to be a common medium of exchange. Differing national currencies that fluctuate against one another inhibit trade flows by increasing uncertainty facing companies which can only be eliminated by hedging techniques that entail additional (though not substantial) costs for small to medium-sized companies. This argument for a currency union in Europe is particularly important; not only are the European economies particularly open to international trade as a percentage of their gross domestic product, but also a large proportion of their trade is with each other, that is there high degree of intra-European trade.

Against this, some have argued that short-run exchange rate uncertainty can be easily hedged and probably has very little adverse effect on trade (see for example IMF, 1984), implying that the benefits from a single currency may be small. However, Peree and Steinherr (1989) have argued that the problem is not really short-term uncertainty which can be easily hedged, but rather medium to long-term uncertainty (one-year-plus horizon) for which well-developed forward markets do not exist. They find that medium to long-run exchange rate uncertainty generally exerts a significant adverse effect on international trade. As a monetary union is by definition a long-term arrangement, the adverse effects of medium to long-run exchange rate uncertainty would presumably be eliminated.

A further boost to intra-EU trade comes from the elimination of the transactions costs involved in converting different currencies for intra-EU trade. These costs involve the time and resources used up by firms acquiring and selling the requisite currencies, and banks' commission charges. The European Commission has estimated the cost savings from elimination of these transaction costs to be around 0.4% of EU GDP per annum. It should be noted, however, that this would involve smaller profits for banks. **Box 16.1** describes controversial research on the impact of monetary unions on trade flows.

The impact of a monetary union on trade

In a recent and controversial paper, Rose (2000) estimated that the effects of a currency union could increase trade by as much as 300% in the countries he studied where currency unions had come into being, comparing the volumes of trade to countries that did not have a common currency. The Rose paper has come in for much criticism since it was focused on relatively poor and/or small nations that had formed currency unions and its applicability to the case of the European Union is doubtful, although it nonetheless suggests that the effects of creating a single currency in Europe could be quite significant. In a follow-up paper, Glick and Rose (2001) examine the impact of a currency union on those countries that adopt a common currency using panel data (a mix of cross-sectional and time-series data) and find that it doubles the volume of trade, a considerably lower impact than in the original Rose paper yet still highly significant. In a recent paper, Micco, Stein and Ordonez (2003) using post-1999 data argue that the euro has already increased trade in the region by 4% to 16% depending upon the particular methodology used. These estimates while significantly lower and more realistic than those of Rose (2000) and Glick and Rose (2001) are nonetheless significant and suggestive that the creation of the euro has already had a significant economic impact. They also find that the creation of the euro, as well as stimulating intra-Eurozone trade, has also increased extra-Eurozone trade (that is trade with non-Euro members). Another interesting finding is that the impact of the euro on trade flows actually really began in 1998, a whole year prior to the actual permanent fixing of exchange rates!

A more efficient allocation of factors of production within the EU

EMU involves not only the creation of a single European currency, but also the removal of capital controls and distortions to the treatment of financial capital among EU countries. There is no doubt that the free movement of capital within the EU has in the past been distorted by capital controls and differing national treatments of financial capital leading to a sub-optimal allocation within the Union. Capital controls have typically restricted capital from moving to countries where it has a low marginal productivity to countries where it has a high marginal productivity. The permanent abolition of exchange rate controls and the absence of uncertainty created by exchange rate fluctuations has undoubtedly led to a more efficient allocation of capital within the Union. Similarly, with wages and salaries expressed in terms of a common currency, EMU will result in a better allocation of labour, as labour moves from areas of low-marginal to high productivity regions.

Economizing of foreign exchange reserves and seigniorage benefits

Dollar Treasury bonds held in EU member reserves typically earn low rates of interest and their purchasing power in terms of US goods is eroded over time by US inflation. Economizing on the amount of reserves held would reduce the seigniorage benefits accruing to the USA (see Chapter 11). Some argue that EMU will reduce the total foreign exchange reserve holdings of EU countries, since there is no need to hold reserves to manage intra-EU exchange rates. Furthermore, there is a good chance that the euro will tend to fluctuate less against third-country currencies than the individual EU currencies. The reasoning is that the average economic performance of many countries with the same currency is likely to be more stable than that of the individual countries with their own currencies, implying less need to hold foreign exchange reserves. In addition, the euro will inevitably become a major world currency, leading to an increase in the European currency component of non-EU countries' reserves primarily at the expense of the US dollar, resulting in corresponding seigniorage benefits accruing to the EU. Cohen and Wyplosz (1989) have estimated that the gains accruing to the EU from this latter effect could amount to around 0.75% of European Union gross national product.

Additional benefits are:

- **Savings in administrative costs for businesses.** This is potentially significant benefit for firms involved in managing their exchange risk and operating their businesses in many different European currencies. Different European currencies and fluctuations between them have meant that firms use up resources in having to monitor their exchange-risk exposure and in revising their pricing strategies in the different European markets. The existence of the euro has considerably reduced these costs.
- **Greater liquidity and rationalization of financial markets.** This is less talked about but potentially important benefit of EMU for the eurozone area. Prior to the euro, national government bond and equity markets, while generally very liquid, were to some extent segmented from one another. Post-EMU, all government debt of the member countries has been denominated in euros and this has made the government bond markets even more liquid and resulted in a lowering of transaction costs. Furthermore, there has already been a significant rationalization of equity markets; now company stocks are all quoted in euros with more equity business done on the most efficient exchanges. The access to cheaper sources of finance and improved liquidity for both governments and companies is a potentially significant benefit from EMU.
- **Greater price transparency.** Another gain from having a single currency is that consumers and businesses benefit from price transparency. Now that all prices in the eurozone countries are quoted in euros it is more difficult for manufacturers to maintain significant price differentials in different markets. Consumers buying from the cheapest sources will, over time, help ensure that a single pricing policy biased towards the lower end of the prices charged in different countries is adopted by many multinationals. This implies a potential benefit for consumers and businesses at the expense of reduced profits for some multinational companies.

16.13 Costs of European Monetary Union

Most of the perceived costs of EMU are not so much associated with the final attainment of monetary union, but rather with the transitional costs associated in achieving it.

- **Loss of monetary autonomy.** The use of a common currency with a European Central Bank charged with determining monetary policy and the short-term interest rate on the euro is the most visible sign of the main cost associated with EMU.

Since EMU has involved the introduction of a single currency with no capital controls, then a single short-term interest rate has prevailed in the eurozone countries. This means real dilemmas for the European Central Bank when setting interest rates, as it has to reconcile the needs of booming member states with those of member states suffering from recession. In the absence of EMU, national central banks in booming countries would typically raise the short-term interest rate to dampen economic activity, while national central banks of countries in recession would usually reduce the short-term interest rate to boost economic activity. A common interest rate in the post-EMU era may be insufficiently high to curtail economic activity in booming countries while too high to help countries in recession.

- **Loss of national macroeconomic policy autonomy.** A major argument against EMU is that the acceptance of a single currency means that countries are no longer free to determine their own monetary policies and inflation rates. In economics it is widely believed that in the short run a trade-off exists between inflation and unemployment known as the Phillips curve. Some countries prefer to have low inflation rates and are prepared to accept relatively high unemployment, while others prefer low unemployment and relatively high inflation. With floating exchange rates these different inflation preferences can be reconciled by an appreciating currency for low-inflation countries. Since a monetary union requires common inflation rates, countries with differing preferences with respect to any unemployment–inflation trade off will lose from monetary union. This argument is illustrated in **Figure 16.1** that compares the UK and eurozone Phillips curves.

  Assume that UK policy makers prefer relatively high inflation, while the Eurozone prefers less inflation. The optimal inflation-unemployment trade-off for the UK is given by P_{UK*} and U_{UK*}, while the optimal trade-off for Eurozone area

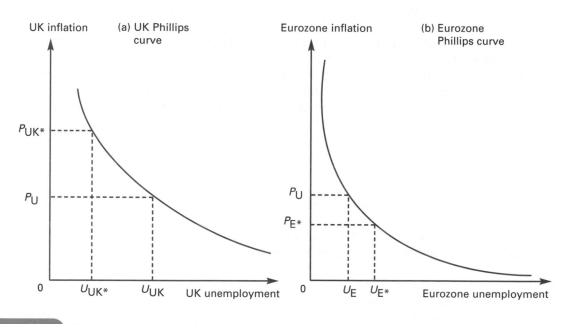

Figure 16.1   UK and eurozone Phillips curves

is P_{E*} and U_{E*}. In a monetary union both have to accept a common inflation rate P_{U*}, which implies higher UK unemployment than UK policy-makers prefer, and higher eurozone inflation than the eurozone countries prefer. However, there is much debate in economics over whether Phillips curve trade-off exists. Most economists accept that in the short run such a trade-off usually exists but in the long run no such trade-off exists, with each country having a vertical Phillips curve at its natural rate of unemployment. Hence, the costs associated with the loss of national policy autonomy are probably confined to the short run.

- **Loss of inflation tax**. German agreement to EMU was crucially dependent upon guarantees of a low inflation rate in the union. For some governments, especially the 2004 Accession countries, the move to EMU is potentially costly because it is necessary to bring their inflation rates down and into line with the low eurozone rate. This undermines their implicit inflation tax revenue. In countries where there is a large amount of outstanding public debt and a large holding of the monetary base, as opposed to interest-earning bank accounts, inflation by reducing the real value of both the outstanding debt and the purchasing power of the authorities' monetary base liability effectively constitutes a tax. The lower EMU inflation rate implies a smaller inflation tax revenue for high-inflation countries meaning that their governments will have to replace the lost inflation tax with explicit direct and indirect taxes. In an analysis of this argument, Cohen and Wyplosz (1989) calculated that the taxation of the monetary base was far more significant for some countries than others. In particular, assuming a constant 5% inflation rate, the inflation tax as a percentage of GDP was 2.1% for Ireland, 3.9% for Italy and 3.5% for Spain, but only 1% for Germany, 1.1% for France and 0.7% for the UK and the Netherlands. Furthermore, since Italy and Spain are among the most heavily indebted countries, the temptation to inflate and reduce the real value of outstanding debt was higher in those countries. It should be noted that although explicit taxes tend to be politically more unpopular than hidden taxes, such as 'inflation taxes', from an economic viewpoint the replacement of inflation tax by more explicit taxes is not necessarily a bad thing!

- **Regional disparities**. Another concern over EMU is that while it will probably lead to gains for the EU as a whole, some countries could gain while others could lose. The increased movements of capital and labour associated with EMU, as factors move from low marginal productivity areas towards high productivity areas, could manifest as a regional problem with undesirable social effects. This may be particularly important with respect to labour movements, because labour that leaves low productivity areas is usually the most mobile and productive part of a region's workforce. To mitigate such adverse regional effects may require a corrective EU regional policy, with those regions and countries that gain, funding compensatory measures in regions that have lost from EMU. Although some regional disparities may emerge as a result of EMU, it is very much open to debate as to whether regional policy is the best means of alleviating the problem. Regional policies have fallen out of favour in recent years for a whole host of reasons; these include political manipulation, the diversion of funds to inefficient industries and the delaying of desirable economic adjustments. In practice, it is difficult to assess whether a region is in decline because of EMU or for other reasons.

- **Loss of the exchange rate policy instrument**. Another argument employed against EMU is that the member countries, by agreeing to a fixed exchange rate within the union, are depriving themselves of both the exchange rate policy instrument and monetary policy instruments. Tinbergen's instruments–target rule (see Chapter 4) argued that policy-makers generally require as many independent instruments as they have targets. The loss of the exchange rate policy instrument and ability to pursue an independent monetary policy does not matter if the authorities have only one objective, because they could use fiscal policy to achieve internal balance. However, this leaves the problem of external balance. The question of whether or not the authorities are really losing a policy instrument for dealing with external equilibrium is not clear-cut. This is because for the Eurozone as a whole, there is nothing to prevent the euro floating *vis-à-vis* currencies of the rest of the world to ensure that the balance of payments of the Eurozone is kept in equilibrium. Nevertheless, overall external equilibrium for the Eurozone disguises the fact that some member countries of the Eurozone may experience persistent deficits and others persistent surpluses. The loss of the exchange rate policy instrument is therefore applicable to the individual Eurozone countries.

- **Transition costs**. There are inevitably some transition costs involved in EMU. These range from the costs of calling-in existing national notes, the printing of new notes, education and training, changing information technology systems to cope with the new currency, and altering existing automated telling machines and vending machines. The European Banking Federation (1995) estimated the costs of the transition to be 25–40 billion ECUs or roughly 2% of bank costs. These are largely 'one-off' costs, and against these we need to offset certain future benefits such as economies of scale that will result from manufacturers having to deal with only one currency and banks having to deal with less currencies, and so on.

Overall, it is clear that there are some advantages and some disadvantages attached to EMU. Even if the overall benefits of EMU exceed the overall costs this does not necessarily imply that EMU is in any sense optimal. The number of countries that would form an optimal EMU remains an open question. Another point to bear in mind is that there may well be winners and losers from EMU, and/or the benefits may be spread thinly over many millions of people throughout the Union while the losses are heavily concentrated in particular sectors. Another very important point when considering the benefits and costs associated with EMU concerns the characteristics of the new European currency. If the euro turns out to be a low-inflation and well-managed currency with responsibility for its issue in the hands of a credible, independent, well-managed European Central Bank (ECB), then the case for EMU is strengthened. If, however, the euro turns out to be a weak, inflation-prone currency run by a poorly managed European Central Bank then the case for EMU is correspondingly weakened. Finally, for past and future potential member states the precise costs and benefits depend partly on the conversion rates of their currency against the euro – to the extent that a currency is overvalued in relation to say PPP this increases the real purchasing power of the country, but against this the country may suffer a loss of competitiveness which could contribute to a post-EMU recession in that country.

16.14 A history of the road to European Monetary Union

The Rome Treaty of 1957 which created the European Economic Community (EEC) made no explicit mention of monetary union; however, the architects of the treaty no doubt envisaged the EEC eventually developing into a fully fledged economic union with full monetary integration among its members. At the time of signing the Rome Treaty, the priority was the creation a customs union which involved the adoption of a common tariff policy *vis-à-vis* third countries and the removal of trade barriers (especially tariffs) between member countries. By 1968 much progress had been made in these areas and it was believed that a means of further increasing trade between members would be creation of a single European currency. At the Hague Summit of December 1969 the then six member countries of the EEC agreed in principle to establish complete economic and monetary union in stages, commencing in January 1971 and being completed by the end of 1980. Although in retrospect such a target seems absurdly ambitious, it must be remembered that the Bretton Woods system of fixed exchange rates had been operating with only occasional realignments for two decades.

The Werner Report

As a result of the Hague Summit of 1969, a committee was set up to investigate the subject and in 1972 it delivered the so-called Werner Report on Economic and Monetary Union. The report envisaged a fully fledged monetary union between the members of the EEC by 1980. In relation to the free movement of factors of production the report argued for the removal of all impediments and distortions to such movements. The report foresaw the conduct of fiscal and monetary policies being carried out at the community level by community institutions invested with the necessary decision-taking powers. The main aim of such institutions being to regulate the monetary and credit policies of the union and manage the external exchange rate *vis-à-vis* non-EEC currencies. Fiscal policy would be employed to ensure both economic stability and growth. Finally, community institutions would also operate regional and structural policies designed 'to contribute to the balanced development of the community'.

The main result of the Werner Report was the Snake in the Tunnel arrangement of 1972 which, as we have seen, had a very poor track record and was all but finished by 1978. Apart from being over-ambitious, there were more fundamental reasons for the failure to achieve EMU by the target date. In the first instance, the six original members were joined by Ireland, the United Kingdom and Denmark in 1973. Their accession negotiations and ensuring their successful integration into the EEC inevitably took precedence. In addition, as we saw in Chapter 11, the Bretton Woods system of fixed exchange rates broke up in 1971 and was swiftly followed by the first oil shock of 1973/4. The impact of the oil price rise was not spread evenly and coinciding with the new era of floating exchange rates meant that countries were free to adopt different policy responses. Some countries, such as the UK and Italy, adopted expansionary policies in a bid to stave off recession, while others such as Germany were determined to avoid inflation and adopted deflationary policies. With such policy divergences and resulting differential inflation rates any hope of achieving fixed exchange rate parities between European currencies was soon vanquished. During the period 1971–75 French consumer prices rose by 52%, while in Germany they rose by 34.7% and in the UK by 82.5%.

At the end of the day, the principal obstacle to monetary union was that the Heads of State that met at the Hague Summit failed to deliver the political will and commitment necessary for its achievement. To a large extent they misunderstood the full implications required to achieve EMU. Put simply, the declaration to achieve EMU only had a real chance of success if the member states were prepared to sacrifice the macroeconomic control of their national economies to achieve common inflation objectives, and the political will to do this was never present.

EMS and the Delors Report

The EMU project was clearly flagging when in 1978 the President of the European Commission Roy Jenkins suggested that a European Monetary System be set up to provide a zone of currency stability for the European currencies. As we have seen, the EMS had a mixed performance in its early days and was not initially viewed as a vehicle for achieving EMU. However, in 1986 Europe passed the Single European Act with the aim of creating a single market by 1992. This in turn led to an inevitable debate about whether a single market would be best served by a single currency. At a meeting of the European Council in June 1988, the Heads of Government of the member countries of the EEC confirmed the long-run objective of economic and monetary union. A committee of academics and central bankers headed by Jacques Delors, President of the European Commission, was set up to investigate the EMU issue and propose a strategy for achieving EMU. The result of the deliberations was the so-called Delors Report of 1989 which set out a broad outline proposal for achieving EMU. The Delors Report emphasized that member states would have to be prepared to transfer decision-making power to Community institutions in the field of monetary policy and be bound to pre-set procedures and rules in other areas such as fiscal policy. In particular, it emphasized the need not only for convergent monetary policies, but also for convergent fiscal policies. The report argued that monetary union requires a single currency rather than just irrevocably fixed parities. A single currency would demonstrate the irreversibility of the move to monetary union, considerably facilitate monetary management within the community and avoid the transaction costs of converting currencies. An EU Central Bank was viewed as a necessity to operate monetary and credit policy and interest policy rather than close coordination between existing central banks. Full liberalization of capital markets and financial market integration were also viewed as essential.

The Delors Report took it for granted that the benefits of EMU exceed the costs, and it was the remit of the committee to draw up a set of proposals relating to how such a process might be achieved. The report envisaged the attainment of EMU in three stages, each stage representing a significant change with respect to the preceding one. The report did not set out explicit deadline dates, but it was subsequently decided by the European Council meeting in Madrid in June 1989 that Stage 1 would begin on 1 July 1990. Prospective dates for Stage 2 (1 January 1994) and Stage 3 (1 January 1997 or 1 January 1999) were later agreed at Maastricht and by the European Council in Madrid in December 1995. The three stages were as follows:

Stage 1: the convergence phase
The first stage lasted from 1 July 1990 to 31 December 1993 and aimed at providing the necessary foundation upon which to build EMU, especially a greater convergence of economic performance and enhancing economic and monetary coordination between member states within the existing EMS institutional framework. The main features of this stage were the completion of the Single Market project, a strengthening of community policies to iron out regional imbalances, greater cooperation and coordination of monetary and fiscal policies, the removal of obstacles to financial integration including the removal of all obstacles to the private use of the ECU, and all members of the EMS joining the ERM.

Stage 2: the transition phase

The second stage began on 1 January 1994 and represented a transition phase aimed at ensuring the readiness of national economies for the eventual permanent fixing of exchange rate parities. The second stage required amendments to the Treaty of Rome and resulted in the Maastricht Treaty. In this stage the basic organs and structure of economic and monetary union were set up involving both the revision of existing community institutions and establishment of new ones. The major institutional development in this stage was the establishment of the European Monetary Institute (EMI) in Frankfurt on 1 January 1994 to prepare the groundwork for the implementation of the final phase. The EMI had two main tasks: (i) to assist progress on economic convergence by strengthening coordination of monetary polices between EU central banks, the so-called European System of Central Banks (ESCB) with the aim of ensuring price stability, and (ii) to make preparations for the final phase, for example, by working on issues such as the statute of the Central Bank, the European System of Central Banks (ESCB), note and coin design, financial sector issues, dissemination of information, and so on.

The ESCB absorbed the previously existing monetary arrangements (the EMCF and Committee of Central Bank governors). The key task of the ESCB was to begin the transition from the coordination of independent national monetary policies to the formulation and implementation of a common monetary policy by the ESCB itself. Upon EMU in 1999, the ESCB assumed full control over the formulation and implementation of the Community's monetary policy, including day to day decisions on exchange market interventions with respect to third currencies.

Stage 3: the fixing and euro phase

The Maastricht Treaty stipulated two possible starting dates for the permanent fixing of exchange rates, either the 1 January 1997 or 1 January 1999; since the 1997 date was missed the 1 January 1999 date became *de facto* the new starting date. Members that met the so-called Maastricht conditions would move to irrevocably locked exchange rates with national currencies subsequently being replaced by the euro. From 1 January 1999 the members of the currency union became subject to a single monetary policy set by the European Central Bank. In addition, rules and procedures relating to the Community in the macroeconomic and budgetary field became binding. In particular, the Council of Ministers in cooperation with the European Parliament had the authority to take directly enforceable decisions. The European Central Bank was given full control over the formulation and implementation of the Eurozone's monetary policy.

16.15 The Maastricht Treaty

As a follow-up to the Delors Report, the Maastricht Treaty was signed in the Dutch town of Maastricht in December 1991 and, following ratification in the parliaments of all EU countries, came into force on 1 November 1993. The Maastricht Treaty was in part a collection of additions and amendments to the Treaty of Rome covering political and economic reform. It provided the legal basis to establish the institutions required for EMU; for instance, allowing the formation of a European Central Bank. The Treaty also set out the conditions under which a country would be eligible for joining EMU. Only countries that meet all four of the following conditions, the so-called 'convergence criteria' had the right to join in EMU at the outset and these conditions also apply to the prospective new EMU entrants (see section 16.25):

1　Average consumer price inflation in the country should not be more than 1.5% above that of the three countries with the lowest inflation rates.
2　A country should not have an excessive budget deficit, with the reference rate being that it should not exceed 3% of gross domestic product.
3　The outstanding public-sector debt (national debt) of the country should not exceed 60% of gross domestic product.
4　Average nominal long-term interest rates in the year of examination should not be more than 2% above that of the three countries with the lowest inflation rates.

It should be noted that in respect of the Maastricht criteria there was two big let-out clauses. Firstly in respect of fiscal deficits a country might be permitted to join with a fiscal deficit above 3% of GDP if 'the ratio has declined substantially and continuously and reached a level that comes close to the reference value; or, alternatively, the excess over the reference value is only exceptional and temporary and the ratio remains close to the reference value'. In respect of the levels of national debt, a country might be permitted to join in EMU with national debts above 60% if 'the ratio is sufficiently diminishing and approaching the reference value at a satisfactory pace'. The latter let-out clause became very significant when the European Commission made its assessment of eligible entrants in 1998.

In addition to the four criteria, the currency of a country was expected to have respected normal margins of fluctuation and not been devalued within the ERM in the two years prior to a country joining EMU. The United Kingdom and Denmark were in a different position from the other EU countries since they were not required to join EMU even if they met the convergence criteria. The United Kingdom negotiated an 'opt-out' which was set out in a Protocol attached to the Treaty. The Protocol stated that the UK was not obliged to join Stage 3 without a separate decision by its government and Parliament. Denmark decided not to join Stage 3 but had the right to revoke this decision in accordance with its constitution. Subsequently, it was agreed that actual (not forecast!) 1997 data would be used for assessing which countries were eligible to join EMU in conjunction with forecasts for 1998, the decision being taken by a qualified majority vote in May 1998. Sweden effectively made itself ineligible for EMU entrance by not permitting the kronor to participate in the ERM system for the two years prior to EMU.

16.16 An evaluation of the Maastricht criteria

The Maastricht criteria were primarily motivated by a German desire to ensure that the qualifying members for EMU had a strong fiscal and monetary background. Having a European Central Bank with voting members made up from countries with a sound financial background was viewed as an essential foundation for ensuring that the euro would turn out to be a sound currency with similar attributes to the deutschmark. Another way of saying roughly the same thing was that the Germans were keen to exclude countries with a poor economic record and high propensity to print money when faced with economic difficulty (such as Italy and Greece). While the basic idea of including only countries with sound economies and sound fiscal policies as a basis for ensuring a sound monetary union has significant merits, the Maastricht criteria have been subjected to numerous criticisms.

One criticism was that the Maastricht criteria were very arbitrary both in relation to the targets set and the targets chosen. The choice of 3% for the budget deficit to GDP ratio and 60% for the government debt to GDP ratio were clearly arbitrary – the limits could easily be raised to say 3.5% and 80% respectively without creating a confidence crisis and permitting more founding members. In addition, in the run-up to EMU there was evidence that some governments were massaging their fiscal deficits it meet the criteria.

Another major criticism was that the national debt criterion was not really appropriate since it looked only on the liability side, ignoring state-owned assets. A government can have a high national debt but the value of state-owned assets might mean it has a low net liability or even a positive net asset position; whereas a government with a lower national debt might have relatively few state-owned assets and a lower net asset position relative to its GDP. Many have criticized the choice of targets as being only financially oriented, having nothing to say on the real economy such as economic growth, the balance of payments and rate of unemployment. Indeed, the narrow focus on financial criteria may have imposed an excessive degree of fiscal austerity on Europe in the run-up to EMU, implying higher unemployment and lower economic growth than would otherwise have been the case.

A significant critique of the Maastricht conditions was made by De Grauwe (1996) who pointed out that countries like Italy and Belgium would have less of a public debt problem and lower fiscal deficits if they were allowed to join EMU. This is because outside of EMU they had to pay high interest rates on their public debts since financial markets feared that they would resort to printing money to repay their debts, and as such they had a significant inflation risk premium built into their interest rates. In a monetary union they would have a lower inflation premium to pay since they would not be able to print money to redeem their national debts which would be denominated in euros. In turn, lower interest rates would enable them to lower their fiscal deficits since they would reduce the financing cost of the national debt which is part of this year's fiscal deficit. In other words, high government debt countries could more easily meet the Maastricht conditions as members of EMU than if they were excluded.

A further argument against the Maastricht conditions is that the convergence criteria are not really that important and they distract attention from more important fundamental issues. The Maastricht Treaty itself has a so-called 'no-bail-out' clause that makes it clear that government debt is the responsibility of the government that issues the debt; in legal terms other member states are excluded from 'joint and several liability'. As such, it can be argued that the Maastricht conditions were not really necessary since each government that joins EMU is responsible for its own debt and governments will have to be prudent so as to ensure that their debt rating is not undermined by credit-rating agencies.

Another problem with the Maastricht conditions is that there were plenty of 'before' conditions but no 'after' conditions, which to some extent was illogical. A country might behave well before joining the monetary union to qualify for membership and then misbehave after joining. A realization of this problem motivated the Germans to demand that the Maastricht conditions be extended to cover the behaviour of countries after they joined EMU. More specifically, the Germans negotiated a so-called Stability and Growth Pact (SGP) to cover the post-EMU era.

16.17 The Stability and Growth Pact

In the run-up to EMU the German government began to realize that selling the EMU project to a sceptical German public would be extremely hard without any post-EMU guarantees on fiscal deficits. In particular, the Germans feared that countries might get their budget deficits down to meet the Maastricht fiscal criteria, but after EMU fiscal laxity would undermine confidence in the new euro.

At a summit held in Dublin in December 1996, the Germans secured the Stability and Growth Pact (SGP) designed to ensure that fiscal prudence remained in place following the start of EMU. The pact subjects countries running 'excessive' fiscal deficits (defined as a deficit above 3% of GDP) to fines unless they take action to get their deficits down. Each member state of the monetary union has to prepare a multi-annual stability programme setting out its budgetary position which requires endorsement by the Council of Economic and Finance Ministers (ECOFIN) and is made public. Implementation of the programme is monitored by the Commission and ECOFIN which can recommend policy adjustments if the plans are not adhered to.

If a country is deemed to have an 'excessive deficit' the Commission prepares a report and sends it to ECOFIN and if the Council believes the deficit to be excessive it will recommend that the member state take corrective action within four months with a view to correcting the deficit within 12 months of its occurrence. If the measures are not implemented or are deemed to be insufficient, the member state must make a non-interest-rate bearing deposit with the European Central Bank ten months after the notification. If the deficit remains excessive the deposit is converted into a fine two years later.

There are exceptions in which a deficit may be above 3% of GDP without incurring a fine. Most importantly, if the member state has suffered a sharp economic downturn defined as an annual fall of real GDP of 2%, then the deficit is considered exceptional and does not trigger any action. In general, a fall of less than 0.75% in GDP is not considered exceptional, while a fall of between 0.75% and 2% in GDP is subject to the judgment of the Council. Other exceptions include unusual events outside of the Country's control such as a national catastrophe which has a major impact on the member state's financial position.

The penalty initially takes the form of a deposit to be placed in a special Community budget account, which is convertible into a fine after two years if the country fails to bring down its annual budget deficit. The maximum penalty in any one year is 0.5% of GDP, in the first year the deposit is a fixed portion of 0.2% of GDP and a variable portion of 0.1% for every 1% above the 3% threshold. If the deficit persists in the second year, additional variable portion sanctions can be levied up to a ceiling of 0.5% of GDP. Ironically, as **Box 16.3** explains, the Germans themselves have been in breach of the SGP!

16.18 The changeover to the single currency

In November 1995 the European Monetary Institute published a document entitled 'The changeover to the Single Currency', setting out the transition process. The document envisaged three periods for the transition:

1 The first period (originally scheduled for May 1998) involved the selection of the countries that met the Maastricht criteria and were therefore eligible to join EMU.

2 A second period (1 January 1999), the permanent fixing of the bilateral rates between the member currencies and announcement of their conversion rates to the euro. At the start of the second period the European Monetary Institute was to be liquidated and be replaced by the European Central Bank and the European System of Central Banks (ESCB) comprising the ECB and existing national central banks; the purpose of the ESCB being to conduct a single monetary policy for the euro area and to maintain price stability by setting appropriate short-term interest rates for the euro. The ESCB would be responsible for both money-market and foreign-exchange operations for the euro. The Euro was to be used in banking operations alongside the existing national currencies, but one of the guiding principles of the second period was 'no compulsion, no prohibition', that is, no company/bank was to be compelled to use or prevented from using the euro or existing national currencies. This meant that banks were free to make transactions and offer services in the Euro but would only be compelled to do so in the final period. In addition all contracts denominated in ECUs were to be legally replaced by the euro on the basis of one ECU being equal to one euro.

3 A final period (starting on 1 January 2002) was the introduction of euro banknotes and coins alongside existing national notes and coins for a maximum period of six months. Both being legal tender and anyone able to exchange on demand at commercial banks or the national central banks national currency for euros. At the end of the six months and no later than 1 July 2002, it was planned that national notes would cease to be legal tender (although exchangeable for euros at national central banks) with the euro becoming the sole legal tender in the participating countries.

By and large, the timetable envisaged in the changeover plan was successfully followed. On 25 March 1998 the European Commission and European Monetary Institute published their convergence reports recommending that 11 countries, Austria, Belgium, Finland, France, Germany, Ireland, Italy, Luxembourg, Netherlands, Portugal and Spain be admitted to EMU. Then in May 1998 during a meeting of the Heads of State held in Brussels the formal decision was taken to admit the 11 countries and the bilateral exchange rate parities were fixed at the central rates prevailing in the ERM as shown in **Table 16.2**. It was not possible to announce the rates against the euro since the pound sterling was floating against the currencies, and since the pound was part of the ECU then the currencies were still fluctuating against the ECU. On 1 June 1998 the ECB formally came into being replacing the EMI.

On 31 December 1998 the conversion rates to the euro were announced based on the then prevailing exchange rates of the currencies against the ECU. Hence the ECU moved from being a mere calculation to a real currency called the euro at a parity of one ECU to one euro. The final announced conversion rates of the national currencies to the euro are shown in **Table 16.6**, and are the permanently irrevocably fixed rates that prevailed from that point onwards for financial market transactions and for when the national currencies were to be replaced by actual euro notes and coins as from 1 January 2002. On 19 June 2000 the Council of Ministers judged that Greece had fulfilled the convergence criteria and approved its accession to the euro area as the twelfth member starting 1 January 2001. **Box 16.2** looks at some of the logistical matters associated with bringing actual euro notes and coins into existence.

Table 16.6 Irrevocable euro conversion rates

Austria schilling	13.7603	Ireland punt	0.787564
Belgium franc	40.3399	Italy lira	1936.27
Finland markka	5.94573	Luxembourg franc	40.3399
France franc	6.55957	Netherlands guilder	2.20371
Germany deutschmark	1.95583	Portugal escudo	200.482
Greece drachma	340.750	Spain peseta	166.386

Source: European Commission.

Box 16.2

The practicalities of introducing the euro

Although EMU commenced in January 1999 with the irrevocable fixing of exchange rate parities, euro notes and coins were only actually introduced at street level on 1 January 2002. Approximately €132 billion worth of notes and €37.5 billion of euro coins were brought into circulation. The distribution of the coins required the equivalent of 1,000 one tonne trucks making the equivalent of 100,000 journeys. Some 3.2 million vending machines needed converting requiring at least one man-hour to convert each to accept new notes and coins. However, the actual introduction of euro notes and coins went surprisingly smoothly, and within 20 days there was a near 90% usage of the euro in the eurozone area.

16.19 The performance of the euro in the foreign exchange market

When the euro first came into existence it had a parity of approximately $1.17/€1 against the US dollar, and many economists expected it to strengthen. But contrary to expectations the first few years of its existence the euro exhibited a marked decline against the US dollar in the foreign exchange market. However, as **Figure 16.2** shows, the euro has since made a dramatic recovery and the US dollar has declined in value in part due to concerns about the need to correct an ever-widening US current account deficit. The euro's future looks to be bright because of the various safeguards that have been put in place to ensure that it will be a sound low-inflation currency.

16.20 The eurosystem

The overall decision-making structure and control of monetary policy in the eurozone is carried out in the framework of the eurosystem. The eurosystem comprises the ECB and the 12 national central banks (NCBs); the governing bodies of the eurosystem are the Executive Board and the Governing Council. The Executive Board consists of the president, vice-president and four directors of the ECB while the Governing Council is made up of the six members of the Executive Board and

$/€ rate

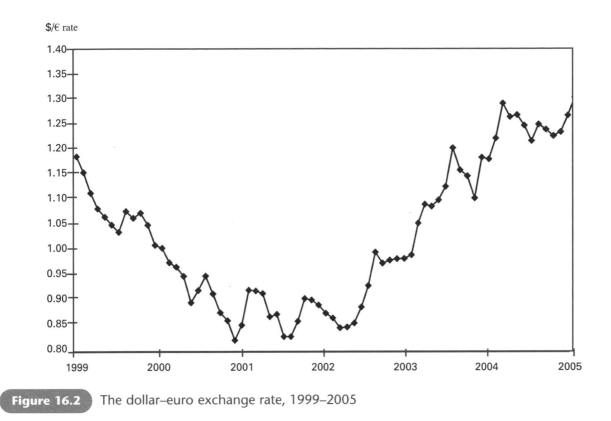

Figure 16.2 The dollar–euro exchange rate, 1999–2005

governors of the 12 NCBs. The Governing Council is the main decision-making body and formulates monetary policy for the eurozone area taking decisions on interest rates, reserve requirements and the provision of liquidity to financial markets and institutions. The Governing Council meets every two weeks in Frankfurt and each of its 18 members has one vote; the Executive Board implements decisions taken by the Governing Council including giving instructions to the 12 NCBs. So while the decision-making process is highly centralized, the implementation process is in fact quite decentralized with the NCBs carrying out the decisions in their national money markets.

The independent ECB has been set up basically modelled on the Bundesbank. Indeed, Paul De Grauwe (2003) argues that the language used by the drafters of the statutes on the ECB is tougher on inflation and political independence than the statutes of the Bundesbank. The ECB has a statutory duty to ensure price stability, and it was left to the European Central Bank to define what was meant by price stability and in its *Monthly Report* of January 1999 it defined this as keeping inflation within the range of 0–2% for the euro area as a whole, using a harmonized index of consumer prices (HICP). The objectives of the ECB are laid out in the Maastricht Treaty, in particular Article 105 makes it clear that the prime objective is price stability but it permits the ECB to 'without prejudice to the objective of price stability' to take into account general economic policies within the Eurozone area including levels of employment, but these are very much secondary to the main objective and from its *Monthly Report* it is quite clear that the ECB itself regards its sole objective as being the maintenance of price stability. The Maastricht Treaty is very clear on the political independence of the ECB, and Article 107 states that:

> When exercising the powers and carrying out the tasks and duties conferred upon them by this Treaty . . . neither the ECB nor a national central bank, nor any member of their decision making bodies shall seek or take instructions from Community institutions or bodies, from any Government of a Member State or from any other body.

The independence of the ECB has been secured by several means. Firstly, the Maastricht Treaty conditions which can themselves only be modified by unanimous approval of all EU member states. Secondly, the minutes of its Governing Council meeting when it sets the target level of short-term interest rate for the euro are not published and neither is the voting record of its members; this protects national central bank governors from fear of job losses for not voting the way that their national governments would like. Finally, the ECB is also prohibited from printing money to finance any member state's fiscal deficit. There have been criticisms about the potential lack of accountability of the ECB, but it has made some moves to dispel such criticisms, for instance the President of the Bank holds a press conference after every meeting of the Governing Council to explain its interest rate policy and the ECB also publishes it *Monthly Report* which explains in some detail the basis of its policies.

While the ECB has a target rate of inflation between 0–2%, it has made it clear that this is a medium-term target (the precise time period is not defined) and as such it can permit this target to be exceeded in the short run. Indeed, in the first 72 months of the euro the 2% inflation target was exceeded in 36 of the months (that is, 50% of the time); however, the deviations were not generally substantial except for a period during late 2000 when in November an annual inflation rate of 2.9% was recorded. In fact in the first 72 months the annualized rate of inflation was exactly 2.01%. The ECB uses an intermediate monetary targeting system to achieve its inflation target, and in particular it has set a reference value for the rate of growth of the M3 money supply in the eurozone of 4.5% per annum, but it permits the reference value to be exceeded or undershot so long as the inflation target is likely to be met over the medium term. The main policy decision of the Governing Council is to set the *refinancing rate* which is the rate of interest at which it will provide liquidity to the banking system in exchange for eligible reserves such as euro-denominated Treasury bills.

Authors such as De Grauwe (2003) have made a number of criticisms of the inflation target; in particular, it is regarded as too low since the actual reported inflation rate may overstate the real inflation rate by anywhere from 0.5–1.5% because of quality improvements. Also, since it is an inflation target for the eurozone area as a whole there may be widely divergent inflation rates between members of the eurozone, with deflation in some and inflation above 2% in others. For further details the reader is referred to De Grauwe (2003) which provides a comprehensive analysis of many issues relating to EMU and the ECB.

Box 16.3

The Stability and Growth Pact in practice

The Stability and Growth Pact (SGP) came about very much because of German insistence that there would be fiscal restraint after the commencement of EMU, and in particular to reassure a sceptical German public that countries such as Italy, Greece, Spain and Portugal would not destabilize the new currency by running large fiscal deficits post-EMU. In practice, however, the German economy has been experiencing slow growth, high unemployment and large fiscal costs associated with reunification of West and East Germany, all of which have meant fiscal problems. In addition, the French economy has been growing relatively slowly combined with high levels of unemployment, and the result has been that, ironically, both countries have been exceeding the fiscal deficits of the SGP is shown in **Table 16.7**.

The fact that German and French fiscal deficits have exceeded the SGP requirements has led to a number of problems, the first being that initial deposit fines should have been levied on France and Germany who successfully blocked such attempts, and this has to a large extent undermined the credibility of the SGP. Fines can be imposed only when a two-thirds majority of the Council of Ministers (finance ministers) approve their imposition, and France and Germany blocked attempts by smaller countries and the Commission to impose the fines. The failure to enforce the SGP on the big countries and a feeling that the SGP imposes an unduly harsh fiscal straightjacket upon countries that need to stimulate economic growth by running larger than 3% fiscal deficits for a certain period of time, has led to an intense debate on how to reform the SGP. One suggestion is to pay attention to the size of public debt; if a country has a low level of national debt then it could be permitted to exceed the 3% fiscal deficit criterion for a period of time, whereas a country with a high national debt would be expected to keep to the 3% limit. Another suggestion is to pay more attention to the cyclically adjusted fiscal deficit; in the case where an economy is growing below trend its headline deficit may be above 3% but its cyclically adjusted deficit might be below 3%, whereas when the economy is growing above trend its headline figure may below 3% while its cyclically adjusted figure might be above 3%. Other proposals include raising the fiscal deficit above 3% to say 4%, or permitting it to average 3% over the economic cycle, thereby allowing a country to temporarily exceed 3% without necessarily incurring a fine.

Table 16.7   Fiscal deflicits post-EMU of euro members

	1999	2000	2001	2002	2003	2004	2005
Austria	2.0	0.8	−0.8	0.3	0.8	0.5	0.5
Belgium	−0.5	1.0	0.5	0	0.2	−0.2	−0.7
Finland	2.2	7.1	5.2	4.3	2.1	1.6	2.1
France	−1.8	−1.4	−1.5	−3.3	−4.1	−3.8	−3.6
Germany	−1.5	1.3	−2.8	−3.5	−3.9	−3.7	−3.1
Greece	−1.8	−2.0	−1.4	−1.5	−3.0	−3.2	−2.9
Ireland	2.3	4.4	1.1	−0.1	0.2	−0.5	−0.8
Italy	−1.8	−0.7	−2.7	−2.4	−2.5	−3.1	−3.9
Luxembourg	3.7	6.3	6.3	2.7	−0.1	−1.8	−2.5
Netherlands	0.7	2.2	0	−1.6	−3.2	−3.1	−2.9
Portugal	−2.9	−2.9	−4.4	−2.7	−2.9	−3.8	−3.2
Spain	−1.2	−0.9	−0.4	−0.1	0.3	0.3	0.5
euro area	−1.3	0.1	−1.7	−2.3	−2.7	−2.8	−2.7

Source: OECD. The figures for 2005 are forecasts.

Table 16.8	Exchange Rate Mechanism II member countries	

Currency	Joined in	Central rate per euro
Danish krone	Jan 1999	7.46038 ± 2.25%
Estonian krone	June 2004	15.6466 ± 15%
Lithuanian litos	June 2004	3.45280 ± 15%
Slovenian tolar	June 2004	239.640 ± 15%

Note: The Greek drachma was a member of ERM II for the period January 1999–December 2000 at a parity of 340.75 drachmas per euro, the parity at which it converted to the euro on 1 January 2001.
Source: European Commission.

16.21 The Exchange Rate Mechanism II

When the ERM I ceased to exist on 1 January 1999, ERM II came into being principally so that Greece that had not qualified for EMU and Denmark that had decided not to join EMU could continue to maintain stable currencies against the euro members. The ERM II is also relevant to the accession countries that joined the European Union in May 2004, as joining ERM II for two years is an essential precondition for participation in EMU itself. Despite having the same fluctuation bands as ERM I of ±15%, ERM II is not a carbon copy. ERM II has four key features: (1) it is based on central rates fixed for participating currencies *vis-à-vis* the euro and therefore has no parity grid – the normal band of fluctuation being ±15%, (2) obligatory interventions once margins are met, (3) the ECB and all participating 'pre-in' central banks have the right to initiate procedures to review the central rates, and (4) access to short-term financing facilities with the ECB having the right to suspend intervention and financing operations. In practice, a country that joins ERM II can request a lower margin of fluctuation, and such has been the case with Denmark that currently operates a ±2.25% band against the euro. It is envisaged that the new accession countries will spend a *minimum* of two years in ERM II prior to their adoption of the euro, and it is possible that *some* might use the narrower ±2.25% band and it is likely that they will join at central rates which will ideally be their conversion rates to the euro once they go for permanent fixing. Three of the accession countries joined ERM II, and **Table 16.8** shows the members that at the time of writing had joined ERM II; Greece was a member for two years prior to its entrance into EMU.

Box 16.4

The United Kingdom and the euro

There has been an intense debate between politicians and increasingly among the British public about whether the UK should join EMU; all three major political parties have committed themselves to holding a referendum on the matter. As well as the traditional debate about the economic costs and benefits, there is an intensely political element to the debate in the UK with many opposed to EMU on the grounds of a loss of national sovereignty. While the Labour government is committed in principle to joining the EMU, it is ambivalent on the timing →

→

and the government decided to assess the suitability of UK entrance in relation to the so-called 'five economic tests':

(1) **Convergence** – are business cycles and economic structures compatible so that we and others could live comfortably with euro interest rates on a permanent basis?
(2) **Flexibility** – if problems emerge is there sufficient flexibility to deal with them?
(3) **Investment** – would joining EMU create better conditions for firms making long-term decisions to invest in Britain?
(4) **Financial services** – what impact would entry into EMU have on the competitive position of the UK's financial services industry, particularly the City's wholesale markets?
(5) **Growth, stability and employment** – will joining EMU promote higher growth, stability and a lasting increase in jobs?

In June 2003 the UK Treasury published 'UK membership of the single currency: An assessment of the five economic tests', based on the outcome of 18 extensive EMU studies into the above issues. The assessment argued that intra-euro area trade has increased strongly in recent years as a result of EMU by as much as 3 to 20%; that the UK could enjoy a significant boost to trade with the euro area of up to 50% over 30 years; and that UK national income could rise over a 30-year period as a result of EMU entrance by between an additional 5 to 9%. A 9% increase in national income translates into a boost to potential output of around 0.25% a year, sustained over a 30-year period. However, despite this, at the time of the assessment the UK failed the convergence criteria even though meeting the Maastricht criteria, partly because of concerns over its housing market. The flexibility criterion was also failed; even though more flexibility of labour markets has been achieved there is still quite a divergence between the UK and EU labour markets. The investment test was nearly passed with the report noting that there had been some loss in inward foreign direct investment into the UK since the start of EMU. The financial services test was met with the report believing the UK would prosper even more inside the eurozone than it currently does outside. Despite the potential for increased trade and output, the growth, stability and employment objective was not met in the short term with it being judged that the UK would be better outside of EMU than inside. In particular, a common interest rate set by the ECB and the potential constraints on the use of fiscal policy under the Stability and Growth Pact were noted. The executive summary concludes:

> Overall the Treasury assessment is that since 1997 the UK has made real progress towards meeting the five economic tests. But, on balance, though the potential benefits of increased investment, trade, a boost to financial services, growth and jobs are clear, we cannot at this point in time conclude that there is sustainable and durable convergence or sufficient flexibility to cope with any potential difficulties within the euro area. So, despite the risks and costs from delaying the benefits of joining, a clear and unambiguous case for UK membership of EMU has not at the present time been made and a decision to join now would not be in the national economic interest.

I am frequently asked by students, policy-makers and people working in the financial sector of the City of London for my views on the subject of EMU and UK entry, and in the hope of influencing a few votes I should state that I am strongly in favour of UK participation in EMU. No-one would be in favour of UK participation in EMU if the euro was to prove to be a high-inflation and low-confidence currency, but there have been numerous safeguards put →

> →
>
> in place to ensure that it will be a sound low-inflation currency that over time will acquire cred-ibility in financial markets and with EU citizens. In addition, there is plenty of theoretical and empirical evidence that shows that monetary policy is not that powerful a tool in anything but the very short run at influencing output and employment, this means that giving up monetary sovereignty is not that big a deal. In addition, the medium to long-term prosperity in an econ-omy is determined by the productivity, ingenuity, education, flexibility and other 'real things' not by the unit of money that we use in the shops! Finally, there are real savings in transaction and hedging costs for economic agents and businesses, and while the UK remains outside of the euro area there is a real risk of a loss of foreign direct investment due to the exchange risk specific to the UK. In the UK the debate tends to be very polarized and one should not exag-gerate the importance of the issue; the UK economy will certainly not fall apart because it remains outside the euro area and will certainly not fall apart or boom because it joins the euro area. As for the appropriateness of the five economic tests, the less I say the better!

16.22 The accession countries and EMU

When the eight Central Eastern European Countries (CEEC) (Czech Republic, Estonia, Hungary, Latvia, Lithuania, Poland, Slovakia, Slovenia) along with Malta and Cyprus joined the European Union in May 2004 they also agreed in principle to the adoption of the euro as their national currency at some time in the future, and none have an 'opt-out' arrangement such as the one negotiated by the UK. According to the European Commission and European Central Bank, the monetary integration of the CEEC economies into the euro area should be multilateral (that is involve the ECB, existing and new entrants), successive (that is in stages dependent on economic reform and progress prior to ERM II entrance) and phased (some join before others). The CEEC countries need to meet the Maastricht Treaty criteria as a precondition for joining EMU, but in addition they are also expected to achieve some real convergence which entails catching up with the rest of Europe in the process of economic develop-ment by speeding up the processes of transition and structural reform. As Ottmar Issing stated in a speech in Budapest in February 2003:

> It is important that any decision to join ERM II is consistent with an adequate level of nominal and real convergence with the euro area . . . Once in ERM II, countries will be expected to continue their convergence process until the sustainable achievement of the Maastricht criteria . . . For some countries the benefits of staying longer in ERM II could more than offset the opportunity costs . . . Optimally choos-ing the timing of adoption of the euro also implies reducing the differences in per capita income levels.

The addition of the real convergence criteria is interesting and it is understood to involve the catching-up of their real GDP per capita towards the community average, the implementation of structural reform and the termination of their process of transi-tion towards market-based economies. However, the real convergence criteria have not been clearly defined although it is possible that the community will define this at some point. Lavrac and Zumer (2003) suggest that the real convergence criteria have been added so as to give the existing eurozone countries the right to delay the entrance of some of the CEEC that might quickly have fulfilled the nominal (Maastricht) criteria should the need arise. They point out that the concept of real convergence is potentially dangerous since it could be misused to keep the CEEC out of EMU indefinitely since catching up will be a lengthy process; transition and structural reform can likewise be never-ending. For example, in 2002 only Slovenia, Cyprus and the Czech Republic had a PPP per capita GDP above 60% of the EU average, Hungary and Malta were above 50%, Estonia, Lithuania and Poland slightly above 40% and Latvia around 35%. In addition, there is a potential for a conflict between real and nominal (that is Maastricht) convergence, the latter in particular by requiring fiscal discipline and low inflation means that tight macro-polices may conflict with economic growth and employment and the process of real convergence.

The first phase of this process was the pre-accession phase prior to their admittance into the European Union in May 2004. During this phase the CEEC adopted the *acquis communautaire* in respect of EMU – this involved removal of capital controls, making their central banks independent and prohibiting their central banks from printing money to finance their fiscal deficits. During the pre-accession phase the CEEC countries were free to pursue their own independent exchange rate policies.

The second phase started with their accession to the EU in May 2004 and ends with their inclusion in the eurozone. During this phase the CEEC give up some of their monetary autonomy since their exchange rates are a matter of common concern as are their macro-economic policies (fiscal and monetary). During this period they need to avoid excessive fluctuations of their currencies and also misaligned exchange rates (such as undervaluations which would give them a competitive advantage). Prior to joining EMU they will need to have spent at least two years with their currencies inside the ERM II arrangement and not have devalued their currencies during their membership. When they are assessed to be ready to join EMU they will have no option but to join, although this is not a major concern since all CEEC countries have already expressed a commitment to join.

The third and final phase – the adoption of the euro – starts when the CEEC meet the criteria to join the eurozone, adopt the euro and cease to use their national currencies. Once they join they have similar rights and obligations as other eurozone member countries and they will need to respect the fiscal requirements of the Stability and Growth Pact and their national central banks will join in the ESCB arrangements.

While all accession countries have committed themselves to joining EMU, at the time of writing Cyprus, Lithuania, Malta, Slovenia and Estonia have committed themselves to a fast-track route of entrance, possibly 2007/08, while the others particularly those with more difficult fiscal projections are thinking more in terms of 2009/10. In terms of the Maastricht Treaty conditions, as **Table 16.9** shows it is noticeable that the accession countries do not fare too badly in term of the criteria, the main problem area is with respect to the fiscal deficit criteria where the performance of the individual countries exhibits quite a bit of variability and there is likely to be problems for some of them in meeting the criteria. The addition of some real convergence criteria might potentially present a problem, but in practice it is unlikely to be significant. The countries will attract more investment and growth once they are inside the eurozone which will actually help with the process of real convergence in the medium term.

A point of more than academic interest is that the Maastricht criteria require the

| Table 16.9 | The accession countries and the Maastricht criteria |

	Harmonized index of consumer prices	Fiscal balance % of GDP	Public debt % of GDP	Long-term yields
Cyprus	2.8	–3.5	59.7	5.1
Czech Republic	1.4	–6.7	26.9	4.8
Estonia	3.6	1.3	5.8	7.4
Hungary	5.2	–9.2	56.3	7.1
Latvia	2.0	–3.0	14.6	5.3
Lithuania	0.4	–1.7	22.7	5.2
Malta	2.2	–6.2	66.6	5.4
Poland	1.9	–3.8	41.8	7.3
Slovakia	3.3	–7.2	44.3	7.0
Slovenia	7.5	–2.4	27.8	6.7
AC-10	2.7	–5.1	39.9	6.6
Reference value	2.9	–3.0	60.0	6.9

Notes: (a) Figures are for 2002. (b) The AC-10 figure is the accession countries' weighted average according to their GDPs. (c) The long-term bond yields are 5 or 10-year bonds or relevant proxies.
Source: Backe and Thinman (2004).

accession countries to achieve convergence of price inflation and interest rates to within 1.5% and 2% of the 'three best-performing' EU countries. Some commentators such as Kenen and Meade (2003, p. 9) are concerned that this criterion is overly burdensome and inappropriate now that EMU is in existence; they suggest that:

> The European Commission should recast the benchmarks used to assess compliance with the inflation-rate and interest-rate requirements. These should be based on the inflation rate and average long-term interest rate prevailing in the euro area, not those prevailing in the 'three best-performing' EU countries.

In addition there is the issue of whether when assessing exchange rate stability in the two years prior to joining EMU to apply the 2.25% band or the 15% band; the Commission has indicated that it would likely use the 2.25% band. However, Kenen and Meade (2003) argue that the new members need more flexibility and that the Commission should apply the 15% standard band of ERM II. The currencies will otherwise be vulnerable to speculative attacks and at risk of crisis should their currencies approach or exceed the 2.25% band.

There are important issues posed by CEEC entry into EMU for both the CEEC and the existing eurozone countries. Too-early entry of the weaker CEEC currencies into the euro could undermine confidence in the euro and require a looser European monetary policy than would otherwise be the case. There is also no doubt that with more member states joining the euro at very different levels of economic development compared to the existing members that the design of the optimal monetary and exchange rate policy becomes a more complicated task for the ECB. The CEEC will be exposed to the same sort of cost–benefit analysis that we have outlined earlier in this chapter. However, these risks should not be exaggerated, the CEEC economies are only a small part of EU GDP and there are plenty of safeguards in place to ensure the euro will remain a low inflation currency.

16.23 Conclusions

Although the EMS was originally envisaged as a zone of monetary stability, it differed from a simple agreement to peg exchange rates in a number of important respects, such as the central role of the ECU, the setting up of a common pool of reserves, the individualization of divergence thresholds and the theoretically symmetric responsibilities for surplus and deficit countries. However, the EMS was certainly far from a monetary union. There was no European Central Bank to supply the ECU which was a mere calculation and far from a medium of exchange. The EMS transformed itself from a zone of currency stability into a credible anti-inflation zone, and its final transformation was to become a framework for achieving EMU. Its success as an anti-inflation zone can be partly explained by the fact that following the experience of the 1970s there was a greater commitment by governments to control inflation. Furthermore, the associated cost in terms of higher unemployment levels did not prove to be politically disastrous for the governments concerned. While EMS members did bring down their inflation rates, especially in the cases of Italy and France, this does not establish causality. It may well have been the case that Italy and France would have engaged in an anti-inflationary set of policies even if they had not joined the EMS.

During the 1980s and 1990s the balance of benefits and costs tipped increasingly favourably towards EMU. In the way of benefits, the single market project by tackling non-tariff barriers to trade and requiring the removal of capital controls made the usage of differing national currencies look increasingly inefficient; while the main cost associated with EMU, namely the loss of monetary policy sovereignty, had already largely been given up by members of the ERM who accepted the monetary discipline of the Bundesbank. For this reason, France and Italy became increasingly interested in EMU partly because it would give them a greater say in the conduct of monetary policy as members of the board of the European Central Bank.

The implications of EMU extend beyond the boundaries of the European Union. The euro, backed by a credible European Central Bank, is likely to acquire an important role as a major reserve currency. In 2003 the enlarged EU-25 GDP at €9,715 billion was slightly larger than the US GDP of €9,616 billion, but GDP per capita in the USA is €33,017 which is substantially higher than the EU-25 average of €21,232. In 2002 the eurozone area accounted for 15.7% of world output, lower than the 21.1% share of the United States. In addition, the eurozone area accounted for around 31.2% of world exports (excluding intra-Eurozone trade) while the USA accounted for approximately 12.4% of world exports. Against this, US capital markets are approximately twice the size of the combined EU markets, and the dollar dominance may take some time to be overcome, and some authors such as Cohen (2003) are sceptical about whether the euro will challenge the dollar as the major international currency in the foreseeable future. However, a significant shift towards the euro as a reserve currency and less holdings of dollar reserves is likely to occur over time.

There are a number of safeguards designed to ensure that the euro proves to be a sound low-inflation currency: the Maastricht convergence criteria, the Stability and Growth Pact, the independent status of the ECB with its 0–2% inflation target, and the 'no-bail-out' Maastricht clause being among the most significant. With such safe-guards in place it is somewhat surprising that the first few years of the euro were char-acterized by noticeable weakness in the foreign exchange market. However, despite breaches of the SGP by two of the key countries and the ECB tending to exceed its 2% inflation target, the euro has made a substantial comeback on the foreign exchange market showing that it will likely become a major reserve currency. There are still many challenges ahead for the euro and the ECB, the most pressing being the poten-tial admission of the UK and the accession countries.

Further reading

Artis, M.J. and Taylor, M.P. (1988) 'Exchange Rates, Interest Rates, Capital controls and the European Monetary System: Assessing the Track Record', in F. Giavazzi, S. Micossi and M. Miller (eds), *The European Monetary System* (Cambridge: Cambridge University Press).

Artis, M.J. and Taylor, M.P. (1994) 'The Stabilising Effect of the ERM on Exchange Rates and Interest Rates', *IMF Staff Papers*, vol. 41, no. 1, pp. 123–48.

Backé, P. and Thinman, C. (2004) 'The Acceding Countries Strategies Towards ERM II and the Adoption of the Euro: An Analytical Review', European Central Bank, Occasional Papers no. 10.

Canzoneri, M.B. and Rogers, C.A (1990) 'Is the European Community an Optimal Currency Area? Optimal Taxation Versus the Cost of Multiple Currencies', *American Economic Review*, vol. 80, pp. 419–33.

Cheung, Y., Fung, H., Lain, K. and Lo, W. (1995) 'Purchasing Power Parity Under the European Monetary System', *Journal of International Money and Finance*, vol. 14, no. 2. pp. 179–89.

Cohen, B.J. (2003) 'Global Currency Rivalry: Can the Euro ever Challenge the Dollar?', *Journal of Common Market Studies*, vol. 41, pp. 575–95.

Cohen, D. and Wyplosz, C. (1989) 'The European Monetary Union: An Agnostic Evaluation', in R.C. Bryant, D.A. Currie, J.A. Frenkel, P.R. Masson and R. Portes (eds), *Macroeconomic Policies in an Interdependent World* (Washington: IMF).

Collins, S. (1988) 'Inflation and the European Monetary System', in F. Giavazzi, S. Micossi and M. Miller (eds), *The European Monetary System* (Cambridge: Cambridge University Press).

De Grauwe, P. (1996) 'The Economics of Convergence to EMU', *Welwirtschaftliches Archiv*, vol. 132, pp. 1–27.

De Grauwe, P. (2003) *Economics of Monetary Union*, (Oxford: Oxford University Press).

Emerson, M. (1990) 'The Economics of EMU', in *Britain & EMU*, Centre for Economic Performance, London School of Economics, London.

European Banking Federation (1995) *Survey on the Introduction of the Single Currency: A First Contribution*.

Giavazzi, F. (1989) 'The Exchange Rate Question in Europe', in R.C. Bryant, D.A. Currie, J.A. Frenkel, P.R. Masson and R. Portes (eds), *Macroeconomic Policies in an Interdependent World* (Washington: IMF).

Giavazzi, F. and Giovannini, A. (1988) 'The Role of the Exchange Rate Regime in a Disinflation: Empirical Evidence on the European Monetary System', in F. Giavazzi, S. Micossi and M. Miller (eds), *The European Monetary System* (Cambridge: Cambridge University Press).

Giavazzi, F. and Pagano, M. (1988) 'The Advantage of Tying One's Hands: EMS Discipline and Central Bank Credibility', *European Economic Review*, vol. 32, pp. 1055–75.

Glick, R. and Rose, A. (2001) 'Does a Currency Union Affect Trade? The Time Series Evidence', NBER Working Paper no. 8396.

Kenen, P. and Meade, E. (2003) 'EU Accession and the Euro: Close Together or Far Apart?', International Economic Policy Brief, no. PB 03-9 (Washington: Institute for International Economics).

Lavrac, V. and Zumer, T. (2003) 'Accession of CEE Countries to EMU: Nominal Convergence Real Convergence and Optimum Curremncy Area Criteria', *Bank of Valetta Review*, no. 27.

Lucas, R.E. Jnr (1976) 'Econometric Policy Evaluations: A Critique', in K. Brunner and A.H. Meltzer (eds), *The Phillips Curve and Labour Markets*. Carnegie-Rochester Conference Series on Public Policy no. 1 (Amsterdam: North-Holland), pp. 19–46.

Mastropasqua, C., Micossi, S. and Rinaldi, R. (1988) 'Intervention Sterilization and Monetary Policy in the European Monetary System Countries 1979–87', in F. Giavazzi, S. Micossi and M. Miller (eds), *The European Monetary System* (Cambridge: Cambridge University Press).

Melitz, J.A. (1988) 'Monetary Discipline and Cooperation in the European Monetary System: A Synthesis', in F. Giavazzi, S. Micossi and M. Miller (eds), *The European Monetary System* (Cambridge: Cambridge University Press).

Micco, A., Stein, E. and Ordonez, G. (2003) 'The Currency Union Effect on Trade: Early Evidence on EMU', *Economic Policy*, vol. 37, pp. 315–56.

Padoa Schioppa, T. (1985) 'Policy Cooperation and the EMS Experience', in W.H. Buiter and R.C. Marston (eds), *International Economic Policy Coordination* (Cambridge: Cambridge University Press).

Peree, E. and Steinherr, A.(1989) 'Exchange Rate Uncertainty and Foreign Trade', *European Economic Review*, vol. 33, pp. 1241–64.

Rose, A. (2000) 'One Money One Market: Estimating the Effects of Common Currencies on Trade', *Economic Policy*, vol. 30, pp. 7–46.

Rose, A. (2001) 'Currency Union and Trade: The Effect is Large', *Economic Policy*, vol. 33, pp. 46–62.

Torres, F. (ed.) (1996) *Monetary Reform in Europe* (Lisbon: Universidade Catolica Editora).

Urenger, H., Evans, O., Mayer, T. and Young, P. (1986) 'The European Monetary System: Recent Developments', IMF Occasional Papers no. 48, Washington.

17

Currency Crises and the East Asian Financial Crisis

17.1 Introduction

The 1990s and early part of this century were characterized by a number of currency and financial crises. The turmoil started with major speculative attacks against the European Monetary System in 1992–93 which led to devaluations of the pound sterling and the Italian lira (see Chapter 16), followed by the Mexican crisis of December 1994; then, starting with the Thai baht devaluation on 2 July 1997, the so called East Asian financial crisis is generally agreed to have started. The Asian crisis was characterized by major economic and financial turmoil in many of the East Asian economies with large falls in the values of their currencies, stockmarkets and property prices. The crisis continued into 1998, a year in which there were very significant falls in output in many of these previously fast-growing economies. Fortunately, there was a sharp recovery of those economies in 1999 and 2000 by which time the crisis was largely over.

The Asian financial crisis was swiftly followed by other crises such as the Russian default on its debt in August 1998, and the collapse of the hedge fund Long-Term Capital Management in late September 1998. Other noticeable crises have followed: in January 1999 the Brazilian real was forced to devalue and eventually to float, and it quickly depreciated a further 35%; in January 2001 there was a major banking crisis in Turkey leading to the floating of the Turkish lira; and, more spectacularly, in December 2001 Argentina declared a default on its external debt and had to abandon its currency board on 7 January 2002 with a devaluation from 1 peso to 1.4 pesos, swiftly followed by a dramatic fall in the Argentinian peso to a low of 3.75 pesos per dollar by the end of October 2002.

These periodic crises have stimulated a great deal of theoretical and empirical literature that looks at the causes of currency and financial crises, and in this chapter we look at some of the theoretical models that have been developed to analyse such crises. In particular, we look at what have been termed first, second and third-generation models of currency crises, explaining some of their basic features and differences. We also briefly mention some of the other models that have been developed. We then concentrate on the causes and details surrounding the East Asian financial crisis which was one of the most significant events to confront the international financial community in the last 40 years. We focus attention on eight of the countries most directly involved in the crisis, namely Hong Kong, Indonesia, Philippines, South Korea, Singapore, Malaysia, Taiwan and Thailand, and as such exclude any detailed analysis of other countries affected by the crisis such as China and India. A great deal of money can be made by predicting crises in advance of them happening, and early warning of such crises may help policy-makers avert them; we conclude the chapter by looking at some of the recent literature that attempts to find what economic and financial indicators may be useful to predict currency and financial crises.

17.2 First-generation models of currency crises

First-generation models refer to a strand of literature that builds upon an article by Krugman (1979) and which has been extended and developed in various directions; see for example Flood and Garber (1984). In his article, Krugman assumed that a government operates a fixed exchange rate and runs a budget deficit financed by the government selling bonds in exchange for money from the central bank; that is, its fiscal deficits are financed by domestic credit expansion. However, this increases the supply of money and puts downward pressure on the interest rate leading to capital outflows and pressure for a devaluation of the currency. As such, it is necessary for the central bank to defend the currency by using its foreign exchange reserves. At a certain point, the reserves reach a critically low level and a speculative attack is made on the currency forcing a devaluation. In the so-called 'first generation models of speculative currency attacks' there is a fundamental inconsistency between the fiscal (and with it monetary) policy pursued by the government and the commitment to a fixed exchange rate which is spotted by speculators and precipitates a speculative attack.

The assumptions of the Krugman (1979) model are: perfect competition in the economy; domestic and foreign goods are perfect substitutes; perfect capital mobility and uncovered interest parity holds at all times; and also that purchasing power parity holds. In the Krugman model money demand is assumed to be fixed at some constant value and the exchange rate is assumed to be fixed so that $\dot{s} = 0$, where $\dot{s}$ is the rate of change of the exchange rate. A final important feature of the model is that once the fixed exchange rate regime breaks down, the new regime that replaces it is a fully floating exchange rate regime.

The first assumption is that the money market is kept in continual equilibrium, that is:

$$md_t = \bar{m}s_t \tag{17.1}$$

where md_t is the log of money demand, and $\bar{m}s_t$ is the log of the fixed money supply.

The demand for real money balance is assumed to be inversely related to the domestic interest rate:

$$md_t - p = -\sigma r \tag{17.2}$$

where p is the log of the domestic price level and r is the domestic interest rate.

The log of the money supply is given by a log linearization of the domestic credit and foreign exchange reserves:

$$\bar{m}s_t = D + R \tag{17.3}$$

where D is the log of domestic credit and R is the log of the reserve component of the monetary base. (note equation (17.3) is strictly true only in *levels* but is an acceptable log-linearization approximation in the literature).

The domestic credit is assumed to expand at a constant rate per annum $\dot{D} = \mu$, where $\dot{D}$ is the rate of change of domestic credit; the increase in domestic credit is assumed to come about because of the government printing money to buy domestic bonds that are being sold to finance its fiscal deficit.

The exchange rate is assumed to follow PPP so that:

$$s = p - p^* \tag{17.4}$$

where s is the log of the exchange rate defined as domestic currency units per unit of foreign currency, p is the log of the domestic price level and p^* is the log of the foreign price level.

Uncovered interest parity is assumed to hold at all times so:

$$r = r^* + E\dot{s} \tag{17.5}$$

where r is the domestic interest rate, r^* is the foreign interest rate and $E\dot{s}$ is the expected rate of depreciation of the domestic currency.

Since money demand is a constant, any increase in domestic credit will as in the monetary model lead to a fall in reserves of an equivalent amount, which implies that the rate of fall of reserves $\dot{R}$ is the same as the rate of increase of domestic credit; that is:

$$\dot{R} = -\mu \qquad\qquad\qquad\qquad\qquad\qquad\qquad\qquad (17.6)$$

Finally, assuming the exchange rate is fixed at $\bar{s}$ and $E\dot{s} = 0$, the foreign interest rate at $r^* = r$ and the foreign price level is fixed at p^* we can substitute equations (17.1) to (17.3) and (17.5) into equation (17.4) to obtain:

$$\bar{s} = R + D - p^* + \sigma r^* \qquad\qquad\qquad\qquad\qquad\qquad (17.7)$$

Since we assume that p^* and r^* are fixed, increases in domestic credit lead to equivalent falls in foreign exchange reserves and there is no change in the money supply. It is quite clear that if foreign exchange reserves are falling at the same rate that domestic credit is expanding, at some point they will reach a critically low level. It is not a foregone conclusion that a speculative attack will necessarily follow a decline in the reserves; however, if the central bank announces that once reserves hit a certain level they will abandon the fixed exchange rate then a speculative attack is a foregone conclusion. The interesting thing is that speculators will not wait until the reserves reach the critically low level before mounting the speculative attack since this would imply a large capital loss at that point. Rational speculators will launch the speculative attack before the critical level of reserves is met. Flood and Garber (1984) have shown that the speculative attack will occur when the rate of exchange that would occur if the currency were floating (the so-called shadow exchange rate) is equal to the fixed exchange rate and that the speculative attack will completely drain the foreign exchange reserves of the central bank. The dynamics of the speculative attack are illustrated in **Figure 17.1**.

In **Figure 17.1(a)** it can be seen that the money supply is fixed at the level $M1$ at time $t1$, domestic credit is expanding at a rate $\dot{D} = \mu$ and the reserves are falling by a like amount at the rate $\dot{R} = -\mu$ with the money supply remaining constant. The shadow exchange rate in **Figure 17.1(b)** starts at an overvalued level $S1$ but would, if

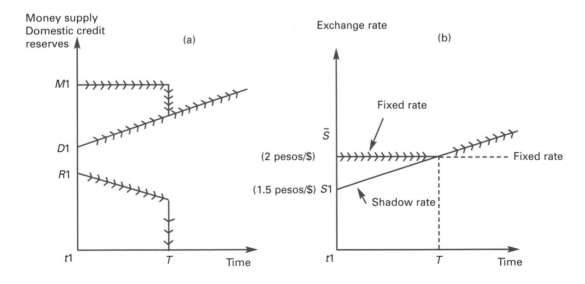

Figure 17.1 The dynamics of a speculative attack in first-generation models

the exchange rate were floating, depreciate at a rate $\dot{s} = \mu$ in line with the rate of increase of domestic credit. While the fixed exchange rate of the peso per dollar is undervalued at, say, 2 pesos per dollar compared to the shadow exchange rate, say 1.5 pesos per dollar, it is possible to maintain a fixed exchange rate without any problems since there is no prospect of a capital gain for speculators. However, once the shadow exchange rate moves above the fixed exchange rate making the latter overvalued at time T, for example 2.01 pesos/$1, a speculative attack is inevitable as it pays speculators to sell unlimited quantities of domestic currency (pesos) to buy the foreign currency (dollars); the authorities' foreign exchange reserves will be exhausted and the currency is forced to float. It should be noted that at the precise time of the speculative attack there is an increase in the domestic interest rate to compensate investors for the fact that after the speculative attack the exchange rate is expected to depreciate at the rate μ, in line with the expansion of domestic credit, this follows from the UIP condition. The timing of the attack is such that there is no discrete jump in the exchange rate as this would imply large capital loss for speculators at that point, but since the inevitable breakdown of the fixed parity is foreseen in advance this would be inconsistent with an efficient market and therefore can be ruled out.

At the time of the speculative attack the reserves are exhausted and fall by an amount dR (negative), hence, there is a discrete fall in the money supply of a like amount dms (negative). There is also a rise in the domestic interest rate given by μ (since this is the rate at which the currency is expected to depreciate in line with the growth of domestic credit) so that r becomes $r + \mu$. Inserting this into the money demand equation (17.2) means there is a fall in money demand given by $dmd = -\sigma\mu$. Since the money market is kept in continual equilibrium the fall in the money supply equals the fall in money demand, so that:

$$dR = -\sigma\,\mu \tag{17.8}$$

Since before the speculative attack reserves were falling at the rate μ, if the initial stock of reserves is given by $R1$ and the time from the base period to the attack is given by T, then the level of reserves just prior to the attack must be $R1 - \mu T$ (positive) which must be equal to the fall in reserves that occurs at the time of the attack $-dR$ (positive since dR is negative). That is:

$$R1 - \mu\,T = -dR \tag{17.9}$$

Substituting (17.8) into (17.9) and rearranging to solve for the timing of the speculative attack T, we find:

$$T = \frac{(R1 - \sigma\mu)}{\mu} \tag{17.10}$$

That is, the timing of the speculative attack is greater (that is, delayed) the higher the initial level of reserves $R1$ and the lower the rate of expansion of domestic credit μ. This condition makes sound intuitive economic sense the higher the level of reserves the greater the ability of the authorities to resist a speculative attack and the lower the rate of domestic credit expansion of domestic credit the slower the drain on the reserves from domestic credit expansion.

There have been several criticisms of the first generation models amongst which:

1   It is unclear why the level of foreign exchange reserves should be so crucial to the timing of a speculative attack, since governments could always resist an attack on their currencies by other means such as raising the domestic interest rate. If they raise interest rates sufficiently this will lead to potential losses for speculators that have borrowed large amounts of the domestic currency so as to sell it in the foreign exchange market.

2   It is not at all clear why a government that is committed to a fixed exchange rate regime would wish to pursue a policy of printing money to finance its fiscal deficit that it knows will ultimately lead to a speculative attack on its currency. In the real world, it is likely that governments are far smarter than assumed in the first-generation models and they look at the costs and benefits of maintaining a fixed exchange rate system and keep the option of allowing their currency to float prior to a speculative attack.

3   There was also an empirical problem in that some of the recent crises were not characterized by large fiscal deficits that had been monetarized as assumed in the first-generation models. There had been no secular change in the fundamentals prior to the ERM crises in 1992–93 as predicted by the first-generation models, and the ERM crises were largely unforeseen. In addition, as we shall see, most of the Asian economies were running fiscal surpluses prior to the outbreak of their crises.

4   A further empirical problem is that in some of the recent crises there was not a secular fall in the foreign exchange reserves as predicted by the first-generation models. In the Asian economies heavy capital inflows in the years prior to the outbreak of the crises had meant that foreign exchange reserves had been increasing as central banks sold their currencies to buy US dollars to offset the excess demand for their currencies from capital inflows. As we shall see, it was in fact an abrupt change from capital inflows to capital outflows that led to the currency and financial crises in these economies.

17.3 Second-generation models of currency crises

Due to the deficiencies of the first-generation models in explaining currency crises, in particular the speculative attack on the ERM that occurred in 1992–93, a new generation of models emerged in the 1990s (see for example Obstfeld, 1994 and 1996, and Jeanne, 1997, which offered an alternative explanation of currency crises). Two key features of the second-generation models are that governments are assumed to be much smarter than in the first-generation models; that is, they continually evaluate the pros and cons of maintaining a fixed exchange rate, and the linkage between macro fundamentals and the timing of speculative attacks is much weaker than in the first-generation models. In fact some authors such as Rangvid (2001) contend that the key distinction between first and second-generation models is that in the latter the government seeks to minimize some sort of loss function, for instance deviations of output or inflation rates from their desired levels. In the second-generation models, a devaluation is seen as an optimal response by the government to speculative pressures against the currency. The second-generation models allow for the possibility that the private sector anticipating a devaluation can increase the costs to the devaluing government of not devaluing such that it becomes rational for the government to devalue. In such models, there is the possibility of *multiple equilibria*; that is, if private agents' expectations of devaluation are low then the costs of maintaining a fixed exchange rate are low and hence the government of the country will not devalue. On the other hand, if private agents' expectations of devaluation are high then the costs of maintaining a fixed exchange rate are high and the government accordingly has a higher incentive to devalue. In such models, private agents' expectations can become self-fulfilling in the sense that if there is an exogenous shock to their expectations such that they move from a low risk of devaluation to a high risk of devaluation, then the probability of a devaluation will rise accordingly. There are usually three key components to the second-generation models:

1   Government preferences – in second-generation models the costs and benefits to the authorities of maintaining a fixed exchange rate are continually reviewed and modelled. The authorities are assumed to attach some weight to exchange rate stability and some weight to a real variable such as output stability or the rate of unemployment.

   For example a possible loss function is:

$$L = (y_t - y^*)^2 + w \, (s_{t+1} - s_t)^2$$

where y_t is the log of current level of output, y^* is the log of desired level of output, s_{t+1} is the log of exchange rate one period hence, s_t is the log of exchange rate today, and w is a weighting parameter.

   Here the idea is that the government attaches some importance to stability of output and some importance to stability of the exchange rate. A link between changes in the exchange rate and deviations of output can then be introduced. For instance, a sudden increase in expectations of a devaluation might lead to higher wage demands (since the price level will rise following a devaluation) and a rise in real wages in the short term which leads to a fall in output below the desired level.

2   Specification of the real variable – different second-generation models specify different real variables that are affected by an expected devaluation; this may be the level of output, the level of unemployment or the real level of public debt. An expected devaluation will likely lead to a fall in output (due to wage rises in anticipation of devaluation) or a rise in unemployment (for example by raising interest rates to compensate for the risk of a devaluation) or the cost of servicing the public debt (since an expected devaluation will raise the required interest rate).

3   There is a fixed cost to devaluation – the second-generation models assume that if a government is forced to devalue then there will be a given cost to it, and this cost might be seen as a loss of political prestige due to a failure to carry out the stated fixed exchange rate policy or a loss of economic credibility.

   In second-generation models, some sort of shock comes along to alter private agents' expectations of a devaluation. If the shock is small then the costs of maintaining the fixed exchange rate will be relatively small and it is likely that the authorities will be able to continue with the fixed exchange rate regime. If, however, the shock is relatively large and private agents' expectations of the size of a potential devaluation become quite large this increases the cost to the government of maintaining the fixed exchange rate; for example the loss of output will rise making it more likely that the government will decide to abandon the fixed exchange rate. One of the key features of second-generation models is the more the expectation of a devaluation the more the cost to the government of maintaining the fixed exchange rate and the higher the actual devaluation that is required. For instance, if agents expect a high rate of devaluation they will then put in high wage demands which leads to a high loss of output; hence, it will pay the government to enact a large devaluation to ensure that realized prices rise by a large amount and that real wages remain constant, so minimizing the loss of output that occurs. The subsequent switch to floating will also permit the authorities to engage in a monetary expansion to cure high levels of unemployment.

Another key feature of second-generation models is that there can be sudden switches in private agents' expectations concerning a devaluation without any apparent change in the economic fundamentals. An economy with sound fundamentals and low expectations of a devaluation can suddenly be exposed to a speculative attack and a high probability of devaluation simply because of a sudden change in private agents' expectations of a devaluation without any significant change in macro fundamentals. It is, however, important to note that an increase in private agents' expectations of a devaluation will not necessarily lead to an actual devaluation in the second-generation models. The government is continually monitoring the costs and benefits of the devaluation and if, for instance, the fixed costs of devaluation are relatively high then the government may decide it is best not to devalue, whereas if the fixed costs of devaluation are relatively low the government might decide to devalue. Nonetheless, the probability of a devaluation in the second-generation models is affected by the state of the fundamentals. If the fundamentals are very bad (for example unemployment is very high) then a devaluation is more likely than when the fundamentals are good (for example unemployment is low), since private agents' rational expectations of the government adopting a devaluation increase when unemployment is high than when it is low.

While the second-generation models have provided some new insights and in particular assume much smarter governments than in first-generation models, there remain several problems which they do not satisfactorily deal with. In particular, the reason why private agents should switch expectations from a low state of probability of devaluation to a high probability is not clear. In addition, the precise state of financial markets prior to the outbreak of the crisis is not fully considered in the second-generation models.

17.4 Third-generation and other models of currency and financial crises

In addition to the first and second-generation models, in an attempt to properly explain the Asian financial crises, so-called third-generation models of currency crises have been developed. Indeed, there have been an extensive range of other models designed to explain financial and currency crises. The third-generation models were developed because it was noted that there had not been severe fiscal problems in the Asian economies prior to the outbreak of the crises as one might have expected from the first-generation models. In addition, there were also no significant monetary expansions after the crisis as might have been expected from the second-generation models. The third-generation models vary greatly in their assumptions, but have a common theme that financial crises (rather than currency crises *per se*) can be caused by a 'moral hazard' problem. Such a problem exists when the existence of an insurance policy makes the insured-against event more likely to occur than if no such insurance policy existed (see **Box 17.1** for a simple example of moral hazard).

Box 17.1

Moral hazard and how a government bailout guarantee can turn a bad investment into a good one

The third-generation financial crisis models focus attention on the problem of 'moral hazard', whereby explicit or even perceived government guarantees to bail out investors can make the probability of such bailouts more likely to occur than if no such explicit/implicit guarantees existed. Consider the following simple numerical example; an investment project requires an investment of $80 million and will generate a profit of $40 million with a probability of 40% and a loss of $40 million with a probability of 60%. The expected return from the project is therefore negative since [($40 million × 0.4) + (–$40 million × 0.6)] = –$8 million. Clearly this investment does not make economic sense and will not therefore be undertaken and will not require any government rescue package. Imagine, however, that a government keen to see the investment go ahead guarantees investors that if the project does not work they will be bailed out by the taxpayer so as not to make any losses on their investment. In this case, the expected return on the project becomes positive since [($40 million × 0.4) + ($0 million × 0.6)] = +$16 million or a 20% return on the $80 million investment. Assume now that the expected rate of return is sufficiently high that the investment takes place, there is now a 60% chance that taxpayers will end up having to stump up $40 million if the project goes wrong. The existence of the bailout package makes a bailout more probable (60%) than if no such bailout promise existed (0%), this is the essence of the problem of moral hazard.

Models such as Akerlof and Romer (1994), Burnside *et al.* (2001), Dooley (2000), McKinnon and Pill (1996), Corsetti *et al.* (1999), Edison *et al.* (1998) and Krugman (1998) argue that a crucial role in the occurrence of a financial/currency crises is played when private agents perceive financial intermediaries' liabilities as having an implicit government guarantee. This enables financial intermediaries in the country to borrow money at relatively low rates of interest and then lend it out in highly risky investments, for example, leading to property and stockmarket bubbles and even outright fraud. When things go wrong agents know/assume that the government will come along to bail out the affected banks. Krugman (1998) has characterized this mentality as 'to play a game of heads I win, tails the taxpayer loses'. As asset prices rise, the lending looks to be sound but eventually the asset bubbles burst and a vicious circle comes into play as the proportion of non-performing loans rises and asset prices decline. Once the bubble appears to be bursting, it can also trigger a large capital outflow from the country and a collapse of the exchange rate of the country involved.

In addition to the models discussed there have been numerous other models designed to explain why financial crises occur. Blanchard and Watson (1982) emphasize the importance of 'rational' financial bubbles, where economic agents continue to buy what are perceived to be overvalued financial assets (or even real assets such as property) in the belief that the prospective capital gain from a continuation of the upward trend will more than compensate for the risk of a sudden collapse. Of course, an eventual collapse does occur resulting in large capital losses for those caught out near the top of the bubble. Other models such as Radlett and Sachs (1998) emphasize the role of financial panic which usually happens out of the blue; an important element of such models is that otherwise solvent borrowers face a liquidity squeeze when short-term liabilities exceed their short-term assets. Another model is that of Sachs (1995) who discusses the role of disorderly workouts in financial crises. A disorderly workout occurs when there is a lack of coordination between creditors who decide to individually withdraw funds from the distressed borrower. The lack of coordination between borrowers may be based on the fact that local bankruptcy laws are absent or ineffective. Another model worthy of mention where current account deficits financed by capital inflows can provoke a crisis is that of Rigobon (1998); excessive optimism leads to massive capital inflows that are suddenly and abruptly reversed when a shock hits the system. In Rigobon's model, to the extent that economic growth fuels unrealistic expectations about long-run economic growth prospects, it can be accompanied by overinvestment, excessive reliance on foreign capital and insufficient monitoring of domestic investments.

Other models emphasize the role of contagion behaviour on the part of investors. Fratzcher's (2003) paper is interesting in this respect. Defining contagion as 'the transmission of a crisis to a particular country due to its real and financial interdependence with countries that are already experiencing a crisis' (p. 110), Fratzcher argues that contagion provides an adequate description of both the Asian crisis of 1997/8 and Latin American crisis of 1994. In the paper, it is proximity of a country to another country under speculative attack that triggers the contagion. Various forms of *financial interdependence* can exist such as cross-border holdings between banks and financial institutions within a region and a common creditor to banks in a region, and should the common creditor withdraw from the region then all the countries in the region will be affected. In addition, *real interdependence* can exist via bilateral trade flows or trade competition between countries so that a crisis in one country might lead to a fall in exports of another or a devaluation of one currency necessitates a devaluation of another currency to maintain its competitive position. Fratzcher finds that the degree of trade linkages and competition in the Asian region was high, as was the degree of financial integration (for example as measured by correlations of their stockmarkets and competition between banks), Fratzcher finds that the degree of interdependence is very much related to their regional proximity to one another. For instance, the Asian economies have much higher degrees of financial and real linkages between each other than with Latin America, and likewise Latin American economies have much higher degrees of financial and real linkages between themselves than with Asia. Fratzcher finds that the main linkage through which contagion is likely to have spread is the financial linkage which is significant in most cases, whereas the real linkages, while important, are generally speaking less significant. In particular, the study shows that bank contagion, the withdrawal of funds and refusal of banks to roll over their loans to the region may have been very significant explanations of the crisis.

Baig and Goldfajn (1999) examine stockmarket, foreign exchange, interest rates and sovereign spreads using high-frequency data and find that correlations between the East Asian economies increased during the crisis as well as their sensitivity to both good and bad news in the other economies, all of which supports the idea of contagion being significant in the crisis. A paper by Caramazza *et al.* (2004) finds a significant role played by financial contagion in the Mexican, Asian and Russian crises, particularly through the common creditor route.

Some theories use herd behaviour as an explanation of currency and financial crises. For example, Calvo (1996) and Calvo and Mendoza (2000) argue that emerging markets are particularly susceptible to a herd mentality on the part of investors. Investors find it costly and potentially risky to examine the state of each economy when there are signs of problems, and so it becomes optimal for them to pull out of a group of related markets simultaneously when they spot signs of nervousness in just one of them. Likewise, Masson (1998) argues that investor psychology can play a role – a small trigger can lead to investors collectively losing confidence and collectively perceiving a higher risk of holding investment in a set of countries. This then leads investors to follow each other and simultaneously pull their funds out of a region causing financial and economic distress to the region. The foregoing overview of the literature is deliberately selective but nonetheless provides us with a useful toolkit with which to study the East Asian financial crisis.

17.5 The run-up to the Asian crisis

One of the most fascinating things about the Asian financial meltdown is that it was largely unforeseen, and there is plenty of anecdotal evidence for this. The IMF in its *World Economic Outlook* publication of April 1997 predicted strong, albeit marginally slower, economic growth of over 5% for Asia in 1998 (excluding India and Japan); there were some expressions of concern about Indonesia but no real alarm bells seemed to have been ringing at the IMF. Also it seems that international investors remained confident as net capital flows continued into the region right up until the crisis broke; only in Thailand and Korea did capital flows begin to dry up somewhat earlier in 1996. In addition, Cline and Barnes (1997) show the spread between Asian dollar-denominated debt and that on US Treasury bonds was actually falling between mid-1995 and mid-1997 contrary to what one would expect if market participants were expecting a crisis. Furthermore, Standard and Poor's and Moody's sovereign credit ratings remained largely unchanged in the year preceding the outbreak of the crisis and the eventual downgrades happened only three to five months after the crisis had broken out! In addition, many stockmarkets in the region were reaching new peaks as late as July 1997, which indicates that market participants were not forecasting the likely extent of the fall of the markets that subsequently occurred. Finally, currency forecasts by investment banks in the region did not predict any significant moves in exchange rates.

17.6 The macroeconomic fundamentals

The fact that the crisis was largely unforeseen is consistent with the hypothesis that the economic fundamentals, while deteriorating in the run-up to the crisis, were not of a significant enough measure to justify the crisis. To advance this hypothesis a bit further we need to look at the economic performance of the economies in the run-up to the crisis. First, we look at the economic growth rates, second their inflation rates and finally we examine their current account positions. We then proceed to look at what we regard as the key to the crisis which was the excessive lending to the region which fuelled asset bubbles (see for example Sarno and Taylor (1999) who detect asset bubbles in all the affected economies, the inevitable bursting of which then led to a

Table 17.1 Economic growth rates in selected Asian economies

	Hong Kong	Indonesia	Malaysia	Korea	Phillipines	Singapore	Taiwan	Thailand
1990	3.4	7.2	9.0	9.0	3.0	9.7	5.4	11.2
1991	5.6	7.0	9.5	9.2	−0.6	6.4	7.6	8.6
1992	6.6	6.5	8.9	5.4	0.3	6.7	7.5	8.1
1993	6.4	6.5	9.9	5.5	2.1	12.3	7.0	8.3
1994	5.5	7.5	9.2	8.5	4.4	11.4	7.1	9.0
1995	3.9	8.2	9.8	9.2	4.7	8.0	6.4	9.2
1996	4.3	7.8	10.0	7.0	5.8	8.1	6.1	5.9
1997	4.1	4.7	7.3	4.7	5.2	8.6	6.7	−1.4
1998	−5.0	−13.1	−7.4	−6.9	−0.6	−0.1	4.6	−10.5
1999	3.4	0.8	6.1	9.5	3.4	6.9	5.4	4.4
2000	10.1	4.9	8.9	8.5	4.0	9.7	5.9	4.7
2001	0.5	3.5	0.3	3.8	3.4	−1.9	−2.2	2.2
2002	1.9	3.6	4.1	7.0	5.5	2.2	3.6	5.3
2003	3.2	4.5	5.3	3.1	4.9	1.1	3.2	6.9
2004	7.1	6.4	5.7	2.7	5.4	2.5	2.5	5.1

Source: National Statistics Offices.

large degree of panic on the part of foreign banks and investors who decided *en masse* to pull funds out of the region). Once the property and stockmarket bubbles burst, there was a significant deterioration in the quality of the asset side of banks' balance sheets in the region as witnessed by a significant increase in their non-performing loans.

Table 17.1 shows that economic growth rates in the Asian economies were extremely high in the run-up to the crisis, with real growth rates in the region of 6–9%; only the Philippines was suffering from low economic growth in the early 1990s, but from 1996 even it was growing at over 5%. High rates of economic growth are generally speaking a good thing unless they are fuelled by excessive debt and/or deterioration in the external accounts of a country. It is quite possible that the prolonged period of economic prosperity sowed the seeds of its own destruction in that it led economic agents to have unduly optimistic expectations for the future. In the case of Asia this may well have been the case; terms like the 'Asian miracle' had become part of the domestic and international perception of Asia. With respect to the stockmarkets and the property sector the high rates of economic growth may have led to unwarranted extrapolative expectations and to some extent prices were driven up by expectations of further price rises rather than a more realistic appraisal of the relevant economic fundamentals.

Inflation rates

The inflation rate can play a significant part in economic crises especially if the exchange rate is fixed, since higher domestic inflation relative to foreign inflation can cause an appreciation of the real exchange rate and the inflation rate itself can be taken as a sign of economic mismanagement. However, there is relatively little evidence (**Table 17.2**) that inflation was a significant factor in the run-up to the crisis. Given the strong economic growth in the region inflation was surprisingly benign,

Table 17.2 Inflation rates in selected Asian economies

	Hong Kong	Indonesia	Malaysia	Korea	Phillipines	Singapore	Taiwan	Thailand
1990	10.3	7.8	2.6	8.6	13.2	3.5	4.1	5.9
1991	11.2	9.4	4.4	9.3	18.5	3.4	3.6	5.7
1992	9.6	7.5	4.7	6.3	8.6	2.3	3.4	4.1
1993	8.8	9.7	3.5	4.8	6.9	2.3	4.6	3.4
1994	8.8	8.5	3.7	6.2	8.4	3.1	2.6	5.1
1995	9.0	9.4	3.5	4.4	8.0	1.7	4.6	5.8
1996	6.4	8.0	3.5	5.0	9.0	1.4	2.5	5.8
1997	5.8	6.2	2.7	4.4	5.9	2.0	0.3	5.6
1998	2.9	58.4	5.3	7.5	9.7	−0.3	2.1	8.1
1999	−4.0	20.5	2.7	0.8	6.7	0	0.1	0.3
2000	−3.7	3.7	1.5	2.2	4.4	1.4	1.7	1.6
2001	−1.6	11.5	1.4	4.1	6.1	1.0	−5.5	1.6
2002	−3.0	11.9	1.8	2.7	3.0	−0.4	0.8	0.6
2003	−2.6	6.6	1.1	3.6	3.0	0.5	−0.1	1.8
2004	−0.4	6.2	1.5	3.6	5.5	1.7	2.3	2.8

Source: National Statistics Offices.

although there may well have been some masking of the underlying inflation due to the existence of price controls in Malaysia and Indonesia.

The inflation rate is more likely to lead to real exchange rate appreciation so undermining the competitiveness of countries when a country has a fixed exchange rate. In Asia the exchange rate policies varied in their degree of fixity with regard to the US dollar. Thailand, Malaysia, Hong Kong and the Philippines had more or less fixed parities, while Korea and Thailand had less rigid crawling peg systems whereby the exchange rate was adjusted on occasion to maintain external competitiveness. Indonesia had a policy of targeting the real exchange rate allowing its currency to depreciate to the extent that its inflation rate was higher than that of its trading partners.

Table 17.3 shows the value of the real exchange rate in the countries in the run-up to the crisis. What is clear is that four of the currencies – the Hong Kong dollar, the Malaysian ringgit, the Indonesian rupiah and the Philippines dollar – all appreciated in real terms prior to the crisis, and as such might have been vulnerable to a speculative attack. However, the picture is not uniform since four of the currencies had depreciated in real terms, so there is little evidence that real exchange rate appreciation played any significant role in the crisis by providing speculators with the prospect of a discrete fall in some of the Asian currencies. It seems that by 1997 only Hong Kong, the Philippines and Singapore were potentially vulnerable, while real exchange rates in the other six countries were not significantly different from those in 1991 or had depreciated in real terms.

The current account

The role of current account imbalances in provoking financial crises appears in numerous models such as Dornbusch *et al.* (1995), Mishkin (1996), Roubini and Wachtel (1998) and Sachs *et al.* (1996). Lawrence Summers presciently noted in *The*

Table 17.3 Real effective exchange rate (average of year)

	Hong Kong	Indonesia	Malaysia	Korea	Phillipines	Singapore	Taiwan	Thailand
1991	100.0	100.0	100.0	100.0	100.0	100.0	100.0	100.0
1992	103.0	97.5	106.9	92.9	110.6	101.9	103.9	98.4
1993	106.4	97.2	108.0	89.1	110.3	102.8	96.4	95.8
1994	109.6	96.6	103.8	89.2	116.1	106.7	94.5	95.9
1995	112.2	95.6	103.7	89.7	119.1	108.4	90.0	95.4
1996	112.9	101.2	108.6	92.0	129.6	112.2	93.9	96.3
1997	125.8	92.6	107.1	85.6	128.9	114.4	93.5	96.8
1998	132.1	42.9	85.1	62.6	105.4	110.0	82.6	79.4
1999	121.0	60.4	87.5	71.5	114.6	103.1	83.0	81.2
2000	117.3	56.6	89.7	78.3	106.9	103.4	88.1	77.7
2001	122.8	52.7	94.6	73.8	101.7	104.2	81.0	74.4
2002	113.8	83.7	94.7	78.2	102.1	101.2	78.4	75.6
2003	101.2	69.0	87.1	79.9	91.8	97.0	73.2	74.5
2004	94.2	66.2	84.6	83.6	87.6	96.0	72.7	74.0

Source: dbresearch.com.

Economist (23 December 1996) that 'close attention should be paid to any current account deficit in excess of 5% of GDP, particularly if it is financed in a way that could lead to rapid reversals'. It is noticeable that a number of Asian economies were becoming more vulnerable in this regard as shown in **Table 17.4**.

The table shows that many of the countries were experiencing large or deteriorating current account deficits as a percentage of their GDP in the 1990s and in the run-up to the crisis in 1997. This was especially the case for Thailand, Malaysia, the Philippines and Korea. In the case of Thailand it was running at an unsustainable rate

Table 17.4 Current account surplus/deficit as % of GDP

	Hong Kong	Indonesia	Malaysia	Korea	Phillipines	Singapore	Taiwan	Thailand
1990	8.9	−1.6	−2.0	0.9	−6.1	8.5	6.5	−8.5
1991	7.1	−1.5	−8.5	−3.0	−2.3	11.3	6.8	−7.7
1992	5.7	−0.1	−3.7	−1.4	−1.9	11.9	4.2	−5.6
1993	7.4	−0.3	−4.5	0.1	−5.6	7.2	3.1	−5.1
1994	1.6	−1.1	−6.1	−1.1	−4.6	16.1	2.7	−5.6
1995	−3.9	−2.4	−9.7	−1.8	−2.7	17.8	2.1	−8.1
1996	−1.1	−1.8	−4.4	−4.4	−4.8	13.9	4.0	−6.7
1997	−3.2	−1.5	−5.9	−1.7	−5.4	18.8	2.5	−2.0
1998	2.4	4.7	13.1	12.5	2.4	24.1	1.3	12.7
1999	6.5	3.1	16.5	5.5	9.5	18.4	2.9	10.2
2000	4.3	4.5	9.5	2.4	8.4	14.3	2.9	7.6
2001	6.1	4.2	8.1	1.7	1.8	16.8	6.4	5.4
2002	7.7	4.4	7.5	1.1	5.5	17.7	9.1	5.5
2003	9.7	3.8	12.7	2.0	4.0	29.2	10.1	5.6
2004	8.2	1.2	8.9	4.4	4.2	26.1	6.6	4.4

Source: National Statistics Offices.

of over 8% of GDP a year in 1995 and 6.7% in 1996. In the case of Hong Kong large surpluses were being run up until 1994 but thereafter there was a significant deterioration in the run-up to the crisis. Nonetheless, the picture is far from uniform; for example, Singapore had large surpluses which actually steadily increased in the 1990s, and likewise Taiwan also remained in surplus throughout the 1990s. To some extent given the high economic growth rates some weakness in the current account was to be expected. Interestingly, what may have been more significant as an early-warning signal was that the deterioration in the current accounts in the immediate run-up to the crisis from 1994 to 1996 coincided with a slowdown in economic growth rates over that period (with the notable exception of Malaysia). As we shall see later, there was some weak linkage between the size of the current account deficit and the fall in the nominal exchange rate that subsequently occurred.

Economics makes a distinction between current account deficits due to domestic investment being greater than domestic savings and/or government taxes exceeding government tax revenues. Generally speaking, where a current account deficit is caused by high domestic investment then the current account deficit is usually regarded as less worrying than in the case where it is caused by low savings, which is suggestive of a consumption boom. One has to be careful, however, because even if investment is higher than domestic savings, this investment needs to be productive. Also it needs to give a sufficient boost to the traded sector to improve the future current account performance of the economy. To the extent that the investment is directed to the non-traded sector, for example the property sector, then it may not help improve the current account in the longer run. It is instructive to look at the government finances and the private-sector balances in this regard; **Table 17.5** shows the government fiscal balances as a percentage of GDP and **Table 17.6** shows the excess of private investment over private savings as a percentage of GDP.

From **Table 17.5** it becomes apparent that it is very difficult to argue that the cause of the crisis lay in the pursuit of imprudent fiscal policies. Most governments were

Table 17.5 Government fiscal balances (% of GDP)

	Hong Kong	Indonesia	Malaysia	Korea	Phillipines	Singapore	Taiwan	Thailand
1990	−0.9	na	−2.9	−0.7	−4.6	9.7	–	4.6
1991	0.6	na	−1.0	−1.6	−1.5	10.2	−7.9	4.7
1992	2.8	1.3	0	−0.5	−1.8	6.9	−5.5	2.8
1993	2.1	−1.0	0.8	0.6	−2.0	8.2	−5.1	2.1
1994	1.1	0.4	2.9	0.3	−2.0	8.5	−3.7	1.9
1995	−0.3	1.2	1.5	0.3	−1.3	7.8	−4.5	2.9
1996	2.2	1.0	1.5	0.2	−0.1	6.8	−5.3	2.3
1997	6.1	−0.7	2.8	−1.4	−1.3	3.3	−3.9	−0.9
1998	−2.3	−5.3	−1.4	−3.9	−2.9	0.6	−3.4	−2.5
1999	0.8	−1.6	−2.8	−2.5	−3.1	3.3	−6.0	−3.4
2000	−0.4	−1.1	−5.8	−1.4	−4.3	2.5	−4.7	−2.9
2001	−5.0	−3.2	−5.5	−1.7	−4.1	−1.7	−6.7	−2.9
2002	−4.9	−1.7	−5.6	0.7	−5.3	0.1	−4.4	−2.6
2003	−3.1	−1.9	−5.6	0.2	−4.4	−1.1	−2.9	−2.3
2004	−3.1	−1.9	−5.3	−0.9	−4.3	−0.4	−3.3	−1.6

Source: dbresearch.com.

Table 17.6 Domestic savings less domestic investment (% of GDP)

	Hong Kong	Indonesia	Malaysia	Korea	Phillipines	Singapore	Taiwan	Thailand
1990	8.0	–	–4.9	0.2	–10.7	18.2	–	–3.9
1991	7.7	–	–9.5	–4.6	–3.8	21.5	–1.1	–4.0
1992	8.5	1.2	–3.7	–1.9	–3.7	18.8	–1.3	–2.8
1993	9.5	–1.3	–3.7	0.7	–7.6	15.4	–2.0	–3.0
1994	2.7	–0.7	–3.2	–0.8	–6.6	24.6	–1.0	–3.7
1995	–4.2	–1.2	–8.2	–1.5	–4.0	25.6	–2.4	–5.2
1996	1.1	–0.8	–2.9	–4.2	–4.9	21.7	–1.3	–4.4
1997	2.9	–2.2	–3.1	–3.1	–6.7	22.1	–1.4	–2.9
1998	0.1	–0.6	11.7	8.6	–0.5	24.7	–2.1	10.2
1999	7.3	1.5	13.7	3.0	6.4	21.7	–2.1	6.8
2000	3.9	3.4	3.7	1.0	4.1	16.8	–1.8	4.7
2001	1.1	1.0	2.6	0	–2.3	15.1	–0.3	2.5
2002	2.8	2.7	1.9	1.8	0.2	17.8	4.7	2.9
2003	6.6	1.9	7.1	2.2	–0.4	28.1	7.2	3.3
2004	5.1	–0.7	3.6	3.5	–0.1	25.2	3.3	2.8

Source: dbresearch.com.

running fiscal surpluses and only in Taiwan was the size of its fiscal deficits significant, and even then it was actually being reduced in the run-up to the crisis. Hence, *prima facie*, the evidence suggests that there was not a significant fiscal root to the crisis. However, one has to be careful; in an influential paper, Burnside, Eichenbaum and Rebelo (2001) argue that the size of fiscal deficits/surpluses masked the potential dangers to public debt levels of implicit bailout guarantees.

What is more apparent from **Table 17.6** is that in many of the economies there was an excess of private investment over private savings, which ominously widened prior to the crisis. Only in Singapore was there a persistent large excess of private savings over private investment. Hence, the net capital inflows into the Asian economies were driven primarily by the fact that private investment was exceeding private savings in the region.

It is worthwhile considering also whether the exceptionally high rates of investment throughout the 1990s of over 30% of GDP in most of these countries were sustainable, even in the case of the Philippines and Taiwan the rates were in the 20–25% range. Although the official figures may overstate actual investment by including in certain instances elements of consumption, there is some evidence presented by Corsetti *et al.* (1998) that such investment was beginning to become less productive in the run-up to the economic crisis (1993–96) compared to the earlier period (1987–93). In the case of Korea, some 20 of the 30 largest conglomerates had rates of return on capital below their costs of capital, and seven of them were close to bankrupt. Indeed, in Korea the 1996 debt/equity ratio of the top 30 *chaebols* was estimated to be in excess of 300% in the run-up to the crisis, with some of them having debt–equity ratios as high as 3,000%.

Table 17.7 shows some interesting data concerning capital flows into the Asian region in the run-up and during the crisis. There were high net capital inflows into the region right up until the crisis broke in mid-1997. It is important to note that many of the capital inflows were of a short-term nature, but by the end of 1996 the

Table 17.7 International bank and securities financing of five Asian economies ($ billions)

1990–95 (Average)	1996	1997 (Q1+Q2)	1997 (Q3)	1997 (Q4)	1998 (Q1+Q2)	1998 (Q3)	1998 (Q4)
28	56	49	–39	–96	–96	–59	–43

Note: The five countries are Indonesia, Korea, Malaysia, Philippines and Thailand.
Source: Bank for International Settlements.

share of short-term debt to total debt was typically above 50% in the region. Indeed, the ratio of short-term liabilities to foreign exchange reserves was above 100% in the cases of Korea, Thailand and Indonesia. It was the sudden and dramatic reversal of these flows that lay at the root of the crisis that then ensued. Our analysis of the macro fundamentals suggests that a sudden reversal could not have been easily predicted from the macro data, and we thus need to investigate in more detail the background to the crisis and make some attempt to account for the sudden withdrawal of foreign capital.

17.7 The role of external factors in the crisis

There can be little doubt that a number external factors also played an important background role to the economic crisis:

1 Following the collapse of its property and stockmarket bubbles at the end of the 1980s, Japan spent most of the 1990s in economic recession. Interest rates were kept at very low levels and this encouraged a capital outflow from Japan into the Southeast Asian economies enabling them to finance excessive investment projects with relative ease.
2 Some argue that a loss in the cost-competitiveness of the Asian economies can be traced back to a 50% devaluation of the Chinese renminbi in 1994. However, this has been disputed by authors such as Edison *et al.* (1999) who argue that many business transactions were carried out at the new parity long before the actual devaluation occurred.
3 Financial deregulation had attracted large foreign banks to invest heavily in the region. International banks believed that their loans were effectively underpinned by the governments in the region thus leading to a moral hazard problem. The belief that loans were guaranteed either by the governments or by the potential for IMF bailout packages may have contributed to a climate of excessive lending that ultimately made a crisis more likely to occur than if the perceived insurance schemes had not been in place.
4 In April 1997 the Japanese government imposed a consumption tax that is widely credited with leading to an abrupt decline in consumer expenditure in Japan. This in turn had a noticeable impact on the exports of its Asian trading partners. The tax was also widely credited with stalling Japan's fragile economic recovery.
5 From mid-1995 onwards there was a sharp effective appreciation of the US dollar in relation to the Japanese and European currencies, which led to a deterioration

in the competitiveness of those Asian economies that had pegged their currencies to the US dollar. Given the lags between exchange rate effects and trade this began to impact upon their export performance in 1996/97.

A combination of the above factors meant that the Asian economies were vulnerable to changes in market sentiment. Before we proceed to examine the factors that were of more immediate concern in causing this change in sentiment we need to examine the crucial role of the financial sector in the crisis. In particular, we need to examine the linkage between the capital flows outlined in **Table 17.7** and the expansion of domestic credit that fuelled the stockmarket and property boom in the region in the run-up to the crisis.

17.8 The role of the financial system

The role of the banking system in financial crises in emerging economies has been noted in a number of studies such as Kaminsky and Reinhart (1997) and Goldfajn and Rodrigo (1997). The occurrence of financial crises has often occurred with a lag following a period of financial liberalization. For instance, Jeffrey Sachs in the *Financial Times* (18 September 1997) has argued that:

> Throughout . . . South East Asia banks have been deregulated and privatized in recent years, allowing them much greater latitude to borrow from abroad. Banks and near-banks such as Thailand's now notorious financial trusts – become intermediaries for channelling foreign capital into the domestic economy. The trouble is that the newly liberalized banks and near-banks often operate under highly distorted incentives. Under-capitalized banks have incentives to borrow abroad and invest domestically with reckless abandon. If the lending works out, the bankers make money. If the lending fails, the depositors and creditors stand to lose money, but the bank owners bear little risk themselves because they have little capital tied up in the bank. Even the depositors and the foreign creditors may be secure from risk, if the government bails them out in the case of bank failure.

The pivotal role of the banking system and its relationship with the government and the corporate structure in the East Asian crisis is perhaps far more important to an understanding of the economic crisis than any deterioration in the macroeconomic fundamentals. The governments in the Southeast Asian economies had tried to foster high rates of economic growth and they applied political pressure on domestic banks to lend to corporations and on the corporations themselves to undertake heavy investment programmes to achieve this. To induce firms to undertake such investment programmes governments provided direct subsidies, tax concessions and in many cases public guarantees. More importantly, state-run banks were directed to extend credit to corporations largely without a proper evaluation of the risk–return nature of the investment being undertaken. The domestic banks obtained easy finance from a mixture of domestic residents and from foreign banks and investors who thought that their loans were effectively guaranteed by the governments of the Southeast Asian economies.

It is also important to appreciate in this context that the Asian banking system suffered from many weaknesses (see Mishkin, 1999), including lax supervision, weak regulation, insufficient skills in the regulatory bodies, low capital adequacy ratios, poor project selection schemes and even corruption in lending practices. The banks used inadequate credit-scoring mechanisms and were subject to political manipulation in their lending criteria resulting in credit being extended to firms without any proper regard to profitability. This resulted in non-performing loans (NPLs) taking up an ever-increasing proportion of their loan book. In addition, governments were heavily enmeshed in the corporate culture with political favouritism, a history of government 'bailouts' of failing firms and little real concern for profitability. This severe structural weakness in the Asian banking systems meant that the foreign capital inflows were not efficiently intermediated.

Given the generally underdeveloped nature of the bond and equity markets in the Southeast Asian countries, the banks have a very significant role in the Asian financial systems. For example, in Indonesia the banks were responsible for around two-thirds of corporate finance, while the stockmarket provided only a third in the run-up to the crisis. Most capital inflows were therefore intermediated one way or another by local banks. It was when the loans intermediated by local banks and financial houses started to become non-performing that foreigners became eager to pull their money out of the region. As **Table 17.8** shows, NPLs were particularly high in the countries most heavily affected by the crisis, namely Indonesia, Malaysia, Korea and Thailand.

One of the major impetuses for the foreign capital inflows into Asia was the financial liberalization that took place in the 1990s. The flows of capital were also encouraged by fixing exchange rate parities *vis-à-vis* the US dollar, which lowered the perceived exchange risk premium on investment in these countries. It seems that international banks believed that should their lending go sour, they would either be bailed out by the local government or obtain an indirect bailout due through IMF involvement in the event of any problems in the region. Such beliefs were to some extent fostered by declarations such as those made by the Indonesian Finance Ministry which announced in 1994 that it would not permit a state bank to default and the government supported 'forced' mergers in instances where a private bank was in trouble. McKinnon and Pill (1996) argue that international banks in the run-up to the crisis had lent huge amounts of funds to the region's domestic banks with little

Table 17.8 Estimates of non-performing loans and non-performing credits

	Non-performing bank loans (% of all loans)		Non-performing credits % GDP, 1997
	End of 1996	**End of 1997**	
Hong Kong	3	1	3.6
Indonesia	13	15	9.7
Malaysia	10	15	18.7
Korea	8	30	25.7
Philippines	14	7	6.5
Singapore	4	4	4.9
Taiwan	4	na	6.0
Thailand	13	36	35.1

Source: Burnside *et al.* (2001).

Table 17.9 Bank lending to the private sector (% of GDP)

	1991	1992	1993	1994	1995	1996	1997
Hong Kong	142	134	140	149	155	162	174
Indonesia	50	50	50	52	54	55	69
Korea	53	53	54	57	57	62	70
Malaysia	75	75	74	75	85	93	107
Philippines	18	20	26	29	38	50	56
Singapore	83	85	84	84	91	96	100
Taiwan	109	126	137	147	149	146	146
Thailand	67	72	80	91	98	102	116

Sources: Various.

regard to any detailed risk-assessment. Evidence of a lending boom fuelled by foreign capital inflows is documented in Corsetti *et al.* (1998), and **Table 17.9** shows a significant upward movement in bank lending to the private sector in all of the countries studied.

In all the countries under study we can see that there was a significant increase in bank lending to the private sector as a percentage of GDP, and the fact that GDP was rising strongly in this period must also be borne in mind. In the three countries where the lending boom was the greatest – namely the Philippines, Thailand and Malaysia – it is noteworthy that these were the countries most hard hit by the crisis in 1997.

That a great deal of the inflow of funds helped fuel a stock and property market boom in the East Asian economies is not really in dispute. As **Tables 17.10** and **17.11** reveal there was a significant rise in both the overall stockmarket indices and an even more marked increase in the value of the property sector of the index in all of the economies during the period 1991 to 1996 which seems to have started to come to an end in 1997. The concentration of foreign loans to the property sector and the financing of speculation in the equity markets meant the banking systems were particularly vulnerable to any asset deflation.

That there was an asset and property bubble in these economies cannot be easily refuted – see for example Sarno and Taylor (1999). The Hong Kong market quadrupled in 1990–96, the Indonesia and Philippine markets rose by over 250% and speculation drove property and land values to unsustainable levels.

17.9 The immediate causes of the crisis

It is not completely clear what was the spark that ignited the crisis. The first major corporate failure took place in Korea in January 1997, when Hanbo Steel collapsed under the weight of $6 billion of debts; it was soon followed by Sammi Steel and Kia Motors. The collapse of these companies meant problems for the local merchant banks that had either borrowed significantly from foreign banks to finance lending to these companies or who had provided guarantees to foreign investors that had made direct loans to the companies.

Pressure on the Thai baht had begun to emerge at the back end of 1996 fostered by

Table 17.10 Stockmarket indices (end of year)

	Hong Kong (Hang Seng)	Indonesia (Jakarta composite)	Malaysia (Kuala Lumpur composite)	Korea (KOSPI)	Philippines (Manilla composite)	Singapore (Times straight)	Taiwan (composite)	Thailand (SET)
1990	3025	417	505	696	653	947	4530	612
1991	4297	247	556	610	1154	1214	4600	711
1992	5512	274	643	678	1272	1240	3327	888
1993	11888	588	1275	866	3241	2086	6070	1682
1994	8191	469	1210	1027	2785	1853	7124	1360
1995	10073	513	995	882	2594	1917	5173	1280
1996	13451	673	1237	651	3170	1991	6933	831
1997	10722	396	594	376	1869	1507	8187	372
1998	10488	398	586	562	1968	1392	6418	355
1999	16962	676	812	1028	2142	2479	8488	481
2000	15095	416	679	504	1494	1926	4739	269
2001	11397	392	969	963	1169	1623	5551	303
2002	9321	424	646	627	1018	1341	4452	356
2003	12575	691	793	810	1442	1764	5890	772
2004	14230	1000	907	895	1822	2066	6139	668

Notes: (a) KOSPI stands for Korean Stock Price Index, and SET is the Stock Exchange Thailand index. (b) The figures are the end of year closing prices of the indices.

Table 17.11 Stockmarket highs and lows

	Date of 1997 high	Stock index	Date of 1998 low	Stock index	% decline from 1997 high to 1998 low
Hong Kong	7/8/97	16,673	13/8/98	6,660	60%
Indonesia	7/7/97	738	21/9/98	256	65%
Korea	17/6/97	792	16/6/98	280	65%
Malaysia	25/2/97	1,271	11/9/98	262	79%
Philippines	3/2/97	3,447	11/9/98	1,082	69%
Singapore	17/2/97	2,129	4/9/98	805	62%
Taiwan	31/7/97	10,066	3/9/98	6,251	38%
Thailand	22/1/97	858	4/9/98	207	76%

Notes: (a) The above indices are based on closing prices of the index (not intra-day high/lows). (b) Note in three countries the pre-crisis peaks were recorded before 1997; Korea (8 Nov. 1994) 1,138; Singapore (5 Feb. 1996) 2,163; Thailand (5 Jan. 1994) 1,753. (c) Note that in the case of Taiwan the ultimate low for the index was 3,811 recorded on 15 Jan. 2001.

concern about its large current account deficit and increasing reliance on short-term foreign capital. In addition the Thai stockmarket had begun a steep decline as early as February 1996; the market fell over 30% in 1996 and a further 30% by mid-1997. The Korean market fell 26% in 1996 and the Malaysian market began to decline in February 1996, but other markets did not show any sign of weakness right up to July/August 1997 (see **Table 17.11**). Pressure had been mounting on the Thai baht as early as July 1996 when, following the collapse of the Bangkok Bank of Commerce, there had been a large injection of liquidity into the financial system by the Bank of Thailand. In February 1997, Samprasong Land (a Thai property company) missed debt payments due to foreign creditors and in so doing signalled the start of a collapse in the local property market and serious trouble for local finance companies with heavy loan exposure to property companies. While the Bank of Thailand committed some $8 billion of loans to assist financial institutions facing difficulty, this proved insufficient to deal with the magnitude of the debts. The pressures on the financial system continued through to 14 May 1997, when the Thai stockmarket fell nearly 7%, and on 19 June following the resignation of the Finance Minister, a staunch supporter of the currency peg, the stockmarket fell nearly 11% in a single day. In a bid to save the Thai baht from devaluation the Bank of Thailand engaged in substantial forward purchases of the baht representing a massive drain on its foreign exchange reserves. The battle to save the baht from devaluation ultimately proved unsuccessful when, following the withdrawal of support from the Thai authorities, Finance One (a major finance company) announced that it would not be able to meet payments to foreign or domestic creditors. This announcement came as a major shock to foreign creditors and led to such a massive withdrawal of funds that the baht was forced to devalue on 2 July 1997.

The Thai devaluation then seems to have triggered international investors' concerns about the entire region. A successful speculative attack was launched against the Philippines peso which was forced to float on 11 July. The crisis soon spread to Malaysia where the property sector had been experiencing a speculative bubble. Local banks had lent significant sums of money to fuel speculative equity and real-estate investments and the party started to come to an end in March 1997 when the central bank announced restrictions on lending for real estate and property purposes. The announcement came as a shock to foreign investors and led to a sharp drop in the Malaysian Stock Exchange which had a heavy weighting to the property and financial sector. The speculative pressure against the ringgit came to a crescendo following the Philippine devaluation, and the ringgit was forced to float on 14 July. The Malaysian Prime Minister Mahathir Mohammmed launched a vitriolic attack against 'rogue speculators' and introduced controls on capital outflows and against the short-selling of equities and the ringgit in the forward exchange market.

The contagion element of the crisis is perhaps best illustrated by the case of Indonesia. Although Indonesia had many weaknesses such as a poorly regulated financial system, 'crony capitalism' characterized by political nepotism and a persistent current account deficit, things were not that bad either. Indonesia had avoided any major corporate bankruptcies, the government had been running fiscal surpluses and the exposure of the commercial banking system to foreign creditors at around 6% of GDP was well below that of other countries in the region, although corporate debts to foreign creditors were fairly significant. Despite this, the rupiah came under intense speculative pressure and was forced to float on 14 August 1997. The resulting depreciation of the rupiah, combined with a rise in interest rates designed to protect the rupiah, resulted in Indonesia being dragged into the crisis, and September to December saw a plunge into a severe crisis situation in Indonesia. Although a letter of intent was signed with the IMF on 31 October that secured a $40 billion support package it had little impact on the crisis, and in November the Indonesian stockmarket fell some 20%. The illness of President Suharto in December only added to the crisis atmosphere and by the beginning of 1998 Indonesia had become the investment pariah of the region.

Political instability in the region also played a background role in the crisis; there were major cabinet reshuffles in Thailand; the Malaysian Prime Minister Mahathir Mohammed attacked 'rogue speculators'; and elections in Indonesia, combined with the ill-health of its President Suharto and his unpredictable policies, combined with presidential elections in Korea, all added to the sense of political and economic instability in the region.

In November 1997 the Hong Kong dollar came under intense speculative attack, since speculators felt its peg to the US dollar was no longer sustainable given the other devaluations that had occurred within the region. Thereafter, for the best part of a year is seems that there was a continual battle between the Hong Kong Monetary Authority (HKMA) and speculators over the sustainability of the Hong Kong dollar peg. Speculators simultaneously shorted the Hang Seng index and sold the Hong Kong dollar forward. The bet proved very lucrative for the speculators since the HKMA was forced to raise interest rates to defend the Hong Kong dollar parity, which depressed the Hong Kong property and stockmarket. The battle between the speculators and the HKMA was only finally resolved in October 1998 when the HKMA started to buy shares to boost the Hang Seng index.

By November 1997 South Korea had been dragged into the crisis and speculative attacks were launched against the Korean won, and even a Korean rescue package with the IMF announced on 21 November failed to end the speculative pressure, as the terms of the deal which included tax rises and spending cuts were viewed by the markets as likely to worsen the plight of the economy. Rumours also surfaced in December that Korea would declare a debt moratorium and on 11 December the Korean markets suffered significant declines following a Moody's downgrade of its foreign-currency-denominated bonds. For a while Japan also became a subject of concern following the closure on 24 November of the fourth-largest securities house Yamaichi Securities, and on 19 December foodstuff trader Toshoku filed for bankruptcy leading to concerns that more would follow. Indonesia added to the sense of panic by reneging on promised structural reforms.

By mid-January 1998, somewhat calmer markets returned on the news that international banks had agreed to roll-over much of Korea's short-term debt, and on 19 January Indonesia's agreement to a tough IMF package was also welcomed. However, once again the calm was short-lived as Indonesia started to flirt with the idea of introducing a currency board and the IMF made it clear that it was not going to support the Indonesian plans to peg the rupiah to the dollar. From February up until the end of May, markets did not stage a comeback nor did they collapse, rallying somewhat on the announcement of trade surpluses in Thailand (13 March) and tumbling on news of unrest and looting in Indonesia which eventually led to the resignation of President Suharto in May 1998.

17.10 An analysis of the crisis

Mishkin (1999) argues that the weak position of the Asian banking system with regard to the increasing percentage of non-performing loans (NPLs) when combined with their fixed exchange rate systems made speculative attacks far more likely to succeed. When banks' balances sheets are weak, speculators know that central banks' attempts to defend the currency via interest rate hikes are likely to fail since they increase the percentage of NPLs and weaken still further the banks' balance sheets eventually making devaluation inevitable. In 1996 it has been estimated that NPLs as a proportion of total lending was 8% in Korea, 13% in Indonesia, 10% in Malaysia, 14% in the Philippines, 13% in Thailand and 4% each in Singapore and Taiwan and 3% in Hong Kong. Exposure to the property market was particularly high in Hong Kong, Malaysia, Singapore and Thailand, whilst in Korea and Indonesia most of the bank exposure was to manufacturing companies. For instance, in 1996 the Malaysian banking system's exposure to the property and equity sector was some 42.6%, while exposure to the manufacturing sector was around 21%. Once the crisis got under way it had a dramatic impact on the proportion of NPLs, which reached an estimated high of over 30% in Korea and Thailand at the peak of the crisis.

Once devaluations and drops in property prices and stockmarkets got under way in the region, the crisis took on a life of its own. The devaluations meant large foreign exchange losses for domestic banks and firms whose liabilities to foreign banks were largely unhedged since they had believed in their government's pledges to maintain fixed exchange rates. The drop in property and equity prices also caused substantial losses and outright defaults by many property companies and those playing the markets with margin accounts. In sum, local banks were hit simultaneously on many fronts – the withdrawal of foreign funds, substantial foreign exchange losses, a sharp rise in the percentage of non-performing loans and losses on equity holdings. The resulting rapid rise in the proportion of non-performing loans further accelerated the withdrawal of foreign funds which in turn led to further falls in the local currencies, property sector prices and stockmarkets, so completing the vicious circle. The erosion of the banking system's capital bases due to all of these factors severely constrained their ability to lend to even solvent companies in the midst of the crisis.

The withdrawal of foreign capital also meant a severe liquidity crisis. The liquidity squeeze forced up local interest rates and meant that meant that local firms had considerable difficulty in obtaining finance just when they needed it to cover their foreign exchange losses and service higher debt payments. The rise in NPLs of the local banking systems made foreign banks even more reluctant to roll-over any loans. There can be little doubt that this reluctance was reinforced by the absence of any effective local bankruptcy laws and concerns that local lenders would receive preferential treatment as compared to foreign creditors.

It is also apparent there was very little discrimination made between the various countries in the region as international banks and foreign investors (including mutual funds) decided *en masse* to pull funds out of the region. The crisis was thus characterized by contagion and herding behaviour on the part of foreign investors and banks, and there were many ways in which the so-called contagion effect came into play during the Asian crisis. As we have mentioned in section 17.4, when one currency was devalued it raised questions about the sustainability and credibility of other fixed parities within the region. The competitive advantage conferred to the devaluing country also raised the prospect of a slowdown in the export growth of competitor countries so calling into question other exchange rate pegs. Similarly as capital was pulled out of one country so forcing it to raise its interest rate, this had the effect of forcing up the interest rates in competing countries. When local companies get into difficulty it is generally the case that domestic banks recall loans lent to foreign businesses in the region first, so spreading the credit squeeze across borders. Furthermore, a downturn in the local economy directly impacts on the exports of other countries in the region.

There also seems to have been a problem of imperfect information; foreign investors faced with insufficient information were unable to distinguish the bad from the not so bad countries and so reacted in a fairly uniform manner by removing capital from all of them. The role of speculators including hedge funds in foreign exchange crises cannot be underestimated; having made a great deal of money by successfully betting against the Thai baht it was only natural for speculators to switch their attention to testing the sustainability of other currency pegs in the region.

It is important to understand that it was not just US and European banks that scaled back their lending to the region. In particular, Japanese banks who were facing further erosion to their already weak capital bases as a result of losses from their Asian exposure decided to call in many of their loans to the region. Similarly, Korean banks that were faced with extensive problems due to their exposure to the heavily indebted *chaebols* started to call in loans they had extended to the rest of Asia. The attempt by speculators to force a devaluation of the Hong Kong dollar led to the raising of interest rates by the HKMA, and apart from placing pressure on the already beleaguered Hong Kong stockmarket and property sector by raising the interest payable on deposits, some Hong Kong banks were forced to recall loans they had made to the rest of Asia.

In retrospect, there were also policy errors conducted by the local governments that probably exacerbated the crisis. For example, the Thai authorities might have been better off allowing the baht to float freely rather than exhausting their foreign exchange reserves trying to defend the parity. Both the Thai and Korean authorities initially spent huge amounts of money trying to keep afloat companies that were clearly headed for liquidation. In the case of Thailand the authorities' refusal in late June 1997 to save Finance One contrary to previous promises brought into question the credibility of all their other guarantees. Indeed, it can be plausibly argued that the

Table 17.12 Currency declines in the crisis and parities at the start of 2005 (domestic currency units per US dollar)

	1 July 1997	1998 low (date)		% decline	3 Jan 2005
Hong Kong dollar	7.7455	7.734	(30/6/98)	0.1	7.7779
Indonesia rupiah	2431	15200	(16/6/98)	84.0	9278
Korea won	886	1806	(9/1/98)	50.9	1037
Malaysia ringgit	2.5240	4.6805	(8/1/98)	46.1	3.7995
Philippines peso	26.35	44.55	(23/9/98)	40.9	56.11
Singapore dollar	1.4296	1.79	(12/198)	20.2	1.6393
Taiwan dollar	27.78	34.83	(31/8/98)	20.2	31.83
Thailand baht	24.35	53.55	(29/1/98)	54.5	38.88

Notes: (a) The percentage decline is measured by comparing 98 low with original exchange rate prevailing at 1 July 1997.
Source: Globalfindata.com.

reneging on the commitment to save Finance One was the crucial match that ignited the Asian crisis. The existence of 'crony capitalism' was seen to be in play in Indonesia where IMF and state funds were directed at trying to save the business interests of President Suharto's relatives. The early imposition in August 1997 by the Malaysian and Thai authorities of foreign exchange controls once the crisis began only heightened the desire of foreign investors to get out of the region and probably contributed to subsequent downgrades by the credit-rating agencies.

The currencies that fell most during the crisis (**Table 17.12**) were currencies of countries with the largest current-account deficits. The Hong Kong dollar parity was successfully defended by the HKMA against speculative attacks throughout the crisis. Most noticeably, the two surplus countries, Singapore and Taiwan witnessed their currencies fall by relatively modest amounts of around 25%; indeed during the crisis the decline of the last two currencies was far more orderly. Hence, there is some evidence that there was a link between current accounts and the exchange rate turmoil.

17.11 The IMF handling of the crisis

Once the crisis was under way economic agents were generally very keen to exit the region and the initial IMF plans were signed but not adhered to by the governments. This was particularly the case in Indonesia where the Suharto regime ignored virtually all of its commitments and only reversed policy once the rupiah went into freefall. Likewise, initially the IMF package for Korea was only grudgingly accepted, and in Thailand it was only the onset of a new government that was committed to economic reform that finally stabilized the baht. The overall IMF programme to the region had a number of objectives:

1 Prevention of default on the part of the Asian countries.
2 Prevention of a freefall in their exchange rates.
3 Prevention of the emergence of inflation.

4 Maintenance of sound fiscal discipline.
5 Restoration of investor confidence in the region.
6 Structural reform of the financial sector and banking system.
7 Structural reform of the corporate sector, in particular the ending of so-called 'crony capitalism'.
8 Rebuilding of foreign exchange reserves.
9 Limiting the decline of output.

The key instruments used by the IMF to achieve these objectives were:

- **Bank closures**. The IMF was very keen to ensure that the least-viable banks were closed down. Those banks that remained open were expected to restore their capital ratios to above the 8% required by the Basle Accord. In Thailand some 58 out of 91 finance companies were suspended of which over 55 were eventually liquidated. In its agreement with the IMF the Thai banks were expected to have a capital adequacy ratio of 10% by the end of 1997 and 12% by 2001. Similarly, in Korea 14 out of 30 merchant banks were suspended in a move designed to restore confidence in the banking system. In the case of Indonesia the IMF insisted on the closure of some 16 banks. The IMF policy focused on closing down the banks with the highest proportion of non performing loans.
- **Fiscal discipline**. The IMF regarded the maintenance of fiscal discipline as crucial to the successful management of the crisis. In its programme for Thailand it stated that 'Fiscal policy is the key to the overall credibility of the programme'. In its initial packages it required that the Asian economies actually run budget surpluses equivalent to 1% of GDP. The IMF viewed the maintenance of fiscal discipline as crucial since government funds would be needed to assist in the eventual recapitalization of the banking systems, restoring foreign confidence and helping to improve the balance of payments position of the deficit countries.
- **Monetary discipline**. As is typical of IMF packages, limits were set on the creation of domestic credit, and interest rates were raised in an attempt to reduce capital outflows and relieve pressures on the currencies. The IMF recognized that the higher interest rates would harm the corporate sector in the economies but judged that the benefits from exchange rate stability would more than offset this. For instance, the Deputy Managing Director Shigemitsu Sugisaki on 30 January 1998 stated:

   We know that higher interest rates are likely to hurt the corporate sector, but an appreciation of the currency that follows a tightening of monetary conditions would greatly benefit those corporations indebted in foreign currency. There is no alternative in the short term. A relaxation of monetary policy would only lead to further depreciations of the currencies.

- **Structural reform of the banking and corporate sector**. While IMF programmes are usually concentrated on ensuring the pursuit of fiscal and monetary restraint on the part of the crisis country, they are usually limited with regard to financial sector and corporate reform. However, in the Asian crisis this was not the case; the IMF believed that in the longer term there was a need to reform the banking and corporate structure in the Asian economies by a more radical policy of restructuring and liberalization, which involved the closing of numerous banks, reducing

tariffs, reducing state aid and the opening-up of the region to foreign direct investment in the economies. As Michel Camdessus, the Managing Director of the IMF,
emphasized:

> In view of the nature of the crisis, these programmes had to go far beyond
> addressing the major fiscal, monetary or external balances. Their aim is to
> strengthen financial systems, improve governance and transparency, restore
> economic competitiveness, and modernize the legal and regulatory environ-
> ment.

17.12 An evaluation of the IMF programmes

Authors such as Radlett and Sachs (1998) have criticized the IMF programmes as being
unduly harsh and indeed exacerbating the crisis, the policy on bank closures coming
in for particular criticism. They argue that the requirements to close many of the
banks added to the credit squeeze on the private sector, created a sense of panic on
the part of international investors and led to a series of bank runs as local residents
sought to safeguard their savings. For instance, by the end of November 1997 two-
thirds of Indonesian banks had suffered a run on their deposits. The policy of recapitalization is also harshly criticized; they argue that the raising of capital adequacy
ratios greatly and unnecessarily added to the credit crunch on the corporate sector.
However, in the IMF's defence it regarded structural reform as absolutely essential
since problems in the banking sector lay at the heart of the crisis. The IMF also
believed that without structural reform, the chance of restoring foreign confidence
and capital flows back to the region would remain low. Moreover, the major bank
runs that had occurred in Indonesia were not repeated on anything like the same scale
in Thailand and Korea.

The fiscal and monetary programmes have also come in for quite a lot of criticism,
most notably from the Nobel Prize-winning economist Joseph Stiglitz (2002), who has
argued that the tough fiscal discipline combined with higher interest rates meant that
the contraction in economic output was greater than would otherwise have been the
case. As we have seen, at the time of the crisis the Asian economies were actually
running fiscal surpluses or relatively small deficits and their national debt to GDP
ratios were also not excessively high. However, as noted previously the IMF believed
that fiscal restraint was essential, partly as a corrective mechanism for helping the
current account to return to surplus and partly as a means of preventing further
wastage of scarce government resources on low marginal return projects. The contain-
ment of government expenditure was regarded as particularly important, given that
public funds would be needed to recapitalize and restructure the banking systems.

On the monetary front the rise in interest rates which should in theory have helped
strengthen the currencies did not succeed in doing so. The currencies in fact depreciated even more heavily following the initial IMF packages, despite the steep rise in
interest rates and the exchange rate targets set. It appears to be the case that the
squeeze on local companies and the increase in non-performing loans on the books of
the banking system probably added to the sense of crisis and may have further exacerbated the withdrawal of foreign capital. However, this argument is not as clear-cut as
it seems; if the countries had not raised their interest rates, it may well have been the
case that their currencies would have depreciated even more than they did, which

would have exacerbated the losses for domestic banks and companies that had unhedged foreign currency debts. Furthermore, larger falls in the currencies of the region could well have led to hyperinflation and even more disruption to economic activity than actually occurred.

While there is no doubt that the initial IMF policy programmes were quite tough, the policies became somewhat softer as the extent of the economic downturn in the Asian economies became evident. For example, the original Indonesian package negotiated in October 1997 required Indonesia to run budget surpluses equivalent to 1% of GDP in the fiscal years 1997/98 and 1998/99, but a subsequent agreement reached in June 1998 permitted the government to run a budget deficit of up to 8.5% of GDP.

The moral hazard problem is a recurrent theme with respect to IMF interventions; the argument being that IMF bailouts actually make crises more likely than if the IMF did not intervene. However, this argument should clearly not be taken too far, since in most economic crises investors are probably not expecting an IMF intervention when investing their funds. Indeed, most investors would probably be very reluctant to lend funds if they felt that there was a reasonable chance that the country might need to seek emergency assistance from the Fund in the near future. Furthermore, during crises most investors do end up losing substantially – in the Asian crisis it is estimated that foreign investors in the bond and equity markets in the affected countries lost in the region of 50–80% of their capital as the value of their investments in the region plummeted. In addition, the idea that governments will be more inclined to pursue imprudent policies knowing that the IMF will likely come to the rescue cannot be taken too seriously. Anecdotal evidence suggests that most governments are extremely reluctant to go to the IMF as it is taken as a clear sign of economic policy failure and usually results in the government falling or failing to get re-elected. It is also important to bear in mind here that if there was no IMF to act as a lender of last resort, then there would be a significant danger of even greater panic. The IMF programmes and loans also act as an institutional buffer to limit potential contagion effects. In the absence of the IMF the risk of even greater regional dislocations, disorderly markets and possibly a more significant global financial crisis has to be considered.

17.13 The crisis and post-crisis performance of the economies

As can be seen in **Table 17.1** there were very significant falls in economic output in many of the crisis-hit countries during 1998, with real GDP falling 13.1% in Indonesia, 10.5% in Thailand, 7.4% in Malaysia and 6.9% in Korea. These output falls were dramatic, especially as these economies had been used to growing at the rate of 5–8% per year. However, fortunately, the slump in economic activity proved to be relatively short-lived and during 1999 and 2000 the economies rebounded strongly, although their growth rates during the first few years of the new century having generally been significantly lower than in the early 1990s. What is also clear from **Table 17.4** is that there was a dramatic improvement in their current accounts during 1998, but this was driven primarily by a massive fall in imports induced by the dramatic fall in output in the afflicted economies, and the effects of the large exchange rate depreciations which encouraged exports and made imports more expensive. In general it seems that the real depreciations of the effective exchange rates that have occurred in all the economies since 1997 has led to an improved current account position in all the economies post-1997 compared to the current account deficits in the run up to the crisis.

The fiscal situation, however, seems to have undergone a significant deterioration as shown in **Table 17.5**; fiscal surpluses of the early to mid-1990s have since been replaced by fiscal deficits in most of the economies. These fiscal deficits have come about partly because of the costs of the crisis itself in terms of bailout of some of the financial institutions and companies, repayment of loans to international institutions, the increased unemployment and also the slower economic growth rates the economies have experienced since the crisis. In addition, the savings and investment data depicted in **Table 17.6** – which changed quite dramatically during the crisis as savings rose and investment collapsed – seem to have undergone a marked change compared to the pre-crisis era with savings rates generally higher and investment rates somewhat lower than before the crisis.

In sum, the output effects of the crises were quite dramatic but the recession itself, while sharp, was relatively short-lived. There does, however, appear to have been a more significant change in some of the crucial economic relationships in these economies, most noticeably the improved current account balances and deterioration in the fiscal balances, meaning that private savings and investment relationship seems to have undergone a quite significant change due to higher savings and lower investment rates than before the crisis. The depreciation of the real effective exchange rates of the economies has made them significantly more competitive in 2004 than in 1997.

17.14 Early-warning systems

Given the number of currency and financial crises that have occurred in recent years, economists, policy-makers and market participants have been keen for different reasons to develop early-warning systems (EWSs) that may be useful in predicting the timing and probability of a financial crisis; Kaminsky, Lizondo and Reinhart (1998) is one of the pioneering papers in this respect. The aim of an early-warning system is to look at various economic and financial indicators for signs prior to outbreak that a crisis is highly likely to occur in the near future (say within 12–18 months). Ideally, of course, an EWS as well as detecting potential crises should avoid giving out false signals, that is predict a crisis when one does not in fact occur. An EWS would be useful for financial market participants in that it would give them a chance to reduce their potential risk exposure (and of course take speculative positions!) and also provide useful information to policy markets who, forewarned of a crisis, could be expected to take preemptive measures to prevent an actual outbreak of a crisis.

The Kaminsky et al. (1998) paper uses a 'signal' approach to devising an early-warning system. This involves looking at a selection of various economic and financial indicators that may exhibit unusual behaviour prior to the outbreak of a crisis; each time an indicator exceeds a predetermined threshold a signal is generated predicting a crisis. It is essential that the thresholds are not set too low or the EWS will generate too many false signals, that is predict a currency crisis when no crisis occurs. On the other hand, the thresholds should not be set so high that too few signals are generated and the EWS fails to predict a crisis when a crisis actually occurs. The aim of an EWS is to predict a currency crisis within one to two years of the actual crisis occurring. A signal can be considered useful on the basis of three alternative metrics: (1) its probability of predicting a crisis (the higher its success rate the better), (2) the length of time in advance of a crisis that it predicts a crisis (the more in advance the better), and (3) the persistence with which it predicts a crisis (the more often it warns of a crisis that actually occurs the better). The following matrix can be used to evaluate the usefulness of a variable in predicting a crisis:

	Crisis (with 24 months)	No crisis (within 24 months)
Signal was issued	A	B
No signal was issued	C	D

where A is the number of months in which the indicator predicts a crisis and a crisis subsequently occurs, B is the number of months the signal provides a false signal of a forthcoming crisis, C is the number of months the indicator fails to produce a signal and a crisis occurs, and D is the number of months the indicator produces a no signal and no crisis occurs. A good indicator is one that has lots of A and D observations and relatively few C and B observations. A useful measure is the ratio $A/(A + C)$ which shows the number of good signals that the indicator issued as a percentage of the total number of signals that it could have produced, since a good indicator will have a relatively high percentage of predicting a crisis when a crisis actually occurs.

In their paper, which is essentially empirical in nature, Kaminsky *et al.* look at a variety of potential indicators of a currency crisis informed partly by the literature on speculative attacks. For instance, the first-generation models predict that the level of the money supply relative to the level of foreign exchange reserves, the size of fiscal deficits and also of current account deficits can provide useful early-warning signals, whilst the second-generation models argue that deviations of output below trend or high levels of unemployment or high levels of public debt may be useful indicators since they weaken the resolve of the authorities to defend a fixed exchange rate parity. The paper also reviews a large range of studies that have looked at numerous currency crises covering both developed and developing countries, and at a huge range of potentially useful indicators.

Kaminsky *et al.* in surveying the literature of currency crises place variables into one of six categories: (1) the external sector, (2) the financial sector, (3) the real sector, (4) public finances, (5) institutional and structural variables, and (6) political variables. A variable is only considered to have some usefulness if the ratio of false to good signals that it generates is below unity. In their empirical analysis, Kaminsky *et al.* find that output levels, deviations of the real exchange rate from trend, banking crises indicators, exports, the ratio of broad money supply to reserves, the inflation rate and equity prices provide useful EWS signals. More surprisingly, current account deficits, fiscal deficits and the differential in real interest rates between the domestic and foreign economies do not provide useful signals for the EWS. Kaminsky *et al.* conclude that a good system needs to consider a variety of economic and financial variables.

We should perhaps not expect too much from an EWS, since no two crises are exactly alike and the economic, financial and political variables which provoke a crisis can vary greatly and interact with each other in often unpredictable ways. Just as a butterfly flapping its wings can provoke a hurricane in another part of the world in chaos theory, so too can a minor event provoke a full-grown speculative crisis which was largely unforeseeable. In addition, Flood and Marion (1999) make the point that currency crises are in practice largely unforeseen by market participants, and they are unforeseen because macro and financial fundamentals are not indicating an impending crisis as seems to have been the case in Asia, hence an EWS based on such indicators is likely to have only a limited success rate. As they put it, '. . . the more unpredictable the crises, the less likely they are to be significantly correlated with the information variables selected as possible crises determinants. Moreover, if the potential determinants of currency crises differ across countries and across time, panel regressions that look for consistent patterns may perform poorly' (p. 18).

17.15 Conclusions

Our interpretation of the Asian financial crisis has been informed by a mixture of the three generations of currency crisis models. There are, however, reasons to believe that none of these models alone is sufficient to explain the crisis, although elements of each were to a greater or lesser extent present during the crisis. For instance, the devaluation of many of the currencies was preceded by current account deficits and a depletion of the foreign exchange reserves of the Asian countries, which is a characteristic of the Krugman model, but the necessary fiscal deficits in the Krugman model were not evident. It is probably fair to say that the second-generation models do somewhat better than the first-generation models at explaining the Asian financial crisis. Indeed, Krugman (1999, pp. 8–9) has acknowledged as much, 'I hereby capitulate. I cannot see any way to make sense of the contagion of 1997–1998 without supposing the existence of multiple equilibria.' Likewise, Masson (1998, p. 6) states, 'the fact that the optimistic view about East Asian economies prevailed for so long (in the face of some reports of banking sector problems), the rapidity of the change of view, and the suddenness and severity of the resulting crises all argue in favour of the multiple equilibria story.' There is also no doubt that there was an explosion of risky lending to the region prior to the crisis and many of the foreign banks that lent to domestic banks and companies in the region felt that there were explicit or implicit government guarantees on their loans which led to the 'moral hazard' problem which is a characteristic of the third-generation models. While it can be disputed whether the bubbles in the local property and stockmarkets were rational or irrational, the proposition that bubbles were present cannot be easily refuted. Finally, the withdrawal of foreign capital when the crisis arrived was both sudden, disorderly and characterized by a high degree of panic which is characteristic of the Sachs (1995) model.

We have argued that although there were signs of a deterioration in the macroeconomic fundamentals, these were not of a sufficiently large order to explain the magnitude of the financial crisis that subsequently erupted. Far more significant in explaining the crisis was the lax lending by the local banking systems fuelled by excessive speculative foreign capital inflows to the region. Much of the foreign capital was used in either unproductive investments or to fuel an unsustainable boom in asset prices, most notably in stockmarket and property valuations. The need to reestablish fair values for property and equity prices then triggered the crisis by undermining the quality of the loan portfolio of the domestic banks. The magnitude of the financial crisis that followed can then also partly be explained in the context of contagion theory and herding behaviour, particularly on the part of foreign banks and international investors exposed to the region. Some of the blame for the magnitude of the crisis can also be apportioned to policy errors by the affected national governments and the initial IMF response.

A central contention of this chapter is that the Asian financial crisis was predominantly a financial crisis caused by excessive foreign-financed credit expansion which resulted in unsustainable asset bubbles rather than any significant macroeconomic weaknesses in the Asian economies. The resulting financial crisis would have been far less severe if international investors had rolled over their loans and not all tried to exit simultaneously from the region. Once this happened, a self-reinforcing crisis was set in motion. As Radlett and Sachs (1998) have put it, 'A combination of panic on the part of the international investment community, policy mistakes at the onset of the crisis by Asian governments, and poorly designed international rescue programs have led to a much deeper fall in (otherwise viable) output than was necessary or desirable.'

In the context of the recent crises it is worth bearing in mind that many of them have been regional in nature. One can think of the Latin American debt crises of the 1980s, the ERM crisis of 1992–93 and the East Asian financial crises of 1997/98. Research by Glick and Rose (1999) suggests that there may be good reasons for crises to become regional in character. Firstly, the economies often compete with one another in international trade so that a devaluation of one country's currency will give it a competitive advantage over other countries, and this may then mean speculators will target the other countries' currencies adversely affected by the initial devaluation. Secondly, devaluations are often followed by recessions which slow down intra-regional trade and growth making other currencies in the region ripe for speculative attack. Their empirical estimates show that trade linkages between the country that is initially subjected to a speculative attack and its trading partners is a statistically significant explanatory variable in regional currency crises. Nevertheless there is mounting empirical evidence (see for example Fratzcher, 2003) that financial linkages between countries are perhaps more important in explaining contagion and regional currency crises.

A recurring theme in financial crises is that extensive dependence on foreign capital leaves a country especially vulnerable since foreign banks are less likely to be willing to renew lines of credit in the event of a crisis than domestic banks. The question of whether the imposition of capital controls on the outflow of capital during a crisis can help to mitigate the crisis is very controversial. The main argument in favour of controls on the outflow of capital is that it would enable the authorities to get away with a lower domestic interest rate than would otherwise be the case, and limiting the sales of the domestic currency would help restrict the depreciation of the local currency which in turn would restrict foreign exchange losses and the risk of uncontrolled inflation. Authors such as Krugman (1998b) have argued that China was largely able to ride out the Asian crisis because the yuan was inconvertible. Economic theory gives little guidance on the subject, since in a second-best world the addition of a further distortion such as capital controls may or may not raise economic welfare. There are, of course, longer-term adverse consequences from deploying capital controls, such as inefficiency, the potential for a misallocation of capital and lower economic growth, but it is not too clear that these outweigh the short-term benefits in times of economic crisis especially when many of the capital movements are driven by panic and contagion effects. However, even during a crisis the imposition of capital controls may not always be beneficial. Once one country imposes capital controls this can lead to foreign investors accelerating capital flight from other countries before they too decide to impose controls. Indeed, capital might be pulled out of otherwise sound emerging market economies so that the crisis is amplified. Some commentators have suggested that the imposition of capital controls by Malaysia in August 1998 may have been a factor in spreading the Asian crisis to Latin America.

The Asian crisis certainly did show that the speed and sequencing of capital account liberalization is an important issue. Capital account liberalization as had occurred in the region needs to be done gradually and be accompanied by strong supervision of the domestic banking system and indeed the corporate sector aimed at avoiding a build-up excessive short-term foreign liabilities on the part of domestic banks and the domestic corporate sector.

The signs of financial and economic recovery that started in 1999 in the East Asian economies may be taken as evidence that the 1997–98 financial crisis was an overreaction on the part of market participants. The speed and size of the recovery has been partly achieved by a return of confidence induced by the adoption of more realistic IMF programmes and a recognition by market participants that the deterioration in economic fundamentals was not of a sufficient magnitude to warrant the fall in currency and asset prices that actually occurred. Indeed, with the benefit of hindsight the exaggerated currency depreciations and falls in equity markets created an excellent buying opportunity for foreign investors seeking to gain exposure to the region.

Further reading

Akerlof, G. and Romer, P. (1994) 'Looting the Economic Underworld of Bankruptcy for Profit', National Bureau of Economic Research, Working Paper no. 1869.

Baig, T. and Goldfajn, I. (1999), 'Financial Market Contagion in the Asian Crisis', *IMF Staff Papers*, vol. 46, no. 2, pp. 167–95.

Blanchard, O. and Watson, M.W. (1982) 'Bubbles, Rational Expectations, and Financial Markets', in P. Wachtel (ed.), *Crisis in the Economic and Financial Structure* (Cambridge, Mass.: Lexington Books).

Burnside, C., Eichenbaum, M. and Rebelo, S. (2001) 'Prospective Deficits and the Asian Crisis', *Journal of Political Economy*, vol. 109, no. 6 pp. 1155–97.

Calvo, G. (1996) 'Capital Inflows and Macroeconomic Management: Tequila Lessons', *International Journal of Finance and Economics*, vol. 1, pp. 207–23.

Calvo, G. and Mendoza, E. (2000) 'Rational Contagion and the Globalization of Securities Markets', *Journal of International Economics*, vol. 51, no. 1, pp. 79–113.

Caramazza, F., Ricci, L. and Salgado, R. (2004) 'International Financial Contagion in Currency Crises', *International Journal of Finance and Economics*, vol. 23, pp. 51–70.

Cline, W.R. and Barnes, J.S. (1997), 'Spreads and Risks in Emerging Markets Lending', Institute of International Finance Research Paper no. 97–1.

Corsetti, G., Pesenti, P. and Roubini, N. (1998) 'What Caused the Asian Currency and Financial Crisis? Part 1: A Macroeconomic Overview', National Bureau of Economic Research, Working Paper no. 6833.

Corsetti, G., Pesenti, P. and Roubini, N. (1999) 'Paper Tigers: A Model of the Asian Crisis', *European Economic Review*, vol. 43, pp. 1211–36.

Dooley, M. (2000) 'A Model of Currency Crises in Emerging Markets', *The Economic Journal*, vol. 110, pp. 256–72.

Dornbusch, R., Goldfajn, I. and Valdes, R.O. (1995) 'Currency Crises and Collapses', *Brookings Papers on Economic Activity*, vol. 2, pp. 219–93.

Edison, H., Fernald, J. and Loungani, P. (1999) 'Was China the First Domino? Assessing Links between China and the Rest of Emerging Asia', *Journal of International Money and Finance*, vol. 18, pp. 515–35.

Flood, R.P. and Garber, P.M. (1984) 'Collapsing Exchange Rate Regimes: Some Linear Examples', *Journal of International Economics*, vol. 16, pp. 1–13.

Flood, R.P. and Marion, N.P. (1999) 'Perspectives on the Recent Currency Crisis Literature', *International Journal of Finance and Economics*, vol. 4, pp. 383–90.

Fratzcher, M. (2003), 'On Currency Crises and Contagion', *Journal of International Money and Finance*, vol. 8, pp. 109–29.

Glick, R. and Rose, A. (1999) 'Contagion and Trade: Why Are Currency Crises Regional', *Journal of International Money and Finance*, vol. 18, pp. 613–87.

Goldfajn, I. and Rodrigo, O.V. (1997) 'Capital Flows and the Twin Crises: The Role of Liquidity', International Monetary Fund Working Paper 97/87.

Jeanne, O. (1997) 'Are Currency Crises Self Fulfilling? A Test', *Journal of International Economics*, vol. 43, pp. 263–86.

Kaminsky, G. and Carmen, M.R. (1997) 'The Twin Crises: The Causes of Banking and Balance of Payments Problems', mimeo, Federal Reserve Board.

Kaminsky, G., Lizondo, S. and Reinhart, C. (1998) 'Leading Indicators of Currency Crises', *IMF Staff Papers*, vol. 45, pp. 1–48.

Krugman, P. (1979), 'A Model of Balance of Payments Crises', *Journal of Money Credit and Banking*, vol. 11, no. 3, pp. 311–25.

Krugman, P. (1998a) 'What Happened to Asia', mimeo, MIT.

Krugman, P. (1998b) 'Saving Asia: It's Time to Get Radical', *Fortune Investor*, September.

Krugman, P. (1999) 'Balance Sheets. The Transfer Problem and Financial Crises', mimeo, MIT.

Masson, P. (1998) 'Contagion: Monsoonal Effects, Spillovers, and Jumps Between Multiple Equilibria', International Monetary Fund Working Paper 98/142.

McKinnon, R. and Pill, H. (1996) 'Credible Liberalization and International Capital Flows: The 'Overborrowing' Syndrome', in T. Ito and A. Krueger (eds), *Financial Deregulation and Integration in East Asia* (Chicago: The University of Chicago Press).

Mishkin, F.S. (1996) 'Understanding Financial Crises: A Developing Country Perspective', National Bureau of Economic Research, Working Paper no. 5600.

Mishkin, F.S. (1999) 'Lessons from the Asian Crisis', National Bureau of Economic Research, Working Paper no. 7102.

Obstfeld, M. (1994) 'The Logic of Currency Crises', *Cahiers Economiques et Monetaires*, vol. 43, pp. 189–213.

Obstfeld, M. (1996) 'Models of Currency Crisis with Self-fulfilling Features', *European Economic Review*, vol. 40, pp. 1037–48.

Obstfeld, M. and Rogoff, K. (1996) *Foundations of International Macroeconomics* (Cambridge, Mass.: MIT Press).

Radlett, S. and Sachs, J. (1998) 'The East Asian Financial Crisis: Diagnosis, Remedies, Prospects', *Brookings Papers on Economic Activity*, vol. 28, no. 1, pp. 1–74.

Rangvid, J.A. (2001) 'Second Generation Models of Currency Crises', *Journal of Economic Surveys*, vol. 15, pp. 613–46.

Rigobon, R. (1998) 'Informational Speculative Attacks: Good News Is No News', mimeo, MIT.

Rodrick, D. (1998) 'Who Needs Capital Account Convertibility', in S. Fischer *et al.* (eds), *Should the IMF Pursue Capital Account Liberalization?* Essays in International Finance, Princeton, no. 207.

Roubini, N. and Wachtel, P. (1998) 'Current Account Sustainability in Transition Economies', National Bureau of Economic Research, Working Paper no. 6468.

Sachs, J. (1995) 'Do we need an International Lender of the Last Resort?' mimeo, Harvard.

Sachs, J., Aaron, T. and Andres, V. (1996) 'Financial Crises in Emerging Markets: The Lessons of 1995', *Bookings Papers on Economic Activity*, no. 1, pp. 147–217.

Sarno, L. and Taylor, M. (1999) 'Moral Hazard, Asset Price Bubbles, Capital Flows, and the East Asian Crisis: The First Tests', *Journal of International Money and Finance*, vol. 18, pp. 637–57.

Stiglitz, J. (2002) *Globalization and its Discontents* (New York: W.W. Norton & Company).

Bibliography

General texts in the field of international finance

Argy, V. (1981) *The Postwar International Money Crisis: An Analysis* (London: George Allen & Unwin).

Batchelor, R.A. and Wood, G.E. (1982) *Exchange Rate Policy* (London: Macmillan).

Bhandari, J.S. and Putnam, B.H. (1983) *Economic Interdependence and Flexible Exchange Rates* (Cambridge Mass.: MIT Press).

Bhandari, J.S. (1985) *Exchange Rate Management Under Uncertainty* (Cambridge Mass.: MIT Press).

Bigman, D. and Taya, T. (1982) *The Functioning of Floating Exchange Rates; Theory, Evidence and Policy Implications* (Cambridge, Mass.: Ballinger).

Bilson, J.F.O. and Marston, R.C. (1984) *Exchange Rate Theory and Practice* (Chicago: University of Chicago Press).

Brooks, S., Cuthbertson, K. and Mayes, D.G. (1986) *The Exchange Rate Environment* (Beckenham: Croom Helm).

Bryant, R.C., Currie, D.A., Frenkel, J.A., Masson, P.R. and Portes, R. (1989) (eds) *Macroeconomic Policies in an Interdependent World* (Washington: IMF).

Buiter, W.H. and Marston, R.C. (1985) *International Economic Policy Coordination* (Cambridge: Cambridge University Press).

Chipman, J.S. and Kindleberger, C.P. (1980) *Flexible Exchange Rates and the Balance of Payments* (Amsterdam: North-Holland).

Claassen, E.M. and Salin, P. (1983) *Recent Issues in the Theory of Flexible Exchange Rates* (Amsterdam: North-Holland).

Cooper, R.N., Kenen, P.B., Macedo, J.B. and Ypersele, J.V. (1982) The *International Monetary System Under Flexible Exchange Rates* (Cambridge, Mass.: Ballinger).

Copeland, L.S. (2004) *Exchange Rates and International Finance*, 3rd edn (New York: Prentice-Hall).

Corden, W.M. (1985) *Inflation, Exchange Rates and the World Economy*, 3rd edn (Oxford: Clarendon Press).

De Grauwe, P. (1983) *Macroeconomic Theory for the Open Economy* (London: *Gower*).

De Grauwe, P. (1989) *International Money* (Oxford: Clarendon Press).

De Grauwe, (2003) Economics of Monetary Union (Oxford: Oxford University Press).

De Grauwe, P., Fratiani, M. and Nabli, M. (1985) *Exchange Rates, Money and Output. The European Experience.* (London: Palgrave Macmillan).

Dornbusch, R. (1980) *Open Economy Macroeconomics* (New York: Basic Books).

Dornbusch, R. and Frenkel, J.A. (1979) *International Economic Policy* (Baltimore: John Hopkins University Press).

Eltis, W.A. and Sinclair, P.J.N. (1981) *The Money Supply and the Exchange Rate* (Oxford: Clarendon Press).

Frenkel, J.A. (1983) *Exchange Rates and International Economics* (Chicago: University of Chicago Press).

Frenkel, J.A. and Johnson, H.G. (1978) *The Economics of Exchange Rates* (Reading: Addison-Wesley).

Gandolfo, G. (2002) *International Finance and Open Economy Macroeconomics* (New York: Springer-Verlag).

Grossman, G.M. and Rogoff, K. (eds) (1995) *Handbook of International Economics, Vol. III* (Amsterdam: Elsevier).

Hallwood, P. and MacDonald, R. (2000) *International Money: Theory Evidence and Institutions* (Oxford: Basil Blackwell).

Jones, R.W. and Kenen, P.B. (eds) (1985) *Handbook of International Economics, Vol. II* (Amsterdam: Elsevier).

Kane, D.R. (1988) *Principles of International Finance* (Beckenham: Croom Helm).

Kenen, P.B. (1988) *Managing Exchange Rates* (London: Routledge).

Kenen, P.B. (2000) *International Economy* (Cambridge: Cambrige University Press).

Krueger, A.O. (1983) *Exchange Rate Determination* (Cambridge: Cambridge University Press).

Krugman, P.R. and Obstfeld, M. (2002) *International Economics*, 6th edn (Reading: Addison-Wesley).

Levi, M. (1990) *International Finance* (New York: McGraw-Hill).

Levich, R.M. (2001) *International Financial Markets: Prices and Policies*, 2nd edn (New York: McGraw Hill).

Llewellyn, D.T. and Milner, C. (eds) (1990) *Current Issues in International Monetary Economics* (London: Palgrave Macmillan).

MacDonald, R. (1988) *Floating Exchange Rates: Theories and Evidence* (London: Unwin Hyman).

MacDonald, R. and Taylor, M.P. (1989) *Innovations in Open Economy Macroeconomics* (Oxford: Basil Blackwell).

Mark, N.C. (2001) *International Macroeconomics and Finance: Theory and Empirical Methods* (Oxford: Basil Blackwell).

McKinnon, R.I. (1979) *Money in International Exchange* (Oxford: Oxford University Press).

Miller, M., Eichengreen, B. and Portes, R. (1989) (eds) *Blueprints for Exchange Rate Management* (London: Academic Press).

Niehans, J. (1984) *International Monetary Economics* (Oxford: Philip Allan).

Pentecost, E.J. (1993) *Exchange Rate Dynamics* (Aldershot: Edward Elgar).

Pilbeam, K.S. (1991) *Exchange Rate Management: Theory and Evidence* (London: Palgrave Macmillan).

Pilbeam, K.S. (2005) *Finance and Financial Markets* (London: Palgrave Macmillan).

Rivera-Batiz, F.L. and Rivera-Batiz, L. (1993) *International Finance and Open Economy Macroeconomics*, 2nd edn (New York: Prentice Hall).

Salvatore, D. (2004) *International Economics*, 8th edn (New York: John Wiley).

Sarno, L. and Taylor, M.P. (2002) *The Economics of Exchange Rates* (Cambridge: Cambridge University Press).

Shone, R. (1989) *Open Economy Macroeconomics* Hemel Hempstead: Harvester Wheatsheaf).

Walmsley, J. (2000) The Foreign Exchange and Money Markets Guide (New York: Wiley).

Williamson, J. and Milner, C. (1991) *The Open Economy and the World Economy*, 2nd edn (New York: Basic Books).

Yeager, L.B. (1976) *International Monetary Relations: Theory, History and Policy* (New York: Harper & Row).

Useful journals for international finance

American Economic Review
Brookings Papers on Economic Activity
European Economic Review
IMF Staff Papers
International Journal of Finance and Economics
Journal of International Economics
Journal of International Money and Finance
Journal of Money Credit and Banking
Journal of Political Economy

Useful theory and policy analysis publications

Bank for International Settlements, Economic Papers, Basle
European Central Bank Working Paper Series, Frankfurt
Group of Thirty Occasional Papers, New York
IMF Occasional Papers, Washington
IMF Working Papers, Washington
Institute for International Economics, Policy Analyses. MIT Press, Cambridge, Mass.
Princeton Essays in International Finance, Princeton University, Princeton
Princeton Studies in International Finance, Princeton University, Princeton
(the last 2 series were discontinued in 2002 but many of these classics are available on the web)

Sources of statistical information

Country Studies, Organisation for Economic Cooperation and Development, Paris. Published bi-annually.
Main Economic Indicators, Organisation for Economic Cooperation and Development, published monthly.
International Financial Statistics, International Monetary Fund, Washington, published monthly.
International Capital Markets: Developments Prospects and Key Policy Issues, International Monetary Fund, Washington, published annually.
Economic Outlook, Organisation for Economic Cooperation and Development, Paris, published bi-annually.
Global Development Finance (previously World Debt Tables), World Bank, Washington, published annually.
World Development Report, World Bank, Washington, published annually.
World Economic Outlook, International Monetary Fund, Washington, published bi-annually.

Selection of useful websites

There are thousands of useful sites on the web, so this is only a small but useful start. Many of them contain links to numerous other sites.

Institutions and central banks

www.imf.org (International Monetary Fund)
www.bis.org (Bank for International Settlements)
www.oecd.org (Organisation for Economic Cooperation and Development)
www.worldbank.org (World Bank)
www.federalreserve.gov (the site of the Federal Reserve)
www.ecb.int (European Central Bank)
www.boj.or.jp/en (English version of Bank of Japan)
www.bankofengland.co.uk (Bank of England's website)
www.iie.com (Institute for International Economics)

News sites

www.bloomberg.com (Bloomberg)
www.economist.com (*The Economist* magazine)

www.reuters.com (Reuters)
www.thestreet.com (a financial news website)
www.ft.com (the *Financial Times*)
www.wsj.com (*Wall Street Journal*)
www.abyznewslinks.com (Abyz news links to newspapers from around the world)

Economic and financial data

www.finance.yahoo.com – great for stock quotes and finance news.
www.economagic.com – plenty of US data.
www.globalfindata.com – a commercial data provider.
www.econ-datalinks.org – provides links to numerous economic and data sites.
www.econstats.com – free data on the US and global economy and plenty of links.
www.fedstats.gov – US federal government statistics.
www.research.stlouisfed.org – St Louis Federal Reserve Bank data on US and other economies.
www.dbresearch.com – Deutsche Bank macro and financial data, covering differing countries and regions of the world.

Education and search

www.financewise.com – a good search engine for finance sites.
www.investopedia.com – a good site with plenty of definitions and information.

Author Index

Subject Index